**Expository Outlines
on the
Whole Bible**

Expository Outlines on the Whole Bible

Charles Simeon

Volume 1

Genesis
Exodus
Leviticus

BAKER BOOK HOUSE
Grand Rapids, Michigan 49516

Reprinted 1988 by Baker Book House

Originally published as *Horae Homileticae*

This reprinting from the eighth edition
published by Henry G. Bolm, London, 1847

Twenty-one Volumes

ISBN: 0-8010-8281-1

Printed in the United States of America

TO HIS GRACE

WILLIAM

LORD ARCHBISHOP OF CANTERBURY,

PRIMATE OF ALL ENGLAND,

AND METROPOLITAN

My Lord Archbishop,

In offering this work to your Grace's patronage, I beg permission to state what occasion there is for such a work, and what I have aimed at in the composition of it.

It is to be regretted, that, whilst the education we receive in our Universities is admirably adapted to lay a good foundation for us to build upon, there is no subsequent instruction given us to fit us for the employment of the ministry. Before men are called to the public exercise of both in the Old and New Testament, avoiding carefully all peculiarities of human systems, and all unprofitable controversies; and I have done this in such a way, as to exemplify what appeared to me the most simple and edifying mode of stating divine truth. Throughout the whole I have laboured to maintain that spirit of moderation which so eminently distinguishes the Established Church, giving to every revealed truth, as far as I was able, its proper place, and that precise measure of consideration which it seemed to occupy in the Inspired Volume. At the same time, every thing has been brought forward with an especial view to its *practical improvement,* so as to lead the minds of my Younger Brethren to that which was pre-eminently necessary for them in their public ministrations. This has been my object *invariably:* and *in that view* I would hope the Discourses here offered to the public will prove of some little service to the Church of Christ.

To render them the more useful, I have studied conciseness, compressing into every separate Discourse all that was needful for an elucidation of the subject, and confirming every part of it with such references to Scripture, as should leave no reasonable doubt of its accordance with "the mind of the Spirit" of God. In every one of the Discourses also I have so clearly marked the method, that the entire scope of the passage may be seen with the glance of an eye; and the young Minister may be able to prosecute his work with ease according to his own judgment, making no other use of what is contained within the brackets, than to enlarge or confirm his own views of the subject.

These my best endeavours, such as they are, I lay before your Grace for your approbation, and commend to God for his divine blessing, without which they can be of no avail.

I am,

My Lord Archbishop,

Your Grace's most obliged

And devoted Servant,

CHARLES SIMEON.

King's College, Cambridge,
May 20, 1833.

the medical or legal profession, they have an appropriate line of study assigned them : nor does any one expect to succeed in either of those professions, till he has, with much labour and study, qualified himself for the discharge of the duties pertaining to it. But for the service of the Established Church no such preparatory studies are required; nor are any great facilities afforded for the acquisition of that knowledge, which ought to be possessed before we become stated and accredited teachers in the Church of Christ. Even that species of composition which is peculiarly proper for an edifying exposition of God's blessed Word, is never made a subject of specific instruction; or, at least, is never marked out with such clearness as to render the attainment of it easy to persons at their first entrance on their clerical duties. Hence considerable discouragement is felt by the Younger Clergy, and a great temptation is thrown in their way, to avail themselves of the labours of others, instead of striking out at first a path for themselves.

To remedy this defect, as far as was in my power, I have endeavoured to unfold the most important and instructive parts of Holy Writ,

PREFACE

INSTRUCTION relative to the Composition of Sermons is of great importance, not only to Ministers, but, eventually, to the community at large. And it were much to be wished that more regard were paid to this in the education of those who are intended for the ministry. It has sometimes been recommended to the younger Clergy to transcribe printed Sermons for a season, till they shall have attained ar ability to compose their own. And it is to be lamented, that this advice has been too strictly followed: for, when they have once formed this habit, they find it very difficult to relinquish it: the transition from copying to composing of Sermons is so great, that they are too often discouraged in their first attempts, and induced, from the difficulty they experience in writing their own Sermons, to rest satisfied in preaching those of others. To remove, as far as possible, these difficulties from young beginners, is the intent of these Skeletons. The directions given in Mr. Claude's *Essay on the Composition of a Sermon*, which is annexed to these Skeletons, cannot fail of being helpful to every one who will study them with care: but there appears to be something further wanted; something of an intermediate kind, between a didactic Essay like Claude's, and a complete Sermon; something which may simplify the theory, and set it in a practical light.

The following Skeletons[a] are not intended particularly to exemplify Mr. Claude's rules. There are indeed all his different kinds of discussion contained in the Skeletons. But instead of illustrating *particular* rules, they are *all* intended rather to

---

[a] For this use of the word "Skeleton," see Johnson's Dictionary

illustrate one *general* rule; namely, to shew how texts may be treated in a *natural* manner. The author has invariably proposed to himself three things as indispensably necessary in every discourse; UNITY in the design, PERSPICUITY in the arrangement, and SIMPLICITY in the diction.

It may perhaps be not unuseful to point out *the manner in which these discourses are formed.* As soon as the subject is chosen, the first inquiry is, *What is the principal scope and meaning of the text*[b]? Let us suppose, for instance, that the text of Jer. xxxi. 18—20, were the subject. Upon examination, it appears to be a soliloquy of the Deity, expressing what He had seen to be the workings of Ephraim's mind, and declaring the emotions which the sight of his penitent child had occasioned within his own bosom. Having ascertained this, nothing is to be introduced into any part of the discourse, which does not, in some way or other, reflect light upon the main subject. The next inquiry is, *Of what parts does the text consist, or into what parts may it be most easily and naturally resolved?* Here an obvious division occurs: it is evident that the text contains, 1st, The reflections of a true penitent; and, 2dly, The reflections of God over him. This division being made, the discussion of the two parts must be undertaken in their order. But how shall we elucidate the first head? Shall we say, that the penitent is roused from his lethargy, humbled for his transgressions, stimulated to prayer? &c. &c. Such a distribution would, doubtless, contain many useful truths; but they are truths which may be spoken from a thousand other texts as well as this; and after they had been spoken, the people would still be left without any precise knowledge of the portion of Scripture which should have been opened to them. If the text did not contain any important matter, it would *then* be proper, and even necessary, to enter in this general manner into the subject: but if the text itself afford ample means of elucidating the point that is under discussion, it is always best to adhere to that. In order then to enter fully into the subject, we examine more carefully, *what are the particular reflections which God noticed in*

---

[b] I BEG EVERY YOUNG MINISTER VERY ESPECIALLY TO REMEMBER THIS.

the penitent before us. And here we observe a further discrimination: the penitent's experience is delineated at two different periods; one in the beginning, and the other in the progress, of his repentance. This distinction serves to open an easy method for arranging what shall be spoken.

Upon investigating still more accurately his expressions, it appears that he laments his past incorrigibleness in the ways of sin, and, with an humble expression of his hope in God, implores converting grace. Soon afterwards, reflecting with a kind of joyful surprise upon the progress he has made, he thankfully ascribes the honour to God, through whose illuminating and converting grace he has been enabled to make such attainments. This experience being not peculiar to Ephraim, but common to all true penitents, we illustrate and confirm it by suitable passages of Holy Writ. *A similar process is then pursued with respect to the second head:* and *when that is arranged and discussed* in like manner, we *proceed to the application.* The nature of the application must depend in some measure on the subject that has been discussed, and on the state of the congregation to whom it is addressed. Where there are many who make a profession of godliness, it will be necessary to pay some attention to them, and to accommodate the subject *in part* to their state, in a way of conviction, consolation, encouragement, &c. But where the congregation is almost entirely composed of persons who are walking in " the broad way" of worldliness and indifference, it may be proper to suit the application to them *alone*. In either case it may be done by inferences, or by address to distinct characters, or by a general address: but, for the most part, either of the former methods is preferable to the last. As for the exordium, *that* is the last part to be composed; and Mr. Claude's directions for it cannot be improved.

Here then is an example of a discourse made on a text that affords an abundance of useful and important matter. But this is not the case in all texts: take Matt. xvi. 26, for instance. In that, the general scope of the text is, to declare the value of the soul; the distribution of it into its leading parts might be varied in many ways: but whatever distribution were adopted, one must of necessity supply from one's own invention matter for the illustration of it; because the text itself, though very important, does not limit one to any particular considerations.

By the adoption of such a plan as this, many good ends are attained: for not only is unity preserved, and a perspicuity diffused through the whole, but a variety of ideas suggest themselves which would not otherwise occur to the mind: an hackneyed way of treating texts will be avoided: the observations will be more appropriate: they will arise in a better order, and be introduced to more advantage: the attention of the audience will be fixed more on the word of God: their memories will be assisted: and the very reading of the text afterwards will bring to their minds much of what they have heard: besides, they will be more enabled to discern beauties in the Scripture when they peruse it in their closets. But it may be thought, that, on this plan, it will be always necessary to use divisions. This, however, is by no means the case: every text drawn up after this manner, must of necessity have an unity of *design;* and wherever *that* is, the *divisions may be either mentioned or concealed, as the writer shall choose.* Let the forementioned text in Jer. xxxi. be treated without any division at all; and the same arrangement will serve exactly as well as if the divisions were specified. It will stand thus—

" A true penitent in the beginning of his repentance reflects on his incorrigibleness in the ways of sin, and pleads with God to turn and convert his soul—

" When he has advanced a little in his repentance, he reflects with gratitude on the progress he has made, and he gives to God the glory of it—

" In such a state he is most acceptable to God—

" Whilst he can scarcely find terms whereby to express his own vileness, God accounts no honours too great for him—

" He owns him as a pleasant child; expresses his compassionate regard for him, promises to manifest his mercy towards him, and grants him all that he himself can possibly desire."—

Divest the Skeleton of Matt. xvi. 26, of its divisions, and it will be equally clear.

" By ' the world' we are to understand pleasure, riches, and honour—

PREFACE.

"This, if considered *in itself*, is vile; if, *as estimated by the best judges*, worthless—

"The soul, on the contrary, if considered *in itself*, is noble; and if, *as estimated by the best judges*, invaluable—

"Such being the disparity between the value of the world, and that of the soul, we cannot but see what must be the result of a comparison between them—

"We suppose, for argument sake, that a man may possess the whole world, and that after having possessed it for a while, he loses his own soul; what in the issue would he be profited?—

"Whether we enter generally or particularly into this subject, the result will be still the same."—

These two Skeletons are selected in order to exemplify this, idea, 1st, In a subject where the whole matter is contained in the text; and, 2dly, In a subject where nothing but the general idea is suggested: and if the Reader will give himself the trouble to examine, he will find that *every one of the other Skeletons may, with equal ease, be drawn out in the same manner.* This is a point of considerable importance: for if the mind were necessarily cramped and fettered by this method of composition, it would be inexpedient to adopt it. But it is manifest that it leaves the mind at most perfect liberty: and while many advantages arise from it, there is no room at all for the principal objection, which might at first sight appear to lie against it. But though these observations are made to shew that discourses might be formed from the Skeletons as easily without divisions as with them, it is not to be thought that the mention of the divisions is a matter of indifference: the minds of the generality are not capable of tracing the connexion and coherence of a discourse: their attention will flag; they will lose much of what they hear; and have no clew whereby to recover it: whereas the mention of an easy and natural division will relieve their minds, assist their memories, and enable them to "mark, learn, and inwardly digest" the word.

If any student, who has a view to the ministry, should choose to employ a part of his Sabbath in perusing any of these compositions, he would do well first to get a clear view of the great outlines of the discourse, and then to consider, under each part, what is contained in the brackets; consulting, as he proceeds, the passages of Scripture that are quoted. After this, if he will write over the whole, interweaving those passages, *or such parts of them as refer immediately to the subject*, adding only a few words here and there to connect the whole, he will find that every Skeleton will make a discourse, which, if read distinctly, will occupy the space of nearly half an hour. In this way he may attain, without any great difficulty, a considerable knowledge of the Scriptures, together with an habit of thinking clearly and connectedly on the principal doctrines contained in them. If any one, who has entered upon the sacred office, should think them worthy of his attention, a different method of using them should be adopted. He, having finished his academical studies, has his time more at his own command: he should therefore make himself perfect master of the Skeleton before him, and then write in his own language, and according to his own conceptions, his views of the subject: and he will find that "verba provisam rem non invita sequentur." It is proper however to observe, that those parts, which have three marks after them — — — should be more fully opened.

But there is *one caution* which requires peculiar attention. In the Skeletons many passages of the Holy Scriptures are quoted, partly for the conviction of the Reader's own mind, and partly to furnish him with the proper materials for confirming his word. These passages, if they were *all formally* quoted, would make the sermon a mere rhapsody, a string of texts, that could not fail to weary and disgust the audience. But if they be glanced at, if the proper parts only be selected, and interwoven with the writer's own language, they will give a richness and variety to the discourse, at the same time that they will be peculiarly grateful to those who delight in the word of God. There is however another extreme, which would be no less pernicious: if no passages be *formally* adduced, many parts of the discourse will appear to want confirmation. The proper medium seems to be, to quote them expressly when there is reason to apprehend that any doubt is entertained respecting the truth that is insisted on, or where the citing of them will give peculiar weight to the point in hand: in all other places the language of Scripture should be used rather to enrich and adorn our own.

PREFACE.

It cannot be but that a Work of this nature should be liable to many objections. Persons will vary in their judgment with respect to it, according as they affect or disregard order; according as they relish or disapprove the use of Scripture language; according as they have been habituated to close thinking, or have been accustomed to a desultory way of communicating their ideas; and, lastly, according as they acquiesce in the unsophisticated doctrines of Scripture, or fondly attach themselves to human systems.

But the Author begs leave to observe, that the very plan of suggesting the whole substance of a Sermon in a few pages, of shewing in so small a space how to *introduce, divide, discuss,* and *apply* every subject, and of referring to the most important passages of Scripture that can reflect light upon it, necessarily precludes all the ornaments of language, and induces somewhat perhaps of obscurity. But if there be found some reason for that complaint, "brevis esse laboro, obscurus fio," it is hoped the candid Reader will consider it as a fault incident to the plan itself; and if he meet with any expression which appears too unqualified, he is requested to remember, that a thousand qualifying clauses might be introduced into a full discourse, which could not possibly find place in such compositions as these: if he would regard these in their proper view, he must consider them only as rough materials prepared to his hand, that out of them he may construct an edifice, modelled and adorned to his own taste.

There is another objection indeed, which has been mentioned to the Author by some of his most judicious friends. It is feared that these Skeletons may administer to sloth and idleness. But he apprehends they are so constructed, that they cannot possibly be used at all, unless a considerable degree of thought be bestowed upon them. Nor does he think that any person, who has ever found the pleasure of addressing his congregation in his own words, will be satisfied with reciting the compositions of another. On the other hand, if some, who would otherwise have preached the sermons of others, be drawn gradually to compose their own, and if others, who have been rude and incoherent, be assisted in the exercise of their judgment, it will tend to wipe off disgrace from the Established Church, and eventually, it is hoped, to benefit the souls of many.

It is not possible to say what is the best mode of preaching for every individual, because the talents of men are so various, and the extent of their knowledge so different. It seems at all events expedient that a young Minister should for some years pen his sermons, in order that he may attain a proper mode of expressing his thoughts, and accustom himself to the obtaining of clear, comprehensive, and judicious views of his subject: but that he should always continue to write every word of his discourses, seems by no means necessary. Not that it is at any time expedient for him to deliver an unpremeditated harangue: this would be very unsuitable to the holy and important office which he stands up to discharge. But there is a medium between such extemporaneous effusions and a servile adherence to what is written: there is a method recommended by the highest authorities, which, after we have written many hundred sermons, it may not be improper to adopt: the method referred to is, to draw out a full plan or skeleton of the discourse, with the texts of Scripture which are proper to illustrate or enforce the several parts, and then to express the thoughts in such language as may occur at the time. This plan, if it have some disadvantage in point of accuracy or elegance, has, on the other hand, great advantages over a written sermon: it gives a Minister an opportunity of speaking with far more effect to the hearts of men, and of addressing himself to their passions, as well by his looks and gesture, as by his words.

Archbishop Secker, in his last Charge, after observing, in reference to *the matter* of our sermons, " We have, in fact, lost many of our people to sectaries by not preaching in a manner sufficiently evangelical," (p. 299,) adds, in reference to *the manner* of our preaching, " There is a middle way[c], used by our predecessors, of setting down, in short notes, the method and principal heads, and enlarging on them in such words as present themselves at the time: perhaps, duly managed, *this is the best.*" (p. 315.) He then proceeds to express his disapprobation of what is called Mandating of Sermons, or repeating them from memory. This custom obtains much among foreign Divines, and throughout the whole Church of

---

[c] *i. e.* Between written discourses, and unpremeditated addresses.

PREFACE.

Scotland; and in the Statute Book of our University there is an order from King Charles II., that this should be practised by all the Clergy, as well when preaching before the University and at Court, as before any common audience[d]. This shews at least, that if a Minister had thoroughly studied his discourse, it was deemed no objection against him that he delivered it without book. But the way proposed by Archbishop Secker seems far preferable, on account of the unnecessary increase of labour to the Minister, and because the repeating of a sermon will most generally appear, as the Archbishop justly expresses it, like " the saying of a lesson." Many other authorities of the greatest note might be adduced (as those of Bishop Wilkin, Bishop Burnet, Archbishop of Cambray, &c.) if it were the Author's wish to vindicate this mode of preaching: but he is far from thinking it proper for all persons, or in all places. He considers it however as extremely useful, where a Minister's talents will admit of it. But, after all, the great concern both of Ministers and private Christians is, to enjoy the blessing of God upon their own souls. In whatever manner the truth may be delivered, whether from a written discourse or memoriter, or from a well-digested plan, they may expect that God will accompany it with a divine energy, if they be looking up to him in the

---

[d] " Mr. Vice-Chancellor, and Gentlemen,

" Whereas his Majesty is informed, that the practice of reading Sermons is generally taken up by the Preachers before the University, and therefore continued even before himself, his Majesty hath commanded me to signify to you his pleasure that the said practice, which took beginning with the disorders of the late times, be wholly laid aside, and that the aforesaid Preachers deliver their Sermons, both in Latin and English, by memory or without book, as being a way of preaching which his Majesty judgeth most agreeable to the use of all foreign Churches, to the custom of the University heretofore, and the nature and intendment of that holy exercise.

" And that his Majesty's commands in the premises may be duly regarded and observed, his farther pleasure is, that the names of all such ecclesiastical persons, as shall continue the present supine and slothful way of preaching, be from time to time signified unto me by the Vice-Chancellor for the time being, upon pain of his Majesty's displeasure. MONMOUTH."

" *October* 8, 1674."   (Page 300 of the Statute Book.)

exercise of faith and prayer. In this hope, the Sermon, on Mark xvi. 15, 16, and the four Skeletons annexed to it, are sent forth into the world: and if, by means of them, the excellency of the Gospel may be more clearly seen, its importance more deeply felt, and its strengthening, comforting, sanctifying efficacy more richly experienced, the Author's labours will be abundantly repaid. They are annexed to Claude's Essay; and the Author recommends those who could thoroughly understand Claude, to consult them.

In the discussion of so many subjects, it cannot fail but that every doctrine of our holy religion must be more or less canvassed. On every point the Author has spoken freely, and without reserve. As for names and parties in religion, he equally disclaims them all: he takes his religion from the Bible; and endeavours, as much as possible, to speak as that speaks[e]. Hence, as in the Scriptures themselves, so also in this Work, there will be found sentiments, not really opposite, but apparently of an opposite tendency, according to the subject that is under discussion. In writing, for instance, on John v. 40, "*Ye will not come to me, that ye might have life,*" he does not hesitate to lay the whole blame of men's condemnation on the obstinacy of their own depraved will: nor does he think it at all necessary to weaken the subject by nice distinctions, in order to support a system. On the contrary, when he preaches on John vi. 44, "*No man can come unto me, except the Father who hath sent me draw him,*" he does not scruple to state in the fullest manner he is able, "That we have no power to do good works pleasant and acceptable to God, without the grace of God by Christ preventing us that we may have a good will, and working with us when we have that good will[f]:" nor does he judge it expedient on any account to soften, and palliate, and fritter away this important truth. While too

---

[e] If in any thing he grounded his sentiments upon *human* authority, it would not be on the dogmas of Calvin or Arminius, but on the Articles and Homilies of *the Church of England*. He has the happiness to say, that he does *ex animo*, from his inmost soul, believe the doctrines to which he has subscribed: but the reason of his believing them is not, that they are made the Creed of the Established Church, but that he finds them manifestly contained in the Sacred Oracles.

[f] The Tenth Article.

many set these passages at variance, and espouse the one in opposition to the other, he dwells with equal pleasure on them both; and thinks it, on the whole, better to state these apparently opposite truths in the plain and unsophisticated manner of the Scriptures, than to enter into scholastic subtleties, that have been invented for the upholding of human systems. He is aware, that they who are warm advocates for this or that system of religion, will be ready to condemn him as inconsistent: but, if he speak in exact conformity with the Scriptures, he shall rest the vindication of his conduct simply on the authority and example of the Inspired Writers. He has no desire to be wise above what is written, nor any conceit that he can teach the Apostles to speak with more propriety and correctness than they have spoken.

It may be asked perhaps, How do you *reconcile* these doctrines, which you believe to be of equal authority and equal importance? But what right has any man to impose this task on the preachers of God's word? God has not required it of them; nor is the truth or falsehood of any doctrine to be determined absolutely by this criterion. It is presumed, that every one will acknowledge the holiness of God, and the existence of sin: but will any one undertake to reconcile them? or does any one consider the inability of man to reconcile them, as a sufficient ground for denying either the one or the other of these truths? If then neither of these points are doubted, notwithstanding they cannot be reconciled by us, why should other points, equally obvious in some respects, yet equally difficult to be reconciled in others, be incompatible, merely because we, with our limited capacity, cannot perfectly discern their harmony and agreement?

But perhaps these points, which have been such a fruitful source of contention in the Church, are not so opposite to each other as some imagine: and it is possible, that the truly scriptural statement will be found not in an exclusive adoption of either, nor yet in a confused mixture of both, but in the proper and seasonable application of them both; or, to use the language of St. Paul, " in rightly dividing the word of truth."

Here the Author desires to speak with trembling. He is aware that he is treading upon slippery ground; and that he has but little prospect of satisfying any who have decidedly ranged themselves under the standard either of Calvin or Arminius. But he wishes to be understood: he is not solicitous to bring any man to pronounce his Shibboleth; much less has he any design to maintain a controversy in support of it: he merely offers an apology for the sentiments contained in his publication, and, with much deference, submits to the public his views of scripture truth: and, whether they be perfectly approved or not, *this* he hopes to gain from all parties, a favourable acceptance of what they approve, and a candid forbearance in the points they disapprove.

This being premised, he will proceed to state the manner in which these apparently opposite tenets may, in his judgment, be profitably insisted on.

It is supposed by many, that the doctrines of grace are incompatible with the doctrine of man's free-will; and that therefore the one or the other must be false. But why so? Can any man doubt one moment whether he be a free agent or not? he may as well doubt his own existence. On the other hand, will any man who has the smallest spark of humility, affirm, that he has made himself to differ; and that he has something which he has not received from a superior power[g]? Will any one refuse to say with the Apostle, "By the grace of God I am what I am[h]?"

Again; as men differ with respect to the first beginnings of a work of grace, so do they also with respect to the manner in which it must be carried on; some affirming, that God has engaged to "perfect that which concerneth us;" and others, that even St. Paul had reason to fear " lest he himself should become a cast-away." But why should these things be deemed incompatible[i]? Does not every man feel within himself a

---

[g] 1 Cor. iv. 7.   [h] 1 Cor. xv. 10.

[i] Benhadad *might* have recovered from his disease, though God had decreed that, by Hazael's device, he should die of it; (2 Kings viii. 10.) so we *may* (for aught that there is in us) die in our sins, though God has decreed that he will save us from death. In both cases the decree of God stands; but the possibility of the event, *as considered in itself*, remains unaltered. Neither our liableness to perish prevents the execution of God's decree; nor does his decree alter our liableness (*in ourselves*) to perish.

liableness, yea, a proneness to fall? Does not every man feel, that there is corruption enough within him to drive him to the commission of the greatest enormities, and eternally to destroy his soul? He can have but little knowledge of his own heart who will deny this. On the other hand, who that is holding on in the ways of righteousness, does not daily ascribe his steadfastness to the influence of that grace, which he receives from God; and look daily to God for more grace, in order that he may be "kept by *his* power through faith unto salvation[k]?" No man can in any measure resemble the scripture saints, unless he be of this disposition. Why then *must* these things be put in opposition to each other, so that every advocate for one of these points must of necessity controvert and explode the other? Only let any *pious* person, whether Calvinist or Arminian, examine the language of his prayers after he has been devoutly pouring out his soul before God, and he will find his own words almost in perfect consonance with the foregoing statement. The Calvinist will be confessing the extreme depravity of his nature, together with his liability and proneness to fall; and the Arminian will be glorifying God for all that is good within him, and will commit his soul to God, in order that HE who has laid the foundation of his own spiritual temple, may also finish it[l].

[k] Zech. iv. 9.
[l] 1 Pet. i. 5.

A circumstance within the Author's knowledge reflects so much light upon this subject, that he trusts he shall be pardoned for relating it.

A young Minister, about three or four years after he was ordained, had an opportunity of conversing familiarly with the great and venerable leader of the Arminians in this kingdom; and, wishing to improve the occasion to the uttermost, he addressed him nearly in the following words: "Sir, I understand that you are called an Arminian; and I have been sometimes called a Calvinist; and therefore I suppose we are to draw daggers. But before I consent to begin the combat, with your permission I will ask you a few questions, not from impertinent curiosity, but for real instruction." Permission being very readily and kindly granted, the young Minister proceeded to ask, "Pray, Sir, do you feel yourself a depraved creature, so depraved, that you would never have thought of turning unto God, if God had not first put in into your heart?"—"Yes," says the veteran, "I do indeed."
—"And do you utterly despair of recommending yourself to God by

Doubtless either of these points may be injudiciously stated, or improperly applied. If the doctrines of Election and Predestination be so stated as to destroy man's free agency, and make him merely passive in the work of salvation, they are not stated as they are in the Articles and Homilies of our Church, or as they are in the Holy Scriptures. On the other hand, if the doctrines of free-will and liableness to final apostasy be so stated as to rob God of his honour, and to deny that he is both "the *Author* and the *Finisher* of our faith," they are equally abhorrent from the sentiments of our Established Church, and from the plainest declarations of Holy Writ.

The Author humbly apprehends, that there is a perfect agreement between these different points; and that they are equally salutary or equally pernicious, according as they are properly or improperly implied. If, for instance, on hearing a person excuse his own supineness by saying, "I can do nothing, unless God give me his grace;" we should reply, "This is true; it is God who alone can give you either to will or to do;"—what would be the consequence? we should

any thing that you can do; and look for salvation solely through the blood and righteousness of Christ?"—"Yes, solely through Christ." —"But, Sir, supposing you were first saved by Christ, are you not somehow or other to save yourself afterwards by your own works?" —"No; I must be saved by Christ from first to last."—"Allowing then that you were first turned by the grace of God, are you not in some way or other to keep yourself by your own power?"—"No."— "What then, are you to be upheld every hour and every moment by God, as much as an infant in its mother's arms?"—"Yes; altogether."—"And is all your hope in the grace and mercy of God to preserve you unto his heavenly kingdom?"—"Yes; I have no hope, but in him."—"Then, Sir, with your leave, I will put up my dagger again; for this is all my Calvinism; this is my election, my justification by faith, my final perseverance: it is, in substance, all that I hold, and as I hold it: and therefore, if you please, instead of searching out terms and phrases to be a ground of contention between us, we will cordially unite in those things wherein we agree."

The Arminian leader was so pleased with the conversation, that he made particular mention of it in his journals; and notwithstanding there never afterwards was any connexion between the parties, he retained an unfeigned regard for his young inquirer to the hour of his death.

confirm him in his sloth, and encourage him to cast all the blame of his condemnation upon God himself. But if we should bring before him the apparently opposite truths, and bid him arise and call upon God; we should take the way to convince him, that the fault was utterly his own, and that his destruction would be the consequence, not of God's decrees, but of his own inveterate love of sin.

Let us suppose, on the other hand, that a person, having "tasted the good word of life," begin to boast, that he has made himself to differ, and that his superiority to others is the mere result of his own free-will: if, in answer to him, we should immediately descant on our freedom to good or evil, and on the powers with which God has endued us for the preservation of our souls, we should foster the pride of his heart, and encourage him, contrary to an express command, to glory before God[m] : whereas, if we should remind him, that " by the grace of God we are what we are," and that all must say, " Not unto us, O Lord, not unto us, but unto thy name be the praise," we should lower his overweening conceit of his own goodness, and lead him to acknowledge his obligations to God.

Let us illustrate the same in reference to the two other doctrines we mentioned, namely, The perseverance of the saints, and our liableness, in ourselves, to " make shipwreck of the faith." Suppose a person say, " I need not be careful about my conduct;" for "God has begun the good work within me, and has engaged to perform it till the day of Christ :" if we were to begin extolling the covenant of grace, and setting forth the truth of God in his promises, we should countenance his error, at the very time that he was turning the grace of God into licentiousness. But if we should warn him against the danger of being given over to a reprobate mind, and of perishing under an accumulated load of guilt, we should counteract his sinful disposition, and stimulate him to flee from the wrath to come.

On the other hand, if a humble person should be drooping and desponding under a sense of his own corruptions, and we should spread before him all our difficulties and dangers, we

[m] 1 Cor. i. 29. Rom. iii. 27.

should altogether " break the bruised reed, and quench the smoking flax:" but if we should point out to him the fulness and stability of God's covenant; if we should enlarge upon the interest which Christ takes in his people, and his engagements that none shall ever pluck them out of his hand[n]; it is obvious, that we should administer a cordial to his fainting spirit, or (as God requires of us) we should " strengthen the weak hands, and confirm the feeble knees, and comfort the fearful heart."

These sentiments may perhaps receive some confirmation from the conduct of the Apostle Paul. In administering the word, he consulted the state of his auditors, and apportioned to them either " milk or strong meat," according to their ability to digest and improve it[o]. In reference to this we may say, that the doctrines of human liberty, and human frailty, together with the other first principles of Christianity, are as milk, which those who are yet " babes in Christ," must have set before them: but that the doctrines of grace, or " the deep things of God," are rather as strong meat, which none can digest, unless they have grown to some stature in the family of Christ, and have had their spiritual senses long exercised in discerning good and evil[p]: and that, as strong meat, which would nourish an adult, would destroy the life of an infant; and milk that would nourish an infant, would be inadequate to the support of a man oppressed with hard labour; so it is with respect to the points which we have been considering. Or, if we may be permitted a little to vary this illustration, the one sort of truths are as food proper to be administered to all; whereas the other are rather as cordials for the support and comfort of those who need them.

In a word, there seems to be a perfect correspondence between God's works of providence and grace: in the former, " he worketh all things according to the counsel of his own will," yet leaves men perfectly free agents in all that they do; so in the latter, he accomplishes his own eternal purpose both in calling, and in keeping, his elect; but yet he never puts upon them any constraint, which is not perfectly compatible with the freest operations of their own will.

The Author well knows that these doctrines *may be*, and

---

[n] John x. 27, 28.   [o] 1 Cor. iii. 1, 2.   [p] Heb. v. 12—14.

alas! *too often are,* so stated as to be really contradictory. But that they *may be* so stated as to be profitable to the souls of men, he hopes is clear from the illustrations that have been just given[q].

He trusts he shall be pardoned if he go yet further, and say, that, in his judgment, there not only is no positive contradiction in this statement, but that there is *a propriety* in it, yea, moreover, *a necessity* for it, because there is *a subserviency in these truths, the one to the other.* God elects us; but he carries his purpose into effect by the free agency of man, which is altogether influenced by rational considerations. So also he carries on and completes his work in our souls, by causing us to feel our proneness to apostatize, and by making us cry to him daily for the more effectual influences of his grace. Thus, while he consults his own glory, he promotes our greatest good, in that he teaches us to combine humility with earnestness, and vigilance with composure.

The Author would not have troubled the Reader with this apology, were it not that he is exceedingly desirous to counteract that spirit of animosity, which has of late so greatly prevailed against those who adhere to the principles of the Established Church. Not that he has himself any cause to complain: but he would wish his Work to be brought to this test—Does it uniformly tend

TO HUMBLE THE SINNER?
TO EXALT THE SAVIOUR?
TO PROMOTE HOLINESS?

If in one single instance it lose sight of any of these points, let it be condemned without mercy. But, if it invariably

---

[q] Many have carried their attachment to system so far, that they could not endure to preach upon any passage of Scripture that seemed to oppose their favourite sentiments; or, if they did, their whole endeavour has been to make the text speak a different language from that which it appeared to do. In opposition to all such modes of procedure, it is the Author's wish in this preface to recommend a conformity to the Scriptures themselves, without any solicitude about systems of man's invention. Nor would any thing under heaven be more grateful to him than to see names and parties buried in eternal oblivion, and primitive simplicity restored to the Church.

VOL. I.

pursue these ends, then let not any, whatever system they embrace, quarrel with an expression that does not quite accord with their views. Let them consider the general scope and tendency of the book: and, if it be, as he trusts it is, not to strengthen a party in the Church, but to promote the good of the whole; then let smaller differences of sentiment be overlooked, and all unite in vindicating the great doctrines of SALVATION BY GRACE THROUGH FAITH IN CHRIST.

Why these Discourses have been multiplied to such an extent the Author will briefly explain. The Reformers of the Church of England, by the publication of HOMILIES on some of the fundamental topics of religion and morals, have rendered an inestimable service to all classes of society. But it is obvious, that these Homilies embrace only a few of the subjects to which it is essential to call the attention of mankind. It is also a known fact, that the Reformers themselves designed considerably to enlarge the number of these truly Scriptural addresses. The Ministers of the Church, accordingly, have never considered their private labours as superseded by the Homilies; but have, from age to age, supplied to the nation Discourses of the highest value.

It has not, however, as the Author believes, occurred to any divine, *to supply a regular series of Discourses on the most important parts of the whole volume of Scripture; and to adapt those Discourses, by their general construction, their simplicity, and their brevity, to the especial service of the younger orders of the Clergy.* But, perhaps, a young Minister may find it not an unprofitable exercise, to take some of the texts here treated, and to make an arrangement of them for himself in the first instance from his own mind, and then to compare that arrangement with what is here set before him.

To supply this deficiency in theological writings, is the particular object of the volumes which the Author now humbly presents to the public.[r] And he trusts this labour of love will be regarded by his Brethren in the Ministry, not as an act of presumption, but as a humble and affectionate attempt to

---

[r] For the TITLE, Horæ *Homileticæ*, see Acts xx. 11. *in the* **Greek.** This book contains *short discourses on divers subjects.*

render their entrance on their holy and honourable calling more easy, and their prosecution of it more useful. And, by embracing so many subjects which have a different aspect in *systematic* divinity, he hopes that he has paved the way for their rising superior to *human* systems of every kind.

The Author is no friend to systematizers in Theology. He has endeavoured to derive from the Scriptures alone *his* views of religion; and to them it is his wish to adhere, with scrupulous fidelity; never wresting any portion of the word of God to favour a particular opinion, but giving to every part of it that sense, which it seems to him to have been designed by its great Author to convey.

He is aware that he is likely, on this account, to be considered, by the zealous advocates of human systems, as occasionally inconsistent: but if he should be discovered to be no more inconsistent than the Scriptures themselves, he will have reason to be satisfied. He has no doubt but that there is a system in the Holy Scriptures; (for truth cannot be inconsistent with itself:) but he is persuaded that neither Calvinists nor Arminians are in *exclusive* possession of that system. He is disposed to think that the Scripture system, be it what it may, is of a broader and more comprehensive character than some very exact and dogmatical Theologians are inclined to allow: and that, as wheels in a complicated machine may move in opposite directions and yet subserve one common end, so may truths *apparently opposite* be perfectly reconcilable with each other, and equally subserve the purposes of God in the accomplishment of man's salvation. The Author feels it impossible to repeat too often, or avow too distinctly, that it is an invariable rule with him to endeavour to give to every portion of the word of God its full and proper force, without considering one moment what scheme it favours, or whose system it is likely to advance. Of this he is sure, that there is not a decided Calvinist or Arminian in the world, who equally approves of the whole of Scripture. He apprehends, that there is not a determined votary of either system, who, if he had been in the company of St. Paul, whilst he was writing his different Epistles, would not have recommended him to alter one or other of his expressions.

But the Author would not wish one of them altered: he

finds as much satisfaction in one class of passages as in another; and employs the one (he believes) as often, and as freely, as the other. Where the Inspired Writers speak in unqualified terms, he thinks himself at liberty to do the same; judging, that they needed no instruction from *him* how to propagate the truth. He is content to sit as a *learner* at the feet of the holy Apostles, and has no ambition to teach them how they ought to have spoken. And as both the strong Calvinists and Arminians approve of some parts of Scripture and not of others, such he expects will be the judgment of the partisans of these particular systems on his unworthy comments;—the Calvinists approving of what is written on passages which have a Calvinistic aspect; and the Arminians, of what is written on passages that favour their particular views. In like manner, he has reason, he fears, to expect a measure of condemnation from the advocates of each system, when treating of the passages which they appear to him to *wrest*, each for the purpose of accommodating them to his own favourite opinions. He bitterly regrets that men will range themselves under human banners and leaders, and employ themselves in converting the Inspired Writers into friends and partisans of their peculiar principles. Into this fault he trusts that he has never fallen. One thing he knows, namely, that pious men, both of the Calvinistic and Arminian persuasion, approximate very nearly when they are upon their knees before God in prayer;—the devout Arminian then acknowledging his total dependence upon God, as strongly as the most confirmed Calvinist; and the Calvinist acknowledging his responsibility to God, and his obligation to exertion, in terms as decisive as the most determined Arminian. And what both these individuals are upon their knees, it is the wish of the Author to become in his writings. Hence it is that he expects to be alternately approved by both parties, and condemned by both. His only fear is, that each may be tempted to lay hold of those parts of his work only which *oppose* their favourite system, and represent them as containing an entire view of his sentiments. He well knows the force of prejudice, and the bitterness of the *odium Theologicum;* and he cannot hope to be so fortunate as completely to escape either. But, even if assailed on all sides, he shall have the satisfaction of reflecting, that it has been his wish simply to follow the Oracles of God. The Scriptures and the Church of England have been claimed, by each of these two parties, as exclusively favouring their peculiar system; and if the same comprehensive and liberal character be found in his writings, he shall consider it, whatever may be the judgment of mere partisans, as no small presumption in his own favour.

There is another point also, in respect to which it has been his aim not to offend; and that is, in not so perverting the Scripture as to make it refer to Christ and his salvation, when no such object appears to have been in the contemplation of the inspired writer. He regrets to observe, in some individuals, what he knows not how to designate by any more appropriate term than that (which however he uses with much hesitation) of an *ultra-Evangelical* taste; which overlooks in many passages the *practical* lessons they were intended to convey, and detects in them only the leading *doctrines* of the Gospel. This error he has laboured earnestly to avoid; being well assured, that lessons of morality are, in their place, as useful and important as the doctrines of grace. In a word, it has been his endeavour faithfully to deliver, in every instance, what he verily believed to be the mind of God in the passage immediately under consideration: and in the adoption of this principle of interpretation, he trusts for the approbation of all, who prefer the plain and obvious comments of sobriety to the far-fetched suggestions of a licentious fancy. He wishes much that the practice of *expounding* the Scriptures, which obtained so generally, and with such beneficial effects, at the time of the Reformation, were revived. He has in his present work introduced many Discourses constructed upon this model; and he cannot but earnestly recommend it to his Younger Brethren in the Ministry, especially those who preach three times in the week, to reserve at least one of these seasons for exposition. It is his wish, however, to guard them against a desultory manner of explaining the Scripture; and to advise, that the leading point of the whole passage be the point mainly regarded; and the subordinate parts only so far noticed, as to throw additional light upon that. If this caution be not attended to, the minds of the people are likely to be distracted with the diversity and incoherence of the matter brought before them. But if an unity of subject be preserved, the discourse will come with ten-fold weight to the minds of the audience; who will be led, under the guidance of the Holy Spirit, to search the Scriptures for themselves, and to read them with more profit at their own homes. To this it may be added, that it is not necessary the whole passage should be read for the text: let the most striking part of it alone be introduced in the first instance; and then the whole explained, with such remarks as are suited to impress on the mind the truths contained in it. This will be found to have been the course pursued in many of the following Discourses, to a greater extent perhaps than at first sight appears.

In order to render the work useful as a COMMENTARY ON THE HOLY SCRIPTURES, the Author has made it his object carefully to consider the context, and, in every passage which he undertook to examine, has uniformly limited his consideration of every distinct subject to the view of it presented in the context. The Author thinks it expedient, that discourses delivered before mixed assemblies should present a complete view of a subject, without reference to any preceding or following discourse: and to this he has directed his attention throughout the whole work; so that any single Discourse will present to the Reader all that was judged necessary for the elucidation and improvement of the subject in hand. And, if in some few instances there be an idea repeated in two consecutive Discourses, it may well be accounted for, from the circumstance, that, though standing together here, many, so placed, were preached at the distance of twenty or thirty years from each other.

The Author has also sought to render the work useful FOR FAMILIES. It has often been a matter of complaint, that there existed few Sermons sufficiently plain and concise for the instruction of Servants: he has therefore filled up the outline of many of these sketches somewhat fully, hoping that Clergymen and others may find them not altogether useless as *a Family Instructor*.

The texts cited in the New Testament from the Old, or occurring more than once in the volume of Scripture, are treated only once in the volume, and that generally in the

PREFACE.

place where it seems to the Author to occupy the most important station. This he particularly mentions, in order that the Reader may not be led to imagine, that a passage occurring in any one Gospel is left unnoticed, because no Discourse upon it is found in that particular place; or that a prophecy is not examined, because it is not considered in the book of the particular Prophet where it originally occurs. Some passages in the Prophets are cited in the New Testament no less than six different times, (particularly Ps. cxviii. 22, 23, and Isai. vi. 9, 10); but of course such passages are investigated only once.

In order that the agreement between the Author's views, and what he conceives to be the views of the Church of England, may be ascertained, he begs leave to refer the Reader to the Four Sermons on Deut. v. 28, 29, in which "The Excellency of the Liturgy" is delineated; and to that on 2 Cor. i. 13, wherein "The Churchman's Confession" is considered. And to any who may wish to become acquainted with the Author's views of what is called "*Evangelical Religion*," he begs to recommend the perusal of the Sermons on 1 Cor. ii. 2, and Psalm cxix. 128; which were *written for the express purpose of exhibiting, in as clear and comprehensive a manner as he was able, his opinions upon that important subject.* More especially, with this object, he would entreat their candid consideration of what he has called an "Appeal to Men of Wisdom and Candour:" (on 1 Cor. x. 15.) All these Sermons, together with those on the Liturgy, and those on the Offices of the Holy Spirit, were delivered before the University of Cambridge. These Discourses, it may be added, comprehend all the topics which he considers as of primary and fundamental importance to mankind. On many other points there exists, and will probably continue to exist, a diversity of opinion : and in writing upon the *whole* Scriptures, it would not be expected but that he should occasionally touch on such topics, as they presented themselves to him in his course. But as he has endeavoured, without prejudice or partiality, to give to every text its just meaning, its natural bearing, and its legitimate use, he hopes, that those who dislike his expositions of the texts which oppose their particular views, will consult what he has written on the texts which they regard as the sheet-anchors of their system; and that, finding him, as he trusts they will, free from party spirit, they will themselves endeavour to shake off party prejudices, and co-operate with him in maintaining and extending that comprehensive, and generous, and harmonious, as well as devout spirit in the Church, which, he ventures to say, it has been one of the great objects of his life to promote.

The Author has only to add, that by compressing thus every subject into the smallest space, he has given in this work, what, if a little dilated and printed in the usual way, would have occupied ONE HUNDRED VOLUMES. And if the Reader peruse *one discourse every day of his life*, the whole will occupy him exactly SEVEN YEARS.

CONTENTS TO VOL. I

Discourse.	Text.	Subject.	Page.
	GENESIS		
1.	i. 26.	Creation of Man	1
2.	ii. 2, 3.	Appointment of the Sabbath	6
3.	ii. 16, 17.	Covenant made with Adam	12
4.	iii. 4.	The Serpent beguiling Eve	19
5.	iii. 6, 7.	The Fall of Man	24
6.	iii. 11—13.	Excuses made by our first Parents, after their Fall	31
7.	iii. 15.	The Seed of the Woman	36
8.	iii. 21—24.	The Way of Salvation illustrated to our first Parents	40
9.	iv. 8—10.	The Death of Abel	46
10.	iv. 26.	Institution of Public Worship	51
11.	v. 24.	Enoch's Walking with God	56
12.	vi. 3.	Strivings of the Spirit	60
13.	vi. 5.	Extent of Man's Wickedness	66
14.	vi. 6, 7.	God's Determination to destroy Man	70
15.	vi. 22.	Noah's Obedience	75
16.	vii. 1.	Preservation of Noah	78
17.	ix. 12—16.	God's Covenant with Noah	85
18.	xi. 4—8.	Confusion of Tongues	90
19.	xii. 1—4.	Call of Abram	96
20.	xii. 5.	Abram's Journey to Canaan	100
21.	xiii. 8—11.	Separation of Abram and Lot	105
22.	xiv. 18—20.	Melchizedec blessing Abram	110
23.	xv. 1.	Encouragement to the Fearful	116
24.	xv. 5, 6.	Abram justified by Faith	118
25.	xv. 8.	Covenant confirmed to Abram	125
26.	xvi. 13.	The Omniscience of God	131
27.	xvii. 9, 10.	Circumcision of Abraham	133
28.	xviii. 13, 14.	Sarah reproved for her Unbelief	139
29.	xviii. 19.	Abraham's Care of his Family	144

Discourse.	Text.	Subject.	Page.
	GENESIS		
30.	xviii. 32.	Abraham's Intercession for Sodom	150
31.	xix. 17.	Lot delivered out of Sodom	157
32.	xx. 9.	Abraham reproved for denying his Wife	163
33.	xxi. 9, 10.	Abraham casting out Hagar and Ishmael	169
34.	xxii. 6—10.	Isaac a Type of Christ	175
35.	xxii. 12.	Importance of Evidences	179
36.	xxii. 14.	Jehovah-jireh, the Lord will provide	183
37.	xxii. 18.	Abraham's promised Seed	190
38.	xxiii. 17, 18.	Abraham purchasing a Burying-Place in Canaan	193
39.	xxiv. 2—4.	Marriage of Isaac	198
40.	xxv. 23.	Jacob preferred before Esau	205
41.	xxv. 32.	The Birthright typical of the Christian's Portion	211
42.	xxvii. 35.	Jacob obtaining the Blessing	215
43.	xxviii. 12, 13.	Jacob's Vision a Type of the Ministration of Angels to Christ	222
44.	xxviii. 15.	The Manner in which God dispenses his Favours	225
45.	xxviii. 16—19.	Jacob's Pillar at Beth-el	229
46.	xxviii. 20—22.	Jacob's Vow	239
47.	xxxii. 26.	Jacob pleading with God	245
48.	xxxiii. 4.	Reconciliation of Esau and Jacob	251
49.	xxxiv. 31.	Slaughter of the Shechemites	256
50.	xxxvii. 4.	Joseph envied by his Brethren	260
51.	xxxix. 9.	The Need of fleeing from Sin with Abhorrence	264
52.	xl. 23.	Ingratitude of Pharaoh's Butler	269
53.	xli. 41.	Joseph's Advancement	273
54.	xlii. 21.	The Power of Conscience	276
55.	xlii. 36.	Jacob's unbelieving Fears	282
56.	xlv. 8.	God viewed in Joseph's Advancement,	286
57.	xlv. 27, 28.	Jacob's Resolution to visit Joseph in Egypt	291
58.	xlvii. 7—10.	Jacob's Interview with Pharaoh	297
59.	xlviii. 15, 16.	Jacob blessing the Sons of Joseph	300
60.	xlix. 10.	Christ the true Shiloh	305

Discourse.	Text.	Subject.	Page.
	GENESIS		
61.	xlix. 22—24.	Joseph a Type of Christ	309
62.	l. 15—17.	Joseph's Brethren fulfilling the Prophecy respecting them	314
	EXODUS		
63.	iii. 2, 3.	The Burning Bush	319
64.	iii. 12.	God's Presence with his People	322
65.	iii. 14.	The Self-Existence and Immutability of God	327
66.	iv. 10—14.	Moses declining the Commission given him	330
67.	v. 2.	Pharaoh's Impiety	334
68.	v. 17, 18.	The Opposition that is made to Religion,	339
69.	vi. 9.	The Despondency of Israel	343
70.	vii. 3.	God hardening Pharaoh's Heart	347
71.	ix. 16.	Pharaoh's Elevation to the Throne of Egypt	352
72.	ix. 20, 21.	The Danger of disregarding the Word of God	358
73.	x. 3.	On delaying our Repentance	362
74.	x. 23.	Distinguishing Privileges of the Lord's People	367
75.	xi. 7.	God puts a Difference between his People and others	371
76.	xii. 41, 42.	Redemption celebrated	373
77.	xii. 3—11.	The Passover	377
78.	xii. 21—23.	Deliverance of the Israelites from the Destroying Angel	381
79.	xiii. 14—16.	Redemption of the First-born	385
80.	xiii. 17, 18.	God's Condescension to his People's Weakness	389
81.	xiii. 21, 22.	The Pillar and the Cloud	394
82.	xiv. 15.	The Command given to the Israelites in their Straits	398
83.	xiv. 31.	Israel's Deliverance at the Red Sea	403
84.	xv. 11.	The Character of God	407
85.	xv. 24, 25.	The Waters of Marah sweetened	410
86.	xv. 26.	Christ the Healer of his People	414
87.	xvi. 16—18.	Scriptural Equality	419

CONTENTS.

Discourse.	Text.	Subject.	Page.
	EXODUS		
88.	xvi. 35.	Sending of the Manna	426
89.	xvii. 5, 6.	Moses striking the Rock	429
90.	xvii. 11.	The History of the Jews typical of Christian Experience	432
91.	xix. 3—6.	Moses' Message to the Israelites	436
92.	xx. 18, 19.	The Giving of the Law	441
93.	xxiii. 13.	On Circumspection	444
94.	xxiii. 20—22.	The Danger of wilful and obstinate Disobedience	449
95.	xxiii. 29, 30.	The Victories of Israel gradual and progressive	452
96.	xxiv. 6—8.	God's Covenant with Israel	458
97.	xxiv. 11.	A Sight of God is a Feast to the Soul	463
98.	xxv. 8, 9.	The Command to build the Tabernacle	467
99.	xxviii. 29, 30.	Aaron's Breast-Plate	471
100.	xxviii. 36—38.	Aaron's Mitre	475
101.	xxx. 7—10.	The Altar of Incense	478
102.	xxx. 14—16.	The Atonement-Money	484
103.	xxx. 25—31.	The Anointing Oil	488
104.	xxxi. 6.	God the Source of all Wisdom	492
105.	xxxii. 19, 20.	Moses' Indignation against the Worshippers of the Golden Calf	497
106.	xxxii. 26.	The Lord's People to be decided and firm	503
107.	xxxii. 31—33.	Moses intercedes for Israel	508
108.	xxxiii. 5, 6.	Repentance of the Israelites	514
109.	xxxiii. 12, 13.	Past Mercies pleaded before God	519
110.	xxxiii. 14.	God's Presence with his Church	524
111.	xxxiii. 18, 19.	God's Goodness his Glory	527
112.	xxxiv. 5—7.	The Perfections of God	533
113.	xxxiv. 14.	Jehovah a jealous God	540
114.	xxxiv. 23, 24.	The three yearly Feasts at Jerusalem	543
115.	xxxiv. 35.	The Veil of Moses	548
116.	xxxvi. 5—7.	The Offerings for the Tabernacle	553
117.	xl. 1, 2.	The Tabernacle Service commenced	556
118.	xl. 33, 34.	Erecting of the Tabernacle	560

CONTENTS.

Discourse.	Text.	Subject.	Page.
	LEVITICUS		
119.	i. 3, 4.	The Burnt-Offering	565
120.	ii. 1—3.	The Meat-Offering	570
121.	ii. 13.	The Meat-Offering a Type of Christ .	576
122.	ii. 14—16.	Green Ears of Corn to be offered . .	581
123.	v. 5, 6.	The Sin and Trespass-Offerings compared	586
124.	v. 17—19.	The Trespass-Offering a Type of Christ	592
125.	vi. 13.	Fire on the Altar not to go out . .	598
126.	vii. 11.	The Peace-Offering	604
127.	ix. 23, 24.	God's Acceptance of the Sacrifices .	608
128.	x. 1—3.	Death of Nadab and Abihu . . .	613
129.	xiii. 45, 46.	The Laws relating to Leprosy . . .	616
130.	xiv. 4—9.	Purification of the Leper	621
131.	xiv. 14—18.	The Cleansing of the Leper . . .	625
132.	xvi. 21, 22.	The Scape-Goat a Type of Christ .	631
133.	xvi. 29, 30, 33.	Duties required on the great Day of Atonement	634
134.	xvii. 10—12.	The Prohibition to eat Blood . . .	639
135.	xxiii. 15—17.	Feast of First-Fruits	644
136.	xxiii. 23—25.	The Feast of Trumpets	648
137.	xxiii. 39—43.	Feast of Tabernacles	652
138.	xxiv. 1—3.	The Golden Candlestick	657
139.	xxiv. 5—9.	The Shew-Bread	661
140.	xxiv. 13—15.	The Blasphemer stoned	665
141.	xxv. 9—11.	The Jubilee a Type of the Gospel .	669
142.	xxv. 20—22.	The Sabbatical Year	674
143.	xxvi. 40—42.	God's Promises to Penitents . . .	679

GENESIS

OUTLINE NO. 1

CREATION OF MAN.

Gen. i. 26. *And God said, Let us make man in our image, after our likeness.*

THOUGH men constantly trace their origin to their immediate parents, and frequently to their remoter ancestors, yet they rarely consider When, or How they first came into existence, or Whether any change has taken place in their nature since they came out of their Creator's hands. That there was a period when no such creature as man existed, even reason itself would teach us; for every effect must proceed from some cause: and therefore the formation of man, however remotely we trace his origin, must, in the first instance, have been the product of some intelligent Being, who was eternally self-existent. But we are not left to the uncertain deductions of reason: God has been pleased to reveal unto us (what could not otherwise have been known [a]) the time and manner of our creation, together with the state in which we were created. And these are the subjects which we would now propose for your consideration:

I. The circumstances of our creation—

---

[a] Heb. xi. 3.

We may not unprofitably notice somewhat respecting *the time*—

[Five days had been occupied in reducing to order the confused chaos, and in furnishing the world with whatever could enrich or adorn it. On the sixth, God formed man, whom he reserved to the last, as being the most excellent of his works; and whose formation he delayed, till every thing in this habitable globe was fitted for his accommodation. It is not for us to inquire why God chose this space of time for the completion of his work, when he could as easily have formed it all in an instant: but one instructive lesson at least we may learn from the survey which he took of every day's work; it teaches his creatures to review their works from day to day, in order that, if they find them to have been good, they may be excited to gratitude; or, if they perceive them to have been evil, they may be led to repentance. At the close of every day, God pronounced his work to be "good:" but when man was formed, and the harmony of all the parts, together with the conduciveness of each to its proper end, and the subserviency of every part to the good of the whole, were fully manifest, then he pronounced the whole to be "*very* good." From this also we learn, that it is not one work or two, however good in themselves, that should fully satisfy our minds; but a comprehensive view of all our works, as harmonizing with each other, and corresponding with all the ends of our creation.]

In *the manner* of our creation there is something worthy of very peculiar attention—

[In the formation of all other things God merely exercised his own sovereign will, saying, "Let there be light," "Let such and such things take place." But in the creation of man we behold the language of consultation; "Let us make man." There is not the least reason to suppose that this was a mere form of speech, like that which obtains among monarchs at this day; for this is quite a modern refinement: nor can it be an address to angels; for they had nothing to do in the formation of man: it is an address to the Son, and to the Holy Ghost, both of whom co-operated in the formation of Him who was to be the master-piece of divine wisdom and power[b]. This appears from a still more striking expression, which occurs afterwards; where God says, "Now man is become like *one of us*, to know good and evil[c]." And it is confirmed in a variety of other

---

[b] The work of Creation is ascribed to Jesus Christ, John i. 1—3. and to the Holy Ghost, Gen. i. 2. Job xxvi. 13. and xxxiii. 4.

[c] Gen. iii. 22.

passages, where God, *under the character of our " Creator,"* or *" Maker,"* is spoken of in the plural number [d].

We must not however suppose that there are three Gods: there certainly is but One God; and His unity is as clear as his existence: and this is intentionally marked in the very verse following our text; where the expressions, *" us "* and *" our "* are turned into *" he"* and *" his:"*—" God created man in *his* own image; in the image of God created *he* him."

Here, then, we may see an early intimation of the *Trinity in Unity;* a doctrine which pervades the whole Bible, and is the very corner-stone of our holy religion. And it is deserving of particular notice, that, in our dedication to our Creator at our baptism, we are expressly required to acknowledge this mysterious doctrine, being " baptized in the name of the Father, and of the Son, and of the Holy Ghost [e]."]

The text informs us further respecting,

II. The state in which we were created—

There was some " likeness" to God even in the nature of man. " God is a spirit," who thinks, and wills, and acts. Man also has a spirit, distinct from his body, or from the mere animal life: he has a thinking, willing substance, which acts upon matter by the mere exercise of its own volitions, except when the material substance on which it operates is bereft of its proper faculties, or impeded in the use of them. But the image of God in which man was formed, is, properly, two-fold:

1. Intellectual—

[" God is a God of knowledge." He has a perfect discernment of every thing in the whole creation. Such, too, was Adam in his first formation. Before he had had any opportunity to make observations on the beasts of the field and the birds of the air, he gave names to every one of them, suited to their several natures, and distinctive of their proper characters. But it was not merely in things natural that Adam was so well instructed: he doubtless had just views of God, his nature and perfections: he had also a thorough knowledge of himself, of his duties, his interests, his happiness. There was no one thing which could conduce either to his felicity or usefulness, which was not made known to him, as far as he needed to be instructed in it. As God is light

---

[d] See Job xxxv. 10. Isaiah liv. 5. Eccl. xii. 1. These are all plural *in the original.*

[e] Matt. xxviii. 19.

without any mixture or shade of darkness[f], so was Adam, in reference to all those things at least which he was at all concerned to know.]

2. Moral—

[Holiness is no less characteristic of the Deity than wisdom. He loves every thing that is good, and infinitely abhors every thing that is evil. Every one of His perfections is holy. In this respect, also, did man bear a resemblance to his Maker. "God made him upright[g]." As he had a view of the commandment in all its breadth, so had he a conformity to it in all his dispositions and actions. He felt no reluctance in obeying it: his will was in perfect unison with the will of his Maker. All the inferior appetites were in habitual subjection to his reason, which also was in subjection to the commands of God. We are told respecting the Lord Jesus Christ, that he was "the image of God[h]," "the image of the invisible God[i]," "the express image of his person[k]." What the Lord Jesus Christ, therefore, was upon earth, *that* was man in Paradise—"holy, harmless, undefiled[l]."

That man's resemblance to his Maker did indeed consist in these two things, is manifest; because our renewal after the divine image is expressly said to be in knowledge[m], and in true holiness[n]. Well, therefore, does the Apostle say of man, that "he is the image and glory of God[o]."]

INFER

1. What an awful change has sin brought into the world!

[Survey the character before drawn: and compare it with men in the present state: "How is the gold become dim, and the fine gold changed!" Men are now enveloped in darkness, and immersed in sin. They "know nothing as they ought to know," and do nothing as they ought to do it. No words can adequately express the blindness of their minds, or the depravity of their hearts.———Yet all this has resulted from that one sin which Adam committed in Paradise. He lost the divine image from his own soul; and "begat a son in his own fallen likeness:" and the streams that have been flowing for nearly six thousand years from that polluted fountain, are still as corrupt as ever. O that we habitually considered sin in this light, and regarded it as the one source of all our miseries!]

[f] 1 John i. 5.   [g] Eccl. vii. 29.   [h] 2 Cor. iv. 4.
[i] Col. i. 15.   [k] Heb. i. 3.   [l] Heb. vii. 26.
[m] Col. iii. 10.   [n] Eph. iv. 24.   [o] 1 Cor. xi. 7.

2. What a glorious change will the Holy Spirit effect in the hearts of all who seek Him!

[In numberless passages, as well as in those before cited [p], the Holy Spirit is spoken of, as "renewing" our souls, and making us "new creatures [q]." What Adam was in Paradise, *that* shall we be, "according to the measure of the gift of Christ." "Instead of the thorn shall come up the fir-tree, and instead of the brier shall come up the myrtle-tree [r]." He will "open the eyes of our understanding," and cause us to "know all things" that are needful for our salvation [s]: and at the same time that he "turns us from darkness unto light, he will turn us also from the power of Satan unto God:" "He will put his laws in our *minds*, and write them in our *hearts* [t]." Let not any imagine that their case is desperate; for He who created all things out of nothing, can easily create us anew in Christ Jesus: and he will do it, if we only direct our eyes to Christ: "We all beholding as in a glass the glory of the Lord, are changed into the same image from glory to glory, even as by the Spirit of the Lord [u]."]

3. What obligations do we owe to the ever-blessed Trinity!

[If we looked no further than to our first creation, we are infinitely indebted to the sacred Three, for making us the subject of their consultation, and for co-operating to form us in the most perfect manner. But what shall we say to that other consultation, respecting the restoration of our souls? Hear, and be astonished at that gracious proposal, "Let us *restore* man *to* our image." "I," says the Father, "will pardon and accept them, if an adequate atonement can be found to satisfy the demands of justice." "Then on me be their guilt," says his only dear Son: "I will offer myself a sacrifice for them, if any one can be found to apply the virtue of it effectually to their souls, and to secure to me the purchase of my blood." "*That* shall be my charge," says the blessed Spirit: "I gladly undertake the office of enlightening, renewing, sanctifying their souls; and I will "preserve every one of them blameless unto thy heavenly kingdom." Thus, by their united efforts, is the work accomplished; and a way of access is opened for every one of us through Christ, by that one Spirit, unto the Father [x]. O let every soul rejoice in this Tri-une God! and may the Father's love, the grace of Christ, and the fellowship of the Holy Ghost, be with us all evermore! Amen.]

[p] See notes [m] and [n]   [q] 2 Cor. v. 17.   [r] Isai. lv. 13.
[s] 1 John ii. 20, 27.   [t] Heb. viii. 10.   [u] 2 Cor. iii. 18.
[x] Eph. ii. 18.

OUTLINE NO. 2

APPOINTMENT OF THE SABBATH.

Gen. ii. 2, 3. *On the seventh day, God ended his work which he had made: and he rested on the seventh day from all his work which he had made. And God blessed the seventh day, and sanctified it; because that in it he had rested from all his work, which God created and made.*

THOUGH we know no reason on God's part why he should proceed in the work of creation by slow and gradual advancement, instead of perfecting the whole at once; yet we may conceive a reason on the part of man, who is enabled thereby to take a more minute and deliberate survey of all its parts, and from every fresh discovery of the creation to derive fresh themes of praise to the Creator. This idea seems to be countenanced by the institution of a Sabbath immediately after the completion of the sixth day's work. At all events, this is the improvement which it becomes us to make of the Sabbath: in speaking of which we shall shew,

I. The reason of its appointment—

God, after finishing his work, " rested, and was refreshed[a]." Whether this expression be merely a figure taken from what is experienced by us after any laborious and successful exertion, or whether it intimate the complacency which God felt, as it were, on a review of his works, we cannot absolutely determine. But his sanctifying of the seventh day in consequence of that rest, shews, that he consulted,

1. His own glory—

[As "God made all things for himself," so he instituted the Sabbath in order that his rational creatures might have stated opportunities of paying him their tribute of prayer and praise. If no period had been fixed by him for the solemnities of public worship, it would have been impossible to bring mankind to an agreement respecting the time when they should render unto him their united homage. They

---

[a] Exod. xxxi. 17.

2.] APPOINTMENT OF THE SABBATH. 7

would all acknowledge the propriety of serving him in concert; but each would be ready to consult his own convenience; a difference of sentiment also would obtain respecting the portion of time that should be allotted to his service: and thus there would never be one hour when all should join together in celebrating their Creator's praise. But by an authoritative separation of the seventh day, God has secured, that the whole creation shall acknowledge him, and that His goodness shall be had in everlasting remembrance. In this view, God himself, speaking of the Sabbath *which he had instituted at the creation*, and the observance of which he was, with some additional reasons, enforcing on the Jews, calls it "*a sign*" between him and them, that they might know that he is the Lord[b].]

2. His people's good—

[Though men might have worshipped God in secret, yet the appointment of a certain day to be entirely devoted to His service, had a tendency to spiritualize their minds, and to make every one in some respect useful in furthering the welfare of the whole community. Sympathy is a powerful principle in the human breast: and the sight of others devoutly occupied in holy exercises, is calculated to quicken the drowsy soul. The very circumstance of multitudes meeting together with raised expectations and heavenly affections, must operate like an assemblage of burning coals, all of which are instrumental to the kindling of others, while they receive in themselves fresh ardour from the contact.

A further benefit from the appointment of the Sabbath is, that the attention of all must necessarily be directed to the eternal Sabbath, which awaits them at the expiration of their appointed week of labour. Each revolving Sabbath, freed from the distractions of worldly care, and attended, not merely with bodily rest, but with a rest of the soul in God, must be to them an earnest and foretaste of heaven itself. Well therefore does Nehemiah number the Sabbath among the richest benefits which God had conferred upon his chosen people[c].]

But as some have thought the Sabbath to be a mere Jewish institution, which, like the rest of the ceremonial law, is abrogated and annulled, we shall proceed to shew,

II. The continuance of its obligation—

That there was something *ceremonial* in the Jewish Sabbath, we readily acknowledge: but there was

[b] Exod. xxxi. 13, 17.   [c] Neh. ix. 14.

something *moral* also; and therefore, as to the moral part of it, it must, of necessity, be of perpetual obligation. To remove all doubt on this important subject, consider,

1. The time of its institution—

[Some have thought that the mention which is made of the Sabbath in the words before us, was merely by anticipation; and that the appointment never took place till the days of Moses. But if this were the case, how came Moses to specify the circumstance of God's resting on the seventh day as the reason of that appointment[d]? It would have been a good reason for our first parents and their immediate descendants to hallow the seventh day; but it could be no reason at all to those who lived almost five-and-twenty hundred years after the event; more especially when so obvious and cogent a reason as their deliverance out of Egypt was assigned at the very same time[e]. But if the command given to the Jews was a repetition of the injunction given to Adam, then there is an obvious propriety in assigning the reason that was obligatory upon all, as well as that which formed an additional obligation on the Jewish nation in particular.

Besides, there are traces of a Sabbath from the beginning of the world. For, if no Sabbath had ever been given, whence came the practice of measuring time by weeks? Yet that custom obtained both in the patriarchal[f] and antediluvian ages[g]: and therefore, since it accords so exactly with what was afterwards instituted by divine authority, we may well infer its original appointment by God himself. And if its obligation existed so many ages before the ceremonial law was given, then must it continue to exist after that law is abolished.]

2. The manner of its re-establishment—

[Notwithstanding the long continuance of the Jews in Egypt, the remembrance of the Sabbath was not effaced: for Moses, *before the giving of the law*, speaks of the Sabbath as an institution known and received among them[h]. And, *without any express direction*, they gathered on the sixth day a double portion of manna to serve them on the Sabbath; which they would not have done, if they had not thought the observance of the Sabbath to be of the first importance[i].

---

[d] Exod. xx. 11.   [e] Deut. v. 15.   [f] Gen. xxix. 27, 28.
[g] Gen. viii. 10, 12.   [h] Exod. xvi. 23.
[i] Exod. xvi. 22. That they did this without any direction from Moses, is evident from the complaint which the Rulers made on the occasion; for which complaint there could have been no ground, if any direction had been given.

APPOINTMENT OF THE SABBATH.

Nevertheless, for the more effectual maintenance of its authority, God judged it necessary to publish it to them again, both upon the original grounds, and on other special grounds peculiar to that people. And how did he publish it? Did he deliver it to Moses in the same manner as he did the *ceremonial* law? No: he wrote it with his own finger in tables of stone, and embodied it with the *moral* law [k]. Surely this affords a very strong presumption that God himself considered its duties, not as ceremonial, limited, and transient, but as moral, universal, and permanent.]

3. The confirmation of it by the Prophets—

[That its obligations should be sanctioned by the prophets, we might well expect; because they lived under the authority of the Jewish law. The mere circumstance, therefore, of their insisting on the observation of the Sabbath would prove nothing. But their speaking of the Sabbath, as to be observed under the Christian dispensation, very strongly corroborates the perpetuity of its obligations. Now the prophet Isaiah does speak of the Sabbath in such a connexion, that we cannot doubt of its referring to the times of the Gospel: and he represents the "keeping of the Sabbath" as no less necessary to our happiness, than the laying hold of Christ's righteousness and salvation [l]. We can scarcely think that the prophet would have so strongly marked the continuance of the Sabbath, if its obligations were to cease with the ceremonial law.]

4. The observation of it by the Apostles—

[The precise day on which the Jews kept their Sabbath, was indeed changed; and the first day of the week was substituted for the seventh. This was done in order to commemorate the resurrection of our blessed Lord; an event, the most interesting that ever occurred from the foundation of the world; an event which proved, beyond all doubt, the Messiahship of Jesus, and has served from that time as the corner-stone of all our hopes [m]. When Israel was brought out of Egypt, God, in order to commemorate that deliverance, changed the commencement of the year from the Autumn to the Spring [n]: can we wonder then, that, in remembrance of an infinitely greater deliverance, he should alter the day on which the Sabbath had been observed? It was in the appropriation of a seventh part of our time to God, that the morality of the Sabbath consisted; and that is preserved under the Christian, as much as under the Jewish economy.

---

[k] Deut. x. 3, 4.
[m] Acts iv. 10—12.
[l] Isai. lvi. 1, 2.
[n] Exod. xii. 2.

This change was sanctioned by our blessed Lord, who *repeatedly selected that day* for the more public exhibition of himself to his disciples°; and on that day sent down the Holy Ghost upon them ᵖ; in order that the application, as well as the completion of his redemption, might give a further sanctity to the new-appointed day.

From that time the first day of the week was invariably observed for the public services of the church ᵍ; and, to stamp peculiar honour upon it, it was distinguished by that endearing name, "The Lord's day ʳ."

Who that weighs all these arguments, can doubt the continued obligation of the Sabbath?]

For the regulation of our conduct on the Sabbath, we should inquire into,

III. The nature of its requirements—

The same *kind* of strictness is not required of us as was enjoined under the law—

[We have before said, that there was something of a ceremonial nature in the Jewish Sabbath. The Jews in the wilderness were not permitted to leave their habitations on the Sabbath-day ˢ, except to assemble for divine worship; and the portion of manna which they gathered on the preceding day for the consumption of that day, was, for the space of forty years, kept fit for their use upon the Sabbath by a constant miracle, on purpose that they might have no excuse for transgressing the divine command ᵗ. They were forbidden even to kindle a fire on the Sabbath-day ᵘ, or to do any species of servile work. But all this rigour is not necessary now: it was suited to the burthensome dispensation of the law; but not to the more liberal dispensation under which we live. Indeed, our blessed Lord has shewn us clearly that works of necessity ˣ, or of mercy ʸ, may be performed on that as well as any other day. Being himself "the Lord of the Sabbath-day," he dispensed with those rites which were merely temporary, and requires of us such services only as a spiritual mind will most delight in.]

Our sanctification of the Sabbath should consist rather in mental than in bodily exercises—

° Luke xxiv. 13, 33, 36, 40, 45. John xx. 19, 26.

ᵖ This is ascertained by calculators, as well as from its being the seventh Sabbath after his resurrection.

ᵍ Acts xx. 7.   1 Cor. xvi. 1, 2.   ʳ Rev. i. 10.

ˢ Exod. xvi. 29.   ᵗ Exod. xvi. 24.   ᵘ Exod. xxxv. 3.

ˣ Matt. xii. 1—8.   ʸ Matt. xii. 10—13.

APPOINTMENT OF THE SABBATH.

[What are the proper employments for our minds, the prophet Isaiah has plainly told us: "We should account the Sabbath a delight, the holy of the Lord, honourable; and should honour him, not doing our own ways, nor finding our own pleasure, nor speaking our own words[z]." We should endeavour to have our thoughts abstracted from the world, and to fix them with intenseness and delight on heavenly objects. On every day we should present to God our sacrifices of prayer and praise: but as, under the law, the accustomed sacrifices, both of the morning and evening, were doubled upon the Sabbath[a], so, under the Gospel, we should have our minds doubly occupied in the service of our God.]

The subject before us suggests ample matter,

1. For reproof—

[Many, very many there are who hate the duties of the Sabbath; and, breaking through all the restraints of conscience, follow without remorse their usual occupations. Others, complying with the established forms, cry, "What a weariness is it[b]!" When shall the Sabbath be over, that I may prosecute more pleasing or more profitable employments[c]? When they come up to the house of God, they find no pleasure in his service, but are rather, like Doeg, "detained before the Lord[d]." Some, indeed, conceiving that they are doing somewhat meritorious, spend without reluctance the time allotted for public service; but, though they draw nigh to God with their lips, their hearts are far from him[e]. It is not such worshippers that God seeks or approves; nor is such the sanctification of the Sabbath that he requires. On the contrary, he is indignant against all such profaneness or hypocrisy; and declares that such persons "worship him in vain.[f]" Whatever such persons may imagine, they indeed profane the Sabbath. And what the consequence will be, they may form some judgment, from the punishment inflicted on the man who gathered sticks upon the Sabbath-day. By God's express command, he was stoned to death[g]. If, then, so heavy a sentence was executed upon him by the direction of the Most High, can we suppose that God is more indifferent about the conduct of his creatures now? or that he has loaded them with mercies for no other end than to give them a greater licence to sin? Let us well consider this: for "if they, who despised Moses' law, died without mercy," surely a far sorer punishment awaits us, if, with our additional obligations, we disregard the wonders of redeeming love[h].]

[z] Isaiah lviii. 13.   [a] Numb. xxviii. 9, 10.   [b] Mal. i. 13.
[c] Amos viii. 5.   [d] 1 Sam. xxi. 7.   [e] Matt. xv. 8.
[f] Matt. xv. 9.   [g] Numb. xv. 32—36.   [h] Heb. x. 28, 29.

2. For encouragement—

[Not only personal, but even national judgments may be expected for the violation of the Sabbath[i]. But, on the other hand, every blessing may be expected, both by individuals[k] and the community[l], if the Sabbath be habitually and conscientiously improved. Indeed, it seems almost impossible that any one who sets himself in earnest to improve the Sabbath-day, should ever perish. God would bless to such an one the ordinances of his grace; and rather send him instruction in some extraordinary way, than suffer him to use the means in vain[m]. We can appeal to all who have ever laboured to sanctify the Sabbath, whether they have not found their labour well repaid? Surely " God has never said to any, ' Seek ye my face in vain ': " and the more diligently we keep his Sabbaths below, the more shall we be fitted for our eternal rest.]

[i] Jer. xvii. 27.   [k] Isaiah lvi. 4—7.   [l] Jer. xvii. 24—26.   [m] Acts viii. 27—35. and x. 1—21.

OUTLINE NO. 3

COVENANT MADE WITH ADAM.

Gen. ii. 16, 17. *And the Lord God commanded the man, saying, Of every tree of the garden thou mayest freely eat: but of the tree of the knowledge of good and evil thou shalt not eat of it: for in the day that thou eatest thereof thou shalt surely die.*

WHEN the creation was formed, it was proper that every part of it should shew forth the Creator's glory, and, as far as its peculiar nature and capacity would admit of, fulfil his will. The sun and moon and stars being inanimate bodies, it was sufficient for them to move with regularity in their respective orbits. The creatures that were endued with life, were to follow their respective instincts, and, according to their abilities, to yield obedience to man, who was God's vicegerent over them. To man more had been given: of him, therefore, was more required. He was endued with understanding and will: he was capable of knowing what he owed to his Maker, and of exercising discretion in performing it. To him therefore, in addition to the moral law which was written on his heart, and from which he could not deviate without opposing all his innate propensities, a positive precept was given: the will of his Creator was enacted into a law: and that which was indifferent in itself, was made a test of its obedience. All the trees in Paradise were given to him for the nourishment and support of his body. But that he might have an opportunity of acknowledging his dependence on God, and his ready submission to the divine will, one tree was excepted; and the use of it was prohibited under the severest penalties. This prohibition is to be the subject of our present consideration: and, in order that it may be understood in all its bearings and relations, we shall endeavour to explain,

I. Its import—

The name given to the forbidden tree strongly marked the importance of abstaining from it—

[Adam was created in the perfect image of his God. He knew every thing that was good, but nothing that was evil. This was his honour and his felicity. The knowledge of evil would have marred, rather than augmented, his happiness. Such knowledge, if speculative, would be only vain; if practical, be ruinous. We have no reason to think that the fruit of the tree was at all noxious in itself; but, as being forbidden, it could not be eaten without guilt: and therefore the designation given to the tree itself was a standing memorial to Adam on no account to touch it; since by eating of it he would attain the knowledge of evil, which, through the perfection of his nature, he was hitherto unacquainted with.]

The necessity of abstaining from it was yet more awfully inculcated in the penalty annexed to disobedience—

[The death which, in the event of his transgressing the command, was denounced against him, was three-fold; it was temporal, spiritual, eternal. His body, which had not in it naturally the seeds of dissolution, was to be given up a prey to various diseases, and at last to return to the dust from which it sprang. His soul was to lose both the image and enjoyment of God, and to be consigned over to the influence of every thing that was earthly, sensual, and devilish. And, after a certain period, both his body and soul were to be "cast into the lake which burneth with fire and brimstone; which is the second death."

That such was the penalty, appears from the event: for, upon transgressing the divine command, he became mortal: a change also instantly took place in his intellectual and moral faculties; as he shewed, by attempting to hide himself from God, with whom he had hitherto maintained the most familiar converse. The eternal duration of his punishment may be inferred from the penalty annexed to sin at this time: for if the wages of sin be eternal death *now*, there can be no doubt but that it was so *then*[a].

There was, however, an *implied* promise, that, if he persevered in his obedience, he should live for ever. In the law which God has since published, and to which the same penalty is annexed for disobedience, we are assured, that whoso doeth the things which are commanded, shall live in them[b]: from whence we may conclude, that there was a similar reward prepared for Adam, if he should continue to obey his God. It is true that the law can not give us life now[c]; but that is not owing to any change in God's regard for obedience, but to our incapacity to render that obedience which his law requires[d]. If we could keep all the commandments, we should, by keeping them, enter into life[e]. And it is manifest that the same reward would have been given to Adam; since we are told, that "the law was ordained to life[f]."]

The import of the prohibition being made clear, let us consider,

II. Its nature—

It could not be expected that in so brief a history as that before us, every minute particular should be explained: indeed, it was intended that the subsequent revelations of God's will should clear up things which were left in a state of obscurity. Now from other parts of scripture we find, that this prohibition was, in reality, *a covenant;* in which, not Adam only, but all his posterity were interested. In this covenant, Adam was the head and representative of all his seed; and *they*, to the remotest generations, were

---

[a] In Rom. vi. 23. death, which is the wages of sin, and the life which is the gift of God, are contrasted; both being of the same duration. Compare also Matt. xxv. 46.

[b] Compare Deut. xxvii. 26. and Gal. iii. 10. with Lev. xviii. 5. and Rom. x. 5. and Gal. iii. 12.   [c] Gal. iii. 21.

[d] Rom. viii. 3, 4.   [e] Matt. xix. 17.   [f] Rom. vii. 10.

to stand or fall in him. In proof of this we may observe that,

1. In this prohibition are contained all the constituent parts of a covenant—

[Here are *the parties;* God on the one side; and Adam, for himself and all his posterity, on the other. Here are *the terms* expressly declared: there was a condition prescribed, namely, that Adam should obey the divine mandate; on his performance of which condition, he had a promise of life; but on his neglecting to perform it, a threatening of death. Lastly, there was also *a seal* annexed to the covenant: as the rainbow was a seal of the covenant made with Noah; and circumcision and baptism were the seals of the Abrahamic and Christian covenants; so "the tree of life" was a seal of the covenant made with Adam[g]; it was a pledge to Adam, that, on his fulfilling the conditions imposed upon him, he should participate the promised reward.]

2. The consequences flowing from the transgression of it, prove it to have been a covenant—

[Death and condemnation were the immediate consequences of Adam's sin. Nor were these confined to the immediate transgressor; they were entailed on his remotest posterity: by that one act of his all his children are constituted sinners, and are consigned over to death and condemnation. Both scripture and experience attest this melancholy truth[h]. Now how can we account for so many millions of persons being involved in his punishment, if they were not in some way or other involved also in his guilt? Surely " the Judge of all the earth will do right;" and therefore, when we behold punishment inflicted on so many beings, who were once formed after the divine image, we may be sure that in the sight of God they are considered as guilty; and, as infants cannot have contracted guilt in their own persons, they must have derived it from Adam, by whom they were represented, and in whom they died.]

3. It is represented as exactly corresponding with the covenant which God made with Christ on our behalf—

[Nothing can be more laboured than the parallel which St. Paul draws between Adam and Christ in the passage we have just referred to. Not content with tracing all evil to

---

[g] Gen. ix. 8—17. Rom. iv. 11.

[h] How often is it repeated, that all these evils proceeded from the offence of *one* man! See Rom. v. 12—19.

the offence of one, he declares that that one person, even Adam, was "a type or *figure of Him who was to come;*" and that *as* death and condemnation came by the offence of ONE, that is, Adam; *so* righteousness and life come by the obedience of ONE, even Christ[i]. In another place he draws precisely the same parallel, representing Christ as "the second man," "the last Adam[k];" and affirming, that "*as* in Adam all died, *so* in Christ shall all be made alive[l]."

These things collectively, clearly prove, that the prohibition was not a mere personal concern with Adam, but that it was a covenant made with him on behalf of himself and all his posterity.

If it be thought strange that God should make other persons responsible for Adam's conduct; we answer, that, amongst ourselves, the happiness of children is greatly involved in the conduct of their parents; and that God expressly avows, on another occasion, that he did make a covenant with some on behalf of others who were yet unborn[m]: and if he did it on one occasion, he might with equal propriety do it on another.]

But lest there should lurk in the mind any dissatisfaction with this mysterious appointment, we proceed to shew,

III. Its reasonableness—

Consider its reasonableness,

1. As a prohibition—

[If the will of the Maker were to be enacted into a law, for the purpose of trying the obedience of man, we cannot conceive a more easy and simple method than the prohibiting the use of one single tree amidst the thousands which were laden with the choicest fruits. If God had prohibited all except one, it would have been highly reasonable that He should be obeyed, seeing that they were all the works of His hands, and He was at liberty to give or withhold, as it seemed to Him good. But when He gave the free enjoyment of all, and denied him only one, certainly nothing could be more reasonable than that His will should be honoured by a cheerful compliance.

Nor was it less reasonable that the prohibition should be enforced with so severe a penalty: for the object of the penalty was, to keep Adam from transgression, and to shut him up under a necessity of continuing holy and happy: and

---

[i] Rom. v. 12—19.
[l] 1 Cor. xv. 22.
[k] 1 Cor. xv. 45, 47.
[m] Deut. xxix. 14, 15.

therefore the more awful the sanctions were, the more likely they were to answer the desired end; and the more gracious was God in annexing them to the prohibition.]

2. As a covenant—

[It is but a small thing to say concerning the covenan , that it was just: we go much further; and affirm, that it was in the highest degree favourable and advantageous to all who were interested in it. Consider the state in which Adam was, when subjected to the temptation; and compare with it the state in which *we* should meet temptation, supposing every one of us to be called forth to the trial as soon as ever we entered into the world: *he* was perfect; *we* are imperfect: *he* was in full possession of all his faculties; *we* should begin our conflict while all the powers of our souls were in a state of infantine weakness: *he* was exposed to only one temptation, and that apparently easy to be withstood, on account of his having no evil disposition to close with it; *we* should be assaulted with ten thousand temptations, with every one of which we have a proneness to comply: *he* conflicted with his enemy who was yet unskilled in the work of beguiling souls; *we* should engage him after his skill has been augmented by the experience of six thousand years: *he* was fortified by the consideration that not his own happiness only, but that also of all his posterity, depended on him; whereas *we* should have no other motive to stedfastness than a regard to our own personal welfare. Let any one compare these states, and then say, whether Adam or We were more likely to fall: and if it appear that his situation was far more conducive to stability than ours, then must it be considered as a great advantage to us to have had such a person for our covenant-head. If it be said, that eventually we are sufferers by it; we may well be satisfied with it; since if he, with all his advantages, was overcome, there is no hope at all that we, under all our disadvantages, should have maintained our integrity. Nor can we doubt, but that if all the human race had been summoned before God at once to hear the proposal of having Adam for their covenant-head, every one of them would have accepted it, as a signal token of the divine goodness.]

INFER,

1. What folly is it to seek for happiness in sin!

[Depraved as every thing is by means of sin, yet is there all that we can wish for in this transient state, together with a liberty " richly to enjoy it." We have not a sense for which God has not provided a suitable and legitimate indulgence. Survey the number, brightness, magnitude, and order of the heavenly bodies; or the innumerable multitude of animate and inanimate beings, with all their variegated hues, the exquisite formation of their parts, their individual symmetry, their harmonious configuration, their wonderful adaptation to their respective ends. Can we conceive a richer feast for our eyes? Behold how the earth is strewed with flowers, that cast their perfumes to the wind, and regale us with their odours! Where, amongst all the contrivances of art, will any thing be found to equal the fruits of the earth, in the variety and richness of their flavour? or where will the sons of harmony produce such exquisite notes as the feathered tribes gratuitously afford to the meanest cottager? Take the feelings for which so many myriads of mankind sacrifice their eternal interests; and we will venture to affirm, that even those are called forth with keener sensibility and richer zest in the way of God's appointment, than they ever can be in a way of licentious and prohibited indulgence. What need have we then of forbidden fruit? If nothing were left us in this world but the favour of God and the testimony of a good conscience, we should have a feast which nothing but heaven can excel: but when, together with these, we have all that can conduce to the comfort of the body; when we have " the promise of the life that now is, as well as of that which is to come," is it not madness to seek for happiness in sin; to relinquish " the fountain of living waters, and to hew out to ourselves cisterns, broken cisterns, that can hold no water?" Let us but learn to enjoy God in every thing, and every thing in God, and we shall find that this world, polluted as it is, is yet a Paradise: with God's favour, pulse is better than royal delicacies, and the meanest dungeon is a palace.]

2. With what abhorrence should sin be viewed by us!

[Look through the creation which God pronounced to be very good, and see how all things are out of course: the earth that should nourish us, struck with barrenness; the elements that should administer to our comfort, armed against us for our destruction. See the smallest insects in the creation invading us with irresistible force, and by their united efforts desolating our fairest prospects. Look at man himself, once the image of his Maker; see with what malignant dispositions he is filled. See him passing his time here in labour and sorrow, and generation after generation swept away from the face of the earth. Follow him into the eternal world, and behold him banished from the presence of his God, and cast into a lake of fire and brimstone, there to endure the full penalty of all his crimes. Behold all this, I say, and consider that this is the work of sin. One sin introduced it all; and successive generations have lived only to complete what our first parents began. O that we could view sin in this light! O that we could bear in mind the judgment denounced against it, "In the day that thou eatest thereof thou shalt surely die!" We have warnings sufficient to intimidate the stoutest heart: "The wrath of God is revealed against all ungodliness and unrighteousness of men[n]:" "The soul that sinneth, it shall die[o]:" "Sin, when it is finished, bringeth forth death[p]." Only let sin be stripped of its deceitful attire, and be viewed in all its naked deformity, and we shall shudder even at the thought of it, and flee from it as from the face of a serpent.]

3. How thankful should we be for the tree of life!

[Blessed be God, the tree of life yet grows in the midst of us[q]. No cherubim with flaming swords obstruct our way to it; on the contrary, all the angels in heaven are ready to exert all their influence to conduct us to it; and God, even our Father, invites and intreats us to gather its life-giving fruits. This tree of life is no other than the Lord Jesus Christ: "it bears twelve manner of fruits," suited to all our various necessities; and its very "leaves are for the healing of the nations[r]." Let us then flock around this tree: let us with humble boldness stretch forth our hands to gather its fruits. We may see around us many who have already experienced its efficacy to heal the sick, and to revive the dead. Let us view the Saviour as God's instituted ordinance for this very end: and now that he is accessible unto us, let us approach him; lest haply the accepted time be terminated, and we eat for ever the bitter fruits of our transgression.]

OUTLINE NO. 4

THE SERPENT BEGUILING EVE.

Gen. iii. 4. *And the serpent said unto the woman, Ye shall not surely die.*

IN reference to the fact before us, St. Paul says, "The serpent beguiled Eve through his subtilty." And great is the subtilty which appears throughout the whole of his conduct on this occasion. He took an opportunity of addressing himself to Eve when she was alone, that so she might become an easier victim to his wiles. He insinuated his temptation

[n] Rom. i. 18.   [o] Ezek. xviii. 20.   [p] Jam. i. 15.
[q] Rev. ii. 7.   [r] Rev. xxii. 2.

first in a way of inquiry only; "Hath God said, Ye shall not eat of every tree in the garden?" By this he intimated, that she had made some mistake respecting the supposed prohibition, since it was scarcely probable that her Maker, who had granted her every thing else in the garden, should impose such an unnecessary restriction upon her. When, in answer to this, Eve informed him, that not only was the restriction really given, but that it was enforced with the most tremendous sanction that could possibly be imagined, he again insinuated that she must be under a mistake, since it could not be that so good a God should inflict so heavy a judgment for so slight an offence: "Ye shall not surely die."

Now this is the very temptation with which he has ever since, even to this present hour, assaulted unwary men, and by which he is yet daily ruining millions of the human race. We will therefore endeavour to put you on your guard against it, by shewing,

I. The falsehood of the suggestion—

Two things were here insinuated, namely, That the threatening was not of such a terrific import as she imagined; and that, whatever it might import, it should not be eventually executed. But in both these things "he lied unto her;" for,

1. God will fulfil his threatenings to whatsoever they may relate—

[See his threatenings to individuals—Ahab, in dependence on his false prophets, and on Satan who inspired them, thought to come off victorious: but, notwithstanding his device to escape the notice of the Syrians, he was slain, according to the prediction of the prophet Micaiah. Hiel the Bethelite would rebuild the city of Jericho: but did he escape the judgment denounced, many hundred years before, against any person who should presume to make the attempt? Did he not lay the foundation in the death of his first-born, and raise up the gates in the death of his youngest son[a]? See his threatenings against the whole nation of Israel: Were they not carried captive to Babylon, according to His word? and

[a] Josh. vi. 26. with 1 Kings xvi. 34.

is not the dispersion of the Jews at this day a proof, that no word of God shall ever fall to the ground? See his threatenings against the whole world—Did not the deluge come according to the prediction, and sweep away every living creature (those only excepted that were in the ark) from the face of the earth? Let us be sure that God is true: and that whatever He has spoken shall surely come to pass.]

2. He will fulfil them in the extent that is here declared—

[Death temporal, spiritual, and eternal were included in the sentence denounced against transgression: and on our first parents it came, the very day that they ate of the forbidden tree. They did not, it is true, cease on that day to live, because God had purposes to serve by their continuance in life: but the seeds of death were that day implanted in their constitution; and in due time they returned to their native dust. That they died at that very moment a spiritual death, is evident from their conduct: for they foolishly hoped to hide themselves among the trees of the garden from the eyes of the omniscient God; and offered vain excuses for their transgression, instead of humbling themselves for it before God. To eternal death also they were subjected; and to it they would have been consigned, had not God, of his infinite mercy, provided a way of deliverance from it, through that seed of the woman, who was in due time to bruise the serpent's head. If it be doubted whether God will execute so heavy a judgment on the sinners of mankind, I hesitate not to declare, that he most assuredly will; since he has himself declared it in terms that admit of no reasonable doubt [b]—and "he is not a man that he will lie, nor the son of man that he will repent."]

But since so many are deceived by this suggestion, I will endeavour to shew, more distinctly,

II. The danger of listening to it—

The effect of this sad delusion is visible in all around us. It is entirely owing to this that Satan retains so many in bondage, and leads them captive at his will.

1. Hence it is that men make so light of sin—

[Whence is it, I would ask, that men are drawn aside by every temptation, and that for a momentary gratification they will offend their God? Is it not from a secret persuasion, that God will not fulfil his threatenings, and that they may

---

[b] See Matt. xxv. 46. the Greek — and Mark ix. 43—48.— and Rev. xiv. 10, 11.

sin against him with impunity? If men saw before their eyes the instruments of torture whereby the violators of a law were to be put to a lingering and cruel death, and knew at the same time that there was no possibility of escape to any one who should transgress the law, would they incur the penalty with the same indifference that they now transgress the laws of God? How much less then would they rush into wretchedness, if they saw hell open before them, and heard the groans of those who are now suffering under the wrath of God? No verily: they would not then "make a mock at sin," but would tremble at it, and flee from it as from the face of a serpent. If then you would be preserved from sin, listen not a moment to this accursed suggestion: and if the whole world should unite in saying, "Ye shall not surely die," reply to them, "Get thee behind me, Satan," for "thou art a liar from the beginning."]

2. Hence it is also that men make so light of salvation—

[Salvation by Christ is offered to a ruined world. But who believes our report? Who receives it with that gratitude which it might well be expected that a perishing sinner should feel towards his reconciled God and Saviour? With the exception of a few, the whole world regard the Gospel as little better than a cunningly devised fable; so faint are the emotions it excites, and so transient the effects which it produces. And what is the reason of this? Is it not that men do not feel their need of such a Saviour, and that they do not believe that God's threatenings will ever be executed upon them? Yes: to this source must it be traced: for if they verily believed, that the wrath of God, which is revealed against all ungodliness and unrighteousness of men, would fall upon them, and that all their hope of escaping it was by embracing the Gospel, they would flee to Christ with their whole hearts, and cleave unto him with their whole souls, and not rest a moment till they saw themselves within the gates of the city of refuge. Were they duly sensible of their danger, even a hope, a mere peradventure that God *might* have mercy upon them, would be sufficient to make them weep before him day and night. Not a word of mercy was mixed in Jonah's message to Nineveh: yet the most distant hope of mercy was sufficient to encourage that whole city to repent in dust and ashes. What then would not all the promises of the Gospel effect, if men really felt the greatness of their guilt and danger? It is evident, that all the indifference of men about the Gospel must be traced to this one source, their believing of Satan's lie in preference to the truth of God: and, if ever the Gospel is to have a saving influence on our hearts, we must begin by rejecting this suggestion of the devil, and by believing that all the threatenings of God against sin and sinners shall assuredly be accomplished.]

OBSERVE then, on the whole,

1. What need there is of fidelity in ministers—

[Satan at this time, no less than formerly, suggests to men, " Ye shall not surely die:" and his emissaries all the world over are re-echoing the delusive sound. Every friend we have, father, mother, brother, sister, husband, wife, the very instant we begin to dread the wrath of God, unite their endeavours to compose our minds, by saying, ' There is no such penalty against sin as ye suppose, nor have you any reason to fear that it shall be inflicted on you.' Our own wicked hearts also are but too ready to adopt a sentiment so gratifying to the mind, and to speak peace to us on insufficient grounds. And what would be the consequence if ministers also favoured such delusions, and, through fear of alarming you, neglected to warn you of your danger? Would not Satan triumph to a far greater extent than he already does? Would he not be secure of his prey? Is not this the very effect produced, wherever the Gospel, instead of being preached with apostolic fidelity, is kept upon the back ground, and modified to the taste of a deluded world? Be thankful then if you hear your guilt and danger faithfully set before you: be thankful, as you would be if a man, seeing your house on fire, roused you from your slumbers, and saved you from death. And, if God have vouchsafed to you this mercy, improve it with all diligence, by fleeing from the wrath to come, and laying hold on eternal life.]

2. What a mercy it is, that, notwithstanding the truth of God in his threatenings, there is a way of salvation opened for us in the Gospel—

[Yes; God can be true, and yet absolve the sinner from his guilt: for, in Christ Jesus, "Mercy and truth are met together, righteousness and peace have kissed each other." The penalty of death has been inflicted upon the Lord Jesus Christ, as the surety and substitute of sinners: and, if we believe in him, all that he has done and suffered for us shall be so imputed to us as to be accepted of God in our behalf, so that God shall be " a just God, and yet a Saviour," yea " just, and yet the justifier" of sinful man. O blessed tidings! amply sufficient to pacify the most afflicted mind, and to warrant in our hearts the most joyful hope! Brethren, only believe in the Lord Jesus Christ, and I will adopt with confidence the very words of Satan, and say, " Ye shall not surely die." I will go further still, and from a doubtful suggestion turn them to a direct affirmation, and say, 'Surely ye shall not die.' So says our blessed Lord himself: "My sheep shall never perish:" St. Paul also says, "There is no condemnation to them that are in Christ Jesus." On this, therefore, you may rely, with the fullest possible assurance: for, if the threatenings of God shall be fulfilled, so shall also His promises be: not one of them shall ever fail, as long as the world shall stand. Fear not then to see the worst of your state: fear not to acknowledge the extent of your guilt and danger, since the provision for you in Christ Jesus is fully commensurate with your necessities, and suited to your wants. Only believe in Him, and you shall not be ashamed or confounded world without end.]

OUTLINE NO. 5

THE FALL OF MAN.

Gen. iii. 6, 7. *And when the woman saw that the tree was good for food, and that it was pleasant to the eyes, and a tree to be desired to make one wise, she took of the fruit thereof, and did eat, and gave also unto her husband with her; and he did eat. And the eyes of them both were opened.*

THE happiness of our first parents in Paradise must have far exceeded any thing which we can conceive. Formed in the image of God, they had not a desire or thought contrary to His holy will. There was no cloud upon their understanding, no undue bias on their will, nothing inordinate in their affections. With respect to outward comforts, they possessed all that they could wish. God himself had planted a garden for them, and given them the whole produce, except one tree, for their support. Above all, they enjoyed the freest intercourse with their Maker, and conversed with Him as a man converseth with his friend. But this happiness, alas! was of short continuance: for Satan, who had left his first estate, and, from being a bright angel before the throne of God, was become an apostate spirit and a wicked fiend, he, I say, envied their felicity, and sought to reduce them to the same misery with himself. An opportunity for making his attempt soon occurred. He saw the woman near the forbidden tree, and at a distance from her husband. So favourable an occasion was not to be lost. He instantly took possession of a serpent; which being confessedly the most subtle of all animals, was least likely to create suspicion in her mind, and fittest to be employed in so arduous a service. Through the instrumentality of this creature, Satan entered into conversation with her; and, as we learn from the history before us, succeeded in withdrawing both her and her husband from their allegiance to God. In the text we have a summary of the fatal tragedy: in it, as connected with the context, the whole plot is developed, and the awful catastrophe declared.

That we may have a just view of the conduct of our first parents, we shall consider,

I. Their temptation—

The scope of Satan's conversation with Eve was to persuade her that she might partake of the forbidden tree,

1. With safety—

[With this view, his first attempt was to raise doubts in her mind respecting *the prohibition*. And here his subtilty is very conspicuous; he does not shock her feelings by any strong assertion; but asks, as it were for information, whether such a prohibition as he had heard of had been really given. Nevertheless, his mode of putting the question insinuates, that he could scarcely credit the report; because the imposing of such a restraint would be contrary to the generosity which God had shewn in other respects, and to the distinguished love which he had professed to bear towards them.

Now, though he did not so far prevail as to induce her to deny that God had withheld from her the fruit of that tree, yet he gained much even in this first address: for, he led her to maintain a conversation with him: he disposed her also to soften the terms in which the prohibition had been given[a]: and though she might intend nothing more than to prevent

---

[a] God had said, "In the day that thou eatest thereof thou shalt surely die:" and she, in reporting it, said, "Ye shall not eat of it or touch it, *lest* ye die;" thus converting a most positive threatening of instant and certain death, into a gentle caution against a possible, or probable, misfortune: "Touch not, *for fear* ye die."

his entertaining any hard thoughts of God, she hereby emboldened him to prosecute his purpose in a more direct and open manner.

Improving the advantage he had already gained, he proceeded to question in direct terms the grounds of her fears, in relation to *the penalty:* "Ye shall not surely die." He here intimates, that she must be mistaken with respect both to the *extent* and *certainty* of the penalty. God could never threaten "death" for such an offence as that: he could threaten nothing worse even for the most heinous transgression that could be committed: how then could he annex that to so small a matter as the eating of a piece of fruit? At least, if he did put forth his threat, he certainly would never execute it; "Ye shall not *surely* die:" it could not be, that a just and good God should ever proceed to such rigorous measures on so slight an occasion. By this daring assertion, he quite disarmed her; and persuaded her, that she must have misunderstood the divine declaration, or, at least, that it never could be carried into effect.]

2. With advantage—

[Finding that Eve did not revolt at his impious assertions, he went on to direct and open blasphemy. He knew, that to an intelligent and holy being nothing was so desirable as knowledge: he therefore affirmed, that there was in the fruit of that tree a virtue capable of wonderfully enlarging her views, so that she and her husband should "become as gods," and possess a self-sufficiency and independence suited to that high character. In confirmation of this, he appeals to God himself; and blasphemously insinuates, that God, in withholding the fruit from them, had been actuated by nothing but envy, and a jealousy, lest they should become as wise and happy as himself.

Such was the temptation with which that "old serpent" assaulted Eve; hoping that, if he could prevail with her, he might, through her influence, overcome her husband also.]

Happy would it have been, if we could have reported of them, as we can of the second Adam, that they repelled the Tempter. But, in following the course of their history, we are constrained to notice,

II. Their sin—

Eve, overpowered by the alluring aspect of the fruit, and the hope of attaining a knowledge as superior to what she already possessed, as this serpent's was to that of all the rest of the creation, ate of the fruit, and prevailed upon her husband to partake with her[b].

Without inquiring how she prevailed with him, or what would have been the effect if she alone had fallen, let it suffice to know, that Adam transgressed in eating the forbidden fruit, and that this was the sin whereby he and all his posterity were ruined. That the offence may not be thought trivial, let us consider of what malignant qualities it was composed:

1. What pride!

[Our first parents were endowed with faculties unknown to any other creatures. While, in common with all the rest, they possessed a beautifully constructed frame of body, they had a rational soul also, which assimilated them to God; so that they were a connecting link between God and the brute creation, a kind of compound of both. Moreover, they were constituted lords of this lower world; and all other creatures were subjected to their dominion. None was above them but God himself. But they chose to have no superior: they affected to be as gods. What daring presumption! What criminal ambition! It was time indeed that "their loftiness should be bowed down, and their haughtiness be made low."]

2. What unbelief!

[God had spoken with a perspicuity which could not admit of misconstruction, and an energy that precluded doubt. Yet they listen to the suggestions of a wicked fiend, and believe the lies of Satan in preference to Jehovah's word. Can any thing be conceived more insulting to the Majesty of heaven than this? Can an offence be deemed light which offers such an indignity to the God of truth?]

3. What ingratitude!

[What could God have done more for them than he had done? What could they have, to augment their felicity? And, if any restraint at all was to be laid upon them for the purpose of trying their fidelity and obedience, what smaller restraint could be conceived than the prohibition of one single tree amidst ten thousand? Was one tree too much for *Him* to reserve, who had created all the rest for their use?

---

[b] A variety of questions might be asked respecting different parts of this history; but where God has not been pleased to inform us, we should be contented to be ignorant: and where no certainty can be attained, we judge it better to pass over matters in silence, than to launch out into the boundless and unprofitable regions of conjecture

Were they to think much of so small an act of self-denial, where so much was provided for their indulgence? Were they to be so unmindful of all which He had done for them, and of all the good things which He had in store for them, as to refuse Him so small a testimony of their regard? Amazing! Incredible! that such favours should be so requited!]

4. What rebellion!

[God had an undoubted right to command; and, whatever His injunctions were, they were bound to obey them. But how do they regard this single, this easy precept? They set it at nought: they transgress it: they violate it voluntarily, immediately, and without so much as a shadow of reason. They lose sight of all the considerations of duty, or interest: they are absorbed in the one thought of personal gratification; and upon that they rush, without one moment's concern, how much they may displease their Friend and Benefactor, their Creator and Governor, their Lord and Judge. Shall not God visit for such rebellion as this?]

After their transgression, we are naturally led to inquire into,

III. Their recompence—

Satan had told them, that "their eyes should be opened:" but little did they think in what sense his words should be verified! "Their eyes were now opened;" but only like the eyes of the Syrian army when they saw themselves in the heart of an enemy's country[c], or those of the rich man when he lifted them up in hell torments.[d] They beheld now, what it was their happiness not to know, the consequences of sin. They beheld,

1. The guilt they had contracted—

[Sin, while yet they were only solicited to commit it, appeared of small malignity: its present pleasures seemed to overbalance its future pains. But when the bait was swallowed, how glad would they have been if they had never viewed it with desire, or ventured to trespass on what they knew to have been forbidden! Now all the aggravations of their sin would rush into their minds at once, and overwhelm them with shame. It is true, they could not yet view their conduct with penitence and contrition, because God had not yet vouchsafed to them the grace of repentance:

[c] 2 Kings vi. 20.   [d] Luke xvi. 23.

they could at present feel little else than self-indignant rage, and self-tormenting despondency: but their anguish, though not participating the ingenuous feelings of self-lothing and self-abhorrence, must have been pungent beyond all expression: and they must have seemed to themselves to be monsters of iniquity.]

2. The misery they had incurred—

[Wherever they cast their eyes, they must now see how awfully they were despoiled. If they lifted them up to heaven, there they must behold the favour of their God for ever forfeited. If they cast them around, every thing must remind them of their base ingratitude; and they would envy the meanest of the brute creation. If they looked within, O what a sink of iniquity were they now become! The nakedness of their bodies, which in innocence administered no occasion for shame, now caused them to feel what need they had of covering, not for their bodies merely, but much more for their souls. If they thought of their progeny, what pangs must they feel on their account; to have innumerable generations rise in succession to inherit their depravity, and partake their doom! If they contemplated the hour of dissolution, how terrible must that appear! to be consigned, through diseases and death, to their native dust; and to protract a miserable existence in that world, whither the fallen angels were banished, and from whence there can be no return! Methinks, under the weight of all these considerations, they wept till they could weep no more [e]; and till their exhausted nature sinking under the load, they fell asleep through excess of sorrow [f].]

INFER,

1. How deplorable is the state of every unregenerate man!

[Any one who considers the state of our first parents after their fall, may easily conceive that it was most pitiable. But their case is a just representation of our own. We are despoiled of the divine image, and filled with all hateful and abominable dispositions: we are under the displeasure of the Almighty: we have nothing to which we can look forward in this world, but troubles, disorders, and death; and in the eternal world, indignation and wrath, tribulation and anguish for evermore. Why do we not endeavour to get our minds suitably affected with this our melancholy condition? Why do we not see ourselves, as in a glass; and apply to ourselves that commiseration which we are ready to bestow on our

---

[e] 1 Sam. xxx. 4. [f] Luke xxii. 45.

first parents? Alas! "the god of this world hath blinded our minds:" else we should smite upon our breasts with sorrow and anguish, and implore without delay the mercy which we so much need.]

2. How astonishing was the grace of God in providing a Saviour for us!

[It is needless to say that our first parents could do nothing to repair the evil which they had committed. And how far they were from attempting to make reparation for it, we see, when they fled from God, and cast the blame on others, yea even on God himself, rather than acknowledge their transgressions before him. But God, for His own great name sake, interposed, and promised them a Saviour, through whom they, and their believing posterity, should be restored to his favour. To this gracious promise we owe it, that we are not all involved in endless and irremediable misery. Let heaven and earth stand astonished at the goodness of our God! And let all the sinners of mankind testify their acceptance of his proffered mercy, by fleeing for refuge to the hope set before them.]

3. How vigilant should we all be against the devices of Satan!

[He who "beguiled Eve under the form of a serpent," can assume any shape, for the purpose of deceiving us. He is sometimes "transformed into an angel of light," so that we may be ready to follow his advice, as if he were a messenger from heaven. But we may easily distinguish his footsteps, if only we attend to the following inquiries:—Does he lessen in our eyes the sinfulness of sin? Does he weaken our apprehensions of its danger? Does he persuade us to that which is forbidden? Would he make us think lightly of that which is threatened? Does he stimulate our desires after evil by any considerations of the pleasure or the profit that shall attend it? Does he calumniate God to us, as though He were unfriendly, oppressive, or severe? If our temptations be accompanied with any of these things, we may know assuredly that "the enemy hath done this," and that he is seeking our destruction. Let us then be on our guard against him. Let us watch and pray that we enter not into temptation. However remote we may imagine ourselves to be from the love of evil, let us not think ourselves secure: for if Satan vanquished our first parents under all the advantages they enjoyed, he will certainly overcome us, unless "we resist him," "strong in the Lord, and in the power of his might."]

OUTLINE NO. 6

EXCUSES MADE BY OUR FIRST PARENTS, AFTER THEIR FALL.

Gen. iii. 11—13. *Hast thou eaten of the tree whereof I commanded thee that thou shouldest not eat? And the man said, The woman whom thou gavest to be with me, she gave me of the tree, and I did eat. And the Lord God said unto the woman, What is this that thou hast done? And the woman said, The serpent beguiled me, and I did eat.*

THE immediate effects of sin are not easily discovered by us at this time: for if we look for them in ourselves, our partiality and self-love conceal them from us; and if we look for them in others, the universal prevalence of those effects prevents us from ascribing them to their proper cause. To see them in their true colours, we should be able to contrast the habits of some person during a state of innocence with those which he manifests after the commission of sin. Doubtless there are glaring instances of iniquity, from the investigation of which we may gather instruction: but we shall make our observations to the greatest advantage, if we examine the records respecting the conduct of our first parents after their unhappy fall. The accounts given of them are not indeed very full and circumstantial; yet the narration, brief as it is, is sufficient to elucidate the immediate influence of sin upon the mind, as well as its remoter consequences in the destruction of the soul. There are two things in particular which we shall be led to notice from the words before us;

I. The way in which men betray their consciousness of guilt—

Mark the conduct of our first parents. While they were innocent, they were strangers either to shame or fear: but instantly after their transgression, they made coverings for themselves of fig-leaves, and fled from the presence of their God. Here we may behold ourselves as in a glass: they have set a pattern to us which all their posterity have followed:

however men may affect to be innocent, they all betray their consciousness of guilt in these two things;

1. They conceal themselves from themselves, and from each other—

[Knowing that their hearts are depraved, and that, if narrowly inspected, they would exhibit a most disgusting appearance, men will not turn their eyes inwards. They will not examine the motives and principles of their actions: they cast a veil over the workings of pride and ambition, of envy and malice, of falsehood and covetousness, of carnality and selfishness: and then, because they see no evil in their actions, they hastily conclude there is none. And so successful are they in hiding from themselves their own deformity, that when all around them are even amazed at the impropriety of their conduct, they take credit to themselves for virtuous principles and laudable deportment.

If we should attempt to open their eyes, and to set before them their own picture, they would not even look at it, but would be offended with our fidelity, and condemn us as destitute of either charity or candour.

Now, would men act in this manner if they had not a secret consciousness that all was not right within? Would they not rather be glad of any assistance whereby they might discover any latent evil; or, at least, be glad to "come to the light, that their deeds might be made manifest that they were wrought in God?"

There is the still greater anxiety in men to hide their shame from each other. The whole intercourse of mankind with each other is one continued system of concealment. All endeavour to impose on others, by assuming the appearances of virtue; but no one will give credit to his neighbour for being as guiltless in his heart as he seems to be in his conduct. A thorough knowledge of a person whose principles have been tried, will indeed gain our confidence: but who has so good an opinion of human nature in general as to commit his wife or daughter to the hands of a perfect stranger; or to give him unlimited access to all his treasures; or even to take his word, where he can as easily obtain a legal security? But, if men were not conscious of depravity within themselves, why should they be so suspicious of others? The fact is, they know themselves to have many corrupt propensities; and justly concluding that human nature is the same in all, they feel the necessity of withholding confidence where they have not been warranted by experience to place it.]

2. They shun, rather than desire, the presence of their God—

[God comes to all of us in his word, and speaks to us in the language of love and mercy: He bids us to draw nigh to Him, and to enjoy "fellowship with him, and with his Son, Jesus Christ." But are these employments suited to the taste of all? or do the habits of the generality evince any regard for these inestimable privileges? Nay, if we endeavour to set God before them, and to make known to them his will, do they consider us as their friends and benefactors? They may bear with us, indeed, in the exercise of our public ministry: but will they be pleased, if we come home to their houses, and labour to bring them, as it were, into the presence of their God? Will they not be ready to say to us, as the demoniac did to Christ, "Art thou come hither to torment us before the time;" or, like the Jews of old, "Prophesy unto us smooth things, prophesy deceits; make the Holy One of Israel to cease from before us?"

Now would this be the conduct of men, if they were not conscious of much guilt within? Would a man who had just received gold from the mint, be afraid of having it tried by a touchstone? or one who was perfectly innocent of a crime, be afraid of being interrogated in relation to it? Would not rather the knowledge of God be desirable to one who had no wish but to perform his will? Would he not account it his highest happiness to gain an increasing acquaintance with his Saviour, and a more entire conformity to his image?]

When the guilt of men can no longer be concealed, they have many refuges of lies to which they flee; to expose which, we shall shew,

II. The way in which they endeavour to palliate and excuse it—

Our first parents confessed indeed their transgression, but in a way which clearly shewed, that they were not humbled for it. Thus, when we cannot deny our guilt,

1. We cast it upon others—

[Doubtless we all are accessary to the production of much guilt in others: and it is well to take shame to ourselves in that view. But to take occasion from this to excuse our own wickedness, is only to add sin to sin. Yet who does not betake himself to this refuge? Mark persons in the early stage of life; they will deny their faults as long as there remains for them any hope of concealment; and, when they are clearly detected, they will do their utmost to shift the blame off from themselves: according to the nature of the crime alleged, they will impute it to accident, or inadvertence, or mistake, or, like our first parents, to the instigation and example of their accomplices. What is the disposition which shews itself in persons of riper years, when they are called to account for any evil that they have committed, or when their angry passions have involved them in dispute and quarrel: is it not the endeavour of each to criminate the other, in hopes thereby to exculpate himself? Or when no particular ill-will is exercised towards others, is not the same system prevalent; and do not men justify their own conduct from the habits and examples of those around them? But what folly is this! Did the Serpent *compel* Eve to eat the fruit? or was Adam *necessitated* to follow her example? They were free agents in what they did: and they should have rejected with abhorrence the first proposals of sin, however specious they might be, and by whomsoever they might be made. And in the same manner, it is no excuse to us that the ways of iniquity are crowded; for we are to withstand the solicitations that would allure us from God, and stem the torrent that would drive us from him.]

2. We cast it even upon God himself—

[There is peculiar force in those words of Adam, "The woman *whom thou gavest to be with me,* she gave me of the tree, and I did eat:" it is no less than a reflection upon God himself for giving him the woman; and a casting of the blame upon him as accessary at least to his fall, if not also as the original *cause* of it. It is thus also that we account for our transgressions from the peculiar circumstances in which we are placed, and thus ascribe them rather to the dispensations of Providence, than to our own wilful depravity. One is poor, and therefore has not leisure to consult the welfare of his soul; or is under the authority of others, and cannot serve God without subjecting himself to their displeasure. Another is rich, and cannot deviate so far from the habits of the world, as to conform to the precise rules which God has prescribed. In this manner, persons endeavour to persuade themselves that a life of entire devotedness to God is incompatible with their worldly duties; and that their deviations or defects are rather their misfortune than their fault. Some indeed will be yet more bold in accusing God; and, when condemned for giving the rein to their appetites, will say, 'Why did God give me these passions? I cannot act otherwise than I do.'

How far these excuses will avail in the day of judgment, it becomes every one to consider with fear and trembling. They may stifle the accusations of a guilty conscience now; but there is not a man in the universe so stupid as seriously to believe that his conscience will acquit him at the tribunal of his God.]

We shall conclude with an ADDRESS,

1. To those who are unhumbled for their sins—

[Some are so impious, that "they declare their sin as Sodom: the very shew of their countenance witnesses against them." To such persons we say with the prophet, "Woe unto them[a]!" Nor can we deliver any milder message to those who "cover their transgressions, as Adam, and hide their iniquity in their bosom[b]:" for God's word to them is plain; "He that covereth his sins shall not prosper: but whoso confesseth and forsaketh them shall have mercy.[c]" It is absolutely indispensable that we humble ourselves before God, and that we repent in dust and ashes. God has noted our transgressions, whether we have observed them or not: for "there is no darkness nor shadow of death where the workers of iniquity may hide themselves[d]." God is extremely earnest in endeavouring to impress this thought upon our minds[e]. It is equally certain that we cannot impose upon him by any vain excuses. The day is coming, when he will not only ask in general, "Hast thou eaten of the tree, whereof I commanded thee that thou shouldest not eat?" but will interrogate us, as he did Eve, with holy indignation, saying, "What is this that thou hast done?" Art thou aware of its malignity? art thou prepared to meet the consequences? O let us, every one of us, humble ourselves before him, while yet the effects of his displeasure may be averted from us: but if yet we remain impenitent and stout-hearted, a sudden and irremediable destruction shall come upon us[f].]

2. To those whose hearts are beginning to relent—

[Do not think that a small and transient humiliation is sufficient. If you could weep "rivers of tears," it would be no more than the occasion calls for. You may perhaps comfort yourselves with the thought of not having committed many or great offences: but consider what it was that brought guilt and ruin upon the whole race of mankind; it was not many offences, but one; nor was it what would appear to us a very heinous sin, but only the violation of a positive precept, the eating of a forbidden fruit: reflect on this, and you will derive little consolation from the thought that you are not so bad as others. But, whether your sins have been more or less heinous, there is one Refuge, and only one, to

---

[a] Isai. iii. 9.   [b] Job xxxi. 33.   [c] Prov. xxviii. 13.
[d] Job xxxiv. 22.   [e] Isai. xxix. 15. with Amos ix. 2, 3.
[f] Prov. xxix. 1.

which you must flee for safety. The refuge provided for our first parents was, "The seed of the woman, who was in due time to bruise the serpent's head." The same is provided for you. Jesus was born into the world for this very end: He has made a full atonement for your sin: and if "only you acknowledge your transgressions," and believe in him, they shall be "remembered against you no more for ever."]

OUTLINE NO. 7

THE SEED OF THE WOMAN.

Gen. iii. 15. *I will put enmity between thee and the woman, and between thy seed and her seed: it shall bruise thy head, and thou shalt bruise his heel.*

THIS was the first promise that was ever given to fallen man. The occasion on which it was given was this: Satan had beguiled our mother Eve, and, through her, had prevailed on Adam to transgress: and he had thereby destroyed both them and all their posterity: for, since they were corrupt, nothing but what was corrupt could proceed from them. But God, in his abundant mercy, interposed for our fallen race, who must without such interposition have been involved in all the misery of the fallen angels. Against Satan he denounced a curse suited to his crime: and at the same time informed him, that, though for the present he had prevailed over the woman, a seed should spring from her who should execute on him the vengeance he deserved, and rescue mankind from the misery he had entailed upon them.

Now, as the oak with all its luxuriant branches is contained in the acorn, so was the whole of salvation, however copiously unfolded in subsequent revelations, comprehended in this one prophecy; which is, in fact, the sum and summary of the whole Bible. And on this promise all the Saints lived, during the space of 2000 years: yes, all from Adam to the time of Abraham were encouraged, comforted, and saved by this promise alone, illustrated as it was by sacrifices appointed by the Lord.

In explaining this prophecy, I shall call your attention to,

I. The person here predicted—

[It was the Lord Jesus Christ; who was in a peculiar way " the seed of *the woman:*" for he was formed in the womb simply by the agency of the Holy Ghost, and was born of a pure virgin altogether without the intervention of man. And this was necessary: for, had he been born like other men, he would have been in the loins of Adam, like other men; and therefore would, like them, have been partaker of his guilt and corruption. But, being the sole and immediate workmanship of God, he was absolutely perfect, and therefore capable of sustaining the office of a Saviour for fallen man: whereas, if he had been otherwise formed, he would have needed a Saviour for himself, and been incapable of effecting salvation for others. Thus you see, that when it was impossible for man to restore himself to God, God " laid help for him upon One that was Mighty;" on one who, being God and man in one person, was able to effect for men all that their necessities required. As man, he could atone for sin; and as God, he could render that atonement available for all who should trust in him.]

At the same time that this prophecy announced the Messiah's advent, it declared,

II. The conflicts he should sustain—

[Between Satan and him, God put an irreconcilable enmity; which, without a moment's intermission, has raged from that very time even to the present hour. Satan, having thus introduced sin into the world, instigated every child of Adam to the commission of it. And how far he prevailed, may be seen in this, that he induced the very first-born of man to murder his own righteous brother, for no other reason than because he was more righteous than himself. At times he had so entirely reduced the whole race of man to his dominion, that scarcely a righteous man existed upon earth. And, when God sent prophets to reclaim the world, Satan stirred up the people of every age and place to destroy them. At last, when the promised Seed himself came, Satan only exerted himself the more violently against him, if by any means he might prevail to destroy the Saviour himself. No sooner was Jesus born into the world, than Satan stimulated Herod to destroy all the males around Bethlehem from two years old and under, that so it might be impossible for Jesus to escape. And, when Jesus was entering upon his ministry, he urged him to cast himself down from a pinnacle of the temple, if peradventure he might thus induce him, under an idea of trusting in God, to destroy himself. Afterwards he stirred up Peter to dissuade him from executing the work he had undertaken; saying, "Master, spare thyself." When he could not prevail in any of these ways, he put it into the heart of Judas to betray him, and stirred up all the Priests and Elders to put him to death. In like manner has this wicked adversary still prosecuted his malignant work even to the present hour, blinding the eyes of men, and hardening their hearts, and "leading them captive at his will:" and if any have dared to resist his will, he has stirred up all his own agents, to persecute them, and to put them to death.

On the other hand, Christ has also fought against him from the beginning, rescuing men from his dominion, and "turning millions from darkness unto light, and from the power of Satan unto God." In the days of his flesh especially he shewed his superiority to Satan, by dismissing him from many whom he had possessed, and constraining him to relinquish the hold which he had gained, both of their bodies and their souls. And though he seemed himself to sink under Satan's attacks, yet did he, in fact, defeat Satan by the very means which that adversary had used for his destruction: for by death he overcame death, and "him that had the power of death, that is, the devil[a]:" yes, "on the very cross itself he spoiled all the principalities and powers of hell, triumphing over them openly in it[b]." And in his ascension, "he led captivity itself captive;" and has bound all the hosts of hell, "reserving them in chains of darkness unto the judgment of the great day." In his people, too, he gets the victory from day to day, enabling them to resist him manfully, and to trample both Satan and all his hosts under their feet.

This conflict is still passing from day to day. The God of this world, and the God of heaven, are contending for us, and in us[c]: and as long as the world shall stand, will this contest continue.]

But in our text we are informed, that Jesus will prevail, and enjoy at last,

III. The victory assured to him—

[In the conflict, the Saviour's "heel is bruised:" but "he bruises the head" of his great adversary, and breaks his power for evermore. Behold the Saviour on his throne of glory, far above all the principalities and powers, whether of heaven or hell! Behold the progress of his Gospel in every age! and see in heaven the multitudes which no man can number, continually increased by fresh accessions from every

[a] Heb. ii. 14.   [b] Col. ii. 15.   [c] 2 Cor. iv. 4, 6.

quarter of the globe, from the most blinded votaries of Satan amongst the Heathen, as well as from his more specious servants amongst ourselves! See the weakest of the children of men enabled to triumph over him, and, though persecuted like their divine Master, "made more than conquerors through him that loved them!" This is going forward amongst ourselves: so that you see the most devoted vassals of Satan casting off his yoke, and " brought into the liberty of the sons of God:" and soon shall you behold those whom once he held in the most miserable bondage, seated upon thrones of glory, and actually sitting in judgment upon the angels, as assessors with their divine Master[d]. Yes: it is but a little time, and the seed of Christ, as well as Christ himself, will be seated upon thrones of glory; whilst Satan, and his seed, shall be cast into the lake of fire prepared for the devil and his angels.

Such is the prophecy before us: and in this way is it accomplishing yet daily; and shall be accomplished, till the final destinies of each shall terminate the contest for evermore.]

BEHOLD then, brethren,

1. How marvellous is the grace of God!

[Think under what circumstances he made this promise to man. He had placed our first parents in Paradise, where there was every thing that could conduce to their happiness; and he himself visited and communed with them, as a friend. Yet did they, on the very first temptation, violate his express command: and then, instead of humbling themselves before him, they fled from him; and, when summoned into his presence, excused themselves, and even cast the blame of their iniquity on him:—" The serpent beguiled me, and I did eat: The woman, *whom thou gavest to be with me,* she gave me of the tree, and I did eat." What might we expect now that he should do unto them? surely, that he should consign them over to the misery they deserved. But no: unsought and unsolicited, he promised them a Saviour, even his only dear Son, who should rescue both them and all their believing posterity out of the hands of their great adversary. Now then, I ask, If God, *unsolicited,* bestowed *the Saviour* himself on these *impenitent* offenders, will he refuse *salvation* to any *penitent* who *calls upon him?— — —*Let no sinner in the universe despond: but let every one see in this prophecy how abundant and inconceivable is the grace of God — — —]

2. How complete shall be the victory of all who believe in Christ!

[d] 1 Cor. vi. 2, 3.

[You appear to be in a hopeless condition, because your corruptions are so great and your enemies so mighty. Go, then, to the cross of Christ, and there see the Saviour himself hanging, an helpless and inanimate corpse! What hope has HE of victory? Wait a moment, and you will see. Behold him rising from the grave, ascending to heaven, sending down the Holy Spirit, establishing his kingdom upon earth, surrounded in heaven by myriads of his redeemed, and sealing up his great adversary, with his hosts, in the bottomless abyss of hell! See all this; and then know what shall be the issue of *your* conflicts. You are fighting with a vanquished enemy: and it is but a little time, and HE, your Almighty Saviour, " will bruise Satan under your feet," and will elevate you to thrones of glory, like unto his own. Only follow him in his conflicts, and you shall be partakers with him in all his victories and triumphs for evermore.]

OUTLINE NO. 8

THE WAY OF SALVATION ILLUSTRATED TO OUR FIRST PARENTS.

Gen. iii. 21—24. *Unto Adam also, and to his wife, did the Lord God make coats of skins, and clothed them. And the Lord God said, Behold, the man is become as one of us, to know good and evil: and now, lest he put forth his hand, and take also of the tree of life, and eat, and live for ever: therefore the Lord God sent him forth from the garden of Eden, to till the ground from whence he was taken. So he drove out the man; and he placed at the east of the garden of Eden, cherubims, and a flaming sword which turned every way, to keep the way of the tree of life.*

THE works of God are extremely different from those which are carried on by man. Creatures of limited capacity are compelled to act as unforeseen occasions require; and hence their works are, for the most part, independent and detached, without being regulated by any fixed system: but the works of God are all united and harmonious, as parts of one grand whole. In the structure of the tabernacle and all its diversified rites, there was not any thing, however minute or obscure, which did not shadow forth some mystery. This appears from the strict injunction given to Moses to " make every thing according to the pattern shewn to him in the mount." It is thus also with respect to all the most remarkable events recorded in the Bible, whether they relate to the Jewish, patriarchal, or antediluvian ages; they were all, in some respect, figurative and emblematical. Amongst these we must certainly number the fall of man, with all its attendant circumstances: the covenant made with him, the means by which he was induced to violate it, the way provided for his recovery, were all of lasting and universal importance. In like manner, the facts specified in our text must be regarded, not as mere uninteresting casualties, but as occurrences of most mysterious import. In God's conduct towards our first parents, as it is here related, we may see,

I. The manner in which He illustrated to them his promised salvation—

Our first parents, feeling in themselves the sad effects of their fall, " sewed fig-leaves together and made themselves aprons," or rather, twined together the tender branches of the fig-tree for girdles. But God was pleased to clothe them in another manner, even with the skins of beasts; and thus to direct their attention to,

1. The blood of atonement—

[We are not expressly told, that the animals which were slain on this occasion were offered in sacrifice; but if we duly weigh the reasons for believing that God ordered them to be slain for this purpose, we can scarcely entertain any doubt upon the subject.

In the first place, we may be sure that the offering of sacrifices was not an institution of man's device; and that, if it were, it could not be pleasing and acceptable to God. How could it enter into the mind of man to imagine, that the blood of a beast could make any satisfaction to God for sin? What connexion is there between the blood of a beast and the sin of man? There was much more reason to think that God would be displeased with the unauthorized destruction of his creatures, than that he would be so pleased with it as to forgive the iniquities of mankind on account of it. Moreover, had not God himself enjoined this method of propitiating his anger, we cannot doubt but that he would have answered the presumptuous offerer, as he did the Jews, "Who hath required this at your hands[a]?" But we know that when a bleeding sacrifice was offered to him by Abel, he testified his acceptance of it in a visible manner, probably by sending fire from heaven to consume it. We cannot doubt, therefore, but that the institution of sacrifices was of divine appointment.

In the next place, if sacrifices were not now instituted, we can scarcely account for the slaughtering of the animals, and much less for God's direction respecting it. It is thought indeed by some, that the flesh was given to our first parents for food: but this seems very improbable, because God told Adam at this very time, that he should henceforth subsist, not upon the fruits of the garden as before, but on "the herb of the field," which should be produced only by constant and laborious cultivation[b]. Nor was it till after the flood that God gave to man the liberty of eating the flesh of animals[c]. Hence, if the animals were not offered to God in sacrifice, they were killed merely for their skins, which seems to be by no means an adequate reason for God's interposition. On the contrary, if they were by God's commandment offered in sacrifice, we see, what we are in no other place informed of, the origin of the institution; and at the same time we behold abundant reason for God's special interference. We see what instruction and consolation our first parents must derive from such an ordinance: for while they beheld their own desert in the agonies and death of an unoffending creature, they must be encouraged to look forward to that Seed of the Woman, who was in due time to offer himself a sacrifice for the sins of the whole world.

We cannot doubt therefore but that this was the time when sacrifices were instituted; and that, as they were appointed of God to prefigure the great sacrifice, they were enjoined at this time for the express purpose of directing the views of fallen man to that atonement which Christ should afterwards offer to God upon the cross. In this sense, as well as in the divine purpose, may Christ be called, "The Lamb of God slain from the foundation of the world[d]."]

2. The righteousness of Him who made that atonement—

[When we are told that "the Lord God made them coats of skins, and clothed them," can we suppose that nothing was intended by him but to provide more conveniently for their decency and comfort? Impossible! There

[a] Isai. i. 12.   [b] Gen. iii. 18, 19.
[c] Gen. ix. 3.   [d] Rev. xiii. 8.

was in this a deep stupendous mystery. Adam and Eve thought only of a covering for their bodies: God pointed out to them a covering for their souls. They were despoiled of their original righteousness; and they needed a robe to cover their naked souls, that they might again stand before God "without spot or blemish." All means which they could devise for this purpose would be ineffectual. God therefore was pleased to shadow forth to them the righteousness of Christ; of Him who was " to be the propitiation for their sins," and emphatically to be " called, The Lord our Righteousness[e]." How far they beheld the substance in the shadow, we cannot say: but there is abundant proof that the same means were used in subsequent ages to represent the Saviour to the world. All the vestments of the priests, sprinkled with the blood of sacrifices, clearly shewed in what manner all were to be clothed who would be " an holy priesthood to the Lord." And the language of Prophets, and Apostles, and of Christ himself, has so strict an analogy with the event before us, that we cannot but discern their harmony and agreement. Isaiah speaks of being " clothed with the garments of salvation, and covered with a robe of righteousness[f]:" St. Paul, enjoying the fuller light of the Gospel, says more plainly, " Put ye on the Lord Jesus Christ[g]:" And our blessed Lord more plainly still, " I counsel thee to buy of me gold tried in the fire, that thou mayest be rich; and white raiment, that thou mayest be clothed, and *that the shame of thy nakedness may not appear*[h]."

We need only further observe, that in this marvellous appointment God taught our fallen parents to look to Him through one Mediator, and to make that one object the *only* ground of *all* their hopes; or, in other words, to expect pardon *only* through His atoning blood, and acceptance *only* through His meritorious and perfect righteousness.]

Having seen how strongly God illustrated to them his promised salvation, let us notice,

II. The means he used to secure their acceptance of it—

He banished his guilty creatures from Paradise, and, by the ministration of angels, prohibited effectually their return to it. This he did,

1. Partly in judgment—

[The ironical and sarcastic expressions which purport to be the reason of this dispensation, are certainly strong

[e] Jer. xxiii. 6.   [f] Isai. lxi. 10.   [g] Rom. xiii. 14.   [h] Rev. iii. 18.

indications of his heavy displeasure. The flattering hope of "becoming as Gods," had led Adam and his wife to transgress the divine command. Now therefore God casts it, as it were, in their teeth, with holy indignation, in order that they might see what they had gained by their folly and presumption. And whereas they had hitherto enjoyed the liberty of eating all the fruits of Paradise, and especially that which was a pledge and earnest to them of God's eternal favour, he drives them out from the garden, to live in a far different manner by the sweat of their brow, and to feel that they were cut off from that life, which, had they maintained their innocence, would have been consummated in glory.

Thus we behold them driven as outcasts from God and happiness, and doomed to a life of labour and sorrow which should issue in a painful death, and (if repentance intervened not) in everlasting misery.]

2. Partly in mercy—

[God's judgments in this world have always been tempered with mercy; yea so tempered, as to be capable of being turned into the richest blessings. Thus it was in the case before us. Our first parents had been accustomed to consider the tree of life as a pledge of the divine favour; and would be likely to regard it in the same view after their fall, as they had done before. Under this delusion they would be ready to embrace these means of reconciliation with their offended God, and would be led thereby to neglect the means which God had prescribed. Persisting in this mistake, they would pacify their own consciences; and having lulled themselves asleep under the guilt of their transgressions, they would perish in the midst of all the mercy which God had offered them through the mediation of his Son. To prevent these fatal consequences, God cuts them off from all access to the tree of life, and thus necessitates them to seek for mercy in his appointed way. Precisely as, in destroying the Jewish nation and polity, God punished his people indeed, but at the same time consulted their truest interests, by rendering it impossible for them to fulfil the righteousness of the Mosaic law, and thereby "shutting them up unto the faith of Christ[1];" so did he expel our first parents from Paradise, that they might have nothing to divert their attention from that "Seed of the Woman who was in due time to bruise the Serpent's head."

Thus did God "in judgment remember mercy;" and, in the very hottest exercise of his anger, provide means for the richest display of his unmerited, unsought-for kindness.]

[1] Gal. iii. 23.

From this subject we may LEARN,

1. The antiquity of the Gospel—

[Whenever Salvation by the blood and righteousness of the Lord Jesus is insisted on, it is exclaimed against as a *new* doctrine: but it is none other than "the good old way[k]," which has been pointed out by our Reformers, by the Apostles, by the Prophets, and by God himself from the beginning of the world. God shewed it to our first parents immediately after their fall: he shewed it them not only by a prophetical declaration, but also by an emblematical exhibition. And our very clothing in which we are so apt to pride ourselves, would, if we considered the origin and occasion of it, lead us to that way, even to Jesus, in whom alone we can find righteousness and life. Let us then hold fast the Gospel, without regarding the senseless cavils of the world: and while "the proud make it only a stumbling-block, and the conceited reject it as foolishness," let us receive and glory in it as "the power of God and the wisdom of God."]

2. The necessity of embracing it—

[Like our first parents, we are ready to rest in the seals of the covenant (as baptism and the Lord's supper), instead of fleeing to the Saviour himself. But whatever devices we use for the reconciling of ourselves to God, they will all prove vain and useless: we shall find them "a bed too short to stretch ourselves upon, and a covering too narrow to wrap ourselves in[l]." There was one way appointed from the beginning: that way has been progressively displayed, and illustrated in different ages; but it has never been altered, no not in the slightest degree. "There never has been any other name whereby we could be saved, but that of Jesus Christ[m];" and the only difference between us and the Jews, or us and Adam, is, that we behold in meridian splendour the truths, of which they saw only the early dawn. Let us be persuaded then that all access to life by the first covenant is stopped; and that all plans for covering our own shame will be in vain. We must all be accepted through one sacrifice, and all be clothed in one righteousness; and all comply with that direction of the prophet, "In the Lord shall all the seed of Israel be justified, and shall glory."]

[k] Jer. vi. 16.   [l] Isai. xxviii. 20.   [m] Acts iv. 12.

OUTLINE NO. 9

THE DEATH OF ABEL.

Gen. iv. 8—10. *And Cain talked with Abel his brother: and it came to pass when they were in the field, that Cain rose up against Abel his brother, and slew him. And the Lord said unto Cain, Where is Abel thy brother? And he said, I know not: Am I my brother's keeper? And He said, What hast thou done? The voice of thy brother's blood crieth unto me from the ground.*

IT is scarcely to be conceived how much iniquity there is in the heart of fallen man. That we have passions which incline us occasionally to deviate from the path of duty, is nothing more than what all feel and confess: but that we are ready to perpetrate all manner of evil, not excepting even murder itself, few are sufficiently candid or intelligent to acknowledge. *This* seems an excess of wickedness, of which human nature, unless in very extraordinary circumstances, is not capable. To such a charge most men would be ready to reply, "Is thy servant a dog, that I should do this thing?" But we may behold in Cain a just picture of ourselves. What he was by nature, that are we also. The first-born of Adam, begotten after his own fallen image, shews what all are, till renewed by grace: " they live in malice and envy, hateful, and hating one another:" and their contempt of God is equal to all the other odious qualities that defile their souls. We cannot but be struck with this in the history of Cain, who having murdered his brother Abel, presumed even to insult his God. His conduct will come properly under our review, if we consider,

I. The Murder—

In this awful transaction, there are two things to be inquired into:

1. *The manner* in which it was perpetrated—

[Satan, in his assaults on man, can exert himself only by wiles and stratagems, not being permitted to exercise his power against us in any other way. But when he employs human agents in his service, he stirs them up to combine in their attacks " deceit and violence." Such were the weapons with which the blood-thirsty Cain sought the destruction of his brother Abel. "He *talked with* Abel his brother." What the subject of the conversation was, it would be foolish to conjecture: but that it was of a friendly nature, there can be no doubt. It was evidently with a design to allure him into a place of solitude, where he might effect his murderous purpose without difficulty or detection. Had he disclosed the sentiments of his heart, he would have put his brother on his guard: whereas by feigning affection towards him, he would remove all fear or suspicion from his brother's mind, and facilitate the accomplishment of the fatal deed[a]. To similar means assassins have had recourse in all ages. It was thus that Joab slew both Abner and Amasa: "he sent messengers after Abner, and took him aside in the gate *to speak with him quietly*[b]:" "to Amasa he said, Art thou in health, my brother? and took him by the beard to kiss him[c]:" but his pretences to friendship were only to secure access to them, that he might strike with effect the dagger to their heart. It was thus that Absalom also contrived to murder his brother Amnon: he made a feast for all his family, and expressed particular solicitude to have the company of Amnon: but the whole was a cover, to effect the destruction of his brother in the midst of his convivial mirth[d].

The murder of a brother is such an atrocious act, that it scarcely admits of being aggravated by any circumstances: but if any thing can aggravate it, surely the treachery of Cain must awfully enhance its guilt. Had it been the effect of sudden wrath, it had even then been criminal beyond the power of language to express: but being the result of premeditation and contrivance, of deceit and treachery, its enormity is increased an hundred-fold.]

2. *The motive* to the commission of it—

[Gladly would we, if possible, find somewhat to extenuate the guilt of this transaction: but the more minutely we examine it, the more heinous it appears. The Scripture informs us, that Cain, in the commission of this act, was impelled only by envy and hatred. God had been pleased to testify his acceptance of Abel and of his sacrifice, while no such token of approbation was vouchsafed to Cain. The effect of this should have been, to lead Cain into a close examination of his spirit and conduct, and to make him earnest in prayer, that he might know wherefore this preference had been given to Abel, and how he also might obtain the favour of his God. But, alas! his heart was filled with envy and wrath, insomuch that his whole countenance was changed. In vain did Go

---

[a] Ps. lv. 21. [b] 2 Sam. iii. 26, 27.
[c] 2 Sam. xx. 9, 10. [d] 2 Sam. xiii. 26--28.

expostulate with him on the unreasonableness of his behaviour[e]. "The spirit that dwelt in him lusted to envy[f]:" this malignant passion " was as rottenness in his bones[g]," so thoroughly had it corroded his very inmost soul. The excellence of Abel's character served only to add fuel to the flame. His virtues were his faults; so " impossible is it to stand before envy[h]." Cain *hated in him the divine image*, as much as he *envied him the divine favour*. The light of his brother's example was offensive to his eyes; and on this account he sought to extinguish it. St. John, having told us that Cain slew his brother, asks, " And wherefore slew he him?" he then answers, " Because his own works were evil, and his brother's righteous[i]."

Such were the motives by which Cain was instigated to this infernal deed. The murder was first committed in his heart; and then completed with his hand; according to that saying of the Apostle, " He that hateth his brother is a murderer[k]." Indeed there is such a connexion between " envy, debate, deceit, and murder[l]," that wherever the first is harboured, the rest would follow of course, if God in his infinite mercy did not interpose to limit the operation of our sinful propensities.]

God, who " maketh inquisition for blood," would not suffer the murder to be concealed: he therefore sought out the offender, and commenced,

II. The Inquest—

It is said, that " Whose hatred is covered by deceit, his wickedness shall be shewed before the whole congregation[m]:" and where that hatred has proceeded to murder, God in his providence has generally fulfilled this saying. On this occasion, the Governor of the Universe proceeded exactly as he had done upon the first transgression: He summoned the criminal, and made inquiry at his hands. In the trial we notice,

1. Cain's denial of the fact—

[Being interrogated, "Where his brother Abel was," he answered with consummate effrontery, "I know not: Am I my brother's keeper?" Alas! how inseparable the connexion between guilt and falsehood! But what blindness had sin induced upon his mind, and what obduracy upon his heart!

[e] ver. 6, 7. [f] Jam. iv. 5. [g] Prov. xiv. 30.
[h] Prov. xxvii. 4. [i] 1 John iii. 12. [k] 1 John iii. 15.
[l] Rom. i. 29. [m] Prov. xxvi. 26.

What could he imagine, when he thus flatly denied any knowledge of his brother? Did he suppose that he could deceive his God? Had he forgotten, that omniscience was an attribute essential to the Deity? Yes: such is the atheism which sin produces: he said in his heart, "Tush, God hath not seen: Can he see through the thick clouds[n]?" Not contented with uttering this impious falsehood, he added an insult, which we should scarcely have thought he would have dared to offer to his earthly parent, much less to his Maker and his God. Behold this murderous wretch presuming to criminate his Judge, and to reprove him as unreasonable and unjust! "Am I my brother's keeper?" that is, 'What right hast thou to interrogate me respecting him?' We stand amazed at this effort of impiety: but, in truth, it is no other than what is daily exemplified before our eyes. If we question men respecting the performance of any of their duties, they will not hesitate to condemn our expectations as unreasonable, and the laws on which they are founded, as absurd: and when the authority of God is urged in support of his law, they will not scruple to arraign the wisdom and equity of the Lawgiver himself. The very manner in which Cain attempted to conceal his crime was of itself a strong presumption against his innocence. What need had he to be offended with an inquiry after his brother, if he really knew not where he was? What occasion was there for all this petulance and profaneness? But it was in vain to deny a fact which the all-seeing God was ready to attest[o].]

2. His conviction before God—

[He had effectually silenced his brother's voice; so that no testimony could be borne by *him*. But the blood which he had shed, had a voice, which cried aloud; a voice which reached the throne of Almighty God, and brought him down to plead the cause of injured innocence. Indeed, every sin has a voice, which speaks powerfully in the ears of God, and calls for vengeance on the head of him who has committed it. It was in vain to dispute the testimony of Jehovah. The criminal stands confounded, and waits the sentence awarded by his Judge. Surely now then at least we shall behold him softened: his obdurate heart must now relent; and he will accept with resignation the punishment of his iniquity. Not so indeed: he expresses no contrition: he asks not once for mercy: he complains indeed, but not of himself, not of the guilt he has contracted, not of the deed he has perpetrated, but of the punishment he has incurred; "My punishment is greater than I can bear." But let not this be wondered at:

[n] Job xxii. 14.   [o] Ps. xciv. 7—10.

It is the effect of sin to sear the conscience, and to harden the heart: and the more heinous our transgressions are, the more shall we be disposed to criminate the authority that calls us into judgment for them. Even in hell itself this disposition is exercised, yea, it rages with uncontrolled and incessant fury: the damned spirits " gnaw their tongues for pain, and blaspheme the God of heaven because of their pains, and repent not of their deeds[p]."]

Hence then we may OBSERVE,

1. How soon did " the enmity which God has put between the Serpent's and the Woman's seed[q] begin to shew itself!

[It is an undeniable fact, that " all who live godly in Christ Jesus do suffer persecution[r]:" and the world, yea sometimes Christians themselves also, are ready to think that the opposition made to them is discreditable to their cause. But our Lord and his Apostles taught us to expect precisely the same treatment which they themselves received[s]. They inform us also how all the Prophets were used by those among whom they sojourned[t]: they declare that, in all ages, even from the beginning of the world, " they who have been born after the flesh have persecuted those who were born after the Spirit[u];" and that all " the blood shed from the time of righteous Abel" to the time that Christ himself was nailed upon the cross[x], served to illustrate " the enmity of the carnal mind against God," and the path in which all must walk who would finally attain to glory. Hence persecutors are emphatically said to " go in the way of Cain[y]." " Let none then think it strange that they are called to endure a fiery trial, as though some strange thing happened unto them[z];" but "let them rejoice and glorify God on this behalf[a];" knowing that myriads who are now in heaven " came thither out of great tribulation[b];" and that, "if they also suffer with Christ, they shall in due time be glorified together with him[c]."]

2. How vain is it to cultivate the friendship of the world!

[If, in any situation, fellowship could have been maintained between a carnal and a spiritual man, we may well suppose that it should subsist between the two first men who were born into the world, educated as they must have been with the strictest care, and necessitated as they were to cultivate a

---

[p] Rev. xvi. 10, 11.   [q] Gen. iii. 15.   [r] 2 Tim. iii. 12.
[s] John xv. 18—20.   [t] Acts vii. 52.   [u] Gal. iv. 29.
[x] Matt. xxiii. 35.   [y] Jude 11.   [z] 1 Pet. iv. 12.
[a] 1 Pet. iv. 13, 14, 16.   [b] Rev. vii. 14.   [c] Rom. viii. 17

friendly intercourse on account of the contracted state of society in the world: yet not even these could enjoy spiritual communion with each other. It is true, that all natural men do not give themselves up, like Cain, to the dominion of their lusts: but it is equally true, that all men have in their hearts the same envious and malignant passions[d], and that, till they are renewed by divine grace, they are enemies to true religion[e]. Hence we are told to come out from the world and be separate, because there can be no more true communion between believers and unbelievers, than between light and darkness, or Christ and Belial[f]. And they who, in opposition to this direction, choose the unregenerate for their associates, or form still more intimate connexions with them, are sure to "suffer loss" in their souls; and, if saved at all, they are "saved only so as by fire[g]."]

3. How certainly "will sin find us out" at last!

[We may conceal our iniquities from man; but we can never hide them from God: "There is no darkness nor shadow of death where the workers of iniquity may hide themselves." God does not often interfere to make known our guilt, as in the case before us; (though the interpositions of His providence in the discovery of murder are sometimes extremely marked and visible;) but in the day of judgment "he will make manifest the very counsels of our hearts." It will be in vain then to deny our guilt, or to raise those captious, not to say impious, objections, which now appear to us of so much weight: Every thing will be substantiated by the fullest evidence, and be recompensed according to its desert. O that "in that day we may be found without spot, and blameless!" This may be the state of all, not excepting even murderers themselves, provided they wash in the fountain of Christ's blood, and be renewed by his Holy Spirit. Let us then seek his pardoning and renewing grace. Then shall we be enabled to "stand before our God with boldness," and "give up our account to him with joy, and not with grief."]

[d] Jam. iv. 5.   [e] Rom. viii. 7.
[f] 2 Cor. vi. 14, 15, 17.   [g] 1 Cor. iii. 15.

OUTLINE NO. 10

INSTITUTION OF PUBLIC WORSHIP.

Gen. iv. 26. *Then began men to call upon the name of the Lord.*

OF the various institutions of religion, some were clearly founded on an express appointment from

God himself; others *appear* to have arisen, in the first instance, from the suggestions of holy men, and to have been afterwards authorized and established by divine authority. It is manifest that baptism was practised by the Jews long before it was appointed by Christ as the rite whereby his followers were to be consecrated to his service: but when it was first introduced, or whether by any express command of God, we know not. The change of the Sabbath from the seventh day to the first was sanctioned by the practice of the Apostles: but whether they received any particular direction respecting it, we are not informed. The presumption indeed is, that all the observances which God has sanctioned, originated from him; and that men began to practise them in consequence of some intimations from him: but as this is not declared in Scripture, we must be contented to leave the matter undecided. We are not any where told that God commanded men to meet together for the purposes of public worship. If we take the text in the precise sense that it bears in our translation, it should seem that public assemblies of worship were rather the offspring of necessity; and that they arose out of an increase of population, and a growing neglect of personal and family religion.

The text indeed is, in the margin of our Bibles, rendered differently: "Then began men to *call themselves by* the name of the Lord:" Nor are commentators agreed to which of the versions we should give the preference. We shall therefore include both; and take occasion from the words to shew,

I. In what manner we should *confess* God—

The descendants of Cain, who had become "a fugitive and a vagabond in the earth," soon cast off all regard for God, and addicted themselves to open and shameless impiety. Lamech broke through the restraints which the Creator had imposed in relation to marriage, and "took unto him two wives;" leaving thereby an example, which in process of time effaced the very remembrance of God's original institution.

From these and other abominations arose an imperious necessity for the godly to separate themselves from the ungodly, and to maintain by an open and more visible profession the honour of God in the world. This they did: and in so doing they have taught us,

1. To separate ourselves from the ungodly—
[There is a certain degree of intercourse which must subsist between us and the world. But it is by no means desirable to extend it beyond that which the duties of our calling absolutely require. Our Lord repeatedly declares that his faithful followers "are not of the world, even as He was not of the world[a]:" The Apostles also with one voice guard us against cultivating the friendship of the world;[b] and teach us to come out from among them[c], and to live as a distinct "peculiar people[d]," "shining among them as lights in a dark place[e]." We should go to them, indeed, when duty calls, as the physician enters the infected chambers of the sick: but we should never forget, that "evil communications corrupt good manners[f];" and that an undue familiarity with them is far more likely to weaken the spirituality of our own minds, than to generate a holy disposition in theirs. In us should be verified the prophecy of Balaam, "Israel shall dwell alone, and shall not be reckoned among the nations[g]."]

2. To make an open profession of our attachment to Christ—
[The godly, in the antediluvian world, called themselves Children of God, as distinct from those who were only children of men: and it was foretold that a similar distinction should obtain among the followers of Christ[h]. If in one instance Peter failed in acknowledging his Lord, on other occasions he witnessed a good confession, and manfully withstood the threatenings of his enemies[i]. It may be thought perhaps, that, because Christianity is the established religion of the land, there is no occasion for such boldness now: but the sons of Cain and of Ishmael are yet amongst us[k]: there are in every place those who deride all vital godliness: and it requires almost as much fortitude to withstand their sneers and contempt, as it does to brave more cruel persecutions. There is the same necessity for *us* to "take up our cross and follow Christ," as there was for the primitive Christians: and the

---

[a] John xvii. 16. [b] James iv. 4. [c] 2 Cor. vi. 14—18.
[d] 1 Pet. ii. 9. [e] Phil. ii. 15. [f] 1 Cor. xv. 33.
[g] Numb. xxiii. 9. [h] Isai. xliv. 5. [i] Acts iv. 8, 10, 19, 20.
[k] Jude 11. Gal. iv. 23, 29.

command given to them to "be faithful unto death," is equally to be regarded by *us*: for the same conduct will be observed by the Judge towards men of every age and nation; "he will confess those before his Father who have confessed him in the world," and "deny before his Father those who have denied," or been ashamed of him[1].]

But the text instructs us also,

II. In what manner we should *worship* him—

We cannot doubt but that Adam and his pious offspring maintained the worship of God both in their families and their closets: but till the human race were considerably multiplied, there was no occasion for what may be called *public* worship. But when the families became so numerous that they were obliged to separate, then it was necessary to call them together at stated times and seasons, that, by forming different congregations, they might all receive instruction at once, and keep up in their minds an habitual reverence for God.

The necessity for public ordinances is obvious; and the benefit arising from them is incalculable.

1. They preserve the knowledge of God in the world—

[There is reason to fear, that if there were no public ordinances of religion, the very name of God would be soon forgotten. Notwithstanding the establishment of such institutions, the generality are "perishing for lack of knowledge:" darkness has overspread the land, even a darkness that may be seen and felt[m]. But there is some light shining in the world; and *that* is diffused almost exclusively by the public ministry of the word. Occasionally, God is pleased to instruct men by his word and Spirit, without the intervention of human agents: but, as he has set apart an order of men for the express purpose of propagating his truth, so he delights to honour them as his instruments to convey his blessings to the world[n]. Doubtless he vouchsafes his blessing to those who read and pray in secret, provided they reverence, as far as their circumstances admit, his public institutions: but never did he, from the foundation of the world, impart his blessing to those who

---

[1] Matt. x. 32, 33. Mark viii. 38.
[m] Exod. x. 21. with Isai. ix. 2.
[n] Compare Zech. iv. 11—14. and 2 Cor. iv. 7. with Acts viii. 26—39. and x. 9—44.

continued to live in an avowed contempt of his ordinances: No: "he loveth the gates of Zion more than all the dwellings of Jacob º."]

2. They are the means of perfecting his work in his people's hearts—

[God has told us that this was a very principal end for his ordaining men to preach the Gospel P; but it is by means of the public ordinances chiefly that Ministers can address the people: and consequently the ordinances themselves are the means by which God accomplishes his end. We have said before, that God will also reveal himself to his people in secret: and it sometimes happens that their communion with him in private is more sweet and intimate than in the public assembly: but may we not ask, on the other hand, whether, when the heart has been cold and formal in the closet, it has not often been warmed and animated in the church? And is not much of the enjoyment experienced in secret, the result of instructions administered in the public ordinances? In the one they gather the food; in the other they ruminate and chew the cud: but the pleasure and nourishment derived to their souls must be acknowledged, in part at least, as originating in their public duties. To these has God promised his peculiar blessing q; and therefore we should "reverence his sanctuary," and join with one consent in a public surrender of ourselves to God r.]

Address,

1. Those who have others under their control—

[Parents, and Masters, you are responsible to God for the exercise of your power and influence. Will you then, either by precept or example, encourage a conformity to the world, or a disregard of the worship of your God? O "destroy not their souls, for whom Christ died!" Employ your authority for God: and, whatever opposition you may meet with in the world, learn to say with Joshua, "As for me and my house, we will serve the Lord s."]

2. Those who are acting for themselves—

[If you have "chosen the good part," be careful that it "be not taken away from you," either through the love of this world, or through the fear of man. Be steadfast, and "endure unto the end, that you may be saved at last." If you lose your life for Christ's sake, you shall find it unto life eternal. But if

º Ps. lxxxvii. 2. P Eph. iv. 11—15.
q Exod. xx. 24. Matt. xxviii. 20.
r See Zeph. iii. 9. Zech. viii. 20—22. s Josh. xxiv. 15.

you are "walking in the broad road," think whither it leads: and begin to serve your God in this world, that you may be honoured by him in the world to come[t].]

[t] John xii. 26.

OUTLINE NO. 11

ENOCH'S WALKING WITH GOD.

Gen. v. 24. *And Enoch walked with God: and he was not; for God took him.*

THE cares of a family are by no means incompatible with a life of devotedness to God. The man distinguished for his piety above all others in the antediluvian world, had a very numerous offspring[a], to whom doubtless he paid every attention in his power: yet he was not impeded in his spiritual course; but found time to serve his God, as much as if he had been free from all concern about this present world.

We shall consider,

I. His conduct—

We are told, he "walked with God." Now "walking with God" implies,

1. Agreement—

[Enoch, as a fallen creature, was once alienated from God, like others[b], and, during his unconverted state, was full of enmity against him both in heart and life[c]; "walking after the flesh," according to the course of this world, and altogether contrary to God[d]. But now he was reconciled to God through faith in Christ[e] — — — And was brought by this means to an agreement with him both in mind and will.

[a] His eldest son, Methuselah, was born to him at the age of sixty-five; after which he continued for the space of three hundred years to beget sons and daughters. ver. 21—23.
[b] Eph. iv. 18. [c] Rom. viii. 7. Col. i. 21.
[d] Rom. viii. 1. Eph. ii. 2. Lev. xxvi. 27, 28.
[e] It is said in Heb. xi. 5. that Enoch was "translated by faith:" and though that faith might have more immediate respect to some promise given him relative to his translation, yet we can scarcely conceive but that it had a further respect to the promised Messiah. And this idea is greatly strengthened by the account St. Jude gives of his

Thus must all of us obtain *reconciliation* with God through the blood of Christ, before we can resemble this eminent saint; for it is not possible for "two to walk together except they be *agreed*[f]."]

2. Familiarity—

[Friends who associate much together, contract a familiarity with each other: they open to each other their sorrows and their joys: they consult each other in their difficulties; and maintain with the greatest freedom a mutual intercourse. Thus did Enoch with his God. He considered God as his friend: he had familiar access to him at all times: he opened to him all his wants, all his fears, all his trials: he did nothing without first asking counsel of his friend, and engaging his assistance.

Nor was this an honour peculiar to him: it is the duty and the privilege of all the saints: we may go and knock at the door of our Friend, and he will always open unto us[g]: we may have access to him with boldness and with confidence, even in his most private apartments[h]: we may ask what we will of him, and he will do it for us[i]. He, on the other hand, will come and knock at our door; and will come in and sup with us[k]: he will communicate to us his secrets[l]; and will in ten thousand ways manifest himself unto us as he does not unto the world[m].]

3. Affection—

[Affection is the very essence of friendship: mere agreement or familiarity are of little value without it: where this does not exist, the intercourse cannot be such as is implied in walking with God. Enoch loved his God, if I may so speak, with all his heart, and mind, and soul, and strength: God would never have given him a special testimony of his approbation, if his heart had been destitute of the sacred flame of love. He went forth to meet his God, as Adam was wont to do in his state of innocence: he looked forward with joy to the seasons when he should again renew his fellowship with him: he studied to avoid every thing that might in any respect grieve him; and made it the great object of his life to do what was pleasing in his sight.

It is in this way that we also are to walk with God: we

---

foretelling the very manner of the future judgment (ver. 14, 15.): for if he prophesied of Christ's *second* coming, doubtless he was not ignorant of his *first* advent.

[f] Amos iii. 3. [g] Matt. vii. 7, 8.
[h] James iv. 8. Eph. iii. 12. Heb. x. 19.
[i] John xv. 7. [k] Rev. iii. 20. John xiv. 23.
[l] Ps. xxv. 14. [m] John xiv. 21, 22.

must commune with him not by constraint, but willingly and of a ready mind[n]. We must delight ourselves in him[o]. His loving-kindness must be better to us than life itself[p]: and it must be as marrow and fatness to us to serve and honour him.[q]]

How acceptable to God this conduct was, we may learn from,

II. The reward with which God honoured him—

The manifestations of God's presence and favour which he continually enjoyed, were a rich recompence for any self-denial which he exercised, or any exertions which he used, to please his God. But, besides all these, God,

1. Exempted him from death, the common lot of all men—

[All, the righteous as well as the wicked, must pay the penalty of death, which has been entailed on them by the sin of Adam, and been richly merited by their own personal transgressions. But God has been pleased to exempt from it one in the old world, and one in the new[r]. This testimony of his approbation God vouchsafed to Enoch. He was a bold and faithful witness for God, and doubtless incensed many against him[s] — — — And God took him from a persecuting and ungodly world, who probably enough were seeking to destroy him on account of his pungent admonitions[t]. He took him in the prime of life, without any previous pain or sickness. To some indeed it might appear a calamity to be taken away, in the midst of his useful labours, and while his family were still looking up to him for instruction and support: but he thought it "far better to depart and to be with Christ," than to prolong his days in the midst of a tempting and ungodly world: and God gave him the desire of his heart.

We, however diligent in walking with God, cannot hope to participate in such a reward as this. But death shall be disarmed of its sting, so that it shall be to us rather an object of desire, than of fear and terror[u]: and while the most stout-hearted sinner in the universe trembles at its approach, *we*

---

[n] 1 John i. 3.   [o] Ps. xxxvii. 4.   [p] Ps. lxiii. 3.
[q] Ps. lxiii. 5.   [r] Compare 2 Kings ii. 11. with the text.
[s] Jude 14, 15.
[t] In Heb. xi. 5. before cited, it is said "he was not found." This may refer to some search made by his friends (see 2 Kings ii.16.) or rather by his enemies, (see 1 Kings xviii. 10.)
[u] 2 Cor. v. 4.

2. Exalted him both in body and in soul to a more immediate enjoyment of his presence—

[While Enoch was in the body, he could not endure the full splendour of the divine glory[y]: he could only behold his God through the dark medium of faith[z], or, at most, be permitted to "see his back parts[a]." But God translated him, both in body and soul, to the highest heavens; making him thereby not only an eminent type of Christ's ascension, but an earnest and pledge to us, that our bodies shall hereafter be raised to a participation of the happiness, which our glorified souls shall enjoy at the instant of their departure from the body. To what extent the blessedness of every individual will be advanced by the re-union of the soul and body, it is not possible to say: but it is reasonable to suppose, that that which consummates our reward, will greatly enhance our felicity. This, however, Enoch had not to wait for; he received his full reward at once; and was thereby distinguished from all those disembodied spirits, which, though perfected in glory, waited for their complete happiness till the day of judgment. The happiness of Enoch in communing with God on earth was doubtless exceeding great: but when he arrived at the full fruition of the divine glory, his blessedness as far exceeded all that he had before experienced, as the early dawn is surpassed by the meridian light.

It need not, however, be any matter of regret to us, that we are not to expect this reward; since, on our dismission from the body, we shall instantly be in Paradise; and at the day of resurrection, we shall have our bodies raised to a participation of our bliss.]

3. Made him a most distinguished monument to the whole world, of the love he bears to those who seek communion with him—

[We know but little of the state of those who are gone into the invisible world, though we believe, from the word of God, that they are completely happy. But here is an evidence to our very senses, that none shall be suffered to "seek God's face in vain." Who, after beholding such an interposition of the Deity, such an honour conferred on a "man of like passions with ourselves," can doubt one moment of the acceptance which all shall find, who serve their God in sincerity and truth[b]?

---

[x] 1 Cor. xv. 55.   [y] 1 Tim. vi. 16.   [z] 1 Cor. xiii. 12
[a] Exod. xxxiii. 23.   [b] Isai. lxiv. 5.

In this view then we may consider his reward as an earnest of ours. We shall not be left without many expressions of God's love even in this world, if we endeavour to walk closely with him. But, whether our present state be more or less joyous, we are sure that in the eternal world we shall not lose our reward. We need only to consider the exalted condition of this distinguished saint and we may see in him the blessedness reserved for us.]

INFER,

1. What an *honourable* character is the Christian.

[We consider those as honourable who associate with great men on earth: but the Christian has higher company than earthly monarchs; he walks with God himself; and God is not ashamed to call him his friend[c]. In some sense, the Christian is already translated into God's kingdom[d], and admitted into the heavenly Zion, and joined to the society of glorified saints and angels[e].

Let every one then walk worthy of this high calling; and, in a dignified contempt of all inferior objects, endeavour to attain this sublime privilege in its highest perfection.]

2. What a *happy* character is the Christian!

[His singularity may bring upon him much odium and persecution. But what need he to regard the frowns of men, who enjoys fellowship with God? One smile from his almighty Friend is sufficient to counterbalance all the indignities that can possibly be cast upon him. Yet, after all, his happiness in this world is but as the drop before the shower. When he has filled up the measure of his obedience, God takes him to himself; a band of angels are sent to bear his spirit to the regions of the blest. It must not be said of the Christian, "He dies;" but merely, that "God translates him" from a world of sin and misery, to a world of blessedness and glory. "Such honour have all his saints;" God grant it may be ours for ever and ever! Amen.]

[c] Heb. xi. 16.   James ii. 23.   John xv. 15.
[d] Col. i. 13.   [e] Heb. xii. 22, 23.

OUTLINE NO. 12

STRIVINGS OF THE SPIRIT.

Gen. vi. 3. *And the Lord said, My Spirit shall not always strive with man.*

MAN, at first, was created in the image of his God: but when he fell, he begat children in his own fallen image. His very first-born became a murderer. Some of his posterity, however, were pious: but they, not being careful to connect themselves with those who feared God, were drawn aside from religion by their ungodly wives, insomuch that, in eight or nine generations, " all flesh had corrupted their way," and it repented " God that he had made man[a]." In consequence of this, God determined to destroy the whole earth. But yet, being full of mercy, he would not proceed to this extremity without giving to man space for repentance. Accordingly, he commanded Noah to preach to them; and to declare, that in the space of 120 years the threatened judgments should be inflicted, if the people did not avert those judgments by their penitence. During that period his Holy Spirit should continue to strive with them— but no longer: for " he should not always strive with man, who was now become altogether flesh," and carnal; and who, if he did not repent in the time allotted him, should be left to reap the bitter fruit of his own ways.

That this warning may have a salutary effect on us, I will endeavour to shew,

I. That the Spirit of God, if long resisted, will cease to strive with us.

Certain it is, that the Spirit of God does strive with unregenerate men—

[He strove with the whole antediluvian world, by the ministry of Noah: for " by the Spirit did that holy man preach, during the whole period whilst the ark was preparing, even to the spirits which for their disobedience were condemned, and shut up in the prison" reserved for all impenitent transgressors[b]. " To the whole nation of Israel, also, did the Holy Spirit for ages testify, in and by his Prophets, notwithstanding they dealt proudly, and withdrew their shoulder, and hardened their neck, and would not hear[c]." With us also does he strive, both by the ministry of his word, and by his own immediate agency on the hearts of men. For, what is conscience, but God's vicegerent in the soul? By that, God speaks to us; warning, and inviting us from time to

---

[a] Gen. vi, 6, 7, 12.   [b] 1 Pet. iii. 19, 20.   [c] Neh. ix. 29, 30.

time, if by any means we may be induced to repent and turn unto him. Let any one only look back upon his past life; and he shall find that there have been some periods when he has felt a conviction upon his mind that it was his duty, and would be his happiness, to seek after God, and obtain, whilst yet he might, the remission of his sins.]

But we resist his sacred motions—

[To whom amongst us may not those words of Stephen be applied, (if not in reference to the present moment, yet certainly in reference to some period of our lives,) " Ye stiff-necked, and uncircumcised in heart and ears, ye do always resist the Holy Ghost: as your fathers did, so also do ye[d]." We may not, indeed, have set ourselves in such hostility to the truth as they did; but have we been more practically obedient than they? Have we obeyed the voice of the Lord our God, calling us to repentance, and to a dedication of our whole selves to him? Alas! there has been the same stoutness of heart in us, as in persons of a more profane character; many of whom, perhaps, have " said, I will not, but afterwards have repented, and went" into their Lord's vineyard; whilst we, perhaps, have said, " I go, Sir," but have been as far from executing our acknowledged duty as ever[e].]

And will the Spirit always continue to strive with us?

[No: we are assured he will not. We know that his motions may be resisted, till they are altogether " quenched[f]." And in many instances has he been driven away by the obstinacy of those with whom he had striven. Of Saul we are told, that " the Spirit of the Lord departed from Saul; and an evil spirit from the Lord troubled him[g]." And it was not without reason that David prayed, " Cast me not away from thy presence! and take not thy Holy Spirit from me[h]!" When God saw his ancient people incurably addicted to idolatry, He said, " Ephraim is joined to idols: let him alone[i]." And what else can we expect, if we continue obstinate in our sins? The doom of Israel must of necessity be ours. Of them it is said, " They rebelled and vexed his Holy Spirit; therefore he was turned to be their enemy, and fought against them[k]:" and we verily can expect no other, than that He, whose solicitations we refused to follow, as a Friend, shall send forth his vindictive judgments against us, as an Enemy.]

Let me then proceed to shew,

[d] Acts vii. 51.   [e] Matt. xxi. 28—30.   [f] 1 Thess. v. 19.
[g] 1 Sam. xvi. 14.   [h] Ps. li. 11.   [i] Hos. iv. 17.
[k] Isai. lxiii. 10.

II. What is the state of a soul thus abandoned by the Lord.

Truly its condition is most pitiable. God has said, "Woe unto them, when I depart from them[1]:" and verily it will be a woeful day for any one of us, if God should ever abandon us to ourselves! for the deserted soul is from that moment given up, yes, and given up for ever,

1. To delusion—

[It is surprising what delusions an abandoned sinner will harbour in his heart: "I shall have peace, though I walk in the imaginations of my heart to add drunkenness to thirst, and sin to sin[m]." Refuges of lies he shall have in plenty, to administer to his composure: 'There is no future state: death is but an eternal sleep: or, at all events, God is too merciful to inflict punishment in a future state: or, at any rate, the punishment cannot be eternal. As for the Holy Scriptures, perhaps they are only the writings of fallible men, like ourselves: or, at best, they are so highly figurative, that you cannot depend upon them.' Thus men take refuge in infidelity, that so they may rid themselves of records, which, if credited, would be subversive of their peace. And to these delusions God will give them up; as he has said: "They have chosen their own ways, and their soul delighteth in their abominations: I also will choose their delusions, and will bring their fears upon them[n]." In the New Testament, this judgment is yet more emphatically denounced: "They (the Antichristian powers) received not the love of the truth, that they might be saved," says St. Paul: "and for this cause, God shall send them strong delusion, that they should believe a lie; that they all might be damned who believed not the truth, but had pleasure in unrighteousness[o]." Oh, terrible judgment!—and the more terrible, because they who are subjected to it have no conception that they are lying under it: but it will be the assured portion of all with whom the Spirit of God has ceased to strive.]

2. To bondage—

[To the power of their own lusts will they be given up, so that Satan shall lead them captive at his will. How awful is that declaration of Solomon, "His own iniquities shall take the wicked himself; and he shall be holden with the cords of his own sins[p]!" Yet this must be the fate of all who constrain

---

[1] Hos. ix. 12.   [m] Deut. xxix. 19.   [n] Isai. lxvi. 3, 4.
[o] 2 Thess. ii. 10—12.   [p] Prov. v. 22.

the Holy Spirit to depart from them. If men " will despise and reject all the counsel of the Lord, they will assuredly be left to eat the fruit of their own ways, and be filled with their own devices." It was so with the Heathen, " who liked not to retain God in their knowledge: he gave them over to a reprobate mind[q]." It was so, also, with the Israelites: " My people would not hearken to my voice, and Israel would none of me: so I gave them up unto their own hearts' lust; and they walked in their own counsels[r]." What more common than to see this very judgment inflicted before our eyes? The infidel, the drunkard, the whoremonger, the thief, the covetous man, the profane swearer, what slaves do they become to their respective habits! These shew us the very truth that I am insisting on; and declare, with one voice, that the Ethiopian may as well change his skin or the leopard his spots, as they renounce the habits to which they have been given over by their God.]

3. To obduracy—

[Pharaoh, for his obstinacy, was given up to a state of hardness that is scarcely to be credited. And how many, in every age, when forsaken by the Lord, have had " their consciences seared as with a hot iron," and become altogether " past feeling[s]!" Behold the scoffer, who pours contempt on all religion, and, with daring impiety, cries, " Where is the promise of God's coming to judgment? for since the fathers fell asleep, all things continue as they were from the beginning of the creation[t]." If reproved for their impiety, they will in effect say, " Who is Lord over us[u]?" " We know not the Lord; neither will we obey his voice[x]." Even in death itself, they often evince the very same hardness, and shew how entirely they are given over by the Lord. Their friends around them are ready to say, " They died like lambs:"—and so indeed they did, even like brute beasts that have no understanding, having no conception of the state which awaits them at their departure hence. A terrible judgment this is! and a certain prelude,]

4. To ruin!—

[There is a time wherein God may be found, by every living man: but that season may be passed; and a time arrive, when he will no more be found[y], and when all God's offered mercies shall be for ever withheld. Such a period had actually arrived to the Jewish nation, when they crucified the

[q] Rom. i. 28.
[s] Eph. iv. 19. 1 Tim. iv. 2.
[x] Exod. v. 2.
[r] Ps. lxxxi. 11, 12.
[t] 2 Pet. iii. 4.
[y] Isai. lv. 6.
[u] Ps. xii. 4.

Lord of glory. Our blessed Saviour, previous to his death, took up this lamentation over them: "O Jerusalem, Jerusalem, thou that killest the prophets, and stonest them who are sent unto thee, how often would I have gathered thy children together, even as a hen gathereth her chickens under her wings, but ye would not! Behold, your house is left unto you desolate [z]!" "Oh that thou hadst known, even thou, at least in *this thy day*, the things which belong unto thy peace! but now they are hid from thine eyes [a]." Thus, it is to be feared, there may be, even amongst ourselves, some with whom God will strive no longer: they have so long trifled with the means of grace, and been unprofitable under all the culture that has been bestowed upon them, that they shall be henceforth left only to be gathered, in due season, as fuel for the fire [b]. What an awful thought, To be left only to "fill up the measure of their iniquities," and to "treasure up wrath against the day of wrath [c]!" Better were it for a man that he had never been born, than that ever he should live for such an end as that! But such is the state of the deserted soul: and at the appointed hour, "wrath will come upon him to the uttermost."]

ADDRESS,

1. Those who are yet withstanding the motions of the Holy Spirit—

[Little do you think how greatly you offend your God, or what misery you are entailing on your own souls. But let me ask, Is there one amongst you that does not look back upon his past rebellion with regret? Is there one who is not persuaded in his mind, that he would have been a far happier man, if he had obeyed the voice of the Lord, and followed, instead of resisting, the dictates of his conscience? How long, then, will ye continue this rebellious course? Shall not the declaration in my text affect you? Shall not even the possibility of your day of grace having come to an end, appal you? Do but think how much you have at stake——— and how short is the time which you have to seek the things belonging to your peace.——— I pray you, Arise, ere it be too late, and cry unto your God, "if God peradventure may give you repentance, and you may be recovered out of the snare of the devil, by whom you have been taken captive at his will [d]!" "To-day, while it is called to-day, harden not your hearts, as in the provocation, as in the day of temptation in the wilderness; lest you provoke God to swear, in his wrath, that you shall never enter into his rest [e]."]

---

[z] Matt. xxiii. 37, 38. [a] Luke xix. 42. [b] Heb. vi. 7, 8.
[c] Rom. ii. 5. [d] 2 Tim ii. 25, 26. [e] Ps. xcv. 7—11

2. Those who through grace have obeyed his blessed will—

[Truly this is of the Lord, who alone has "made you willing[f]," and has thus caused you to "differ from those around you[g]." — — — Be thankful for this distinguishing grace; but remember that you still need his gracious influences as much as ever. There is not any part of the divine life that can be carried on within you but by the operation of the Holy Spirit. He must be within you "a Spirit of wisdom and understanding, a Spirit of counsel and of might, a Spirit of knowledge and of the fear of the Lord, and must make you of quick understanding in the fear of the Lord[h]." Seek him, then, for all these gracious ends: and be careful that you "do not grieve him," by any sinful disposition, or any secret neglect[i]. It is by him that you are to be "sealed unto the day of redemption[k]," and by him that you are to be "rendered meet for your heavenly inheritance." To him, therefore, "I commend you, and to the word of his grace, which is able to build you up, and to give you an inheritance among all them that are sanctified[l]."]

[f] Ps. cx. 3.   [g] 1 Cor. iv. 7.   [h] Isai. xi. 2, 3.
[i] Eph. iv. 30.   [k] Eph. iv. 30.   [l] Acts xx. 32.

OUTLINE NO. 13

EXTENT OF MAN'S WICKEDNESS.

Gen. vi. 5. *God saw that the wickedness of man was great in the earth, and that every imagination of the thoughts of his heart was only evil continually.*

THE extent of man's wickedness is far greater than the generality of mankind have any conception of. Whilst a person's words and actions are inoffensive before men, he is supposed to conduct himself acceptably to God. And even when his words and actions are blameworthy, he is judged as having nothing wrong in his intentions, and as possessing, on the whole, a good heart. But God looks chiefly at the heart, which is the fountain from whence every thing that is evil proceeds[a]: and his testimony respecting it is, that "the heart," not of this or that

[a] Matt. vii. 21—23.

EXTENT OF MAN'S WICKEDNESS.

more egregious offender, but of every man by nature, "is deceitful above all things and desperately wicked." In the passage before us, God assigns his reason for destroying the whole world by an universal deluge. And that we may be suitably affected by it, I shall set before you,

I. The testimony of God respecting man—

He speaks more immediately respecting the antediluvian world—

[*In general,* the wickedness of man was great in the earth. No doubt, every species of wickedness was committed, in the most shameless manner. But, *more particularly,* "the hearts" of men were evil; "the thoughts" of their hearts were evil; "the imaginations" of the thoughts were evil, and this too without exception, without mixture, without intermission; for *every* imagination was evil, and "*only*" evil, and that "*continually.*" What an awful statement is here!

But how could this be ascertained? Who could be competent to judge of this? and on what authority is this declared? I answer, It is the declaration of God, who can discern all things; for "all things are naked and opened before him[b];" and he himself says, "I know the things that come into your mind, every one of them[c]." And, as he knows every thing, so he is able to estimate the quality of every thing; for "he weigheth the spirits[d]." And this is his testimony, after a thorough inspection of every human being.]

But the same must be spoken of man at this day—

[God himself repeats the same testimony, in relation to those who survived the deluge, and of all their descendants[e]. And it is as true of us, as it was of them. In proof of this, I will appeal to your own observation and experience. What, from observation, would you yourselves say was the state of the world around you? Do you not see that evil of every kind obtains to a vast extent; and that piety, except in some very narrow circles of persons whom the world regards as weak enthusiasts, is altogether banished; insomuch that you may mix in society for months and years, and yet never once hear them speak with admiration and gratitude respecting all the wonders of Redeeming Love? Of what passes in the hearts of others you are not able to judge; and therefore, in relation to that, I appeal to every man's own experience. What has been the state of your *hearts?* As to your words and actions, I will suppose them to have been correct: but your "*hearts,*"

---

[b] Heb. iv. 13.   [c] Ezek. xi. 5.   [d] Prov. xvi. 2.   [e] Gen. viii. 21.

your *"thoughts,"* " the *imaginations* of your thoughts," what report must you give of them? Have they been all correct? or, could you bear that man should see them as God has seen them? The proud, the envious, the uncharitable, the angry, the vindictive, the impure thoughts, say, (whether carried into effect or not) have they not sprung up within your hearts as their proper soil, and so occupied the ground, that no holy fruits would grow unto perfection? If occasionally a transient thought of good has arisen, how coldly has it been entertained, how feebly has it operated, how soon has it been lost! And, at all events, if compared with what the Law requires, and what God and his Christ deserve at your hands, tell me whether it do not fall so short of your duty, that you cannot venture to call it good, but only evil of a less malignant kind?

Know ye then, all of you, that this is your real state before God: and now learn,]

II. What effect it should produce upon you—

Certainly this view of our state, and especially as attested by the heart-searching God, should produce in us,

1. Humiliation—

[Even on a review of our words and actions, I am convinced there is not any one of us who has not reason to be ashamed, especially if those words and actions be tried by the standard of God's holy Law. But who amongst us could bear to have all his thoughts inspected and disclosed? Who would not blush, and be confounded before God and man, if his heart were exposed to public view, so that every imagination of every thought of it should be disclosed? Yet God beholds it all; and has as perfect a recollection of all that has passed through our minds from our earliest infancy to this present moment, as if it had passed not an hour ago. What then becomes us, but the deepest humiliation? In truth, our religious thoughts, when compared with what they ought to have been in number and intensity, are no less a ground of humiliation, than those which have sprung from a more impure source; since they prove, indisputably, how defective are our conceptions of God's excellency, and how faint our sense of the Redeemer's love. I call on you then, every one of you, my brethren, to "lothe yourselves for your abominations," and to "abhor yourselves," as Isaiah did, and as holy Job did, "in dust and ashes[f]."]

2. Gratitude—

[We have often told you, that God has sent to us a Saviour, even his only dear Son; and that through Him all

---

[f] Isai. vi. 5. and Job xlii. 6.

our iniquities, how great soever they may have been, shall be forgiven. But methinks, this is only " a cunningly-devised fable:" for, how can it be supposed, that God should ever have shewn such mercy, and manifested such love, towards such vile creatures as we? But, brethren, however incredible it may appear, it is true, even the very truth of God. Notwithstanding all you have done amiss, " God is not willing that any of you should perish, but that all should come to repentance and live." Yes, brethren, he has laid all your iniquities on his only-begotten Son; who, agreeably to the Father's will, has expiated them by his own blood, and will take them away from your souls for ever. Tell me, then, whether gratitude do not well become you? Tell me, whether there should be any bounds to your gratitude? What, think you, would the fallen angels feel, if such mercy were shewn to them? And what are millions of the redeemed now feeling before the throne? Oh, let your souls be penetrated with a measure of their love, and your songs of praise abound day and night, even as theirs.]

3. Fear—

[Though your hearts may have been renewed by divine grace, you are renewed, brethren, only in part: you have still the flesh within you, as well as the Spirit; and you carry about with you still " a body of sin and death," from which, to your dying hour, you will need to be delivered. In fact, your whole life must be " a putting-off of the old man, and a putting-on of the new." I need not tell you what precautions people take, when they carry a light in the midst of combustibles, which, if ignited, will spread destruction all around. Know, that ye carry such combustibles about you, wherever you go; and you know not how soon you may come in contact with somewhat that may cause a desperate explosion. You all know how David fell, in an unguarded moment; and what a dreadful tissue of evil was produced by one sinful imagination. Know ye, then, what corrupt creatures ye are: be sensible of your proneness to commit even the vilest abominations: and pray, day and night, to God, to " hold up your goings in his ways, that your footsteps slip not." It was from sad experience that Peter spoke, when he said, " Be sober, be vigilant; for your adversary, the devil, goeth about as a roaring lion, seeking whom he may devour: whom resist, steadfast in the faith [g]." He had indulged self-confidence, and had slept when he should have watched: and hence arose his fall, which speaks loudly to every one of us. " Be ye, then, not high-minded; but fear:" and " what I say unto one, I say unto all, Watch."]

[g] 1 Pet. v. 8.

OUTLINE NO. 14

GOD'S DETERMINATION TO DESTROY MAN.

Gen. vi. 6, 7. *And it repented the Lord that he had made man on the earth, and it grieved him at his heart. And the Lord said, I will destroy man, whom I have created, from the face of the earth.*

THE evil of sin is visible wherever we turn our eyes. Not only has a manifest deterioration taken place in the intellectual and moral qualities of man, but the material world itself, together with all the brute creation, bears marks of God's displeasure, and of the curse inflicted on account of sin. The spring with all its vivifying powers, or the autumn with all its profusion of matured fruits, does not more surpass the desolate appearances of winter, than the earth at its first formation did the state to which it is now reduced. It was the garden of the Lord, replete with beauty, and productive of nothing which did not minister to the comfort of its inhabitants: but it is become a waste howling wilderness, infected with plagues, agitated with storms, and fruitful in occasions of sorrow. Whether any additional curse was inflicted on it at the time of the deluge, we cannot say: but the shortening of man's life from eight or nine hundred years to less than one tenth of that period, seems to indicate, that both the frame of our bodies, and every thing that contributes to their support, have undergone a further change, and "become subject to vanity" in a yet greater degree, than they were before the deluge. However this may be, it is certain that, of all the judgments with which God has ever visited his rebellious creatures, the deluge was the most tremendous. All other expressions of God's anger have been limited to a few individuals, or cities, or nations; but this extended over the face of the whole earth.

That we may view aright this awful dispensation, let us consider,

I. The state of the antediluvian world—

14.] GOD'S DETERMINATION TO DESTROY MAN. 71

The degeneracy of mankind had been advancing with rapid strides from the time that Adam fell, to the time spoken of in our text. Their state was characterized by

1. General supineness—

[Our blessed Lord informs us, that " in the days before the flood they were eating and drinking, marrying and giving in marriage, till the day that Noah entered into the ark[a]." By this he did not mean to condemn the use of those means which God himself had appointed for the maintenance of life and the preservation of our species, but to inform us, that the people were altogether addicted to carnal and sensual indulgences, without paying any regard to their spiritual and eternal interests. The great ends of life were quite forgotten by them; and their only study was, how to dissipate care, and spend their time in pleasure.]

2. Awful depravity—

[The expressions used in the preceding and following context clearly shew, that wickedness of every kind was practised without restraint[b]. The law of God being disregarded, and human laws not having been framed and executed as they are amongst us, the strong and violent oppressed the weak and peaceable; and whatsoever any man's interest or inclination prompted him to do, that he did without shame or remorse. We may form some idea perhaps of the state which then existed, from what still exists among uncivilized nations, and amongst us also, when the restraints of human laws are withdrawn[c].]

3. Obstinate impenitence—

[For a hundred and twenty years did Noah continue to warn that wicked generation[d]. By his practice also as well as by his preaching, did he condemn them. Before their eyes " he prepared (with vast expense and labour) an ark for the preservation of his household[e];" giving them thereby a certain pledge that the threatened judgments should be inflicted on the impenitent and unbelieving: but they, no doubt, ridiculed

---

[a] Matt. xxiv. 37—39.
[b] ver. 5, 11, 12, 13. The words themselves are strong; but the frequent repetition of them greatly increases their energy.
[c] How ready are men to embark their property and risk their lives in privateering expeditions, when they can obtain a licence to rob and plunder their unoffending neighbours! And how terrible are the atrocities committed by victorious armies!
[d] 1 Pet. iii. 19, 20.   [e] Heb. xi. 7.

his precautions as absurd and visionary; and the longer the judgment was delayed, the more bold was their confidence, and the more bitter their derision[f]. Amongst us, the Gospel, though generally, is not universally, despised: some are brought to listen to its benign overtures: but to such a degree did the contemporaries of Noah harden themselves against the gracious messages of Heaven, that in that whole space of time there was not (as far as we know) one single person awakened to a sense of his guilt and danger.]

Fearful indeed must have been their state, when we consider,

II. The regret which it excited in the bosom of Jehovah—

We must understand the language of the text, not in a literal, but figurative sense—

[We are not to suppose that God did not foresee what would happen; for prescience is an essential perfection of His nature: take away his foreknowledge, and you deny him to be God. Nor must we suppose that his happiness was really interrupted by what he saw in his creatures; for he is as immutable in his happiness, as in his nature. The language of the text is accommodated to our feeble apprehensions: it is taken from what passes among men, when they are disappointed in their expectations and endeavours. As a potter, finding that a vessel which he has formed with the utmost care does not answer the desired purpose, regrets his labour, and casts out of his sight the worthless object with indignation and grief; so God represents himself as "repenting that he had made man, and as grieved at his heart" that he had bestowed upon him so much labour in vain.]

Nevertheless the figure conveys to us much plain and solid instruction—

[The same figure occurs in various other parts of holy writ: sometimes it imports a change from anger to pity[g], and sometimes the reverse[h]. In the text, it is intended to intimate, that God is not an unconcerned spectator of human actions— — —that he expects men to answer the end of their creation, by seeking his glory and their own happiness— — — and that he will manifest against sin his heavy displeasure, making all who practise it the objects of his fiery indignation— — —]

[f] 2 Pet. iii. 3—6.   [g] Jonah iii. 10.
[h] 1 Sam. xv. 11. It is used in both senses, and in connexion with the foregoing illustration. Jer. xviii. 3—10.

The feelings of our Creator on account of man's apostasy are more plainly shewn by,

III. The resolution he adopted in consequence of it—

To destroy all the human race was indeed a *terrible* resolve—

[We can form little conception of the distress occasioned through the habitable globe, when once the flood began to rise above its accustomed limits. Every contrivance would be resorted to, and every eminence be made a refuge, in hopes that the waters would subside, and that a premature death might be avoided. When one place was covered, happy would they feel themselves who could flee to some lofty mountain, and carry with them provision for their support. But they would soon find that they indulged a vain hope: a suspense, more painful than death itself, would soon occupy their minds; and the waves, fast approaching, would at last terminate their lives, which fear and terror had already half destroyed. It is probable that many would seek admittance into the ark, and cling to it, when every other refuge had failed. Many too would, doubtless, betake themselves to prayer in the midst of their distress: but the time of judgment was come; and mercy, whether exercised or not in the eternal world, could not be extended to them[i]. Children in vain solicited their parents' aid; in vain did the fond mother clasp them in her arms, or the affrighted husband strive to succour his beloved wife: all, in quick succession, were swept away; and neither man nor beast (those only in the ark excepted) were permitted to survive the wreck of nature.]

But, however terrible this judgment was, it was strictly *just*—

[The punishments inflicted by human governors, of necessity, involve the innocent with the guilty: the children suffer through the misconduct of their parents; yet no one on that account exclaims against the laws as unjust. Why then should that be deemed unjust in the government of God which is approved as just in the governments of men? But God, who is the giver of life, and by whom alone it is maintained, has a right to take it away at any time, and in any manner that he sees fit. Does any one arraign his providence, if numbers both of men and children are carried off by a pestilence, or overwhelmed in a storm? By what authority then do we prescribe limits to God, and say unto him, "Hitherto shalt thou go, and no further?" We might as well condemn the

---

[i] Thus it was with Saul, 1 Sam. xv. 25, 26.

Governor of the Universe for inflicting disease and death upon one single infant, as arraign his justice for destroying many. The lives of all are forfeited: and whether he take them away after a longer or shorter period, or cut them off singly or at once, he is still the same; "a God of truth and without iniquity, just and right is he." The Judge of all the earth will do right: and who are we that we should reply against him? "Whoso reproveth God, let him answer it."]

INFER,

1. We are not at all the more safe for having many on our side—

[No doubt, the antediluvians fortified themselves against the warnings of Noah, by the consideration that they acted only like those around them. They probably replied, as many at this time do, 'If I perish, what must become of all the world? And, Is God so unmerciful as to destroy the whole world?' But the event shewed the folly of all such reasonings: and we should learn from it to expect safety in no other way than in turning from all iniquity, and seeking refuge in Christ Jesus.]

2. There will certainly be a day of future retribution—

[From the judgment executed at the deluge it is manifest, that God will punish sin: but from the indiscriminate manner in which that punishment was inflicted, we may be assured, that there shall be a day in which justice shall be more equitably dispensed[k], or, as it is called in Scripture, "a day of the revelation of the righteous judgment of God." Then shall every one receive according to his deeds, whether they be good or evil: "the wicked shall go away into everlasting punishment, but the righteous into life eternal." May God prepare us all for that great and solemn day!]

3. It becomes us all to grieve and mourn for our past sins—

[Have the sins of men caused God himself to "repent and be grieved at his heart" that ever he formed man; and should not our sins awaken sorrow and contrition in our hearts? O that we could but view them aright! O that we could mourn over them, as it becomes us, and weep in dust and ashes! Surely if we go on impenitent in our sins, the day will come, when we shall *repent that ever we were created;* we shall wish that we had died in our mother's womb; we shall find that "it would have been better for us if we had never been born."]

[k] 2 Pet. ii. 4, 5, 9.

OUTLINE NO. 15

NOAH'S OBEDIENCE.

Gen. vi. 22. *Thus did Noah; according to all that God commanded him, so did he.*

NEVER, from the foundation of the world to this hour, if we except the sacrifice which Christ made of himself upon the cross for the sins of men, was there such a demonstration of God's hatred of sin, as that which was given at the universal deluge. All flesh having corrupted their way, God determined to execute vengeance upon all, and to destroy from the face of the earth every living thing. There was, however, one favoured servant, whom, together with his family, he was pleased to exempt from the general judgment. Noah was a righteous man, and obtained favour in his sight; and, by means prescribed to him by God himself, he was preserved. Let us consider,

I. The obedience rendered by him—

It is not easy to form a just estimate of this—

[Let us contemplate *the circumstances in which he was placed*. He was appointed " a preacher of righteousness," unto all who came within the reach of his ministrations: and he was commanded to declare that God would overwhelm the whole world with a deluge. Of such a judgment there was no appearance whatever for the space of 120 years, during the whole of which period he proclaimed its approach. If at the beginning of his ministrations any were impressed with fear, they soon were led to deride the menace; and to conclude, from the delay, that the threatened calamity should never come upon them.

Let us next notice the *means he was directed to use for the preservation of God's chosen remnant*. He was to build a vessel of stupendous magnitude, capable of holding two of every sort of animals that breathed, and of containing also provision for them. The expense and labour employed in constructing this ark must have been immense: and the ridicule which it must have excited, year after year, must have been almost beyond endurance.

Let us, lastly, observe *his perseverance in the use of those means, till he had completed the work assigned him.* Nothing could induce him to desist from his work, till it was perfected in every part. Then he, with his whole family, entered into the ark, having first assigned to every living creature its place: and then " God shut him in :" and on that very day the rain descended, and the flood commenced, which speedily reached above the highest mountains, and destroyed every living creature from the face of the earth.]

Verily this obedience was of a most exalted character—

[It shewed how firmly he believed the divine testimony, whilst yet there was not only no symptom of any such calamity, but no conceivable mode by which the threatened judgment could be inflicted. It shewed how much he stood in awe of God; and how determined he was, whilst yet the means of safety were within his reach, to avail himself of the opportunity that was afforded him, lest he also should be involved in the general ruin. It shewed, too, how boldly he faced reproach, when cast upon him for executing the divine commands. Had such a conduct been called for during the space of a few days only, we should have been the less astonished at it: but when it continued without intermission or abatement for the space of 120 years, we cannot but reckon it amongst the sublimest acts of obedience ever rendered unto God by fallen man.]

But in perfect accordance with this, is,

II. The obedience required of us—

1. The danger to which we are exposed is similar—

[God has declared that he will call the whole world into judgment; and that in that day " the wicked shall be turned into hell, and all the nations that forget God[a]." We see not, indeed, any preparation for such a judgment; and are ready to think that it never can be executed. But God has denounced it against the whole world; and executed it shall be, whether men will believe it or not. Multitudes who assisted in building the ark, would not believe the declarations of God, till the threatened judgments were inflicted: and so it is with us. Multitudes laugh at the threatenings of God; and will continue to do so, till their day of grace shall have passed, and the wrath of God shall fall upon them to the uttermost.]

2. The means provided for our escape are similar—

[God has provided an ark for us—even his only dear Son; an ark, into which all who believe shall be admitted, but which will speedily be closed against the unbelieving world. Many think it altogether absurd to imagine that such an ark is provided for us: they would prefer one of their own

[a] Ps. ix. 17.

constructing, and for which their own good works shall afford the materials. To enter into Christ by faith, and to look for salvation through faith in him, is in their eyes an unsuitable device: and it is derided accordingly, as an indication of weakness and folly. But this, after all, will be found "the wisdom of God," yea, and "the power of God unto salvation" also to all them that embrace it.]

3. The distinction that will be made between the believing and unbelieving world will also be similar—

[Of those who believed the testimony of Noah, not one perished: of those that disbelieved it, not one was saved. And so it will be at the last day. Those who are "found in Christ," will be monuments of God's sparing mercy; whilst those who have neglected and despised him, will be monuments of his righteous indignation for ever and ever.]

To dilate more, either on the original fact, or on its typical adaptation to our circumstances, will not be necessary: the whole taken together in one combined view will be found, I apprehend, more instructive.

LEARN then, from the whole,

1. The office of faith—

[It was to his faith that Noah's conduct on this occasion must be ascribed[b]. He did not *reason* on the subject that was revealed to him. He did not say, How can such a deluge be produced? or, How can it be supposed that a merciful God should exercise such severity? or, How can it be hoped, that, if all the rest of the world be destroyed, any vessel that I can build will preserve me? It is probable that others argued thus: but *he* believed, and acted upon, the divine testimony. Now it is precisely in that way that we must exercise faith in the divine records. We are not to argue, How can it be, that any should be punished with endless torments in hell? or, that so great a part of mankind should be doomed to that fate? or, that a simple faith in the Lord Jesus Christ should be sufficient to deliver those, who without such faith must inevitably perish? We are to give credit to the divine testimony; and to assure ourselves, that whatever God has spoken shall surely come to pass;—that "he who believeth and is baptized, shall be saved; and that he who believeth not, shall be damned."]

2. The necessity of fear—

[By this also was Noah actuated; and under the influence of it he prepared the ark[c]. And if we believe God's threatenings against sin and sinners, how can we but fear? The

[b] Heb. xi. 7.   [c] Heb. xi. 7.

wrath of God is not to be disregarded, as a matter of no concern: no, in truth, it becomes us to tremble at it, and to flee from it with all imaginable earnestness. Well would it have been for them, if the people whom he warned had feared also: but, because they would not fear, they perished. So will it be with us also[d]. It shall surely be found a truth at last, that "he who, being often reproved, hardeneth his neck, shall suddenly be destroyed, and that without a remedy[e]."]

3. The benefit of obedience—

[Here you behold with your eyes what shall be again realized in the day of judgment. Behold Noah for 120 years an object of universal derision, but now, with his family, borne above the waves in perfect safety, whilst all the rest of the world, not excepting the very builders of the ark, are overwhelmed in one common destruction! Thus let the ungodly world laugh at piety now, if they will: but such will be the issue of their contemptuous proceedings, when those who were the objects of their scorn will be honoured by their God, and be saved with an everlasting salvation. "Say ye to the righteous, that it shall be well with him; for they shall eat the fruit of their doings: but woe unto the wicked! it shall be ill with him, for the reward of his hands shall be given him[f]."]

[d] Matt. xxiv. 37—39.   [e] Prov. xxix. 1. Compare 2 Pet. ii. 5, 9.
[f] Isai. iii. 10, 11.

OUTLINE NO. 16

PRESERVATION OF NOAH.

Gen. vii. 1. *And the Lord said unto Noah, Come thou, and all thy house, into the ark.*

THE Church of God has frequently been at so low an ebb, that its existence cannot now be traced. There have been times, even since the promulgation of Christianity, when the righteous have been but few: they appear to us indeed much fewer than they really were: and, if we had authentic records respecting them, as we have concerning the Jews, it is probable that we should find several thousand worshippers of Jehovah for one whose name has been transmitted to us[a]. But in the patriarchal ages we are

[a] 1 Kings xix. 14, 18.

certain that the knowledge of God was very limited yea, so universal was the degeneracy of man before the flood, that piety was confined to one single family: nor were all of *them* truly religious, though for their parents' sake they were all made partakers of the same deliverance. The history before us presents to our view a most distressing scene; a world of sinners doomed to destruction; and the only righteous family in the world selected out of them, to be monuments of God's sparing mercy. The account given of Noah in the text will lead us to shew,

I. The provision made for his security—

Righteousness is universally an object of God's regard: and though it is not meritorious in his sight so as to justify men before him, yet is it so pleasing and acceptable to him, that he will on account of it bestow many temporal blessings, and in the eternal world will confer a more exalted state of glory[b]. On account of his eminent piety, God distinguished Noah[c], and instructed him to make an ark for the saving of himself and his household.

This ark was typical of the Church of Christ. St. Peter compares it with baptism, by which we are initiated into the Church; and tells us, that as Noah was saved by his admission into the one, so are we by our introduction into the other[d].

To mark the resemblance between the type and antitype, we may observe that the ark was,

1. Divinely appointed—

[As the Tabernacle in the time of Moses, so the Ark in Noah's time, was made according to a pattern devised by God himself.

Noah never could have thought of constructing such a vessel himself: the suggestion originated with God: the model for it was given by God: nor was even the smallest part of it left to be formed after man's device.

And who among the sons of men ever conceived the idea of saving man through the incarnation and death of God's only-begotten Son? Who could ever have imagined that Jehovah's

---

[b] Ezek. ix. 4. with 1 Tim. iv. 8.
[c] See the words following the text.   [d] 1 Pet. iii. 20, 21.

Fellow should become a man; that He should submit to this degradation, yea, moreover should endure the accursed death of the cross, for the purpose of reconciling us to his offended Father, and of " gathering together into one body all things both in heaven and on earth[e]?" Who, I ask, would have ever thought of forming a church in such a way, and of saving man by such means? The whole plan bears the stamp and character of a divine origin, according to what is said by the Apostle, " By grace are ye saved through faith; and *that* not of yourselves; it is the gift of God[f]."]

2. Wisely framed—

[The ark, it must be confessed, did not accord with those principles of navigation which obtain amongst us: it was defective in some of the most essential points: it had no mast, no sails, no rudder. But it was so constructed as to convince all who were saved in it, that their salvation was of God alone, and that to him alone was all the glory due. At the same time it was so formed, that every creature in it found ample accommodation.

The Church too is constituted far otherwise than human wisdom would have framed it. Man would have left room for the display of his own skill, and for the establishment of his own righteousness. He would not have chosen to stand indebted wholly to the righteousness of another: *that* is too offensive to his natural pride: it is " to the Jews a stumbling-block, and to the Greeks foolishness[g]." To have no sails or rudder left for him to manage, would be disgusting; because it would necessitate him to feel his entire dependence on God, and to acknowledge, that " it is not of him that willeth, nor of him that runneth, but of God that sheweth mercy[h]." Yet in all these things God's wisdom is displayed. This way of salvation is justly called, " the wisdom of God, and the power of God[i]." It cuts off all possible occasion for boasting[k], and compels us to say, " Not unto us, O Lord, not unto us, but unto thy name be the praise." At the same time it is the most suitable that can possibly be imagined. While the moral and discreet are constrained to seek refuge in Christ, the vilest prodigal is not left to despair of mercy: he may enter in at the same door with others, and participate the salvation which God has provided for him.]

3. Richly furnished—

[e] Eph. i. 10.
[f] Eph. ii. 8. Τοῦτο, it should seem, refers rather to the sentiment expressed, than to πίστις, which is of the feminine gender.
[g] 1 Cor. i. 23.   [h] Rom. ix. 16.   [i] 1 Cor. i. 24.
[k] Rom. iii. 27.

[There was in the ark an abundant store of provision both for man and beast: so that no creature, from the largest animal to the smallest insect, lacked any thing that was needful for it.

Surely in this respect it beautifully represents the Church of Christ, wherein the ordinances of divine grace are administered, and "exceeding great and precious promises are given" for our support. There is not a person in it, from the greatest to the least, who may not find all that can conduce to his health and comfort. There is milk for babes, and meat for those who are of full age[1]. There is " a feast of fat things" provided for our daily sustenance. There are the richest cordials, " even wines upon the lees well refined," that are dispensed freely to all who desire them. Nothing is lacking: we need never fear lest the store should be exhausted. Nothing is grudged to the meanest servant in the family: all is given to one as well as to another; and to every one, " without money and without price."]

We may yet further trace the typical import of the ark in,

II. The direction given in reference to it—

Noah having finished the ark, waited for further intimations of the divine will, which at length were given him. The direction, as it relates to *us*, implies two things;

1. That we should use the appointed means of salvation ourselves—

[God having formed his church, and provided every thing requisite for the preservation of our souls, now speaks to every one of us, " Enter thou into the ark."

Christ says to us, " I am the door;" " I am the way, the truth, and the life." By Him therefore we are to enter in[m]. By faith in him we shall be placed beyond the reach of harm, and may " rejoice in hope of the glory of God[n]." This is the duty to which we are called.

We are not to amuse ourselves with indulging idle speculations about the fitness of the ark to answer its intended purpose: we have no time to lose: the danger is imminent: if we lose the present moment, we may be undone for ever. We have nothing to do but to " enter in," and to commit ourselves to the care of our heavenly Pilot.]

2. That we should exert ourselves for the salvation of others—

---

[1] Heb. v. 13, 14.   [m] John x. 9.   [n] Rom. v. 2.

[We should not be contented to go to heaven alone: we should say with the church of old, "Draw *me;* and *we* will run after thee°." It is the height of impiety to ask, "Am I my brother's keeper?" We are all appointed to watch over each other: What the Minister is amongst his flock, that every Parent and Master is among his children and servants. We should employ all the influence we possess, for the advantage of those around us. God testified his approbation of Abraham on account of his fidelity in improving this talent; and inflicted signal judgments upon Eli for neglecting to exert his parental authority. If, like Lot, we cannot prevail upon our relatives to follow our advice, we shall not be responsible for them: but if they perish through our neglect, their blood will be required at our hands P. We should therefore warn our children and servants to flee from the wrath to come. We should open to them the way of salvation through faith in a crucified Saviour. We should declare faithfully to them, that there is " no other name given under heaven whereby we can be saved, but the name of Jesus Christ;" and we should urge them with all possible earnestness to embrace his covenant, and seek acceptance through him: In short, we should separate both ourselves and them from an ungodly world, and " seek to be found in Christ, not having our own righteousness, but that which is of God by faith in him."]

We are aware that many OBJECTIONS will arise against this advice: which therefore we will briefly consider.

1. We are in the ark already—

[It is granted, that as far as the ark designates the *visible* Church of Christ, we are all inclosed in it ꟴ. But we must distinguish between the *visible* and the *invisible* church. Our blessed Lord has taught us carefully to distinguish between the fruitful and unfruitful branches; which, though they are both " *in* him," will be very differently dealt with by the great Husbandman ʳ. The Gospel net incloses many fishes; but the good only will be preserved: the bad will be cast away ˢ. In the field, the tares grow together with the wheat: but a separation will be made at last; the one for the fire of hell, the other for the granary of heaven ᵗ. The Jews were the peculiar people

---

º Cant. i. 4.   ᵖ Ezek. xxxiii. 8, 9.

ꟴ In the baptismal service we pray, that, " as Noah and his family were saved in the ark from perishing by water, so we, being received into *the ark of Christ's Church,* may so pass the waves of this troublesome world, that we may be finally brought to the land of everlasting life."

ʳ John xv. 2.   ˢ Matt. xiii. 47, 48.   ᵗ Matt. xiii. 30.

of God: and St. Paul tells us, that "to them pertained the adoption, and the glory, and the covenants, and the giving of the law, and the service of God, and the promises:" Yet "he had great heaviness and continual sorrow in his heart on account of them;" which he would not have had, if he had thought that the possession of those outward privileges was sufficient. But he accounts for his feelings by saying, that "all are not Israel, who are of Israel[u]." And he elsewhere assures us, in still stronger terms, that it is not any outward privilege or profession that constitutes us Christians, but an inward change of heart, which approves itself to the all-seeing God[x]. Let us not then deceive ourselves, or imagine that we must of necessity be saved because we have been baptized: for there was an "accursed Ham" in the ark, as well as a righteous Noah: but let us inquire into the dispositions and habits of our minds: let us examine whether we have given up ourselves unreservedly to God; and whether we are striving to "glorify him with our bodies and our spirits, which are his?"]

2. We do not see that we are in any danger—

[This was the case with the antediluvian world. They saw no appearance of any deluge: they could not persuade themselves that God would ever inflict such a tremendous judgment on the earth: and they imputed the anxiety of Noah to superstition, credulity, and folly. But did their unbelief make void the truth of God? Yea rather, did it not harden them to their own destruction? What security then will our unbelief afford us? We see not any symptoms of that wrath which is threatened against an ungodly world: but will it therefore never come? Will the word of God fail of its accomplishment? Is it safe for us to set up our opinions against the positive declarations of Heaven, and to found all our hopes of salvation upon the presumption that "God will lie?" Seen, or unseen, our danger is the same: and if all perished at the deluge who took not refuge in the ark, so will all perish at the day of judgment who have not "fled for refuge to the hope set before them."]

3. We shall become singular—

[This is an objection which we cannot but allow; and it is with pain and grief that we confess its force. We acknowledge that, if we will seek in earnest the salvation of our souls, we must be singular. But whose fault is this? It was not Noah's fault that he was singular in the old world: it was the

---

[u] Rom. ix. 3—6.   [x] Rom. ii. 28, 29.

fault of those who refused to listen to the voice of mercy, and to obey the commands of God. And surely Noah would have paid a very unbecoming deference to the world, if he had followed their example rather than his own convictions, and consented to perish with them, rather than secure his own salvation. Why then should we carry our complaisance to such a criminal extent, when the everlasting salvation of our souls is at stake? We regret that we are compelled to be singular: but we must confess, It is better to be saved with Noah and his little family, than to perish with an ungodly world: It is better to walk in the narrow and unfrequented way which leadeth unto life, than to go in the broad road which terminates in destruction.]

Dismissing then your objections, "suffer a word of EXHORTATION"—

[To every one we would address the words of our text, "Enter thou, and all thy family, into the ark." Consider, how near the day of mercy may have come to its close! The day of judgment may be far off, as it respects the world at large; but it may be nigh at hand as it respects ourselves. The hour of death may be much nearer to us than we imagine: and that will, in effect, be the day of judgment to us. O what shall we then do, if we be not found in the true ark? What shall we do, if we belong not to Him "of whom the whole family in heaven and earth is named," and be not numbered amongst his "little flock," on whom alone the kingdom of heaven will be conferred? Let us only paint to ourselves the distress we should have felt, if we had seen the waters rapidly surrounding us, and the ark shut against us: yet this would be a very faint image of what we shall feel, when the vials of God's wrath shall be poured out upon us, and no hope of deliverance be afforded. Let us then "not *seek* merely, but *strive*, to enter in." Let us endeavour to bring all we can along with us. It will be a painful sight, if we be saved ourselves, to see our wife, our children, our servants, our friends perishing around us, and swallowed up in "the lake that burneth with fire and brimstone." On the other hand, what a joy will it be to present them unto God, saying, "Here am I, and the children thou hast given me!" Let us then exert our influence while we can; and I pray God that our labours may be crowned with success; and that, instead of going to heaven alone, we may all have some to be "our joy and crown of rejoicing" in that solemn day!]

OUTLINE NO. 17

GOD'S COVENANT WITH NOAH.

Gen. ix. 12—16. *And God said, This is the token of the Covenant which I make between me and you and every living creature that is with you, for perpetual generations: I do set my bow in the cloud, and it shall be for a token of a covenant between me and the earth. And it shall come to pass, when I bring a cloud over the earth, that the bow shall be seen in the cloud: and I will remember my covenant which is between me and you and every living creature of all flesh; and the waters shall no more become a flood to destroy all flesh. And the bow shall be in the cloud, and I will look upon it, that I may remember the everlasting covenant between God and every living creature of all flesh that is upon the earth.*

MAN has no claim whatever upon his God, any more than a vessel has upon the potter who formed it. He is indebted to God for the existence which he has, and depends altogether on his will for the continuance of that existence. But God has been pleased to lay himself under voluntary engagements with his creatures, in order that they may know how gracious he is, and be encouraged to serve him with more lively gratitude. When he had formed man at the first, he entered into a covenant with him to bestow on him blessings to which he could not otherwise have been entitled. And after that the extreme wickedness of the world had provoked him to destroy it, he vouchsafed to make another covenant with Noah, whom he had preserved in the ark. He knew that the severe judgment which he had inflicted on the human race would, for a time at least, strike terror into succeeding generations, and perhaps deter them from cultivating the earth. He therefore gave to Noah an assurance that he would never again destroy all his creatures with a flood; and confirmed this promise by a covenant and an oath.

It will be instructive to mark,

I. The peculiarities of this covenant—

In many things it differs very widely from any

other covenant that God has ever entered into. Its peculiarity is visible,

1. In the parties with whom it was made—

[The covenant made with Adam, included him and his posterity. That with Abraham, extended only to him and his believing Seed. That with Moses, was limited to the Jewish nation. But the covenant with Noah comprehended the whole creation: it embraced the beasts of the field, as well as the human race: every living creature, not excepting the meanest reptile, was interested in it.]

2. In the blessings which it promised—

[All other covenants held forth spiritual and eternal blessings to those who were admitted into them. Even the Mosaic covenant, which dwelt so much upon the enjoyment of the promised land, can by no means be considered as confining the prospects of the Jews to temporal happiness: for the presence of God amongst them was very distinctly promised them, together with the special manifestations of his love and favour: and the very land itself was regarded as typical of a better rest, which they were hereafter to receive. But the covenant made with Noah, promised only that the earth should not any more be destroyed by a flood. It engaged indeed that there should be a constant succession of the seasons till the end of time: but it gave no intimation whatever of spiritual mercies. Being made with the whole creation of beasts as well as men, it promised only such blessings as all the creation could partake of.]

3. In the seal with which it was confirmed—

[Every covenant has a seal affixed to it, as a pledge of its accomplishment. The Adamic covenant was confirmed by the tree of life; the Abrahamic, by circumcision; the Christian, by baptism. In each the seal was significant, either of duties undertaken, or of benefits conferred. But the seal that was chosen for the covenant with Noah, was very peculiar. It was the rainbow. Whenever a rainbow appears, it is a sign that there is rain at that very moment descending on the earth; (for a rainbow is nothing more than the rays of the sun reflected from the drops that fall): consequently, it is in itself rather a ground for apprehending that another deluge may come. Yet God was pleased to appoint that as a token and pledge, that he never will deluge the earth again: he has chosen that, I say, which is an intimation of our danger, to be his pledge for our security.]

Without insisting any longer on these subordinate matters, we proceed to notice,

II. Wherein it accords with the Christian covenant—

There certainly are some striking features in this covenant, which, if not intended absolutely to typify the Christian covenant, are at least well calculated to draw our attention to it.

1. It was founded upon a sacrifice—

[This is particularly deserving of notice. As soon as Noah had come out from the ark, he built an altar, and offered sacrifices upon it. These sacrifices were to God "an odour of a sweet smell:" yea, so acceptable were they to him, that he immediately "said in his heart, I will not curse the ground any more for man's sake[a]." Can we refrain from acknowledging the correspondence which this bears with the covenant of grace? The hopes which God has been pleased to give us of deliverance from the curses of his law, are altogether founded on that great sacrifice which was once offered on the cross. The covenant indeed was made thousands of years before our blessed Saviour became incarnate: but he was, in the divine intention and purpose, "the Lamb slain from the foundation of the world." From the moment he undertook our cause, he engaged to "make his soul an offering for sin[b]:" and it was on that ground that he was to have a people given to him for "a purchased possession[c]."

Let us never forget this glorious truth; "Our curse was removed by Christ being made a curse for us[d]:" Our reconciliation with God was effected solely by the blood of his cross[e]: God smelled the sweet savour of his sacrifice[f], and determined that all who came to him through Christ should find acceptance with him; and that "*through the blood of the everlasting covenant*" he would be a God of peace unto them[g].]

2. It embraced all, without any respect to their moral character—

[In the passage before cited[h] God declares that "he would not any more curse the earth, *though*[i] the imagination of man's heart was evil from his youth." It was not on account of the *merits* of mankind that God made that covenant with Noah, nor would he withhold the blessings of it on account of their *demerits:* yea, though he foresaw that men would still be naturally and universally prone to evil, he voluntarily entered into this covenant, in order that he might display his own grace and mercy towards them. And what did God find in

---

[a] Gen. viii. 20—22.   [b] Isai. liii. 10—12.   [c] Eph. i. 14.
[d] Gal. iii. 13.   [e] Col. i. 20.   [f] Eph. v. 2.
[g] Heb. xiii. 20, 21.   [h] Gen. viii. 20—22.
[i] The marginal version is "*though;*" and it is certainly preferable to the word "*for,*" which stands in the text.

our fallen race that could induce him to enter into covenant with his Son on their behalf? Had he respect to any merit of theirs; or was he prevented by what he foresaw in reference to their demerit? Had he, in short, any other view than that of displaying "the exceeding riches of his grace in his kindness towards us through Christ Jesus?" The parallel *in this respect* is exact. There is indeed a point connected with this, which forms rather a contrast than a parallel: and we the rather specify it, because the mention of it is necessary to guard against all misconception of our meaning. The covenant made with Noah not only extended its benefits to the ungodly, but left them still as ungodly as ever: whereas the covenant of grace makes provision for the change of men's characters[k]: it offers indeed all its blessings to the most unworthy; but when they embrace it, they are made partakers of a new and divine nature[l], which secures the gradual renovation of their souls after the image of their God. " Sin is no longer suffered to have dominion over them, because they are not under the law, but under grace[m]." Nevertheless, we repeat it, the Christian covenant includes none on account of their superior goodness, nor rejects any on account of their more atrocious sinfulness; but embraces all who will accept its benefits, and imparts salvation to them freely " without money and without price."]

3. It was immutable and everlasting—

[It is above four thousand years since the covenant was given to Noah; and no part of it has ever yet failed. There have been partial inundations, and partial suspensions of fruitful seasons: but at no period, from the deluge to this hour, has any thing occurred like the desolation that was inflicted in the days of Noah. And we may rest assured, that the revolutions of night and day, summer and winter, seed-time and harvest, will continue till the day of judgment, when the earth, and all that is therein, shall be destroyed by fire. And can we not affirm the same respecting the covenant of grace? Is not that "ordered in all things and sure?" We are told that "God, in order to shew the immutability of his counsel, confirmed it by an oath; that by two immutable things, in which it was impossible for God to lie, we who have fled to Christ for refuge, might have strong consolation[n]:" And when did He ever violate his solemn engagements? Who that ever sought to lay hold on this covenant, was rejected? Who that firmly trusted in it ever found it to fail him in any one particular? We challenge the whole world to produce a single instance, wherein " God has ever broken his covenant,

[k] Jer. xxxi. 33.
[m] Rom. vi. 14.
[l] 2 Pet. i. 4.
[n] Heb. vi. 17, 18.

or altered the thing that had gone out of his lips°." The comparison between the two covenants in this particular is not forced or fanciful; it is suggested by God himself; who assures us that the covenant of his grace and peace shall be more immovable than rocks or mountains, yea, as unalterable as the covenant which he made with Noah[p].]

We will close the subject with two suitable REFLECTIONS:

1. What reason have we to admire the *forbearance* of God!

[The continuance of the world, considering the state of its inhabitants, is a most astonishing proof of God's mercy and forbearance. Let us only look around, and see whether mankind be not almost universally living as they did before the flood: "they were then eating and drinking, marrying and giving in marriage," and regardless of the warnings of God's righteous Monitor. And this is precisely our state: yet God has spared us, instead of inflicting on us the judgments we have deserved. He has even sent us "fruitful seasons, filling our hearts with food and gladness." What reason then have we to bless and magnify his name! But let us rather turn our eyes inward, and see what reason God has had to make us monuments of his vengeance. Let us contemplate how many of our fellow-creatures are at this moment suffering the just desert of their deeds, while we continue upon mercy's ground, and have all the offers of salvation still sounding in our ears. Let us "account this long-suffering of God to be salvation:" let us "seek him while he may be found, and call upon him while he is near."]

2. What encouragement have we to seek his *grace!*

[Without ever once adverting to it in our minds, we are at this moment enjoying the benefits of the covenant made with Noah: and, notwithstanding all our unworthiness, we are yet daily invited to embrace that better covenant, the covenant of grace. What shall we do then? Shall we continue regardless of God's mercies, till our day of grace is irrevocably past? O let us "not despise the riches of his patience and long-suffering and forbearance; but let his goodness lead us to repentance." Let us "not receive such stupendous grace in vain." Let us intreat him to "look upon the face of his anointed," as he looks continually upon the rainbow; and for the sake of Jesus to pity and pardon us. Then shall we find favour in his sight, and be delivered from the desolations, which must at last come upon the unbelieving world.]

o Ps. lxxxix. 34.   p Isai. liv. 8—10.

OUTLINE NO. 18

CONFUSION OF TONGUES.

Gen. xi. 4—8. *And they said, Go to, let us build us a city, and a tower whose top may reach unto heaven; and let us make us a name, lest we be scattered abroad upon the face of the whole earth. And the Lord came down to see the city and the tower, which the children of men builded. And the Lord said, Behold, the people is one, and they have all one language; and this they begin to do: and now nothing will be restrained from them which they have imagined to do. Go to, let us go down, and there confound their language, that they may not understand one another's speech. So the Lord scattered them abroad from thence upon the face of all the earth: and they left off to build the city.*

THERE are many things observable in the world, of which neither reason nor history enables us to give any account. One would naturally suppose that Noah and his family speaking the same language, their children should speak the same; and that the same would be transmitted to their latest posterity. Small alterations might be expected to arise; but they would only be different dialects of the same language. But instead of this, there are hundreds of different languages in the world. Even in this island there are no less than three. Learned men have indeed endeavoured to trace various languages to one; but though by their efforts they have displayed their own ingenuity, they have never been able to establish their hypothesis. The true origin of this diversity of languages is revealed to us in the Holy Scriptures. In the passage before us we are informed respecting the time and manner and occasion of their first introduction. The descendants of Noah were building a city and tower in order to prevent that dispersion of their families, which God had ordained for the replenishing of the earth: and God, in righteous displeasure, confounded their languages, so that they could not understand each other: by this means they were necessitated to relinquish their project, and to fulfil the designs of his overruling Providence.

In our observations on the history of these builders we shall notice,

I. Their intentions—

It does not appear that they designed to fortify themselves against another deluge; for then they would have built on a mountain rather than a plain.— They had principally two things in view:

1. The advancement of their own honour—

[They said, " Go to, let us make ourselves a name." They thought that by raising this city they should immortalize themselves, and 'be famed for their wisdom and energy to the remotest generations. And here we see the principle which actuates all the world. What is it but the desire of fame which impels the warrior to the field of battle? What has greater influence on the philosopher, or more forcibly animates him in his researches after knowledge? What is it that actuates the rich in constructing and decorating their spacious edifices, but a desire to display their taste and opulence? Even the charitable are too often under the influence of this motive. To this, *in many instances*, must be ascribed the founding of colleges, or endowing of hospitals, or contributing to the support of established institutions. If, in any public charity, the publishing of the names of its supporters were to be discontinued, a difference would soon be found in the amount of the contributions. Would to God we could exempt the professors of religion also from this imputation! Where the heart is really right with God, it is on its guard against this base principle; but there are too many hypocrites, whose chief aim is to be accounted religious, and to be admired either for their talents or their virtues. There will at times be a mixture of principle in the best of men, which it is the labour of their lives to detect and rectify: and there is in all who are truly conscientious a commendable desire to approve themselves to their fellow-creatures in the discharge of their several duties. It is not in reference to either of these that we now speak. It is rather in reference to those in whom the love of fame has a predominant ascendancy: of them we say, as of the builders of Babel, that they are the objects of God's just and heavy displeasure[a].]

2. The gratification of their own wishes—

[God had ordered that the survivors of the deluge should " increase and multiply, and replenish the earth[b]." Of course,

---

[a] See this exemplified in Nebuchadnezzar (Dan. iv. 30, 31.) Herod (Acts xii. 22, 23.) and even the pious Hezekiah (2 Kings xx. 13—18.) [b] Gen. ix. 1.

if the whole earth was to be re-peopled, the rising generations must gradually enlarge their borders, with a view to occupy every quarter of the globe. But the builders of Babel thought that such a dispersion would deprive them of many comforts, and be attended with many inconveniences. As for the divine will, they were not much concerned about it: all they thought of was, their own ease and pleasure: and if obedience to God stood in competition with the gratification of their own wishes, they did not hesitate to sacrifice duty to inclination.

In this respect their example is very generally followed. God has prescribed a line of conduct to us which is difficult and self-denying. He requires us to sit loose to the vanities of this world, and to seek our rest and happiness above. This but ill suits our earthly and sensual dispositions. Hence we choose not to submit to such restraints: we think we are at liberty to please ourselves: we pronounce the commands of God to be unnecessarily strict and severe: we content ourselves with such a conformity to them as will consist with the indulgence of our own desires: and we prosecute our plans without any reference to His will, or any subjection to His control.

Look at the young, the gay, the worldly, the ambitious; and say whether they be not all treading in the steps of these infatuated builders? Say whether they do not systematically shun a life of self-denial, and follow their own inclinations rather than the commands of God?

How offensive such a life is to God we may collect from those declarations of the apostle, That "to be carnally-minded is death," and that "they who are in the flesh cannot please God[c]."]

Since their purpose was directly opposite to God's decree, we shall not wonder at,

II. Their disappointment—

God in this place, as also in several other places, speaks in the plural number; "Let US go down[d]." By this form of expression he gave, it should seem, an early intimation of the mysterious doctrine of the Trinity, which was afterwards to be more clearly revealed. Moreover, speaking after the manner of men, he represents himself as coming down from heaven to inspect their work, and as feeling an apprehension, that, if he did not interrupt its progress, his own plans respecting the dispersion of mankind would be defeated. He then declares his determination to

[c] Rom. viii. 6, 8.   [d] Gen. i. 26. and iii. 22.

frustrate their design, and to accomplish his own purposes, by confounding their language.

Now in this their disappointment it will be profitable to notice,

1. The time—

[*God interrupted them in the midst of all their hopes and projects.* They had made considerable progress in their work, and were, doubtless, anticipating the satisfaction they would feel in its completion. And thus it is that the expectations of those who are seeking their happiness in this world are generally disappointed. They form their plans; they prosecute their designs; they advance in their prospects; partial success animates them to a more diligent pursuit of their favourite object: but sooner or later God stops them in their career, and says to them, " Thou fool, this night shall thy soul be required of thee." " When they are saying, Peace and safety, then sudden destruction cometh upon them, as a thief in the night, or as travail upon a woman with child."]

2. The manner—

[The means which God used to stop the progress of the work was *the most unlooked for* that can be imagined. The people engaged in it might conceive it possible that they should be stopped by quarrels amongst themselves, or by another deluge, or by fire from heaven; but they could never entertain the remotest idea of such an interruption as they experienced. And thus does God generally interpose to disappoint the expectations of worldly men. He has ten thousand ways in which to render their plans abortive, or to embitter to them the very things in which they have sought their happiness. We have laboured for honour and distinction: he suffers us perhaps to attain our wishes; and then makes our elevation a source of nothing but disquietude and pain. Many have looked for enjoyment in the acquisition of a partner or a family; who after a time would give the world perhaps to loose the indissoluble knot, or to have been " written childless in the earth." In short, the Governor of the Universe is never at a loss for means to confound the devices of the wise, or frustrate the counsels of the ungodly.

Moreover, as the disappointment of the builders was *strange and unlooked for*, so was it *in a way that perpetuated their disgrace.* The building which they had raised would, for many centuries perhaps, be a witness against them: every time also that they opened their lips, they would be reminded of their folly and wickedness by the very language which they spoke: and as long as the world shall stand, the different nations of the earth will exhibit the sad effects of their impiety, the indelible records of their shame.

And where can we turn our eyes without seeing memorials of human folly, and evidences, that all creature-confidences are vain? Ask the aged, and they will testify; inquire even of the young, and they will confess; that the creature, however fair its appearance or promising its aspect, is only " a broken cistern which can hold no water." All of them, both rich and poor, " have gone to it with their vessels, and come away ashamed[e]." They renew indeed their applications from time to time; but only to experience repeated disappointments. There are but few who have not found their cup, notwithstanding its occasional sweets, so distasteful on the whole, that they are almost weary of the world by the time that they have half completed their destined course. And the more eager they have been in their pursuit of earthly good, the more painfully have they been made to feel, that it was all " vanity and vexation of spirit."

If we look into the eternal world, what monuments shall we *there* find of disappointed ambition! What multitudes are *there*, who once said, ' I aspire after happiness; I shall find it in the attainment of wealth, and in the gratifications of sense!' They passed their time in dreaming of happiness which they never realized; and knew not that they had been dreaming, till " they awoke to shame and everlasting contempt." And though, while in this world they justified their choice, they themselves will to all eternity be witnesses for God, acknowledging the folly of their former conduct, and the justice of their present doom.]

We cannot conclude without OBSERVING,

1. How awfully do we at this moment suffer under the curse inflicted on them!

[Difference of language has not only placed obstacles in the way of commercial intercourse, but has given occasion to contiguous or distant nations to consider each other as enemies. Moreover, it has been the means of excluding the greater part of the world from all the advantages of revelation. And if a benevolent person, desirous of diffusing the knowledge of Christ among the heathen, engage in the arduous undertaking, he must first lose several years before he can attain a competent knowledge of the languages in which he is to address them: even then he labours under the greatest disadvantages in speaking to them; and, after all, he must limit his exertions to two or three nations at the uttermost. Multitudes

---

[e] Jer. xiv. 3.

there are who would gladly encounter labour and fatigue in the service of their fellow-creatures; but they are discouraged by these difficulties, and are compelled to restrain their benevolent wishes through a conscious incapacity to carry them into effect. Nor is this all: for the unlearned of our own nation sustain incalculable loss through the introduction of foreign words, and foreign idioms, into our own language; insomuch that, if they hear a discourse that has been penned for the edification of the learned, the preacher is, in fact, " a barbarian to them," almost as much as if he spoke in another language.

Suffering thus as we do for the transgression of those builders, we ought at least to shun a repetition of their sins, and to humble ourselves before God for all the pride and worldliness of our hearts.]

2. How graciously has God blended mercy with judgment!

[When the plan of salvation was perfected, and the time for the more extensive propagation of the Gospel was arrived, God inspired holy men, without any previous instruction, to speak all manner of languages, and to diffuse the knowledge of the truth through all nations; that as by the division of tongues he had dispersed men through the earth, so by the gift of tongues " he might gather together in one the children of God that were scattered abroad[f]." The end of that gift having been in a measure attained, and the gift itself withdrawn, he stirred up men of learning and piety in different countries to translate the Scriptures into their respective languages, so that the unlearned might read them in the language which they understood. What do we of this nation owe to God, and, under God, to our Reformers, for giving us the Bible in our own tongue! If the volume of inspiration were locked up in the languages in which it was first written, how deplorable would be our state! Oh, never, never can we be sufficiently thankful that the fountains of divine knowledge are open and accessible to all!

Moreover, though the languages of men are still different, there is a language in which all the children of God throughout the earth agree,—the language of the heart. As far as respects the work of God upon their souls, they all speak precisely the same thing. Sighs and groans and tears are universally the expressions of their sorrow on account of sin. They all agree in exalting Christ as " their wisdom, their righteousness, their sanctification, and their complete redemption." They glory in Him, and in him alone. They are indeed Barbarians to the ignorant ungodly world, who

---

[f] Acts ii. 3—6. with John xi. 52.

are ready to say of them as the Jews did of the Apostles, "These men are full of new wine," they are foolish, they are mad. But they understand each other: though brought from the most distant parts of the earth, there will be found such an agreement between them, as will unite their hearts to each other in the closest bonds of love. What was said of them before their dispersion[g], may be said of them now again, "They are all one, and they have all one language." Though Egyptians by nature, they have learned the language of Canaan[h], and are again united in building an edifice that shall last for ever.

Let us then bless our God for these rich mercies; and from being "strangers and foreigners, let us seek to become fellow-citizens with the saints, and of the household of God."]

[g] ver. 6.   [h] Isai. xix. 18.

OUTLINE NO. 19

CALL OF ABRAM.

Gen. xii. 1—4. *Now the Lord had said unto Abram, Get thee out of thy country, and from thy kindred, and from thy father's house, unto a land that I will shew thee: And I will make of thee a great nation, and I will bless thee, and make thy name great; and thou shalt be a blessing: And I will bless them that bless thee, and curse him that curseth thee: and in thee shall all families of the earth be blessed. So Abram departed, as the Lord had spoken unto him.*

OUR God has been pleased to teach us, no less by example than by precept: and the instruction to be gathered from the life and conduct of his saints, commends itself to us with peculiar force, as being less open to the evasions of criticism, or the objections of prejudice. Doubtless we must exercise a sober judgment in determining *how far* we are to follow the Patriarchs, Prophets, or Apostles; for there were many things in their conduct which were peculiar to their situation and circumstances. But we can never materially err, if we attend to the spirit of their actions: here they were patterns to us: *and as far as relates to this*, we are to be "followers of them who through faith and patience now inherit the promises." We are bidden particularly to "walk in the steps of our father Abraham:" one of the most remarkable of which is that which is mentioned in our text.

We shall endeavour to observe that sobriety of interpretation, while we consider,

I. The Call of Abram—

The command given to him was most extraordinary—

[The world had speedily relapsed into idolatry. Abram was brought up, it should seem, in the common superstition. But it pleased God to separate him from the idolatrous world, in order that he might be a living witness for Jehovah, and preserve in his family the knowledge of the true God. For this end God appeared to him, and commanded him to leave his country and friends, and to go into a land which should afterwards be shewn him.]

But however strange this may appear, a similar command is given to every one of us—

[We are not indeed called to *leave* our country and connexions: but to withdraw our affections from earthly things, and to fix them upon things above, we *are* called[a]. The whole world around us lies in wickedness[b]: and we are expressly forbidden to be of the world, any more than Christ himself was of the world[c]. We are not to love it, or any thing that is in it[d]. We are not to be conformed to it[e], or to seek its friendship[f]: we are rather to come out from it[g], and be altogether crucified to it[h]. We are to regard it as a wilderness through which we are passing to our Father's house; and in our passage through it to consider ourselves only as strangers and pilgrims[i]. If we meet with good accommodation and kind treatment, we are to be thankful: if we meet with briers and thorns in our way, we must console ourselves with the thought, that it is our appointed way, and that every step will bring us nearer home[k]. Nothing good is to detain us; nothing evil to divert us from our path. We are to be looking forward to our journey's end, and to be proceeding towards it, whatever be the weather, or whatever the road[l]. The direction given to the church, is the same in every age; "Hearken, O daughter, and incline thine ear; forget also thine own people and thy father's house; so shall the King have pleasure in thy beauty[m]." There is no exemption, no dispensation granted to any, no difference allowed.

---

[a] Col. iii. 1, 2. [b] 1 John v. 19. [c] John xvii. 14, 16.
[d] 1 John ii. 15, 16. [e] Rom. xii. 2. [f] Jam. iv. 4.
[g] 2 Cor. vi. 17, 18. [h] Gal. vi. 14. [i] Heb. xi. 13.
[k] Acts xiv. 22. [l] Heb. xi. 14—16. [m] Ps. xlv. 10, 11.

Some from their occupations in society must be more conversant with the world than others: but in heart and affection all must be withdrawn from it; "not partaking of its sins, lest they should receive also of its plagues[n]."]

There will not appear to be any thing harsh in the command given to Abram, if we consider,

II. The inducements offered him—

These were far more than equivalent to any sacrifice he could make—

[He was to be *blessed in himself*, and a *blessing to others*. In respect of temporal things, he was *blessed* in a very signal manner to the latest hour of his life[o]. He was loaded also with spiritual and eternal benefits, being justified and accounted righteous before God, and being exalted after death to the highest seat in his Father's house. He was also *a blessing* to many: for his children and household were governed by him in a way most conducive to their best interests. The people amongst whom he sojourned could not but be edified by his instructions and conduct: and to this day the whole of his life affords a stimulus to the church to serve God after his example. But most of all was he a blessing in being the Progenitor of the Messiah, "in whom all the nations of the earth were to be blessed[p]:" and every person will be blessed or cursed according as he accepts or rejects that promised Seed[q].]

Similar inducements are offered to us also—

[Every one who, for Christ's sake, will renounce the world, shall be *blessed*. He may not possess opulence and honour; but "the little that he hath, shall be better to him than all the riches of the ungodly." In his soul he shall be truly blessed. View him in the state least enviable according to *human* apprehension; see him weeping and mourning for his sins; yet *then* is he truly blessed[r]: he shall have pardon and acceptance with his God: he shall experience the renewing and sanctifying influences of the Holy Spirit: he shall have "joys and consolations which the stranger intermeddleth not with:" and in due time "he shall be blessed with faithful Abraham," in the eternal fruition of his God.

He shall be *a blessing* too to all around him. View him in *his family connexions;* view him as a husband, a parent, a master, a friend; who so kind, so benevolent, so anxious to promote the happiness of those connected with him? View him in *the church*, or in *the state;* what blessings does he communicate by the light of his example! what evils does he avert

---

[n] Rev. xviii. 4.   [o] Gen. xxiv. 1, 35.
[p] Acts iii. 25. and Gal. iii. 8, 16.   [q] ver. 3.   [r] Matt. v. 3, 4

by his prevailing intercessions! Suppose the Christian to be instrumental to the salvation of one single soul; the whole world is not equivalent to the good that he has done. Nor is it that individual soul only that shall acknowledge him as its benefactor; for, all the good that shall arise through the medium of that soul to the remotest posterity, shall be traced up to him as its author; and shall occasion thanksgivings to God on his behalf to all eternity.

Let these inducements be duly weighed, and how light will the vanities of this world appear in comparison of them!]

From a believing prospect of these benefits arose,

III. His ready obedience—

Notwithstanding all the obstacles in his way, he without hesitation obeyed the call—

[His friends and relatives would consider his conduct as an indication of consummate weakness and folly: especially, when he could not so much as tell them whither he was going, they would be ready to pity him as insane. But as, on the one hand, he valued not the comforts of their society, so neither, on the other hand, did he regard their contempt and ridicule: every consideration gave way to a sense of duty, and a desire of the promised blessings. He believed, firmly believed, all that God had spoken. He believed especially that the Saviour of the world should spring from his loins; and that, through the merits of that Saviour, he himself, together with all his believing posterity, should possess that good land, even heaven itself, of which Canaan was a type and shadow. Under the influence of this faith he was contented to forego all the comforts that he could lose, and to endure all the sufferings that could come upon him[s].]

In this he was a pattern and example to all believers—

[If we renounce the world for Christ's sake, and set ourselves in earnest to seek the land of promise, we shall be despised and hated, even as Christ himself was[t]. But this we are not to regard. We are " not to confer with flesh and blood;" but instantly and perseveringly to pursue our destined course. What though we have never seen heaven, nor can even tell where it lies? it is sufficient for us to know that it is a land flowing with milk and honey, and that it is " kept for us until the time appointed of the Father." Nor need we doubt but that it will far more than counterbalance all the sufferings that we can endure in our way to it[u]. Let us only exercise the

[s] Heb. xi. 8—10.   [t] John xv. 18—20.   [u] Rom. viii. 18.

faith of Abram, and we shall instantly set out to follow his steps.]

ADDRESS,

1. Those who are at ease in their native land—

[It may appear harsh to say, that, "if you hate not father and mother, and houses and lands, yea and your own life also, you cannot be Christ's disciple[x]:" but this is the word of Christ himself. It is true, we are not to understand it in a *literal* sense; for we are not to "*hate*" even our enemies: but when our friends, or even life itself, stand in competition with Christ, we must *act as if* we hated them; we must sacrifice them all without one moment's hesitation. On lower terms than these Christ never will accept us: " We must forsake all, and follow him."]

2. Those who have set out towards the land of promise—

[Terah the father, and Nahor the brother, of Abram, accompanied him as far as Charran; and there (from what motive we know not) they all abode five years. God then renewed his call to Abram; but alas! his father was dead; and Nahor was weary of a wandering life; so that, on the recommencement of his journey, Abram had no associate but his Wife and Nephew. We pretend not to determine any thing of the spiritual state of Terah or Nahor; but their never entering into the land of Canaan may well be a caution to us to " beware, lest, having received a promise of entering into God's rest, any of us should seem to come short of it[y]." It were better never to have begun our journey heaven-ward, than to turn back, even in our hearts[z].]

[x] Luke xiv. 26.   [y] Heb. iv. 1.
[z] 2 Pet. ii. 20, 21. Heb. x. 38, 39.

OUTLINE NO. 20

ABRAM'S JOURNEY TO CANAAN.

Gen. xii. 5. *They went forth, to go into the land of Canaan: and into the land of Canaan they came.*

THE call of Abram is one of the most instructive subjects that can occupy the human mind; both because the perfections of Almighty God were most gloriously displayed in it; and because, in it, he shewed himself one of the brightest patterns of obedience that ever the world beheld.

He had had a revelation from God whilst yet he was at Ur, in the land of the Chaldees: by that he was directed to leave his native country; which was immersed, as he also and his father were, in idolatry[a]. At Haran (or, as it is also called, Charran) he abode till his father's death; when he received from God a further direction to go into Canaan, with an express assurance that the whole land of Canaan should be given to him and his posterity for an inheritance, and that in his seed should all the nations of the earth be blessed[b]. With this direction he complied: he took his wife and family, and all that he possessed, and set out upon the journey; as it is said in the words before us—" They went forth, to go into the land of Canaan; and into the land of Canaan they came."

Now this call of Abram is very instructive; no less as displaying the glorious perfections of God who called him, than as exhibiting the distinguished virtues of him who obeyed the call. I propose then, in illustrating this subject, to set before you,

I. The perfections of God for your admiration—

To this we are particularly led by that expression of St. Stephen, "The God of glory appeared unto our father Abraham." Observe, then,

1. His sovereignty—

[Why was Abram distinguished above all other of the sons of men, to be so blessed in himself, and such a blessing to the world? He and all his family were idolaters, as also were all around him: yet was he selected by Almighty God from among them, and made the friend and favourite of heaven. Can any account for this? Can it be traced to any thing but the sovereign will and pleasure of Jehovah? However adverse any man may be to the idea of God's sovereignty in the dispensation of his blessings, he cannot deny, he cannot question it, in this case. Yet this is really what is done in the conversion of every soul to God. The Almighty Sovereign of the universe " has saved us, and called us with an holy calling, *not according to our works*, but according to his own purpose and grace which was given us in Christ Jesus before the world began[c]." " It is God, and God alone, that has made any of

---

[a] Josh. xxiv. 2.   [b] ver. 1—4. with Act vii. 2—4.   [c] 2 Tim. i. 9.

us to differ" from our fellows[d]: and every saint, whether in heaven or on earth, must say, " By the grace of God I am what I am[e]."]

2. His power—

[Nothing less than omnipotence could have effected such a sudden and total change in the heart of Abram as was wrought at this time: nor, in truth, could any thing less than omnipotence have sufficed to accomplish for him all that was now promised. And is less power required for the " turning of any man from darkness unto light, and from the power of Satan unto God?" It is a new creation, and is expressly called so by God himself[f]. It is compared by St. Paul to the power which the Father exercised in raising his Son Jesus Christ from the dead, and exalting him to glory far above all the principalities and powers, whether of heaven or hell[g]. From the first awakening of a sinner to his final exaltation to glory, he must say, in reference to the whole work, " He that hath wrought me to this self-same thing is God[h]."]

3. His faithfulness—

[Not one foot of ground had Abram: nor for twenty-five years after the promise was made to him, had he the child to whom the promises were made. The time was past in which, according to the course of nature, it was possible for him and Sarah to have a child. Yet the child was given him; and to his posterity all the land of Canaan; and in due time, the seed also, in whom all the nations of the earth were to be blessed. Thus, in like manner, are all the promises fulfilled to every one who believes in Christ: not one jot or tittle of God's word is ever suffered to fail[i]. " The promises of God in Christ are, not yea and nay, but yea and amen, to the glory of God[k]," and to the everlasting salvation of all who rely upon them. However numerous their dangers be, or great their difficulties, " they shall never be plucked out of God's hands[l]," but shall be " kept by his power unto full and complete salvation[m]."]

Let us now set before you that which is no less conspicuous in our text; namely,

II. The virtues of Abram, for your imitation—

We are told, on divine authority, that if we be

[d] 1 Cor. iv. 7.   [e] 1 Cor. xv. 10.   [f] Eph. ii. 10.
[g] Eph. i. 19—21. See the wonderful force of the original.
[h] 2 Cor. v. 5.   [i] Josh. xxiii. 14.   [k] 2 Cor. i. 20.
[l] John x. 29.   [m] 1 Pet. i. 5.

Abram's seed, we shall do the works of Abram. Behold, then,

1. His simple faith—

[He received implicitly all that God spake unto him. To whatsoever it referred, and however improbable, humanly speaking, the accomplishment of it was, he never for one moment doubted the truth of God's word, "nor ever staggered at any promise through unbelief." Now in this most particularly he is set forth as an example to us; who are required to "walk in the steps of that faith of our father Abraham, which he had whilst he was yet uncircumcised[n]." And more especially are we to imitate him in relation to the faith which he exercised on the Lord Jesus Christ, whom he beheld at the distance of two thousand years as the Saviour of the world. If any person ever could be justified by his works, Abram might have claimed that honour: but, eminent as his obedience to the divine mandates was, "he had nothing whereof to glory before God;" and, sensible of his own utter unworthiness, he believed in the Lord Jesus Christ for righteousness, and was justified solely by faith in him[o]. And why is this so minutely recorded concerning him? Was it for *his* sake, that *he* might be honoured? No: it was altogether for *our* sakes, that we might know how *we* also are to be justified, and may look simply to Christ as our all in all[p].]

2. His prompt decision—

[It is said concerning him, that "when he was called to go out into a place which he should after receive for an inheritance, he obeyed." There was in him no hesitation, no delay. And in this way must we also obey the divine call, when bidden to "forsake all and follow Christ." We must "not confer with flesh and blood[q];" but must, like the Disciples with their nets, and Matthew at the receipt of custom, leave all for Christ. We must be on our guard against specious excuses, "Lord, let me go home and bury my father," or "take leave of my friends:" we must not be looking for "a more convenient season;" our obedience must be prompt, our decision firm and unchangeable: whilst it is called to-day, we must avail ourselves of the opportunity that is afforded us to do the will of God: to hesitate, is treason: to delay, is death. "What our hand findeth to do, we must do it instantly, and with all our might."]

3. His self-denying zeal—

[Doubtless Abram felt that attachment which men

---

[n] Rom. iv. 12.   [o] ib. ver. 1—3.   [p] ib. ver. 22—25.   [q] Gal. i. 16.

usually do to their native country; and found it painful to turn his back upon all his friends, and to forsake all the comforts which he enjoyed in opulence and ease. No doubt, too, he had much to combat with amongst his friends and acquaintance. He was leaving his native country, and yet "he knew not whither he was going." How strange must this appear! yea, what a folly and infatuation! But "he knew in whom he had believed," and had no fear but that the Lord Jehovah, who had called him, would guide his feet, and keep him in all his ways. And shall not *we* also have much to contend with, if we obey the call of God in his Gospel? To renounce the world, to "mortify our members upon earth, to cut off a right hand, to pluck out a right eye, to crucify the flesh with the affections and lusts," is surely no easy work. The very terms in which these duties are expressed sufficiently declare what self-denial is necessary for the discharge of them. From without, also, our difficulties will be increased. We shall have foes without number to obstruct our way; and most of all, "those of our own household." Hence our blessed Lord warned his followers, saying, "If any man will be my disciple, let him deny himself, and take up his cross daily, and follow me." In truth, "if we hate not father and mother, and houses and land, yea, and our own lives also in comparison of him, we cannot be his disciples." Let not this appear a hard saying: obey it, like Abram; and, like him, you shall find it "a light burden and an easy yoke."]

4. His prudent care—

[Abram collected together all the substance which he could conveniently carry with him, and took it along with him for his support. To have acted otherwise, without necessity, would have been to tempt God, rather than to trust in him. He had many dependent on him; and it became him, as far as with propriety he could, to provide for their support. And the same prudent care becomes us also. It is one thing to improve the means we possess, and another to trust in them. We must never say to gold, "Thou art my hope; or to the fine gold, Thou art my confidence:" but at the same time we are to employ the talents which God has committed to us, that we may support ourselves, and not be chargeable to others. That is a remarkable expression of Solomon, "I wisdom dwell with prudence[r]." And a prudent attention to our worldly circumstances tends rather to honour, than disgrace, religion. Abram, as the head of a family, provided for his own: and he did right in this: yea, if he had not done it, he would have "denied the faith, and been worse than an

---

[r] Prov. viii. 12.

infidel." Whatever, then, be your situation in life, endeavour to discharge the duties of it in a becoming manner; and let your determination through grace be like that of David, " I will behave myself wisely in a perfect way[s]."]

5. His persevering diligence—

[In stopping at Haran till his father's death, I suppose, he judged that to be, or rather, that it was for the time, his proper destination. But being afterwards directed to go to Canaan, he went forth, and turned not aside till he came thither: and there he abode for many years. Indeed, to the very end of his life he held on in the good way which God had directed him to pursue. And thus it is that we also must approve ourselves to God. We must " not turn back : for, if we do, God's soul will have no pleasure in us." If we " turn back" at any time, it is to certain " perdition." Let us " remember Lot's wife." In fact, it were better for us never to have " known the way of righteousness, than, after having known it, to depart from it." Go on then, like Abram, " as pilgrims and sojourners here," " shewing plainly, that you are seeking a better country[t]." And be assured, that " if, by patient continuance in well-doing, you seek for glory and honour and immortality, you shall in the end attain eternal life[u]."]

[s] Ps. ci. 2.   [t] Heb. xi. 9, 10, 13—16.   [u] Rom. ii. 9.

OUTLINE NO. 21

SEPARATION OF ABRAM AND LOT.

Gen. xiii. 8—11. *And Abram said unto Lot, Let there be no strife, I pray thee, between me and thee, and between my herdmen and thy herdmen; for we be brethren. Is not the whole land before thee? Separate thyself, I pray thee, from me: if thou wilt take the left hand, then I will go to the right; or if thou depart to the right hand, then I will go to the left. And Lot lifted up his eyes, and beheld all the plain of Jordan, that it was well watered every where, before the Lord destroyed Sodom and Gomorrha, even as the garden of the Lord, like the land of Egypt as thou comest unto Zoar. Then Lot chose him all the plain of Jordan.*

WEALTH is almost universally considered as a source of happiness, and in that view is most eagerly desired. That it may conduce to our happiness in some respects, especially when it is improved for the relief of our fellow-creatures, we admit: but it is much oftener a source of trouble and vexation than of satisfaction and comfort. "If goods increase, (says Solomon,) they are increased that eat them[a]." A multitude of servants augments our care. Their disagreements among themselves, or disputes with the servants of others, frequently become an occasion of disquietude to ourselves. The envy also and jealousy that are excited in the breasts of others, operate yet further to the disturbance of our peace. In how many families have contentions arisen from this source! How many who have spent years together in love and harmony, have been distracted by feuds and animosities as soon as ever they were called to share the property that has been bequeathed them! Even piety itself cannot always prevent that discord, which the pride or covetousness of others is forward to excite. Abram and Lot had lived together in perfect amity, while their circumstances were such as to preclude any jarring of interests; but when their opulence increased, occasions of jealousy arose; their servants, espousing too warmly their respective interests, quarrelled among themselves; and it became expedient at last, on account of the difficulty of finding pasturage for such numerous flocks and herds, and for the sake of preventing more serious disputes, that a separation should take place between them. The manner in which this separation was effected will afford us much instruction, while we consider,

I. The proposal of Abram—

His conduct on this occasion was indeed such as became his exalted character. It was,

1. Conciliatory—

[Abram well knew the value and blessedness of peace. He knew that "the beginning of strife is as when one letteth out water;" the breach, however small at first, being quickly widened by the stream that rushes through it, and speedily defying all the efforts of man to prevent an inundation. He had learned that valuable lesson, "To leave off contention before it be meddled with[b];" knowing that when it is once

[a] Eccl. v. 11. [b] Prov. xvii. 14.

begun, no man can tell *when* or *how* it shall terminate. Hence he was desirous of promoting peace between the herdmen, and more especially between himself and Lot. The consideration of the relation subsisting between himself and Lot, rendered the idea of contention still more hateful in his eyes; " Let there be no strife, I pray thee, between me and thee, and between my herdmen and thy herdmen; for we be brethren." How amiable was this spirit, how engaging was this address! and how happy would the world be, if all were thus studious to prevent contention, and to "keep the unity of the Spirit in the bond of peace!"]

2. Condescending—

[Abram, as standing in the superior relation of an Uncle, and as being the person peculiarly called of God, while Lot was only a Nephew and an attendant, might well have claimed the deference and submission that were due to him. But, instead of arrogating to himself any authority or asserting his own rights, he was ready to act the part of an inferior; rightly judging, that condescension is the truest honour, and that to be the servant of all is to imitate most nearly the character of our blessed Lord[c]. Accordingly the proposal came from him, that, since circumstances imperiously required a separation, they should separate in a manner that became their holy profession. How many angry disputes, and bitter quarrels, and bloody wars might be avoided, if the contending parties, instead of proudly requiring the first advances from each other, would strive who should be foremost in making proposals for peace!]

3. Generous—

[Common justice required that the partition of land should be such as to secure to Abram equal advantages with Lot. But Abram waved his rights, and cheerfully conceded to his Nephew whatever portion he chose to take. Though he could not but know that there was a great difference between the lands on either side of him, the one being far more fertile and better watered than the other, he desired Lot to occupy whichever he preferred, and to leave the other to him. What a noble, disinterested, generous mind did this manifest! Would to God that such an indifference about carnal interests were more prevalent in the world, and especially among the professors of religion! This would shew a becoming deadness to the world: it would give an evidence, that our hearts were set on things above, and not on things below: it would illustrate, more strongly and convincingly than ten thousand words, the efficacy of faith, and the excellence of true religion.]

[c] Matt. xx. 26—28.

Admirable as was the example of **Abram**, we observe a perfect contrast to it in,

II. The choice of Lot—

Whether Lot was at that time a converted man, we cannot say: it is certain that twenty years after this he was a truly righteous man, and a most distinguished favourite of Heaven[d]: and it is not improbable that the change of heart which he experienced, arose from the troubles which his present choice entailed upon him. But without determining his *general* character, it is very plain that his conduct in the present instance argued,

1. Too great a concern about his temporal interests—

[As far as the history informs us, we have no reason to think that Lot felt any reluctance in parting with Abram. He had now an opportunity of gratifying his covetous desires; and he seems to have embraced it with greediness and joy. If he had not been blinded by selfishness, he would have returned the compliment to Abram, and given him his choice: or, if he had accepted Abram's offer, he would at least have endeavoured to make an equitable division of the lands, so that each might have his proper portion of the more fertile country. But instead of this, he surveyed with pleasure the well-watered plains of Jordan, which were beautiful and fruitful like Eden of old, and took the whole of them for himself; regardless what difficulties his Uncle might experience; and intent only on his own interests. Who does not see the meanness and illiberality of this conduct? Who does not see that worldliness and covetousness were the governing principles of his heart? If the man who requested our Lord to interpose in order to obtain for him his proper share of his father's inheritance, needed that caution, "Take heed and beware of covetousness," much more did the choice of Lot betray a very undue concern about his temporal interests, and a selfishness that was deeply reprehensible.]

2. Too little regard to the interests of his soul—

[Lot could not but know the character of the people of Sodom; for they declared their sin before all, and without the least reserve: and he ought to have considered what a tendency there is in "evil communications to corrupt good manners." But as he left Abram without regret, so he went to

---

[d] 2 Pet. ii. 7, 8.

dwell in Sodom without fear. What benefits he was losing, and what dangers he was about to rush into, he little thought of: his earthly prosperity was all that occupied his mind: and whether the welfare of his soul were forwarded or impeded, he did not care. This conduct every one must blame: yet how many are there who pursue the same heedless and pernicious course! How many for the sake of temporal advantage will leave the places where their souls are nourished with the bread of life, and take up their abode where there is an incessant "famine of the word!" How many will form their connexions even for life upon no better principle than this! Well will it be for them, if the troubles which they bring upon themselves, operate, as they did on Lot, to bring them to repentance.]

Let us LEARN from hence,

1. To guard against the love of this world—

[It is not without reason that St. John says, " Love not the world, neither the things that are in the world: if any man love the world, the love of the Father is not in him[e]." We see in the instance before us what unhappy dispositions the love of this world generated, and what unworthy conduct it produced. Indeed the folly as well as sinfulness of this disposition is strongly illustrated in the present case: for Lot had enjoyed his portion but a little time before he was plundered of all that he possessed, and himself and family were carried into captivity[f]: and, after his restoration to liberty and opulence, he at last was forced to flee for his life, and to leave all his property, and part also of his family, to be destroyed by fire from heaven[g]. Thus shall a love of this world be recompensed to all. If God have designs of mercy towards them, he will either take away from them the objects of their idolatrous regard, or embitter to them the possessions in which they have sought delight. Let us then be on our guard against that "love of money which is the root of all evil; which while some have coveted after, they have erred from the faith, and pierced themselves through with many sorrows: for they that would be rich, fall into temptation and a snare, and into many foolish and hurtful lusts, which drown men in destruction and perdition[h]."]

2. To cultivate an affectionate and self-denying spirit—

[If we look no further than this present life, the exercise of love and self-denial has greatly the advantage of selfishness, even when it is most successful. Let us compare the feelings of Abram and of Lot on this occasion: how refined, how enviable

---

[e] 1 John ii. 15, 16.　　[f] Gen. xiv. 12.
[g] Gen. xix. 14, 17, 25, 26.　　[h] 1 Tim. vi. 9, 10.

were those of Abram in comparison of Lot's! Give to Lot all the joy of successful covetousness, and conceive him to be filled with exultation at the portion he had gained, and at his prospects of increasing opulence : suppose, on the other hand, Abram impressed with thankfulness to God for having enabled him to sacrifice his own interests rather than contend about them, and for having disposed his mind to generosity and love : which of these two had the more solid happiness? No man who has any just notions of happiness, can entertain a doubt. What then we admire in another, let us cultivate in ourselves: and what we cannot but acknowledge to be highly virtuous and laudable, let us labour to attain, let us endeavour to preserve in constant exercise. "Let us be kindly affectioned one to another in brotherly love, in honour preferring one another[i]." Let us "look not on our own things only, but rather and principally on the things of others[k]." Thus "walking in the steps of our father Abraham," we shall approve ourselves his children; yea, we shall resemble that greatest of all patterns, the Lord Jesus Christ, who "came not to be ministered unto, but to minister, and to give his life a ransom for many[l]." And as Abram was immediately visited by God, and refreshed with more assured prospects of the promised land[m], so shall every one who denies himself for God, be recompensed with present consolations, and eternal joys[n].]

[i] Rom. xii. 10.   [k] Phil. ii. 4, 5.   [l] Matt. xx. 26—28.
[m] ver. 14—17.   [n] Luke xiv. 14.

OUTLINE NO. 22

MELCHIZEDEC BLESSING ABRAM.

Gen. xiv. 18—20. *And Melchizedec king of Salem brought forth bread and wine: and he was the priest of the most high God. And he blessed him, and said, Blessed be Abram of the most high God, possessor of heaven and earth: and blessed be the most high God, which hath delivered thine enemies into thy hand. And he gave him tithes of all.*

WAR is a calamity arising out of the state of fallen man. We have innumerable lusts which cannot be satisfied without trespassing on others, and which lead us to retaliate injuries with vindictive ferocity. Hence there is no nation, whether savage or civilized, which is not frequently engaged in war: and if there were any one nation determined to cultivate peace to the uttermost, it would still be necessary for them to learn the art of war, in order that they might be ready, when attacked, to repel aggression, and to maintain their liberties. The first war of which we read in history, was that recorded in the chapter before us. Chedorlaomer king of Elam, with three confederate kings, invaded the cities of the plain, who had combined for their mutual defence; and, having defeated the combined armies, took Sodom and Gomorrha, and plundered them of all that was valuable or useful. Abram, as we have already seen in his conduct to Lot, was a man of peace: and from the history before us it is clear, that he was not under the influence either of covetousness or ambition; but, living in the midst of hostile nations, he had wisely trained his servants, 318 in number, to the use of arms: and finding that his nephew Lot had been carried captive by the victorious invaders, he determined, with God's help, to rescue him. Accordingly he armed his little band, and, with a few allies, pursued the victors. He speedily came up with them, and, by a stratagem suited to the inferiority of his force, prevailed against them. Having dispersed or slain his enemies, he recovered all the captives and the spoil; and returned in triumph to those whose cause he had espoused. In his way to them he received the testimonies of God's approbation mentioned in the text. To elucidate these, together with the circumstances connected with them, we shall consider,

I. The respect which Melchizedec paid to Abram—

Melchizedec was a person of most singular and mysterious character—

[Some have thought that he was the same as Shem: but Shem's parentage was known; whereas Melchizedec's was not. Others have thought that he was Christ, who just for that occasion assumed the appearance of a man: but he was a person "made like unto the Son of God;" and therefore could not be the Son of God himself. Whoever he was, he was certainly a very eminent type of Christ. His name imported that he was king of righteousness, while at the same time, as king of Salem, he was king of peace[a]. He was also "a Priest of the most high God," ministering, not to one peculiar people, as the Levites afterwards did, but to mankind at large without any distinction. In these respects he typified the Lord Jesus, whose "sceptre is a right sceptre[b]," who "maketh peace for us by the blood of his cross[c]," and who is "the great High Priest" that once ministered on earth, and is "now passed into the heavens" to offer incense before the throne of God[d]. In him alone, after Melchizedec, were combined the offices of King and Priest: He and he only is "a Priest upon his throne[e]."

Moreover, Melchizedec was a type of Christ in those things which we do not know concerning him, as well as in those things which we do know: yea, there were many things concealed from us, on purpose that he might be a more illustrious type of Christ. We are not informed of his birth, or parentage, or death. We are not told who preceded him in his office, or who followed him. He is merely introduced on this occasion as "without father, without mother, without beginning of life or end of days," that he might fitly represent that adorable Jesus, who was without father, as Man, and without mother, as God, and who abideth a priest continually[f].]

As God's servant, he came forth on a remarkable occasion to honour Abram—

[Abram was returning with his victorious bands, laden with the spoil that he had recovered from the slaughtered kings. For the refreshment of his weary troops, Melchizedec brought forth bread and wine. It is certainly a striking coincidence, that this, even bread and wine, is the provision which our great High Priest has appointed to be received by all his people to refresh them after their conflicts: but we do not on the whole apprehend that there was any thing more intended by the bread and wine, than to administer suitable nourishment to Abram and his attendants after their fatigues. But from the other tokens of respect which Melchizedec shewed to Abram, there is much instruction to be derived.

Melchizedec *blessed Abram for the zeal he had manifested*, and *blessed God for the success he had given*. In blessing Abram he shewed what obligations we owe to those who go forth to fight in our defence, and by their valour procure to us the peaceful enjoyment of our possessions. If Abram had not stood forth on that occasion, what misery would have been entailed on those who had been taken captive, and on those who were left behind to bewail the loss of their dearest relatives, and experience the pressure of want and famine! And

---

[a] See Heb. vii. 1, 2.   [b] Ps. xlv. 6.   [c] Col. i. 20.
[d] Heb. iv. 14.   [e] Zech. vi. 13.   [f] Heb. vii. 3.

we also may easily conceive to what a deplorable state we of this nation should soon be reduced by our envious and ambitious neighbours, if we had not fleets and armies ready to maintain our cause. It is to be lamented indeed that all our warriors are not so pacific in their principles, and disinterested in their patriotism, as Abram was; but still they are instruments of good to us; and we ought to acknowledge with gratitude the benefits they confer upon us.

Had Melchizedec rested there, he had ill performed the office of a priest. But he proceeded to bless God also; shewing thereby, that all success must ultimately be traced to God, " the giver of every good and perfect gift." It would have been impiety indeed not to give him the glory of so complete a victory, obtained by so small a force over four confederate and triumphant kings, without the loss of one single follower. But he should be acknowledged in every instance of success, whether more or less complete, and whether more or less dearly purchased: for " it is He who giveth victory unto kings;" " he raiseth up one and casteth down another;" " he saves whether by many or by few."]

Let us now turn our attention to,

II. The return which Abram made him—

Had we been told that Abram gave Melchizedec *a present* in return for his kindness, we should merely have considered it as a proper compliment suited to the occasion. But we are informed that " he gave him *tithes* of all." This circumstance is peculiarly important. If we attend to it, and consider it according to the light reflected upon it in other parts of Scripture, we shall find in it,

1. An acknowledged duty—

[Melchizedec was God's Minister. In the performance of his high office, he had taken a lively interest in the concerns of Abram: he had not merely congratulated him as a friend, but blessed him officially as a priest; and had rendered thanks also to God for him as his Minister and representative. In short, he had been a kind of Mediator between God and Abram, acting, as Priests are ordained to do, for each, with and towards the other [g]. Abram, viewing him in this light, gave him the tithes, not as a friend, but as God's representative. Doubtless Abram accompanied the present with unfeigned expressions of personal respect and gratitude: but still, though he might intend it in some measure as a token of love to man, he

---

[g] Heb. v. 1.

designed it principally as a tribute of piety to God. And herein he has shewn us our duty towards the Priests and Ministers of God. If they perform their office, as Melchizedec did, with a tender concern for those amongst whom they minister, and with real piety towards God, they ought to be " esteemed very highly in love for their work's sake:" " While they serve at the altar, they ought to live of the altar;" and " while they minister unto us of their spiritual things, we should feel happy in imparting to them of our temporal things." What if our property be earned with the sweat of our brow, or purchased, as Abram's was, at the risk of our life; we should account a portion of it due to God, who has enabled us to acquire it; and we should consider the support of his Ministry and his religion as having the first and most urgent demand upon us.]

2. A hidden mystery—

[We should have seen nothing particular in this transaction, if God had not been pleased to reveal it to us. But by the light of the New Testament we see in it nothing less than *the abolition of the whole Jewish polity, and the establishment of Christianity upon its ruins.*

The tribe of Levi were by God's special command ordained to be priests; and the tithes of every thing (which God claimed as his property) were to be given to them for their support. They were to be considered as God's representatives; and therefore they had, in this respect, a superiority above all the other tribes. But Melchizedec ministered in the priesthood four hundred years before they had any designation to the office; and an hundred and fifty years before Levi himself existed: and to him Abram, the father of all the tribes, paid tithes. The same superiority therefore which the tribe of Levi claimed on account of the priesthood above their brethren, Melchizedec claimed above Abram himself, and consequently above Levi also: for " Levi being in the loins of his father Abram, may be considered as paying tithes in Abram." Here then at once we see, that Melchizedec's priesthood was superior to that of Levi. Now the priesthood of Christ was to be, not after the order of Levi, but after the order of Melchizedec; (for God foretold, even while the Levitical priesthood was in all its plenitude of sanctity and power, that another priest should arise after the order of Melchizedec[h].) Christ therefore had a priesthood of a higher order than that of Levi. This further appears from the circumstance of his being appointed to the priesthood with an oath, (" The Lord *sware*, and said, Thou art a priest for ever after the order of Melchizedec:") whereas the Levitical priests were appointed

[h] Ps. cx. 4.

without any such solemnity. Moreover, as we before hinted, there was no successor to Melchizedec in his priestly office; which intimated, that Christ should have none in his; but that his priesthood should be everlasting: whereas the Levitical priests could not continue in their office by reason of death. From all this it appears, that Christ's priesthood was intended to supersede that which was appointed by the law; and consequently, that the law itself, which was so intimately connected with the priesthood, was to yield to the dispensation which Christ should introduce. For if Melchizedec's priesthood, which was only typical, was superior to that of Levi, much more must Christ's priesthood be superior; because the things which exalted the person and office of Melchizedec, were merely figurative and shadowy; whereas those which dignify the person and office of the Lord Jesus, are real and substantial; he is really in his person the eternal God, and will execute to all eternity the office he has undertaken[i].

Behold, then, how deep a mystery is contained in that which appears at first sight so unimportant! O that we may all bear it in mind, and present to him, not a portion of our property only, but " our bodies and our souls also to be a living sacrifice unto God!"]

To IMPROVE this subject, we would earnestly entreat of you these two things:

1. Study the Scriptures with earnest prayer to God for the teaching of his good Spirit—

[In every part of God's word there are many important truths which cannot be discerned, unless God be pleased to " open our eyes to see them, and our understandings to understand them." We do not mean by this observation to refer to mysteries merely, but to great practical truths. We may understand the letter of Scripture, and yet be extremely ignorant of its spirit. Take, for instance, such an expression as this, " God is love:" What, I ask, can we understand of it without humble meditation and prayer? Yet if we have meditated and prayed for ever so long a time, there would still be unsearchable riches in those words to reward our continued search; yea, eternity itself will not suffice to explore their full meaning. Exactly as we might have meditated a thousand years upon the text, and not found out the truths which by the light of subsequent revelations we discover in them, so it is with ten thousand other passages, which we cannot duly comprehend or feel, till God is pleased to reveal them to us by his Spirit. The Bible is " a sealed book;" and neither

---

[i] See the whole seventh chapter to the Hebrews.

the unlearned nor the learned can open it of themselves[k]. It contains inexhaustible "treasures of wisdom and knowledge" which God alone can impart. Let us then search the Scriptures with humility and diligence, lifting up at the same time our voice to God for understanding: for it is God alone who giveth wisdom; "out of his mouth cometh knowledge and understanding[l]."]

2. Let every mercy you receive, lead you to God the giver of it—

[Ungodly men would have been rioting upon the spoil, and abusing the gifts which God had bestowed upon them[m]. But Abram and Melchizedec made this victory an occasion of glorifying God. O that we could learn of them! Our successes too often lead to intemperance and riot: yea, mercies of every other kind have but little effect to solemnize the spirit, or to change the heart. Deliverances from sickness, how little are they improved as they ought to be! Instead of devoting our renewed strength to the service of our God, we too commonly lose the impressions that were upon us, and forget the vows which we made in the day of our calamity. But let it not be thus in future: let the honour of God be dear to us: let it be the first desire of our hearts to render unto him our tribute of praise and thanksgiving: and the more visible his interpositions have been in our favour, the more earnest let our endeavours be to live to his glory.]

[k] Isai. xxix. 11, 12.   [l] Prov. ii. 1—6.   [m] 1 Sam. xxx. 16.

OUTLINE NO. 23

ENCOURAGEMENT TO THE FEARFUL.

Gen. xv. 1. *After these things, the word of the Lord came unto Abram in a vision, saying, Fear not, Abram: I am thy shield, and thy exceeding great reward.*[*]

WE may here observe,

I. The most eminent saints need encouragement—

They are apt at times to feel discouragement,

1. From a review of past difficulties—

[Persons under the immediate pressure of their trials are often not aware of their greatness. God mercifully conceals it from them, lest their energies should be weakened. But

[*] This is only a slight sketch, given extemporaneously to a friend.

when they see, in their calmer moments, what difficulties they have had to encounter, they are amazed at themselves: I had almost said, They are amazed at God: and they tremble, lest there should be a recurrence of similar trials; apprehending nothing but a failure under them. This was the special case with Abram at this time.]

2. From a prospect of augmented trials—

[Trials in prospect are always formidable; and the imagination often paints them in the deepest colours. A sense of weakness gives rise to fears; and the most eminent saints are apt to be appalled.]

3. From an apprehension of disappointed hopes—

[Confidence in a time of ease is apt to fail when the hour of trial comes: *e.g.* Peter, on the waves; and Moses[a]; and Joshua[b]. And you too, my brethren, who have hoped that sin should be entirely slain, are apt to be discouraged when you find it still working in you.]

II. The encouragement which God affords them—

God affords them the richest encouragement:

1. He assures them of protection—

[He provides armour for his people: and that armour shall be effectual. But he himself is in the place of armour: and our enemies must break through him, to reach us. He is "a wall of fire," that devours the assailants. See how this is represented by St. Paul (Col. iii. 3): "Your life is hid with Christ in God." Who can fear, that has such a protection as this? The weakest may laugh all his enemies to scorn.]

2. He gives himself to them, as their portion—

[Happiness too, as well as protection, will he afford them: happiness here; happiness hereafter. Conceive of all the glory of heaven—how rich a reward! But heaven is nothing in comparison of the reward provided: it is *the God* of heaven that is our portion. See him in all his perfections, in all his glory, in all his blessedness: HE is yours; THAT is yours, for ever—your eternal portion, your indefeasible inheritance. Say, fearful saint, whether here is not sufficient encouragement?]

And now, is there here *a timid saint?*

[Come with me, and survey *your enemies*. Who are they? what are they? They are "crushed before the moth." And look at *your Friend:* survey HIM, *his* power, *his* goodness, *his*

---

[a] Exod. v. 22, 23. [b] Josh. vii. 7—9.

fidelity. Have you *now* any cause for fear? Be strong: fear not. See 1 Tim. iv. 10.]

To *the careless unbeliever* let me also speak—

[Tell me, Have not *you* cause to fear? Think of the danger to which you are exposed. And where will *you* find "a shield?" Think of the recompence that awaits you: how different from that of the believing soul! Exceeding bitter will be "thy reward"— — — O that I could awaken *you* to *fear!* The world and the devil say, "Fear not." But I say, "Fear, and tremble." Yet will I say, that Abram's God may still be thine: *he* was once an idolater, as thou art: the sovereign grace that elected him, may fix on thee: the covenant made with him is open to thee; and all the blessings of it will be thine, if, like him, thou wilt be "strong in faith, giving glory to God." The seed for whom he waited, is come: the blessings, to which he looked forward, are poured out upon all the families of the earth. Look to the Lord Jesus Christ, and they shall all be thine.]

OUTLINE NO. 24

ABRAM JUSTIFIED BY FAITH.

Gen. xv. 5, 6. *And he brought him forth abroad, and said, Look now toward heaven, and tell the stars, if thou be able to number them. And he said unto him, So shall thy seed be. And he believed in the Lord; and he counted it to him for righteousness.*

THE enjoyment of the divine presence is truly satisfying to the soul. In having the light of God's countenance we have all that we can desire: we are elevated above earthly things; the possession of them cannot add to our happiness; the want of them cannot diminish it. Yet, in another sense, the soul is not satisfied: the more it has of God, the more it desires; nor will it ever be satisfied, till it shall have attained the full, uninterrupted, everlasting fruition of him. Unspeakably blessed was the state of Abram, when God, in return for his active and disinterested zeal in rescuing Lot from captivity, gave him that promise, " I am thy shield, and thy exceeding great reward." This was sufficient to dissipate all fear with respect to confederacies that might be formed against him, and to confirm that contempt of lucre which he had shewn in refusing to accept even a thread of a shoe-latchet of all the spoil that he had taken. But was Abram contented with this promise? No. God had before promised that he should have a child, from whom in due time the Messiah should spring. He had waited already ten years, and had no child: and as he and his wife were far advanced in years, the prospect of issue became, daily, more dark and discouraging. He therefore could not be completely happy till he could see this great point accomplished. Hence, notwithstanding the declaration which God had just made to him, he expressed his regret at not having an offspring to inherit his substance, and to confirm his expectations of the promised Messiah; " Lord God, what wilt thou give me, seeing I go childless, and the steward of my house is this Eliezer of Damascus? Behold, to me thou hast given no seed: and lo, one born in my house is mine heir." We cannot suppose that it was merely an anxiety to have an heir to his fortune, that produced this reply to God: *that*, though natural enough, would have been unworthy of so eminent a saint, and especially at the very moment when he was receiving such communications from God. But, if we suppose his anxiety to have respect chiefly to the Messiah, then was it every way worthy of his high character. Indeed the answer which God gave to him in the text, clearly shews that Abram's views extended not to an immediate progeny, so much as to a remote posterity, who should " be blessed through him." And in this view the conduct of Abram strongly exemplifies our introductory observation.

We do not apprehend that he doubted whether the promise formerly given him would be fulfilled; but, that he began to be impatient for its accomplishment. The repetition of the promise, however, with all its attendant circumstances, confirmed his faith; in the exercise of which he obtained renewed testimonies of his acceptance with God.

We shall endeavour to set before you,

I. The faith he exercised—

The promise which was now given him, was very extensive—

[It being early in the morning before sun-rise, God "brought him forth abroad, and bade him count, if he could, the stars of heaven;" and then told him that "his seed should be, like them," innumerable. This doubtless respected, in the first instance, his natural seed: and though he waited fifteen years longer for the birth of that child from whence that numerous progeny was to spring, yet it was accomplished, as Moses repeatedly declared, previous to their taking possession of the promised land[a]. But the promise, taken as it must be in connexion with that which had been before given him[b], and that which was afterwards given[c] (for they were all either different parts, or only repetitions of the same promise), had an ulterior, and more important view. It assured to him, that he should have a spiritual seed; that the Messiah himself should spring from his loins; and that multitudes, both of Jews and Gentiles, should, through faith in the Messiah, become his spiritual children.

That the promise had this extensive meaning, we cannot doubt: for we are told, that the seed promised to Abram, was Christ[d]; and that in this promise the Gospel was preached unto him[e]. Now the Gospel includes every thing respecting the work and offices of Christ, and the call of the Gentiles to believe in him: and therefore these were the things to which Abram was taught to look forward when this promise was given him.]

The faith which he exercised, had respect to the promise in all its parts—

[He believed that he should have a numerous progeny: yea, fifteen years afterwards, when it was more plainly declared that he should have a child by Sarah, notwithstanding he was about an hundred years old, and Sarah ninety, and both the deadness of his own body and of Sarah's womb forbade all hope that a child should be born to him in the natural way, "he, against hope, believed in hope:" God had said to him, "SO SHALL THY SEED BE;" and "he staggered not at the promise through unbelief, but was strong in faith, giving glory to God; being fully persuaded, that what he had promised he was able also to perform[f]." At the same time, in this progeny he beheld the promised seed, the Lord Jesus Christ. Of this we can have no

[a] Deut. i. 10. and x. 22.
[b] Gen. xii. 2, 3.
[c] Gen. xvii. 4—7. and xxii. 17, 18.
[d] Gal. iii. 16.
[e] Gal. iii. 8.
[f] Rom. iv. 18—21.

We have before shewn, that Christ and his salvation were contained in the promises made to Abram; and that Abram's faith had respect to them. Now we say that by his faith Abram became interested in all that Christ did and suffered, precisely as we do at this day. The only difference between Abram and us is this: Abram believed in a Saviour that *should* come; and we believe in a Saviour that *is* come. As to the efficacy of Christ's death, there is no difference at all between those who preceded, or those who followed him: he was "the Lamb slain from the foundation of the world." The righteousness of Christ also availed as much for the justifying of believers under the Old Testament, as of those who were his more immediate followers. The parallel drawn by St. Paul between the sin of the first Adam and the righteousness of the second Adam, is equally just, whether it be referred to Abram or to us: it designates the way in which Abram was justified, as well as the way in which we are justified: " By one man's offence death reigned by one: much more they which receive the gift of righteousness, shall reign in life by one, Jesus Christ." " As by the offence of one, judgment came upon all men to condemnation, even so by the righteousness of One the free gift comes upon all men to justification of life." " As by one man's disobedience many were made sinners, so by the obedience of One shall many be made righteous[o]." In a word, " Christ, who had no sin of his own, became a sin-offering for" Abram, just as he did for us: and Abram, by believing in Christ, became, as all other believers do, " the righteousness of God in him[p]."]

APPLICATION—

We intreat you, Brethren,

1. To bear in mind in what way you yourselves are to be saved—

[You have heard how Abram's faith " was counted to him for righteousness." But was this only an historical fact; a fact in which you have no personal interest? Far from it: St. Paul assures us, that "it was not recorded for Abram's sake only, but for ours also, to inform us, in what manner we are to be justified, and to assure us that righteousness shall be imputed to us also, if we believe on him that raised up Jesus our Lord from the dead; who was delivered for our offences, and raised again for our justification[q]." Now in this passage there is an express parallel drawn between the manner of Abram's justification, and of ours. While therefore it proves on the one hand that Abram had respect to the death

[o] Rom. v 17—19. [p] 2 Cor. v. 21. [q] Rom. iv 23—25.

and resurrection of Christ, it shews us, on the other hand, that we must seek for justification, not by our works, but by faith in Christ Jesus. For if so eminent a man as Abram, who had forsaken his country and kindred, and sojourned willingly in a strange land where he had not the smallest possession, and even offered up his own son, at the command of God, if *he* was not justified by his works, but by his faith in the promised Messiah, then it must be madness indeed for us to dream of justification by works, or to hope for acceptance in any other way than through the blood and righteousness of the Lord Jesus.

It is worthy of observation also, that as his being justified by his faith before he had performed any of the good works for which he was so eminent, proves that he was justified by faith only; so its being spoken of him after he had performed these acts, proves that he was justified by faith *only* from first to last. This it is of great importance to notice: for it shews us, that we also must be justified from first to last in the very same way. It is true that God will reward our works; but the reward will be of grace, and not of debt: the *only meritorious* ground of our acceptance from first to last must be the righteousness of the Lord Jesus. We must exercise the faith of Abram, if we would be numbered amongst his children[r].

It may be objected indeed that St. James says, "Abram was justified by works, when he had offered Isaac his son upon the altar[s]." But Abram was justified by faith twenty-five years before Isaac was born[t]: which alone is an absolute demonstration that St. James did not speak of the same justification that St. Paul did, since that mentioned by St. Paul had taken place at least fifty years before. The truth is, St. James speaks of Abram's works as manifesting the truth and excellence of his faith: for the whole scope of his argument is to shew, that we are not saved by a dead faith, but by a living and operative faith: in confirmation of which he observes, that the perfection of Abram's faith was displayed by that consummate act of his obedience: and that it was *this* faith, and not a dead faith, that was imputed to him for righteousness. There is therefore no real opposition between the two apostles, nor any argument to be derived from St. James that can in the smallest degree invalidate the foregoing statement.

We recur then to what we have before said, and urge you to believe in Christ for the salvation of your souls[u].]

2. To be concerned about nothing so much as the manifestation of Christ to your souls—

[Nothing dwelt so much upon the mind of Abram as the promise given to him relating to the Messiah: Nor could any

---

[r] Gal. iii. 7, 9.   [s] Jam. ii. 21.   [t] See notes [b] and [c].   [u] Heb. x. 39.

thing that God himself could say to him allay the thirst which he had after that unspeakable gift. His longing after Christ arose, *as we should think,* even to impatience and ingratitude. But God approved of it; and instantly renewed his promises to him in a more plain and express manner than before. And thus will he do towards us, if we manifest the same holy ardour after the knowledge and enjoyment of Christ. He will permit us to say to him, 'What are all thy gifts to me, or all thy promises, if I go *Christless*[x], or have not assured hopes of an interest in him!' Yes, he would be pleased with such *apparent* ingratitude; and would speedily return unto us an answer of peace. Let then every thing which you possess, appear as nothing in your eyes in comparison of Christ: let nothing comfort you while you are destitute of Christ: let it not satisfy you to have embraced the promises which relate to Chsist; but endeavour to obtain brighter prospects of their approaching accomplishment. Like the holy Patriarch of old, entreat of God that you may not die till you have embraced Jesus in your arms, and can confidently say, "Mine eyes have seen his salvation[y]." This is the boldness which Jacob exercised when he wrestled with the angel[z]: and similar importunity shall surely be crowned with similar success.]

[x] See ver. 2. [y] Luke ii. 28—30. [z] Gen. xxxii. 26.

OUTLINE NO. 25

COVENANT CONFIRMED TO ABRAM.

Gen. xv. 8. *And he said, Lord God, whereby shall I know that I shall inherit it?*

THE innumerable instances of God's condescension which occur in the holy Scriptures, familiarize the idea of it so much to our minds, that we cease to wonder at it even on occasions the most stupendous. In the history before us we are ready to conceive of God as if he was a man like ourselves. His appearances to Abram are so frequent, his intercourse with him so intimate, his regard for him so tender and affectionate, that we really lose sight of *the Deity* in *the Friend.* Every fresh manifestation of himself seems only introductory to still higher exercises of his condescension and grace. In the preceding verses God had been pleased to allay the fears of

Abram, and confirm his hopes of a numerous posterity: but, Abram being still desirous of receiving stronger assurances respecting his possession of the promised land, God graciously complied with his request in this respect also, and confirmed his expectations of it in a manner that deserves particular attention.

Let us consider,

I. The inquiry which Abram made—

We may perhaps be disposed to blame this inquiry, as savouring of vain curiosity, or sinful distrust. To obviate such misconceptions, we shall distinctly state,

1. Its nature—

[The very same act may be good or evil, according to the principle from which it proceeds. Had this inquiry arisen from unbelief, it would have been decidedly sinful. It would have resembled the question which Zacharias asked, when the angel told him from God, that he should have a child; "Whereby shall I know this? for I am an old man, and my wife well stricken in years[a]:" for which unbelieving question he was immediately struck dumb. If, on the other hand, it expressed a wish to be informed more clearly respecting the divine purposes, or to receive those superabundant testimonies which God himself was willing to communicate, then it was perfectly innocent, and consistent with the strongest faith. It was for the purpose of instruction only that the blessed Virgin inquired of the angel, how she should have a child, since she was a Virgin[b]. The question did not materially differ from that of Zacharias; but the principle was different; and therefore the one received a gracious answer; the other a severe rebuke. Many instances are recorded where God has been graciously pleased to give signs to his people for the confirmation of their faith, when there was not any doubt upon their minds respecting either his faithfulness or power. When he appeared to Gideon, and told him that he should deliver his country from the yoke of Midian; Gideon said, "If now I have found grace in thy sight, then shew me a sign that thou talkest with me:" in answer to which, God caused fire to come out of the rock, and consume the kid and cakes which Gideon had prepared for him[c]: and presently afterwards, he gave him another sign, making the dew to fall alternately on the fleece and on the ground, while the other remained perfectly dry[d].

[a] Luke i. 18.   [b] Luke i. 34.
[c] Judg. vi. 14, 17, 21.   [d] Judg. vi. 36—40.

In the same manner he gave to Hezekiah a choice of signs, offering to make the shadows on the sun-dial to go backward or forward ten degrees, according as he should desire[e]. From hence it appears that the inquiries which proceed from faith, are good and acceptable to God: and that Abram's was of this nature is manifest; because his faith on this occasion was specially commended by God himself.]

2. Its importance—

[If we were to limit the inquiry to the mere circumstance of Abram's inheriting Canaan in his own person, it would be indeed of very little importance: for he never did possess (except the burying-ground which he purchased) one single foot of ground in the country[f], nor, as far as appears, had he any expectation of gaining any permanent settlement in it. But, viewed in its just extent, the inquiry comprised in it nothing less than the happiness of Abram and of all mankind. We are willing to allow that the prospect of having a posterity so numerous and so renowned, must be gratifying to flesh and blood: but that was, at best, but a very small part of Abram's hope: he regarded the promised land as the scene of all those wonderful transactions, where God should be honoured and enjoyed by his posterity; where the redemption of mankind should be effected by the Messiah; and where the final rest of the redeemed should be typically exhibited: in the possession of that, all his hopes centred; yea, all his happiness in time and in eternity was bound up. If by any means that were prevented from taking place, the day of Christ, which he had foreseen, would never arrive; and consequently all his own prospects of salvation, as also of the salvation of the whole world, would be altogether annihilated. Canaan was in his estimation the pledge and earnest of heaven[g]: and if he failed of the one, both he and all mankind must fail of the other also. Surely when so much depended on that event, the most reiterated assurances respecting it were no more than what it became him to desire.]

We shall be yet more fully convinced that Abram's inquiry was proper, if we notice,

II. The way which God took to satisfy him respecting it—

God commanded Abram to take of every animal that was proper to be offered in sacrifice, whether of beasts or birds; each beast was to have attained its full age and perfection (for nothing but an

---

[e] 2 Kings xx. 8—11.   [f] Acts vii. 5.   [g] Heb. xi. 10, 13, 16.

absolutely perfect sacrifice could avail for ratifying of God's covenant with man), and, after being slain, their parts were to be divided and placed opposite to each other, so that a sufficient space should be left for a man to pass between them. Whether this way of making covenants had obtained before, or whether it was first suggested by God on this occasion, we cannot tell: but we have notices of it in the heathen world, both among the Greeks and Romans; and it was certainly practised by the Jews also[h]. But, whatever was its origin, God appointed it now for the purpose of satisfying Abram's mind. The sacrifice being prepared, God accompanied it,

1. With significant emblems—

[God designed to give Abram a just conception of *the manner* in which the desired object should be accomplished; and by various emblems shewed him that it should be *against much opposition—after many troubles—*and *long delays.*

The opposition was signified to Abram by "the fowls that came down upon the carcases," and that were with difficulty driven away. It is no uncommon thing for the enemies of our salvation, whether men or devils, to be represented by this figure[i]. And it was indeed verified by the efforts which the Egyptians made to detain them in bondage, and the confederacies which the nations of Canaan formed to obstruct their entrance into the land, or to dispossess them of it when they were there.

"The horror of great darkness that fell upon Abram when he was in a deep sleep[k]," denoted *the heavy troubles* that his posterity should endure in Egypt; such troubles as made them groan for anguish of spirit, and made "the soul of God himself to be grieved for the misery of Israel[l]." Perhaps too the judgments inflicted on them through the various oppressions of the Midianites and Philistines, the Assyrians and Chaldeans, might be represented to his mind.

The long interval of time that passed between the promise and the ratification of it, even from the earliest dawn, while the stars were yet shining bright, to the return of darkness after the setting of the sun—all this time had Abram to wait: and though part of it would be consumed in the preparing of the sacrifices, yet a considerable part was occupied in his

[h] Jer. xxxiv. 18, 19.
[i] ver. 11. with Jer. xxxiv. 20. and Matt. xiii. 19.
[k] ver. 12.   [l] Judg. x. 16.

endeavours to drive away the fowls, and in the preternatural sleep and horror that came upon him. This lapse of time, I say, intimated *the delay* that should take place before the promise should be fulfilled, or his wishes receive their final completion.

If in deciphering these emblems we seem to have gone beyond the line of sober interpretation, let us turn to the explanation which God himself gives us of them, and we shall see all these particulars distinctly enumerated;—the opposition they should encounter, the troubles they should endure, and the delay they should experience, even four hundred years[m]. And so far from exceeding the limits of sobriety, we are by no means certain that much more is not intended under these emblems, even to designate the trials and conflicts which the children of Abraham shall experience in their way to the promised land.]

2. With demonstrative attestations—

[After the parts of the sacrifice were properly disposed, it was customary for the parties who covenanted with each other, to pass between them[n]; intimating, if not expressing, their willingness to be cut asunder in like manner, if they should ever violate their engagements. God therefore, assuming the appearance of a smoking furnace and a burning lamp, passed visibly between the pieces that were placed opposite to each other; and thereby ratified the covenant on his part, as Abram, in all probability, did on his part. Why God assumed these diversified appearances, we cannot absolutely determine. But at all times, if he did not assume the human or angelic shape, he revealed himself in the likeness of fire. It was in a burning bush that he was seen by Moses[o]; and in a burning mountain by Israel[p]; and in a pillar of smoke and fire that he went before his people in the wilderness[q]: from whence we are disposed to think that, though the appearances were diverse, the intent was one; namely, to represent himself to Abram, as he did to his descendants, as "the Glory and Defence" of all his people[r]. Under this character he shewed himself to Abram, and, passing between the pieces of the sacrifice, pledged himself for the accomplishment of all that he had promised.]

Let us LEARN from hence,

1. To make a similar inquiry relative to the inheritance which we seek—

[We profess to be looking for heaven and eternal glory. Ought we not then, every one of us, to ask, "Whereby shall I know that I shall inherit it?" Surely the inquiry is as

---

[m] ver. 13.   [n] Jer. xxxiv. 18, 19.   [o] Exod. iii. 2.
[p] Exod. xix. 18. with Heb. xii. 18.
[q] Exod. xiv. 19, 20. and xxiv. 17.   [r] Isai. iv. 5.

important to us, as Abram's was to him: and we have more encouragement to ask the question, because God has provided us with such ample means of solving it. As for any thing to confirm the veracity of God, nothing can be added to what he has already done: he has sent his only dear Son into the world to die for us; he has given his Holy Spirit to instruct us; he has already brought myriads, of Gentiles as well as Jews, to the possession of the inheritance; so that nothing remains but to inquire into the marks whereby he has taught us to judge of our own character. Am I "poor in spirit?" Then is the kingdom mine, and I shall surely inherit it[s]. Am I living daily upon Christ, as the Israelites did upon the manna? Then I have, and shall have, everlasting life[t]. Am I "keeping his commandments diligently and without reserve?" Then I may know from hence my interest in his favour[u]. We are not to expect visions, such as were vouchsafed to Abram: "we have a more sure word of prophecy; and to that it behoves us to take heed[x]." Let us then "examine ourselves whether we be in the faith:" let us "prove our own selves[y]:" thus shall we "make our calling and election sure[z]," and be enabled to say with confidence, "I know that when the earthly house of this tabernacle shall be dissolved, I have an house, not made with hands, eternal in the heavens[a]."]

2. To look forward to the full possession of our inheritance without regarding any difficulties that we may have to encounter in our way to it—

[Abram was not discouraged either with the difficulties or delays which he was instructed to expect. He never once regretted the losses he had sustained in leaving his native country; nor was he wearied with the inconveniences of a pilgrim's life. He steadily pursued the path of duty in expectation of the promised blessings[b]. Let us then "walk in the steps of our father Abraham." Let our prospect of the inheritance reconcile us to the hardships of our pilgrimage; and our view of the prize animate us throughout the whole of our course. If enemies oppose us, and troubles come upon us, and our possession of the inheritance be delayed, it is no more than what God has taught us to expect. But God has said, "He that endureth to the end, the same shall be saved." Let us therefore confide in that promise, and expect its accomplishment to our souls. Let us not be weary in well-doing; "for in due season we shall reap, if we faint not."]

[s] Matt. v. 3.　　[t] John vi. 53—58.
[u] 1 John iii. 24. with 1 Thess. i. 3, 4.　　[x] 2 Pet. i. 19.
[v] 2 Cor. xiii. 5.　　[z] 2 Pet. i. 10.　　[a] 2 Cor. v. 1.
[b] Heb. vi. 15.

OUTLINE NO. 26
THE OMNISCIENCE OF GOD.

Gen. xvi. 13. *She called the name of the Lord that spake unto her, Thou God seest me.*

AFFLICTIONS sanctified are amongst our greatest mercies. Hagar would have known less of herself, and less of God, if she had not experienced domestic trouble. She had indulged an exceeding bad spirit in despising her mistress on account of her barrenness; and, when she had thereby provoked the resentment of her mistress, she could not bear it; but fled away towards her own country. The gracious and seasonable visit however which she received from God, brought her to a better temper: it led her to return to that station which she had left; and to adore that God, whom as yet she had altogether neglected.

The person that appeared to her is called " an angel;" but he was " the Angel of the Covenant," the Lord Jesus Christ, under the semblance of an angel. This appears from the promise which he gave her, " I will multiply thy seed;" and, still more clearly, from the discovery which was made to her, that it was " the Lord Jehovah who spake to her;" and from the name by which she called him, " Thou God seest me."

From this name of God we shall be naturally led to speak of his Omniscience: but we will not occupy our time with proofs that this attribute belongs to God, or with uninteresting speculations respecting it: we will rather endeavour to impress the consideration of it upon our minds, and to mark its aspect upon the different states and conditions of men.

The consideration then of the Omniscience of God is suited to produce in us,

I. Conviction and sorrow—

[Men commit iniquity under an idea that God does not notice them[a] — — — Hence, though they know that they have sinned, they are regardless of the consequences of their

---

[a] Ps. lxxiii. 11. Job xxii. 13, 14.

sin[b] — — — But God has indeed been privy to every one of their most secret thoughts[c] — — — And he has noticed them in order that he may bring them into judgment, and make them the foundation of his own decisions at the last day[d] — — — What a fearful thought is this! and what a necessity does it impose on every one to search out his iniquities, and to humble himself for them in dust and ashes[e]! — — —]

II. Circumspection and fear—

["God will not judge according to appearance, but will judge righteous judgment." If he saw only our outward actions, we might hope perhaps to find a favourable acceptance with him: but he discerns the motives and principles of our actions[f]: he sees whether they flow from a regard to his authority;—whether they be done in the precise manner that his word requires;—and whether, in doing them, we seek the glory of his name. If we do the best things under the influence of a corrupt principle, they are no better in his sight than splendid sins[g] — — — What self-examination then is requisite, to ascertain the secret springs of our actions, and to guard against the delusions which we are so prone to foster! — — —]

III. Consolation and hope—

[In seasons of temporal affliction, we may be ready to think that our state is altogether desperate[h]. Under false accusations especially, we may be incapable of establishing our own innocence, and of vindicating our character from the vilest aspersions[i]. But it is consoling to reflect, that "all things are naked and open before God[k]:" and that he can, whensoever it shall seem good to him, extricate us from all the miseries that we either feel or fear[l].

Under spiritual trouble also, O how consolatory is it to know, that God is thoroughly acquainted with the inmost

---

[b] They are afraid of being detected by man, but not of being judged by God, Job xxiv. 15—17. with Prov. xxx. 20.

[c] Jer. xxiii. 24. Ezek. xi. 5. This is not only asserted by God, but acknowledged by men. Job xxxiv. 21, 22. and xlii. 2. Ps. cxxxix. 1—12. and exemplified in Achan, Gehazi, and Ananias.

[d] Jer. xvii. 10.   [e] Ps. cxxxix. 23, 24.

[f] 1 Sam. xvi. 7. Ps. xi. 4. Job xxvi. 6. Prov. xvi. 2.

[g] Isai. i. 11—15. and lxvi. 3. Ezek. xxxiii. 31, 32. Matt. xii. 8.

[h] This was certainly the state of Hagar under the harsh treatment of her mistress; and was probably so when the angel appeared to her.

[i] This was David's case, when fleeing from Saul, and accused by him of treason. Ps. xxxv. 11—14, 22.

[k] Heb. iv. 12, 13.   1 Cor. iv. 3—5.

[l] 2 Chron. xvi. 9.   Ps. xxxiii. 18, 19.

desires of our souls: that if, on the one hand, he has seen our corruptions, he has, on the other hand, beheld our conflicts, and can bear witness to the ardour and sincerity of our exertions [m]! —— What a comfort is it to know, that he sees us striving after universal holiness, and plunging daily and hourly, as it were, into "the fountain that was opened for sin," and relying, as the very chief of sinners, upon his covenanted mercy in Christ Jesus [n]! —— In this view, the most desponding soul may cast itself at the foot of the cross, and may say, "If I perish, I will perish here."]

ADDRESS—

[Endeavour to realize the thought of God's presence with you, wherever you are; and to behold, as it were, the name of God inscribed on every place, "Thou, God, seest me"—— Endeavour also to "set the Lord always before you," and to order all your actions, words, and thoughts with a direct reference to his approbation in the future judgment [o] ——]

[m] He testified that there was some good thing in the heart of young Abijah; 1 Kings xiv. 13. and will bear witness even for those who only "*think*" upon his name." Mal. iii. 16, 17.
[n] John i. 47, 48.   [o] Ps. xliv. 20, 21. with 1 Chron. xxviii. 9.

OUTLINE NO. 27

CIRCUMCISION OF ABRAHAM.

Gen. xvii. 9, 10. *And God said unto Abraham, Thou shalt keep my covenant therefore, thou, and thy seed after thee, in their generations. This is my covenant, which ye shall keep between me and you, and thy seed after thee; Every man-child among you shall be circumcised.*

TO a Jewish auditory the subject before us would be so familiar, that it might be treated without any difficulty. But as it is otherwise with us, we shall wave every thing relative to the right of circumcision, and fix our attention upon the ends for which it was instituted. The writings of the New Testament, as well as of the Old, abound with references to this ordinance: and a just knowledge of its original design is necessary to a due understanding of the corresponding ordinance under the Christian dispensation. Let us then state to you,

I. What were the great ends of circumcision—

The importance attached to this rite under the Jewish dispensation clearly shews, that it was not a mere arbitrary imposition, but an ordinance fraught with instruction. It was imposed on Abraham and all his posterity,

1. As a seal of their privileges—

[Abraham had from the first believed the promises which God had given him relative to a numerous posterity, and to "that seed in particular, in whom all the nations of the earth were to be blessed:" and, in consequence of that faith, he was justified before God; or, to use the expressive language of Scripture, "his faith was counted to him for righteousness." But when five and twenty years had elapsed, and it was more distinctly made known to him that the promised seed was to spring from Sarah, he had some pledges given him that God's word, however improbable, should be fulfilled. His name was changed from Abram, which means *high father;* to Abraham, *the high father of a multitude.* His wife's name also was changed, from Sarai, *my princess,* to Sarah, *the princess of a multitude* [a]. Now also circumcision was enjoined on him and all his posterity: and St. Paul expressly says, that it was "a seal of the righteousness of the faith which he had being yet uncircumcised[b]." To Abraham and his *believing* seed, this seal assured the certain enjoyment of "God as their God" and Portion for ever[c]: but as administered to infants, it assured only that they should participate all the blessings of God's covenant, as soon as ever they exercised the faith of Abraham, and "walked in his steps[d]." But towards all, it had the same force as a seal has when annexed to a covenant: it was God's seal impressed on their flesh[e], that he would fulfil to them all the promises which he had given.]

2. A memorial of their engagements—

[In the verse following our text, God calls circumcision "*a token* of the covenant between him and his people." It was designed by God that his people should be separated from all the world, and that they should be constantly reminded of their engagements to him. When they submitted to that rite, whether it were in infancy or at an adult age, they were no longer to consider themselves as at their own disposal, but as dedicated to the service of their God. St. Paul, in reference to the scars and bruises with which his body had been covered in the service of his Lord, said, "I bear in my body the marks of the Lord Jesus[f]." The same language might with propriety

---

[a] ver. v. 15. [b] Rom. iv. 11. [c] ver. 7, 8.
[d] Rom. iv. 12. [e] See ver. 13, latter part. [f] Gal. vi. 17.

be used by every Jew in reference to this sacred memorial: for, having in his own person the appointed sign of his relation to God, he must be continually reminded "whose he was, and whom he was bound to serve."]

3. An emblem of their duties—

[We cannot doubt but that this painful rite was intended to represent the mortification of sin. The Scripture speaks much of the "putting off the whole body of sin;" "the crucifying of the flesh with the affections and lusts;" "the putting off the old man, and putting on the new:" which expressions exactly coincide with the chief intent of this ordinance: they shew, that we bring a corrupt nature into the world with us; and that it must be the labour of our lives to put away sin, both original and actual, both root and branch. Indeed St. Paul explains the ordinance in this way, and calls it "a putting off of the body of the sins of the flesh." But there are also other expressions of Scripture which shew that this rite imported the highest degrees of sanctification and holiness. Moses repeatedly speaks of "the circumcising of the heart to love the Lord with all our heart and all our soul [g]." And the prophet Jeremiah's language is singularly emphatic: "Circumcise yourselves to the Lord, and take away the foreskins of your heart, lest my fury come forth like fire, and burn that none can quench it [h]." From all these passages we learn, that the ordinance was figurative, and designed to instruct the Lord's people in the nature and extent of their duties towards him.]

This rite however being dropped, it will be proper to shew,

II. How those ends are attained under the Christian dispensation—

The rite of circumcision has been superseded by the rite of baptism, just as the passover has given way to the supper of our Lord. The dispensations being changed, a change was made of the two great ordinances which were adapted to Judaism; and others were introduced more immediately suited to Christianity. St. Paul, in reference to the ordinances which we are now comparing, distinctly draws the parallel; and shews that, though different in their nature, they were of precisely the same import: "In Christ," says he, "ye are circumcised with the circumcision made without hands, in putting off the

---

[g] Deut. x. 16. and xxx. 6.   [h] Jer. iv. 4.

body of the sins of the flesh by the circumcision of Christ: buried with him in baptism, wherein also ye are risen with him through the faith of the operation of God, who hath raised him from the dead[i]."

Now in BAPTISM we have,

1. A seal of our privileges—

[When Christianity was first preached, the ordinance was principally administered to adults, because they alone were capable of that instruction which the Apostles were sent to convey. To them the baptismal rite was administered *after they had believed* in Christ, and after "their faith had been imputed to them for righteousness:" and to them it was, precisely what circumcision had been to Abraham, "a seal of the righteousness which they had being yet unbaptized." It assured them, that they were "accepted in the Beloved;" that, "they had redemption through His blood, even the forgiveness of sins;" that "grace and glory should be given them;" and that while the inheritance of heaven was kept for them, they also should by the mighty power of God be preserved for it[k]. But to their infant offspring the ordinance of baptism assured nothing more than an external right to these blessings, and a certainty of possessing them as soon as they believed. It was of the unbelieving and impenitent Jews that St. Paul said, "Theirs is the adoption, and the glory, and the covenants, and the giving of the law, and the service of God, and the promises[l]." This therefore must be understood of the title to these things which they enjoyed by means of their admission into covenant with God. The actual enjoyment of these things they could not have, till they became obedient to the commands of God. It is exactly in the same manner that our Church instructs children to say, that in their baptism they were made "members of Christ, children of God, and heirs of the kingdom of heaven." They have a title to these privileges, as a woman has to the estate of her deceased husband, which yet she cannot legally possess, till she take out administration: so these cannot attain the actual enjoyment of their privileges, till they sue them out by believing.]

2. A memorial of our engagements—

[The effects of the baptismal water are not indeed long visible upon the body; but the name given to us at our baptism (emphatically called our *Christian* name) continues with us until death: and the name of the society into which we are introduced (that of *Christians*) is an indelible badge of our

---

[i] Col. ii. 11, 12.   [k] 1 Pet. i. 4, 5.   [l] Rom. ix. 4.

profession, and of the solemn engagements that we have entered into. It is worthy of observation that, when the sacred historian says, "They were called Christians first at Antioch," he uses a word, which, with one only exception, *always* implies *a divine appointment*[m] : and in the passage that we except, it may very properly be so interpreted[n]. Now, in this view of the subject, the divine appointment of the name *Christian*, to those who had before no right or title to it, is exactly equivalent to the change of Abram's and of Sarai's names: and in thus being brought to "name the name of Christ, we are taught to depart from all iniquity." We can never recollect to what society we belong, or hear ourselves addressed by our Christian name, but we have a striking memorial, that "we are not our own; and that, having been bought with a price, we are bound to glorify God with our body and our spirit which are his[o]."]

3. An emblem of our duties—

[In our Catechism we are told that baptism is "an outward and visible sign of an inward and spiritual grace:" nor are we at any loss to declare what that grace is which it was intended to represent: the symbol is clear enough of itself; but it is explained by God himself; who informs us, that it is "not the putting off of the filth of the flesh, but the answer of a good conscience towards God[p]." In this, of course, the cleansing of ourselves from outward pollutions is intended: but there is also much more implied, even a life of entire devotedness to God: for thus it is said in another place; "We are buried with Christ by baptism into death; that like as Christ was raised up from the dead by the glory of the Father, even so we also should walk in newness of life[q]." While our blessed Lord sojourned upon earth, he set us a perfect example of the divine life: but in his resurrection and ascension to heaven he left us, if I may so speak, a visible exhibition of our duty: he shewed us that it consists in "a death unto sin, and a new birth unto righteousness;" and in having "our conversation henceforth, as much as possible, in heaven."]

The INSTRUCTION which we would further suggest as arising from this subject, is comprised in two things. We learn from it,

---

[m] It is used nine times in the New Testament; Matt. ii. 12, 22. Luke ii. 26. Acts x. 22. and xi. 26. Heb. viii. 5. and xi. 7. and xii. 25. See also Rom. xi. 4.

[n] Rom. vii. 3. If it be considered that our Lord abolished the polygamy which obtained by divine connivance, and in some cases, as it should seem, by divine appointment, the excepted case will perhaps be thought no exception at all.

[o] 1 Cor. vi. 19, 20.   [p] 1 Pet. iii. 21.   [q] Rom. vi. 4.

1. Why infants ought to be baptized—

[The great argument for not baptizing infants is, that they are incapable of performing the duties of the Christian covenant, and therefore they ought not to have the seal of that covenant applied to them. Now if children had never been admitted into covenant with God at all, this argument would have had some weight. But under the Jewish dispensation they were admitted into covenant with God at eight days old; and the seal of that covenant was applied to them. Moreover, this was done by the absolute command of God; who ordered, that a contemner of this ordinance should be *cut off* from his people. This objection therefore can be of no validity under the Christian dispensation. It is further objected, that God does not particularly order children to be baptized. True, he does not; nor was it necessary that he should: for there was no change of the persons who were to be admitted into covenant with him, but only of the rite by which they were to be admitted. If there was to be a change of the persons as well as of the rite, we might well expect that he should have revealed his will to us respecting it. But there is not one syllable in the whole New Testament that will admit of any such construction: and if God has not deprived children of the honour and privilege of being admitted into covenant with him, who are we, that we should take it away from them? By thus robbing them of their privileges, we represent Jesus Christ as less merciful to children now, than he was to the children of Jewish parents: and we put an almost insurmountable obstacle in the way of the Jews; who, though convinced of the truth of Christianity, might justly keep back from embracing it, on account of their children; seeing that, while they remain Jews, their children are partakers of the covenant; but, when they become Christians, their children are cut off from all interest in it.

Some indeed are superstitiously anxious about the early administration of this ordinance to their children, as if their salvation entirely depended upon it. That it should not be needlessly delayed we grant: but the command to circumcise the children on the eighth day sufficiently shews, that the children who died under that age, did not perish for the mere want of that ordinance: and Christian parents may be equally assured, that, if their infants die before they have been initiated into the Christian covenant by baptism, the want of that ordinance will not at all affect their eternal welfare. It is the avowed contempt of the ordinance, and not the providential seclusion from it, that makes us objects of God's displeasure.]

2. How baptized persons ought to live—

[Though this idea has been in part anticipated, it may very properly be repeated in our practical application of the subject.

The persons whom we address, have all been devoted to God in their infancy. But have all remembered the obligations which their baptism entailed upon them? Have all experienced " the washing of regeneration, and the renewing of the Holy Ghost[r]?" Are all walking worthy of Him into whose sacred name they have been baptized? Are not many at this hour still " uncircumcised in heart and ears?" If we be not conformed to the death and resurrection of Christ, to what purpose are we called Christians? We are told by St. Paul, that " he is not a Jew who is one outwardly; neither is that circumcision which is outward in the flesh: but he is a Jew who is one inwardly; and circumcision is that of the heart, in the spirit, and not in the letter; whose praise is not of men, but of God[s]." All this is true in reference to those who have been baptized. Our baptism is, in fact, no baptism[t], if we be not washed from our " filthiness, both of flesh and spirit." " Neither circumcision nor uncircumcision is any thing; but the keeping of the commandments of God[u]." St. Paul, in holy contempt and indignation, calls the ungodly Jews, " the concision," as being unworthy of the name by which the more pious among them were designated[x]. Let us know then, that even the heathen themselves are in a better state than we, if we " walk not worthy of our high vocation[y]:" and that, if we would be Christians indeed, we must answer to the character given of them by the apostle; we must " worship God in the spirit, and rejoice in Christ Jesus, and have no confidence in the flesh[z]."]

[r] Tit. iii. 5.   [s] Rom. ii. 28, 29.
[t] Rom. ii. 25.   [u] 1 Cor. vii. 19. and Gal. v. 6.
[x] Phil. iii. 2.   [y] Eph. iv. 1.   [z] Phil. iii. 3.

OUTLINE NO. 28

SARAH REPROVED FOR HER UNBELIEF.

Gen. xviii. 13, 14. *And the Lord said unto Abraham, Wherefore did Sarah laugh, saying, Shall I of a surety bear a child, which am old? Is any thing too hard for the Lord? At the time appointed I will return unto thee, according to the time of life, and Sarah shall have a son.*

THERE is no time, no situation, no circumstance wherein we are not in danger of falling into sin. Whether we be in good company or in bad, we have need to be on our guard against the influence of our indwelling corruption. We may be engaged in the most sacred duties, and yet be assaulted by the most horrible temptations: we may be performing the kindest offices to others, or be receiving the most important instructions from them; and the things which in their own nature tended only to good, may through the depravity of our hearts become occasions of sin.

Abraham and Sarah were occupied in a way truly pleasing to God. The aged Patriarch, seeing three strangers at a distance, ran and invited them to his tent; and having brought them thither, gave immediate directions for their hospitable entertainment. He desired his wife to make ready some cakes; and ran himself and fetched a young calf from the herd; and, when it was dressed, he set it with butter and milk before them. In this he is proposed as a pattern to us; and we are told for our encouragement that "he entertained angels unawares." No doubt, Sarah also performed her part with as much alacrity as Abraham himself: yet behold, the very kindness with which her hospitality was rewarded, called forth the latent evil of her heart; and occasioned her to commit a sin, which brought down upon her a severe rebuke.

We propose to consider,

I. The reproof given to Sarah—

Sarah, occupied in her domestic engagements, was not present while these illustrious strangers partook of the refreshment provided for them: but, being close at hand, she overheard the inquiries made after her, and the assurance given to Abraham that she should bear him a son. Not able to credit these tidings, she "laughed within herself." But the Lord (for he was one of the guests in human shape) knew what passed in her heart, and testified his displeasure on account of it. In his reproof, we notice,

1. A just expostulation—

[Sin of every kind is unreasonable; but unbelief in particular: because it questions every perfection of the Deity, and contradicts all the records both of his providence and grace. However secret may be its actings, or however specious its appearances, God will not fail to notice and reprove it. Sarah might have said, that she had done nothing but what Abraham himself had done, the very last time that the divine purpose respecting a son had been announced to him[a]: but though the external act of laughing was the same both in her and in him, the principle from which it sprang was widely different: Abraham's was a laugh of admiration and joy; Sarah's was a laugh of unbelief and distrust. But instead of attempting to extenuate her fault, she denied the fact altogether. Alas! how awfully prolific is sin! it never comes alone: it generally brings a multitude of others to justify or conceal it. But it is in vain to cover our iniquities: God sees through the cobweb veil, and will charge upon us the aggravated guilt which we thus foolishly contract. And sooner or later he will call every one of us to account, 'Wherefore we did so or so?' and especially, 'Wherefore we disbelieved his word?']

2. A convincing interrogatory—

[Unbelief has not respect so much to the veracity, as to the power of God. "He has given water indeed, but *can* he give bread also; *can* he provide flesh for his people?" Even Moses doubted how God could supply the Israelites with flesh in the wilderness, since it would require all the flocks and herds that they possessed, to feed them one single month[b]. But God has given abundant evidence of his power, so that no apparent impossibilities ought at all to shake the steadfastness of our faith. Did he not form the universe out of nothing, by a simple act of his will? Did he not give laws to all the heavenly bodies; and does he not still preserve them in their orbits? Does he not also supply the wants of every living creature upon earth? Is he not moreover the true and proper Father of all who are born into the world, and especially "the Father of their spirits?" How absurd then was it to suppose, that her age, together with that of her husband, was any effectual obstacle to the accomplishment of God's word? "Can *any thing* be too hard for the Lord?" One moment's reflection on his omnipotence should banish unbelief from the heart for ever.

3. A reiterated assurance—

[It is most humiliating to think what a necessity our unbelief imposes upon God to repeat and renew his promises to us: and the earnestness with which the promise so often given, is here repeated, shews the just displeasure which Sarah's unbelief had excited in the bosom of her God. We cannot indeed but be filled with amazement that he did not rather say 'Since you treat my promises with profane derision, you shall never be made a partaker of them.' But God well knows the weakness of the human heart; and therefore, in condescension

---

[a] Gen. xvii. 17.   [b] Numb. xi. 22.

to it, he has confirmed his promise with an oath, that we might have the fuller assurance, and the stronger consolation[c]. It is thus that he tenderly reproved the church of old; "Why sayest thou, O Jacob, and speakest, O Israel, saying, My way is hid from the Lord, and my judgment is passed over from my God? Hast thou not known? hast thou not heard, that the everlasting God, the Lord, the Creator of the ends of the earth, fainteth not, neither is weary? there is no searching of his understanding[d]." Were he to suffer our unbelief to make void His truth, no one of his promises would ever be fulfilled. But he has assured us that this shall not be the case[e]. If any thing will put to shame our unbelief, surely this must. Such tenderness cannot but prevail upon us more forcibly than ten thousand menaces.]

While we contemplate the reproof so long since administered, let us consider,

II. The instruction to be gathered from it—

In truth, it sets before us many an instructive lesson. Amongst many others, it teaches us,

1. What need we have to guard against the workings of unbelief—

[Sarah, fifteen years before, had betrayed her unbelief, in giving her servant Hagar into Abraham's bosom, in order that she might obtain through her the child which she despaired of obtaining in her own person. She had waited ten years, and began to think, that the promise would fail, if she did not resort to such an expedient as this[f]. And though she had been deservedly punished for her unbelief by the petulance and contempt of Hagar, and by the workings of envy and wrath in her own heart, yet she still yielded to the same evil principle as soon as a fresh occasion for its exercise arose. It is astonishing what deep root this malignant principle has taken in our fallen nature. From the moment that our first parents questioned the fulfilment of that word, "In the day that thou eatest thereof thou shalt surely die," man has been prone to doubt the veracity of God. There is not a promise or a threatening, to which we do not find some objections, and some fancied ground for doubting its accomplishment. If we do not directly contradict the declarations of God, we still entertain a secret suspicion, that they will not be verified. But let us be on our guard: for though the sin of unbelief is

[c] Heb. vi. 17, 19. [d] Isai. xl. 27, 28. Then see the additional promises, 29—31. See also Isai. xlix. 13—16.
[e] Rom. iii. 3, 4. with 2 Tim. ii. 13.
[f] Similar to this was Rebekah's policy, Gen. xxvii. 6—10.

but small in human estimation, it is exceedingly offensive to God, and will, if allowed to gain an entire ascendency over us, assuredly exclude us from his heavenly kingdom[g].]

2. How ready God is to mark the good that is in our actions, while he casts a veil over the evil with which it is accompanied—

[At the very time that Sarah yielded to unbelief, she exercised a reverential regard for her husband: and though our duty to man is certainly inferior to our duty to God, God has passed over in silence the unbelief she betrayed, and recorded with peculiar approbation the terms in which she spake of Abraham: " After I am waxed old, shall I have pleasure, *my Lord* being old also?" St. Peter, I say, records this, and proposes her as a pattern to all married women; saying, " In this manner in the old time the holy women who trusted in God adorned themselves, being in subjection to their own husbands; even as Sarah obeyed Abraham, calling him *Lord.*" We see in the Scriptures many instances wherein God has manifested the same condescension to his frail and sinful creatures. In the reproof which our blessed Lord gave to Peter, he acknowledged that he had a little faith, at the very time that he had been yielding to unbelieving fears. And because there was *some good thing* towards the Lord God of Israel in the heart of young Abijah, God was pleased to distinguish him from all the family of Jeroboam by giving to him a peaceful death, and an honourable interment[h]. This is a great encouragement to us amidst all the weakness that we feel: and we may be assured that if, on the one hand, the evils of our heart will be disclosed, so, on the other hand, there is not a good purpose or inclination that shall not be made manifest, in order that every one may have his due proportion of praise from God[i].]

3. What a mercy it is to have our secret sins detected and reproved—

[From this time we hear no more of Sarah's unbelief: on the contrary, the reproof given her on this occasion was effectual for the confirming and establishing her faith. In the account given of the most eminent Saints who were distinguished for their faith, Sarah herself is mentioned; and her faith is said to have been instrumental to the accomplishment of that very promise, which in the first instance she had disbelieved[k]. And how many have found similar reason to bless God for the fidelity of their friends, or for the inward rebukes

[g] Heb. iii. 19. and iv. 11.   [h] 1 Kings xiv. 13.
[i] 1 Cor. iv. 5.   [k] Heb. xi. 11, 12.

of their own conscience! Had their sin passed without notice, they had lived and died under its dominion: but by a timely discovery of it they have been led to repentance, and stirred up to the exercise of the virtue they had overlooked. Let us then " in any wise rebuke our brother, and not suffer sin upon him." And let us be studious to improve the instructions we receive, that we may be radically amended by them, and " make our profiting appear unto all."]

4. How essential to our best interests is a right knowledge of God—

[Had Sarah duly adverted to the omnipotence of God, she had escaped the shame and the reproof which her unbelief drew down upon her. And what is it that is really at the root of all our sin? Is it not an ignorance of God? If we duly considered how great he is, should we not be afraid to provoke his displeasure? If we reflected properly on his goodness, should we not be shamed into a sense of our duty? If we were mindful of his truth and faithfulness, should we not expect the certain completion of every word that he has ever spoken? We are told, that the Jews "would not have crucified the Lord of Glory if they had really known him:" in like manner we may say of every sin we commit, We should not have committed it, if we had known what a God we sinned against. Let us then endeavour to obtain just views of God, and of all his perfections. Let us not limit either his power or his grace: but knowing him to be " God Almighty, let us walk before him, and be perfect[1]."]

[1] Gen. xvii. 1.

OUTLINE NO. 29

ABRAHAM'S CARE OF HIS FAMILY.

Gen. xviii. 19. *I know him, that he will command his children and his household after him, and they shall keep the way of the Lord.*

WONDERFUL is the condescension of Almighty God. His attention to his own peculiar people surpasses almost the bounds of credibility. Who would think that He " whose ways are in the great deep" should yet so far humble himself as to " do nothing without first revealing his secret unto his servants the prophets[a]!" He had in his righteous judgment

[a] Amos iii. 7.

determined to take signal vengeance on Sodom and Gomorrha for their horrible iniquities. But he had a favoured servant who was particularly interested in the fate of those cities; and he knew not how to proceed in the work of destruction until he had apprised him of his intention, and given him an opportunity of interceding for them: " The Lord said, Shall I hide from Abraham that thing which I do?" No; I will not: " for I know him," how faithful he is in the discharge of all his duties to me: and since he so delights to honour me, I also will delight to honour him.

The duties, for the performance of which Abraham was so highly commended, were of a domestic nature: " I know him, that he will command his children and his household after him, that they keep the way of the Lord." He eminently excelled in the observance of what may be called, family religion. And this being of such incalculable importance to the maintenance of piety in the world, I will propose him as an example to you; and with that view will shew,

I. The use we should make of influence—

Influence, of whatever kind it be, should be diligently improved;

1. To enforce the commands of God—

[Nothing should be of importance in our eyes in comparison of the honour of God. To uphold it should be our chief aim. The power given us, of whatever kind it be, is bestowed for this end. It is, in fact, God's own power, delegated to us; and, so far as we possess it, we are responsible to him for the use of it. Magistrates are invested with it by him, and are therefore called " his Ministers" and Vicegerents upon earth[b]. Masters in like manner bear his authority, and are his Representatives in the exercise of it[c]. To encourage virtue, to repress vice, to enforce the observance of "justice and judgment," and to make men " keep the way of the Lord," *this*, I say, is the true end of authority, whether it be official or personal, civil or religious. In particular, every thing that dishonours God, no less than that which is injurious to society, must be opposed with determined vigour. The violation of

[b] Rom. xiii. 1—6.   [c] Col. iii. 24.

the Sabbath, and all kinds of profaneness, must be discountenanced to the utmost: and all the maxims and habits of the world, as far as they are contrary to the commands of God, must be held up to decided reprehension. The Gospel too, which above all things most exalts the honour of God, must be patronized, inculcated, enforced. The utmost possible exertion should be made to diffuse the knowledge of a crucified Saviour, " in whom all the fulness of the Godhead dwells," and " in whose face all the glory of the Godhead shines." In a word, the legitimate use of power is, so to exercise it " that God in all things may be glorified through Christ Jesus[d]."]

2. To promote the best interests of men—

[Were this world our only state of existence, it would be sufficient so to use our authority as most to subserve the present happiness of mankind. But men are immortal beings; and their chief concern in this life is to prepare for a better. In this work then we should aid them to the utmost of our power. To this should all our instructions and exhortations tend. We should, as far as we are able, make known to them " the way of the Lord," and especially the way in which they may find acceptance with Him in the last day. With this view we should enable, and indeed require, them to attend upon the ordinances of religion. We should inquire from time to time into their proficiency in divine knowledge, and their progress in the heavenly road. This is not the duty of Ministers only, but of all, according to their ability, and to the measure of influence which they possess. Parents should pay this attention to their children; and Masters to their servants, and apprentices. They should not be content to see those whom God has committed to their care prospering in a worldly view, but should be anxious for the good of their souls, praying for them, and praying with them, and using every effort for their eternal welfare. St. Paul speaks of his " power as given to him for edification[e]:" and the same may be said of all influence whatever: it is a talent committed to us for the benefit of others: and we are not to hide it in a napkin, but to improve it for the good of all around us. Of course, the nearer any are to us, the stronger claim they have upon us for our exertions in their behalf: and hence our domestic duties are of primary obligation. But we are not to say in reference to any man, " Am I my brother's keeper?" but to do him good in every way that we can, and to the utmost extent of our ability. As our blessed Lord did all imaginable good to the bodies of men, yet did not neglect their souls, so in relation to

[d] 1 Pet. iv. 11. [e] 2 Cor. x. 8.

these more important duties we must say, "These ought we to do, and not to leave the other undone."]

That we may be stirred up to exert our influence in this way, let us consider,

II. The benefit of using it aright—

This is great,

1. To those who exercise it—

[So Abraham found it: he was approved of his God, and had the most astonishing testimonies of Divine approbation given to him. 'I know him,' says God; 'and he shall know that I know him. Go, ye my angels, and make known to him my purposes respecting Sodom and Gomorrha. He has a zeal for my honour, and a love for his fellow-creatures: go, give him an opportunity of exercising both. He has Relations too in Sodom: go and deliver them. This holy man shall never want a testimony of my love: I will fulfil to him in their utmost extent all the promises of my covenant[f].'

And shall any other person "give unto the Lord, and not be recompensed again[g]?" The ungodly have indeed said, "What profit is there that we should serve him[h]?" but he never gave occasion for such an impious charge. Say, ye who have endeavoured to live for His glory, has he not favoured you with his visits, and "lifted up upon you the light of his countenance?" Has he not shed abroad his love in your hearts, and "by the witness of his Spirit enabled you to cry, Abba, Father?" Yes, his promise to you is this; "Because he hath set his love upon me, therefore will I deliver him: I will set him on high, because he hath known my name. He shall call upon me, and I will answer him. I will be with him in trouble: I will deliver him, and honour him. With long life will I satisfy him, and shew him my salvation[i]." This, I say, is his promise to his faithful servants; and the whole of it shall be fulfilled to you in its season. "Faithful is He that hath called you; who also will do it[k]."]

2. To those over whom it is exercised—

[It is said, "Train up a child in the way he shall go, and when he is old he will not depart from it[l]." This is not to be understood as an *universal* truth: for it is in many instances contradicted by experience: but it is a *general* truth: and there is ample ground to hope for its accomplishment. At all events some benefit must accrue to those who are brought up in the fear of God. Innumerable evils, which under a different

---

f ver. 20.   g Rom. xi. 35.   h Mal. iii. 14.
i Ps. xci. 14—16.   k 1 Thess v. 24.   l Prov. xxii. 6

education would have been committed, are prevented; and good habits are, for a time at least, induced. And though afterwards the force of temptation may prevail to draw them aside from the good way, yet in a season of trouble they may be brought to reflection, and the seed long buried in the earth may spring up, and bring forth fruit to their eternal welfare. The prodigal son is no uncommon character. The advantages of a father's house may be forgotten for a season; but in a day of adversity may be remembered, and be realized to an extent greater perhaps in proportion as they were before neglected and despised.]

That this subject may be more deeply impressed on our minds, let us PURSUE it,

1. In a way of inquiry—

[Are we, Brethren, "walking in the steps of our father Abraham?" Can God say respecting each of us, "I know him:" 'I know *his principle:* he regards all that he possesses, his wisdom, his power, his wealth, his influence altogether, as a talent committed to him by me, to be improved for the good of others, and the glory of my name. I know *his inclination:* he has a zeal for my honour, and longs to be an instrument of exalting and magnifying my name: he has also a love to his fellow-creatures, and desires to benefit them in every possible way to the utmost of his power. I know *his practice* too: he calls his family together from day to day, to unite in worshipping and serving me. He catechises his children; he instructs his servants; he labours steadily and affectionately to guide them all into the way of peace. His heart is set upon these things: he enters into them as one who feels his responsibility, and has no wish but to approve himself to me, and to give up a good account of his stewardship at last.'

Say, Brethren, whether the heart-searching God can testify these things respecting you? Must he not rather, respecting many of you say, "I know him," that he cares no more for the souls committed to him than he does for his flocks and herds, or for the cattle which are employed in his service? If only they are well, and subserve his interest, and do his work, it is all he is concerned about. Even his very children are not regarded by him as immortal beings: if they do but get forward in their respective callings, and prosper in relation to the present world, he is satisfied, and leaves all the rest to "time and chance." Alas! alas! what an account will such persons have to give at the judgment-seat of Christ, when the Lord Jesus shall say to them, 'Is this the way in which you dealt with the souls committed to you, the souls which I purchased with my own blood?' Beloved brethren, if ye are so unlike to Abraham in this world, do you think that you can be numbered amongst his children in the world to come? O judge yourselves, that ye may not be judged of the Lord in that great and fearful day.]

2. In a way of reproof—

[Surely this subject administers a severe reproof not only to *those who never employ their influence at all for God*, but *those* also *who exert it only in a tame and timid ineffectual way*.

Think, ye who have children, servants, apprentices, have ye no responsibility on their account? Has not God constituted you watchmen to give them warning of their subtle enemy, and to shew them how they are to escape from his assaults? And, if they perish through your neglect, shall not their blood be required at your hands? Did God intrust them to you for your comfort and advancement only, and not at all for their benefit? And the many Sabbaths which he has given you to be improved for them, shall not a fearful account be given of them also? Is it pleasing to Him, think you, that you suffer the ordinances of divine worship to be neglected by them, and the Sabbaths to be wasted in idle vanities, instead of being employed by them and you for their welfare?

But perhaps you will say, 'I do occasionally give them good advice.' What is that? Abraham did not satisfy himself with giving good advice to his children and his household, but " commanded them:" he maintained authority in his family, and exercised that authority for God. And thus should you do also. Eli could say to his sons, " Nay, my sons, this is no good report that I hear of you: ye make the Lord's people to transgress." He even went further, and reminded them of the day of judgment: " If one man sin against another, the judge shall judge him: but if a man sin against the Lord, who shall entreat for him?" But was this all that his situation called for? No: he should have " commanded them," and have thrust them out from the priestly office, *if* they did not obey his injunctions: and because he neglected to do this, God sent him a message that " made the ears of all that heard it to tingle." And some awful message shall you also have, if you neglect to employ for God the authority you have received from God: for " them that honour him he will honour; and those who despise him shall be lightly esteemed[m]."]

3. In a way of encouragement—

[True it is, that though you may command, you cannot ensure obedience to your commands: and notwithstanding your utmost care, there may be much amiss among those who are under your control. In Abraham's family there was a mocking

[m] 1 Sam. ii. 22—30.

Ishmael, in Isaac's a profane Esau, and in Jacob's many a sinful character. But still, if you fail in many instances, and succeed in only one, will not one soul repay you for all your trouble? — — — The testimony of your own conscience too, confirmed by the witness of God's Spirit—is this no recompence? Will not this amply repay every effort you can make, even though you should never succeed in one single instance? Reflect too on the testimony which God himself will give you in the last day: "I know him:" I know how he persevered under the most discouraging circumstances: I know the battles he fought for me: I know the contempt he endured for me: but he was determined to persevere: and "he was faithful unto death: and therefore I award to him a crown of life." Say, Brethren, is there not enough in such a prospect as this to carry you forward, though your difficulties were ten thousand times greater than they are? Say not, 'I am not able to conduct family worship, and to instruct my family.' If this be the case, as doubtless in many instances it is, are there not helps sufficient to be obtained from books of instruction and from forms of prayer? Do your best; and beg of God to bless your endeavours: and you shall not labour in vain nor run in vain: for "out of the mouth of babes and sucklings God will ordain strength, and perfect praise."]

OUTLINE NO. 30

ABRAHAM'S INTERCESSION FOR SODOM.

Gen. xviii. 32. *And he said, Oh let not the Lord be angry, and I will speak yet but this once: Peradventure ten shall be found there. And he said, I will not destroy it for ten's sake.*

THE selection of this chapter as one of the Lessons for this day* intimates, that the doctrine of a Trinity of persons in the Godhead derives some confirmation from it. That one of these strangers who visited Abraham in the likeness of men, was God, cannot admit of any doubt: for He is called The LORD, that is Jehovah, above ten times in this and the following chapter; and Abraham's address to him clearly shews, that he knew him to be God. Moreover there is reason to think that it was the Second Person in the Trinity, who thus conversed with Abraham; because Abraham calls him "the Judge of all the earth."

* Trinity Sunday.

Now " the Father judgeth no man; but hath committed all judgment to the Son[a]:" and therefore we conclude, that this was not God the Father, but God the Son. But it is by no means clear that the other two strangers were the other Persons in the Trinity. Many of the ancients indeed thought they were so; and there is *some* foundation for their opinion: for Lot addressed them in terms which seem more properly applicable to God than to angels; " Behold now, thy servant hath found grace in thy sight, and thou hast magnified thy mercy, which thou hast shewed unto me in saving my life[b]." And one of the angels (for so those two are called[c]) answered him in language almost too exalted for a creature to use, " See, I have accepted thee concerning this thing[d]." But if we consider the peculiar nature and extent of their commission, we may account for the use of this language without supposing either of them to be God. And indeed there is clear evidence that they were only angels, attendant on the Son of God, and sent by him; for they themselves say, " *The Lord hath sent us* to destroy Sodom[e]." Nevertheless, if we admit, as we must, that the person who is here so frequently called Jehovah, was God the Son (for no man hath seen the Father at any time[f]), the chapter clearly marks a plurality of persons in the Godhead; and therefore is properly read on this day, when the Trinity in Unity is the peculiar subject to which our attention is called.

To Him, even to our adorable Emmanuel, did Abraham address his intercession on behalf of Sodom and Gomorrha: an intercession the most instructive of all that are recorded in the sacred volume. When Abraham understood that this divine Person with his attendant angels was come to destroy those wicked cities, he entreated that, if fifty righteous persons could be found in them, the wicked might be spared for their sake. Having prevailed thus far, he in five successive petitions reduced the number to *ten*, and

---

[a] John v. 22.   [b] Gen. xix. 18, 19.   [c] Gen. xix. 1.
[d] Gen. xix. 21.   [e] Gen. xix. 13.   [f] John i. 18.

obtained a promise that if only ten could be found, the rest should be spared for their sake. What an astonishing idea does this give us of GOD's REGARD FOR HIS PEOPLE!

Let us observe,

I. How dear to Him are their persons!

We forbear to notice the honourable appellations which he gives them (as his jewels, his peculiar treasure, &c.) or the great and precious promises made to them, or the blessings of *grace* bestowed upon them: we shall confine our attention solely to the interpositions of his *providence* in their behalf: because it is in that view only that they are noticed in the text. But in marking God's kindness to them, we shall notice it as manifested,

1. To them personally—

[We cannot conceive any thing so great, but God has actually done it for his people.

He has controlled *the elements*. *The earth* has opened at his command to maintain the authority of his chosen prophet, and to swallow up his insolent competitors[g]. *The air* has raised itself into tempests, and shot forth its lightnings, and shaken the foundations of the earth, with its thunders, in order to punish the enemies of his people[h], or vindicate their injured honour[i]. *Fire* also has suspended its destructive energies, in order to defeat the persecuting rage of a tyrant, and rescue from his hands the children of oppression[k]. Nor has *the water* been backward to obey his will, when any signal benefit was to be conveyed to his favourite people. It has repeatedly stood as a wall, to open an avenue for them through the rivers[l], and through the sea[m].

God has compelled all classes of *the brute creation* also to consult their benefit. *The birds*, though of the most voracious kind, have served up the stated meals of bread and meat to his prophet in a time of dearth and necessity[n]. *The beasts*, though fierce and hunger-bitten, have shut their mouths before the saint, whom they were invited to destroy[o]. *The fishes* have swallowed up a drowning prophet, to discharge him again in safety upon the dry land[p]; or taken into their mouth a bait

---

[g] Numb. xvi. 32. [h] Exod. ix. 23—25.
[i] 1 Sam. xii. 16—18. [k] Dan. iii. 27.
[l] Josh. iii. 15, 16. 2 Kings ii. 8, 14. [m] Exod. xiv. 21, 22.
[n] 1 Kings xvii. 6. [o] Dan. vi. 22. [p] Jonah ii. 17. and iii. 10.

unsuited to their appetite, that the Saviour in his humiliation might be enabled to pay his tax[q]. *The insects* too have united their irresistible efforts to punish a proud and cruel nation, and to assert the liberties of God's oppressed people[r].

We may add also, that even *the heavenly bodies* have been overruled by God for the purpose of aiding, or comforting, or honouring those who were dear to him. The *sun* and *moon* stood still for the space of a whole day, to witness the triumphs of his chosen servants[s]. "The stars in their courses fought against Sisera[t]." And the shadow on the sun-dial of Ahaz returned ten degrees, that a pious and afflicted monarch might be assured of the deliverance which his soul desired[u].

How dear to God must they be to whom the whole creation is thus made subservient, and for whose benefit the government of the universe is administered!]

2. To others for their sake—

[For their sakes *blessings have been imparted* to the undeserving, and *judgments averted* from the wicked. For Jacob's sake God multiplied the flocks of Laban[x]; and from respect to Joseph he prospered the house of Potiphar[y]. If ten righteous could have been found in Sodom, the impending destruction would have been turned from all the cities of the plain[z]: and notwithstanding the extreme wickedness of its inhabitants, the city of Zoar was exempted from the common fate, at the intercession of Lot[a]; nor could the storm be poured out upon Sodom, till Lot was placed beyond its reach[b]. The mercy shewn to a whole ship's company on account of Paul, deserves peculiar notice. There were 276 souls on board: the storm was so violent that there was no hope left for their preservation; they were just ready to be swallowed up in the tempestuous waves. But there was one saint on board; a saint, hated of men, but beloved of God: and for his sake the whole were preserved from death, and not a hair of their heads suffered to perish[c]. When God was about to send the Jews into captivity, he told them, that if they could find one righteous man in Jerusalem, he would spare them all[d]: and after he had inflicted his judgments upon them, he assigned as his reason for it, that not one had been found to stand in the gap, and to intercede for them[e]. After the murder of the Messiah, the Jewish nation was devoted to utter destruction: but when the days of vengeance came, "they were shortened for

[q] Matt. xvii. 27.   [r] Exod. viii. 17, 24.   [s] Josh. x. 13.
[t] Judg. v. 20.   [u] Isai. xxxviii. 6—8.   [x] Gen. xxx. 27.
[y] Gen. xxxix. 5.   [z] The text.   [a] Gen. xix. 21.
[b] Gen. xix. 22.   [c] Acts xxvii. 24, 34.   [d] Jer. v. 1.
[e] Ezek. xxii. 30, 31.

the elect's sake;" yea, it was out of respect to them alone that there was not an utter excision of the whole human race [f].

What stronger proofs can be given of God's love to his chosen people?]

But we shall have a further insight into this subject, if we consider,

I. How acceptable are their prayers!

Who can contemplate one single individual interceding, as Abraham did, for all the cities of the plain, and not admire the condescension of God to his praying people? He has heard and answered them, for whomsoever they made their supplications; whether,

1. For themselves—

[No limits whatever, except those which were necessarily fixed by a concern for his own honour, have been assigned by God to the exercise of his own grace in answer to his people's prayers. God has said to them, "Open thy mouth wide, and I will fill it:" "Ye shall ask what ye will, and it shall be done unto you." Agreeably to these promises he has done for them not only what they have asked, but exceeding abundantly above their most sanguine hopes. The prayer of Jonah ascended up even from the bottom of the sea, and brought him a deliverance unprecedented in the annals of the world. The situation of the Canaanitish woman may be considered in some respects still more desperate, because her request had been repeatedly refused: but by persisting in her supplications she obtained the desire of her heart [g]. No kind of blessing has ever been denied to the prayer of faith. David sought information whether the men of Keilah would betray him; and God told him that they would [h]. He desired direction, when and in what manner he should attack the Philistine armies: and God pointed out to him the precise time and place for making his attack successfully [i]. Thus also when they have implored mercy after the most heinous transgressions, God has shewn the same readiness to hear and answer their requests [k]. "He has never said to any of them, Seek ye my face in vain."

2. For each other—

[Mutual intercession is a duty which has been expressly enjoined, and to which we have been encouraged by the most signal tokens of God's acceptance. The deliverance vouchsafed to Peter deserves particular attention. He was secured in prison with all the care that human foresight could devise.

[f] Matt. xxiv. 22. [g] Matt. xv. 22—28. [h] 1 Sam. xxiii. 11, 12.
[i] 2 Sam. v. 19, 23, 24. [k] Ps. xxxii. 5. 2 Chron. xxxiii. 12, 13.

He was chained between two soldiers, and guarded by many others. Prayer was made for him by the church; but apparently to no purpose. The day appointed for his execution was almost arrived. But at midnight God returned an answer; an answer which as much surprised the suppliants, as it confounded their enemies: his chains fell off, the iron gates opened to him of their own accord, and his adversaries were put to shame[l]. It was from a full persuasion of the efficacy of intercession, that St. Paul was so earnest in requesting the prayers of others for him[m], and that he was so unwearied in his prayers for them[n]. And it is particularly in reference to intercession for the saints, that St. James says, "The effectual fervent prayer of a righteous man availeth much[o]."]

3. For the ungodly—

[The iniquities of a nation may indeed arrive at such a height, that if Noah, Daniel, and Job were in it, those holy men should not prevail, except for the preservation of themselves[p]. But the instances wherein God has heard prayer on behalf of the ungodly are very numerous, and very encouraging. How speedily did the supplications of Amos remove the threatened judgment from his country[q]! And how irresistible, if we may so speak, were the intercessions of Moses! God had determined to execute vengeance on his people for making and worshipping the golden calf. He therefore, fearing, as it were, that Moses would interpose in their behalf, and prevent the execution of his purpose, said to him, "Let me alone, that my wrath may wax hot against them, and that I may consume them;" that is, 'If thou intercedest for them, thou wilt bind my hands; therefore let me alone, that I may inflict upon them the judgments they have deserved.' But Moses would not "let him alone:" he instantly "besought the Lord," and, as it were, prevailed against him: for "the Lord repented of the evil which he had thought to do unto his people[r]."

While in such instances as these we contemplate the condescension of our God, we cannot fail to notice the love which he bears to his chosen people, and the peculiar delight which he feels in hearing and answering their prayers.]

OBSERVE,

1. What blessings are God's people in the places where they live!

[Our blessed Lord represents them as "the lights of the world," and "the salt of the earth;" because, without them,

---

[l] Acts xii. 4—19.   [m] Rom. xv. 30.
[n] 1 Thess. iii. 10. Phil. i. 4. Col. iv. 12.   [o] Jam. v. 16.
[p] Ezek. xiv. 14.   [q] Amos vii. 1—6.   [r] Exod. xxxii. 10, 11, 14.

the world would be immersed in total darkness, and speedily become one mass of corruption. Little do the world think how much they are indebted to the saints. They are ready to traduce the characters of God's people, and to represent them as "the troublers of Israel:" but, were they viewed aright, they would be considered rather as "the shields of the earth," who ward off from it the judgments of the Almighty. Only let us duly notice the tokens which God has given them of his regard, and the mercy he has shewn to others for their sake, and we shall know how to appreciate their value, and ardently pray for their increase in the earth.]

2. What encouragement have the ungodly to pray for themselves!

[Has God shewn himself so willing to hear the prayers of a single individual in the behalf of populous cities, and will he not hear the prayers of individuals for themselves? Never from the foundation of the world has he rejected the petitions of a real penitent: nor, as we have before observed, has he prescribed any limits to our petitions for spiritual blessings. "The Lord will not be angry," however frequently we renew, or however largely we extend, our supplications: "If we ask, we shall have; if we seek, we shall find;" yea, if we ask for all the glory of heaven, it shall be given to us. O that men were duly sensible of the privilege of prayer! and that they would plead for mercy while yet a throne of grace is open to them!]

3. How diligently should the godly improve their interest in the behalf of others!

[We can scarcely conceive a person so obdurate, but that if, by speaking to another, he could obtain health for the sick, and relief for the indigent, he would avail himself of such an opportunity to benefit his fellow-creatures. Yet is there amongst us a lamentable backwardness to the work of intercession, notwithstanding our almighty Friend is at all times accessible, and the blessings which he will bestow are infinitely greater than words can express. O let all of us stir up ourselves to this blessed work! Let us consider how much we ourselves need the prayers of others; and let a sense of our own necessities stimulate us to "labour fervently in prayer" for others. We are sure at least that, if we prevail not for them, we shall bring down a blessing upon our souls, and "our prayer shall return into our own bosoms." Let us consider also that to neglect to pray for others, is to sin against our God[s]; and that, if we have no heart to sigh and cry for the abominations or the miseries of others, we have great reason to fear and tremble for ourselves[t].]

[s] 1 Sam. xii. 23.   [t] Ezek. ix. 4. with Amos vi. 6, 7.

OUTLINE NO. 31

LOT DELIVERED OUT OF SODOM.

Gen. xix. 17. *And it came to pass, when they had brought them forth abroad, that he said, Escape for thy life; look not behind thee, neither stay thou in all the plain: escape to the mountain, lest thou be consumed.*

IT is extremely profitable to observe how ready God is to honour those who honour him. Lot had been a very distinguished character in Sodom. He had seen and heard with much concern the iniquities that were committed by those around him: " he had vexed his righteous soul with their unlawful deeds from day to day;" and had set them a pattern of piety and virtue. Nor was he inattentive to the welfare of strangers: he was ready at all times to exercise the rights of hospitality, and to shew to others the same liberality which he would wish to meet with at their hands. Indeed his sense of honour in this respect carried him beyond the bounds of prudence or propriety: for when he was protecting his guests from the assaults of those who would have injured them, he even preferred the sacrificing of his daughters, to the suffering of the laws of hospitality to be so grossly violated. That he erred in this matter, we have no doubt; because he had no right to commit one sin in order to prevent another. But he meant well: and probably was so agitated with fear and horror, as scarcely to be aware of the impropriety of his proposal. His zeal for God, and his attention to his guests, were well rewarded. He was informed that the persons whom he had received under his roof were angels in human shape; that they were sent to destroy the cities of the plain; and that they were commissioned to rescue him and his family from the common ruin. In what manner they executed their commission, we may judge from the urgent advice which they gave him in our text; and which we shall consider,

I. As given to Lot—

If we consider the circumstances of Lot, the advice given him was,

1. Most salutary—

[The measure of this people's iniquities was now full: and God had determined utterly to destroy them. This determination had already been announced to Lot; and he had been sent to his friends and relatives to declare it to them; though, alas! they had only treated his message with contempt and derision. His own mind indeed was convinced that the wrath of God would fall upon those devoted cities: but yet *he was disposed to linger,* and defer his flight. Whether he felt regret at leaving so many relatives behind him, or was grieved at the thought of losing all his substance, or had an idea that some time would elapse before the threatened judgments should be inflicted, he was not sufficiently earnest to escape the impending danger. The angels therefore took him and his wife and daughters by the hand, and led them forth without the city; and gave them the counsel which is contained in the text.

The time for executing vengeance was just at hand—There was no safety but in flight; nor any refuge but that which God had appointed—A little longer delay would prove fatal to them all—Though they were out of Sodom, they were at a considerable distance from the mountain—To reach it, required their utmost exertions: it became them therefore to strain every nerve in order to secure the proffered mercy—

To promote this was the direct tendency of the advice: so suited was it to their condition, and so conducive to their welfare.]

2. Most benevolent—

[It is obvious that the extreme earnestness expressed by the angels, together with the whole tenour of their advice, was exceedingly alarming. It was calculated to inspire Lot himself with terror, and to extinguish in the weaker females all the powers of reason and reflection. But shall we therefore say that these divine Monitors were impertinently officious, or needlessly severe? Suppose that, having received a commission to warn Lot, they had yielded to a mistaken tenderness, and forborne to alarm his fears: suppose they had gently admonished him of his danger, and suggested the expediency of providing against it: suppose that, when they saw him lingering, and knew that one hour's delay would involve him and his family in the common ruin, they had contented themselves with hinting in a distant manner that more expedition would be desirable: would such conduct have become them? Would they have acted the part of friends? Yea, would they not have been awfully responsible to God for their unfaithfulness, and been really chargeable with the death of all the family? Assuredly, the more faithful and earnest they were in the discharge of their duty, the more real benevolence they exercised: nor could they have displayed their love in any better way, than by seizing hold of them to quicken their pace, and urging them by the most powerful considerations to secure their own safety.]

We shall not depart from the real scope of the advice, if we regard it,

II. As applicable to ourselves—

Our condition is certainly very similar to Lot's—

[God has declared that he will destroy the whole world of the ungodly, as soon as ever they shall have filled up the measure of their iniquities: and the judgments that he will execute upon them were typified by those that were inflicted upon Sodom. "The cities of the plain were set forth for an example, suffering the vengeance of eternal fire[a]." And it is doubtless in reference to the destruction with which they were visited, that the place of torment is described as "a lake that burneth with fire and brimstone[b]." But there is a place of refuge provided for us; a mountain where no storms can assail us, no judgments ever hurt us. This refuge is the Lord Jesus Christ; "whose name is a strong tower, to which the righteous runneth and is safe." On the other hand, there is no salvation for us, unless we flee to him. While we continue of the world, we must take our portion with the world: we must "come out of it, if we would not be partakers of its plagues[c]." We must "bear our testimony against it, that its ways are evil," and must in the whole of our spirit and conduct be separate from it[d].]

The same advice therefore is proper for us, as for him—

[Two things are indispensably necessary for us, if we would enjoy the benefits which God has offered us in his Gospel; and these are *personal exertion* and *persevering diligence*.

It had been declared to Lot, that the threatened destruction could not be executed till he should have arrived at the place provided for him[e]. But could he therefore say, I am in no danger; I may take my leisure; I may leave myself in God's hands? Surely if he had acted in so presumptuous a manner, he would have perished with the ungodly multitude. When he had come out of Sodom, his exertions were no less necessary than before. He must flee to the mountain: he must escape as for his life:

---

[a] Jude, ver. 7.   [b] Rev. xx. 10.   [c] Rev. xviii. 4.
[d] 2 Cor. vi. 17.   [e] Gen. xix. 22.

he must not delay a moment, lest he should be consumed. Thus it is with us. We cannot say, God has sent his only dear Son to save me, and therefore I have nothing to do: we must rather say, God has offered to have mercy on me, and therefore I must "work out my salvation with fear and trembling." To found our hopes upon the secret purposes of God, would be to delude ourselves, and to ensure our eternal ruin. We might as well hope to win a race without running, or to gain a battle without fighting, as to get to heaven without *personal exertion*. We must seek; yea not only seek, but *strive*, to enter in at the strait gate, if ever we would find admittance into it.

Nor will it avail us any thing to put forth our strength to the uttermost, unless we maintain a constant, vigorous, *persevering diligence* in the course that we have begun. Lot's wife was a partner of his flight, but not of his preservation: for she looked back, and was therefore made a lasting monument of God's displeasure[f]. And if Lot himself had remitted his endeavours, he also would have perished in like manner. We may "run well for a season, and yet be hindered:" we may "begin in the spirit, and yet end in the flesh:" we may "escape the pollutions of the world, and yet be again entangled therein, and overcome." We may come out of Egypt, and yet never reach the promised land. It is not he who begins well, but "he that endureth unto the end, that shall be saved." "If we put our hand to the plough, and look back, we are not fit for the kingdom of heaven."]

ADDRESS,
1. Those who are at ease in Sodom—

[We would not willingly speak reproachful words, or address you in terms that are needlessly offensive: but we are sanctioned by the prophet Isaiah in saying, "Hear the word of the Lord, ye Rulers of Sodom, and ye people of Gomorrha[g]." We bless our God that the abomination referred to in the context, is held in universal abhorrence; and that the very thought of it excites as general indignation amongst us, as it did in Sodom a general concurrence and approbation[h]. But in all other respects those wicked cities are a glass wherein we may behold ourselves. "This," says the prophet, "was the iniquity of thy sister Sodom; pride, fulness of bread, and abundance of idleness was in her[i]." And what can be conceived more characteristic of our state? Our pride, our luxury, our love of ease are not a whit inferior to theirs. Again, our Lord says, "As it was in the days of Lot; they did eat, they drank, they bought, they sold, they planted, they

---

[f] ver. 26.   [g] Isai. i. 10.   [h] ver. 4.   [i] Ezek. xvi. 49.

builded; but the same day that Lot went out of Sodom it rained fire and brimstone from heaven, and destroyed them all; even thus shall it be in the day when the Son of Man shall be revealed[k]:" and let me ask whether it is not so at this day? We are attending to our temporal concerns, our cares and pleasures, with avidity: but notwithstanding we are warned continually of our guilt and danger, how backward are we to flee from the wrath to come! Know ye then that the wrath of God is about to be poured out upon you: and that if ye flee not with all earnestness to the Lord Jesus Christ, ye must inevitably and eternally perish. Perhaps in warning you thus we appear " as persons who mock[1]," or, at best, as needlessly harsh and severe: but we affirm, that what we speak will soon be found true; and that in discharging our duty thus, we perform an office worthy of an angel. We believe God's denunciations, and therefore we speak: and if we should " speak smooth things to you, and prophesy deceits," we should prove your bitterest enemies. In this urgent matter, concealment is treachery, and fidelity is love. Arise then, every one of you; and " escape for your lives."]

2. Those who are lingering, and deferring their flight—

[Many, we doubt not, are convinced of the necessity of taking refuge in Christ, yet are so immersed in worldly cares or pleasures that they know not how to commence their heavenly course. They think that a more convenient season will present itself; and that they shall carry their purposes into effect before the day of vengeance shall arrive. But how many have grown grey with age, while their convictions have led to nothing but abortive wishes and ineffectual resolutions! And how many have been overtaken with the storm, while they were thinking and intending to escape from it! There are indeed many, who have come out of Sodom so as no longer to participate in its grosser abominations; and are, in profession at least, advancing to the place of refuge; while yet in their hearts they are attached to the things that they have renounced. To such persons we would say, with our blessed Lord, " Remember Lot's wife[m]." She looked back, while she was following her husband's steps. We inquire not what her motives were; it is sufficient, she looked back; and for *that* she was struck dead upon the spot; for *that* she was made a monument to all future ages, to assure us, that if our heart be in Sodom, we shall perish like Sodom: whatever be our professions, or whatever our progress, if our heart be not right with God, " we shall take our portion in the lake of fire and

[k] Luke xvii. 28—30. [1] ver. 14. [m] Luke xvii. 32.

brimstone, which is the second death[n]." "Make haste then, and delay not, to keep God's commandments[o]," and to "lay hold on eternal life." Rest not in any purposes, professions, or attainments. Turn not back even in thought: but "forgetting what is behind, press forward toward that which is before." It will be time enough to "rest from your labours," when you are got safe to heaven.]

3. Those who are daily running in the way prescribed—

[Faint not, dearly Beloved, "neither be weary in well doing." For your encouragement you are told to regard Lot's deliverance as a proof, that "God knoweth how to deliver the godly out of temptations, as well as to reserve the ungodly for punishment[p]." Whatever difficulties therefore you have to encounter, fear not. And do not unbelievingly wish that your way were shorter than God has appointed it. This was Lot's weakness and folly. God did indeed graciously condescend to his request; and spared Zoar for his sake: but his unbelief was punished, not only in the fears which harassed him in Zoar, but in the awful dereliction that he afterwards experienced. From this time we hear nothing of him except his drunkenness and incest: and, if St. Peter had not given us reason to believe that he became truly penitent, we should have had ground to apprehend that he was, after all, an outcast from heaven. Plead not then for any other refuge, or for the indulgence of any sin. Say not of any thing that God has proscribed, "Is it not a little one?" A little one it may be in comparison of others; but, whether little or great, it must be renounced: we must abandon for ever our connexion with it, and let our regards terminate in God alone.

But let not those who are hastening towards heaven, be contented to go alone: let them seek to take all they can along with them. Let them exert their influence to the uttermost over all their friends and connexions, in order that they may be instrumental to their salvation also. Let them especially manifest their conjugal and parental affection in this way. Yet if, after all, they be derided as visionaries by some, and be forsaken in their progress by others, let them not for one moment intermit their diligence in the preservation of their own souls. If their labours prove effectual only to one or two, it will be a rich consolation to them in the day of judgment, that, though many who were once dear to them have reaped the fruits of their supineness, there are others for whom they have "not laboured in vain, nor run in vain."]

[n] Rev. xxi. 8.   [o] Ps. cxix. 60.   [p] 2 Pet. ii. 6—9.

himself, he has recourse to this expedient of denying his wife. But was not God still able to protect him? or could the Philistines touch an hair of his head without God's permission? In what had God failed him, that now at this time he should begin to doubt his faithfulness or power? It was the limiting of these perfections that in after ages brought down upon the whole nation of Israel the heaviest judgments[a]: and it could not but greatly aggravate the offence of Abraham in the present instance.]

2. Its natural and necessary tendency—

[We shudder while we contemplate the tendency of this shameful expedient. It was calculated to ensnare the people among whom he sojourned; while it exposed the virtue of Sarah to the extremest hazard. Had she been acknowledged for Abraham's wife, every one would have known the unlawfulness of entertaining a desire after her, and would have abstained from shewing her any undue attention, or from cherishing in his bosom an inclination towards her. But when she passed for an unmarried woman, every one was at liberty to insinuate himself into her affections, and to seek to the uttermost an honourable connexion with her. The event indeed shews what might reasonably have been expected from such a plot. What other catastrophe could well be looked for? Terrible as it might have proved, both to her and to Abimelech, it was no other than the natural consequence of the deceit which was practised.

But what was its aspect and tendency with respect to the Messiah? We tremble to relate. Surely the whole human race combined could not have devised or executed any thing more injurious to his honour. It was but just before, perhaps a week or two, that God had promised to Abraham, that within the year he should have a son by Sarah. Suppose then that matters had proceeded according to Abimelech's intention, and that God had not miraculously interposed to prevent the execution of his purpose, it would have remained a doubt at this moment whether the promises were ever fulfilled to Abraham, and whether the Messiah did indeed descend from his loins. Consequently, the covenant made with Abraham, and all the promises made to him and his seed, would be left in an awful uncertainty. If it would have been criminal in Abraham and Sarah to concert such a plan under any circumstances whatever, how much more criminal was it to do so under the peculiar circumstances in which they then were!]

3. Its having been before practised by him, and reproved—

[a] Ps. lxxviii. 20—22, 40—42.

OUTLINE NO. 32

ABRAHAM REPROVED FOR DENYING HIS WIFE.

Gen. xx. 9. *Then Abimelech called Abraham, and said unto him, What hast thou done unto us? and what have I offended thee, that thou hast brought on me and on my kingdom a great sin? thou hast done deeds unto me that ought not to be done.*

WE admire the fidelity of Scripture history. There is not a saint, however eminent, but his faults are reported as faithfully as his virtues. And we are constrained to acknowledge, that the best of men, when they come into temptation, are weak and fallible as others, if they be not succoured from above. We are habituated to behold Abraham as a burning and shining light: but now we are called to view him under an eclipse. We see the father of the faithful drawing upon himself a just rebuke, and that too, not for some slight defect in his obedience, but for a great and heinous transgression. It will afford us a salutary lesson to consider,

I. The offence which Abraham committed—

He was guilty of dissimulation in calling Sarah his sister, when she was in reality his wife. It is true, she was also his sister, in the same sense that Lot was his brother; she was his niece, the daughter of Haran, who was his brother by the father's side. But was there nothing wrong in this concealment? We do not hesitate to declare, that it was a very grievous sin. Consider,

1. The principle from which it sprang—

[He had been called out from his country to sojourn in a strange land: and, depending upon God for direction and support, "he went forth, not knowing whither he went." For the space of twenty-five years he had experienced the faithfulness and loving-kindness of his God. And he had recently received the most express promises that he should have a son by Sarah, who should be the progenitor of the Messiah. Yet behold, when he comes to Gerar, a city of the Philistines, he is afraid that the people will kill him, in order to gain possession of his wife, who, though ninety years of age, still retained a considerable measure of her former beauty: and, in order to secure

[Had the Philistines come suddenly upon Abraham, and threatened to put him to death for his wife's sake, we should the less have wondered that they were prevailed upon to conceal their relation to each other. But he had committed this same offence many years before; and had thereby ensnared Pharaoh king of Egypt; nor was he then delivered without a divine interposition, and a just rebuke from the injured monarch[b]. Surely he ought to have profited by past experience: he should have been sensible of the evil of such a proceeding; and, having been once rescued, as it were by a miracle, he should never have subjected himself again to such danger, reproach, and infamy. The repetition of so heinous a crime, after such a warning and such a deliverance, increased its malignity an hundred-fold.]

If we consider the offence of Abraham in this complicated view, we shall not wonder at,

II. The rebuke given him on account of it—

Abimelech, admonished by God in a dream to restore Abraham his wife, sent for him, and reproved him for the imposition he had practised. In this rebuke we observe,

1. Much that was disgraceful to Abraham—

[It was no little disgrace that Abraham, a saint, a prophet of the most high God, should be reproved at all by a heathen: but, when we reflect how much occasion he had given for the reproof, it was disgraceful indeed.

The *uncharitableness* which he had manifested was very dishonourable to his character. He had indeed just heard of the horrible impiety of Sodom; and he concluded perhaps, that if a whole city so virulently assaulted Lot for the purpose of gratifying their diabolical inclinations with the men that were his guests, much more would some individual be found in Gerar to destroy him, for the purpose of gaining access to a female that was so renowned for her beauty. Glad should we be to offer this excuse for him: but he had before acted in the same manner without any such considerations to influence his conduct; and therefore we cannot lay any material stress on this recent occurrence. But supposing he had been actuated by such reflections, what right had he to judge so harshly of a people whom he did not know? Abimelech justly asked him, "What sawest thou that thou hast done this thing?" He had no other grounds than mere surmise: "I thought, Surely the fear of God is not in this place." But why should he think so?

[b] Gen. xii. 12—20.

Could not that God who had brought him out from an idolatrous country, and preserved Lot and Melchizedec in the midst of the most abandoned people, have some "hidden ones" in Gerar also? Or, supposing that there were none who truly feared God, must they therefore be so impious as to murder him in order to possess his wife? It is a fact, that many who are not truly religious, have as high a sense of honour, and as great an abhorrence of atrocious crimes, as any converted man can feel: and therefore the reproach which he so unjustifiably cast on them, returned deservedly upon his own head.

In what a disgraceful manner too was his wife restored to his hands! How must he blush to be told, that he who should have been her protector, had been her tempter; that, in fact, he had put a price upon her virtue; and that, instead of being willing, as he ought to have been, to die in her defence, he had sacrificed her honour to his own groundless fears. It must not be forgotten, that Sarah was actually given up to Abimelech, and that Abraham had forborne to claim her: so that he was answerable, not only for the consequences that did ensue, but for those also which, according to the common course of things, were to be expected.

Further, in what light must he appear to himself and all around him, when he was informed, that he had brought on Abimelech and all his household some very severe judgments, and had actually exposed them all to instantaneous death! What Abimelech had done, "he had done in the integrity of his heart:" and, if he and all his family had died for it, Abraham would have been the sole author of their ruin.

We need add no more to the humiliating picture that has been exhibited. Methinks we see Abraham before our eyes ashamed to lift up his head, and with deepest penitence accepting the punishment of his iniquity.]

2. Much that was honourable to Abimelech—

[If we were to judge from this portion of sacred history, we should be ready to think that Abraham had been the heathen, and Abimelech the prophet of the Lord. In the reproof this offended king administered, he was a most eminent pattern of *moderation*, of *equity*, and of *virtue*.

Considering what injury he had sustained, it is truly wonderful that he should express himself with such mildness and composure. The occasion would almost have justified the bitterest reproaches: and it might well be expected that Abimelech would cast reflections on his religion; condemning *that* as worthless, or *him* as hypocritical. But not one reproachful word escaped his lips. The only word that has at all that aspect, is the gentle sarcasm in his address to Sarah; "I have given *thy brother* a thousand pieces of silver;"

admonishing her thereby no more to call him by that deceitful name.

On restoring Sarah to her husband, he endeavoured to make all possible reparation for the evil which he had unwittingly committed. He loaded Abraham with presents, and permitted him to dwell in any part of his dominions; and gave him a thousand pieces of silver to purchase veils for Sarah and her attendants, that they might no longer tempt his subjects by their beauty[c].

Finally, we cannot but admire the utter abhorrence which this heathen prince expressed of a sin, which is too lightly regarded by the generality of those who call themselves Christians. It is observable that he never once complained of the punishment which he and his family had suffered, nor of the danger to which they had been exposed, but only of their seduction into sin. He considered *this* as the greatest injury that could have been done to him: and inquired what he had done to provoke Abraham to the commission of it: "What have I offended thee, that thou hast brought on me and my kingdom *a great sin?*" Surely a more striking refutation of Abraham's sentiments concerning him it was not in the power of language to express.]

On this subject we would found " a word of EXHORTATION"—

1. Shun every species of equivocation and deception—

[They are rarely to be found who will under all circumstances rigidly adhere to truth. Many who would not choose to utter a direct and palpable falsehood, will yet put such a colour upon things as to convey an idea quite contrary to truth. To magnify another's faults or to extenuate their own, to raise or depreciate the value of some commodity, to avoid persecution or obtain applause, are temptations which forcibly operate to produce either exaggeration or concealment. In disagreements especially, no person can be fully credited in his own statement. But this is dishonourable to religion. There is scarcely any thing that affords a greater triumph to the enemies of religion, than to find instances of disingenuousness in those who profess it. And it requires constant watchfulness and self-command to speak the truth at all times. O let us beg of God to "put truth in our inward parts:" and let none of us think it beneath him to use that humiliating prayer of David, "Remove from me the way of lying[d]."]

---

[c] This seems to be the sense of ver. 16. "*It* (the silver) is to thee, &c." [d] Ps. cxix. 29.

2. Guard against relapses into sin—

[We may have repented of a sin, and for a long time forsaken it, and yet be in danger of falling into it again. Indeed our besetting sin, however repented of, will generally continue our besetting sin: and the power of divine grace will appear, not so much in taking away all temptation to it, as in enabling us to withstand and vanquish the temptation. The Spirit of God may form the contrary grace in our hearts, and even cause us to exercise it in a very eminent degree: but still we are not beyond the reach and influence of temptation. If we had all the strength of Abraham's faith, we might fall, like him, through cowardice and unbelief. Let us then watch in all things, but especially in those things wherein we have once been overcome: and let our falls be constant monitors before our eyes, to shew us our weakness, and to stimulate us to prayer. More particularly, if we imagine that we have so forsaken our sin as to be in no danger of committing it again, let us beware: "let him that thinketh he standeth, take heed lest he fall."]

3. Be thankful to God for his protecting and preserving grace—

[If God had taken no better care of us than we have done of ourselves, how many times should we have dishonoured our holy profession! Who that knows any thing of his own heart, is not conscious, that he has at some times tampered with sin; and laid such snares for his own feet, that nothing but God's gracious and unlooked-for interference has preserved him? While we were in our unconverted state, "God has withheld us" on many occasions, as he did Abimelech, "from sinning against him." And since God has been pleased to call us by his grace, we have frequently been rescued by his providence from dangers, to which the folly and depravity of our own hearts have exposed us. Let us then magnify the grace of God: and, if we are enabled to maintain a holy and consistent conduct, let us say with David, "My foot standeth fast; in the congregations will I praise the Lord."]

4. Strive to the uttermost to cancel the effects of your transgressions—

[Abraham by his prevarication had brought distress on Abimelech and all his household. But when he was humbled for his transgression, he prayed to God to remove his judgments from the persons whom he had so seduced. By this means, as far as in him lay, he counteracted and reversed the evil that he had done. It is but seldom that we can cancel in any degree the evil that we have committed: but, if any way whatever present itself to us, we should embrace it gladly, and pursue it eagerly. At all events, the measure adopted by Abraham is open to us all. We may pray for those whom we have injured. We may beg of God to obliterate from their minds any bad impression, which either by our words or actions we have made upon them. And, if we find in them a kind forgiving spirit, we should so much the more redouble our exertions, to obtain for them the blessings of salvation, which will infinitely overbalance any evils which they may have suffered through our means.]

OUTLINE NO. 33

ABRAHAM CASTING OUT HAGAR AND ISHMAEL.

Gen. xxi. 9, 10. *And Sarah saw the son of Hagar the Egyptian, which she had borne unto Abraham, mocking. Wherefore she said unto Abraham, Cast out this bond-woman and her son: for the son of this bond-woman shall not be heir with my son, even with Isaac.*

SIN, even in this world, almost always brings its own punishment along with it: and not unfrequently the sin itself is marked in the punishment that follows it. We can have no doubt but that Sarah erred when she gave Hagar into Abraham's bosom, in hopes of having the promised seed by her. And scarcely had her device been carried into execution before she began to suffer for it. As soon as Hagar had a prospect of becoming a mother, she began to despise her mistress. Her contempt excited vehement indignation in the breast of Sarah; insomuch that she made Abraham himself also a party in the quarrel, and accused him of encouraging Hagar in her insolence. When Abraham, to vindicate himself, empowered her to use her own discretion with respect to Hagar, she began to retaliate on her contemptuous bond-maid, and to treat her with excessive severity. Thus was domestic harmony interrupted by those very means which Sarah had adopted to increase her happiness. Hagar, unable to bear the unkind treatment of her mistress, fled from her face; and returned to her only in consequence of being commanded to do so by an angel of the Lord[a]. We cannot suppose that her forced

[a] Gen. xvi. 3—9.

submission was attended with much comfort either to herself or her mistress: where there was no love, there would be found many occasions of vexation and dispute. At last, after about eighteen years, a quarrel arose, which determined Sarah to expel from her family both Hagar and her son. This domestic occurrence is replete with instruction: we propose therefore to make some observations upon,

I. The history itself—

The expulsion of Hagar and her son, who was now about seventeen years of age, was a strong measure. Let us inquire into,

1. The grounds and reasons of it—

[Sarah had seen Ishmael mocking Isaac. From the resolution adopted by Sarah in consequence of it, we apprehend, that Ishmael had derided the pretensions of Isaac to inherit his father's substance. No doubt, Isaac was instructed as early as possible to regard God as *his* God, and to expect both from his earthly and his heavenly Father the accomplishment of all that God had promised him. Ishmael, on the other hand, would but ill brook the idea of being excluded from the birthright; and therefore would be ready to dispute Isaac's title to it. Possibly too the very name *Isaac*, which signifies *laughter*, would afford Ishmael many occasions of profane banter. Had this " mocking " been nothing more than idle jest, attended with a foolish pleasure in teazing her child, we take for granted that Sarah would have deemed it sufficient to reprove the fault, and to point out to Ishmael the impropriety of his conduct. But she saw that it proceeded from profaneness; that it argued a rebellious spirit against God; that it would become his daily practice; and that his mother encouraged him in it, glad to avenge in that way the wrongs that she supposed herself to suffer. On these accounts Sarah despaired of accomplishing her ends by correction, and determined to prevent a recurrence of such offences by an immediate and final expulsion of the offenders.]

2. The manner in which it was carried into execution—

[Sarah, though right in her judgment respecting the means of obtaining domestic peace, seems to have been too precipitate, and too peremptory in her demands for their expulsion: and Abraham demurred about the carrying it into execution. He indeed had different feelings from Sarah. Sarah's regards were fixed exclusively on Isaac: she did not consider Ishmael as a son, but rather as an intruder, and a rival. But Abraham, being the father of both, felt a paternal affection towards each of them: nor was he indifferent towards Hagar, whom he had considered, and lived with, as a legitimate wife. Perhaps too he suspected that Sarah's proposal originated in an irritation of temper, and that less severe measures would in a little time satisfy her mind. He was grieved exceedingly at the thought of proceeding to such extremities: but finding how resolutely she was bent upon it, he committed the matter to God, and sought direction from above. God directed him to acquiesce in Sarah's wishes; and reminded him, that her proposal, however grievous it might be to him, accorded exactly with his repeated declarations, that "in Isaac should his seed be called," and that all the blessings of the covenant exclusively belonged to *him*[b]. The divine will being thus made known to him, he deferred not to comply with it, but dismissed them early the very next morning. The provision which he gave them for their journey, was not such as might have been expected from a person of his opulence; but we can have no doubt but that he acted in this by the divine direction, and that the mode of their dismission, as well as their dismission itself, was intended for their humiliation and punishment, and probably too for the shewing unto us, that the natural man has no claim upon him for even the most common blessings of his providence. That Hagar and Ishmael were reduced to straits, was owing to their having "wandered" out of their way in the wilderness of Beersheba: had they prosecuted their journey in the direct path to Egypt, where Hagar's friends were, we take for granted that they would have found their provision adequate to their support.]

Hitherto we have seen nothing but a domestic occurrence: we must next contemplate,

II. The mystery contained in it—

Here, as in multitudes of other passages, we are entirely indebted to the New-Testament writers for the insight which we have into the meaning of the Old Testament. Here also we see the advantage that is to be derived from the study of the Old-Testament history: since in very many instances the incidents that are recorded, are not mere memoirs of what has passed, but types and shadows of better and more important things. This family quarrel was designed to instruct the whole world; and to shew us,

1. That the children of promise would always be objects of hatred and contempt to the natural man—

[b] Gen. xvii. 19, 21.

[We should not have ventured to deduce such a position as this from an altercation that took place between two children so many hundred years ago, if an inspired Apostle had not put this very construction upon it. But the disagreements of Cain and Abel, and of Ishmael and Isaac, are recorded on purpose to shew us what is in the heart of man. The principles upon which they acted are common to the whole human race; and will operate in a similar manner whenever circumstances arise to call them forth into action. On this ground we might have formed a reasonable conjecture, that every one who resembled Ishmael, would be hostile to those who resembled Isaac. But the Scriptures supersede all conjecture about the matter: for they affirm, in reference to this very history, that " as *then* he that was born after the flesh, persecuted him that was born after the Spirit, even so it is *now*[c]." Indeed the very same things are grounds of offence to the carnal man in this day, as were in the days of Ishmael. He cannot endure that any persons should be marked by God as his favoured and peculiar people. Our blessed Lord says, " Because ye are not of the world, but I have chosen you out of the world, *therefore* the world·hateth you[d]." The very name of "*saints*" and "*elect*" is as offensive to the world, as that of *Isaac* was to Ishmael, because it imports a preference in the Father's estimation of them. Some indeed will say, that there is no persecution in this day: but St. Paul expressly calls Ishmael's conduct towards Isaac "*persecution:*" and let it be remembered, that to be mocked and despised by our relations and friends is as bitter persecution, and as difficult to bear, as almost any other injury that men can inflict. The Apostle thought so when he numbered "*mockings* and scourgings with bonds and imprisonment[e]." And if those who profess religion are not imprisoned and put to death for their adherence to Christ, sure I am that they are mocked and derided as much as in any age; and that, in this sense at least, "all who will live godly in Christ Jesus must suffer persecution[f]."]

2. That they alone are members of the true church—

[St. Paul explains this whole history as an allegory[g]. He tells us that Hagar, the bond-woman, typified the Mosaic covenant entered into at Mount Sinai, which brought forth children in a state of bondage: but Sarah, the free woman, typified the Christian covenant, which brings forth children in a state of liberty. The natural seed of the former represents all who are born after the flesh: the spiritual seed of the latter, that is, the child of promise, represents those who are born

[c] Gal. iv. 29.   [d] John xv. 19.   [e] Heb. xi. 36.
[f] 2 Tim. iii. 12.   [g] Gal. iii. 24—28.

after the Spirit. Hence it appears that we must be children of promise, in order to belong to the church of Christ. We must have embraced the promise of life which is in Christ Jesus; we must, "by means of the promises, have been made partakers of a divine nature[h];" and been led by them to "purify ourselves from all filthiness both of flesh and spirit[i]." These things are the inseparable attendants of a spiritual birth; and are therefore necessary to make us real members of the church of Christ. The mere circumstance of being descended from Christian parents, or having received the seal of the Christian covenant, or making a profession of the Christian faith, will not constitute us Christians. St. Paul, in reference to this very history, makes this distinction, and leaves no doubt respecting the truth or importance of it: "All," says he, "are not Israel, who are of Israel: neither, because they are the seed of Abraham, are they all children: but In Isaac shall thy seed be called: that is, They who are the children of the flesh, *these are not the children of God;* but *the children of promise are counted for the seed*[k]."]

3. That they alone shall finally possess their Father's inheritance—

[Whether there was an undue mixture of warmth in Sarah's spirit, or not, we are sure that, as far as respected the words that she uttered, she spake by a divine impulse: for St. Paul, quoting her words, says, "What saith *the Scripture?* Cast out the bond-woman and her son; for the son of the bond-woman shall not be heir with the son of the free woman[l]." And this he declares to be a *general* sentence; a sentence of expulsion passed on all who remain under the covenant of works, and an exclusive grant of heaven and happiness to the children of promise. It is not the persecuting son only, but the bond-woman herself, the mother, the whole Jewish Church, the collective body of natural and unconverted men, wherever they be, all must be "cast out:" no regard will be shewn either to their privileges or professions: if they live and die in their natural state, they can have no part or lot with the children of God. They only who in this world rested on the promises as the one ground of their hope and joy, shall experience their accomplishment in the world to come. Doubtless, if we may so speak, it will be grievous to our heavenly Father to disinherit so many of his professed children; for he swears that "he has no pleasure in the death of a sinner, but rather that he turn from his wickedness and live:" but still his decree is gone forth, and cannot be reversed: we must be living members of Christ's church below, before we can inherit his kingdom above.]

[h] 2 Pet. i. 4.   [i] 2 Cor. vii. 1.   [k] Rom. ix. 6—8.   [l] Gal. iv. 30.

From this subject we may gather some HINTS:

1. For the regulating of the conduct of earthly parents—

[It can scarcely be expected in this state of imperfection, but that disagreements will arise between some individuals of a large family. The imperiousness of a master or mistress, the petulance or idleness of a servant; the severity of a parent, or the frowardness of a child; the want of brotherly kindness in children towards each other; and especially the jealousies which subsist, where either the husband or wife is called to exercise authority over the children of the other by a former marriage; any of these things, I say, may soon produce dissatisfaction, and turn our "*laughter*" into an occasion of sorrow: nor is this ever more likely to arise, than when a husband and his wife differ in their judgment respecting the mode of conducting themselves towards their children. But in all cases it is desirable to avoid precipitancy and passion. Authority must be maintained by those whose right it is to govern: and when occasion calls for it, correction must be administered. But it should always be grievous to us to proceed to extremities: nor should we ever exercise very severe discipline without having first spread the case before God, and implored his direction and blessing. There is an excessive lenity which is as injurious in its effects as the contrary extreme. We should inquire at all times, "What saith the Scripture?" And, when we have once ascertained the will of God, we should neither come short of it through a foolish fondness, nor exceed it through vehement irritation. There is one thing which above all should be checked with a strong hand; I mean, profaneness. Parents in general are too strongly impressed with things which relate to themselves, and too little affected with what relates to God. But a scoffing at religion, or impiety of any kind, ought to be an object of our heaviest displeasure. And though nothing but the most incorrigible impiety can warrant us to proceed to such extremities as those which were enjoined in the instance before us, yet we do not hesitate to say, that an incurable member should rather suffer amputation, than that all the other members should be incessantly tormented, and the life itself endangered, by its union with the body. Nevertheless we say again, No chastisement should ever be given "for our pleasure," that is, for the gratification of our spleen or anger, but solely "for the profit" of the individual chastised, and the benefit of all connected with him.]

2. For the perpetuating of the regards of our heavenly Parent—

[Thanks be to God, we materially differ from Ishmael and Isaac in this, that whereas Ishmael could not become a child of promise, we may: for the Scripture says, "If ye be Christ's, then are ye Abraham's seed, and heirs according to the promise[m]." Moreover, if we be indeed Christ's, then shall we never be disinherited: for "he hateth putting away[n];" nor will he suffer any to "pluck us out of his hands[o]," or to "separate us from his love[p]." If we offend, he will chastise with suitable severity: but he will not cast off his people[q]: whom he loveth, he loveth to the end[r]. Behold then the way of securing to yourselves the heavenly inheritance; lay hold on the promises, especially "the promise of life which is in Christ Jesus[s]." Rely on the promises; plead them at a throne of grace; take them as your portion and your heritage; seek to experience their renovating, cleansing efficacy[t]. Be not satisfied with any outward privileges or professions; but "live the life which you now live in the flesh, entirely by faith on the Son of God, as having loved *you*, and given himself for *you*[u]." Thus, though "once ye were aliens, and strangers from the covenants of promise, ye shall become fellow-citizens with the saints, and of the household of God[x]," and shall "inherit the kingdom prepared for you from the foundation of the world[y]."]

[m] Gal. iii. 29.
[n] Mal. ii. 16.
[o] John x. 28, 29.
[p] Rom. viii. 35—39.
[q] Ps. lxxxix. 30—35.
[r] John xiii. 1.
[s] 2 Tim. i. 1.
[t] See notes [h] and [i].
[u] Gal. ii. 20.
[x] Eph. ii. 19.
[y] Matt. xxiv. 34.

OUTLINE NO. 34

ISAAC A TYPE OF CHRIST.

Gen. xxii. 6—10. *And Abraham took the wood of the burnt-offering, and laid it upon Isaac his son: and he took the fire in his hand, and a knife: and they went both of them together. And Isaac spake unto Abraham his father, and said, My father: and he said, Here am I, my son. And he said, Behold the fire and the wood; but where is the lamb for a burnt-offering? And Abraham said, My son, God will provide himself a lamb for a burnt-offering. So they went both of them together. And they came to the place which God had told him of: and Abraham built an altar there, and laid the wood in order; and bound Isaac his son, and laid him on the altar upon the wood. And Abraham stretched forth his hand, and took the knife to slay his son.*

MANY and wonderful are the instances of faith and obedience recorded in the Scriptures. But no action whatever (those only of our Lord himself excepted) has at any time surpassed or equalled that related in the text. It justly obtained for him who performed it, the honourable title of The Father of the Faithful, and, The Friend of God[a]. We shall find it profitable to consider,

I. The history itself—

Abraham had often enjoyed intimate and immediate communion with the Deity. But now he heard the command which was of a most singular and afflictive nature—

[God in some way clearly intimated to Abraham his will: nor left him to doubt one moment, whether it were his voice or not. He commanded Abraham to take his only, his beloved son, Isaac, and to offer him up as a burnt-offering in a place that should afterwards be pointed out. How strange the order! How difficult to be complied with! How well might Abraham have said, "Would God I might die for thee, O Isaac, my son, my son!"]

Instantly, however, and without reluctance, he arose to execute the will of God—

[Had he presumed to reason with God, what specious arguments might he have adduced for declining the way of duty! The certainty of his being reproached by Sarah, "A bloody husband art thou to me[b]:" the offence that would be taken by all the neighbouring nations against him, his religion, and his God: the counteracting and defeating of all the promises which had been made by God himself, and which were to be accomplished solely in and through his son Isaac[c]: all this, with much more, might have been offered in excuse for his backwardness, if indeed he had been backward, to accomplish the will of God. But he conferred not with flesh and blood[d].]

Nor was he diverted from his purpose during the whole of his journey—

[Having prepared the wood, he proceeded instantly, with Isaac and his servants, towards the place that God had pointed out. Nor did he open his intentions to Sarah, lest she should labour to dissuade him from his purpose. But what must have been his thoughts every time that he looked on Isaac? Yet never for one moment did he relax his determination to

[a] Jam. ii. 21, 23.   [b] Exod. iv. 25, 26.
[c] Gen. xvii. 19.   [d] Gal. i. 16.

execute the divine command. Having come in sight of the mountain, he ordered his servants to abide in their place, lest they should officiously interpose to prevent the intended offering. He put the wood on his son, and carried the fire and the knife in his own hands. Affecting as these preparations must have been to a father's heart, how must their poignancy have been heightened by that pertinent question, which was put to him by his son[e]! His answer, like many other prophetical expressions, conveyed more than he himself probably was aware of at the moment. Without giving a premature disclosure of his intention, he declares the advent of Jesus, that Lamb of God, who in due time should come to take away the sin of the world[f]. Thus for three successive days did he maintain his resolution firm and unshaken.]

Having arrived at the spot determined by God, he with much firmness and composure proceeded to execute his purpose—

[He built the altar, and laid the wood upon it in due order. Then with inexpressible tenderness announced to Isaac the command of God. Doubtless he would remind his son of his preternatural birth; and declare to him God's right to take away, in any manner he pleased, the gift he bestowed[g]. He would exhort him to confide in God as a faithful and unchangeable God; and to rest assured, that he should, in some way or other, be restored, after he was reduced to ashes, and have every promise fulfilled to him. Having thus gained the consent of his son, he binds him hand and foot, and lays him on the altar; and, with a confidence unshaken, and obedience unparalleled, holds up the knife to slay the victim. Whether shall we more admire the resolution of the father, or the submission of the son? O that there were in all of us a similar determination to sacrifice our dearest interests for God; and a similar readiness to yield up our very lives in obedience to his will!]

Nothing but the interposition of God himself prevented the completion of this extraordinary sacrifice—

[God had sufficiently tried the faith of his servant. He therefore, by a voice from heaven, stopped him from giving the fatal blow; ordered him to substitute a ram in the place of Isaac; renewed to him with an oath his former promises; rendered him a pattern to all succeeding generations; and, no doubt, is at this instant rewarding him with a weight of glory, proportioned to his exalted piety.]

[e] ver. 7.   [f] ver. 8. John i. 29.   [g] Job i. 21.

Almost every circumstance in this narrative deserves to be considered in,

II. Its typical reference—

Waving many less important points, we may observe that Isaac was a type of Christ:

1. In his appointment to be a sacrifice—

[Isaac was a child of promise, born in a preternatural way, of a disposition eminently pious; yet him did God require for a burnt-offering: it must not be Abraham's cattle, or his son Ishmael, but his beloved Isaac. Thus was Jesus also, the promised seed, named, like Isaac, before he was conceived in the womb: he was born, not after the manner of other men, but of a pure virgin: He was that only, that beloved Son, in whom the Father was well pleased: yet him did God appoint to be a sacrifice. A body was given him for this very purpose[h]. He was ordained from eternity to be a propitiation for sin[i]: nor did the Father recede from his purpose for four thousand years. Having set apart his Son for this end, he changed not: and Jesus, at the appointed time, became obedient unto death, even the death of the cross[k].]

2. In the manner of being offered—

[Isaac bore the wood on which he was afterwards to be lifted up; and voluntarily yielded up his body to be bound, and his life to be destroyed in God's appointed way. Thus did Jesus bear his cross to the place of his crucifixion; and, having been bound, was lifted up upon it. On the very spot where Isaac had been laid upon the altar, was Jesus (most probably) offered in sacrifice to God[l]. And by whose hand was Isaac to bleed, but by that of his own Father? By whom too did Jesus suffer, but by Jehovah's sword[m]? It was not *man*, who made him so to agonize in the garden; nor was it man, that caused that bitter complaint upon the cross[n]. Nevertheless it was with the perfect concurrence of his own will that he died upon the cross; "He *gave himself* an offering and a sacrifice to God, for a sweet smelling savour[o]."]

[h] Heb. x. 4, 5.   [i] Rom. iii. 25.   [k] Phil. ii. 8.

[l] Mount Calvary was one of the mountains in that small tract of country called the land of Moriah: and from ver. 2. it can scarcely be doubted, but that it was the very spot pointed out by God. It could not possibly be far from the spot; and therefore, when the place for the sacrifice of Isaac was so accurately marked, it can scarcely be thought to be any other, than the very place where Jesus was offered two thousand years afterwards.

[m] Zech. xiii. 7. Isai. liii. 10.   [n] Luke xxii. 44. Mark xv. 34.
[o] Eph. v. 2.

There is one point, however, wherein the resemblance does not appear—

[For Isaac was found a substitute; for Jesus none. Neither the cattle on a thousand hills, nor all the angels in heaven, could have stood in his place. None but Jesus could have made a full atonement for our sins. He therefore saved not himself, because He was determined to save us.]

INFER—

1. How marvellous is the love of God to man!

[We admire the obedience of Abraham: but God had a right to demand it: and Abraham knew, that he was about to give his son to his best and dearest friend. But what claim had we on God? Yet did he give up his Son for us, for us sinners, rebels, enemies; nor merely to a common death, but to the agonies of crucifixion, and to endure the wrath due to our iniquities[p]. What stupendous love! Shall any soul be affected with a pathetic story, and remain insensible of the love of God? Let every heart praise him, trust him, serve him: and rest assured, that He, who delivered up his Son for us, will never deny us any other thing that we can ask[q].]

2. What an admirable grace is faith!

[The faith of Abraham certainly had respect to Christ, the promised seed[r]. And, behold how it operated! So will it operate in all who have it. It will keep us from staggering at any promise, however dark or improbable; and will lead us to obey every precept, however difficult or self-denying. Let us seek his faith: and, while we are justified by it from the guilt of sin, let us manifest its excellence by a life of holiness.]

[p] Isai. liii. 6.   [q] Rom. viii. 32.   [r] Heb. xi. 17—19.

OUTLINE NO. 35

IMPORTANCE OF EVIDENCES.

Gen. xxii. 12. *Now I know that thou fearest God, seeing thou hast not withheld thy son, thine only son, from me.*

THERE are in the Holy Scriptures many expressions, which, if taken in the strictest and most literal sense, would convey to us very erroneous conceptions of the Deity. God is often pleased to speak of himself in terms accommodated to our feeble apprehensions, and properly applicable to man only. For instance; in the passage before us, he speaks as if from Abraham's conduct he had acquired a knowledge of something which he did not know before: whereas he is omniscient: there is nothing past, present, or future, which is not open before him, and distinctly viewed by him in all its parts. Strictly speaking, he needed not Abraham's obedience to discover to him the state of Abraham's mind: he knew that Abraham feared him, before he gave the trial to Abraham: yea, he knew, from all eternity, that Abraham would fear him. But it was for our sakes that he made the discovery of Abraham's obedience a ground for acknowledging the existence of the hidden principle from which it sprang: for it is in this way that we are to ascertain our own character, and the characters of our fellow-men. And this is the point which it is my intention chiefly to insist upon at this time. I shall not enter upon the circumstances of the history, but confine myself rather to the consideration of two points; namely,

I. The general importance of evidences for ascertaining our state before God—

Many are ready to pour contempt on marks and evidences, as though they were *legal*. They imagine that the direct agency of the Spirit on the souls of men is quite sufficient to satisfy our minds respecting our real state. Now, though we deny not that there is a direct agency of the Holy Spirit on the souls of men, and that " God's Spirit does witness with our spirits, that we are his[a]," yet is this not of itself sufficient; because it may easily be mistaken, and can never, except by its practical effects, be discovered from the workings of our own imagination. Indeed, the greater our confidence is, when independent of evidences, the more questionable it is; because there is the more reason to suspect that Satan has made the impression in order to deceive us. Evidences in confirmation of this persuasion are necessary,

1. For the satisfaction of our own minds—

[a] Rom. viii. 16.

[The Scriptures suggest innumerable marks whereby to discover our true character. St. John seems to have written his First Epistle almost for the very purpose of informing us on this head, that he might leave us altogether inexcusable if we erred respecting it: "Hereby we do know that we know God, if we keep his commandments. He that saith, I know him, and keepeth not his commandments, is a liar, and the truth is not in him: but whoso keepeth his word, in him verily is the love of God perfected. Hereby know we that we are in him[b]." (Some of the other passages referred to may also be cited.) And St. Paul particularly exhorts us to consult these marks and evidences, just as we would in the assaying of gold: "Examine yourselves whether ye be in the faith: prove your own selves."]

2. For the satisfaction of others—

[What can others know of our state, any farther than it is discoverable in our lives? Our blessed Lord teaches us to bring all, even though they may call themselves prophets, to this test: "Ye shall know them by their fruits: do men gather grapes of thorns, or figs of thistles? even so every good tree bringeth forth good fruit; but a corrupt tree bringeth forth evil fruit. Wherefore by their fruits ye shall know them[c]." And to this test must we ourselves be brought: "By this shall all men know that ye are my disciples, if ye have love one to another[d]."]

3. For the honour of our God—

[Men will judge of our principles by our practice. Now the Gospel is represented as "a doctrine according to godliness." But how shall men know it to be so? Our mere assertions will carry no conviction with them, if they be not confirmed by manifest and substantial proofs. Men will naturally say to us, "Shew me your faith by your works:" and, if our works be unworthy of our profession, "the name of God and his doctrine will be blasphemed[e]." It is by our works that we are to shine as lights in the world: and we are therefore bidden to let our light shine before men, that they, seeing our good works, may glorify our Father that is in heaven[f]."]

From the text we learn,

II. What is that evidence which alone will prove satisfactory to God or our own souls—

---

[b] See 1 John ii. 3—5. and iii. 6—10. ib. 14, 15. ib. 18—21. and iv. 13. ib. 20. and v. 1—4. ib. 10. ib. 18.
[c] Matt. vii. 15—20.   [d] John xiii. 35.
[e] 1 Tim. vi. 1.   [f] Matt. v. 16.

Never was there a more glorious act of obedience than that which Abraham performed in offering up his son, his only son, Isaac. But it will be asked, Is any thing like that required of us? I answer,

1. A full equivalent to this is required of us—

[True, indeed, we are not called to that very act of offering up our own son: but we are expressly commanded to "hate father and mother, and wife and children, and brethren and sisters, yea, and our own life also, in comparison of Christ[g]:" and our blessed Lord declares, that "whosoever cometh not after him, and forsaketh not all that he hath, he cannot be his disciple[h]." This may be deemed a hard saying; but so it is; and the declaration is irreversible: and further still, our blessed Lord has decreed, that "he who saveth his life shall lose it; and he only who loseth his life for his sake, shall find it unto life eternal[i]." There is no difference between either persons or times: the same is true respecting all his followers, in every age and place. On no lower terms will any human being be acknowledged as a friend of Christ; nor will any child of man that is unwilling to comply with them, find acceptance with him in the day of judgment.]

2. Without a compliance with this, we in vain pretend to have the fear of God—

["The fear of God" is the lowest of all graces: yet must that, no less than the highest, be tried by this test. The truth is, that the new creature, even in its lowest state, is complete in all its parts. A little infant has all the parts of an adult: there is nothing added to him even to his dying hour: the only difference between him in the different periods of his life is, that his parts are more matured by age, and capable of greater exertion when he arrives at manhood than they were in the earlier stages of his existence. The different rays of light may be separated by a prism, and so be brought under distinct and separate consideration: but it is the assemblage of all the rays that constitutes light. In like manner, we may separate in idea the graces of a Christian: but where there is *one* truly operative, there is, and must be, *all.* One particular grace may shine more bright in one person, and another in another; but when "Christ is formed in us[k]," not one of his graces can be absent. Hence then I say, that *the fear* of God, no less than *the love* of him, must be tried by this test: and by this alone will "God know that you *fear him,* if you withhold not your son, your only son, from him."]

[g] Luke xiv. 26.   [h] Luke xiv. 33.
[i] Matt. xvi. 25.   [k] Gal. iv. 19.

JEHOVAH-JIREH, THE LORD WILL PROVIDE.

Now, let me ASK, What testimony must God bear respecting *you?*

[He knows every one amongst you, and every secret of your hearts: yet will he not proceed in judgment without adducing the proofs which you had given of your true character. If he say to you, "Come, ye blessed," or, "Go, ye cursed," he will assign his reasons for it, and thereby approve the equity of his sentence before the whole universe[1]. Let me ask, then, What sacrifices have you made for him? and what duties have you performed? Have you "plucked out the right eye, and cut off the right hand, that has offended you?" If not, you know the sad alternative, that "your whole body and soul will be cast into hell fire[m]." Examine yourselves, then, and inquire, whether God can bear this testimony respecting you? Must he not rather, with respect to the greater part of you, say, 'I know you, that "you have not the fear of God before your eyes[n]!" You have made no sacrifice for me; nor have you paid any attention to my commands. Abraham consulted not even his own wife, lest she should prove a snare to him: but you have been ready to follow any adviser that would counsel you to disregard me.' Well, know of a surety that the time is shortly coming, when God will call every one of you into judgment, and when he will put an awful difference between his friends and his enemies; between those who feared his name, and those who feared him not[o].]

---

[1] Matt. xxv. 34—43.   [m] Mark ix. 43—48.   [n] Rom. iii. 18.
[o] Mal. iii. 18.

OUTLINE NO. 36

JEHOVAH-JIREH, THE LORD WILL PROVIDE.

Gen. xxii. 14. *And Abraham called the name of that place, Jehovah-jireh: as it is said to this day, In the mount of the Lord it shall be seen.*

THE Saints of old took special care to remember the mercies of their God. Hence they scarcely ever received any remarkable deliverance from evil, or communication of good from him, but they erected some memorial of it, and gave either to the place or to the memorial itself, some name, that should transmit to posterity a remembrance of the blessing vouchsafed unto them. Such was "Beth-el," where Jacob was favoured with a special vision[a]; and "Peniel," where he wrestled with the angel[b]; and "Eben-ezer," the stone erected by Samuel in remembrance of Israel's victory over the Philistines[c]. Frequently the name of Jehovah himself was annexed to some word expressive of the event commemorated; as, "Jehovah-nissi, meaning, The Lord my banner;" a name given to an altar raised by Moses, to commemorate the total discomfiture of the Amalekites[d]; and "Jehovah-shalom, The Lord send peace;" being the name given to another altar, which Gideon erected in remembrance of a special visit which he had received from the Lord in Ophrah of the Abi-ezrites[e]. The Father of the Faithful set an example in this respect. He had been ordered by God to sacrifice his son Isaac; but in the very act of offering him up, God had arrested his uplifted arm, and directed him to offer in the stead of his son a ram caught in the thicket which was close at hand. This was in fact an accomplishment of what Abraham himself had a little before *unwittingly* predicted. For, in answer to Isaac's question, "My father, behold the fire and the wood, but where is the lamb for a burnt-offering?" he replied, "My son, God will provide himself a lamb for a burnt-offering." By this answer he merely intended to satisfy his son's mind for the present, till the time should arrive for making known to him the command which he had received from God; in which command that provision was actually made: but through the miraculous intervention of Divine Providence and the substitution of the ram in Isaac's place, it had now been literally verified in a way which he himself had never contemplated. And it was in reference to this expression which he had used, that he called the name of the place, "Jehovah-jireh," which means, "The Lord will provide."

This circumstance, occurring on Mount Moriah at the very instant when Abraham's hand was lifted up to slay his son, passed immediately into a proverb,

[a] Gen. xxviii. 19.   [b] Gen. xxxii. 30.   [c] 1 Sam. vii. 12.
[d] Exod. xvii. 15.   [e] Judg. vi. 24.

and has been handed down as a proverb through all successive generations even to this very day: the proverb is, "In the mount of the Lord it shall be seen;" or, as it should rather be translated, "In the mount the Lord shall be seen." To enter fully into this most instructive proverb, it will be proper to shew,

I. What it supposes—

Much important truth lies concealed in it. It supposes,

1. That God is the same in all ages—

[It may be thought that this is a truth which no one will controvert. I grant that no one will controvert it in theory: but practically it is denied every day. The God who is revealed in the Scriptures is evidently a God of infinite condescension and grace; as appears in all his mercies to the children of men. He is also a God of inflexible justice and holiness; as appears by the awful judgments he has executed on account of sin. But, if we now hold him forth in either of these points of view, and inculcate the necessity of our regarding him with hopes and fears suited to these perfections, we are considered as either derogating from his Majesty on the one hand, or from his goodness on the other hand. The notion, that "the Lord will not do good, neither will he do evil," though not openly avowed, is yet the secret persuasion of almost every heart. But if there were any foundation for this Epicurean sentiment, what room could there be for this proverb? But know assuredly, that "He changeth not;" "with Him is no variableness neither shadow of turning:" "He is the same yesterday, to-day, and for ever."]

2. That the privileges of his people in all ages are the same—

[To imagine this, is thought by many to be the height of presumption. But what privilege had Enoch, or Noah, or Abraham, or Moses, or any other of the children of men, which we have not? No one of them enjoyed any thing which was not contained in the covenant of grace. And what was the great promise in that covenant? Was it not, "I will be their God, and they shall be my people?" Was there any thing that was not comprehended in that? or could any thing whatever be added to it? Yet behold, that covenant is as much in force at this day as it was at any period of the world: and those who lay hold on that covenant are as much entitled to its blessings, as any ever were from the foundation of the world. Were this not so, we should have been injured, rather than benefited, by the coming of Christ. But our interest in it is not only as great as theirs was in the days of old, but, I had almost said, greater: for in the mention of this part of the covenant in the New Testament there is this remarkable difference: in the Old Testament God says, "I will be their God;" but in the New Testament he says, "I will be a God unto them[f]." This *seems* to convey a stronger and more determinate idea to the mind. We all know what it is to be a friend or a father to any person: but oh! what is it to be a God unto him? *This* none but God can tell: but the least it means is this; that, whatever situation a believer may be in, all that infinite wisdom, unbounded love, and almighty power can effect, shall be effected for him. Of the believer therefore now, no less than in former days, it may be said, "All things are yours: whether Paul, or Apollos, or Cephas, or the world, or life, or death, or things present, or things to come; all are yours; and ye are Christ's; and Christ is God's[g]."]

3. That whatsoever God at any time has done for the most favoured of his saints, may be expected by us now, as far as our necessities call for it—

[Of all the circumstances related in the Old Testament, scarcely any one was so particular and so exclusive as this which we are considering. Who besides him was ever called to sacrifice his own son? Who besides him was ever stopped by a voice from heaven in the execution of such a command, and directed to another offering which God himself had provided? Yet *behold, this very event was made the foundation of the proverb before us;* and *from this,* particular and exclusive as it was, *all believers are taught to expect, that God will interpose for them in like manner, in the hour of necessity!* If then we may expect such an interposition as this, what may we not expect?

But let us take some other events, to which nothing parallel exists. The passage of Israel through the Red Sea; the striking of the rock, in order to supply them with water in the wilderness; and the feeding of them with daily supplies of manna for forty years: can we expect any interpositions like these? Yes: and an express reference is made to these in the Holy Scriptures in order to raise our expectations to the highest, and to assure us that we shall receive from God every thing that our necessities may require. Were "the depths of the sea made a way for the ransomed to pass over?" With similar triumph may all the "redeemed of the Lord hope to return and come to Zion[h]." What was done "in the ancient

---

[f] Heb. viii. 10.   [g] 1 Cor. iii. 21—23.
[h] Isai. li. 9—11. Cite the whole.

days, in the generations of old," is there made the very pattern of what shall be done for all the Lord's people. A similar assurance is given in reference to the water that issued from the rock; and we are told "not even to remember or consider the former things," since God will repeat them again and again, doing them "anew," so that "every body shall know" and observe it: "I will give waters in the wilderness, and rivers in the desert, to give drink to my people, my chosen[i]." As for the manna, you all are taught by our blessed Lord to pray, "Give us *day by day* our daily bread[k]." The matter then is plain: for, if such things as these are to be realized in *our* experience, there is nothing which was ever done for mortal man, which we are not authorized to expect, *as far as our necessities require it.* Miracles indeed we are not to expect: but what was formerly done by visible exercises of a miraculous power, shall now, *in effect*, be done by the invisible agency of God's providential care. *The mode* of effecting our deliverance shall be varied; but the deliverance itself shall be secured.]

Now we come to,

II. What it affirms—

The proverb is express: " In the mount the Lord shall be seen:" that is,

1. He will interpose for his people in the hour of necessity—

[This is its plain import: and to the same effect it is elsewhere promised, "The Lord will judge his people, and repent himself for his servants; when he seeth that their power is gone, and that there is none shut up or left[l]." If it be asked, ' In what way will he interpose?' I answer, ' This must be left to him: he is not limited to any particular means: he can work *by* means, or *without* them, as he seeth fit: the whole creation is at his command: *the wind* shall divide the sea; and *the sea* shall stand up as a wall on either hand, when he is pleased to make a way through it for his people: and the waters shall resume their wonted state, when he gives them a commission to overwhelm his enemies: and both the one and the other shall be done *at the precise moment of Israel's necessity*[m]. If confederate armies come against his people, *his enemies* shall defeat their own sanguinary purpose, and be the executioners of God's vengeance on each other[n]. Is the destruction of a faithful servant menaced and expected by blood-thirsty persecutors? *an angel* becomes the willing agent

---

[i] Isai. xliii. 18—20. Cite the whole.   [k] Luke xi. 3. See the Greek.
[l] Deut. xxxii. 36.   [m] Exod. xiv. 10—14.
[n] 2 Chron. xx. 1, 10—13, 16, 17, 22—24.

of Jehovah for his deliverance[o]. Sometimes he will defeat the enterprises of his enemies by the very means which they use to carry them into effect. This was the case with respect to Joseph, whose exaltation sprang from the very means used by various instruments for his destruction[p]. As for means, we may safely leave them to God. Two things we certainly know; namely, that he will interpose seasonably; and that he will interpose effectually: for he is, and ever will be, a *very present* help in trouble[q].]

2. We may confidently trust in Him in seasons of the greatest darkness and distress—

[God may not come to our help at the moment that our impatient minds may desire. On the contrary, he may tarry, till we are ready to cry, like the Church of old, "The Lord hath forsaken us, and our God hath forgotten us[r]." But he has wise and gracious purposes to answer by such delays. He makes use of them to stir us up to more earnest importunity[s]; to render us more simple and humble in our dependence upon him[t]; to display more gloriously before our eyes the riches of his power and grace[u], and to teach both us and others to wait his time[x]. Sometimes he suffers the enemy so far to prevail as that to all human appearance our case shall be irremediable: whilst yet those very enemies are instruments in his hands to accomplish unwittingly the very ends which they are labouring to defeat; disappointing thus the devices of the crafty, and taking the wise in their own craftiness[y]. The history of Joseph will of necessity occur to every mind in illustration of this point[z]. But what does all this say to us? Its language is precisely that of the prophet: "The vision is yet for an appointed time; but at the end it shall speak, and not lie: though it tarry, wait for it; because it will surely come, it will not tarry[a]."]

ADDRESS,

1. Those who have never yet been brought into deep waters—

[Do not imagine that because you have hitherto experienced but little trouble, your path shall always be smooth and easy. No: it is a thorny wilderness that you have to pass through, and a troubled ocean that you have to navigate, ere you can reach the desired haven. The mariner when scarcely launched upon the deep does not expect that the breeze shall be alike gentle to the end of his voyage: he prepares for

[o] Acts xii. 4—10.   [p] Gen. l. 20.   [q] Ps. xlvi. 1.
[r] Isai. xlix. 14.   [s] Matt. xv. 22—27.   [t] 2 Cor. i. 8—10.
[u] John xi. 6, 15, 40.   [x] Ps. xl. 1—3. Luke xviii. 1.
[y] Acts xxiii. 12—17.   [z] Gen. l. 20.   [a] Hab. ii. 3.

storms, that he may be ready to meet them when they come. In like manner you also will do well to prepare for seasons of adversity and trial. The seaman takes with him his compass, his chart, his quadrant; and makes his daily observations, that he may know where he is, and not be driven from his course. So likewise do you take with you this proverb; which will ever be of use to you in the most trying hour, and enable you to steer your course with safety to the haven of rest.]

2. Those who are under any great and heavy calamity—

[The Lord's people are no more exempt from trouble than others. When most in the path of duty, storms and tempests may overtake you, and menace your very existence: yea, and in the midst of all, your Lord and Saviour may seem regardless of your trouble. But remember, that, embarked as you are with him, you can never perish. In the fittest moment, he will arise and rebuke the storm; and both winds and waves shall obey him[b]. Go forward, as Abraham did, in the path of duty, and leave events to God. Do not be impatient because God does not appear for you so soon as you could wish. Perhaps you have not gone above one day's journey yet in the path assigned you: if so, you have another and another day yet to go. Possibly you may have been long tried, and are got to the very mount: but you are not yet got to the top of that mount: much less have you bound your Isaac, and lifted up your hand to slay him. If not, the time for the Lord's interposition is not yet come. See how it was with David. He fled from Saul—The Ziphites came and informed Saul of the place where he was hid—Saul blessed them for the intelligence they had brought him: and set out immediately and encompassed with his army the very spot where David was. Alas! David, thy God hath forsaken thee! No: not so: in that critical moment, "a messenger comes to Saul, saying, Haste thee, and come; for the Philistines have invaded the land." And thus was the snare broken, and the persecuted saint delivered[c]. Thus also shall it be with you. Only stay till the critical moment has arrived, and you shall find the proverb true: "In the mount the Lord shall be found." Whatever you may imagine, the Lord is not an inattentive observer of your state. He may suffer you to be cast into the tempestuous ocean, and to be swallowed up by a whale, and yet bring you up again from the very depths of the sea, and advance his own glory the more in proportion to the greatness of your deliverance[d]. Trust then in the Lord, and let your mind be stayed on him.

[b] Mark iv. 35—39.   [c] 1 Sam. xxiii. 19, 21, 26, 27.
[d] Jon. ii. 1—9.

This is the direction which he himself gives you: "Who is among you that walketh in darkness, and hath no light? Let him trust in the name of the Lord, and stay upon his God[e]." And if the time for your deliverance seem to be utterly passed, go with the Hebrew youths into the fiery furnace, taking God's express promise with you[f], and say with Job, "Though he slay me, yet will I trust in him[g]."]

[e] Isai. l. 10.   [f] Isai. xliii. 2, 3.
[g] Job xiii. 15. See the whole subject illustrated in Ps. xxx. 1—12.

OUTLINE NO. 37

ABRAHAM'S PROMISED SEED.

Gen. xxii. 18. *In thy seed shall all the nations of the earth be blessed.*

THERE is nothing in man which can merit the divine favour: the promises of God to us are altogether free, resulting wholly from his sovereign grace: yet does God frequently *manifest* his love towards us in consequence of something done by us. Abraham, it should seem, was an idolater, when God first made himself known to him in his native land: and *then* did the Almighty promise, that in him should all the families of the earth be blessed. But, in the passage before us, Abraham is recorded to have performed the most extraordinary act of obedience that ever was known from the foundation of the world: and God takes occasion from that to renew his promise, and, for his more abundant consolation, to confirm it with an oath. To ascertain the full import of this glorious prophecy, it will be proper to inquire,

I. Who is the seed here spoken of—

It is not to all the natural descendants, or to that part of them that composed the Jewish nation, or even to the spiritual seed of Abraham, that these words refer: they speak of one particular individual, the Lord Jesus Christ.

1. To him all the types direct our attention—

[The temple with all its utensils, the priests with all their habits and services, the sacrifices and oblations of every kind, all shadowed forth his work and offices. The principal events in the Jewish history, together with the great persons engaged in them, their lawgiver, their commanders, judges, kings, and prophets, prefigured him in different points of view, and, as so many lines, meet in him as their common centre. On this account we have reason to think that the prophecy before us relates to him.]

2. In him all the prophecies receive their accomplishment—

[However some of the prophecies might be partially fulfilled in Solomon or others, it is certain that all of them together were never accomplished in any one but Jesus. They were intended to designate HIM, that, when he should arrive, there might be no doubt of his being the very person fore-ordained of God to be the Saviour of the world. The minute description of the promised Messiah, together with the marvellous combination of circumstances that marked Jesus as the person foretold, lead us further to believe that the text had particular respect to him.]

3. To him *exclusively* the text is applied by God himself—

[St. Paul tells us that *the blessing of Abraham* was to come on the Gentiles through Jesus Christ[a]; and that the words of the text related, not to others, but to Christ alone[b].]

This point being ascertained, let us inquire,

II. In what respect all nations are blessed in him—

The full accomplishment of the text will not take place till that glorious period when the knowledge of the Lord shall cover the earth, as the waters cover the sea. Yet, in a limited sense, all nations have experienced the truth of this prophecy already.

1. They are reconciled to God through him—

[Christ died not for one nation only; he was a propitiation for the sins of the whole world. Many of all nations have already believed in his name, and rejoiced in his salvation: and in every place they who believe in him shall find acceptance with their God[c].]

2. They are united in one body in him—

[He has broken down the middle wall of partition that divided the Jewish and Gentile world, and, having reconciled both unto God in one body by the cross, he has slain the

---

[a] Gal. iii. 14.   [b] Gal. iii. 16.   [c] Col. i. 20—22.

enmity thereby [d]. All mankind are now brought into one family, and are taught to regard each other as brethren: and in proportion as the religion of Jesus gains the ascendant over our hearts, we are united in love to every member of his mystical body.]

3. They are blessed with all spiritual blessings—

[There is not any thing that can conduce to our present or future happiness which Jesus will not bestow on his believing people. Adoption into his family, peace in our consciences, holiness in our hearts, and an eternity of glory in the Father's presence, are the certain portion of all his faithful followers. There is no difference between Jew and Gentile; all are admitted to the same privileges, and all shall participate the same enjoyments.]

INFER,

1. The antiquity of the Gospel—

[The sum and substance of the Gospel is, that Christ is the only source of all spiritual and eternal blessings. Wherever this truth is strongly urged, men are ready to cry out against it as a *new* doctrine. But we can trace it, not only to the Reformers of our church, but to the Apostles, yea to Abraham also: for St. Paul declares, that when God spake the words to Abraham, he "*preached the Gospel to him*," even that very Gospel whereby he and all the nations of the earth must be saved.[e] Let this truth then no longer be reviled as novel, but be received as the one ground of all our hopes.]

2. The importance of faith—

[Abraham's faith in this Gospel was imputed to him for righteousness [f]; and by believing the same divine record we also must be justified [g]. No doctrine whatever is more explicitly declared in Scripture than this. Let us then acknowledge the necessity of faith, and look to the Lord Jesus Christ as that promised seed, through whom alone the blessings of Abraham can flow down upon us.]

3. The connexion between faith and works—

[Faith was that principle which produced in Abraham such exemplary obedience [h]: and the same root will bear similar fruits wheresoever it exists [i]. Indeed the pardon of past sins would be utterly insufficient to make us happy, if it were not accompanied with the renovation of our natures. To this effect St. Peter expounded, as it were, the very words of the text, declaring to the Jews, that conversion from sin

---

[d] Eph. ii. 14—16.   [e] Gal. iii. 8.   [f] Gal. iii. 6.
[g] Gal. iii. 7, 9.   [h] Heb. xi. 17.   [i] Acts xv. 9.

was one of the first blessings which the Lord Jesus was sent to bestow[k]. Let us then not consider faith and works as opposed to each other, but as possessing distinct offices, the one to justify our souls, the other to honour God, and to manifest the sincerity of our faith.]

[k] Acts iii. 25, 26.

OUTLINE NO. 38

ABRAHAM PURCHASING A BURYING-PLACE IN CANAAN.

Gen. xxiii. 17, 18. *And the field of Ephron, which was in Machpelah, which was before Mamre, the field, and the cave which was therein, and all the trees that were in the field, that were in all the borders round about, were made sure unto Abraham for a possession, in the presence of the children of Heth, before all that went in at the gate of his city.*

THERE is something in a holy life which wonderfully conciliates the minds of men. At first indeed, like a strong influx of light, it offends their eyes; and the beholders, unable to bear the effulgence of its beams, turn away from it, or perhaps desire its utter extinction. But when it has shone for a long time before them, and they have had sufficient opportunity to contemplate its worth, they are constrained to acknowledge, that "the righteous is more excellent than his neighbour:" and they begin to venerate the character, whose virtues at first were occasions of offence. We have a striking instance of this in the chapter before us. The children of Heth were not acquainted with Abraham's principles: but they had seen his exemplary deportment for many years: and when the death of his wife necessitated him to ask a favour at their hands, they were as glad to confer it, as he could possibly be to receive it. The purchase of a burying-place does not indeed appear at first sight to be an incident worthy of notice: but in the present instance there is much that deserves attention. We would make some remarks upon,

I. The manner in which the agreement was made—

No records, human or divine, afford us a more

admirable pattern for transacting the common business of life than the history before us. All parties seemed to be penetrated with the same spirit: they vied with each other in all that was amiable and praiseworthy. We may notice in particular,

1. Their courteousness—

[Abraham, in his address to the chief persons of the city, testified all the respect due to their character, " standing up before them, and bowing to them:" and they, on the other hand, addressed him as " a mighty prince," whom they were forward and happy to oblige. It were well if, in all our intercourse with mankind, we were careful to maintain a similar deportment. But there are many Christians who seem almost to forget that God has said unto them, "Be courteous[a]." They are arrogant and assuming towards their superiors; they are haughty and imperious towards their inferiors; they are ready to claim as their right what they ought to ask as a favour; and, if they grant a favour, they confer it in so ungracious a way, as to destroy all sense of obligation in him who receives it. Some allowance indeed must be made for natural disposition, and for defects of education: yet, after all, the Christian ought to be the most polite of men, because he ought to feel in his heart all that others express in their conduct: he should "esteem others better than himself[b]," and "prefer them in honour before himself[c]," and make himself the servant of all for his Master's sake[d]. He should have in subjection all that pride and selfishness, that stimulates to contention[e]; and maintain in exercise that divine philanthropy, which is the foundation and cement of all civilized society[f]. "Whatsoever is lovely and of good report," he should revolve it in his thoughts, and manifest it in his actions[g].]

2. Their equity—

[Gladly would Ephron have *given* to Abraham both the sepulchre which he desired, and the field in which it was contained: but Abraham entreated that he might be permitted to pay for it a valuable consideration. Accordingly the price was fixed on the one part with perfect equity, and paid, on the other, with perfect cheerfulness. Would to God that all men would adopt this mode of dealing, and buy and sell according to this pattern! Would to God that even professed Christians would copy after this example! How much falsehood, how much imposition, would then be avoided! Solomon has drawn to the life the characters of many, who depreciate every

[a] 1 Pet. iii. 8. [b] Phil. ii. 3. [c] Rom. xii. 10. [d] 1 Cor. ix. 19.
[e] Eph. iv. 31, 32. [f] Col. iii. 12—14. [g] Phil. iv. 8.

thing which they wish to buy, and then go away boasting of the advantageous bargains they have made; " It is naught, it is naught, saith the buyer; and when he is gone his way, he boasteth[h]." But this is beneath the character of a good man. We should not wish to obtain more, or to pay less, for a thing, than it is worth. We should not advance the price on account of the purchaser's necessity, or refuse what is right on account of the necessity of the seller: but, whether we buy or sell, should act towards our neighbour as we in a change of circumstances would have him do to us.]

3. Their prudence—

[To Abraham especially it was of importance that the purchase should be known and ratified. Had he accepted the sepulchre as a present, or bought it in a private way, his title to it might at some future period have been disputed, and his descendants been deprived of that which he was desirous of securing to them. But all fears of this kind were effectually prevented by the publicity of the transaction. The chief persons of the city were not only witnesses of it, but agents, by whose mediation Ephron was induced to conclude the bargain[i]. Moreover, all who went in or out of the gate of the city, were witnesses; so that, after possession was once taken, no doubt could ever arise respecting the transfer of the property, or the title of Abraham's descendants to possess it.

How unlike to Abraham are many who call themselves his children! They embark in business, and enter into contracts, without due consideration: they transact their affairs without order, and leave them in confusion: and thus by their indiscreet conduct they involve their names in disgrace, and their families in ruin. Let us learn from him: let us act with caution: let not even affliction itself render us inattentive to the welfare of our posterity: let us conduct ourselves conformably to that sage advice of Solomon, " Prepare thy work without, and make it fit for thyself in the field; and afterwards build thine house[k]." In other words, Let deliberation and foresight so regulate our conduct, that they who succeed us may applaud our wisdom, and reap the benefit of our care.]

If the manner of forming this agreement is profitable, much more shall we find it profitable to consider,

II. The ends for which it was made—

There was much more in the mind of Abraham than was known to the people among whom he sojourned. Besides the immediate and ostensible

[h] Prov. xx. 14.   [i] ver. 8.   [k] Prov. xxiv. 27.

reason of making that purchase, he had others that were no less important. We shall mention them in their order. He bought the field,

1. To bury his wife—

[Sarah had lived with him to a good old age. But the dearest relatives, how long soever their union may continue, must part at last[1]. And when the time of separation is come, the most beloved object ceases to please. The soul having taken its flight, the body hastens to putrefaction; and we are as glad to have it removed out of our sight, as ever we were to enjoy communion with it. To give it a decent interment, and drop a tear over it at the grave, is the last office of love which we are able to shew to our dearest friend: and he who lives the longest, has only to perform this painful office the more frequently, till he sees himself, as it were, forsaken by all, and left desolate, unknowing, and unknown. O that we could all bear this in mind! We are born to die: the moment we drew our breath, we had one breath less to draw. Every hour we live, we approach nearer and nearer to our grave. If we continue our course, like the sun, from its rise to the meridian, and from its meridian to the close of day, still every moment shortens our duration; and while we are speaking to you now, we are hastening to the chambers of death. Let husbands and wives, parents and children, and friends who are to each other as their own soul, remember this. Let them sit loose to each other; and let the time that they enjoy the society of their friends, be regarded by them as the interval allotted to prepare for their interment.]

2. To express his confidence in the divine promise—

[God had promised to him and to his seed the land wherein he sojourned. But Abraham had continued there above sixty years without gaining in it so much as one foot of land[m]. But was the promise therefore to be doubted? No. It was not possible that that could fail. Abraham was as much assured that the promise should be fulfilled, as if he had seen its actual accomplishment. Under this conviction, he purchased the field as a pledge and earnest of his future inheritance. In the prophecies of Jeremiah we have a similar compact made with precisely the same view. The prophet had foretold the speedy desolation of Jerusalem by Nebuchadnezzar, and the restoration of the Jews to their own land after a captivity of seventy years. His uncle's son, alarmed, as it should seem, by the

---

[1] This idea is judiciously put into the mouths of both the parties at the time they betroth themselves to each other at the altar; "*Till death us do part.*" [m] Acts vii. 5.

approach of the Chaldean army, determined to sell his estate; and offered it to Jeremiah first, because the right of redemption belonged to him. By God's command Jeremiah bought the inheritance; and had the transfer signed and sealed in a public manner; and buried the writings in an earthen vessel; that, being preserved to the expiration of the Babylonish captivity, they might be an evidence of his title to the estate. This was done, not that the prophet, or his heirs, might be enriched by the purchase, but that his conviction of the truth of his own prophecies might be made manifest[n].]

3. That he might perpetuate among his posterity the expectation of the promised land—

[It was to be four hundred years before his seed were to possess the land of Canaan. In that length of time it was probable that the promise itself would be forgotten; and more especially during their Egyptian bondage. But their having a burying-place in Canaan, where their bones were to be laid with the bones of their father Abraham, was the most likely means of keeping alive in every succeeding generation the hope of ultimately possessing the whole land. Accordingly we find, it did produce this very effect: for as Abraham and Sarah were buried in that cave, so Isaac and Rebekah were, and Jacob and Leah, notwithstanding Jacob died in Egypt[o]. And Joseph also, though buried in Egypt, gave commandment, that when the Israelites should depart out of Egypt to possess the land of Canaan, they should carry up his bones with them, and bury them in the sepulchre of his progenitors[p].]

ADDRESS—

1. Let us seek an union that shall never be dissolved—

[All earthly connexions must sooner or later be dissolved: and when once they are broken by death, they are terminated for ever. But an union formed with the Lord Jesus Christ shall never cease. If we are grafted into him as the living vine, we shall never be broken off: if we are made living members of his body, he will suffer nothing to separate us from him. Death, so far from destroying that union, shall confirm it, and bring us into a more intimate enjoyment of it. Let us then seek that union which is effected by faith in the Lord Jesus. If we consider only the *present* happiness arising from it, it infinitely transcends all other: but if we regard its *continuance*, the longest and dearest connexions upon earth are not worthy a thought in comparison of it.]

[n] Jer. xxxii. 6—16, 42—44.
[o] Gen. xxv. 9, 10. and xlv. 29, 30. and xlix. 30—32. and l. 13,
[p] Gen. l. 24, 25. with Heb. xi. 22.

2. Let us look forward to the possession of the heavenly Canaan—

[There is " a promise left us of entering into rest," even into " that rest which remaineth for the people of God." But we may experience many difficulties and trials in our way thither. Nevertheless " the promise is sure to all the seed:" and " our Forerunner is already entered" into heaven, to take possession of it for us. Nay more, he has given us his " Holy Spirit to be a pledge and earnest of our inheritance." Let us then be contented to live as pilgrims and sojourners in this world; and make it our chief labour to keep our title to that inheritance clear. Let us be anticipating the time when the promise shall bring forth, and all the seed of Abraham rejoice together in its full accomplishment.]

3. Let all our intercourse with men be worthy of our professions and expectations—

[If we have indeed been chosen of God to an eternal inheritance, we should shew a deadness to the things of this world, and an amiableness in the whole of our deportment. It is a shame to be outdone by heathens in any thing. We should excel in courteousness and generosity, in prudence and equity, as well as in heavenly-mindedness and devotion. In short, we should endeavour in all things to "walk worthy of our high calling," and to " shew forth the virtues, as well as the praises, of him who hath called us to his kingdom and glory." Such behaviour will go far towards conciliating our enemies. It will " put to silence the ignorance of foolish men;" and " make those ashamed, who falsely accuse our good conversation in Christ:" and, our light shining thus with uniform and engaging splendour, will constrain many to " glorify our Father that is in heaven."]

OUTLINE NO. 39

MARRIAGE OF ISAAC.

Gen. xxiv. 2—4. *And Abraham said unto his eldest servant of his house, that ruled over all that he had, Put, I pray thee, thy hand under my thigh: and I will make thee swear by the Lord, the God of heaven, and the God of the earth, that thou shalt not take a wife unto my son of the daughters of the Canaanites, among whom I dwell; but thou shalt go unto my country, and to my kindred, and take a wife unto my son Isaac.*

THE great events which take place in the world, such as the rise and overthrow of kingdoms, are disregarded by God as unworthy of notice; whilst the most trivial things that appertain to his church and people, are recorded with the minutest exactness. The whole chapter from whence our text is taken relates to the marriage of Isaac. We are introduced into the most private scenes, and made acquainted with the whole rise, progress, and consummation of a matter, which might as well, to all appearance, have been narrated in a few words. But nothing is unimportant in God's eyes, that can illustrate the operations of his grace, or tend to the edification of his church. In discoursing on this part of sacred history we shall notice,

I. Its peculiar incidents—

Abraham commissioned his servant to go and seek a wife for his son Isaac—

[That holy man could not endure the thought of his son forming a connexion with the Canaanites, who would be likely to draw him aside from the worship of the true God. He therefore ordered his old and faithful servant, Eliezer[a], to go to the country where his father's relations lived, and where, though idolatry obtained in part, Jehovah was still known and worshipped, to bring for his son a wife from thence. As Isaac was forty years of age, it might have seemed more proper for him to go himself: but Abraham had been called out from thence, and would on no account either go back thither himself, or suffer his son to go, lest he should appear weary of his pilgrimage, or countenance his descendants in going back to the world from whence they have been brought forth. On this account, when his servant asked whether, in the event of the woman, whom he should fix upon, being unwilling to accompany him, he should take Isaac thither to see her, Abraham in the most peremptory manner imaginable forbade any such step; and declared his confidence, that while he was thus jealous for the honour of his God, God would overrule the mind of any person who should be selected as a partner for his son[b]. But not contented with charging him in this manner, he imposed an oath upon him, and bound him by the most solemn obligations to execute his commission with fidelity and care[c].

[a] It is not absolutely said that this was the servant; but the confidence placed in him sixty years before, renders it most probable. Gen. xv. 2.   [b] ver. 6—8.

[c] The more customary mode of swearing was by lifting up the hand to heaven (Gen. xiv. 22.): but here it was by putting his hand under Abraham's thigh; which was afterwards required by Jacob for the same purpose of his son Joseph. Gen. xlvii. 29.

How admirable a pattern is this for parents, in reference to the forming of matrimonial connexions for their children! The generality are influenced chiefly by the family and fortune of those with whom they seek to be allied: and even professors of godliness are too often swayed by considerations like these, without adverting sufficiently to the interest of their immortal souls. But surely the religious character of a person ought to operate upon our minds beyond any other consideration whatever. To what purpose has God told us, that the believer can have no communion with an unbeliever, any more than light with darkness, or Christ with Belial[d]? To what purpose has he enjoined us to marry "*only in the Lord*[e]," if we are still at liberty to follow our carnal inclinations and our worldly interests, without any regard to our eternal welfare? Let the example of Abraham and of Isaac have its due weight on all, whether parents or children: and let a concern for God's honour regulate our conduct, as well in choosing connexions for ourselves, as in sanctioning the choice of others.]

The servant executed his commission with fidelity and dispatch—

[Never was there a brighter pattern of a servant than that which this history sets before us. In every step that Abraham's servant took, he shewed how worthy he was to be intrusted with so important a mission. In his first setting-out he acted with great prudence: for, if he had gone alone without any evidences of his master's wealth, he could not expect that he should obtain credit for his assertions. Therefore, without any specific directions from his master, he took ten camels richly laden, and, with them, a proper number of attendants; who, while they evinced the opulence of his master, would be witnesses also of his own conduct. His dependence indeed was upon God, and not on any devices of his own: nevertheless he rightly judged that a dependence upon God was not to supersede the exercise of wisdom and discretion.

Having reached the place of his destination, he earnestly implored direction and blessing from God: and in order that he might ascertain the will of God, he entreated that the woman designed for him might of her own accord offer to water all his camels. A better sign he could not well have asked: because such an offer, freely made to a stranger, would indicate a most amiable disposition: it would demonstrate at once the humility, the industry, the affability, the extreme kindness of the female; and would be a pledge, that she who could be so courteous and obliging to a stranger, would certainly conduct herself well in the relation of a wife. Scarcely had he

[d] 2 Cor. vi. 14, 15.   [e] 1 Cor. vii. 39.

presented his silent ejaculations to God, when Rebekah came, according to the custom of those times, to draw water; and, on being requested to favour him with a draught of water, made the very reply which he had just specified as the sign that was to mark the divine appointment. And no sooner had she made the offer, than she set herself (though it was no inconsiderable labour) to perform it. Amazed at the merciful interposition of his God, he stood wondering, and adoring God for the mercy vouchsafed unto him: nor did he suffer any of the inferior servants to assist her; that, by leaving her to complete the work alone, he might see more clearly the hand of God ordering and overruling the whole matter. When she had finished, he inquired her name and family: and finding that they were his master's nearest relations, he made her a present of some valuable ornaments; and proposed, if her father could accommodate him, to spend the night at his house. She went home immediately to inform her friends, who came to the well, and invited him to return with them. Having brought him to their house, and shewn him the greatest hospitality, he refused to partake of any refreshment till he had made known to them the design of his coming. He then began to relate the wish of Abraham his master, the oath that he had imposed upon him, the prayer which he himself had silently offered to God, and the miraculous answer he had received to it; informing them at the same time of the opulence of Abraham, and that Isaac, on whose behalf he was come, was to be his sole heir. Immediately they all agreed, that the matter proceeded from the Lord; and they testified their willingness to accede to the proposal. They wished however for a few days' delay; but the servant, having succeeded in the object of his mission, was impatient to be gone, and to deliver his master from the suspense in which he must of necessity have been kept. And Rebekah declaring her readiness to proceed with him, he took her and her nurse (after having given presents to all her relations, and thereby increased their esteem for his master), and brought her in safety to Isaac; who gladly received her as a present from the Lord, and was thenceforth united to her with the most affectionate regard.

In all this transaction we cannot but admire, on the one hand, the wisdom, the zeal, and the piety of the servant; and, on the other hand, the condescension and goodness of Jehovah. And though we are not warranted by this history to expect precisely the same interposition in our behalf, yet we are warranted to confide in God, and to expect his direction and blessing in all the things which we humbly commit to him.]

As a mere history, this is replete with instruction but it is still more so, if considered in,

II. Its emblematic import—

Fearful as we would be, exceeding fearful, of imposing any sense upon the Holy Scriptures, which God himself has not plainly sanctioned, we will not take upon ourselves *absolutely to affirm* that the marriage of Isaac was allegorical: but when we consider that some of the most striking parts of Isaac's history are explained by the inspired writers as emblematical of some mystery; that as the promised seed, born in a preternatural way, he was certainly a type of Christ; and that, as being the heir in opposition to Ishmael, he shadowed forth that spiritual seed who should inherit the promises; when we consider too the marvellous circumstances attending his marriage; we cannot reasonably doubt, but that it was a figure or emblem of some mysterious truth. If this ground of interpretation be admitted, we do not then hesitate to say, what that point is which it was intended to prefigure: it was certainly the marriage of God's only dear Son to his bride, the church.

1. God, like Abraham, sends forth his servants to obtain a bride for his Son—

[The object nearest to the heart of our heavenly Father is to bring souls into connexion with his dear Son. This connexion is often represented under the idea of a marriage. Not to mention the innumerable places in the Old Testament where this image is used, we would only observe, that Jesus Christ is expressly called "the Bridegroom;" that his servants are called "the friends of the bridegroom, who hear his voice, and rejoice" in his prosperity[f]; and that the church is called "the Lamb's wife[g]." Ministers are sent forth to prevail on persons to unite themselves to him by faith, so as to become one flesh, and one spirit[h], with him. And when they are successful in any instances, "they espouse their converts to one husband, that they may present them as a chaste virgin to Christ[i]." To this office they are sworn in the most solemn manner: they are warned, that they shall be called to an account for their discharge of it; that if any through their neglect remain unimpressed with his overtures of mercy, their souls shall be required

[f] John iii. 29.   [g] Rev. xxi. 9.   [h] Eph. v. 30. 1 Cor. vi. 15, 17.
[i] 2 Cor. xi. 2. Who that weighs these words, can doubt the propriety of interpreting Isaac's marriage as emblematical of Christ's union with the Church?

at the hands of him who neglected them. At the same time they are informed, that if their want of success is not owing to their own negligence, but to the obstinacy of the people to whom they are sent, it shall not be imputed to them; but "they shall receive a recompence according to their own labour[k]," and "be glorious in God's eyes though Israel be not gathered[l].']

2. His servants execute their commission in the very way that Abraham's servant did—

[They look unto God for his direction and blessing; knowing assuredly, that, though "Paul should plant and Apollos water, God alone can give the increase." They endeavour to render the leadings of his providence subservient to their great end. They watch carefully for any signs which may appear of God's intention to render their message effectual; and they are forward to set forth the unsearchable riches of Christ, together with his suitableness and sufficiency for his church's happiness. They declare that He is "appointed heir of all things;" and that out of His fulness all the wants of his people shall be abundantly supplied. They exhibit in their own persons somewhat of that "salvation wherewith he will beautify the meek;" and to every soul that expresses a willingness to be united to him, they are desirous to impart pledges and earnests of his future love. And if in any instance God blesses their endeavours, they labour to accelerate that perfect union which is the consummation of all their wishes. To any thing that would divert their attention or retard their progress, they say, "Hinder me not, seeing the Lord hath prospered my way[m]."]

3. Their labours are crowned with similar success—

[No faithful servant labours altogether in vain[n]. Some doubtless are far more successful than others; but all who endeavour earnestly to "win souls to Christ," have the happiness of seeing some who obey the call, and cheerfully "forsake all to follow him." These are to them now their richest recompence; and in the last day will also be "their joy and crown of rejoicing:" for "when the marriage of the Lamb is come, and his wife hath made herself ready," then shall they also be "called to the marriage supper of the Lamb," and be eternally blessed in his presence. "These are the true sayings of God[o]."]

To make a suitable IMPROVEMENT of this history,

1. Let us have respect to God in all our temporal concerns—

[k] 1 Cor. iii. 8.   [l] Isai. xlix. 5. with ver. 41.
[m] ver. 56.   [n] Jer. xxiii. 22.   [o] Rev. xix. 7—9.

[We have seen how simply and entirely God was regarded by all the parties concerned in this affair; by Abraham who gave the commission, by Isaac who acquiesced in it, by the servant who executed it, by Rebekah's friends who submitted to the proposal as proceeding from God, and by Rebekah herself, who willingly accompanied the servant to his master's house. Happy would it be if all masters, children, servants, families, were actuated by such a spirit! We need not limit our thoughts to the idea of marriage; for we are told that "in *all* our ways we should acknowledge God, and that he will direct our paths." There is not a concern, whether personal or domestic, which we ought not to commit to him. And if all our "works were begun, continued, and ended in him," we should find that God would "prosper the work of our hands upon us:" "being in his way, he would most assuredly lead us" to a happy and successful issue[p].]

2. Let us execute with fidelity every trust reposed in us—

[It is the privilege both of masters and servants to know, that "they have a Master in heaven;" who accepts at their hands the most common offices of life, provided his authority is acknowledged, his honour consulted, and his will obeyed, in the execution of them. This is God's own direction to them: "*Servants*, be obedient to them that are your masters according to the flesh, with fear and trembling, in singleness of your heart, as unto Christ; not with eye-service, as men-pleasers; but as the servants of Christ, doing the will of God from the heart; with good will doing service, as to the Lord, and not to men: knowing that whatsoever good thing any man doeth, the same shall he receive of the Lord, whether he be bond or free. And, ye *masters*, do the same things unto them[q]." Whatever be our particular calling, it is that to which God himself has called us, and which ought to be exercised with a view to him, and as in his immediate sight. O that when we come into the presence of our Lord in the last day, we may be able to give as good an account of ourselves to him, as this servant did to his master Abraham!]

3. Let us accept the offers which are sent to us in Jesus' name—

[The great concern typified in the history before us, is that in which we are this moment engaged. We are the servants of the most high God; and you are the people to whom we are sent. We are ambassadors from him; and we beseech you, in Christ's stead, to be reconciled to him, and to accept

---

[p] ver. 27. [q] Eph. vi. 5—9.

his overtures of love and mercy. We declare to you, that now he will adorn you with a robe of righteousness and the graces of his Spirit, which were but faintly shadowed forth by the raiment and the jewels that were given to Rebekah[r]. You shall be "all glorious within, and your raiment of wrought gold[s]." O let us not go away ashamed: let us not return and say, that those whom we have solicited, "refuse to come with us." This is the message which he has sent to every one of you: *"* Hearken, O daughter, and consider, and incline thine ear; forget also thine own people and thy father's house; so shall the King have pleasure in thy beauty[t]." May God of his mercy incline you to accept his invitation, and make you willing in the day of his power!]

[r] ver. 53.   [s] Ps. xlv. 13.   [t] Ps. xlv. 10, 11.

OUTLINE NO. 40

JACOB PREFERRED BEFORE ESAU.

Gen. xxv. 23. *The elder shall serve the younger.*

THE common gifts of Providence are bestowed in such a regular and ordinary way, that the hand of God is scarcely seen or acknowledged in them. They are considered as resulting from a settled order of things, and are placed to the account of an imaginary cause, called *Nature*. But it pleases God sometimes to mark his dispensations in so plain a manner, that his agency cannot be overlooked. He withheld from Abraham the promised seed, till there was not the most remote hope of a child being born to him of his wife, Sarah, according to the common course of nature; and thus evinced, beyond a possibility of doubt, that the child was a special and miraculous gift from him. In the same manner he kept Isaac also twenty years childless; and then at last condescended to his repeated supplications, and granted him the desire of his heart. On that occasion God further manifested, that, as " children are a fruit and heritage that cometh of the Lord," so all that relates to them, even to the remotest period of time, is ordered by him. Rebekah, who had been twenty years barren, at last found in herself symptoms of a very extraordinary kind; and being unable to account for them, consulted the Lord. God answered her, that twins were in her womb; that they should be fathers of two distinct nations; that their characters, as also that of their descendants, should be extremely different; that they should contend with each other for the superiority; that the younger should be victorious; and that "the elder should serve the younger." This was not fulfilled in the children themselves; for Esau was stronger than Jacob; being at the head of a warlike band[a] while Jacob was only a poor shepherd, and having many generations of great and powerful men, while Jacob's posterity were oppressed with the sorest bondage. But in the time of David the prophecy began to be accomplished[b] (we may indeed consider Jacob's obtaining of the birthright as a partial fulfilment of it), and in after ages it was fulfilled in its utmost extent; Edom being made a desolation, while the kingdom of Judah was yet strong and flourishing[c]. We must not however imagine that *this* is all that is contained in the words of our text. This prophecy is referred to by the inspired writers both of the Old and New Testament; and that too in such a way, as to shew that it is of singular importance. The prophet Malachi adduces it in proof of God's partiality towards the Jewish nation[d]: and St. Paul quotes it, to confirm the idea he has suggested of God's determination to reject the Jews, who were the elder part of his family; and to receive the Gentiles, who were the younger[e]. The whole train of the Apostle's argumentation in that chapter shews, that he had even an ulterior view, which was, to vindicate the sovereignty of God in the disposal of his favours, whether temporal or spiritual; and to make every one sensible that he was altogether indebted to the free grace of God for his hopes of mercy and salvation.

To confirm the words in this view, we may observe,
I. That God has a right to dispense his blessings according to his own sovereign will—

[a] Gen. xxxvi. Ezek. xxv. 12—14. [b] 2 Sam. viii. 14. [c] Obad. 6—10, 17, 18; [d] Mal. i. 2, 3. [e] Rom. ix. 10—13.

God, as the Creator of all things, has an unlimited right over all—

[It was of his own good pleasure that he created the world at all: there was nothing that had any claim upon him to call it into existence. When he had formed the chaos, no part of matter had any claim above the rest: that which was left inert had no reason to complain that it was not endued with vegetative power; nor vegetables, that they were not enriched with animal life; nor animals, that they were not possessed of reason; nor our first parents, that they were created inferior to angels. Nothing had any claim upon its Maker. He had the same right over all as "the potter has over the clay, to make one vessel to honour, and another to dishonour;" nor could any presume to say, "Why hast thou made me thus [f]?" If this then be true, what claim can man have upon his Maker *now*? If he had none when innocent, has he acquired any by his fall? Does a loyal subject acquire new rights by rising in rebellion against his prince?]

As the Lord and Governor of all things too, he may dispose of them as he sees fit—

[An earthly monarch does not consider himself accountable to his subjects for disposing of that which is properly, and in all respects, his own. He obliges those who are the objects of his favour, but does no injury to those who participate his bounty only in a less degree. Indeed every individual thinks himself at liberty to bestow or withhold his gifts, according as his inclination or judgment may dictate. And shall we deny to God what we concede to men? Shall we bind Him by a law from which we ourselves are free? If any one were to blame us for using our own discretion in conferring obligations, we should ask without hesitation, "Is it not lawful for me to do what I will with mine own [g]?" Shall we then presume to negative that question when put to us by the Governor of the Universe?

Let this idea be well fixed in our minds, that God has a right to bestow his blessing on whom he will; and it will root out that arrogance which is the characteristic of fallen man: it will bring us to the footstool of the Deity, and constrain us to say, "Let him do what seemeth him good:" "I was dumb, because thou didst it."]

We cannot doubt but that God possesses this right, since it is clear,

II. That he actually exercises it—

---

[f] Rom. ix. 20, 21.   [g] Matt. **xx.** 15.

We may daily see this,

1. In the dealings of his providence—

[He consulted not any of his creatures how long a space of time he should occupy in completing the work of creation; or how many orders of creatures he should form. He could as easily have perfected the whole at once, as in six days; or have endued every thing with a rational or angelic nature, as he could diversify their endowments in the marvellous way that he has done. But he acted in all things "according to the counsel of his own will." When it pleased him to destroy the works of his hands on account of their multiplied iniquities, why did he preserve a wicked Ham, when millions no worse than he were overwhelmed in the mighty waters? But to speak of things that have passed since the deluge—Who has ordered the rise and fall of *nations?* Who has raised or depressed the *families* of men? Who has given to *individuals* their measure of bodily or intellectual strength, or ordered the number of their days on earth? Is not this the Lord? Who is it that gives us fruitful seasons, or causes drought and pestilence and famine to oppress the world? "Is there either good or evil in the city, and the Lord hath not done it?"

If it be thought that these different events are regulated according to the moral state of mankind, and that therefore they exemplify rather the equity than the sovereignty of God; we would ask, What was the foundation of the distinction put between Esau and Jacob, together with their respective families? St. Paul particularly notices, that, when the prophecy in our text was delivered, "they were not yet born, nor had done any species of good or evil;" and that the decree was delivered at that time, in order "that the purpose of God according to election might stand, not of works, but of him that calleth[h]." It is clear therefore and indisputable that "he doeth according to his will in the armies of heaven, and among the inhabitants of the earth, and that none can stay his hand, or say unto him, What doest thou[i]?"]

2. In the dispensations of his grace—

[In the call of Abraham, and the separation of his seed for a peculiar people; in distinguishing between his immediate sons, Ishmael and Isaac, as also between Isaac's sons, Esau and Jacob; in giving to their posterity the revelation of his will, while the whole world were left to walk in their own ways; in making yet further distinctions at this present moment, sending the light of his Gospel to a few of the Gentile nations, while all the rest are permitted to sit in darkness and the shadow of

---

[h] Rom. ix. 11.   [i] Dan. iv. 35.

death; in all this, I say, has not God clearly shewn, that "he will have mercy on whom he will have mercy, and that whom he will he hardeneth, or giveth over to the blindness and obduracy of their own hearts[k]?" But, as among Abraham's seed "all were not Israel who were of Israel," so it is now in the Christian world: there is a great and visible distinction made between the different hearers of the Gospel: some have "their hearts opened," like Lydia's of old, to receive and embrace the truth, or, like Saul, are arrested in their mad career of sin, and made distinguished monuments of grace; whilst thousands around them find "the word, not a savour of life unto life, but of death unto death." "Who is it that makes these persons to differ[l]?" To whom is it owing that "the deaf hear, the blind see, the lepers are cleansed, the dead are raised?" We answer, It is all of God: "It is not of him that willeth, nor of him that runneth, but of God that sheweth mercy[m]." The favoured objects "are born, not of blood, nor of the will of the flesh, nor of the will of man, but of God[n]."]

The existence of this right being thus incontrovertibly manifest, we observe,

III. That all in whose favour it is exercised, are bound to acknowledge it with most ardent gratitude—

Impious indeed would it be to arrogate the glory to ourselves—

[We have not of ourselves a sufficiency for the smallest thing, even for the forming of a good thought: what folly then is it to suppose that we can create ourselves anew, and renovate our souls after the divine image! This is the work of God alone. If then we have any reason to hope that God has wrought this great work within us, what base ingratitude is it to rob him of his glory! Is it for this end that he has shewn to us such unmerited regard? or is it such an use that we ought to make of his distinguishing mercy? Surely, what he has done, he has done "for the praise of the glory of his own grace[o]:" and if we have been made partakers of his grace, we should strive to the uttermost to answer the ends for which he has bestowed it.]

Those who have been the most highly favoured by God, have always been most forward to acknowledge their obligations to him—

---

[k] Rom. ix. 18.   [l] 1 Cor. iv. 7.   [m] Rom. ix. 16.
[n] John i. 13.   [o] Eph. i. 6.

[Ask of St. Paul, To whom he owed his eminent attainments? and he will answer, "By the grace of God I am what I am[p]." Ask him, To whom all Christians are indebted for every grace they possess? he will answer, "He that hath wrought us for the self-same thing is God[q]." Ascend to the highest heavens, and inquire of the saints in glory: you will find them all casting their crowns at their Redeemer's feet, and singing, " Unto Him that loved us, and washed us from our sins in his own blood, and hath made us kings and priests unto God and our Father, to him be glory and dominion for ever and ever." To imitate them is both our duty and happiness. Our daily song therefore should be, " Not unto us, O Lord, not unto us, but unto Thy name be the praise:" "Salvation to our God which sitteth upon the throne, and unto the Lamb for ever."]

To guard this deep subject against the abuses to which it is liable, and to render it conducive to its proper and legitimate ends, we shall add a word,

1. Of caution—

[If, as the Apostle says, "there is a remnant according to the election of grace[r]," we are ready to suppose that those who are not of that number are not accountable for their sins, and that their final ruin is to be imputed rather to God's decrees than to their own fault. But this is a perversion of the doctrine. It is a consequence which our proud reason is prone to draw from the decrees of God: but it is a consequence which the inspired volume totally disavows. There is not in the whole sacred writings one single word that fairly admits of such a construction. The glory of man's salvation is invariably ascribed to the free, the sovereign, the efficacious grace of God: but the condemnation of men is invariably charged upon their own wilful sins and obstinate impenitence. If, because we know not how to reconcile these things, men will controvert and deny them, we shall content ourselves with the answer which St. Paul himself made to all such cavillers and objectors; "Nay but, O man, who art thou that repliest against God[s]?" And if neither the truth nor the authority of God will awe them into submission, we can only say with the fore-mentioned apostle, " If any man be ignorant, let him be ignorant[t]." As for those, if such are to be found, who acknowledge the sovereignty of God, and take occasion from it to live in sin, we would warn them with all possible earnestness to cease from their fatal delusions. In comparison of such characters, the people who deny the sovereignty of God are innocent. We

[p] 1 Cor. xv. 10.   [q] 2 Cor. v. 5.   [r] Rom. xi. 5.
[s] Rom. ix. 19, 20.   [t] 1 Cor. xiv. 38.

believe there are many persons in other respects excellent, who, from not being able to separate the idea of absolute reprobation from the doctrine of unconditional election, are led to reject both together: but what excellence can he have, who " turns the very grace of God into licentiousness," and " continues in sin that grace may abound?' A man that can justify such a procedure, is beyond the reach of argument: we must leave him, as St. Paul does, with that awful warning, " His damnation is just[u]."]

2. Of encouragement—

[To one who feels his utter unworthiness of mercy, we know not any richer source of encouragement than the sovereignty of God. For, if he may dispense his blessings to whomsoever he will, then the very chief of sinners has no need to despair: the person who is most remote from having in himself any ground to expect the birthright, may be made a monument of God's grace; while the person who by nature seems to have had fairer prospects, may be left, like the rich youth, to perish in his iniquities. The obstacles which appear to stand in the way of his acceptance may even be turned into grounds of hope; because the more unworthy he feels himself to be, the more he may hope that God will glorify the riches of his grace in shewing mercy towards him. We do not mean that any person should rush into wickedness *in order to* increase his prospects of salvation; for, abstractedly considered, the more sinful any man is, the greater prospect there is of his perishing for ever: we only mean to say, that, *in the view of God's sovereignty*, that which would otherwise have been a ground of despondency, may be turned into a ground of hope. Let the subject then be thus improved: and while some dispute against it, and others abuse it, let us take occasion from it to make our supplication to God, saying with David, " Be merciful unto my sin, *for* it is great!"]

[u] Rom. iii. 8.

OUTLINE NO. 41

THE BIRTHRIGHT TYPICAL OF THE CHRISTIAN'S PORTION.

Gen. xxv. 32. *And Esau said, Behold, I am at the point to die: and what profit shall this birthright do to me?*

IT may be considered as a general rule, that no man abstains from any thing which he has purposed to do, for want of some excuse of expedience or necessity to justify it. A melancholy instance of infatuation we have in the history before us; an instance singular indeed as to the immediate act, but common, and almost universal, as to the spirit manifested in it. Esau, having come home from hunting unusually oppressed with fatigue and hunger, set his heart upon his brother's pottage; and not only agreed to sell his birthright for it, but confirmed with an oath the alienation of that inheritance, to which, by primogeniture, he was entitled. To justify his conduct he offered this vain and false apology, "Behold, I am at the point to die; and what profit shall this birthright do to me?" But the fact is, as the historian informs us, he "despised his birthright."

Let us then consider,

I. Esau's contempt of his birthright—

There were many important privileges attached to primogeniture among the Jews—

[The first-born was by God's appointment to have dominion over his brethren[a], and to enjoy a double portion of his father's inheritance[b]. But besides these *civil*, there were also some *sacred* privileges, which he possessed. The Messiah, of whom he was to be a type, and who, in reference to the ordinances of birthright, is called "the first-born among many brethren[c]," was to spring from his loins[d]. Yea, in some sense, the firstborn had a better prospect even of heaven itself, than the rest of his brethren; because the expectation of the Messiah, who was to descend from him, would naturally cause him to look forward to that great event, and to inquire into the office and character which the promised seed should sustain.]

But these privileges Esau despised—

[He accounted them of no more value than a mess of pottage: nor did he speedily repent of his folly and wickedness. If he had seen the evil of his conduct, he would surely have endeavoured to get the agreement cancelled; and if his brother Jacob had refused to reverse it, he should have entreated

---

[a] Gen. xxvii. 29, 37. and xlix. 3.
[b] This was not optional with the parent in any case. Deut. xxi. 15, 17.
[c] Rom. viii. 29.
[d] In one instance this privilege was separated from the foregoing one; and both were alienated from the first-born; the former being given to Joseph, and the latter to Judah, as a punishment of Reuben's iniquity in lying with his father's concubine. 1 Chron. v. 1, 2.

the mediation of his father, that so he might be reinstated in his natural rights. But we read not of any such endeavours: on the contrary, we are told, " He did eat and drink, and rose up, and went his way;" so little did he value, or rather, so utterly did he " despise, his birthright." On this account is he stigmatized by the Apostle, as a profane person[e]: had he disregarded only temporal benefits, he had been guilty of *folly;* but his contempt of spiritual blessings argued *profaneness.*]

Jacob's conduct indeed in this matter was exceeding base: but Esau's was inexpressibly vile. Yet will he be found to have many followers, if we examine,

II. The analogy between his conduct and our own—

The birthright was typical of the Christian's portion—

[The true Christian has not indeed any temporal advantages similar to those enjoyed by right of primogeniture: but he is made an heir of God, and a joint-heir with Christ. He has a distinguished interest in the Saviour, and an indisputable title to the inheritance of heaven. And hence they who have attained the full possession of their inheritance are called, " The general assembly and Church of the first-born[f]."]

But the generality are like Esau, having,

1. The same indifference about spiritual blessings—

[Some excuse may be offered for Esau, because he knew not what a Saviour, or what an inheritance, he despised. But we have had the Saviour fully revealed to us; and know what a glorious place the heavenly Canaan is. Yet too many of us think as lightly of Christ and of heaven, as if neither he nor it were worth our attention: yea, we are ready at any time to barter them away for the most trifling gratification: and what is this, but to imitate the profaneness of Esau?]

2. The same insatiable thirst after earthly and sensual indulgence—

[Though Esau pretended that he was near to die, it was only an excuse for his profane conduct; for it cannot be conceived, but that, in the house of an opulent man like Isaac, there either was, or might easily be procured, something to satisfy the cravings of nature. But he was bent upon having his brother's pottage, whatever it might cost[g]. And is it not

[e] Heb. xii. 16.   [f] Heb. xii. 23.

[g] His extreme eagerness may be seen in his words, " Give me that *red, red.*" Being captivated with the colour, he determined to get it, whatever it might be, and whatever it might cost: and from thence the name Edom, which signifies *red*, was given him. ver. 30.

so with those who yield to uncleanness, intemperance, or any base passion? Do they not sacrifice their health, their reputation, yea, their very souls, for a momentary indulgence? Do they not say, in fact, 'Give me the indulgence of my lust; I must and will have it, whatever be the consequence: if I cannot have it without the loss of my birthright, be it so; let my hope in Christ be destroyed; let my prospects of heaven be for ever darkened; let my soul perish; welcome hell; welcome damnation; only give me the indulgence which my soul longs after.' This sounds harsh in words; but is it not realized in the lives and actions of the generality? Yes; as the wild ass, when seeking her mate, defies all endeavours to catch and detain her, so these persist in spite of all the means that may be used to stop their course; no persuasions, no promises, no threatenings, no consequences, temporal or eternal, can divert them from their purpose[h].]

3. The same want of remorse for having sold their birthright for a thing of nought—

[Never did Esau discover any remorse for what he had done: for though, when the birthright was actually given to Jacob, he "cried with an exceeding bitter cry, Bless me, even me also, O my father[i]," yet he never humbled himself for his iniquity, never prayed to God for mercy, nor endured patiently the consequences of his profaneness: on the contrary, he comforted himself with the thought, that he would murder his brother, as soon as ever his father should be dead[k]. And is it not thus also with the generality? They go on, none saying, What have I done? Instead of confessing and bewailing their guilt and folly, they extenuate to the utmost, or perhaps even presume to justify, their impieties. Instead of crying day and night to God for mercy, they never bow their knee before him, or do it only in a cold and formal manner. And, instead of submitting to the rebukes of Providence, and kissing the rod, they are rather like a wild bull in a net, determining to add sin to sin. Even Judas himself had greater penitence than they. Alas! alas! what a resemblance does almost every one around us bear to this worthless wretch, this monster of profaneness!]

ADDRESS,

1. Those who are still despising their birthright—

[Reflect a moment on your *folly* and your *danger*. Place yourselves a moment on a death-bed, and say, 'I am at the point to die; and what profit do my past *lusts and pleasures* now do me?' Will ye then justify yourselves as ye now do,

---

[h] Jer. ii. 23, 24.   [i] Gen. xxvii. 34.   [k] Gen. xxvii. 41, 42.

or congratulate yourselves on having so often gratified your vicious inclinations? Suppose on the other hand that ye were dying, like Isaac, in the faith of Christ; would ye then say, What profit shall my *birthright* do to me? Would it then appear a trifling matter to have an interest in the Saviour, and a title to heaven? Consider further, how probable it is that you may one day, like Esau, seek earnestly the inheritance you have sold, and yet find no place of repentance in your Father's bosom! We mean not to say that any *true penitent* will be rejected: but the Apostle intimates, what daily experience proves true, that, as Esau could not obtain a revocation of his father's word, though he sought it carefully with tears, so we may cry with great bitterness and anguish on account of the loss we have sustained, and yet never so repent as to regain our forfeited inheritance[1]. At all events, if we obtain not a title to heaven while we are here, we may come to the door and knock, like the foolish virgins, and be dismissed with scorn and contempt. Having " sown the wind, we shall reap the whirlwind." Let us then " seek the Lord while he may be found, and call upon him while he is near."]

2. Those who value their birthright above every thing else—

[Amidst the multitudes who pour contempt on spiritual blessings, there are some who know their value and taste their sweetness. But how often will temptations arise, that divert our attention from these great concerns, and impel us, with almost irresistible energy, to the commission of sin! And how may we do in one moment, what we shall have occasion to bewail to all eternity! Let us then watch and pray that we enter not into temptation: and, however firm we may imagine our title to heaven, let us beware lest our subtle adversary deprive us of it: Let us fear, lest a promise being left us of entering into the heavenly rest, any of us should seem to come short of it[m].]

[1] Heb. xii. 17.   [m] Heb. iv. 1.

OUTLINE NO. 42

JACOB OBTAINING THE BLESSING.

Gen. xxvii. 35. *And he said, Thy brother came with subtilty, and hath taken away thy blessing.*

IT is not within the reach of our limited capacity to conceive how many and how great events depend upon causes apparently unimportant. We can have no doubt but that parents so pious as Isaac and Rebekah, and who excelled all the patriarchs in the conjugal relation, endeavoured to discharge their duty towards their children in a becoming manner. But each of them felt a partiality for one of their children in preference to the other. Esau, the first-born, who was " a cunning huntsman," and supplied his father with venison, was Isaac's favourite: Jacob, on the other hand, who was of a more domestic turn, and had from the womb been designated by God himself as the inheritor of the birthright, was the favourite of Rebekah. To this circumstance, as it should seem, we must refer all the most important events of Jacob's life. Isaac, in his partiality for Esau, had either misconstrued the intimations which God had given him respecting the birthright, or perhaps had forgotten them. He therefore, when he apprehended himself to be near death, told Esau to go out and bring him some venison, and to receive from his hands the blessings of primogeniture. Rebekah, alive to the interests of Jacob, and afraid that her wishes, as well as the counsels of the Deity, would be thwarted, suggested an expedient to Jacob, which, though adopted with reluctance, was conducted with art, and crowned with the desired success. She bade him fetch her two kids, which she dressed so that they might appear like venison. She moreover clothed him in an odoriferous garment belonging to his elder brother, and put the skins of the kids upon his hands and neck, in order that he might as nearly as possible resemble Esau. And then she sent him in to deceive his aged father, and, by personating Esau, to obtain the blessing. Jacob acted his part with more skill and confidence than could have been expected from a person unaccustomed to deceit: he hesitated not to accumulate falsehoods in support of his claim, and even to represent God himself as having interposed to expedite his wishes. His greatest difficulty was to imitate the voice of Esau. Isaac was blind; and therefore no discovery was dreaded from the difference which there must have been in their appearance.

The taste of Isaac, as well as his sight, was easily deceived. His ear however was more capable of discernment, and excited strong suspicions, that the person who addressed him was not the person he professed to be, but Jacob in disguise. To satisfy his mind, he determined to call in the evidence of his other senses: and by these, as well as by the firmness of Jacob's asseverations, he was deceived. He smelt the rich odours of Esau's garment (which probably was preserved in the family as the distinguishing property of the eldest son), and he felt, as he thought, the roughness of Esau's hands and neck; and therefore imputing his suspicions to his own infirmities, he proceeded without further hesitation to bestow his benediction, together with all the privileges of the birthright, on this treacherous impostor. When Esau, who had been thus defrauded, came to him, the unhappy father found out the treachery that had been practised upon him, and announced to his bereaved son the melancholy tidings; "Thy brother came with subtilty, and hath taken away thy blessing."

Much is to be learned from this extraordinary portion of Holy Writ. Let us consider,

I. The event referred to—

The circumstances being so universally known, we need not go particularly into them. The fraud practised in order to obtain the birthright is that which more immediately calls for our attention—

1. In reference to the end, it was unnecessary—

[It is certainly true, that God had, while Esau and Jacob were yet in the womb, promised the birthright to Jacob the younger son: and no doubt, the birthright was a blessing greatly to be desired. It was also true that Isaac, either through forgetfulness or partiality for his favourite son, was about to bestow the birthright upon Esau. But were there no other means to be used in order to the accomplishment of the divine counsels? Why could they not have reminded Isaac of the promise which God had made, which, as it had been made seventy-six years before, might now well be supposed to have been forgotten by him, especially in his present infirm and dying state? Isaac was a pious man, and would not have dared knowingly and intentionally to thwart the revealed purposes of his God. But supposing, what indeed cannot be reasonably supposed, that this holy man could have so far declined from God as to set himself in deliberate and determined opposition to his will, was not God able to overrule his actions, and to constrain him, as he afterwards did Jacob himself, to cross his hands, and, even against his will, to transfer the blessing to him for whom it was designed[a]? At all events, if they could see no means of preventing the dreaded event, was God unable to effect it? and might not he be safely left with the execution of his own purposes? Was it necessary for them to resort to fraud and lying, in order to prevent his decrees from being superseded and defeated?]

2. As means, it was most unjustifiable and base—

[We are perfectly astonished when we see a person of Rebekah's exemplary character devising such a plot, and a plain man like Jacob executing it in such a determined way; a plot to deceive a holy and aged man, a husband, a parent, in the very hour of his expected decease, and in reference to a point of such importance. We know from the whole of their lives that this was not their ordinary mode of acting: but from the address they shewed throughout the whole of it, we should have thought them the greatest proficients in the arts of dissimulation and fraud. Every difficulty seems to have been foreseen and guarded against with consummate skill: and where Rebekah's experience had not suggested a precaution, the subtilty of Jacob supplied a ready remedy. Lies, when once begun, were multiplied without fear or shame: and because they were not sufficient, God himself was called in as aiding the deception. It was in vain to think that the circumstance of God's having made known his will respecting the birthright could sanction any such means as these; or that they were at liberty to do evil in order that good might come. The whole transaction was vile and hateful in the extreme: and, as long as fraud, and lying, and hypocrisy before God, and uncharitableness and undutifulness to man, are odious, so long must this action merit the execration and abhorrence of all mankind.]

But that we may have a more complete view of this event, let us consider,

II. The reflections it suggests—

Truly profitable is it to the contemplative mind. Methinks, the most superficial observer cannot but remark from hence,

1. How mysterious are the ways by which God accomplishes his own purposes!

[a] Gen. xlviii. 8—20.

[He had determined that Jacob should have the blessing: but who could have thought that he should ever confer it in such a way? Who would have thought that he should employ all this treachery and deceit and falsehood in the bestowment of it? Let not any one however imagine, that the divine conduct is vitiated by overruling thus the wickedness of men; or that Jacob's conduct was justified by accomplishing thus the purposes of Heaven. Evil ceases not to be evil because God overrules it for good: for, if it did, then would the crucifiers and murderers of the Lord of glory be innocent, because by their instrumentality God accomplished the redemption of the world. But as it was "with wicked hands that the Jews crucified and slew Jesus, notwithstanding he was delivered into their hands by the determinate counsel and foreknowledge of God[b]," so were Jacob and Rebekah most criminal, whilst God, who wrought by them, was holy, and just, and good. We must say respecting all the ways of men, of whatever kind they be, they shall eventually "praise God;" and, however contrary to his commands, shall assuredly both accomplish his will and glorify his name[c].]

2. How weak are the best of men when they come into temptation!

[It is not to be supposed that either Jacob or Rebekah would have acted thus on any common occasion: but the importance of the occasion seemed to them to justify the expedients they used. Thus are even good men sometimes betrayed into the commission of evil. They are not aware how much they may be biassed by interest or passion. They have an object to attain: that object is in itself desirable and good: how to attain it in a *direct* way, they know not. Therefore they incline to an *indirect* way, conceiving that the end will justify the means. It was thus that Peter brought upon him the rebuke of Paul. He doubtless wished to soften the prejudices of his Jewish brethren; and he thought that a little sacrifice of liberty on the part of the Gentiles might well be made for so good an end. Hence he required the Gentiles to make the sacrifice: and so plausible were his reasonings on the occasion, that even Barnabas was drawn away by his dissimulation. What wonder then if even good men be sometimes deceived by the specious reasonings of others, or of their own minds, especially when there is some great interest to serve, and when our tempters are those on whose judgment we rely? Let every man then stand on his guard, and beware how he be drawn by any authority whatever to the commission of evil. It will be of little avail to say, My adviser was my father or my mother: there is a plain path, from which no authority under heaven

[b] Acts ii. 23. [c] Ps. lxxvi. 10.

should induce us to deviate. We must walk always as in the immediate presence of God. We must not for a moment allow ourselves in guile of any kind. Little do we know whither we may be drawn, if once we depart from the path of truth and honesty. Who would have thought that Jacob should have been drawn from dissimulation and falsehood to the most horrid blasphemy, even that of making God himself his confederate in sin; and that Rebekah should go farther still, even to the very braving of the curse and wrath of God[d]? Beware then of evil in its very first approaches. Pray to God that you may not be led into temptation of any kind. "Cease from man;" and learn not to follow him, any further than he follows Christ. If Satan can assume the form of "an angel of light," and "his ministers appear as ministers of righteousness," so may our relations and friends appear. Not that this consideration should induce us to disregard good advice; but it should lead us to try all counsels by the word and testimony of God: for "if men speak not according to the written word, there is no light in them."]

3. How vain is it to hope for happiness in the ways of sin!

[Jacob was successful in his impious device. But what fruit had he of his success? "He sowed the wind, and he reaped the whirlwind." Soon was he forced to flee from his brother's wrath: and years of trouble followed his departure from his father's house. Similar measure too was meted out to him both by Laban and his own children. Say, Jacob, what didst thou not suffer from the thought that thy beloved Joseph was devoured of wild beasts: yet was that only a deception of thine own sons for the purpose of gaining thy favour to themselves. Nearly did they bring thy grey hairs with sorrow to the grave; and thou deservedst it all, for thy treachery to thy father, and thy cruelty to thy brother. And let all know, that the sin which they roll as a sweet morsel under their tongue, shall prove gall in their stomach. Thou didst succeed, Gehazi; and thoughtest thyself exceeding rich when thou hadst deposited thine ill-gotten wealth in the house. But what was thy gain at last? or who envies thee thy newly-acquired wealth? So it will be with all who seek their happiness in the ways of sin. They behold, and covet, the bait: but ere long they shall feel the hook. Jacob for the space of twenty years was still under alarm and terror for the consequences of his deceit. In the first instance he was forced to flee in haste, and to go, unprovided, and unprotected, a journey of four hundred miles; and, when he got there, was doomed to

[d] ver. 13.

experience evils to which in his father's house he was an utter stranger. But where will your evils end, if you live and die impenitent and unrenewed? Consider this, Brethren, ere it be too late: and beg of God to keep your feet in the ways of holiness and peace.]

ADDRESS,

1. Those who despise their Birthright—

[Esau had despised his birthright, and sold it for a mess of pottage: and now " he could not recover it, though he sought it carefully with tears[e]." Nor was it any mitigation of his grief that he had been defrauded of it. So neither will it be any comfort to the sinners of mankind that Satan has beguiled them, or that they have been brought to ruin by the fraudulence of others. Dear brethren, what will it avail you to say, My mother, and my brother, were the instruments of my destruction? the loss is still your own, and must be your own to all eternity. If you duly value your Birthright, God will watch over you, and will preserve both *it for you*, and *you for it*[f]——— But, if you make light of God's promised blessings, whatever may be the immediate means of your privation, you shall never enjoy them, nor ever so much as taste the banquet which your Lord and Saviour has prepared[g].]

2. Those who desire the Birthright—

[Seek it in a humble simple dependence upon God. In this both Jacob and Rebekah failed: they could not leave God to accomplish his promises in his own time and way. Hence they resorted to such unworthy expedients. But as Abraham felt assured, that, though the promised seed should be slain and reduced to ashes, the promises should yet be verified in him, so should we expect assuredly the fulfilment of God's promises to us. Happy had it been for Jacob if he had thus believed: he might have enjoyed the birthright without any of the subsequent afflictions. Let us then guard against an unbelieving and impatient spirit. Let us commit our every concern to God, and expect, that in the mount of difficulty his interposition shall be seen. This is our wisdom and our happiness: for " His counsel shall stand, and he will do all his will," even though earth and hell should be confederate against him. Let us comply with that important precept, " He that believeth shall not make haste[h]," and we shall secure beyond the possibility of failure the blessing we seek after: for " he that believeth in God shall not be ashamed or confounded world without end."]

---

[e] ver. 38. with Heb. xii. 16, 17. [f] 1 Pet. i. 4, 5.
[g] Luke xiv. 18, 24. [h] Isai. xxviii. 16.

OUTLINE NO. 43

JACOB'S VISION A TYPE OF THE MINISTRATION OF ANGELS TO CHRIST.

Gen. xxviii. 12, 13. *And he dreamed, and behold a ladder set upon the earth, and the top of it reached to heaven: and behold the angels of God ascending and descending on it. And, behold, the Lord stood above it.*

NOW that God has given to the world a complete revelation of his mind and will, we are no longer to expect any extraordinary and personal communications with him: but, in former days, he frequently instructed his more favoured servants by dreams and visions. The particular vision recorded in the passage before us is almost universally considered as typical, though few, if any, have given any satisfactory account wherein the type consists. We shall endeavour therefore to put the subject in a just point of view; and for that purpose shall consider,

I. The immediate end of the vision—

When so remarkable a revelation is vouchsafed to man, we may conclude that some end, worthy of the divine interposition, is to be answered by it. The intent of the vision here given to Jacob, seems to be,

1. To dispel his fears of merited evils—

[Jacob could not but be conscious that he had acted a base and treacherous part: and that therefore he had incurred the divine displeasure, at the same time that he had excited a murderous rancour in the breast of his injured brother. He was now fleeing to avoid the effects of his brother's wrath, and had but too much reason to dread some righteous judgment from the hand of God. But God, who is altogether sovereign in the distribution of his favours, and frequently bestows them at seasons, when, according to our conceptions, they could be the least expected, appeared to him, with expressions of love and mercy. He assured the unhappy fugitive, that he was reconciled towards him, and would give his angels charge over him to keep him in all his way, to protect him from all danger, and to supply his every want[a]. Thus were all his apprehensions at once removed, and his mind restored to perfect peace.]

[a] ver. 15.

2. To confirm his hope of promised blessings—

[He had received a promise of the birthright, while yet he lay in his mother's womb; and doubtless he had expected its accomplishment. But when he saw his father dying, and knew that the rights of primogeniture were about to be confirmed to his elder brother, his faith failed him; and, instead of waiting like David for the throne of Saul, he yielded to the solicitations of his mother, and sought to obtain by craft, what, if he had waited God's time, he would have received in a fair and honourable way. And now he had good reason to doubt, whether he had not forfeited his interest in God's promise, and entailed a curse upon himself instead of a blessing. But God, on this occasion, renewed his promise to him, almost in the very terms, in which, but a few hours before, it had been declared by his father[b]; and thus assured to him, not only a numerous seed, and the inheritance of Canaan, but (which was infinitely the dearest right of primogeniture) the descent of Christ from his loins. From henceforth therefore we behold him walking steadfastly in the faith of Abraham, looking forward with joy to the day of Christ, and maintaining a conduct suitable to his profession.]

While the vision was replete with personal benefit to Jacob, it conveyed instruction also to the Church, by,

II. Its typical reference—

Instead of supposing, with all writers upon this subject, that the ladder was a type of Christ in his divine and human nature mediating between heaven and earth (which is fanciful, and without any warrant from Scripture), we rather think that the vision itself was the type (if it was indeed a type), and that it prefigured,

1. The testimony which angels were to give to Christ—

[Our Lord himself has cast the true light on this passage. In his conversation with Nathanael, he tells the young convert, that he should one day see that *realized* in him, which had been *shadowed forth* in Jacob's vision[c]. Accordingly we find that as, from the first conception of Christ in the womb to that very hour, the angels had deeply interested themselves in every thing that related to him, so they continued on all occasions to wait upon him, to soothe his sorrows, to animate his courage, to fulfil his will, and to bear testimony on his behalf[d]. More than twelve legions of them would have come

---

[b] Compare ver. 13, 14. with ver. 3, 4.   [c] John i. 51.
[d] Matt. iv. 11 Luke xxii. 43. and xxiv. 4, 5, 6, 7, 23.

to his succour if he had desired their aid[e]. Here then is a correspondence between the type and antitype: Jesus was a man of sorrows, and cast out by his brethren, who said, "This is the heir, come let us kill him, and the inheritance shall be ours[f]." But God would not leave his beloved Son without witness, or without support; and therefore opened a communication between heaven and earth, that the angels might have continual access to him, whilst " he himself stood, as it were, at the top of the ladder" to direct their operations.]

2. The confirmation which his people's faith was to receive from that testimony—

[The circumstances of Nathanael and his other disciples, to whom this *ocular* demonstration was to be given, were not unlike to those of Jacob, to whom the *vision* was vouchsafed. They had believed in Jesus; but their faith was to be sorely tried, so that they should be reduced almost to despair. There was however a seasonable support to be afforded them by the intervention and agency of angels. It was the repeated testimony of angels that first inspired them with hope[g], and that, afterwards, at the time of Christ's ascension into heaven, filled them all with a pleasing expectation, that they should one day see him come again in power and great glory[h]. In consequence of their declarations, no less than of the declarations of Christ himself, "they returned to Jerusalem with great joy," and waited for the promised effusion of the Holy Ghost, " knowing in whom they had believed, and assured, that he would keep that which they had committed to him." Thus in this respect also did the type receive a suitable accomplishment.]

For our further IMPROVEMENT of this history, we may observe,

1. There is no person so guilty, but God is willing and desirous to shew mercy to him—

[We cannot but admire the extent and freeness of that mercy with which God revealed himself to this guilty fugitive. We have a similar instance in the mercy shewn to Saul, at the very instant he was " breathing out threatenings and slaughter against the disciples of Christ[i]." And, has not the Apostle told us, that he was intended of God to be in this respect a monument of God's long-suffering, and a pattern to those who should hereafter believe on him[k]?" Let none then despair; but, whatever evils they have brought upon themselves by their iniquities, and whatever reason they may have

---

[e] Matt. xxvi. 53.   [f] Luke xx. 14.   [g] John xx. 12.
[h] Acts i. 11.   [i] Acts ix. 1—6.   [k] 1 Tim. i. 16.

to dread the wrath, either of God or man, let them call to mind the example before us; and turn unto him, who has promised " that he will in no wise cast them out."]

2. There is no distress so great, but God is able and willing to deliver us from it—

[God has thousands of angels at his command, and has appointed them to " minister unto those who shall be heirs of salvation[1]." These he orders to " encamp round about his people, and deliver them[m]." Let us then suppose ourselves as destitute as Jacob himself, having only the earth for our bed, a stone for our pillow, and no other canopy than the heavens; still, a vision of God, with the ministry of his angels, shall render our situation both comfortable and happy; yea, shall make it appear to us as " the very house of God, the gate of heaven[n]." And such a confirmation will these " visions of the Almighty" give to our faith and hope, that we shall be fitted for all future trials, and be enabled to testify on God's behalf, that " he will never leave his people, till he has fulfilled to them his promises in their utmost extent[o]."]

[1] Heb. i. 14. [m] Ps. xxxiv. 7. [n] ver. 17. [o] ver. 15.

OUTLINE NO. 44

THE MANNER IN WHICH GOD DISPENSES HIS FAVOURS.

Gen. xxviii. 15. *Behold, I am with thee, and will keep thee in all places whither thou goest, and will bring thee again into this land: for I will not leave thee, until I have done that which I have spoken to thee of.*

THE study of profane history is exceeding profitable, inasmuch as it brings us into an acquaintance with human nature in all its diversified forms, and thereby qualifies us to discharge all our own duties with more wisdom and propriety. But sacred history, besides that it sets before us incomparably brighter examples of virtue, has this peculiar advantage, that it brings God himself to our view, and exhibits him to us in all the dispensations of his providence and grace. The account which is here given us of his intercourse with Jacob, will serve to shew us, in a very striking point of view, in what manner he dispenses his favours.

I. He bestows them sovereignly—

[Jacob had grievously sinned both against God and man, in personating his brother, in imposing on his father, in blasphemously ascribing to God what was the fruit of his own device, and in fraudulently obtaining his brother's birthright. Having incensed his injured brother, he was now fleeing, to avoid the effects of his indignation. And in what manner should we suppose that God would meet him, if indeed he should deign to notice such a miscreant? Would he not say to him, as he afterwards did to the fugitive prophet, "What dost thou here, Elijah?" Or rather, instead of noticing him at all, may we not suppose that he would send a lion to destroy him[a]? But behold, for the displaying of the riches of his own grace, he revealed himself to him in a most instructive vision; he confirmed to him all the promises that had been made to Abraham and to Isaac; and even extended beyond all former bounds the manifestations of his favour.

A similar instance we have in the Apostle Paul; whom, at the very instant that he was labouring to extirpate the followers of Christ, God was pleased to stop, not, as might have been expected, with some signal judgment, but with singular expressions of his regard, conferring on him the highest honours, and communicating to him the richest blessings.

And may not we also admire the sovereignty of God in the exercise of his mercy towards ourselves? Wherefore is it that we are favoured with the light of his Gospel, when so many myriads of our fellow-sinners are left in darkness and the shadow of death? If we have experienced in our souls the efficacy of divine grace, may we not look back with wonder to the period of our conversion, when we were either drinking iniquity with greediness, or proudly establishing our own righteousness in opposition to the righteousness of Christ? Let us deliberately consider our state when God first caused a ray of light to shine into our minds, and implanted his grace in our hearts, and we shall esteem ourselves no less indebted to the electing love of God, than Jacob, or Saul, or any other whom he has ever chosen[b].]

II. He times them seasonably—

[The fugitive patriarch was now in a very desolate and forlorn condition, wearied in body[c], and distressed in mind. Probably his conscience now smote him, and he was saying with himself, as Joseph's brethren afterwards did, "I am verily guilty concerning my brother[d]." How welcome then must the tokens of God's regard be to him at that season! What

---

[a] 1 Kings xiii. 24.   [b] 2 Tim. i. 9.
[c] From Beersheba to Beth-el was about forty miles.
[d] Gen. xlii. 21.

justify those, who open the sacred records, and expect that the portion of Scripture, on which they cast their eye, shall be a kind of *literal* direction to them; (a most unwarranted and delusive method of ascertaining the mind of God!) but this we must affirm, that, whatever we want, whether wisdom, or strength, or grace of any kind, it shall be given us, if we ask in faith. And the experience of all the saints attests the truth of that promise, " Ye shall ask what ye will, and it shall be done unto you."]

IV. He continues them faithfully—

[God had given promises, not to Abraham only and to Isaac, but to Jacob also, while he was yet in his mother's womb. But instead of fulfilling them to him after this flagrant instance of misconduct, he might well have said to him, as he did to his unbelieving posterity, " Thou shalt know my breach of promise[h]:" " I said indeed, that thy house and the house of thy father should walk before me for ever: but now it shall be far from me: for them that honour me I will honour; and they that despise me shall be lightly esteemed[i]." But he had spoken, and would not go back: for his word's sake he would not cast off his offending child, or even suffer one jot or tittle of his promises to fail.

Thus to his descendants in future ages did God manifest his fidelity; insomuch that Joshua, after eighty years' experience, could appeal to the whole nation, saying, " Ye know in all your hearts and in all your souls, that not one thing hath failed of all the good things which the Lord your God spake concerning you; all are come to pass unto you, and not one thing hath failed thereof[k]."

To us also will he approve himself faithful. " He will not cast off his people, because it hath pleased him to make us his people[l]." He has said, I will never leave thee, I will never, never forsake thee[m]. " He may indeed hide his face from us for a moment; but with everlasting kindness will he have mercy on us: the mountains may depart, and the hills be removed; but the covenant of my peace," says he, " shall not be removed: for like as I have sworn that the waters of Noah shall no more cover the earth, so have I sworn that I would not be wroth with thee, nor rebuke thee[n]."]

IMPROVEMENT—

1. For caution—

[We have seen that Jacob inherited the blessing which he had gained by treachery; and that, where sin had abounded,

[h] Numb. xiii. 34.   [i] 1 Sam. ii. 30.   [k] Josh. xxiii. 14.
[l] 1 Sam. xii. 22.   [m] Heb. xiii. 5.   [n] Isa. liv. 7—10.

a support under his present trials! what an antidote against any future calamities!

Thus it is that God interposes on the behalf of his people, and " repents himself for them, when their strength is gone, and there is none shut up or left[e]." When the contrite soul is bowed down under a sense of guilt, and ready to say, There is no hope; then does God speak peace unto it, saying, " Be of good cheer, I am thy salvation." Just as, in Hagar's extremity, God sent his angel to point out to her a spring, whereby the life of her child was unexpectedly preserved, so in ten thousand instances he appears for us, when we are ready to despair of help: and though his interpositions on our behalf are less visible than these, yet every one of us has reason to acknowledge the truth of that proverb, " In the mount of the Lord it shall be seen[f]." Let us but review our lives, and call to mind the aids of his Spirit under temptations, trials, difficulties; let us see how marvellously we have been upheld when conflicting with sin and Satan, and we shall confess indeed, that " he is a present, a very present, help in trouble."]

III. He imparts them suitably—

[It is probable that Jacob's reply to the advice of his mother was now, in his apprehension, about to be verified; and that he expected a curse rather than a blessing. His evil conscience now might well suggest to him such thoughts as these: 'God has forsaken me, and some great evil will come upon me. I can never hope to return again to my father's house in peace, or to enjoy the blessing which I have so treacherously gained.' To remove these apprehensions, God vouchsafed to him exactly such tokens of his regard, as were best calculated to allay his fears. *In the vision,* God shewed to him both his providential care, and his redeeming love: for doubtless, while he discovered to him the ministry of angels who were commissioned to protect him, he also shewed him that promised Seed, who was in due time to spring from him, and whom at that very instant he typically represented[g]. *In the promise,* he assured him, that his presence should follow him; that his power should preserve him; that he would bring him back again to that very land; and that not one of all the promises that had been ever made to him, should fail of accomplishment.

In this respect also we may trace the tender mercies of our God towards all his people. His manifestations of himself to them, and his application of promises to their souls, are wonderfully suited to their several necessities. We cannot indeed

[e] Deut. xxxii. 36.   [f] Gen. xxii. 14.
[g] This is more fully opened in the preceding Discourse.

grace did much more abound. But shall *we* do evil that good may come; or commit sin that grace may abound? God forbid. We must never expect the blessing of God but in the way of duty.]

2. For encouragement—

[If through temptation we have fallen into sin, let us not flee from God, like Adam, but go to him in humble hope that he will magnify his mercy towards the chief of sinners.]

OUTLINE NO. 45

JACOB'S PILLAR AT BETH-EL.

Gen. xxviii. 16—19. *And Jacob awaked out of his sleep; and he said, Surely the Lord is in this place; and I knew it not. And he was afraid, and said, How dreadful is this place! this is none other but the house of God; and this is the gate of heaven. And Jacob rose up early in the morning, and took the stone that he had put for his pillows, and set it up for a pillar, and poured oil upon the top of it. And he called the name of that place Beth-el: but the name of that city was called Luz at the first.* *

ON whatever side we look, we see abundant evidence that "God's ways are not as our ways, nor his thoughts as our thoughts." With us, there are laws of equity prescribed for the regulation of our conduct in the whole of our intercourse with men; and on our strict observance of them the welfare of society depends. But God is not restrained by any such rules in his government of the world: men having no claims whatever upon him, he has a right to dispose of them, and of all that pertains unto them, according to his own sovereign will and pleasure. This right too he exercises in a way, which, though inexplicable to us, is manifest to all. In the conversion of St. Paul we see this in as striking a point of view as it can possibly be placed. St. Paul,

---

* Preached at the chapel erected and endowed by the Rev. Lewis Way, in Stansted Park (Sussex), on the day previous to the consecration of it by the Right Rev. Lord Bishop of St. David's, and the Hon. and Right Rev. Lord Bishop of Gloucester, on January 24th, 1819: the day on which is annually commemorated *the Conversion of St. Paul.*

even to the very moment of his conversion, was breathing out threatenings and slaughter against the disciples of our Lord, having voluntarily enlisted himself in the service of the high-priest to execute against them his cruel decrees. He was, as he himself tells us, " a blasphemer, and injurious, and a persecutor;" nor had so much as one penitential pang, till he was arrested by the grace of God, and favoured with a sight of that very Jesus, whose interests he was labouring to destroy. Somewhat of a similar display of God's grace may be seen in the history before us. Jacob had been guilty of base deceit in relation to his brother's birthright. He had even represented God himself as confederate with him in that wicked act, and as facilitating by an extraordinary exercise of divine power the attainment of his object. By this treacherous conduct he had greatly incensed his brother against him, and rendered any longer continuance under his father's roof unsafe. Rebekah, who had instigated him to this wickedness, recommended him to flee: and, to reconcile Isaac to his departure, proposed that he should go to his uncle Laban, and take a wife from amongst his own relatives, and not connect himself with any of the daughters of Canaan, as his brother Esau had done. This however was a mere pretext: the true reason of his departure was, that he feared the wrath of Esau, and fled to avoid the effects of his merited indignation. Thus circumstanced, it could not fail but that he must at this time be in a state of much disquietude, not only as being driven from his family at the very time that his pious and aged father was supposed to be dying, but as having brought this evil on himself by his own base and treacherous conduct, and as having provoked God to anger, as well as man, by his impiety. Wearied with fatigue of body and anxiety of mind, he laid himself down to rest under the open canopy of heaven, with nothing but the bare ground for his bed, and a stone for his pillow. If it be asked, why he did not go into the adjacent city to seek a more comfortable lodging there; I answer, that it was altogether owing to the state of his mind: and his conduct in this respect was perfectly natural; the pain of a guilty conscience uniformly indisposing men, not only for society, but even for any corporeal indulgence.

Who would have thought that under such circumstances he should so speedily be honoured with one of the most wonderful manifestations of God's love that ever were vouchsafed to mortal man? Yet on this very night did God draw nigh to him as a reconciled God, and pour into his bosom all the consolations which his soul could desire.

Well might Jacob express surprise at this marvellous display of God's love and mercy: and I pray God that somewhat of the same holy feelings may be engendered in us, whilst we consider,

I. His unexpected discovery, and

II. The grateful acknowledgments which it drew from him.

I. We notice his unexpected discovery—

There were two things with which Jacob was favoured on this occasion; a *vision,* and a *voice. In the vision,* he saw a ladder reaching from earth to heaven, and angels ascending and descending upon it, whilst God himself stood above it to regulate their motions. This imported, that, however destitute Jacob at this time was, there was a God, who ordered every thing both in heaven and earth, and who by means of ministering angels would effect in behalf of his believing people whatsoever their diversified necessities might require. *By the voice,* he was informed, that all which had been promised to Abraham and to Isaac, respecting the possession of Canaan by their posterity, and the salvation of the world by the promised Seed, should be fulfilled, partially in his own person, and completely in his posterity. Thus did God exhibit himself to him on this occasion as a God of providence and of grace, and, under both characters, as his God for ever and ever.

Such a revelation, at such a time, and such a place, a place where the grossest idolatry prevailed to the utter exclusion of the only true God, astonished him beyond measure, and constrained him to exclaim, "Surely the Lord is in this place; and I knew it not." He now saw that God was not confined to any place or country; and that wherever he should reveal himself to man, there was "the house of God, and there the gate of heaven," through which the vilest sinner in the universe might gain access to him.

To prosecute this subject further in reference to Jacob is unnecessary. It is of more importance to consider its bearing on ourselves. Know ye then, that, though the vision and the voice had a special respect to Jacob, and the circumstances in which he was more immediately interested, they are eminently instructive to us also, and *that,* not merely as prophecies that have been fulfilled, but as illustrations of the way in which God will yet magnify the riches of his grace towards his believing people.

How wonderful on many occasions have been the dispensations of his providence! Circumstances as much unlooked for as Jacob's possession of the land of Canaan, have not unfrequently occurred; and, though perhaps small in themselves, have led to results, which have been of the utmost importance through our whole lives. Had we been more observant of the leadings of providence, and marked with more precision the time and the manner in which the different events of our lives have occurred, we should be no less struck with wonder and amazement than Jacob himself. And how extraordinary have been the communications of his grace! Perhaps when we have been surrounded on every side by men immersed in the cares and vanities of this world, ourselves also destitute of all holy principles, and under the guilt of all our past sins, we have been brought to hear the word of God, and to feel its power, yea and to taste its sweetness also, through the manifestations of the Saviour's love to our souls. Possibly, even the enormity of some particular sin has, as in the case of Onesimus, been the very means which God has made use of for bringing us to repentance, and for converting our souls to him. It may be that, like Zaccheus, we have gone to some place, where we contemplated nothing but the gratification of our curiosity; and have been penetrated beyond all expectation by a voice from heaven, saying, "Come down, Zaccheus; for this day is salvation come to thy soul." Perhaps some heavy affliction has been made the means of awakening us to a sense of our lost estate; and through a manifestation of Christ to our souls we have found a heaven, where we anticipated nothing but accumulated and augmented sorrow. Yes verily, there are witnesses without number, at this present day, that God still acts in a sovereign way in dispensing blessings to mankind; and that those words are yet verified as much as ever, "I am found of them that sought me not; I am made manifest to them that asked not after me[a]!"

And now let me ask, Whether the effect of such manifestations be not the same as ever? Have we not on such occasions been ready to exclaim, "This is the house of God! this is the gate of heaven?" Yes: it is not in the power of outward circumstances, however calamitous, to counterbalance such joys as these. Even the terrors of a guilty conscience are dissipated in a moment; and peace flows in upon the soul like a river.

The practical effects upon the life which will result from this experience may be seen in,

II. The grateful acknowledgments which it drew from Jacob.

"He rose up early in the morning, and took the stone which he had put for his pillows, and set it up for a pillar, and poured oil upon the top of it. And he called the name of that place Beth-el; but the name of the city was called Luz at the first." He determined to erect a memorial of the stupendous mercy that had been vouchsafed to him, and to serve

[a] Rom. x. 20.

his God in that very place which had been so commended to him by the providence and grace of God. Accordingly he took the stone on which he had reclined his head, and erected it for a pillar, and poured oil upon it, in order to consecrate it to the special service of his God. We have no account of any express command from God that oil should be applied to this purpose by him: but in after-ages it was particularly enjoined to Moses to be used in consecrating the tabernacle, together with all the holy vessels and instruments that were employed in God's service[b]; as also to be used in all the peace-offerings that were presented to the Lord: "This is the law of the sacrifice of peace-offerings, which he shall offer unto the Lord. If he offer it for a thanksgiving, then he shall offer with the sacrifice of thanksgiving unleavened cakes *mingled with oil*, and unleavened wafers *anointed with oil*, and cakes *mingled with oil*, of fine flour, fried[c]." Thus not only under the law, but long before the law, we behold the solemn rite of consecration performed by one of God's most highly-favoured servants; and a place that was common before, rendered holy to the Lord by the administration of this ordinance. And how acceptable to God this service was, may be judged from hence, that, twenty years afterwards, God again appeared to Jacob, and reminded him of this very circumstance, saying, "I am the God of Beth-el, *where thou anointedst the pillar,* and where thou vowedst a vow unto me[d]." "Arise, and go up to Beth-el, and dwell there; and make there an altar unto God, that appeared unto thee when thou fleddest from the face of Esau thy brother[e]." And in obedience to this command, we are told, "Jacob came to Luz, that is, Beth-el, and built an altar there, and called the place El-beth-el, because God there appeared unto him, when he fled from the face of his brother[f]."

Do we not then see in this record how we also should mark the interpositions of God in our behalf? Does it not become us to remember them, and to

[b] Numb. vii. 1.   [c] Lev. vii. 11, 12.   [d] Gen. xxxi. 13.
[e] Gen. xxxv. 1.   [f] Gen. xxxv. 6, 7.

perpetuate the remembrance of them for the instruction and encouragement of others? Should not the honour of God be dear to us; and, if the place which God has signalized in so remarkable a way, have hitherto been distinguished by the name of Luz (a place of *almonds,* and of carnal delights), should we not labour to convert it to a Beth-el, and to render it to all future generations a house of God, and, if possible, the very gate of heaven? Let the idea be derided as it may by them that know not God, this is an action worthy of a child of Abraham, a service acceptable and well-pleasing unto God.

In the verses following my text we have the vow of Jacob respecting this place recorded: "This stone, which I have set for a pillar, shall be God's house; and of all that thou shalt give me, I will surely give the tenth unto thee." Thus, whilst he consecrated here an altar to the Lord, he provided for the service of that altar by an actual endowment. What might be his circumstances, or the circumstances of his family, in future life, he knew not: yet he bound himself by this solemn and irrevocable vow. What any ignorant and ungodly man might think of this, it is easy to imagine: but I find not in all the inspired volume one single word that discountenances such a conduct. I find, on the contrary, the whole people of Israel contributing according to their power towards the erection of the tabernacle, and stripping themselves of their ornaments in order to furnish it with vessels for the service of their God—I find David, the man after God's own heart, even when not permitted to build the temple himself, devoting not less than eighteen millions of money to the preparing of materials for it—I find similar exertions made by others, at a subsequent period, for the rebuilding of the temple—and I find a poor widow, who had but one farthing in the world, commended for casting it into the treasury, to be expended for the Lord. In whatever light then the lovers of this world may view such an appropriation of wealth, I have no hesitation in saying, that it will never be condemned by our God.

What if, by means of it, God's salvation be made known, and his name be glorified? What if many who have immortal souls, now sunk in ignorance and sin, "be turned by means of it from darkness to light, and from the power of Satan unto God?" What if, by the erection of an altar here, there be in this place somewhat effected towards the accomplishment of that promise, "In that day shall there be an altar to the Lord in the midst of the land of Egypt, and a pillar at the border thereof to the Lord: and it shall be for a sign and for a witness to the Lord in the land of Egypt; for they shall cry unto the Lord because of the oppressors, and he shall send them A SAVIOUR, and A GREAT ONE, and he shall deliver them[g]?" Should God so honour this place, and so testify his acceptance of the sacrifices that shall here be offered, how will *they* bless him, who have been born to God in this place! and how will *they* bless him, who have been his honoured instruments of erecting an altar here, and of consecrating it to his service!

What now remains, but that I endeavour to improve this joyful occasion for the benefit of those who hear me?

Are there any here who are *bowed down under a sense of sin?* Peradventure, though you may have come hither only to witness a novelty, God has brought you hither to speak peace unto your souls, and to anoint you to the possession of a kingdom, when you have no more contemplated such an event than Saul did, when he was in the pursuit of his father's asses. Know ye of a truth, that God is in this place, though ye may not be aware of it. Know, that he is a God of love and mercy, as much as ever he was in the days of old. Know that he has still the same right to dispense his blessings to whomsoever he will, even to the very chief of sinners. Know that he has not only the same communication with men as ever through the instrumentality of angels, but that he has access to the souls of men by his Holy Spirit, who is ready to impart unto you all

[g] Isai. xix. 19, 20.

the blessings of grace and glory. Know that the Seed promised to Jacob has come into the world, even the Lord Jesus Christ; and that he has fulfilled all that is necessary for our salvation. He has expiated our guilt by his own blood upon the cross; and has made reconciliation for us with our offended God; so that through Him all manner of sin shall be forgiven unto men, and "all who believe in him shall be justified from all things." O Beloved, only look unto Him, and whatever were the load of guilt under which you groaned, you should find rest and peace unto your souls: "Where sin had abounded, His grace should much more abound:" and "though your sins were as scarlet, they should be as wool; though they were red like crimson, they should be white as snow."

It may be that some one may have come hither, who, though not particularly bowed down with a sense of guilt, is *oppressed with a weight of personal or domestic troubles.* Who can tell? God may have brought such an one hither this day, in order to fill his soul with heavenly consolations. O that, if such an one be here, God may now appear unto him as a reconciled God, and "say unto him, I am thy salvation!" O that by the word now spoken in God's name, there may this day be "given unto him beauty for ashes, the oil of joy for mourning, and the garment of praise for the spirit of heaviness; that he may become a tree of righteousness, the planting of the Lord, and that God may be glorified!" You have done well that you have come hither; for it is in the house of prayer that God pours out more abundantly upon men the blessings of grace and peace: "He loveth the gates of Zion more than all the dwellings of Jacob." Thousands and millions of afflicted souls have found in God's house such discoveries of his love, and such communications of his grace, as they before had no conception of: and you at this hour, if you will lift up your soul to God in earnest prayer, and cast all your burthens upon him, shall say before you go hence, "This is the house of God: this is the gate of heaven." Know of a truth, that one ray of the Sun of Righteousness is sufficient to dispel all the gloom and darkness of the most afflicted soul: and, if only you will direct your eyes to Him, however your afflictions may have abounded, your consolations shall much more abound.

I trust there are not wanting here some who can bear testimony to the truth of these things by their own experience; and who, from the discoveries which they have received of the Saviour's love, "are *filled with peace and joy in believing.*" To such then will I say, Bless and magnify your God with all the powers of your souls: "let the children of Zion be joyful in their King;" let them "rejoice in the Lord alway;" "let them "rejoice in Him with joy unspeakable and full of glory." At the same time, even whilst they are, as it were, "at the very gate of heaven," let me particularly caution them against that kind of joy which is tumultuous, and that kind of confidence which borders on presumption. There is a holy fear, which is rather increased than dissipated by heavenly joy; and a solemn awe, that always accompanies the manifestations of God to the soul. Observe the state of Jacob's mind on this occasion: "He was afraid; and said, How dreadful is this place! this is none other but the house of God; this is the gate of heaven." Thus blended in its nature, thus tempered in its exercise, thus chastised in all its actings, should our joy be. It is of great importance that we should all remember this: for there is amongst the professors of religion much joy that is spurious, much confidence that is unhallowed. We may have great enlargement of heart; but we must "fear and be enlarged:" we may possess much joy; but we must "rejoice with trembling." Even in heaven itself the glorified saints, yea, and the angels too, though they have never sinned, fall upon their faces before the throne, whilst they sing praises to God and to the Lamb. Let such then be your joy, and such your sacrifices of praise and thanksgiving.

But let not all your gratitude evaporate in unsubstantial, though acceptable, emotions. Think with yourselves what you can do for Him, who has done so much for you. Say with yourselves, "What shall I render unto the Lord for all his benefits?" Think how you may improve your mercies for the good of your fellow-creatures, and the honour of your God. Of Jacob it is said, "*He rose up early in the morning,* and took the stone and raised it for a pillar." Let it be thus with you also : lose no time in honouring your God to the utmost of your power. Account all you have, whether of wealth or influence, as given to you for that end. Determine that those who are around you shall have before them the evidences of true piety, and such memorials as shall, if possible, lead them to the knowledge of the true God. Jacob had it not in his power at that time to do all that his heart desired : but he did what he could; and twenty years afterwards, when his means of honouring God were enlarged, he executed all his projects, and performed the vows which he had made. Thus let your desires be expanded to the uttermost; and then fulfil them according to your ability. So shall you have within yourselves an evidence that God is with you of a truth; and having been faithful in a few things, you shall be rulers over many things in the kingdom of your God.

OUTLINE NO. 46

JACOB'S VOW.

Gen. xxviii. 20—22. *And Jacob vowed a vow, saying, If God will be with me, and will keep me in this way that I go, and will give me bread to eat, and raiment to put on, so that I come again to my father's house in peace; then shall the Lord be my God: and this stone, which I have set for a pillar, shall be God's house: and of all that thou shalt give me, I will surely give the tenth unto thee.*

IT is thought by many, that it is wrong to make any kind of vows. But the propriety of making them depends on the manner in which they are made. If, for instance, we make them in our own strength; or hope that by them we can induce God to do for us what he is otherwise unwilling to perform; or imagine that the services which we stipulate to render unto God will be any compensation to him for the mercies he vouchsafes to us; we are guilty of very great presumption and folly. Vows are not intended to have the force of a bargain or compact, so as to involve the Deity in obligations of any kind; but merely to bind ourselves to the performance of something which was before indifferent, or to impress our minds more strongly with the necessity of executing some acknowledged duty. Of the former kind was Hannah's vow, that if God would graciously give unto her a man-child, she would dedicate him entirely, and for ever, to his immediate service[a]. Independently of her vow, there was no necessity that she should consecrate him to the service of the tabernacle: but she greatly desired to bear a son; and determined, that if God heard her prayer, she would testify her gratitude to him in that way. Of the latter kind was the vow which Israel made to destroy both the Canaanites and their cities, if God would but deliver them into their hands[b]. God had before enjoined them to do this; and therefore it was their bounden duty to do it: and their vow was only a solemn engagement to execute that command; which however they could not execute, unless he should be pleased to prosper their endeavours. That such vows were not displeasing to God, we are sure; because God himself gave special directions relative to the making of them, and the rites to be observed in carrying them into execution[c]. Even under the New-Testament dispensation we find Aquila vowing a vow in Cenchrea[d]; and St. Paul himself uniting with others in the services, which the law prescribed to those who had the vows of Nazariteship upon them[e].

The first vow of which we read, is that contained in our text: and extremely instructive it is. It shews us,

[a] 1 Sam. i. 11.   [b] Numb. xxi. 2.   [c] Numb. vi. 2, 21.
[d] Acts xviii. 18.   [e] Acts xxi. 23, 24.

I. Our legitimate desires—

Man, as compounded of soul and body, has wants and necessities that are proper to both: and whatsoever is necessary for them both, he may reasonably and lawfully desire. We may desire,

1. The presence and protection of God—

[The Israelites in their journeys from Egypt to the promised land passed through a "great and terrible wilderness, wherein were fiery serpents, and scorpions, and drought, where there was no water[f]:" and such is this world wherein we sojourn. Dangers encompass us all around: and, if left to ourselves, we never can reach in safety the land to which we go. Well therefore may we adopt the language of Moses, when Jehovah threatened to withdraw from Israel his own immediate guardianship, and to commit them to the superintendence of an angel; " If thou go not up with us, carry us not up hence[g]." " It is not in man that walketh to direct his own steps[h]:" nor will any created aid suffice for him: " his help is, and must be, in God alone." If God guide us not, we must err; if He uphold us not, we must fall; if He keep us not, we must perish. We may therefore desire God's presence with us, and so desire it, as never to rest satisfied one moment without it. " As the hart panteth after the waterbrooks," says David, " so panteth my soul after Thee, O God. My soul thirsteth for God, for the living God[i]." And, when he had reason to doubt whether God was with him or not, his anguish was extreme: " I will say unto God my rock, Why hast thou forgotten me? As with a sword in my bones, mine enemies reproach me, while they daily say unto me, Where is thy God[k]?" This was the language of the man after God's own heart; and it should be the language also of our souls.]

2. A competent measure of earthly comforts—

[These also are necessary in this vale of tears. Food we must have to nourish our bodies, and raiment to cover us from the inclemencies of the weather: these therefore we may ask of God: beyond these we should have no desire: " Having food and raiment we should be therewith content[l]." To wish for more than these is neither wise[m], nor lawful[n]. Nor even for these should we be over-anxious. We should rather, like the fowls of the air, subsist on the providence of God, and leave it to Him to supply our wants in the way and measure that he

---

[f] Deut. viii. 15.   [g] Exod. xxxiii. 1—3, 12—15.
[h] Jer. x. 23.   [i] Ps. xlii. 1, 2.   [k] Ps. xlii. 9, 10.
[l] 1 Tim. vi. 8.   [m] Prov. xxx. 8, 9.   [n] Jer. xlv. 5.

shall see fit°. Yet it is proper that we make it a part of our daily supplications; " Give us this day our daily bread."]

3. The final possession of the promised land—

[Canaan was desired by Jacob not merely as an earthly inheritance, but chiefly as an earnest of that better land which it shadowed forth. None of the patriarchs regarded it as their *home:* " they dwelt in it as *sojourners,* and looked for a city which hath foundations, whose builder and maker is God [p]." There is for us also " a rest" which that land typified [q], and to which we should look as the end of all our labours [r], and the consummation of all our hopes [s]. It is " the inheritance to which we are begotten [t]," and " the grace which shall surely be brought unto us at the revelation of Jesus Christ [u]." To be waiting for it with an assured confidence, and an eager desire [x], is the attainment to which we should continually aspire; yea, we should be " looking for it and hasting to it" with a kind of holy impatience [y], " groaning within ourselves for it, and travailing as it were in pain," till the period for our complete possession of it shall arrive [z].]

All these things God had previously promised to Jacob [a]: and he could not err, whilst making God's promises the rule and measure of his desires. The engagement which he entered into, and to which he bound himself in this vow, shews us further,

II. Our bounden duties—

Though the particular engagement then made by Jacob is not binding upon us, yet the spirit of it is of universal obligation—

1. We must acknowledge God as our God—

[" Other lords have had dominion over us:" but they are all to be cast down as usurpers; and God alone is to be seated on the throne of our hearts [b]. No rival is to be suffered to remain within us: idols, of whatever kind they be, are to be " cast to the moles and to the bats." We must avouch the Lord to be our only, our rightful, Sovereign, whom we are to love and serve with *all* our heart, and *all* our mind, and *all* our soul, and *all* our strength. Nor is it sufficient to submit to him merely as a Being whom we are unable to oppose: we must claim him with holy triumph as our God and portion,

Matt. vi. 25, 26. [p] Heb. xi. 9, 10, 13—16. [q] Heb. iv. 8, 9.
[r] Heb. xi. 26. [s] 2 Tim. iv. 8. [t] 1 Pet. i. 3, 4.
[u] 1 Pet. i. 13. [x] 1 Cor. i. 8. Phil. i. 23. [y] 2 Pet. iii. 12.
[z] Rom. viii. 22, 23. [a] ver. 15. Isai. xxvi. 13.

saying with David, " O God, thou art my God; early will I seek thee[c]." It is remarkable that this very state of mind, which was yet more conspicuous in Jacob in his dying hour, is represented as characterizing the people of God under the Christian dispensation: " It shall be said in that day, Lo, this is our God; we have waited for him, and he will save us: this is the Lord; we have waited for him; we will rejoice and be glad in his salvation[d]."]

2. To glorify him as God—

[The two particulars which Jacob mentions, namely, the building of an altar to the Lord on that very spot where God had visited him, and the consecrating to his especial service a tenth of all that God in his providence should give unto him, were optional, till he by this vow had made them his bounden duty. With those particulars we have nothing to do: but there are duties of a similar nature incumbent on us all. We must maintain in our families, and promote to the utmost in the world, the worship of God; and must regard our property as his, and, after we have "laboured with all our might" to serve him with it, must say, " All things come of Thee, and of Thine own have we given thee[e]." There must be one question ever uppermost in the mind; What can I do for God; and " what can I render to him for all the benefits that he hath done unto me?" Can I call the attention of others to him, so as to make him better known in the world? If I can, it shall be no obstacle to me that I am surrounded with heathens; nor will I be intimidated because I stand almost alone in the world: I will confess him openly before men: I will " follow my Lord and Saviour without the camp, bearing his reproach:" I will " esteem the reproach of Christ greater riches than all the treasures of Egypt:" whether called to forsake all for him, or to give all to him, I will do it with alacrity, assured, that his presence in time, and his glory in eternity, will be an ample recompence for all that I can ever do or suffer for his sake. He has bought me with the inestimable price of his own blood; and therefore, God helping me, I will henceforth " glorify him with my body and my spirit, which are his[f]."]

ADDRESS—

1. To those who are just entering upon the world—

[Be moderate in your desires after earthly things. You can at present have no conception how little they will contribute to your real happiness. Beyond food and raiment you can have nothing that is worth a thought. Solomon, who

---

[c] Ps. lxiii. 1.   [d] Isai. xxv. 9. with Gen. xlix. 18.
[e] 1 Chron. xxix. 2, 14.   [f] 1 Cor. vi. 19, 20.

possessed more than any other man ever did, has pronounced it all to be vanity; and not vanity only, but vexation of spirit also. And, whilst it is so incapable of adding any thing to your happiness, it subjects you to innumerable temptations[g], impedes in a very great degree your progress heaven-ward[h], and greatly endangers your everlasting welfare[i]. " Love not the world then, nor any thing that is in it[k]:" but " set your affections altogether on things above." In your attachment to them there can be no excess. In your desire after God you cannot be too ardent: for " in his presence is life, and his loving-kindness is better than life itself." Set before you the prize of your high calling, and keep it ever in view: and be assured that, when you have attained it, you will never regret any trials you sustained, or any efforts you put forth, in the pursuit of it. One hour spent in " your Father's house" will richly repay them all.]

2. To those who have been delivered from trouble—

[It is common with persons in the season of deep affliction to make vows unto the Lord, and especially when drawing nigh to the borders of the grave. Now you perhaps in the hour of worldly trouble or of spiritual distress regretted that you had wasted so many precious hours in the pursuit of earthly cares and pleasures, and determined, if God should accomplish for you the wished-for deliverance, you would devote yourselves henceforth entirely to his service. But, when delivered from your sorrows, you have, like metal taken from the furnace, returned to your wonted hardness, and forgotten all the vows which were upon you. Even " Hezekiah rendered not to God according to the benefits conferred upon him," and by his ingratitude brought on his whole kingdom the heaviest judgments, which would have fallen upon himself also, had he not deeply " humbled himself for the pride of his heart[l]." Do ye then, Brethren, beware of trifling with Almighty God in matters of such infinite concern: " it were better never to vow, than to vow and not pay[m]." God forgets not your vows, whether you remember them or not. At the distance of twenty years he reminded Jacob of his vows; and then accepted him in the performance of them[n]. O beg of him to bring yours also to your remembrance! and then " defer not to pay them," in a total surrender of yourselves to him, and a willing consecration of all that you possess to his service[o].]

3. To those whom God has prospered—

[In how many is that saying verified, " Jeshurun waxed

[g] 1 Tim. vi. 9.   [h] Hab. ii. 6.   [i] Matt. xix. 23, 24.
[k] 1 John ii. 15, 16.   [l] 2 Chron. xxxii. 25.   [m] Eccl. v. 4, 5.
[n] Gen. xxxv. 1, 3, 6, 7, 9—12.   [o] Rom. xii. 1. 1 Cor. viii. 3. 5.

fat and kicked." But, Beloved, let it not be so with you. It were better far that you were spoiled of every thing that you possess, and driven an exile into a foreign land, than that you should "forget God who has done so great things for you," and rest in any portion short of that which God has prepared for them that love him. Who can tell? your prosperity may be only fattening you as sheep for the slaughter: and at the very moment you are saying, "Soul, thou hast much goods laid up for many years; eat, drink, and be merry;" God may be saying, "Thou fool, this night shall thy soul be required of thee." Know that every thing which thou hast is a talent to be improved for thy God. Hast thou wealth, or power, or influence of any kind, employ it for the honour of thy God, and for the enlargement and establishment of the Redeemer's kingdom. Then shalt thou be honoured with the approbation of thy God; even with the sweetest manifestations of his love in this world, and the everlasting enjoyment of his glory in the world to come.]

OUTLINE NO. 47

JACOB PLEADING WITH GOD.

Gen. xxxii. 26. *And he said, I will not let thee go, except thou bless me.*

SOME have thought that the circumstances here recorded were a mere vision; and others a reality: but they seem to have been neither the one nor the other; but a real transaction under a figurative representation. The "wrestling" was not a corporeal trial of strength between two men, but a spiritual exercise of Jacob with his God under the form of an angel or a man. That it was not a mere man who withstood Jacob, is clear, from his being expressly called "God," and from his taking upon him offices which none but God could perform[a]. And that it was a spiritual, and not a corporeal, exercise on the part of Jacob, is evident, from what the prophet Hosea says respecting it; "By his strength Jacob had power with God; yea, he had power over the Angel, and prevailed: *he wept, and made supplication unto him*[b]." Such manifestations of God under the

[a] ver. 29, 30. [b] Hos. xii. 3, 4.

angelic or human form were not uncommon in the earlier parts of the Jewish history: and it is generally thought, that the Lord Jesus Christ was the person who assumed these appearances; and that he did so in order to prepare his people for his actual assumption of our nature at the time appointed of the Father. His appearance to Jacob at this time was for the purpose of comforting him under the distressing apprehensions which he felt on account of his brother Esau, who was "coming with four hundred men" to destroy him[c]. Jacob used the best means he could devise to pacify his brother, and to preserve as many as he could of his family, in case a part of them should be slain. But he was not satisfied with any expedients which he could use. He well knew, that none but God could afford him any effectual succour: he therefore "remained alone" all the night, that he might spread his wants and fears before God, and implore help from him. On this occasion God appeared to him in the shape and form of a man, and apparently withstood him till the break of day. Then the person would have departed from him: but Jacob would not suffer him; but held him fast, as it were, saying, " I will not let thee go, except thou bless me."

From these words I shall take occasion to shew,

I. The constituents of acceptable prayer—

These are beautifully displayed in the prayer of Jacob:

1. A renunciation of all dependence on ourselves—

[With this acknowledgment Jacob began his prayer: " O God of my father Abraham, I am not worthy of the least of all the mercies and of all the truth which thou hast shewed unto thy servant[d]." And such is the feeling that must influence our hearts whensoever we attempt to draw nigh to God. If we think ourselves deserving of the divine favour, not one word can we utter with becoming humility; nor have we the smallest prospect of acceptance with God: " The hungry he will fill with good things; but the rich he will send empty away[e]." It is " he who humbleth himself, and he alone, that shall ever be exalted." In this respect the returning prodigal is a pattern

[c] ver. 6, 7.   [d] ver. 10.   [e] Luke i. 50.

for us all. He takes nothing but shame to himself, and casts himself wholly on the mercy of his father. O that there were in us also such a heart! for not the Pharisee who commends himself, but the Publican who smites on his breast and cries for mercy, shall obtain the blessings of grace and glory.]

2. A simple reliance on the promises of God—

[Jacob puts God in remembrance of the promise which had been made to him twenty years before; " Thou saidst, I will surely do thee good[f]." And this is the true ground on which alone we can venture to ask any thing of God. He has " given us exceeding great and precious promises[g]," which he has also " confirmed with an oath, on purpose that we may have consolation" in our souls[h], and be encouraged to spread before him all our wants. Behold how David laid hold of the promises, and pleaded them before God in prayer: " O Lord God, thou hast promised this goodness to thy servant: do as thou hast spoken; do as thou hast said[i]"———— Again, and again, and again does he in this passage remind God of the promises he had made; and declares, that on them all *his prayers*, and all his hopes, were founded. In this manner then are we also to come before him; " Put me in remembrance," says God: " let us plead together: declare thou, that thou mayest be justified[k]." Are we anxious to obtain the forgiveness of our sins? we should take with us such promises as these; " Whosoever cometh unto me I will in no wise cast out:" " Though your sins be as crimson, they shall be as white as snow." Do we want deliverance from some grievous temptation? we should remind the Lord, Hast thou not said, " There shall be no temptation without a way to escape, that thou mayest be able to bear it?" So, whatever our want be, we should take a promise suited to it, (for what trial is there that is not provided for amongst the promises of God?) and plead it, and rest upon it, and expect the accomplishment of it to our souls.]

3. A determination to persevere till we have obtained the desired blessing—

[This is the particular point mentioned in our text. And it is that without which we never can prevail. Jacob, though lamed by his antagonist, still held him fast. And thus must *we* do also: we must " pray, and not faint." A parable was delivered by our blessed Lord for the express purpose of teaching us this invaluable lesson[l]. It should be a settled point in our minds, that " God cannot lie," and " will not

---

[f] ver. 12. [g] 2 Pet. i. 4. [h] Heb. vi. 17, 18.
[i] 2 Sam. vii. 25—29. [k] Isai. xliii. 26. [l] Luke xviii. 1—8.

deny himself." He has said, "Ask, and ye shall have; seek, and ye shall find; knock, and it shall be opened unto you." He has not determined any thing indeed with respect to the time or manner of answering our petitions: but answer them he will, in the best manner and the fittest time. He may not grant the particular thing which we ask for, because he may see that the continuance of the trial will answer a more valuable end than the removal of it: but in that case he will give us, as he did to Paul, what is far better[m]. In the confidence of this we should wait for him. "If the vision tarry, still we must wait for it, assured that it will come at last[n]." And if at any time our soul feel discouraged by the delay, we must chide it, as David did: " Why art thou cast down, O my soul; and why art thou disquieted within me? Hope thou in God; for I shall yet praise him, who is the health of my countenance, and my God[o]." In a word, we must hold fast our blessed Lord, though under the greatest discouragements[p], and must say, " I will never let thee go, except thou bless me."]

Where such prayer is offered up before God, no tongue can tell,

II. The blessings it will bring down into the soul—
It will ensure to us,

1. The effectual care of God's providence—

[The danger to which Jacob was exposed was imminent: but his prayer averted it, so that the brother whom he feared as an enemy, was turned into a friend. And what interpositions will not persevering prayer, when offered with humility and faith, obtain? It matters not what situation we are in, if God be our God. We may have seas of difficulty in our way; but they shall open before us: we may be destitute of food; but the clouds shall send us bread, and the rocks gush out with water for our use. Even though we were at the bottom of the sea, from thence should our prayers ascend, and thither should they bring to us effectual help. We read of such things in the days of old: but we are ready to think that no such things are to be expected now. But has God ceased to govern the earth? or is he changed in any respect, having " his hand shortened, that he cannot save, or his ear heavy, that he cannot hear?" What if God do not repeat his former miracles now, has he no other way of accomplishing his will, and of fulfilling his gracious promises? If our hairs are all numbered, and not so much as a sparrow falls to the ground without him, shall it be in vain for us to call upon him? No: he is still " a God that heareth prayer:" and " whatsoever we

[m] 2 Cor. xii. 8, 9.   [n] Hab. ii. 3.   [o] Ps. xlii. 11.   [p] Cant. iii. 4.

shall ask of him, believing, he will do:" yea, " we may ask what we will, and it shall be done unto us."]

2. The yet richer blessings of his grace—

[The new name which God gave to Jacob was a standing memorial of God's love[q], and a pledge of all that should be necessary for his spiritual welfare. And what will he withhold from us, if we seek him with our whole hearts? Recount all the necessities of your soul: express in words all your wants: and when you have exhausted all the powers of language, stretch out your thoughts to grasp in all the ineffable blessings of his grace; all that the promises of God have engaged; all that the covenant itself contains; and all that an almighty and all-gracious God is able to bestow: and, when you have done this, we will not only assure it all to you, but declare that "he will do for you, not this only, but exceeding abundantly above all that ye can ask or think[r]." However "wide you open your mouth, he will fill it." Make what attainments ye will, ye shall still find, that "he giveth more grace." And, whatever difficulties ye may have to encounter, you shall find "that grace sufficient for you." Only "continue instant in prayer," and God will give you, not a new *name* only (for that also will he give, even a name better than of sons and of daughters[s],) but a new *nature* also, like unto his own[t], that shall progressively transform you into his perfect image "in righteousness and true holiness.[u]"]

3. The full possession of his glory—

[The answer which God gave to Jacob's prayer is more fully recorded in a subsequent chapter. There, after declaring plainly who he was, "I AM GOD ALMIGHTY," he promises, "The land which I gave Abraham and Isaac, to thee will I give it, and to thy seed after thee[x]." This was typical of that better inheritance, to which all the Lord's Israel are begotten, and for which they are reserved[y]. And thither shall the prayer of faith carry us: for "God will never leave us, till he has done all for us that he has spoken to us of[z]," and brought us to "his presence, where there is fulness of joy, and to his right hand, where there are pleasures for evermore[a]." Hear the dying thief preferring his petitions; "Lord, remember me when thou comest into thy kingdom!" And now hear the Saviour's answer; "To-day shalt thou be with me in Paradise[b]." Thus he speaks also to all who seek him in humility

[q] ver. 28. with Hos. xii. 5.
[s] Isai. lxii. 2, 12. and lvi. 5.
[u] Eph. iv. 24. 2 Cor. iii. 18.
[y] Heb. xi. 16. 1 Pet. i. 3—5.
[a] Ps. xvi. 11.
[r] Eph. iii. 20.
[t] 2 Pet. i. 4.
[x] Gen. xxxv. 11, 12.
[z] Gen. xxviii. 15.
[b] Luke xxiii. 42, 43.

and faith. It is curious to observe how often, without any apparent necessity, he repeats this promise to us. After saying, "He that cometh to me shall never hunger, and he that believeth on me shall never thirst," he repeats no less than *four times,* "I will raise him up at the last day;" and repeatedly also adds, "He shall have everlasting life; he shall not die; he shall live for ever[c]." And whence is all this but to assure us, that, "Whatsoever we ask in prayer, believing, we shall receive[d];" yea, that he will "give us, not to the half, but to the whole, of his kingdom[e]?"]

Let me ADD in conclusion,

1. A word of inquiry—

[What resemblance do we bear to Jacob in this particular? I ask not whether we have ever spent a whole night in prayer, but whether we have ever wrestled with God at all; and whether, on the contrary, our prayers have not for the most part been cold, formal, hypocritical; and whether we have not by the very mode of offering our prayers rather mocked and insulted God, than presented to him any acceptable sacrifice? Say whether there be not too much reason for that complaint, "There is none that calleth upon Thy name, that *stirreth up himself to lay hold of Thee*[f]?" Dear Brethren, I know nothing which so strongly marks our departure from God as this. To an earthly friend we can go, and tell our complaints, till we have even wearied him with them; and in the prosecution of earthly things we can put forth all the energy of our minds: but when we go to God in prayer, we are straitened, and have scarcely a word to say; and our thoughts rove to the very ends of the earth. The prophet Hosea well describes this: "They have not cried unto me with their heart. They return, but not to the Most High: they are like a deceitful bow[g]," which, when it promises to send the arrow to the mark, causes it to fall at our very feet. O let us not fancy that we are of the true Israel, whilst we so little resemble Him whose name we bear, and bear as a memorial of importunity in prayer. The character of the true Israel ever has been, and ever will continue to be, that they are "a people near unto their God[h]."]

2. A word of caution—

[On two points we are very liable to err; first, in relation to *the fervour that we exercise* in prayer; and next, in relation to *the confidence that we maintain.* Many, because they are ardent in mind, and fluent in expression, imagine that they are offering to God a spiritual service; when, in fact, their devotion

---

[c] John vi. 35—58. [d] Matt. xxi. 22. [e] Mark vi. 23.
[f] Isai. lxiv. 7. [g] Hos. vii. 14, 16. [h] Ps. cxlviii. 14.

is little else than a bodily exercise. Whoever has made his observations on the way in which both social and public worship is often performed, will have seen abundant cause for this caution. In like manner, the confidence of many savours far more of bold presumption, than of humble affiance. But let it never be forgotten, that tenderness of spirit is absolutely inseparable from a spiritual frame. When our blessed Lord prayed, it was "with strong crying and tears[i]:" and when Jacob wrestled, "he *wept*, and made supplication." This then is the state of mind which we must aspire after. Our fervour must be a humble fervour; and our confidence, a humble confidence. And whilst we look to God to accomplish all things for us, we must at the same time use all proper means for the attainment of them. Jacob, though he relied on God to deliver him from his brother's wrath, did not omit to use all prudent precautions, and the most sagacious efforts for the attainment of that end[k]. So likewise must we "labour for the meat which the Son of man will give us[l]," and "keep ourselves in the love of God[m]," in order to our being "kept by the power of God through faith unto salvation[n]."]

3. A word of encouragement—

[It is said of Jacob, that "God blessed him *there*[o]," even in the very place where he lamed him. Thus shall you also find that your greatest discouragements are only a prelude to your most complete deliverance. To his people of old he said, "Thou shalt go even to Babylon: *there* shalt thou be delivered: *there* shall the Lord redeem thee from the hand of thine enemies[p]." Go on, therefore, fully expecting that God will interpose in due season, and that your darkest hours shall be only a prelude to the brighter day[q].]

[i] Heb. v. 7.   [k] ver. 3—8.   [l] John vi. 27.
[m] Jude, ver. 21.   [n] 1 Pet. i. 5.   [o] ver. 29.
[p] Mic. iv. 10.   Jer. xxx. 7.   [q] Isai. liv. 7, 8. Ps. xxx. 5.

OUTLINE NO. 48

RECONCILIATION OF ESAU AND JACOB.

Gen. xxxiii. 4. *And Esau ran to meet him, and embraced him, and fell on his neck, and kissed him: and they wept.*

SUCH are the dispositions of men in general, that they cannot pass any considerable time without feeling in themselves, and exciting in others, some malignant tempers. The more nearly men come in contact with each other, the more do they disagree. Nations are most inveterate against those who are most in their vicinity. Societies are for the most part distracted by opposing interests. Families are rarely to be found, where the demon of Discord has not raised his throne: yea, even the dearest friends and relatives are too often filled with animosity against each other. Happy would it be, if disagreements were found only among the ungodly: but they not unfrequently enter into the very church of God, and kindle even in good men a most unhallowed fire. Paul and Barnabas were a lamentable instance of human weakness in this respect. But on the present occasion we are called to consider, not a quarrel, but a reconciliation. The quarrel indeed had been rancorous in the extreme; but the reconciliation, as described in the text, was most cordial and most affecting.

We would call your attention to a few observations arising from the circumstances before us—

I. The resentments of brethren are usually exceeding deep—

[If a stranger injure us in any respect, the irritation produced by the offence is, for the most part, of very short duration. But if a brother, or a friend, and more especially a person with whom we have been united in the bonds of the Spirit, provoke us to anger, the wound is more severe, and the impression more lasting. In many cases the difficulty of effecting a reconciliation is so great, as almost to preclude a hope of restoring the former amity. One who was thoroughly conversant with human nature, has told us, that " a brother offended is harder to be won than a strong city." We should be ready to imagine that in proportion as the previous union was close and affectionate, the restoration of that union would be easy; and that the spirits which had suffered a momentary separation, would, like the flesh which has been lacerated, join together again readily, and, as it were, of their own accord. But the reverse of this is true: nor is it difficult to be accounted for. *The disappointment of the two parties is greater.* From strangers we expect nothing: and if we find rudeness or selfishness or any other evil quality, though we may be offended at it, we are not disappointed. But from friends, and especially religious friends, we expect all that is kind and amiable; and therefore we are the more keenly affected when any thing of a contrary aspect occurs. Moreover *the aggravating circumstances are more numerous.* Between friends there are a thousand little circumstances taken into the account, which could find no place among strangers, and which, in fact, often operate more forcibly on the mind than the more immediate subject in dispute. Above all, *the foundations of their regard are overthrown.* Each thinks himself in the right. Each thought highly of the honour, the integrity, the friendship, or perhaps the piety of the other: and behold, each imagines that the other's conduct towards him has violated all these principles, and given him reason to fear, that he was deceived in his judgment of the other; or at least, that he was not deserving of that high opinion which he had entertained of him.

From some such considerations as these, the alienation of the parties from each other, if not more fierce and violent, is usually more fixed and settled, in proportion to their previous intimacy and connexion.]

But,

II. However deep the resentment of any one may be, we may hope by proper means to overcome it—

We cannot have a better pattern in this respect than that which Jacob set before us. The means we should use, are,

1. Prayer to God—

[God has access to the hearts of men, and "can turn them whithersoever he will." The instances wherein he has exerted his influence upon them, to induce them either to relieve his friends, or to punish his enemies, are innumerable. By prayer his aid is obtained. It was by prayer that Jacob prevailed. He had experienced the seasonable and effectual interposition of the Deity when Laban pursued him with such wrath and bitterness: he therefore again applied to the same almighty Friend, and again found him "ready to save." Prayer, if fervent and believing, shall be as effectual as ever: there is nothing for the obtaining of which it shall not prevail. To this then we should have recourse in the first instance. Nothing should be undertaken without this. We should not neglect other means; but our chief dependence should be placed on this; because nothing but the blessing of God can give success to any means we use.]

2. A conciliatory conduct to man—

[Nothing could be more conciliatory, nothing more ingenious, than the device of Jacob, in sending so many presents to his brother, in so many distinct and separate parts, and with the same information so humbly and so continually repeated in his ears. Vehement as Esau's anger was, it could not withstand all this kindness, humility, and gentleness. The submission of his brother perfectly disarmed him: and "the gift in his bosom pacified his strong wrath[a]."

Thus we may hope to "overcome evil with good[b]." As stones are melted by being subjected to the action of intense heat, so are the hardest of men melted by love: it "heaps coals of fire upon their head[c]," and turns their rancorous hostilities into self-condemning accusations[d]. We say not indeed that the victory shall be certain and uniform in all cases; for even the Saviour's meekness did not prevail to assuage the malice of his enemies: but, as a means, we may reasonably expect it to conduce to that end. As a proud, distant, and vindictive carriage serves to confirm the hatred of an adversary, so, on the other hand, a kind, gentle, and submissive deportment has a direct tendency to effect a reconciliation with him.]

Not that a short and transient care will suffice: on the contrary,

III. When once a reconciliation is effected, extreme caution is necessary to preserve and maintain it—

A wound that has been lately closed, may easily be rent open again: and friendship that has been dissolved by any means, does not speedily regain its former stability. To cement affection, much attention is required. We must aim at it,

1. By mutual kindnesses and endearments—

[Exceeding tender was the interview between the brothers, after their long absence, and alienation from each other. Nor should we deem it beneath us to yield thus to the emotions of love, or to express our regards by salutations and tears. These may possibly be counterfeited by a consummate hypocrite: but, in general, they are the involuntary effusions of a loving heart. And as denoting cordiality, they have the strongest tendency to unite discordant minds, and to efface from the memory all painful recollections.]

2. By abstaining from all mention of past grievances—

[The revival of things which have been matters in dispute, generally revive the feelings which the dispute occasioned. And, as few are ever found to acknowledge that the fault or error has been wholly on their own side, recriminations will

[a] Prov. xxi. 14. [b] Rom. xii. 21.
[c] Rom. xii. 20.   [d] 1 Sam. xxiv. 16, 17.

arise from accusations, and the breach perhaps be made wider than ever. To bury matters in oblivion is the readiest way to the maintenance of peace. In this respect the reconciled brothers acted wisely: explanations would only have led to evil consequences; and therefore they avoided them altogether. And we in similar circumstances shall do well to follow their example.]

3. By guarding against that kind or degree of intercourse that may rekindle animosities—

[There are some whose dispositions are so opposite, that they cannot long move in harmony with each other: "not being agreed, they cannot walk comfortably together." It is thus particularly with those whose spiritual views are different: for, "what communion hath light with darkness, or Christ with Belial?" It was prudent in Jacob to decline the proffered civilities of Esau, when he saw the mutual sacrifices that would be necessary in order to carry them into effect: it was prudent that Esau with his four hundred armed men should prosecute their journey without needless incumbrances and delays; and that Jacob should be left at liberty to consult the comfort of his children, and the benefit of his flocks. Had the two endeavoured to make concessions, and to accommodate themselves to each other, neither would have been happy; and their renewed amity would have been endangered. Thus, where the dispositions and habits are so dissimilar as to bid defiance, as it were, to mutual concessions, the best way to preserve peace is to interfere with each other as little as possible.]

APPLICATION—

[Are there any *who are involved in disputes and quarrels?* Follow after peace: and be forbearing and forgiving to others, if ever you would that God should be so to you[e]. Are there any *who desire reconciliation with an offended friend?* Be willing rather to make, than to exact, submission: and let generosity and kindness be exercised to the uttermost, to soften the resentments which have been harboured against you. And lastly, are there any *who have an opportunity of promoting peace?* Embrace it gladly, and exert yourselves with impartiality. And instead of widening a breach, by carrying tales, endeavour to heal it by all possible offices of love. Let the quarrels of brethren be regarded as a fire, which it is every one's duty and desire to extinguish. Thus shall you yourselves have the blessing promised to peace-makers, and be numbered among the children of God[f].]

[e] Matt. xviii. 35   [f] Matt. v. 9.

OUTLINE NO. 49

SLAUGHTER OF THE SHECHEMITES.

Gen. xxxiv. 31. *And they said, Should he deal with our sister as with an harlot?*

THE life of man is continually exposed to trouble; and not unfrequently waves follow waves with little intermission. It was thus in Jacob's case, who, from the time that he fled from the face of Esau, met with a continued series of difficulties and distresses. Having terminated his hard service under Laban, and miraculously escaped the vindictive assaults both of Laban and of Esau, he seemed to have obtained a respite. But his peace was of very short duration; for his own children, to whom he looked for comfort in his declining years, became to him a source of the most poignant sorrows. It appears indeed, from various circumstances in this short history, that he did not maintain sufficient authority over his own house. Had he taken the direction of matters into his own hands, instead of waiting to consult his young, inexperienced, and headstrong sons, he had prevented those horrible crimes which they perpetrated without fear, and vindicated without remorse.

In considering the petulant answer which they made to his reproofs, we shall be led to notice,

I. The provocation they had received—

We apprehend that Leah herself was in part accessary to the evils that befell her daughter—

[Dinah, like other young people, wished to see, and be seen; and on some festive occasion went to visit the daughters of the land of Canaan. She would probably have been displeased, if her mother had imposed restraints upon her. But it was her parent's duty to consult, not so much her inclination, as her safety: and it was highly blameable in Leah to suffer her daughter, scarcely fifteen years of age, to go into scenes of gaiety and dissipation unprotected and unwatched.

Perhaps by this calamity Leah herself was punished for the prostitution of herself (for what else can it be called?) in compliance with her father's wishes. Personating her sister Rachel, she had yielded to what might be justly termed, an incestuous commerce: and now she lives to see the humiliation and defilement of her only daughter.]

But, whatever degree of blame attached either to Dinah or her mother, the provocation given by Shechem was doubtless exceeding great—

[To take advantage of a thoughtless unprotected female was exceedingly base: and the distress brought by it upon her whole family was most deplorable. Ah! little do the gay and dissipated think, what sacrifices they require for the gratification of their lusts. Here was the happiness, not of an individual only, but of a whole family, destroyed. That her seducer endeavoured afterwards to repair the injury, is true: and in this he differed from the generality, who, as soon as they have accomplished their vile purposes, have their love turned into indifference or aversion: but the injury was absolutely irreparable; and therefore we do not wonder that it excited a deep resentment in the breasts of her dishonoured relatives.]

But though her brothers were justly indignant at the treatment she had received, they were by no means justified in,

II. The manner in which they resented it—

Shechem, though a prince among the Hivites, instantly made application to Dinah's father to give her to him in marriage. Though he had humbled her, he did not wish to perpetuate her disgrace, but sought, as much as possible, to obliterate it for ever. The terms he proposed were dictated not only by a sense of honour, but by the most tender affection. Happy would it have been if Jacob's sons had been actuated by principles equally honourable and praiseworthy! But they, alas! intent only on revenge, contrived a plot as wicked and diabolical as ever entered into the heart of man. They formed a design to murder, not only the person who had given them the offence, but all the men of his city together with him. In the execution of their purpose they employed,

1. Hypocrisy—

[They pretended to have scruples of conscience about connecting themselves with persons who were uncircumcised. We may admit for a moment, that this did really operate on their minds as an objection to the projected union; and that this objection was sufficient to weigh down every other consideration: still what regard had *they* for conscience when they could deliberately contrive a plan for murdering the whole city? This was indeed to "strain at a gnat, and to swallow a camel."]

2. Profaneness—

[They knew that both the prince and his people were altogether ignorant of Jehovah, and destitute of the smallest wish to be interested in the Covenant which God had made with Abraham: and yet they proposed that all the males should receive the seal of God's covenant in circumcision; and that too, not in order to obtain any spiritual benefit, but solely with a view to carnal gratification. What a profanation was this of God's holy ordinance! and what impiety was there in recommending to them such a method of attaining their ends!]

3. Cruelty—

[One would scarcely have conceived that such cruelty could have existed in the human heart. That a spirit of revenge should excite in the minds of these men the thought of murdering the person who was more immediately implicated in the offence, was possible enough: but that it should prompt them to involve a multitude of innocent persons in the same ruin; and at a time when those persons were making very great sacrifices in order to conciliate their favour; and that it should induce them to make use of religion as a cloak for the more easy accomplishment of their execrable purpose; this almost exceeds belief: yet such was their inhuman plot, which too successfully they carried into effect. And though their brethren did not join them in destroying the lives of any, yet they so far participated in the crime, as to take captive the defenceless women, and to seize upon all the cattle and property for a prey.]

There is nothing so iniquitous, but the perpetrators of it will justify it. This appears from,

III. Their vindication of their conduct—

In their answer to their father's reproof we behold nothing but,

1. Offended pride—

[They would not have felt any displeasure against Shechem, if he had dealt with any other female, or any number of them, as harlots; but that he should offer such an indignity to "*their sister*," this was the offence, an offence that could not be expiated by any thing less than the blood of all that were even in the most distant way connected with him. We are surprised and shocked at the relation of this event; and yet is it very similar to what occurs continually before our eyes. Is an injury done, or an affront offered to us? we feel ourselves called upon by a regard for our own honour to seek the life of the offender. Is a slight encroachment made on the rights of a nation? it is deemed a just cause of war; and the lives of thousands are sacrificed in order to avenge it. But Jacob formed a just estimate of his children's conduct, when he said, " Cursed be their anger, for it was fierce; and their wrath, for it was cruel."]

2. Invincible obduracy—

[We might well expect that, after a moment's reflection, these bloody murderers should relent, and be filled with remorse. But all sense of guilt, yea, and all regard for their own and their father's safety, seemed to be totally banished from their minds. Instead of regretting that they had acted so treacherous and cruel a part, they vindicate themselves without hesitation, and even tacitly condemn their father, as manifesting less concern for his daughter than they had shewn for their sister. We can scarcely conceive a more awful instance than this of the power of sin to blind the understanding and to harden the heart. But daily experience shews, that, when once the conscience is seared, there is no evil which we will not palliate, no iniquity which we will not justify.]

INFER,

1. How astonishingly may the judgment of men be warped by partiality and self-love!

[These men could see evil in the conduct of Shechem, and yet justify their own; though theirs was beyond all comparison more vile and horrible than his. And is it not thus with us? If the world behold any thing amiss in the conduct of a person professing religion, with what severity will they condemn it, even though they themselves are living in the unrestrained commission of ten thousand sins! And even professors of religion too are apt to be officious in pulling out a mote from their brother's eye, while they are inattentive to the beam that is in their own eye. But let us learn rather to exercise forbearance towards the faults of others, and severity towards our own.]

2. How certainly will there be a day of future retribution!

[Here we behold a whole city of innocent men put to death, and their murderers going away unpunished. But let us not on this account arraign the dispensations of Providence. In the last day all these apparent inequalities will be rectified. It will then infallibly go well with the righteous, and ill with the wicked. The excuses which men now make, will be of no avail: but every transaction shall appear in its proper colours; and every man receive according to what he has done in the body, whether it be good or evil.]

OUTLINE NO. 50

JOSEPH ENVIED BY HIS BRETHREN.

Gen. xxxvii. 4. *When his brethren saw that his father loved him more than all his brethren, they hated him, and could not speak peaceably unto him.*

WE are not expressly told in Scripture that the events of Joseph's life were intended to prefigure those which should afterwards be accomplished in the Messiah: but the humiliation and exaltation of each, together with the means whereby both the one and the other were effected, are so much alike, that we can scarcely view them in any other light than as a typical prophecy fulfilled in the Antitype. It is not however our intention to prosecute the history of Joseph in this view: we shall rather notice some of the most striking particulars as tending to elucidate the passions by which mankind in general are actuated, and the changes to which they are exposed. The words of our text describe the dispositions of his brethren towards him; and will lead us to consider,

I. The occasions of his brethren's hatred—

Joseph was pre-eminently marked as the object of his father's love—

[That his father should love him above all his brethren is not to be wondered at: Joseph was born to him of his beloved Rachel; and in him, Rachel, though dead, might be said to live. He was also imbued with early piety, whilst his brethren were addicted to all manner of evil; insomuch that he himself was forced to report their wickedness to his father, in order that they might be corrected and restrained by his parental authority. It is probable also that he stayed at home to minister to his aged father, whilst they were occupied in their pastoral cares; and that he won the affections of his parent by his dutiful and incessant assiduities.

As a general principle, we highly disapprove of partiality in parents towards their children; though we think it justified, when it is founded on a great and manifest difference in their moral character; inasmuch as it is a parent's duty to mark his approbation of religion and morals. But in no case ought that partiality to be shewn by such vain distinctions as Jacob adopted. Joseph's "coat of many colours" was calculated to generate nothing but vanity in the possessor, and envy in those who thought themselves equally entitled to their parent's favour: and indeed this very distinction proved a source of all the calamities which afterwards befell him.]

God himself also was pleased to point him out as destined to far higher honours—

[God revealed to him in dreams that all his family should one day make obeisance to him. The dreams were doubled, as Pharaoh's afterwards were[a], to shew that his exaltation above all his family, and their humblest submission to him, should surely come to pass. These dreams being divulged by Joseph, he became more than ever an object of most inveterate hatred to his brethren. They could not endure that even God himself should exercise his sovereign will towards him. They considered every favour shewn to him (whether by God or man) as an injury done to themselves; and the more he was honoured, the more were they offended at him. They did not consider, that he was not to be blamed for his father's partiality, nor to be condemned for those destinies which he could neither procure nor prevent. Blinded by envy, they could see nothing in him that was good and commendable, but made every thing which he either said or did, an occasion of blame.]

To set his brethren's conduct in its true light, we will endeavour to shew,

II. The evil of that principle by which they were actuated—

Envy is one of the most hateful passions in the human heart:

1. It is most unreasonable in itself—

[It is called forth by the honour or advantages which another enjoys above ourselves. Now if those advantages be merited, why should we grudge the person the possession of them? If they be not acquired by merit, still they are given to him by the unerring providence of God, who "has a right to do what he will with his own. Is our eye then to be evil because he is good[b]?" Besides, the things which we envy a person the possession of, are often snares, which we should

---

[a] Gen. xli. 32.   [b] Matt. xx. 15.

rather fear than covet: and, at best, they are only talents, of which he must soon give an awful account to God. If therefore we are sensible how little improvement we have made of the talents already committed to us, we shall see at once how little reason we have to envy others their increased responsibility.]

2. It is extremely injurious both to ourselves and others—

[Nothing can be more destructive of a person's own happiness than to yield to this hateful passion. It causes him to derive pain from those things which ought to afford him pleasure; and to have his enmity augmented by those very qualities which ought rather to conciliate his regard. It is justly declared to be "the rottenness of the bones[c]." It corrodes our inmost souls, so that we can enjoy no comfort whatever, while we are under its malignant influence. And there is nothing so spiteful, nothing so murderous, which we shall not both devise and execute, when we are subject to its power[d]. Behold Cain, when envying Abel the testimonies of God's approbation: behold Saul, when he heard David celebrated as a greater warrior than himself: how downcast their looks! what wrathful and vindictive purposes did they form! how were they changed into incarnate fiends! Thus it was also with Joseph's brethren, who could be satisfied with nothing but the utter destruction of the envied object.]

3. It renders us as unlike to God as possible—

[See how our God and Saviour acted towards us in our fallen state: instead of rejoicing in our misery, he sought to redeem us from it, and sacrificed his own happiness and glory to re-establish us in the state from which we had fallen. What a contrast to this does the envious person exhibit! He repines at the happiness of others, whilst God is grieved at their misery: he seeks the destruction of others, whilst God labours for their welfare: he breaks through every restraint to effect their ruin, though with the loss of his own soul; whilst God takes upon him all the pains of hell, in order to exalt as to the blessedness of heaven. He is thus hostile to those who have never injured him, whilst God loads with his benefits those who have lived in a constant scene of rebellion against him. What can set the passion of envy in a more hateful light than this?]

4. It transforms us into the very image of the devil—

[c] Prov. xiv. 30. [d] Jam. iii. 16.

[Satan was once an angel of light, as happy as any that are now before the throne: but he kept not his first estate: he sinned; and thereby brought upon himself the wrath of Almighty God. It pleased God afterwards to form another order of beings, who were designed to fill up, as it were, the seats from which the fallen spirits had been driven. But this envious spirit strove to turn them from their allegiance. He knew well enough that he could not thereby mitigate his own misery: but he could not endure to see others happy, whilst he himself was miserable: yea, he was willing even to augment his own guilt and misery, provided he might destroy the happiness of man. With the same view he afterwards strove to set God against his servant Job, in order that he might deprive that holy man of his integrity and bliss. In this mirror let the envious man behold himself, and he will discern every lineament of his own hateful image. Well did Jesus say of such persons, " Ye are of your father, the devil, and the lusts of your father ye will do[e]."]

By way of IMPROVING the subject, let us INQUIRE,

1. Whence it is that persons are so unconscious of this principle within them?

[It is not surely, because they have not this principle in their hearts; for, " Hath the Scripture said in vain, The spirit that dwelleth in us lusteth to envy[f]?" No: all are more or less actuated by it, till it has been conquered by divine grace. But it is confessedly a *mean* principle, and therefore men are averse to acknowledge its existence in them. It is also a principle easily concealed by specious coverings. Its effects are ascribed to just indignation against sin; and the most eminent virtues of a person are blackened by the most opprobrious names, in order to justify the resentment which it excites in the bosom. Other strong passions, as lust and anger, are more determinate in their actings, and therefore less capable of being hid from our own view; but envy, like avarice, is of so doubtful a character, and admits of so many plausible excuses, that those who are most subject to it are unconscious of its existence and operation within them.]

2. How it may be discerned?

[Envy is not excited, except where the advancement or happiness of another appears within our own reach. To discern its workings therefore, we must watch the actings of our mind towards persons whose situation and circumstances nearly accord with our own. The principle is then most strongly operative, when there is a degree of rivalry or competition

[e] John viii. 44   [f] Jam. iv. 5.

existing. People do not like to be excelled in that line wherein they themselves affect distinction. The female that courts admiration, the tradesman that values himself upon the superiority of his goods, the scholar that is a candidate for fame, the statesman that is ambitious of honour, must consider how he feels, when he sees himself outstripped in his course; whether he would not be glad to hear that his successful competitor had failed in his expectations; whether his ear is not open to any thing that may reduce his rival to a level with himself; whether, in short, the fine coat and promised elevation of Joseph do not grieve him? Let persons be attentive to the motions of their hearts on such occasions as these, and they will find that this accursed principle is exceeding strong within them; and that they need to watch and pray against it continually, if they would gain the mastery over it in any measure.]

3. How it may be subdued?

[Doubtless many things might be prescribed which would conduce to this end. We content ourselves however with specifying only two. *First*, Let us endeavour to get a knowledge of our own vileness. When we have thoroughly learned that we deserve God's wrath and indignation, we shall account it a mercy that we are out of hell. We shall not then be grieved at any preference shewn to others. We shall see that we have already far more than we deserve; and we shall be willing that others should enjoy what God has given them, when we see how mercifully he has dealt with us.

Next, Let us get our hearts filled with love to our fellow-creatures. We do not envy those whom we love: the more we love any person, the more we rejoice in his advancement. The Apostle justly says, "Charity envieth not." Let us beg of God then to implant this better principle in our hearts. Then shall our selfish passions be mortified and subdued; and we shall be made like unto him, whose name is Love[g].]

[g] 1 John iv. 8.

OUTLINE NO. 51

THE NEED OF FLEEING FROM SIN WITH ABHORRENCE.

Gen. xxxix. 9. *How can I do this great wickedness, and sin against God?*

THE grace of God is equally necessary for us in every situation of life; in adversity, to support us; and in prosperity, to keep us—We should have been ready indeed to congratulate Joseph on his advancement in the house of Potiphar, as though his trials had been ended: but we see that, if his former path was strewed with thorns, his present station was slippery, and replete with danger—His history is well known, and need not be insisted on: suffice it to say, that when tempted by his mistress, and importuned from day to day to commit sin with her, he resisted her solicitations with unshaken constancy, and rejected her proposals with indignation and abhorrence—The reply, which through the grace of God he was enabled to make, leads us to observe that,

I. Sin is no light evil—

The world in general imagine sin to be of very little moment—

[Sin universally prevails, and, except where it greatly interferes with the welfare of society, is countenanced and approved—The customs of the world sanction the practice of it to a certain extent in every one, whether male or female; though the greater latitude of indulgence is allowed to men—The very education that is given both to our sons and daughters, tends only to foster in them pride and vanity, wantonness and sensuality, worldliness and profaneness: let but these dispositions assume the names of ease, elegance, and gaiety, and they instantly lose all their malignant qualities; and, instead of exciting our abhorrence, endear to us the persons by whom they are indulged—Too many indeed will not submit to any restraints, but will even justify the grossest immoralities—They impose upon their excesses some specious appellation; they call drunkenness, conviviality; and whoredom, youthful indiscretion—Thus they commit sin without fear, persist in it without remorse, and even glory in their shame, when, through age and infirmity, they can no longer follow their former courses—]

But, if viewed aright, it will appear a dreadful evil—

[Can that be light or venial which cast myriads of angels from their height of glory into the bottomless abyss of hell?—Is that of trifling importance which in one moment ruined the whole race of man, and subjected them to an everlasting curse?—But if these effects be not sufficient to convince us, let us behold the Saviour in the garden of Gethsemane, or on the hill of Calvary: let us behold the Lord of glory bathed in blood, and expiring under the curse which our sins have merited; and we shall instantly confess with Solomon, that they are "fools, who make a mock of sin"—]

Not however to insist on this general view of sin, we observe that,

II. Considered as an offence against God, its enormity is exceeding great—

This is the particular light in which it struck the mind of Joseph—Though the iniquity to which he was tempted, would have been a defiling of his own body, and an irreparable injury to Potiphar his master, yet every other consideration seemed to be swallowed up in that of the offence it would give to God[a]—Sin is levelled more immediately against God himself—It is,

1. A defiance of his authority—

[God commands us to keep his law; and enforces his commands with the most awful and encouraging sanctions—But sin says, like Pharaoh, "Who is the Lord, that I should regard him? I know not the Lord, neither will I obey his voice[b]"—And is it a light matter for a servant thus to insult his master, a child his parent, a creature his Creator?—]

2. A denial of his justice—

[God threatens that "the wicked shall not be unpunished"—But what does sin reply? It says like them of old, "God will not do good, neither will he do evil[c]"—And shall it be thought a trifling matter to rob the Deity thus of his most essential perfections?—]

3. An abuse of his goodness—

[It is altogether owing to the goodness of God that we are even capable of sinning against him—It is from him that we receive the bounties which administer to our excess, and the strength whereby we provoke the eyes of his glory—And can any thing be conceived more vile than to make his goodness to us the very means and occasion of insulting him to his face?—]

4. A rejection of his mercy—

[God is continually calling us to accept of mercy through the Son of his love—But sin "tramples under foot the Son of God;" it even "crucifies him afresh, and puts him to an

---

[a] David viewed his sin in this light, Ps. li. 4.
[b] Exod. v. 2. See also Ps. xii. 4. and Jer. xliv. 16.
[c] Zeph. i. 12.

open shame"—It proclaims aloud, that the glory of heaven is not to be compared with the gratification of our lusts; and that it is better to perish by self-indulgence, than to obtain salvation in the exercise of self-denial—What terms then can sufficiently express the enormity of that, which so blinds and infatuates its wretched votaries?—]

It is not possible to behold sin in this light, without acknowledging that,

III. We ought to flee from it with indignation and abhorrence—

Instead of tampering with it we should flee from it—

[Sin is of so fascinating a nature that it soon bewitches us, and leads us astray—As "a man cannot take fire into his bosom without being burnt," so neither can he harbour sin in his heart without being vitiated and corrupted by it—Had Achan fled from the wedge of gold as soon as ever he found a desire after it springing up in his heart; and David turned away his eyes the very instant he saw Bathsheba, how much shame and misery would they have escaped! But the breach, which might easily have been stopped at the first, presently defied the efforts of an accusing conscience; and a flood of iniquity soon carried them away with irresistible impetuosity—Thus also it will be with us; if we parley with the tempter, he will surely overcome us: we must resist sin at the first, if we would oppose it with success—]

Instead of loving it, we should utterly abhor it—

[The grace of God enabled Joseph to reject with abhorrence the offers proposed to him; and to prefer a dungeon with a good conscience before the indulgence of a criminal passion, or the favour of a seducing mistress—Thus should we turn with indignation from the allurements of sin—We should "make a covenant with our eyes," yea, with our very hearts, that we may close, as much as possible, every avenue of ill—Instead of palliating sin, we should view it in all its aggravations; and especially as an offence against a just and holy, a merciful and gracious, God—Nor should we ever forget, that, though it be "rolled as a sweet morsel under the tongue, it will prove gall in the stomach;" and though it flatter us with its innocence, "it will bite as a serpent, and sting like an adder"—]

ADDRESS,

1. Those who think lightly of sin—

[We well know that the generality of men have much to say in extenuation of their guilt; and, if they had been in the situation of Joseph, would have accounted the greatness of the temptation a sufficient excuse for their compliance with it—But to what purpose shall we palliate our guilt, unless we can prevail on the Judge of quick and dead to view it with our eyes? We may indeed weaken our present convictions, but we shall only secure thereby, and enhance, our eternal condemnation—Let us remember that "fleshly lusts war against the soul[d];" and that either we must mortify and subdue them, or they will enslave and destroy us[e]: for, even though the whole universe should combine to justify the commission of sin, not one who yields to its solicitations, shall ever pass unpunished—]

2. Those who begin to see the evil of it—

[It is an unspeakable mercy to have any view of the malignity of sin—To see how much we have deserved the wrath and indignation of God, is the very first step towards repentance and salvation—Let not any then turn away from this sight too hastily, or think they have discovered the evil of sin in its full extent—This is a lesson we are to be learning all our days; and it is only in proportion as we advance in this humiliating knowledge, that we shall be qualified to receive and enjoy the Saviour—It is necessary indeed that, while we look at sin, we look also at Him who made atonement for it; for otherwise, we shall be led to despair of mercy; but, if we keep our eyes fixed upon the Lord Jesus Christ, and see the infinite extent of his merits, we need never be afraid of entertaining too bitter a remembrance of sin—The more we lothe ourselves for past iniquities, the more shall we be fortified against temptations to commit them in future, and the more will God himself be ready to preserve and bless us—]

3. Those who, like Joseph, are enabled to withstand it—

[Blessed be God, there are many living witnesses to prove, that the grace of God is as sufficient at this day, as ever it was, to purify the heart, and to "keep the feet of his saints"—Let those then who are enabled to hold fast their integrity, give glory to him, by whom they are strengthened and upheld—But let them remember, that they are never beyond the reach of temptation, nor ever so likely to fall, as when they are saying, "My mountain stands strong; I shall not be moved"—Let us then continue to watch against the renewed assaults of our great adversary—Never let him find us off our guard, or draw us to a parley with him—Let us suspect him, and he shall not deceive us; let us resist him, and he shall flee from us: and the very assaults that he shall make upon us, shall terminate in our honour and his own confusion—]

[d] 1 Pet. ii. 11. [e] Rom. viii. 13.

OUTLINE NO. 52

INGRATITUDE OF PHARAOH'S BUTLER.

Gen. xl. 23. *Yet did not the chief butler remember Joseph, but forgat him.*

IT was a wise and prudent choice which David made, "Let me fall into the hands of God, and not into the hands of man." Man, when intent on evil, knows no bounds, except those which are prescribed by his ability to execute his wishes. He is easily incensed, but with difficulty appeased. The ties of blood and relationship are not sufficient to bind persons in amity with each other, when once any ground of discord arises between them. It might have been hoped that in such a family as Jacob's, love and harmony would prevail: but to such a degree had envy inflamed his whole family against their younger brother, that they conspired against his life, and only adopted the milder alternative of selling him for a slave, through a horror which they felt at the thought of shedding his blood. Nor will the most amiable conduct always ensure regard, or protect a person from the most cruel injuries. The holy, chaste, and conscientious deportment of Joseph should have exalted his character in the eyes of his mistress: but when she failed in her attempts to ensnare his virtue, her passionate desire after him was converted into rage; and she procured the imprisonment of him whom she had just before solicited to be her paramour. During his confinement, he had opportunities of shewing kindness to his fellow-prisoners. To two of them he interpreted their dreams, which proved to be prophetic intimations of their respective fates. Of Pharaoh's chief butler, whose speedy restoration he foretold, he made a most reasonable request: he told him, that he had been stolen out of the land of the Hebrews; and that there existed no just cause for his imprisonment: and he entreated, that he would make known his case to Pharaoh, and intercede for his deliverance. In making this request, he never once criminated either his brethren who had sold him, or his mistress who had falsely accused him: he cast a veil of love over their faults, and sought for nothing but the liberty of which he had been unjustly deprived. Who would conceive that so reasonable a request, presented to one who had such opportunities of knowing his excellent character, to one too on whom he had conferred such great obligations, should fail? Lord, what is man? how base, how selfish, how ungrateful! Let us fix our attention upon this incident in the history of Joseph, and make some suitable reflections upon it—

We observe then,

I. That gratitude is but a feeble principle in the human mind—

[Corrupt and sinful principles are, alas! too strong in the heart of man; but those which are more worthy of cultivation, are weak indeed. To what a degree are men actuated by *pride — ambition — covetousness — envy — wrath — revenge!* — To what exertions will they not be stimulated by *hope* or *fear!* — — — But the motions of *gratitude* are exceeding faint: in the general, they are scarcely perceptible: and though on some extraordinary occasions, like that of Israel's deliverance at the Red Sea, the heart may glow with a sense of the mercies vouchsafed unto us, we soon forget them, even as the Israelites did, and return to our former coldness and indifference.]

II. That its operations are rather weakened than promoted by prosperity—

[Pharaoh's butler, when restored to his master's service, thought no more of the friend whom he had left in prison. This is the general effect of prosperity, which steels the heart against the wants and miseries of others, and indisposes it for the exercise of sympathy and compassion. It is usually found too that the more we abound in temporal blessings, the more unmindful we are of Him who gave them. That is a true description of us all; "Jeshurun waxed fat, and kicked." On the other hand, adversity tends to bring us to consideration: when we have suffered bereavements of any kind, we begin to feel the value of the things we have lost; and to regret, that we were not more thankful for them while they were continued to us. The loss of a part of our blessings often renders us more thankful for those that remain: and it is no uncommon sight to behold a sick person more thankful for an hour's sleep, or a small intermission of pain, or the services of his attendants, than he ever was for all the ease and sleep that he enjoyed, or the services that were rendered him, in the days of his health. We have a very striking instance of the different effects of prosperity and adversity in the history of Hezekiah. In his sickness he exclaimed, "The living, the living, he shall praise thee, as I do this day:" but when restored to health, he forgat his Benefactor, and "rendered not again according to the benefits that had been done unto him." In this, I say, he is an example of the ingratitude which obtains in the world at large; for we are told, that "God left him to try him, and that he might know all that was in his heart."]

III. That the want of it is hateful in proportion to the obligations conferred upon us—

[We suppose that no man ever read attentively the words of our text without exclaiming (in thought at least, if not in words), What base ingratitude was this! Whether we consider his obligations to Joseph, who had been to him a messenger of such glad tidings, or his obligations to God, who had overruled the heart of Pharaoh to restore him to his place, he surely was bound to render that small service to his fellow-prisoner, and to interpose in behalf of oppressed innocence. And we cannot but feel a detestation of his character on account of his unfeeling and ungrateful conduct. Indeed it is thus that we are invariably affected towards all persons; and more especially those who have received favours at our hands. If we receive an injury or an insult, or are treated with neglect by persons whom we have greatly benefited, we fix immediately on their ingratitude, as the most aggravating circumstance of their guilt: it is that which pains us, and which makes them appear most odious in our eyes. And though this sentiment may be easily carried to excess, yet, if kept within due bounds, it forms a just criterion of the enormity of any offence that is committed against us. It was this which in God's estimation so greatly aggravated the guilt of the Jewish nation; "They forgat God who had done so great things for them[a]." And we shall do well to bear it in mind, as the means of awakening in our own minds a just sense of our condition before God: for ingratitude, above all things, subjects us to his displeasure[b].]

This subject may be fitly IMPROVED—

1. To fill us with shame and confusion before God—

[If we think of our temporal mercies only, they call for incessant songs of praise and thanksgiving: but what do we

[a] Ps. cvi. 7, 13, 21.
[b] Rom. i. 21.   2 Tim. iii. 2.   Isai. i. 3.   Deut. xxviii. 45, 47.

owe to God for the gift of his dear Son—and of his Holy Spirit—and of a preached Gospel?—What do we owe to God if he has rendered his word in any measure effectual for the enlightening of our minds, and the quickening of our souls? "What manner of persons then ought we to be?" How should our hearts glow with love, and our mouths be filled with his praise! Let us prosecute these thoughts, and we shall soon blush and be confounded before God, and lie low before him in dust and ashes.]

2. To keep us from putting our trust in man—

[Many years had Joseph been confined in prison, and now he thought he should have an advocate at court, who would speedily liberate him from his confinement. But God would not let him owe his deliverance to an arm of flesh: yea, he left him two years longer in prison, that he might learn to put his trust in God only: and then he wrought his deliverance by his own arm. "Till his time was come, the word of the Lord tried him." At last, God suggested to Pharaoh dreams, which no magicians could expound; and thus brought to the butler's recollection the oppressed youth who had interpreted his dreams, and who was the only person that could render similar service to the affrighted monarch. Now we also, like Joseph, are but too apt to lean on an arm of flesh, instead of looking simply to the Lord our God: but we shall always find in the issue, that the creature is only a broken reed, which will pierce the hand that leans upon it; and that none but God can render us any effectual assistance. Let us then trust in him only, and with all our heart, and then we shall never be confounded.]

3. To make us admire and adore the Lord Jesus—

[That blessed Saviour is not less mindful of us in his exalted state, than he was in the days of his flesh. Yea, though not at all indebted to us, though, on the contrary, he has all possible reason to abandon us for ever, yet is he mindful of us day and night; he makes intercession for us continually at the right hand of God; he considers this as the very end of his exaltation; and he improves every moment in protecting, comforting, and strengthening those who depend upon him. We challenge any one to say, When did the blessed Saviour forget him? We may have been ready to say indeed, "He hath forsaken and forgotten us;" but "He can no more forget us than a woman can forget her sucking child." Let us then bless his name, and magnify it with thanksgiving. And let us from time to time offer to Him the petition of the dying thief, "Lord, remember me now thou art in thy kingdom:" and not all the glory and felicity of heaven shall divert his attention from us for a single moment.]

OUTLINE NO. 53

JOSEPH'S ADVANCEMENT.

Gen. xli. 41. *And Pharaoh said unto Joseph, See, I have set thee over all the land of Egypt.*

IN the eventful life of Joseph we are particularly struck with the suddenness and greatness of the changes he experienced. One day he was his father's favourite; the next he was menaced with death and sold as a slave: one day at the head of Potiphar's household; the next immured in a prison and laden with fetters of iron. From that state also he was called in a moment by the singular providence of God, and exalted to the government of the first nation upon earth. Of this we are informed in the text; from whence we take occasion to observe,

I. That we can be in no state, however desperate, from whence God cannot speedily deliver us—

[The state of Joseph, though considerably ameliorated by the indulgence of the keeper of his prison, was very hopeless. He had been many years in prison; and had no means of redress afforded him. His cause being never fairly tried, his innocence could not be cleared: and there was every reason to apprehend that his confinement would terminate only with his life. The hopes he had entertained from the kind offices of Pharaoh's butler had completely failed: and God had suffered him to be thus disappointed, in order that, "having the sentence of death in himself, he might not trust in himself, but in God that raiseth the dead." But when God's time was come, every difficulty vanished, and his elevation was as great as it was sudden and unexpected.

It would be well if we bore in mind the ability of God to help us. People when brought into great trials by loss of dear friends, by embarrassed circumstances, or by some other calamitous event, are apt to think, that, because they see no way for their escape, their state is hopeless; and, from indulging despair, they are ready to say with Job, "I am weary of life," and "my soul chooseth strangling, and death rather than my life[a]." But we should remember that there is "a God with whom nothing is impossible:" though human help may fail us, "his arm is not shortened, that it cannot save, nor is his ear heavy,

[a] Job vii. 15.

that it cannot hear:" yea rather he would glorify himself, as he did in rescuing Israel at the Red Sea, if we would call upon him; and our extremity should be the opportunity he would seize for his effectual interpositions: "In the mount, the Lord would be seen."

We may apply the same observations to those who seem to have cast off all fear of God, and to have sinned beyond a hope of recovery. But while the conversion of Saul, and the deliverance of Peter from prison, stand on record, we shall see that there is nothing too great for God to effect, and nothing too good for him to give, in answer to the prayer of faith.]

II. That God is never at a loss for means whereby to effect his gracious purposes—

[He had decreed the elevation of Joseph to the highest dignity in the land of Egypt. To accomplish this, he causes Pharaoh to be disturbed by two significant dreams, which none of his magicians could interpret. The solicitude of Pharaoh to understand the purport of his dreams leads his butler to "confess his fault" in having so long neglected the youth who had, two years before, interpreted *his* dreams; and to recommend him as the only person capable of satisfying the mind of Pharaoh. Instantly Joseph is sent for (not from a sense of justice to an injured person, but from a desire for the information which he alone could give); and, upon his interpreting the dreams of Pharaoh, and giving suitable advice respecting the steps that should be taken to meet the future distress, he is invested with supreme authority, that he may carry his own plans into execution. Thus God, by suggesting dreams to Pharaoh, and to Joseph the interpretation of them, effects in an hour what, humanly speaking, all the power of Pharaoh could not otherwise have accomplished.

If we were duly observant of the works of Providence, we should see, in many instances relating to ourselves, how wonderfully God has brought to pass the most unlooked-for events. Things the most strange have been made to subserve his gracious purposes, and to accomplish what no human foresight could have effected for us. In relation to the concerns of our souls this may perhaps be more visible than in any temporal matters. The history of God's people, if it were fully known, would furnish thousands of instances, not less wonderful than that before us, of persons "raised" by the most unexpected and apparently trivial means "from the dust or a dunghill, to be set among princes, and to inherit a throne of glory." We are far from recommending any one to trust in dreams, or to pay any attention to them whatever: for "in the multitude of dreams are divers vanities." But we dare not say that God never makes use of dreams to forward his own inscrutable designs: on the contrary, we believe that he has often made a dream about death or judgment the occasion of stirring up a person to seek after salvation; and that he has afterwards answered the prayers, which originated in that apparently trifling and accidental occurrence. At all events, there are a multitude of little circumstances which tend to fix the bounds of our habitation, or to bring us into conversation with this or that person, by whom we are ultimately led to the knowledge of the truth. So that we should commit our every way to God, and look to him to order every thing for us according to the counsel of his own gracious will.]

III. We are never in a fairer way for exaltation to happiness than when we are waiting God's time, and suffering his will—

[We hear nothing respecting Joseph but what strongly impresses us with a belief that he was perfectly resigned to the will of God. It is most probable indeed that he had formed some expectation from an arm of flesh: but two years' experience of human ingratitude had taught him that his help must be in God alone. At last, his recompence is bestowed, and ample compensation is given him for all that he endured. With his prison garments, he puts off his sorrows; and, from a state of oppression and ignominy, he is made the Benefactor and the Saviour of a whole nation.

Happy would it be for us if we could leave ourselves in God's hands, and submit ourselves in all things to his wise disposal! We are persuaded, that our want of submission to Divine Providence is that which so often necessitates God to afflict us; and that if we could more cordially say, " Thy will be done," we should much sooner and much oftener be favoured with the desire of our own hearts. Have we an husband, a wife, a child in sick and dying circumstances? our rebellious murmurings may provoke God to inflict the threatened stroke, and to take away the idol which we are so averse to part with: whereas, if we were once brought to make a cordial surrender of our will to His, he would in many instances arrest the uplifted arm, and restore our Isaac to our bosom. At all events, he would compensate by spiritual communications whatever we might lose or suffer by a temporal bereavement.]

We may yet further LEARN from this subject,

1. To submit with cheerfulness to all the dispensations of Providence—

[We may, like Joseph, have accumulated and long-continued trials; the end of which we may not be able to foresee. But, as in his instance, and in that of Job, " we have seen the end of the Lord, that the Lord is very pitiful and of tender mercy," so we may be sure that our trials shall terminate well; and that however great or long-continued they may be, our future recompence, either in this world or the next, will leave us no reason to complain.]

2. To be thankful to God for the Governors whom he has been pleased to set over us—

[It is "by God that kings reign, and princes decree justice." Sometimes, "for the punishment of a land, children (that is, persons weak and incompetent) are placed over it," that their infatuated counsels or projects may bring upon it his heavy judgments. We, blessed be God! have been highly favoured in this respect. By his gracious providence, we have for a long series of years had persons exalted to posts of honour, who, like Joseph, have sought the welfare of the nation, and have promoted it by their wise counsels and indefatigable exertions. Let us thankfully acknowledge God in them, and endeavour to shew ourselves worthy of this mercy, by the peaceableness of our demeanour, and the cheerfulness of our submission to them.]

3. To be thankful, above all, for our adorable Emmanuel—

[" Him hath God exalted with his right hand to be a Prince and a Saviour." " To Him hath he given a name that is above every name; that at the name of Jesus *every knee should bow*[b]." To Him doth our almighty King direct us, saying to every famished soul, " Go to Jesus[c]." In Him there is all fulness treasured up: to Him all the nations of the earth may go for the bread of life: nor shall any of them be sent empty away. They shall receive it too "without money and without price." O what do we owe to God for raising us up such a Saviour! and what do we owe to Jesus, who has voluntarily undertaken this office, and who submitted to imprisonment in the grave as the appointed step to this glorious elevation! Let us thankfully bow the knee to him; and go to him continually for our daily supplies of grace and peace.]

[b] Compare ver. 43. with Phil. ii. 9—11.   [c] ver. 55.

OUTLINE NO. 54

THE POWER OF CONSCIENCE.

Gen. xlii. 21. *And they said one to another, We are verily guilty concerning our brother, in that we saw the anguish of his soul, when he besought us, and we would not hear: therefore is this distress come upon us.*

THE history of Joseph appears rather like a well-concerted fiction than a reality. In it is found all that gives beauty to the finest drama; a perfect unity of design; a richness and variety of incident, involving the plot in obscurity, yet gradually drawing it to its destined end; and the whole issuing happily, to the rewarding of virtue and discouraging of vice. The point to which all tends, is, the fulfilment of Joseph's dreams in the submission of his whole family to him. And here we find his dreams realized through the very means which were used to counteract their accomplishment. Already had his brethren bowed themselves down with their faces to the earth: but this was only the commencement of their subjection to him: they must be brought far lower yet, and be made to feel the guilt they had contracted by their cruelty towards him. With this view Joseph forbears to reveal himself to them, but deals roughly with them, imprisoning them as spies, and menacing them with death if they do not clear themselves from that charge. They had formerly cast him into a pit, and sold him as a slave; and now they are cast into prison and bound: they once were deaf to his cries and entreaties; and now the governor of Egypt is deaf to theirs. This brings to their remembrance their former conduct; and they trace the hand of an avenging God in their sufferings. Their conscience, which had been so long dormant, now wakes, and performs its office.

This is the incident mentioned in our text: and, confining our attention to it, we shall shew,

I. The general office of conscience—

To enter into any philosophical discussion respecting that faculty which we call conscience, would be altogether beside our purpose, and unsuited to the present occasion. It will be sufficient to take the word in its popular sense, as importing that natural faculty whereby we judge both of our actions and the consequences of them. It is given to us by God, to operate as,

1. A guide—

[Of itself indeed it cannot guide, but only according to rules which before exist in the mind. It does not so much tell us what is right or wrong, as whether our actions correspond with our apprehensions of right and wrong. But as we are apt to be biassed by interest or passion to violate our acknowledged obligations, conscience is intended to act as a guide or monitor, warning us against the commission of evil, and inciting us to the performance of what is good. True it is indeed that it often stimulates to evil under the notion of good: for St. Paul followed its dictates in persecuting the Christians, when "he thought he *ought* to do many things contrary to the name of Jesus[a]:" and our blessed Lord informs us, that many who would kill his disciples would do it under an idea that they were rendering unto God an acceptable service[b]. The fault of these persons consists not in following the dictates of their conscience, but in not taking care to have their conscience better informed. A thing which is evil in itself cannot be made good by any erroneous conceptions of ours respecting it: but things which are of themselves innocent, become evil, if they be done contrary to the convictions of our own minds[c]: for we ought to be fully persuaded of the propriety of a thing before we do it[d]; and "whatsoever is not of faith is sin[e]."]

2. A judge—

[Conscience is God's vicegerent in the soul, and authoritatively pronounces in the soul the judgment which God himself will pass on our actions[f]. It takes cognizance not of our actions only, but of our principles and motives, and brings into its estimate every thing that will form the basis of God's judgment. Of course, in this, as well as in its suggestions, it may err: for, if it form a wrong judgment of *the qualities* of our actions, its judgment must be wrong also as to *the consequences* of them. It may promise us God's approbation upon grounds that are very erroneous: but when its apprehensions of our duty are themselves just, its award respecting our performance of it is a prelude of God's final judgment: for St. John says, "If our heart condemn us, God is greater than our heart, and knoweth all things:" but "if our heart condemn us not, then have we confidence toward God[g]."]

But, as its operations are by no means uniform, we proceed to mark,

II. Its insensibility, when dormant—

[a] Acts xxvi. 9. [b] John xvi. 2. [c] Rom. xiv. 14.
[d] Rom. xiv. 5. [e] Rom. xiv. 23. [f] Rom. ii. 15
[g] 1 John iii. 20, 21.

Wonderful was its insensibility in the sons of Jacob—

[When they conspired against their brother Joseph, and cast him into the pit, that he might perish with hunger, they regarded not the cries and entreaties of the youth, but proceeded in their murderous career without remorse. But the seasonable appearance of a company of Ishmaelites suggested to them somewhat of an easier method of ridding themselves of him. At the suggestion of Judah, "What profit is it if we slay our brother, and conceal his blood? Come, and let us sell him to the Ishmaelites, and let not our hand be upon him; for he is our brother, and our flesh;" they acceded to it, and "*were content.*" In the first instance, after putting him into the pit, "they sat down to eat bread," evidently without any compunction: but *now* they were quite "*content*," applauding themselves for their humanity, instead of condemning themselves for their injustice and cruelty[h].

View next their mode of deceiving their aged father. They took Joseph's coat, and dipped it in the blood of a kid which they killed for the purpose; and brought it to their father, in order that he might conclude, that an evil beast had devoured his son. (How far God might design this as a just retribution for the deceit which Jacob himself had practised towards his aged father, when he, by assuming Esau's coat, stole away the blessing that belonged to Esau, we stay not to notice: with this the sons of Jacob had nothing to do.) They behold their aged parent overwhelmed with grief, and absolutely inconsolable for the loss of his son: and these detestable hypocrites "rise up to comfort him[i]." Where is conscience all this time? Has it no voice? Is there not one amongst them all that has any compunctious visitings? not one amongst all the ten? Does no heart relent at the sight of the anguish of an aged and pious parent, sitting from day to day and from month to month "with sackcloth on his loins," and "going down mourning to the grave?" No; not one of them all, as far as we know, ever "repented, saying, What have I done?" *For the space of two and twenty years* they *all* continued in impenitent obduracy; and were not made even at last to feel the guilt they had contracted in selling their brother, till they themselves were brought into somewhat similar circumstances with him, and constrained to read their own crime in their punishment. Such was conscience in *them!*]

Yet this is in reality what we may see in ourselves and in all around us—

[Behold *the profane,* who have not God in all their thoughts, and who never utter the name of God but to blas-

---

[h] Gen. xxxvii. 23—28. [i] Gen. xxxvii. 31—35.

pheme it: they can go on for years and years, and yet never imagine that they have once offended God. Behold *the sensual,* who revel in all manner of uncleanness: they " wipe their mouth, like the adulteress, and say, I have done no wickedness k." Behold *the worldly,* who have no cares whatever beyond the things of time and sense: their idolatrous love to the creature raises no doubts or fears in their minds: yea, rather, they bless themselves as wise, prudent, diligent, and think that they have done all that is required of them. Behold *the self-righteous,* who, from an overweening conceit of their own goodness, will not submit to the righteousness of God: they can make light of all the invitations of the Gospel, and pour contempt upon its gracious overtures, and yet never once suspect themselves to be enemies of Christ. Behold *the professors of religion* who " confess Christ with their lips but in their works deny him:" they will spend a whole life in such self-deceit, and never entertain a doubt but that he will acknowledge them as his in the day of judgment. And whence is this? Is it not that conscience is asleep? If it performed in any measure its office, could it be thus? Yet thus it is sometimes even with those who are well instructed in religion. The sins of David are well known: yet even he, who at one time was smitten with grief and shame at having cut off the skirt of a man who sought his life, now kills the very man who was daily hazarding his life for him, and feels no remorse: yea, after having seduced the wife of his friend, and then murdered him, he continues at least nine months as obdurate as the most profligate of the human race: to such a degree was his " conscience seared as with a hot iron[1]," and to such a degree may our " hearts also be hardened through the deceitfulness of sin [m]."]

But the text leads us to contemplate more particularly,

III. Its power when awake—

God has various ways of awakening a drowsy conscience. Sometimes he does it through some afflictive dispensation, as in the case before us: sometimes through the conversation of a friend[n]: sometimes by the public ministry of the word[o]: sometimes by an occurrence arising out of men's wickedness[p], or in some way connected with it[q]. But by whatever means it is called into activity, it will make us hear when it speaks to us.

[k] Prov. xxx. 20.   [1] 1 Tim. iv. 2.   [m] Heb. iii. 13.
[n] 2 Sam. xii. 7.   [o] Acts xxiv. 25.   [p] 2 Sam. xxiv. 10.
[q] Dan. v. 5, 6. Matt. xiv. 1, 2.

54.] THE POWER OF CONSCIENCE. 281

Some it inspires only with terror—

[Thus it wrought on these: they saw their guilt, and the wrath of God upon them on account of it: "We are verily guilty concerning our brother," said they, "and behold his blood is required of us[r]." Thus it wrought also on the unhappy Judas, who, when he saw what he had done, could no longer endure his very existence[s]. And on how many does it produce no other effect than this! They see how grievously they have offended God: and, not having the grace of repentance given to them, they sink into despondency. Life now becomes a burthen to them: and they choose rather to rush into an unknown state than to endure the stings of an accusing conscience. Hence the suicides that are so frequent in the world. Men live in sin, imagining that no painful consequences shall ever ensue: but at last "their sin finds them out;" and they seek in suicide a refuge from the torments of a guilty mind. But where a sense of guilt does not drive men to this extremity, it makes them tremble, as Felix did; and imbitters to them their whole existence, so that they are utter strangers to peace, according as it is written, "There is no peace, saith my God, to the wicked."]

On others it operates with a more genial influence—

[Thus it wrought on Manasseh, when he was taken among the thorns[t]. And thus on Peter also, when he "went out, and wept bitterly[u]." Happy, happy they, on whom it produces such effects as these! They will have no reason to repine at any afflictions that are productive of such a blessing[x]. What if the intermediate trials be severe? we shall have reason to bless God for them to all eternity, if they lead to this end[y]; and shall have cause to say with David, "It is good for me that I have been afflicted."]

On all, its testimony is as the voice of God himself—

[It speaks with authority. The stoutest man in the universe cannot endure its reproaches: and the most afflicted man in the universe is made happy by its testimony in his behalf[z]. We should therefore keep it tender, and be ever attentive to its voice. On no occasion should we violate its dictates: for though we may silence its voice for a time, or drown it in vanity and dissipation, it will speak at last, and constrain us to hear all that it has recorded concerning us. And when once it does speak, then we may say concerning it, that "he whom it blesses, is blessed; and he whom it curses, is cursed."]

ADVICE—

[r] ver. 22.   [s] Matt. xxvii. 3—5.   [t] 2 Chron. xxxiii. 11—13.
[u] Luke xxii. 61, 62.   [x] Job xxxvi. 8, 9.   [y] Ps. xxxii. 3—6.
[z] 2 Cor. i. 12.

1. Seek to maintain a good conscience before God—

[Let your minds be well instructed in the written word, and your lives be regulated by its dictates. To have always a conscience void of offence towards both God and man is no easy matter: but it is worth the utmost labour and vigilance that you can bestow upon it.]

2. Do not however rest too confidently in testimonies of its approbation—

[It will not always speak the same language that it does when blinded by prejudice or passion. At the time of committing this great evil, the sons of Jacob "*were content;*" and they applauded themselves for their forbearance towards their ill-fated brother. But at a subsequent period, how different were their views of the very same action! So will it be with us. We may now approve and applaud our own conduct: but we must not conclude that we shall therefore always do so. We are now too apt to be partial in our own favour; but at a future period we shall judge righteous judgment, even as God himself will do: and we are no longer certain that our judgment of our own state is correct, than when it manifestly accords with the word of God.]

3. Look forward to the future judgment—

[That will certainly be correct: for God knoweth our hearts, and will bring every secret thing into judgment, whether it be good or evil. But oh! how painful will be the review in that day, if then for the first time we are made sensible of our sins! What a bitter reflection will it be, 'I did so and so; and therefore all this is come upon me: I have procured it all unto myself.' On the other hand, how delightful will it be to look back, and be able to appeal to God and say, "I have walked before thee with a perfect heart!" True it is, this will afford us no ground for boasting: but, if we walk before God in all good conscience now, we shall have its approving testimony in a dying hour, and the approbation of our God in the day of judgment[a].]

[a] Isai. xxxviii. 3.

OUTLINE NO. 55

JACOB'S UNBELIEVING FEARS.

Gen. xlii. 36. *All these things are against me!*

THE best of men are weak when they come into temptation. The trials of Jacob were indeed heavy: and, if we suppose that he had any idea that his sons had been active agents in bereaving him of his beloved Joseph, his grief must have been poignant beyond all expression. Not having been able to bring home to them any proof of such a conspiracy, he seems never to have dropped any hint to them before respecting it; and possibly he did not even now mean to charge it home upon them, but only to say, that he had been bereaved in some measure through them: nevertheless his words seem to betray a lurking suspicion, that they had been accessary to Joseph's death; " Me ye have bereaved; Joseph is not:" and this might well make him averse to trust Benjamin in their hands. But in the complaint he uttered respecting the ultimate end of his trials, he was manifestly wrong. We say not, that we should have shewn more constancy than he: it is more than probable that none of us in his circumstances would have acted better: but from his language on the occasion we may learn, *how we do act in trying circumstances,* and *how we ought to act.*

I. How we do act—

" We are born to trouble as the sparks fly upward:" none therefore can hope to escape it; and least of all they, who, like Jacob, have large families. While our trials are light, we can bear them with composure; but if they become heavy and accumulated, we are then apt to indulge,

1. Murmuring complaints—

[Whether Jacob meant to reflect on his sons or not, he certainly meant to complain of his afflictions; which was, in fact, to complain of God, who, in his all-wise providence, had appointed them. It was thus with his posterity during their sojourning in the wilderness: they always murmured against Moses, and against God, whenever they were involved in any difficulty or distress; and, when they were discouraged by the report of the spies respecting the land of Canaan and its inhabitants, they even proposed to make a Captain over them, and to return unto Egypt[a]. And how many such "murmurers and complainers" are there amongst ourselves! Some will expressly declare, that they think God deals hardly with them: others content themselves with venting their spleen against the instruments of their calamities: but all, in one way or other,

[a] Numb. xiv. 4.

are apt to "charge God foolishly," as if he were unmerciful, if not unrighteous also, in his dispensations towards them.]

2. Desponding fears—

[So filled was Jacob with a sense of his present calamities, that he could not indulge a hope of a favourable issue from them: he thought of nothing but increasing troubles, which should "bring down his grey hairs with sorrow to the grave." Thus also his descendants, whom we have before alluded to: they had seen bread given them from heaven, and water out of the stony rock; but they doubted whether God were able to provide flesh also for their sustenance: and when they were brought to the very borders of Canaan, they doubted whether it were possible for them ever to conquer the inhabitants, and take their fenced cities. And are not we also ready to say, on some occasions, "Our hope is lost; we are cut off for our parts?" Are we not ready to ask with David, whether his "mercy be not come utterly to an end?" Yes; in temporal things we too often sink under our troubles as absolutely irremediable; and in spiritual matters, we doubt almost the ability, and at all events the willingness, of Christ to save us.]

While we condemn the unbelief of this afflicted patriarch, we acknowledge, in fact,

II. How we ought to act—

However dark may be the dispensations of God towards us, we should,

1. Wait his time—

[We are not to be impatient because relief does not come at the first moment that we ask for it. There must be a time for the dispensations of God to produce their proper effects upon our hearts. We do not expect that a medical prescription shall effect in one moment all for which it was administered; we expect its operation to be unpleasant; and we are contented to submit to pain for a season, that we may afterwards enjoy the blessings of health. Now we know that our heavenly Physician prescribes with unerring wisdom, and consults our greatest good: whatever time therefore the accomplishment of his designs may occupy, we should wait with patience, assured that the intended benefits shall ultimately be enjoyed. We should give him credit, if we may so speak, for his wisdom and love; and leave him to display them in his own way: "He that believeth, shall not make haste."]

2. Rest on his promises—

[The promises of God to his people, respecting the issue of their trials, are exceeding great and precious. He declares, that we shall have "no temptation without a way to escape;"

that "all things shall work together for our good," and "work out for us a more exceeding weight of glory." Surely such promises as these should reconcile us to trials, however great. What can we wish for more? And how can we dare to say, "All these things are against me," when God tells us positively that they are working for us? Did we ever know that one of God's promises failed? Why then should we doubt the accomplishment of these, when they have already been fulfilled in so many thousand instances? Let it satisfy us, that God has promised; and that "what he has promised, he is able also to perform."]

3. Hope against hope—

[This was Abraham's conduct under far heavier trials than we have ever experienced[b]. What though we cannot see *how* God can effect our deliverance? Is HE also at a loss? The darker our state, the more simple should be our affiance. We should say with Job, "Though he slay me, yet will I trust in him." How was Jacob reproved at last, when he saw the issue of those things which in his haste he had so deplored! Let us remember that there is the same gracious, almighty God at this time; and that "they who trust in Him shall never be confounded."]

We may further LEARN from this subject,

1. What an excellent grace faith is—

[Faith beholds nothing but paternal love in the heaviest chastisements. Faith "brings meat out of the eater," and tastes sweetness in the bitterest cup. Faith looks to the end of things, and sees them, in a measure, as God sees them. It is the great and sovereign antidote to troubles of every kind. If Jacob had exercised faith as Abraham did, the trials of which he complained would scarcely have been felt at all. But God is pleased to try us on purpose that we may learn to trust in him. In this world "we are to walk by faith, and not by sight." Let us therefore cultivate continually this divine principle, which, while it honours God, tends exceedingly to the advancement of our own happiness.]

2. How blessed a state heaven will be—

[Here God has wisely and graciously hid futurity from our view. But when we are arrived at the heavenly mansions, we shall see all the merciful designs of God developed, and the wisdom of his dispensations clearly displayed. We shall then see that the trials of which we once complained, were not only salutary, but absolutely necessary for us; and that, if they had been withheld from us, there would have been wanting a link

[b] Rom. iv. 18. with Heb. xi. 17—19.

in that chain, by which we were to be brought in safety to heaven. Who will *there* adopt the language of the text? Who will utter it in reference to any one trial of his life? Who will not rather say, "He hath done all things well?" Let us then look forward to that time, and not pass our judgment on present things, till we see and understand the design of God in them.]

OUTLINE NO. 56
GOD VIEWED IN JOSEPH'S ADVANCEMENT.

Gen. xlv. 8. *So now, it was not you that sent me hither, but God.*

BY looking through second causes to the first Cause of all, we learn to trace events to an all-wise Being, who "worketh all things after the counsel of his own will," and whose prerogative it is to bring good out of evil, and order out of confusion. To this view of things we are directed, and in this we are greatly assisted, by the Holy Scriptures; which draw aside the veil of mystery that is on the ways of God, and set before our eyes the most hidden secrets of divine providence. The history before us more especially affords a beautiful illustration of those ways, in which the Governor of the Universe accomplishes his own designs: he suffers, in many instances, such adverse circumstances to occur, as apparently to preclude almost a possibility of their terminating according to his original purpose: yet does he wonderfully interpose in such a manner as to bring them easily, and, as it were, naturally, to their destined issue. If in any thing his intentions could be frustrated, we should have found them fail in reference to the predicted elevation of Joseph above his brethren: yet that event took place at last, and that too through those very means which were used to defeat it: and Joseph, after the event was actually accomplished, referred the whole dispensation to God, as its primary Author and infallible Director.

To elucidate this subject, we shall shew,

I. What part God takes in the actions of wicked men—

Though God cannot be a partaker in *the wickedness* of men, yet he may, and certainly does, bear a part in *those actions which wicked men perform.* We need go no further than the text, to confirm and establish this truth. That the conduct of Joseph's brethren, notwithstanding it was ultimately instrumental to his advancement, was deeply criminal, can admit of no doubt: yet says Joseph, "It was not you that sent me hither, but God." The question is then, What is that part which God takes in the actions of wicked men? To this we answer,

1. He affords them opportunities of perpetrating what is in their hearts—

[The brethren of Joseph were full of envy and malice against him: but while he was under his father's wing, they could not give full scope to their hatred, because they were afraid of their father's displeasure. To remove this difficulty, God so ordered matters that Joseph should be sent to inquire after the health of his brethren when they were at a distance from home. This gave them an opportunity of executing all that was in their hearts. But as the executing of their first intention would have defeated the plans of Providence, it was so appointed that certain Ishmaelite merchants should be passing that way, and that he should be sold to them for a slave instead of being put to death.

That we do not err in tracing these minuter incidents to divine providence, is manifest; for the elevation of Pharaoh to the throne of Egypt is expressly said to have been effected by God for that very purpose, that he might be an instrument on whom the divine power should be exerted, and in whose destruction God himself should be glorified[a].

But in thus facilitating the execution of evil, God does not make himself a partner in the crime: he only affords men power and opportunity to do what their own wicked dispositions prompt them to: and this he does, as in the instances before referred to, so also in every crime that is committed in the world. What our blessed Lord said to his judge who boasted of having power to release or condemn him, we may say to every criminal in the universe, "Thou couldst have no power at all to commit thy crimes, except it were given thee from above."]

2. He suffers Satan to instigate them to evil—

[" Satan is always going about as a roaring lion, seeking whom he may devour:" but he cannot act without divine permission: he could not tempt Job, or even enter into the herd

[a] Rom. ix. 17.

of swine, till he had first obtained leave of God. For the most part, God imposes a restraint on this our inveterate enemy; or, if left to himself, he would soon "sift us all as wheat," and reduce us all to the lowest ebb of wickedness and misery: but at times he leaves the fiend somewhat more at liberty, and permits him to exercise his power over his wretched vassals. On these occasions Satan operates upon their minds with more than usual violence, and not only leads them captive at his will, but instigates them to the commission of the most heinous crimes. Of these acts God is frequently represented as the author, whilst in other parts of Scripture their origin is referred to Satan. We are told that Satan moved David to number the people; and that he sent forth lying Spirits into all the prophets of Baal, that they might induce Ahab to go up to Ramoth-gilead to battle, where he was sure to fall. But both these things are also said to have been done by God[b]. The fact is, that God did these things through the agency of Satan; that is, he permitted Satan to act according to the impulse of his own mind, and left the persons whom he assaulted to comply with his temptations.]

3. He withdraws from them his restraining grace—

[Man needs nothing more than to have the preventing grace of God withheld, and he will as surely fall, as a stone, cast out of the hand, will gravitate to the earth. Now it is in this way that God often punishes the sins of men: he leaves them to put forth the depravity of their own hearts: he withholds those mercies which he sees they despised, and gives them up to follow their own vile propensities without restraint. To this effect, it is often said in Scripture, "So I gave them up;" "So I gave them up." Yea, the sacred records speak yet more strongly, and represent God as "blinding the eyes of men," and "hardening their hearts[c]." But we must not imagine that God ever actively concurs in the production of sin: in fact, there is no occasion for any active exertion on his part; nothing further is necessary than for him to withdraw his preventing grace; and evil will blaze forth, as fire will to consume the stubble, when no counteracting influence is used to extinguish the flames.]

To remove all objection against his participating in the actions of wicked men, we proceed to point out,

II. The benefit arising from acknowledging Him in them—

[b] 2 Sam. xxiv. 1. with 1 Chron. xxi. 1. and 2 Chron. xviii. 20—22.
[c] Exod. vii. 3, 13. Isai. vi. 9, 10, which is quoted six times in the New Testament.

It may be thought that such an acknowledgment, if it did not make God a minister of sin, would at least represent him in a very unamiable light; and that it would tend to justify men in their iniquities. But we affirm, on the contrary, that such an acknowledgment is calculated rather to bring good to man, and honour to our God.

1. It affords us sweet consolation under our troubles—

[Were we to look no further than to second causes, we should be grieved beyond measure at the instruments of our affliction, and be filled with apprehensions at their malevolent desires. But when we reflect that our enemies are no more than the sword in our Father's hand, and the rod with which he corrects us; when we consider that his design in correcting us is widely different from theirs[d], and that after he has made use of them for our good, he will cast them into the fire[e], and receive us to his bosom in an improved state[f], our minds are pacified, and we say, " It is the Lord, let him do what seemeth him good." What a source of comfort was this to Job, when the Sabeans and Chaldeans slew his servants and his cattle! " The Lord gave, and the Lord hath taken away; blessed be the name of the Lord!" It is thus with all the sons and daughters of affliction, when once they can view the hand of God in their trials: they adopt the language of the Psalmist; " I was dumb, and opened not my mouth, because *Thou* didst it."]

2. It disposes us to a ready forgiveness of those who injure us—

[It does not incline us to palliate their faults, as if they were mere unconscious instruments impelled by the force of Him who made use of them; (for in all that they do, they act as freely as if God bare no part at all in their actions:) but it inclines us to pity, to forgive, and pray for them, as slaves to their own passions, enemies to their own welfare, and real, though unwitting, benefactors to our souls. This effect is strongly exemplified in our text: Joseph saw the hand of God overruling the designs of his brethren; and from that consideration, he not only readily forgave them, but entreated them " not to be grieved or angry with themselves;" since, whatever had been their intentions, God had made use of their counsels for the accomplishment of his own gracious purposes: yea, thrice does he repeat this idea as a ground whereon he

---

[d] Isai. x. 4—6.   [e] Isai. x. 12, 16.   [f] Isai. x. 24—27.

would have them satisfied with the dispensation, as he himself also was[g]. We have also a similar effect mentioned in the history of David. Shimei, in the hour of David's adversity, loaded him with execrations; and Abishai, eager to avenge the insult offered to his master, desired permission to go and kill him: but David forbade it, saying, "Let him curse, because the Lord hath said unto him, Curse David: let him alone, and let him curse; for the Lord hath bidden him: it may be that the Lord will requite me good for his cursing this day[h]." Thus shall we also mortify all vindictive feelings, when once we discern that our enemies are agents for Him: we shall say with Stephen and our blessed Lord; "Lay not this sin to their charge:" "Father, forgive them; for they know not what they do."]

3. It fills us with an admiration of the divine wisdom—

[It is impossible to trace all the parts of this history, and not adore the wisdom, whereby the various incidents in Joseph's life were made to concur to the production of one great event, the preservation of Jacob and all his family. If we contemplate the still greater diversity of circumstances, whereby Jesus was made to fulfil the Scriptures, and to effect the redemption of the world; or the astonishingly mysterious designs of God relating to the excision of the Jews, as the means of engrafting the Gentiles into their stock; and the restoration of the Jews, as the means of bringing in all the fulness of the Gentiles; I say, if we contemplate these things, we are necessitated to exclaim with the Apostle, " O the depths of the riches both of the wisdom and knowledge of God! How unsearchable are his judgments, and his ways past finding out[i]!" In like manner, the more we are habituated to trace the mercies of God in our own personal experience, and the numberless instances wherein he has made " the wrath of men" and devils " to praise him," the more heartily shall we join in the adoring language of Moses, " Who is like unto Thee among the gods? Who is like Thee, glorious in holiness, fearful in praises, doing wonders[k]?"]

In prosecuting this subject, we cannot but be struck with the following REFLECTIONS—

1. How happy is the Christian in this world!

[Those that know not God, have no refuge to flee unto; no consolation under the trials they endure, no security against the evils they dread. But the true Christian is persuaded,

[g] ver. 5—8.   [h] 2 Sam. xvi. 5—12.
[i] Rom. xi. 33.   [k] Exod. xv. 11.

that, though he navigates a tempestuous ocean, he has an all-wise, almighty Pilot at the helm: and "therefore he will not fear though the waves thereof roar, and the mountains be carried into the midst of the sea." He knows not indeed what will be the precise issue of impending calamities; but he knows that it shall be precisely such as his heavenly Father sees to be best for him; and with that assurance he is satisfied. Thus is he kept in perfect peace, because he "trusts in God."]

2. How happy will he be in the future world!

[Here "he walks by faith, and not by sight." He believes that things are working for his good, because God has said that they shall do so. But in heaven he will have a perfect discovery of all the links in that chain of providences, whereby he has been brought to glory. He will see the importance of those things which once appeared most trifling, and the necessity of those things which once were most distressing, and the perfect harmony of those things which once were involved in the most impenetrable darkness and confusion. What cause will he then see to bless and adore his God! What views will he then have of the unsearchable depths of wisdom, which ordered every thing for his good! Well may he leave himself at God's disposal now, when such shall be his recompence at last! Let us then commit ourselves entirely to God, and be satisfied with all his dealings towards us: and "what we know not now, we shall know hereafter."]

OUTLINE NO. 57
JACOB'S RESOLUTION TO VISIT JOSEPH IN EGYPT.

Gen. xlv. 27, 28. *And they told him all the words of Joseph, which he had said unto them: and when he saw the waggons which Joseph had sent to carry him, the spirit of Jacob their father revived: and Israel said, It is enough; Joseph my son is yet alive: I will go and see him before I die.*

IT is of very great importance to exercise sound wisdom and discretion in interpreting the Holy Scriptures, lest, by imposing on them a forced or fanciful meaning, we bring the sacred oracles themselves into contempt. Yet is there a certain latitude allowed us, provided we do not set forth the subordinate and accommodated sense as if it were the true and primary import of the passage. The Apostles themselves frequently take this liberty. The prophet, speaking of the Babylonish captivity, says, "A voice was heard in Ramah, lamentation, and bitter weeping: Rachel, weeping for her children, refused to be comforted for her children, because they were not[a]." This passage St. Matthew applies to the slaughter of the children in Bethlehem, to which, in its primary sense, it had no reference[b]: nevertheless, the citation of it was just, and the accommodation beautiful. A similar use the same evangelist makes of a passage primarily referring to the atonement which Christ should offer for the sins of mankind: he applies it to his miraculously healing their bodily disorders[c]. These examples, and others which might be adduced, would justify a considerably greater latitude of observation than we propose to adopt on the present occasion. In considering this portion of sacred history, we do not found upon it any doctrine relating to the Gospel: we do not even insinuate that it was originally *intended* to illustrate any of the peculiar doctrines of Christianity: we shall merely *take occasion from it* to introduce to your notice some useful observations, with which indeed it has no immediate connexion, but with which it has a very striking correspondence.

Joseph having made known himself to his brethren, and cautioned them against "falling out by the way," (an event too probable in their circumstances,) sends them back to their father, with orders to inform him of all that they had seen and heard, and to bring him and their respective families down to Egypt. Jacob, when first he received the information, could not credit it: but upon further conversation with his sons he was convinced of the truth of their report, and determined to accept the invitation which his beloved Joseph had sent him.

Now we propose to notice,

I. The grounds of his doubts—

There seem to have been two reasons for his questioning the truth of the information he received;

1. The report contradicted all that he had before received for truth—

---

[a] Jer. xxxi. 15.   [b] Matt. ii. 17, 18.
[c] Compare Isai. liii. 4. with Matt. viii. 16—18.

['He had above twenty years before had reason to believe that his son Joseph had been torn in pieces by a wild beast; he had even seen his son's coat torn and drenched in blood; nor had the lapse of so many years brought him any other information: how then could this son be the person that presided over the kingdom of Egypt at this time? There might be some one that resembled him in name; but it could not possibly be his darling son: had Joseph been alive, he must long since have heard of him: whoever therefore the person might be, or whatever he might profess to be, he could not be the long-lost son of his beloved Rachel.' Such were Jacob's arguments, and such his reasons for rejecting the testimony of his sons.

And do we not here see one ground on which the testimony of those who preach the Gospel is rejected? We find men rooted in certain sentiments, which, in their opinion, they have adopted on very sufficient grounds. The general acceptance which those sentiments meet with, and the confirmation of them during a long course of years, concur to render them, as it were, fixed principles in their minds. But the doctrines of the Gospel are directly the reverse of those which pass current in the world. The extreme depravity of human nature, the desert and danger of all mankind, the insufficiency of any good works to recommend us to God, the necessity of seeking justification by faith alone, the nature and extent of true holiness, and the impossibility of being saved without an entire consecration of ourselves to the service of God, are as opposite to the doctrines and sentiments of the world, as light is to darkness: and on this account they are rejected by the generality with scorn and contempt. It was on this ground that Nicodemus rejected the doctrine of the new birth; "How can these things be?" 'I have never held this sentiment; therefore it cannot be true.' And on the same grounds it is, that the preaching of the Gospel is at this time, no less than in former ages, accounted foolishness.]

2. The tidings were too good to be true—

[There is a proneness in the human mind to believe evil reports more easily than those which are favourable. Jacob instantly acceded to the idea that his son Joseph had been torn in pieces, notwithstanding, if he had considered the spirit and temper of his brethren towards him, there was very abundant reason to doubt the fact. But, when he is told that Joseph is alive, and at the head of the Egyptian kingdom, he cannot entertain the thought one moment: "his heart even faints" at the mention of the fact, (not because he believed it, but) because he believed it not.

Here again we trace the workings of the human mind in relation to higher things. If we come and tell persons that they must make their peace with God by a long course of repentance and good works, they will believe us readily enough; though, if they duly considered the nature of such tidings, they would have evidence enough of their falsehood. But if we declare to them, that Christ has made a full atonement for our sins; that a free and full salvation is offered them through Him; that they may partake of it " without money and without price," that is, without any thing on their part to merit it; and that their former guilt, however great and aggravated, is no bar to their acceptance with God, provided they simply and unfeignedly believe in Christ; ' all this seems too good to be true: it can never be, that the way to heaven should be so easy.' This is the argument used by all the train of self-righteous Pharisees, who, " being whole, feel no need of a physician;" and by multitudes also of repenting " Publicans, who dare not lift up their eyes to heaven," or entertain a nope, that " grace should ever so abound towards them, in whom sin has so greatly abounded[d]."]

Having canvassed thus his doubts, we proceed to notice,

II. The means of their removal—

Of these we are minutely informed in the words of our text. They were,

1. A fuller recital of Joseph's words—

[Jacob's sons had told him of Joseph's elevation; but not obtaining credit, proceeded to " tell him *all the words* that Joseph had said unto them." Now their testimony became so circumstantial and convincing, that he could resist no longer: his incredulity was borne down by a weight of evidence that could not be withstood.

Thus also it is that the Gospel forces its way into the hearts of thousands, to whom, at its first statement, it appeared no better than an idle tale. Ministers set forth innumerable declarations which Jesus has made respecting us: they report his gracious invitations, his precious promises, his tender expostulations; all of which evince such a perfect knowledge of our state, and are so suited to our necessities, that we cannot any longer doubt from whom they come. They shame us out of our doubts, and constrain us to exclaim, " Lord, I believe; help thou my unbelief! "]

2. An actual sight of the tokens of his love—

[A view of the waggons which Joseph had sent, stored with every thing requisite for his accommodation in his journey,

---

[d] See Isai. xlix. 24, 25.

completed his conviction. All the patriarch's doubts were dissipated, and his "spirit instantly revived."

And what will not give way before the sensible manifestations of God's love to the soul? Let "His love be shed abroad in the heart by the Holy Ghost;" let the promises be applied with power to the soul; let "the Spirit of God once witness with our spirit that we are God's;" and no fears will then remain respecting the truth of the Gospel or the power and grace of Christ: we shall then "have the witness in ourselves," that "Jesus is exalted to be a Prince and a Saviour," and that he is "able to save to the uttermost all that come unto God by him."]

With the removal of his doubts there was an instantaneous change in his determinations. This will appear while we consider,

III. The effect which their removal produced upon him—

He had been hitherto reluctant to leave his home; but now,

1. He desired nothing so much as to see the one object of his affections—

[Joseph was now more dear to him than ever; and if he might but live to enjoy a sight of him, he should consider himself as having attained all for which he wished to live: "It is enough; Joseph my son is yet alive; I will go and see him before I die."

And let us once be persuaded that Jesus is set at God's right hand, far above all principalities and powers, and that he has all heaven at his disposal, and has sent to invite us to come unto him, and has made ample provision for us by the way, and prepared mansions for us at the end of our journey, and engaged that we shall dwell in his immediate presence for ever and ever; let us be persuaded of this, and shall we feel no disposition to visit him? Will it not, on the contrary, be the first desire of our hearts? Shall we not say, "Whom have I in heaven but Thee; and there is none upon earth that I desire in comparison of Thee?" Will not the attainment of this object appear to be the only thing worth living for? And having an assured prospect of this, shall we not say, "Now lettest thou thy servant depart in peace?" Yes; this desire will swallow up, as it were, every other; and to secure this happiness will be the only end for which we shall wish to live.]

2. He disregarded all the difficulties he might encounter in the way to him—

[It was not a pleasing thing for an infirm old man, who was one hundred and thirty years of age, to leave his home, and set out upon so long a journey: but the mountains became a plain, when such an object was to be attained.

Nor is it pleasing for flesh and blood to encounter the difficulties which we must meet with in our journey heaven-ward. But who that loves our exalted Jesus will regard them? who will not welcome reproach, and take up with cheerfulness whatever cross may lie in his way to that blessed kingdom? Suppose that we must suffer the loss of our worldly interests and accommodations; who will not account them mere "stuff," that is unworthy of one moment's notice? who will not readily exchange them for the fulness of the heavenly land, and for the enjoyment of the Saviour's presence? Difficulties become no difficulties, and sacrifices no sacrifices, when by faith we behold the Saviour's glory, and have an assured hope of participating it for ever.]

REFLECTIONS—

1. How amiable is the exercise of unfeigned love!

[Joseph, for peculiar reasons, had imposed a restraint upon his feelings, till the proper time arrived to give them vent: but when he was no longer under any necessity to conceal them, they burst forth in a torrent of affection, as waters that have broken down the dam by which they had been confined. He retained no anger against his murderous brethren, but fell on their necks and kissed them. His charge to them "not to fall out by the way," shewed how ardently he desired that they might maintain, with each other as well as with himself, the unity of the Spirit in the bond of peace. And how animated was his message to his dear aged father! "Haste you, and go up to my father, and say unto him, Thus saith thy son Joseph; God hath made me lord of all Egypt: come down to me; tarry not: and thou shalt dwell in the land of Goshen; and thou shalt be near unto me, thou and thy children, and thy children's children, and thy flocks, and thy herds, and all that thou hast: and there will I nourish thee!" Nor was the aged patriarch's affection less ardent, when once he was persuaded that his Joseph was yet alive. His whole soul was wrapt up in his darling son: and, in his determination to visit him, he lost sight of all his temporal interests: the thought of enjoying plenty in Egypt seems not to have entered into his mind: all that he cared for was a sight of Joseph; and beyond that he had no wish in life.

Would to God it were thus in every church, and every family! Thus indeed it will be, wherever the grace of God reigns in the heart. Instead of "rendering evil for evil," we shall "heap coals of fire on the heads" of those who injure us, to melt them into love. Instead of harbouring envy, or hatred, or a selfish indifference in our hearts, we shall feel the sublimest happiness in the exercise of love: parents will love their children, and children seek to requite their parents, and " brethren delight to dwell together in unity." O let us cultivate such a spirit, which shall be the best evidence, both to ourselves and others, that we are Christ's disciples.]

2. How delightful will be our interview with Christ in heaven!

[If we had beheld the meeting of this aged patriarch with his beloved Joseph, who amongst us could have refrained from tears? —— —— But what must be the meeting of the soul with Jesus, on its first admission into his presence? Who can conceive the tender endearments of the Saviour's love, or the admiration, gratitude, and joy with which the soul shall be overwhelmed in his embrace? Surely such an interview is worth the longest and most arduous journey. Well may we account every thing as dung and dross, to obtain it; more especially because it shall not be transient, like that which Jacob enjoyed, but permanent and everlasting. Behold then, we invite you all to a participation of it. He has said respecting you, " Father, I will that they whom thou hast given me may be with me where I am, that they may behold my glory which thou hast given me." And is there one amongst you that will not add his Amen to that petition? Make haste then, tarry not: " Mind not your *stuff*," but commence your journey instantly: and soon shall death transport you into his presence; and " then shall you be for ever with the Lord. Comfort ye one another with these words."]

OUTLINE NO. 58

JACOB'S INTERVIEW WITH PHARAOH.

Gen. xlvii. 7—10. *And Joseph brought in Jacob his father, and set him before Pharaoh: and Jacob blessed Pharaoh. And Pharaoh said unto Jacob, How old art thou? And Jacob said unto Pharaoh, The days of the years of my pilgrimage are an hundred and thirty years: few and evil have the days of the years of my life been, and have not attained unto the days of the years of the life of my fathers, in the days of their pilgrimage. And Jacob blessed Pharaoh, and went out from before Pharaoh.*

TO acknowledge God in all our ways, and to commit our way to him, secures to us, as we are told, his gracious interposition for the direction of our paths, and the accomplishment of our desires. It is possible that Jacob, after he had set out towards Egypt in the waggons that Joseph had sent for him, felt some doubts about the propriety of leaving the promised land, when, at his advanced age, he could have no reasonable prospect of returning thither with his family. But, knowing from experience the efficacy of prayer, he betook himself to that never-failing remedy: he stopped at Beersheba, and offered sacrifices to the Lord. That very night God vouchsafed to appear to him in a vision, and to dissipate his fears, by an express command to proceed on his journey, and by a promise that he should in due time be brought back again[a]. He then prosecuted his journey in safety, and had a most affecting interview with his beloved Joseph. Soon after his arrival, five of his sons were introduced to Pharaoh; and afterwards he himself. It is this introduction of the aged patriarch to Pharaoh that we are now more particularly to consider. In the account given us of the interview, we notice,

I. The question which Pharaoh put to Jacob—

[It could not be expected that persons so remote from each other in their station, their views, and habits of life, should have many topics in common with each other whereon to maintain a long and interesting conversation. The interview seems to have been very short, and of course the conversation short also. All that is related concerning it contains only one short question. This, *as far as it related to Jacob*, was a mere expression of kindness and respect on the part of Pharaoh. To have questioned him about matters which he did not understand, would have been embarrassing to Jacob, and painful to his feelings: and to have asked him about any thing in which neither party was at all interested, would have betrayed a great want of judgment in Pharaoh. The topic selected by Pharaoh was liable to no such objection: for it is always gratifying to a person advanced in years to mention his age, because the "hoary head, especially if found in the way of righteousness, is always considered as a crown of glory[b]."

As a general question, independent of the history, it cannot fail of suggesting many important thoughts to all to whom it is addressed. "How old art thou?" Art thou far advanced in life? how much then of thine allotted time is gone, and how

---

[a] Gen. xlvi. 1—4.   [b] Prov. xvi. 31. Lev. xix. 32.

little remains for the finishing of the work that is required of thee! how diligently therefore shouldst thou redeem every hour that is now added to thine expiring term! Art thou, on the contrary, but just setting out in the world? how little dost thou know of its snares, temptations, sorrows! what disappointments and troubles hast thou to experience! and how deeply art thou concerned to have thy views rectified, and thy conduct regulated by the word of God! Whatever be thine age, thou shouldst consider every return of thy birth-day rather as a call to weep and mourn, than as an occasion of festivity and joy: for it is the knell of a departed year; a year that might, in all probability, have been far better improved; a year in which many sins have been committed, which are indelibly recorded in the book of God's remembrance, and of which you must shortly give a strict account at his judgment-seat.]

We notice,

II. Jacob's answer to it—

[The patriarch's mind was fraught with zeal for God; and therefore not contenting himself with a plain short answer, he framed his reply in words calculated to make a deep impression on the mind of Pharaoh, without giving him the smallest offence.

He *insinuates*, and repeats the idea, *that life is but a "pilgrimage;"* that we are merely sojourners in a foreign land, and that our home and our inheritance is in a better country. This part of his speech is particularly noticed in the Epistle to the Hebrews, as being an open acknowledgment of his principles as a worshipper of Jehovah, and of his expectations in a better world[c]. He intimates also *that his years*, though they had been an hundred and thirty, *were few*. This age might appear great to Pharaoh; but it was not near equal to that of Jacob's progenitors[d]. On a retrospect, every person's days appear to have been but few. Various incidents of former life seem to have been but recently transacted; the intervening time being lost, as it were, like valleys intercepted by adjacent hills. He further declares, *that these years of his had been replete with evil.* Certainly his life, from the time that he fled from the face of his brother Esau to that hour, had been a scene of great afflictions. His fourteen years' servitude to Laban, the disgrace brought on him and his family by Dinah his only daughter, the murderous cruelty of his vindictive sons, the jealousies of all his children on account of his partiality to Joseph, the sudden loss of Joseph, and all his recent trials, had greatly embittered life to him, and made it appear like a sea of troubles, where wave followed wave in endless succession. And who

[c] Heb. xi. 13, 14, 16.
[d] Terah was 205 years old; Abraham 175; Isaac 180.

is there that does not find, (especially in more advanced life,) that the evil, on the whole, outweighs the good?

These hints, offered in so delicate a manner to a potent monarch, with whom he had only one short interview, afford a beautiful pattern for our imitation, at the same time that they convey important instruction to our minds.]

We conclude with commending to your imitation the whole of Jacob's conduct towards Pharaoh—

[At his first admission into Pharaoh's presence, and again at his departure from him, this holy patriarch blessed him. We do not suppose that he pronounced his benediction in a formal and authoritative manner, as Melchizedec did to Abraham; but that he rendered him his most grateful acknowledgments for the favours he had conferred, and invoked the blessing of God upon him and upon his kingdom on account of them. Such a mode of testifying his gratitude became a servant of Jehovah, and tended to lead the monarch's thoughts to the contemplation of the only true God. And well may it put to shame the greater part of the Christian world, who systematically exclude religion from their social converse, under the idea that the introduction of it would destroy all the comfort of society———True Christians, however, should learn from this instance not to be ashamed of their religion; but, as inoffensively as possible, to lead men to the knowledge of it; and to make the diffusion of it a very essential part of all their intercourse with each other———More especially we should embrace every opportunity of impressing on our own minds and on the minds of others the true end of life; that we may thereby secure that rest which remaineth for us after our short but weary pilgrimage.]

OUTLINE NO. 59
JACOB BLESSING THE SONS OF JOSEPH.

Gen. xlviii. 15, 16. *And he blessed Joseph, and said, God, before whom my fathers Abraham and Isaac did walk, the God which fed me all my life long unto this day, the Angel which redeemed me from all evil, bless the lads!*

THERE are not any more profitable scenes than those which we behold in the chambers of dying saints. There religion is exhibited in the most lively colours, and evinces itself to be, not a visionary phantom, but a real and substantial good. We are bidden to "mark the perfect man, and to behold the upright, because the end of that man is peace." Some instances there are, where persons on their death-bed are transported with unutterable joy: they seem to breathe the very atmosphere of heaven, while they are yet in the body. But it is more frequent to behold them waiting for their dissolution with a peaceful dignified composure; and improving their precious moments for the benefit of their surviving friends. Such was the closing scene of Jacob. We read not of any particular ecstasies that he enjoyed; but we see him with a hope full of immortality, and an affectionate attention to the welfare of all his children. It seems indeed that several of the patriarchs were on these occasions endued with a spirit of prophecy, and directed to pronounce blessings on those, for whom God, of his own sovereign will, had reserved them. They were not left to their own caprice or judgment in this matter; but were overruled, sometimes contrary to their own intentions to convey the blessings of primogeniture to the younger branches of the family in preference to the elder. Thus Isaac, having unwillingly given the blessing to Jacob, was constrained to confirm it to him, notwithstanding Esau laboured with tears to prevail upon him to recall his word. Somewhat similar to that was the transfer of the blessing to the younger of Joseph's sons in preference to the elder. Joseph brought his sons to his dying parent, and placed them so that Manasseh, his first-born, should have the right hand of Jacob placed upon his head: but the dying patriarch was inspired of God to counteract the wish of Joseph in this particular, and, by crossing his hands, to convey the principal blessing to Ephraim, who was the younger son. We might remark upon this subject, that God often, if we may so speak, crosses his hands in bestowing his blessings, since he gives them to those, who, in our eyes, are least worthy of them, and least likely to receive them. But our object at present is rather to inculcate the necessity of attending to the spiritual interests of young people, and especially of those who by the ties of consanguinity are connected with us.

In prosecuting this subject, we observe, that,

I. We should feel a concern for the spiritual welfare of the rising generation—

We should by no means be indifferent to the souls of any: on the contrary, the conveying of religious instruction to children is an occupation well worthy the attention of all, who have leisure and ability to engage in it[a]. But we are more especially bound to instruct those who are related to us and dependent on us: indeed they may justly claim this service at our hands—

1. Their spiritual welfare is incomparably more important than their temporal—

[All persons feel it incumbent on them to consult the temporal welfare of their children, and account themselves happy, if they can bequeath them an inheritance, that shall make them independent of the world; or give them such an education, as shall enable them to make a comfortable provision for themselves. But how much richer is a child that possesses a saving knowledge of Christ, however low he be in outward circumstances, than the heir of a kingdom would be, if destitute of that knowledge! — — — Shall we then be diligent in promoting the temporal prosperity of our relations, and shew no regard for their eternal interests? God forbid! Let rather our care be most bestowed on those things which most of all deserve our care — — —]

2. Their spiritual welfare greatly depends on us—

[Who is to instruct our children, if we do not? or how can they gain knowledge without instruction? We provide for their bodies, because nature, as well as custom, tells us that it is our duty to do so. But is it not equally our duty to provide for their souls? If we educate them in ignorance, what can be expected but that they should grow up in sin? and how can it be thought that they should bestow any pains in cultivating divine knowledge for themselves, when they see us, whom they suppose to have formed a right estimate of things, indifferent whether they possess it or not? On the contrary, if we conscientiously discharge our duty to them in this respect, we have reason to hope, that God will bless our endeavours, and make us instruments of good to their souls.

---

[a] If this were the subject of a sermon for the support of *charity*, or *Sunday Schools*, the idea of relationship should be dropped, and the sentiments a little varied.

For though the best efforts may not *universally* succeed, we may assume it as a *general* truth, that " if we bring up a child in the way he should go, when he is old he will not depart from it."]

3. Their souls will be required at our hands—

[This is a truth acknowledged in reference to Ministers: all agree that *they* must give account of the souls committed to their charge. Why then should not this be the case with those who have the care of children? Methinks every parent, as soon as ever a child is born, should receive it as it were from the hands of God, with this charge, " Bring this child up for me[b]." As for the attention which a parent bestows on the temporal advancement of his children, it will not only not excuse his neglect of their better interests, but will be a fearful aggravation of it. The Judge will say to them as he once did to the hypocritical Pharisees, These things ought ye to have done, and not to leave the other undone.]

If we should feel this concern at all times for the rising generation,

II. We should express it more especially in a dying hour—

Every word acquires weight from the circumstance of its being uttered at the approach of death. We should avail ourselves therefore of that advantage, to impress the minds of young people with a concern for their souls. Two things in particular we should do:

1. We should commend God to them—

[This Jacob did: and we cannot do better than follow his example.

Young people are ready to think, that religion is a *new* thing, and that the exhortations of their parents are the effects of needless preciseness, or of superstitious fear. On this account, it is well to shew them, that all those eminent characters of old, whom they profess to reverence, were devoted to the service of their God: and that, in recommending religion to them, we recommend only what all the wise and good in all ages have approved; that, if God is our God, he was " the God also, before whom Abraham, and Isaac, and Jacob walked." Moreover, though it is not always expedient to be talking of our own experience, yet, at such a season, we may do it to good effect. We may declare to others what we have known of God, both as a God of providence and of grace. It is of great importance to make them entertain right sentiments

[b] Exod. ii. 9.

respecting the providence of God, and to make them know, that whether they become rich by industry or by inheritance, it is "God who feeds them all their life long." It is also indispensably necessary to direct their attention to that "Angel," Jehovah, the Lord Jesus Christ, "the Angel of the Covenant[c]," through whom alone we have redemption, either from the *moral evil* of sin, or from the *penal evil* of damnation. It is "He that redeems us from *all* evil," temporal, spiritual, and eternal. If we can from our own experience bear testimony to Christ in this view, it will avail more than a thousand lectures given in a time of health: for then the surrounding relatives will see, the sting of death is taken away, and that "they are indeed blessed who put their trust in Christ."]

2. We should pray to God for them—

[The prayer of Jacob is short, but sententious. The expression, "God bless you!" is often uttered in a dying hour, but without any just ideas affixed to the petition. But we, in imploring the blessing of God upon our children, should distinctly inform them wherein that blessing consists. We should inform them, that, to enjoy God in the dispensations of his providence, and Christ in the riches of his grace, and to walk before God in Christ, as our God and Saviour, in all holy obedience, is to be truly blessed; and that we are then indeed blessed, when God by his Spirit enables us thus to enjoy and to serve him. Having these things in our own minds, and conveying them to the minds of those whom we desire to instruct, we need not multiply words in prayer: while we entreat of God to *bless* those for whose welfare we are particularly concerned, we shall find acceptance with God, and obtain mercies for them.

It is recorded of Jacob, that in this prayer of his he exercised faith[d]. Now we have not precisely the same grounds for faith that he had; because he was inspired to pronounce over the youths the blessings which God had before determined to bestow: but the more we are enabled to believe in God as a prayer-hearing and promise-keeping God, the more reason we have to hope that our prayers shall be answered, whether for ourselves or others.]

ADDRESS—

1. To those who are advanced in life—

[You see before you the composure of a dying saint. Seek to obtain such for yourselves. And that you may "die

---

[c] The same Person is spoken of as in the former members of the text: nor would Jacob have prayed to him, if he had not been *God*. Compare Gen. xxxii. 24, 28, 30. with Hos. xii. 3—5. and Mal. iii. 1.

[d] Heb. xi. 21.

the death of the righteous," be diligent to live his life. If your own business be not already transacted with God, (so to speak,) you will have little disposition either to speak to others in a dying hour, or to pray for them: but if your own calling and election be made sure, then will your dying exhortations be delivered with ease, and received with benefit.]

2. To those who are coming forward into life—

[You are apt to slight the instructions of your parents, under the idea that they are unnecessary or unsuitable to your state. But you see what has always occupied the minds of dying saints. You know that Jacob's example is commended by God himself. Be thankful then, if you have friends or relatives who walk in the steps of Jacob: and let that, which they above all things desire for you, be your chief desire for yourselves.]

OUTLINE NO. 60

CHRIST THE TRUE SHILOH.

Gen. xlix. 10. *The sceptre shall not depart from Judah, nor a lawgiver from between his feet, until Shiloh come: and unto him shall the gathering of the people be.*

THERE was a series of predictions relative to the Messiah from the very beginning of the world; and, as the time for the accomplishment of the prophecies drew near, the predictions concerning him were more particular and minute. About seventeen hundred years before his appearance, the time of his coming was fixed with great accuracy and precision. At the very first moment that the sons of Jacob were made heads of different tribes, it was foretold, that the continuance of Judah's power should extend beyond that of the other tribes, and that the Messiah should arrive before its expiration. In explaining this prophecy we shall of necessity be led to speak of,

I. The time of his advent—

This, according to the text, was to precede the departure of Judah's sceptre—

[Judah is here represented as a lion gorged with his prey, and couching in his den with a sceptre between his feet; a sceptre, which none should ever wrest from him, until *he* should come, whose right it was[a]. "The sceptre" does not import dominion over the other tribes, but only the same kind of

[a] ver. 9.

separate and independent jurisdiction which was vested in Dan, and in all the other tribes[b]. Nor does the term "lawgiver" mean a person who should enact laws; but rather, one who should execute and enforce them. Moses was the only lawgiver of the Jews; and even the kings were required to write a copy of his law, and to obey it in all things. Now it was here foretold, that this particular power should remain with Judah after that the other tribes should have been deprived of theirs; and that it should continue vested in persons belonging to that tribe till the Messiah should come. The precise import of the term "Shiloh" is not certainly known; but it is thought by most to mean, The Peacemaker. All however are agreed that it is a name for the Messiah, whose advent was to precede the dissolution of the Jewish polity.]

The event exactly corresponded with the prediction—

[The ten tribes were spoiled of their power when they were carried captive to Assyria. But the tribe of Judah retained both their ecclesiastical and civil polity even in Babylon. If they did not exercise it to the same extent as before, they had by no means wholly lost it. As they had possessed it in Egypt, and retained it the whole time of their Egyptian bondage[c], so they still nominated their chiefs and elders, yea and appointed fasts and feasts, while they were oppressed with the Chaldean yoke[d]. Their bondage in Babylon was indeed, on the whole, exceeding heavy; but many of them were suffered to build houses and plant gardens, and to live rather as a colony than as slaves[e]. On their return from Babylon, their own chiefs and elders were appointed to superintend the execution of Cyrus' decree[f]; and, after that period, they continued to enjoy their privileges till the time of our Lord's advent. Soon after that, they were reduced to the state of a Roman province; but still exercised the same powers, only in a more limited manner[g]. But, forty years after the death of Christ, when his Gospel had been fully preached, and people of all nations had been gathered to him, their city and temple were utterly destroyed; and they themselves were dispersed into all lands. From that time their sceptre has utterly departed from them; nor can the smallest vestige of their former power be traced. They are therefore *living* proofs throughout the whole world that their Messiah is indeed come.]

[b] ver. 16.   [c] Exod. xxxiv. 31, 32.

[d] Moses and Aaron were sent to *the elders* of the people, Exod. iii. 16. and iv. 29; and these were *heads of houses*, Exod. vi. 14; and rulers of the congregation, Exod. xvi. 22. Compare Numb. i. 3, 16. See Sherlock's third Dissertation, pp. 342, 346, 6th edition.

[e] Jer. xxix. 5, 7.   [f] Ezra i. 5, 8.

[g] Compare John xviii. 3, and 31.

The time of Christ's advent being thus clearly ascertained, let us consider,

II. The consequences of it—

The last clause of the text is by some applied to Judah, to whom the tribe of Benjamin was attached, and the few of the other ten tribes, who returned after their dispersion by the Assyrians, were gathered[h]. But the sense of that clause is both more clear, and infinitely more important, as applied to Shiloh. And, if it be understood, as it may well be, as a further limitation of the time beyond which Judah should not retain this power, it will mark, with most astonishing accuracy, the precise period at which his sceptre was to depart.

But, taking it according to its general acceptation, it declares the calling of the Gentiles to the knowledge of Christ—

[The Scriptures speak much upon this glorious subject. Without noticing the innumerable passages that declare God's intention to convert the Gentiles, we will confine our attention to two or three that speak of it almost in the very same terms as those in the text. Isaiah, representing Christ as standing for an ensign to the people, says, " To him shall *the Gentiles seek*, and his rest shall be glorious[i]." There was a remarkable prophecy to the same effect unwittingly uttered by Caiaphas the high-priest. While he designed nothing more than to instigate the Jews to destroy Jesus, God overruled his mind to declare that Jesus should die for the whole world, and should *gather together in one* the children of God that were scattered abroad[k]. Our Lord himself also, foretelling the same glorious event, said, " I, if I be lifted up, will *draw all men* unto me[l]." Nor is only the mere circumstance of their conversion declared in the text; the *manner* also of their coming to him is strongly intimated. They " shall be a willing people in the day of God's power," and as the prophet describes at large, shall fly to him as a cloud, or as doves to their windows[m].]

This part of the prediction also has received, and is daily receiving, its accomplishment—

[No sooner had our Lord given up the Ghost, than the centurion, the first fruits of the Gentiles, was led to acknowledge him as the Son of God. Presently, not Judea only, but

---

[h] 1 Chron. ix. 3.   [i] Isai. xi. 10.   [k] John xi. 52.
John xii. 32.   [m] Isai. lx. 3—8.

the whole Roman empire, was filled with those who were gathered unto him. And, at this moment, "all who are taught of God come unto *him*" as the one foundation of all their hopes, and the only fountain of all their blessings. There is a period still future, when this prophecy shall be fulfilled in its utmost extent; when "all kings shall bow down before him, and all nations shall serve him." Blessed period! may "God hasten it in its time!" may his "Gospel run and be glorified," and "his glory fill the whole earth!"]

Let us now ADDRESS a few words,

1. To those who are yet dispersed, and at a distance from the Lord—

[We need not here turn our eyes to Jews, but reflect how many are there even in this Christian land, who have no more fellowship with Jesus than if he had never come into the world! But what account will they give to him when they shall stand at his tribunal in the last day? Are not the words of our text *a direction*, as well as a prophecy? Are they not equivalent to *an express command*? Has not Christ himself enforced this command by repeated invitations and promises, "Look unto me, and be ye saved;" "Come unto me, and ye shall find rest unto your souls?" Has he not even sworn that all shall come to him, or perish for their neglect[n]? Why then should we not all gather ourselves around him as in the days of his flesh? Why should not the blind, the lame, the leprous, the possessed, come to him for deliverance? Why should not the poor trembling sinner press through the crowd, and "touch the hem of his garment?" Surely none should find it in vain to come unto him; "Virtue should go forth from him to heal them all." O let the prophecy then receive a fresh accomplishment this day; and may God so "draw us by his Spirit that we may run after him," and abide with him for ever!]

2. Those who, through grace, have been gathered to him—

[The sceptre is now passed into the hands of Jesus. He is the true *lion of the tribe of Judah*[o], to whom all power in heaven and in earth has been committed. What then have ye to fear, who are under his protection? Who shall ever pluck you from his hands[p]? When, or to whom shall his sceptre ever be transferred? His *mediatorial* kingdom will indeed be put down, when there shall be no more occasion for it[q]. But though he will cease to mediate between God and man, his

---

[n] Isai. xlv. 22—25.   [o] Rev. v. 5.   [p] John x. 28.
[q] 1 Cor. xv. 24. This relates to the peculiar mode of administering the affairs of his kingdom *as our Mediator*.

sovereign dominion shall exist to all eternity; "Thy throne, O God, is for ever and ever; of thy kingdom there shall be no end[r]." Rejoice then, believers, in your Lord; "let the children of Zion be joyful in their king." Cherish his attractive influences: gather yourselves around him yet daily and hourly: spread before him your every want: commune with him on every occasion: consult him; listen to him; obey him: cleave to him with full purpose of heart: so will he keep you steadfast unto the end, and admit you to the richer fruition of his presence in his kingdom above.]

[r] Isai. ix. 7. Dan. ii. 44. Heb. i. 8.

OUTLINE NO. 61
JOSEPH A TYPE OF CHRIST.

Gen. xlix. 22—24. *Joseph is a fruitful bough, even a fruitful bough by a well; whose branches run over the wall. The archers have sorely grieved him, and shot at him, and hated him. But his bow abode in strength, and the arms of his hands were made strong by the hands of the mighty God of Jacob: from thence is the shepherd, the stone of Israel.*

PECULIAR care is to be used in unfolding the types, lest, by indulging our own imagination, we bring the very truth of God itself into contempt. Where the Scriptures themselves have marked the typical reference, we may proceed without fear; but when once they cease to guide us, we should not venture one step but with fear and trembling. This observation is peculiarly applicable to the subject before us. It does not appear that Joseph is anywhere declared to be a type of Christ, notwithstanding the circumstances wherein they resemble each other are as numerous and remarkable, as in almost any other instance whatever. We forbear therefore to assert any thing on this subject with confidence; while, in compliance with the opinion of the most judicious commentators, and indeed with the almost irresistible conviction of our own mind, we proceed to trace the resemblance of Joseph to Christ, in,

I. His distinguishing character—

Joseph is represented as "a fruitful bough"—

[Every tribe is distinguished by something characteristic, either of the patriarchs themselves, or of their descendants.

The distinction assigned to Joseph, is that of peculiar fruitfulness: and to him it eminently belonged. All his brethren indeed were honoured with being heads of distinct tribes: but Joseph had both his sons chosen of God, and appointed to be heads of separate tribes; and thus two tribes sprang from him, while one tribe only sprang from any of his brethren.]

To our Lord also is a similar title frequently ascribed—

[Jesus was that "beautiful and glorious BRANCH," which was in due time to spring from the stem of Jesse[a], the fruit whereof was to fill the whole earth[b]. It was not one tribe only, or two, that was to acknowledge him as their head, but all the tribes; yea, Gentiles as well as Jews, even all the ends of the earth: his fruit was to shake like the woods of Lebanon, and they, who should spring from him, were to be numerous as the piles of grass[c], the stars of heaven[d], and the sands upon the sea-shore[e]. And so abundantly has this prediction been already verified, that we may say of this Branch as the Psalmist did of *that* which typically represented it, "It has taken deep root, and filled the land: the hills are covered with the shadow of it, and the boughs thereof are like the goodly cedars; it has sent forth its boughs unto the sea, and its branches unto the river[f]."]

But the resemblance will more fully appear, while we consider,

II. His grievous sufferings—

Joseph was for many years very grievously afflicted—

[He was eminently the beloved of his father[g]; and, being utterly averse to sin himself, he would reprove, and lay before his father, the misconduct of his brethren[h]: he also, unreservedly, communicated to them all the repeated intimations, which he had had in dreams, respecting his future exaltation above his whole family[i]. For these reasons he was envied, hated, and persecuted by his brethren[k]. And when he came to them from his father, upon an errand of love, they conspired against him to kill him[l]. An opportunity offering at the moment, they sold him into the hands of strangers for twenty pieces of silver[m]. After that, he was accused of a crime he utterly abhorred, and, without any one to plead his cause, was cast into prison[n], where, for a time at least, "he was laid

---

[a] Isai. iv. 2. and xi. 1.   [b] Isai. xxvii. 6.   [c] Ps. lxxii. 16.
[d] Gen. xv. 5.   [e] Gen. xxii. 17.   [f] Ps. lxxx. 9—11.
[g] Gen. xxxvii. 3.   [h] Gen. xxxvii. 2.   [i] Gen. xxxvii. 5, 9.
[k] Gen. xxxvii. 4, 11.   [l] Gen. xxxvii. 18—20.
[m] Gen. xxxvii. 28.   [n] Gen. xxxix. 12—20

in irons," and galled with heavy fetters°; so "sorely did the archers grieve him, and shoot at him, and hate him."]

And can we err in tracing here the sufferings of our Lord?

[Jesus was, infinitely above all others, the well-beloved of his Father[p]; and, while he faithfully reproved the sins of his brethren, declared to them his future exaltation and glory[q]. Filled with envy and wrath against him, they said, as it were in malignant triumph, "This is the heir; come, let us kill him[r];" so cruelly "did they reward him evil for good, and hatred for his love[s]." When he was come to them from his Father with the most benevolent design, behold, one of his own disciples sold him, and *that* to strangers too, for thirty pieces of silver[t]. He was accused of blasphemy against God, and of rebellion against his king; and, without any one appearing to speak on his behalf[u], was instantly condemned; and thus, though "none could convince him of sin," "was numbered with the transgressors." Could there have been such a coincidence of circumstances between his lot and Joseph's, at least is it probable there would have been, if it had not been particularly ordained of God?]

We may pursue the comparison yet further, in,

III. His unshaken constancy—

Joseph was marvellously upheld under all his trials—

[Though he besought his brethren with cries and tears, we read not of any reproachful language that he used: when he entreated Pharaoh's butler to intercede for him, he did not so much as mention either his brethren, who had sold him, or his mistress, who had falsely accused him[x]: nor, while he was enduring his hard lot, did he once murmur or repine at the providence of God: through the whole of his trial he possessed his soul in patience: nor, when he had it in his power to revenge himself, did he render any thing but love for hatred, and good for evil. The *apparent* unkindness of his deportment, which he adopted for a time, was a violence done to his own feelings, in order that he might discern the real state of their minds, and reveal himself to them afterwards to better effect[y]. When the proper season was arrived, he fully evinced the tenderness of his heart, and the delight he took in the exercise of mercy; and, so far from upbraiding his brethren, he said all he could to extenuate their crime, and referred

---

[o] Ps. cv. 18.   [p] Matt. iii. 17.   [q] John vii. 7. and Matt. xxvi. 64.
[r] Matt. xxi. 38.   [s] Ps. cix. 3—5.   [t] Matt. xxvi. 15, 16.
[u] Isai. liii. 8. See Bp. Lowth's translation and note, and Ps. lxix. 20
[x] Gen. xl. 14, 15.   [y] Gen. xlii. 7, 9, 12.

the whole event to the overruling providence of God[z]. So effectually were "his hands strengthened by the mighty God of Jacob," that in no instance was he "overcome of evil, but at all times overcame evil with good."]

Our blessed Lord also shone like him, only with infinitely brighter lustre—

[Never did an inadvertent word drop from the lips of Jesus under all his persecutions: "When he was reviled, he reviled not again; when he suffered, threatened not; but committed himself to him that judgeth righteously[a]." "As a sheep before her shearers is dumb, so opened he not his mouth[b]" either in menaces, or complaints. His meekness was uniform, his fortitude undaunted, his patience invincible. He sought nothing but the good of those who were daily conspiring against his life: he wept over them, when they resisted all his overtures of mercy[c]: he even prayed for them, and apologized for their crimes, when they were in the very act of putting him to death[d]: and, after his resurrection, commanded that the offers of salvation through his blood should be made *first* to the very people who had so lately shed it[e].]

There is yet one more feature of resemblance to be noticed, in,

IV. His glorious advancement—

After all his trials Joseph was exalted to a throne—

[Through the good providence of God, Joseph was enabled to interpret the dreams of Pharaoh, and was, on that account, brought from the dungeon, and made, next to Pharaoh, the supreme governor of the Egyptian kingdom[f]: all were ordered to bow the knee to Joseph[g]; and all, who came for a supply of corn, received this direction, Go to Joseph[h]. Thus did God exalt him to be both "the shepherd and the stone of Israel," that he might not only provide for Egypt and the neighbouring kingdoms, but be an effectual support to all his kindred, and preserve the lives of those very persons who had sought his destruction.]

Can we reasonably doubt but that in this he was a type of Jesus?

[Jesus was raised from the prison of the grave by the effectual working of God's power: "he was highly exalted; and had a name given him above every name, that at the

---

[z] Gen. xlv. 5. [a] 1 Pet. ii. 23. [b] Isai. liii. 7.
[c] Luke xix. 41. [d] Luke xxiii. 34. [e] Luke xxiv. 47.
[f] Gen. xli. 14, 15, 41. [g] Gen. xli. 43. [h] Gen. xli. 55.

name of Jesus every knee should bow[i]:" "all power was committed to him in heaven and in earth; and all things were put under him, HE only excepted, who did put all things under him[k]." Whatever we want for our souls, we must receive it all out of his fulness[l]: the direction given to every living creature is, Go to Jesus, Look to Jesus[m]. And how does he exercise his power? Behold, he calls his sinful brethren from a land of want and misery, and brings them to his own land of peace and plenty. There he nourishes them with the bread of life, and "reigns over the house of Jacob for ever and ever." Thus, as "the great Shepherd of the sheep," he both feeds and rules his flock, while as "the foundation" and "corner-stone" he supports and connects, confirms and dignifies, all the "*Israel*" of God[n].]

By way of IMPROVEMENT we observe,

1. The purposes of God, whatever may be done to frustrate them, shall surely be accomplished—

[We are amazed at the variety of incidents, that *seemed* to put the elevation of Joseph, and of Christ, *almost* beyond the reach of Omnipotence itself. Yet God's purposes were accomplished by the very means used to defeat them. Thus shall it be with us also, if we confide in the word of God. Whatever means Satan, or the world, may use to "separate us from God," they shall not prevail. "What God has promised, he is able also to perform." Let us therefore trust in him; for He will work, and who shall let it? He hath purposed, and who shall disannul it? His counsel shall stand; and he will do all his pleasure[o].]

2. God's dearest children must expect many trials in their way to glory—

[Joseph, and Christ, endured much before their exaltation. And we also "through much tribulation shall enter into the kingdom." The number and weight of our trials are no grounds of concluding ourselves to be objects of God's displeasure: they should rather, especially if they be sanctified to us, be considered as tokens of his love[p]. As the Captain of our salvation was, so also must we be, made perfect through sufferings[q]. Let us then "arm ourselves with the mind that was in Christ." We shall surely have no reason to regret the difficulties of the way, when we have attained the rest prepared for us.]

---

[i] Phil. ii. 9—11. Ps. lxxii. 8, 9, 11.   [k] 1 Cor. xv. 27.   [l] John i. 16.
[m] Isai. xlv. 22. John vii. 37.   [n] Heb. xiii. 20. 1 Pet. ii. 6.
[o] Isai. xliii. 13. and xiv. 27. and xlvi. 10.   [p] Heb. xii. 6.
[q] Heb. ii. 10.

3. We should not labour to control events, but study rather to accommodate ourselves to the circumstances in which God has placed us—

[How often might Joseph have escaped from the house of Potiphar, or sent to his brethren the news of his exaltation in Egypt! But he left all in the hands of God, endeavouring only to fulfil his duty, whether as a slave or a steward, whether as a jailor or a prince. Thus did our Lord also, when he could in ten thousand ways have changed the course of events. Let us do likewise. Whatever be our circumstances or condition in life, let us be more desirous of glorifying God under them, than of contriving, by any means, to alter them. God's time and manner of accomplishing his own ends will be found infinitely better in the issue, than any we can devise[r]. Let us then tarry his leisure, and leave ourselves wholly to his disposal, and approve ourselves to him as faithful, and obedient children.]

[r] Isai. lv. 8, 9.

OUTLINE NO. 62

JOSEPH'S BRETHREN FULFILLING THE PROPHECY RESPECTING THEM.

Gen. 1. 15—17. *And when Joseph's brethren saw that their father was dead, they said, Joseph will peradventure hate us, and will certainly requite us all the evil which we did unto him. And they sent a messenger unto Joseph, saying, Thy father did command before he died, saying, So shall ye say unto Joseph; Forgive, I pray thee now, the trespass of thy brethren, and their sin; for they did unto thee evil: and now, we pray thee, forgive the trespass of the servants of the God of thy father. And Joseph wept when they spake unto him.*

THE heart of man by nature is vindictive. It was a just observation of Saul to David, "If a man find his enemy, will he let him go well away[a]?" Hence, when men have injured any person, they hate him, because they think he must of necessity have become their enemy: and, if they are within the reach of his power, they fear him, because they conclude that he will avail himself of any favourable opportunity to revenge himself upon them. It was thus with Joseph's brethren. Their father being dead, and they being entirely at the mercy of their brother whom they had sold into Egypt, they concluded, that " he

[a] 1 Sam. xxiv. 19.

62.] JOSEPH'S BRETHREN FULFIL THE PROPHECY.

would requite them all the evil which they had formerly done unto him." It is probable that this apprehension was strengthened by a recollection of what their father Jacob had suffered from the vindictive spirit of Esau: " The days of mourning for my father are at hand; then will I slay my brother Jacob." Full of fear, they sent to Joseph to implore his forgiveness: which, as will be seen, they readily obtained.

The points to which we would direct your attention are,

I. The means they used to conciliate his favour—

These were certainly well adapted to the end proposed.

1. They plead the dying request of their revered father—

[What more cogent argument could be used with a pious mind than this? The dying request of a friend is sacred: and how much more of a parent, a parent of such consummate piety as Jacob! A request too so reasonable in itself, and so conducive to the welfare of his whole family! It is probable indeed that the representation which they gave of their father's request was not altogether correct. We cannot conceive that Jacob should have entertained any suspicions about the subsequent conduct of Joseph; or that, if he had, he would have left a posthumous request to be made through his other children, when he could have urged it himself with so much more effect in his lifetime. The probability is, that he enjoined *them* to act in a submissive spirit towards Joseph, and not by any refractory conduct to bring upon themselves his displeasure. But, however this might be, the plea was very powerful, and could not fail of obtaining for them the favour they implored. True indeed it is, that persons of a headstrong disposition frequently forget, and *that* at no distant period, the dying advices of their parents — — — but it was not probable that Joseph should do so, after having so long evinced a disposition most contrary to that of which he was suspected.]

2. They unite with it their own most humble and earnest entreaties—

[However strong may be our propensity to revenge, the entreaties of a penitent offender will disarm us. It is scarcely possible for a man to revenge himself on one who lies prostrate at his feet. But there is a very peculiar delicacy in this address which they make to Joseph: in speaking to him of Jacob, they do not designate him as *their* father, but as *his;*

"*Thy* father did command." And when they speak to him of themselves, they do not designate themselves either as Jacob's sons, or as Joseph's brethren, but as "the servants of the God of thy father;" thus keeping out of view every thing which might appear presumptuous, and calling to their aid Joseph's love to his parent, and his duty to his God. If this was the result of ingenuity, we admire it; but if of real humility, we greatly applaud it: for there is a delicacy in humility, a beautiful and lovely delicacy, which, though in words it amount to little, as indicating the spirit by which a man is actuated, is extremely valuable. The true point to be aimed at in asking forgiveness is humility: to be open and ingenuous in our confessions, to take shame to ourselves for what we have done amiss, and to make all the reparation in our power, this is the spirit we should cultivate; and it is pleasing to see these long-obdurate men brought at last to a measure of this experience.]

Reserving for a while our further observations on this part of our subject, we pass on to notice,

II. The effect produced on Joseph's mind—

Considering how long they had forborne to humble themselves aright, he might well have upbraided them, both with their former cruelty, and their subsequent impenitence: or he might have imposed conditions upon them, as Solomon afterwards did on Shimei: or he might have pardoned them in kind and condescending terms. But the way in which he expressed his forgiveness was more eloquent and convincing than any words which human ingenuity could ever have devised: "Joseph *wept* when they spake unto him."

His weeping was from mixed emotions in his mind. The human heart is susceptible of greatly diversified impressions even at the same moment. The two Marys, when they had ascertained beyond a doubt the resurrection of their Lord, "departed from the sepulchre with fear and great joy[b]." Thus in the breast of Joseph, we apprehend, there was a mixture both of grief and joy:

1. Of grief—

[It must have been inexpressibly painful to him to have such suspicions entertained respecting him, especially after he had for the space of seventeen years manifested such uniform kindness towards them. A man possessed of a generous mind

[b] Matt. xxviii. 8.

cannot endure that all the love he exercises should be construed as a mere hypocritical pretence, covering a rooted enmity that will break forth as soon as an opportunity shall enable him to manifest it with effect: yea, the more conscious a man feels of his own integrity, the more deeply will he feel such unfounded suspicions. If jealousy is painful to him who harbours it, it is no less painful to him who is undeservedly the object of it. This avowal therefore of their secret fears could not but inflict a deep wound on his tender spirit.

At the same time it must be distressing to Joseph to see, that, after all they had witnessed of piety in their father Jacob, and all the reason they had to believe he was possessed of the same divine principle, they should betray such ignorance of religion, as to suppose, that, where the lowest degrees of it existed, a vindictive spirit could be indulged. If indeed they thought him a determined hypocrite, they might suppose him capable of harbouring such resentment: but, if he had any hope of forgiveness from God himself, he never could suffer such feelings to rankle in his breast. Whilst therefore they doubted the influence of true religion in him, they shewed, that they were in a very great degree strangers to it themselves: and this discovery must have been painful to him, in proportion to the love he bore them, and the desire he felt for their eternal welfare. Hence that expression of his, " Am I in the place of God," to whom exclusively " vengeance belongs," and whose prerogative, if I avenged myself, I should usurp[c]?]

2. Of joy—

[Whilst they thus betrayed an ignorance of genuine religion, they gave by their voluntary humiliation some reason to hope that the seeds of true piety were springing up in their souls. And this hope doubtless filled him with holy joy. Say, any of you, who have wept over an abandoned child, or the impiety of a friend or brother, what joy has not sprung up in your bosom when you have first seen the obdurate heart to relent, and the tears of penitential sorrow to flow down, so as to justify a hope that a work of grace was begun in the soul! How have you secretly lifted up your heart to God in devout aspirations, to entreat, that he would confirm the rising purpose, and perfect in their souls the work he had begun! Doubtless then, in such a pious mind as Joseph's, the very first dawn of piety in his obdurate brethren could not but cause the tear of love and gratitude to start from his eyes.

Another thought too, that could not fail of rushing into his mind, and filling him with adoring gratitude to God, was, that in this act of humiliation his brethren had voluntarily fulfilled those dreams which they had before accomplished only from

[c] Rom. xii. 19. with Gen. l. 19.

necessity and constraint. To trace the ways of Providence, and especially to see how mysteriously God has dealt with us, and made all things to work together for our good, is one of the sublimest enjoyments that we can experience on earth; and I doubt not but that it will constitute in no small degree the blessedness of heaven. Well therefore might Joseph now weep for joy, more especially as the exaltation which all his previous trials had led to, enabled him now to requite, not evil for evil, as they feared, but good for evil, and to " overcome evil with good[d]."]

From hence then we may LEARN,

1. To ask forgiveness of those whom we have injured—

[This is a hard task to an unhumbled spirit: but it is indispensably necessary: nor can any man be upright before God, who will not submit to it. To approach the table of the Lord without first endeavouring to conciliate our offended brother is directly to oppose the command of God, who says, " Leave there thy gift before the altar, and go thy way:" " *Go thy way: first* be reconciled to thy brother, and *then* come and offer thy gift[e]." Many will be the excuses which we shall be ready to offer for our neglect of this duty;— — — but the command of God is plain and express; and a compliance with it is indispensable, to prove that our penitence is sincere: nor can we ever obtain forgiveness from God, if we are too proud to solicit forgiveness from man.]

2. To forgive those who have injured us—

[This is a far easier duty than the other; because, whilst a compliance with the other humbles us, the performance of this elevates and exalts us. Is it asked, " How often shall I forgive an offending brother? till seven times?" I answer, Yes, and "till seventy times seven[f]." Nor is our forgiveness to be merely negative, such as consists in a forbearance from retaliation: no; it must be real, cordial, permanent: for in the parable of the unforgiving servant who is represented as cast into prison till he shall have paid the uttermost farthing, we are warned, " So also shall your heavenly Father do unto you, if ye *from your hearts* forgive not every one his brother their trespasses[g]." Let not any one then say, ' I cannot forgive, or, Though I forgive, I cannot forget:' for we must, in the mercy which we extend towards man, resemble that which we ourselves hope to receive from God; and must " forgive our brother as completely and cordially as God for Christ's sake hath forgiven us[h]."]

[d] Rom. xii. 20, 21. [e] Matt. v. 23, 24. [f] Matt. xviii. 21, 22
[g] Matt. xviii. 35. [h] Eph. iv. 32.

EXODUS.

OUTLINE NO. 63

THE BURNING BUSH.

Exod. iii. 2, 3. *The angel of the Lord appeared unto him in a flame of fire out of the midst of a bush: and he looked, and, behold, the bush burned with fire, and the bush was not consumed. And Moses said, I will now turn aside and see this great sight, why the bush is not burnt.*

IF God have on some occasions revealed himself to persons, when, like Saul, they have been in the very act of committing the most heinous sins[a], he has more generally favoured them when they have been occupied, like the shepherds, in their proper calling[b]. Moses was keeping the flock of Jethro his father-in-law, when God appeared to him in a burning bush, and gave him a commission to deliver Israel from their bondage in Egypt. By this extraordinary appearance God not merely awakened the curiosity of Moses, but conveyed to him some very important instruction; to elucidate which we shall,

I. Shew what was intended by the burning bush—

It was intended to represent the state and condition—

1. Of the Israelites in Egypt—

[They were cruelly oppressed, and every effort was made to destroy them[c]. Nor had they in themselves any more ability to withstand their enemies, than a thorny bush has to resist the action of fire. Yet not only were they preserved from destruction, but they even multiplied in proportion as means were used to prevent their increase.]

2. Of the church of God in the world—

[The church, whose state was typified by that of Israel, has at all times suffered by persecution, though it has enjoyed

---

[a] Acts ix. 4. [b] Luke ii. 8, 9. [c] Exod. i. 9—22.

some intervals of comparative rest. And, considering that all the powers of the world have been confederate against it, we may well be amazed that it has not been utterly consumed. But it has endured the fiery trial to this hour, and still defies the impotent attacks of all its adversaries.]

3. Of every individual in the church—

[The declaration that "all who would live godly in Christ Jesus should suffer persecution," has been verified in every place and every age: "the third part are, and ever will be, brought through the fire." And it is no less than a miracle, that, when the believer has so many enemies, both without and within, he does not "make shipwreck of faith and of a good conscience." But the furnace, instead of destroying, purifies and refines him; and his very graces are perfected by the trials that endanger their existence[d].]

Having pointed out both the primary and more remote signification of this phenomenon, we shall,

II. Account for the miracle which it exhibited—

Well might the sight of a bush burning, but not consumed, excite the astonishment of Moses: but his wonder would cease when he found that *God was in the bush*.

The person here called "the angel of the Lord" was Christ—

[The angel expressly called himself "The God of Abraham, the God of Isaac, and the God of Jacob;" which sufficiently proves that he could not be a *created* angel, seeing that it would be the most daring blasphemy in any creature to assume that incommunicable title of Jehovah: yet it was not God the Father: for St. Stephen, recording this history, informs us, that "God sent Moses by the hand of the angel[e]:" consequently the angel was God the Son, and not God the Father. Indeed Christ, who is elsewhere called "The angel of the covenant," was the person, who, in *all* the appearances of God to man, assumed the human or angelic shape; thereby preparing the world for the fuller manifestation of himself in his incarnate state. And it is on this account that he is called "The image of the invisible God[f]."]

It was his presence with the Israelites that prevented their destruction—

[He was in the bush, and *therefore* the bush was not consumed: so he was in the midst of his oppressed people; and

[d] Rom. v. 3—5.   [e] Acts vii. 30—35.   [f] Col. i. 15.

therefore the Egyptians could not prevail against them. Christ was among them before he gave them any symbol of his presence; for it was he who rendered the assistance of the midwives unnecessary, and emboldened them to withstand the commands of Pharaoh. He was afterwards with them in the pillar and the cloud, protecting them from the Egyptian hosts, and stopping the progress of their enemies till they were overwhelmed in the sea. When, for the punishment of their sins, he refused to go with them, they were sure to be overpowered[g]: but whenever he returned in mercy to them, they prospered and prevailed.]

It is that same presence that preserves the church and every member of it—

[Christ has said, " Lo, I am with you alway, even to the end of the world;" and hence it is that " the gates of hell have never prevailed against the church;" yea, we are assured, they never shall prevail. We are also told that " he dwelleth in the hearts" of all his people[h], and is " their life[i];" and that, whereinsoever they live and act, it is not so much they, as Christ in them[k]. It is by this consideration that he encourages them to " go through fire and water," persuaded that no evil shall happen to them[l]. And to his continued interposition and support they must ascribe their preservation in every danger, and their deliverance from every enemy[m].]

Let us now *"turn aside and behold this great sight"* (let us turn from every worldly thought, and inspect this wonderful appearance, not with curiosity, but profoundest reverence); let us OBSERVE herein,

1. To what state God's most favoured people may be reduced—

[Your afflictions may be heavy. But are any discouraged by reason of their great trials? Be it known that tribulation is the way to the kingdom; and all, who arrive there, have trodden the same path[n]. Nor need we be alarmed at any fire that is kindled for us, since Christ will be with us in the midst of it[o], and " bring us out of it purified as gold."]

2. What they may expect at God's hands—

[In seasons of great trial we are tempted to think that God has forsaken us: but he never was more immediately present with the Hebrew youths, than when they were cast into the furnace; nor did he ever feel more love to his own

---

[g] Numb. xiv. 42—45. Josh. vii. 4, 5.   [h] Eph. iii. 17.
[i] Col. iii. 4.   [k] Gal. ii. 20.   [l] Ps. xlvi. 5.
[m] Ps. cxxiv. 1—5.   [n] Acts xiv. 22. Rev. vii. 14.   [o] Isai. xli. 10.

Son, than in the hour when he cried, "My God, my God, why hast thou forsaken me?" Let us then learn to trust God, and expect that, when we walk through the fire, we shall not be burned[p].]

3. What in the midst of all their trials should be their chief concern—

[Moses in his valedictory address to the twelve tribes, congratulates Joseph on "*the good-will of Him who dwelt in the bush*[q]." And most truly are they blessed who are thus interested in the divine favour. To them God is "a wall of fire" for their protection[r]: but to others he is "a consuming fire" for their destruction[s]. Alas! alas! in what a fearful state are they, who shall be "cast into the lake of fire and brimstone," into "a fire that never shall be quenched," and in which they shall continue unconsumed to all eternity! Oh! "who can dwell with everlasting burnings[t]?" But, if we are reconciled to him in the Son of his love, we have nothing to fear: we have nothing to fear either in time or eternity: for, however painful our state in this world may be, he will support us with his presence; and in the world to come, we shall be for ever beyond the reach of harm, even in "his immediate presence, where is the fulness of joy for evermore." Seek then his favour; yea, seek it with your whole hearts — — —]

[p] Isai. xliii. 2.   [q] Deut. xxxiii. 16.   [r] Zech. ii. 5.
[s] Heb. xii. 29.   [t] Isai. xxxiii. 14.

OUTLINE NO. 64
GOD'S PRESENCE WITH HIS PEOPLE.

Exod. iii. 12. *And he said, Certainly I will be with thee.*

THERE is nothing more amiable in the character of a saint than true and genuine humility. Without that virtue, all graces are defective, and all attainments worthless in the sight of God. But it is no uncommon thing to see other dispositions assuming the garb of humility, and claiming an excellence which they do not possess. The Prophet Jeremiah, when called to the prophetic office, declined it under an idea that he was "a child, and unable to speak." But God said to him, "Say not, I am a child: for thou shalt go to all that I shall send thee, and whatsoever I shall command thee thou shalt speak[a]." His

[a] Jer. i. 4—7.

pretended insufficiency for the work was, in reality, no other than a cover for his dread of the dangers to which it would expose him: and therefore God, in order to remove the impediment, replied, "Be not afraid of their faces; for I am with thee, to deliver thee[b]." Thus Moses, when God said to him, "Come now, and I will send thee unto Pharaoh, that thou mayest bring forth my people, the children of Israel, out of Egypt;" replied, "Who am I, that I should go unto Pharaoh, and that I should bring forth the children of Israel out of Egypt[c]?" This was specious enough, and had the semblance of true humility; but it was only a pretext, and a cover to his fears and unbelief. He had, forty years before, exerted himself with great vigour in behalf of that people, and had even slain an Egyptian who was contending with them: but they had thrust him from them, saying, "Who made thee a ruler and a judge over us?" and Pharaoh had sought his life, as forfeited to the laws of the land. Now, therefore, he was afraid that the people would shew the same disregard of his efforts, and that his slaughter of the Egyptian would be visited with the punishment which the laws of the land denounced against him. This, indeed, did not at first sight appear to be his real motive: but his numerous refusals of the office delegated to him, repeated as they were under a variety of pretexts, clearly discovered at last what was in his heart, and justly excited the displeasure of God against him[d]. But the very first answer of God should have been quite sufficient to remove every apprehension. God said to him, "Certainly I will be with thee:" and, having that assurance, he should without hesitation have gone forth to his destined labours.

Let us consider,

I. The extent of the promise—

As relating to him, it comprehended all that he could wish—

[True, his work was arduous, and to unassisted man

[b] Jer. i. 8. [c] Exod. iii. 10, 11. [d] Exod. iv. 13, 14, 19.

impracticable: but, if God was with him, what could he have to fear? He would be guided by a wisdom that could not err, and be aided by a power which could not be overcome. With such an assurance, what had he to do with discouragements? Could Pharaoh hurt him, whilst he was under such protection; or the Israelites withstand his solicitations, when enforced by such powerful energy on their minds? Every difficulty should have vanished from his mind; and he should have leaped for joy at the prospect of effecting so great and good a work.]

But it relates to us also, and pledges God to an equal extent in our behalf—

[A similar promise was given to Joshua, on an occasion precisely similar[e]: and that is quoted by the Apostle Paul as applicable to every true believer: "God hath said, I will never leave thee, nor forsake thee: so that WE may boldly say, The Lord is MY helper, and I will not fear what man shall do unto me[f]." Here *the very promise made to Moses*, is *renewed to Joshua*, and *declared to belong to us also*. Whatever difficulties, therefore, we may have to encounter in the discharge of our duty to God, we need not fear: his promised presence shall be with us in our efforts, and his almighty power secure to us a successful issue.]

The more minute consideration of the subject will fall under the next head of my discourse, whilst I endeavour to shew,

II. The encouragement it affords to us—

We may properly view it, in the first place, as applicable to Ministers—

[Ministers have, if I may so speak, the very same office delegated to them as was assigned to Moses: they are sent to bring men out of spiritual thraldom, and to deliver them from a bondage far more terrible than that of Egypt. The power that opposes them is far stronger than that of Pharaoh; and the unhappy captives are in love with their chains: they are themselves as averse to leave their hard taskmaster, as he is to lose their services. Were we to go in our own strength, we should soon desert our post; as Moses did, when, in reliance on his own arm, he prematurely proffered to the people his assistance. But with the promise of God's presence, a promise specifically given to us by our Divine Master for our encouragement[g], we go forth with confidence; and to every obstacle that is in our way, we say, "Who art thou, O great

[e] Josh. i. 5.   [f] Heb. xiii. 5, 6.   [g] Matt. xxviii. 18.

mountain? Before Zerubbabel thou shalt become a plain[h]."
We know that the persons to whom we speak are as incapable of hearing our words, as dry bones scattered upon the face of the earth: yet do we not despond, or even doubt the efficacy of our ministrations for those to whom we are sent: and, in dependence on this word, we hope and believe, that the word which we speak shall prove " the power of God to the salvation" of those who hear it. We are not unmindful of the question put by the Apostle, " Who is sufficient for these things?" but, if the rod of Moses wrought effectually in his hand for the deliverance of Israel, we have no fear but that the word of God, by whomsoever administered, shall be alike effectual for all the ends for which it is sent. It is " the rod of God's strength;" and not all the powers of darkness shall be able to withstand it.]

But it is also applicable to God's people generally throughout the world—

[To this extent, as we have before observed, St. Paul applies it: and every believer needs it for his support. Every one is engaged in a great work, for which no finite power is sufficient: every one, therefore, needs to be encouraged with an assurance, that God will be with him in all his endeavours to perform it, and will secure to him the desired success. Believer, hast thou much to *do* for God, even so much as thou couldest have no hope of effecting without the arm of Omnipotence exerted in thy behalf? Hear what God has said for thine encouragement: " Fear thou not, for I am with thee; be not dismayed, for I am thy God: I will strengthen thee; yea, I will help thee; yea, I will uphold thee with the right hand of my righteousness[i]." See here, how God, in every successive part of these promises, accommodates himself to thy weakness and thy fears. When he says, " I am with thee," a thought may perhaps arise, that he will be with thee only to witness thy defeat: he therefore adds, " I will be thy God." Does a sense of thy weakness press upon thee? he further says, " I will strengthen thee." Art thou still discouraged, because the work is left to thee? he adds, " I will help thee." Art thou still dejected, through an apprehension of thy failure at last? he takes the whole responsibility on himself, and declares, for thy comfort, " I will altogether uphold thee with the right hand of my righteousness." This may serve to shew (what we forbore to specify under the former head) *the extent* to which this promise goes, in relation to every thing which our necessities may require.

Again; Hast thou also much to *suffer* for God in thy Christian course? Doubtless thou must have some cross to bear, else thou couldest not be conformed fully to thy Saviour's image. But, whether thy trials be more or less severe, the

[h] Zech. iv. 7.   [i] Isai. xli. 10.

promise in my text secures to thee an effectual help, and a sure deliverance. For thus saith the Lord: "When thou passest through the waters, *I will be with thee;* and through the rivers, they shall not overflow thee: when thou walkest through the fire, thou shalt not be burned; neither shall the flame kindle upon thee: for I am the Lord thy God, the Holy One of Israel, thy Saviour [k]." Here again *the extent* of the promise clearly appears, and its perfect sufficiency for every trial to which thou canst be exposed.

Is there yet a lurking apprehension that *in the extremity of death* thy heart will fail? At this season, also, shall the presence of thy God afford thee effectual support: "Though I walk through the valley of the shadow of death, I will fear no evil; for *thou art with me;* thy rod and thy staff they comfort me[1]." Now, though the valley of this shadow of death may comprehend the whole of the present life as beset with snares and difficulties, yet it must include the closing scenes of life, as well as those that have preceded it; and, consequently, when our flesh and heart fail, we may be assured that "God will be the strength of our heart, and our portion for ever [m]."]

LEARN from hence—

1. To undertake nothing but in dependence on God—

[When God vouchsafed his assistance to Israel, no man could stand before them: but when they went up against the Canaanites in dependence on an arm of flesh, they were put to flight and slain[n]. So it will be with us, if we presume to engage in any thing without first asking counsel, and imploring help, from him. God is jealous of his own honour: and if we place our reliance on any thing but him, we must expect a curse, and not a blessing, on all our labours[o].]

2. To shrink from nothing to which he calls us—

[If Moses was forbidden to shrink from the duties imposed on him, what shall we not willingly and confidently undertake for God? We must not contemplate human means, when the path of duty is clear; but must expect him to "perfect his own strength in our weakness." With him it is alike "easy to save by many or by few:" nor need we doubt a moment, but that "through Christ strengthening us we can do all things." "If God be for us, who can be against us?"]

3. To despair of nothing which we undertake at his command—

[We may be in the path of duty, and yet find many dif-

---

[k] Isai. xliii. 2, 3.   [1] Ps. xxiii. 4.   [m] Ps. lxxiii. 26.
[n] Numb. xiv. 43—45.   [o] Jer. xvii. 5, 6.

ficulties, even such as may appear utterly insuperable. Moses himself was so discouraged by his want of success, that he complained of God as having disappointed and deceived him. But he succeeded at last: and the very difficulties which had discouraged him served but the more to illustrate the power and grace of God. So may we find it for a season: but we should bear in mind, that his word, which he has pledged to us, is immutable, and that his counsel shall stand, though earth and hell should combine to defeat it. Let us then " commit our every way to him;" and, with a holy confidence, advance, " strong in the Lord, and in the power of his might."]

OUTLINE NO. 65

THE SELF-EXISTENCE AND IMMUTABILITY OF GOD.

Exod. iii. 14. *And God said unto Moses,* I AM THAT I AM: *and He said, Thus shalt thou say unto the children of Israel,* I AM *hath sent me unto you.*

IT is of great importance that Ministers should be considered as ambassadors of God. And that they should deliver nothing which they cannot enforce with, Thus saith the Lord. Without this, their word can have but little weight. But ministrations thus supported will produce the happiest effects. Moses was commissioned to offer deliverance to the oppressed Israelites. But he rightly judged that they would ask, from whence he had his authority. He therefore inquired of God, what answer he should return. And received from God the direction recorded in the text.

To understand the words aright, we must consider,

I. The title God assumed—

The Deity had hitherto revealed himself to man by the name of God Almighty. Though he had been called JEHOVAH, he was not fully known by that name, even to his most highly-favoured servants[a]. He now was pleased to assume a title similar to that; but, if possible, of still plainer import—

The name, I AM THAT I AM, represents him to be,

1. Self-existent—

[a] Exod. vi. 3.

[Creatures have only a derived, and therefore a dependent, existence. They are now what they once were not, and may again cease to be. But God from all eternity was precisely what he now is. To him therefore this august title may be properly applied. Nor are there wanting other similar descriptions of him to confirm it[b].]

2. Immutable—

[Every creature in earth and heaven is liable to change. But "with God there is no variableness, neither shadow of turning." He himself claims immutability as his own peculiar prerogative[c]. And in this view, the title assumed in the text must ever belong to him.]

3. Incomprehensible—

[No words can convey, or imagination conceive, an adequate idea of God[d]. Hence God does not endeavour to explain his nature to Moses. But, by declaring himself to be what he is, intimates, that he is what can neither be comprehended nor expressed. His answer, in effect, was similar to that which he afterwards gave to Manoah[e].]

The title thus explained, it will be proper to consider,

II. For what end he assumed it—

The Israelites were extremely debased by means of their long bondage. It was necessary therefore to prepare their minds for the intended deliverance—

[Though they groaned under their oppression, they were too much reconciled to their yoke. They rather affected a mitigation of trouble, than the attainment of liberty. Though the promises made to their fathers were not wholly forgotten, the accomplishment of them was not cordially desired. Indeed, they scarcely conceived it possible that their emancipation should be effected. Hence it was necessary to stimulate their desires, renew their hopes, and confirm their expectations, of a better country.]

The title which God assumed was admirably adapted to this end—

[If God was so incomprehensible a Being, he could easily devise means of executing his own sovereign will and pleasure. If he was the one self-existent, independent Creator of the universe, all creatures must be wholly subject to his control. And if he were absolutely immutable, he could not recede

[b] Ps. cii. 27. Rev. i. 4.   [c] Mal. iii. 6.
[d] Job xi. 7. 1 Tim. vi. 16.   [e] Judg. xiii. 17, 18.

65.] SELF-EXISTENCE AND IMMUTABILITY OF GOD. 329

from the covenant entered into with their fathers. He therefore could not want either inclination or power to deliver them. Yea, He could not but deliver them for his own great name's sake. He could not be I AM, if his promised interposition should be either withheld or defeated. Thus the declaration of his name must inspire them with confidence, and induce them willingly to put themselves under the direction of Moses.]

INFER,

1. What a solemn attention does the Gospel demand!

[The Gospel is a message of mercy to those who are in bondage to sin. And they who preach it are ambassadors from the great I AM. Jesus, who sends them forth, assumes to himself this very title[f]. To the same effect also his character is drawn in the Epistle to the Hebrews[g]. He has commissioned his servants to go forth into all the world[h]; and promised (as God did to Moses) to be always with them[i]. Shall we then make light of the mercy which He offers to us; or doubt his power and willingness to fulfil his promises? Shall we thrust away his servants, saying, Why dost thou interfere with us[k]? Let us remember who it is that speaks to us in the Gospel[l]. Every faithful Minister may say, I AM hath sent me unto you. Nor, though miracles have ceased, shall signs be wanting to confirm the word: the deaf shall hear, the blind see, the lame walk, the lepers be cleansed. And blessed is he whosoever shall not be offended at the Redeemer's voice[m].]

2. What encouragement is here afforded to those who are groaning under spiritual bondage!

[God brought out his people safely, notwithstanding all their difficulties; and in due time put them into possession of the promised land. Shall the spiritual redemption offered by him be less effectual? Are not his power and faithfulness the same as in former ages[n]? Will he not remove our obstacles, supply our wants, and destroy our enemies? Surely there are none so weak but they shall be made to triumph[o]. Nor shall the Prince of Darkness oppose with more success than Pharaoh[p]. Behold, then, I AM hath sent me to proclaim these glad tidings. Let all arise, and cast off their yoke, and burst their bands asunder. Let not unbelief represent the obstacles as insurmountable; nor fear induce you to comply

[f] John viii. 58.   [g] Heb. xiii. 8.   [h] Mark xvi. 15.
[i] Matt. xxviii. 20.   [k] Acts vii. 27.   [l] Luke x. 16.
[m] Matt. xi. 5, 6.   [n] Isai. lix. 1.   [o] Isai. xlix. 24, 25.
[p] Rom. xvi. 20.

with the imperious dictates of the world^q. Behold! the Pillar and the Cloud are ready to conduct your path. The great I AM is for you: who then can be against you? Go forth; and universal nature shall applaud your steps^r.]

q Pharaoh, after many successive plagues, agreed first that they should sacrifice to God *in the land, but not in the wilderness;* then that they should go *into the wilderness, but not far;* then that *the men* should go, but *without the women or children;* then that *the women and children, but not the flocks.* Exod. viii. 25, 28. and x. 11, 24. Thus the world would prescribe limits to the service we shall pay to God. r Isai. lv. 12.

OUTLINE NO. 66

MOSES DECLINING THE COMMISSION GIVEN HIM.

Exod. iv. 10—14. *And Moses said unto the Lord, O my Lord, I am not eloquent, neither heretofore, nor since thou hast spoken unto thy servant: but I am slow of speech, and of a slow tongue. And the Lord said unto him, Who hath made man's mouth? or who maketh the dumb, or deaf, or the seeing, or the blind? have not I the Lord? Now therefore go; and I will be with thy mouth, and teach thee what thou shalt say. And he said, O my Lord, send, I pray thee, by the hand of him whom thou wilt send. And the anger of the Lord was kindled against Moses.*

THAT iniquity should prevail among the blind and ignorant, is no more than might reasonably be expected: but when we behold it in the most eminent saints, we are ready to exclaim, "Lord, what is man, that thou art mindful of him, and the son of man, that thou so regardest him?" It should seem indeed that God has determined to stain the pride of human glory, by recording the faults of his most favoured servants. It is remarkable that those who are most noted in Scripture for their piety, not only fell, but manifested their weakness in those very graces for which they were most distinguished. Abraham yielded to unbelief, Job to impatience, Moses to anger, Peter to fear. The circumstances here related concerning Moses, clearly shew, not only what Moses was, but what human nature is, when put to the trial. The following observations therefore, while they elucidate the text, will lead us to behold our own faces as in a glass.

I. There is in man a backwardness to engage in God's service—

[Who was this man? Moses, *in some respects* the most pious of mankind. What was the service to which he was called? The most honourable and beneficial that could possibly be assigned him ——— Yet, with a pertinacity truly surprising, he persisted in declining it, and desired that any one might be employed in it rather than he [a].

We, it is true, are called to no *such* service. But is there no work committed to us? Has not God appeared to *us* in his word, and commanded us to devote ourselves to his service? Has not the Saviour bidden us to "deny ourselves, and take up our cross daily, and follow him?" And have we not shewn an utter aversion to obey his call? Glorious as his service is, have we not declined it; and, like Moses, been more studious of our own ease than either of God's honour or the benefit of our fellow-creatures? Because we have foreseen difficulties, we have been unwilling to embark in the cause of God and of our own souls; when we ought rather to have gloried in enduring hardships for God, and closed with the proposal at once, saying, "Here am I, Lord; send me [b]."]

II. We are prone to cloke this backwardness with vain excuses—

[Moses would not in plain terms refuse to obey his God; but he tried by every method to excuse himself from undertaking the office assigned him. He first pretends to decline through modesty [c]: and we might have given him credit for real humility, if his subsequent refusals had not shewn that he was actuated by a far different principle. When God has obviated all objections arising from his unworthiness, then, in direct opposition to God's promise, he objects, that the people will not believe his message [d]. To remove all apprehensions on this ground, God works three miracles before him, and commissions him to perform the same in the sight of Pharaoh and the people of Israel [e]. Still averse to engage in this work, he pleads his want of eloquence, and his consequent unfitness for such an undertaking [f]. To obviate this, God asks him, "Who made man's mouth;" and whether He, who had given him the faculty of speech, was not able to give effect to his endeavours? Yea, he promises to "be with him, and to teach him what he shall say." And does not all this overcome his reluctance? No: he still declines the service, and begs that God would employ any other person rather than himself.

Now we say that these were *vain* excuses: for the real

---

[a] ver. 13.   [b] Isai. vi. 8.   [c] Exod. iii. 11.
[d] Comp. Exod. iii. 18. with iv. 1.   [e] ver. 2—9.   [f] The text.

principles by which he was actuated, were unbelief and cowardice. He had failed in this attempt forty years before, when he had run unsent, and acted in his own strength, and striven for the victory with no other than carnal weapons; and now he is apprehensive of another failure, when expressly sent, and furnished with a wonder-working rod, and assured of success by a God of almighty power and unimpeachable veracity. Moreover, as on the former occasion Pharaoh sought his life, he is afraid to put himself within his reach, lest he should execute his threats upon him[g].

And what are the pleas whereby we attempt to justify or extenuate our neglect of God? Have they any solidity? yea, have they any foundation in truth? Are they not mere excuses? and is not an aversion to the service to which we are called, the true reason of our declining to engage in it? We will not say in plain words, 'I hate God; I hate religion; I am determined never to follow the Saviour's steps:' but we pretend that this is not a convenient season, or that the work to which we are called is impracticable. Yes; if we will only suffer our own consciences to speak, they will tell us that our pleas are mere excuses, and that, in fact, we are hypocrites, and dissemblers with God.]

III. However satisfactory our excuses may appear to ourselves, they will only bring upon us the divine displeasure—

[Possibly Moses was unable to discern the true workings of his own heart: but did not God spy them out? and was not God's anger kindled against him? How God manifested his anger, we know not: it is sufficient to know God's "judgment was according to truth."

Who then are we, that we should think to impose upon God, or to hide from him the motives by which we are actuated? Has he not cautioned us sufficiently against such fatal mistakes, saying, "Be not deceived; God is not mocked: whatsoever a man soweth, that shall he also reap?" Has he not warned us, that we shall certainly incur his displeasure, if we suffer any thing to keep us back from his service? He has mentioned the excuses made by those whom he invited to his feast: one had bought a piece of ground; and another a yoke of oxen which he wanted to see; another had married a wife, and therefore could not come. Now these were as weighty excuses for not going to an entertainment, as any that you can urge for not serving your God: and yet he declared that none of them should ever *taste* of his supper[h]. If this was the doom of those who were *invited but once*, do you think that *you*

---

[g] ver. 19.   [h] Luke xiv. 18—24.

shall *sit down at* his supper, who have *rejected ten thousand* invitations? No: you may excuse your supineness by saying, "There is a lion in the way; there is a lion in the streets;" but he will say, "Thou wicked and slothful servant!" "Cast the unprofitable servant into outer darkness." The spies thought they had reason enough for postponing the invasion of the promised land: but they were all excluded from it; as were all others who yielded to their pernicious counsels.]

Advice—

1. Beware of self-deception—

[The heart is deceitful above all things: and we have a subtle adversary, who will not fail to help forward the most fatal delusions. We see how others are biassed, and how empty the pleas are by which they often justify their conduct. Let us see in them an image of ourselves; and learn to suspect the treachery of our own hearts. Let us remember that we cannot deceive our God; and that the time is coming when we shall be judged, not by our professions, but by our practice.]

2. Learn what are the duties to which you are called—

[With respect to particular steps in life, it may be extremely difficult to judge[i]: but about a life of devotedness to God there can be no doubt. Endeavour then to ascertain what the Scriptures require of you; and set yourselves instantly to fulfil it. Do not invent excuses to shift off your duty; but look up to God to direct you in his way, and to strengthen you for the performance of all his will.]

3. Yield not to any discouragements in the way of duty—

[It is not to be expected that you should meet with no difficulties. You must doubtless have conflicts, and many of them severe: but "greater is He that is in you than he that is in the world." You may not improperly, in a view of your own weakness, say, "Who is sufficient for these things?" but you must never forget who has said, "My grace is sufficient for you." Go on then, expecting assuredly that "your strength shall be according to your day of trial;" that the weaker you are in yourselves, the more shall "Jehovah's strength be magnified in your weakness;" and that "you shall at last be more than conquerors through Him that loved you."]

---

[i] For instance, whether one should go to such or such a station; whether one should undertake the office of a Missionary, &c.

OUTLINE NO. 67
PHARAOH'S IMPIETY.

Exod. v. 2. *And Pharaoh said, Who is the Lord, that I should obey his voice, to let Israel go? I know not the Lord, neither will I let Israel go.*

MANY of the characters in the Old Testament are "set forth to us as examples;" and their history is recorded "for our admonition, upon whom the ends of the world are come[a]." Amongst these, Pharaoh holds a very conspicuous place. When he persisted in his rebellion against God, Moses was inspired to declare to him what a monument of God's indignation he should be made to all future generations, and that God had raised him up to his exalted station for that express purpose. Not that God had infused any evil disposition into his mind; but by investing him with regal authority, and continuing him in the exercise of that authority notwithstanding his impious abuse of it, he enabled Pharaoh to display more conspicuously the wickedness of his heart, and to involve himself and his whole kingdom in more awful judgments than he could have done if he had moved in the situation of a private man. St. Paul quotes this declaration, in order to shew, that God disposes of men according to his sovereign will and pleasure, either converting them unto himself, or permitting them to proceed in their wickedness, in such a way as shall ultimately conduce most to the honour of his own name, and to the accomplishment of his own eternal purposes[b]. In this view, the passage before us is commended to us, as of singular importance. It shews us, not only what Pharaoh was, but what human nature itself is, if left to manifest its dispositions without restraint. I shall take occasion from it, therefore, to shew,

I. The impiety of Pharaoh—

I will bring it before you in a brief but comprehensive way. Mark,

[a] 1 Cor. x. 6, 11. [b] Compare Exod. ix. 16. with Rom. ix. 15—18.

1. Its source—

[It arose from *pride* and *ignorance*. Because there was no man of greater eminence than himself on earth, this unhappy monarch imagined that there was none above him even in heaven. Poor foolish worm! swelling with his own importance, whilst the plagues inflicted on him shewed how impotent he was to repel the assaults of the meanest insects. What insufferable arrogance was there in that question, " Who is the Lord, that I should obey his voice?" And what horrible impiety in that declaration, " I know not the Lord; neither will I let Israel go!" True, thou son of Belial, thou hast unwittingly assigned the real cause of thine obstinacy: " I know not the Lord[c]." As St. Paul says of the Jews, " Had they known, they would not have crucified the Lord of glory[d]," so say I to thee: Hadst thou known what a great and holy Being thou wast resisting, thou wouldst not have dared to withstand him thus. No: thou wouldst have bowed before him, and submitted instantly to his commands. Thy profaneness was proof enough of thine ignorance.]

2. Its operation—

[His *obstinacy* was *irreclaimable*, whether by judgments or by mercies. Nine successive plagues, and the removal of them all at thy request, were insufficient to subdue the pride and haughtiness of thy spirit. Not even the tenth, the greatest and heaviest of them all, prevailed on thee to desist from fighting against God. Thy relentings were only momentary: thy hardness returned the very instant thou wast out of the furnace: thine own consent thou didst recall; and follow with murderous rage those thou hadst permitted to go forth from thy land. How blinded wast thou by the wickedness of thine own heart! Thou wast alike insensible to the evil and the danger of thy ways. And in this thou hast shewn what is, in every place and in every age, the sad effect of sin.]

3. Its issue—

[Whither did it lead this devoted monarch, but to shame and ruin? Thou saidst, " Neither will I let Israel go." But when that Jehovah whom thou defiedst put forth his hand against thee, thou didst thrust them forth from thy land: and so anxious were thy whole people to get rid of them, that they loaded them with all their most valuable jewels, and with every thing that could be desired to speed their way.

But when they seemed to be entangled in the land, and an opportunity was afforded thee, as thou thoughtest, for their destruction, thou couldst not forbear: thou wouldst seize the occasion, and summon all thine hosts, and execute upon

---

[c] 1 Sam. ii. 12.   [d] 1 Cor. ii. 8.

them thy vengeance to the uttermost. Thou sawest the sea opening for them a way: but hadst thou yet to learn that God would put a difference between the Israelites and Egyptians? Presumptuous wretch! thou wouldst follow them even through the sea itself, and lead on in passion thine infatuated hosts. I see thee enter within the watery walls which Omnipotence had raised: but there thou hastenest to thy destruction. Now escape from the snare into which thine impiety has led thee. Thou canst not: thy chariot wheels are broken; and too late dost thou find that Jehovah fights for Israel. Of all that followed this infuriated monarch, not one escaped; the sea came upon them, and overwhelmed them all; not so much as one was left, to report to Egypt the calamity they had sustained.]

But, not to dwell any longer on the impiety of Pharaoh, I shall proceed to that which is of more immediate interest to ourselves; namely, to shew,

II. To what an extent a similar spirit prevails amongst us—

To you the messages of heaven are sent—

[We, Brethren, are ambassadors of God to you, and in his sacred name do we bring you the counsels which we offer; and every word that is so delivered, in accordance with his mind and will, must be received, "not as the word of man, but as the word of God himself." To every different class of hearers have we a message suited to their state. We call upon the licentious to forsake their evil ways; the worldling to seek for better things than this world can give; the formal and self-righteous to renounce their self-dependence, and to make the Lord Jesus Christ the ground of all their hopes.]

But who amongst you can be prevailed upon to obey the word?

[The same spirit by which Pharaoh was actuated, pervades the great mass of mankind; every one displaying it in a way suited to his own particular state. Some will openly say, with Pharaoh, "Who is the Lord, that I should obey his voice?" Others, who would not altogether express themselves in such impious terms, will yet *in effect* maintain the same language, and *practically* follow the same ungodly course. The inspired writers give this precise view of the ungodly world. Job speaks of them, as saying to God in his day, "Depart from us; for we desire not the knowledge of thy ways. What is the Almighty, that we should serve him? and what profit should we have, if we pray unto him[e]?" David gives a similar representation of them in his day: "They have said, With

[e] Job xxi. 14, 15.

our tongues shall we prevail: our lips are our own: who is Lord over us[f]?" The Prophet Jeremiah gives exactly the same character of those in his age: all classes of the community said to his very face, in answer to the messages he delivered to them from the Lord, " As for the word that thou hast spoken unto us in the name of the Lord, we will not hearken unto thee: but we will certainly do whatsoever thing goeth forth out of our own mouth, or cometh into our own hearts[g]." Now from these testimonies it is evident that I am not putting an undue construction on the words of Pharaoh, or pressing them too far, when I represent them as characterizing the spirit of the present day. It is clear that men do at this day "reject the word of the Lord," and "cast it behind them," and, in effect, say as he did, "Who is the Lord, that I should obey his voice?" It is obvious, too, that they do this in the midst of all the judgments and mercies with which God is pleased to visit them. There may be in many an occasional relenting, or purpose to amend: but all endeavour to lower the commands of God to the standard that is agreeable to their own minds; nor do any, except those who have been savingly converted to God, through Christ, ever surrender up themselves to God, or yield an unreserved obedience to his commands.]

And in what must your disobedience issue?

[Ask of persons in their career of sin, and they will tell you that they have nothing to fear. The confidence of Pharaoh and all his host exactly represents their state. Behold that whole army: onward they go, in prosecution of their bloody purpose: but little do they think how soon they will rue their folly, and how irretrievable will their ruin be in the space of a few moments. See them pressing forward: how little do they apprehend the fate that awaits them! So behold the various classes of ungodly men: how little do they dream of the destruction to which they are hastening! Wait but a few short moments, and they will all sink into everlasting perdition. But will not their confidence deliver them? No: the greater their confidence, the more certain is their ruin. But surely we may hope that their numbers will be some protection? No: of the whole Egyptian army, not one soul escaped: nor, if the unconverted world were a million times more numerous than they are, should one single soul escape the wrath of God. They are willingly and determinately treasuring up wrath to themselves against the day of wrath: and at the appointed season it shall come upon them to the uttermost. Then they will know who that Lord is, whom

[f] Ps. xii. 4.   [g] Jer. xliv. 16, 17. with xxiii. 17.

now they so despise: and they shall find, to their cost, that "those who walk in pride he is able to abase[h]."]

SEE then, from hence,

1. How great is the folly of ungodly men!

[Were a child to contend in battle with a man, who would not upbraid him for his folly and presumption in entering into so unequal a contest? But what shall we say of those who set themselves in array against the Majesty of heaven? Truly, a contest of briers and thorns against a devouring fire would not be more absurd. And this is the very comparison which is made by God himself: "Who would set briers and thorns against me in battle? I would go through them, and burn them up together[i]." I pray you, Brethren, remember against whom it is that you fight. It is against Him, who by a word spake the universe into existence, and by a word could reduce it in an instant to absolute nonentity. Look at the fallen angels, and see the consequence of rebelling against God! Look at the antediluvian world, and say, whether it be not an evil and bitter thing to sin against him, and to provoke his displeasure. Were it possible for you to withstand his power or to elude his search, you might have some excuse for casting off his light and easy yoke: but indeed you must, ere long, be summoned to his tribunal, and receive at his hands a doom which can never be reversed. And "will ye be strong in the day that he shall deal with you, or will ye thunder with a voice like his?" I pray you, lay down the weapons of your rebellion without delay, and implore mercy at the Saviour's hands, whilst yet "the day of salvation lasts, and the accepted time is continued to you."]

2. How greatly are they to be pitied!

[See how secure they are in their own apprehensions, and how confidently they expect a successful termination of their conflicts! Unhappy men! Methinks I see you in the agonies of death, and behold you at the instant of your entrance into the presence of your God. Oh! could we but conceive your terrors, and hear your cries, and witness your unavailing lamentations, how should we pity you! Could we further behold the triumphant exultations of that cruel fiend, who was once your tempter, and will then be your tormentor to all eternity, how should we weep over you! And lastly, if we could behold you suffering the vengeance of eternal fire, under the wrath of Almighty God, methinks it would be too much for us to endure: the very sight would overwhelm us, even though we had no fears for ourselves. Verily, it was with good reason that

[h] Dan. iv. 37.   [i] Isai. xxvii. 4.

the Saviour wept over the devoted city of Jerusalem: and we would that "our eyes also were a fountain of tears, to run down day and night" on account of your present obduracy, and on account of the miseries that await you in the eternal world!]

3. How desirable is the knowledge of God, as revealed in the Gospel!

[Never was there one who sought the face of God in vain. No: however long ye may have rebelled against God, there is mercy for you, if you turn to him with your whole hearts. Think how many of those who crucified the Lord of glory obtained mercy at his hands: and so shall you also, if you will humble yourselves before him, and seek for mercy through his atoning blood. "Not so much as one of you should perish, if you would but go to him." No truly, "there is no condemnation to them that are in Christ Jesus." "All that believe in him shall be justified from all things." "Acquaint, then, yourselves with God, and be at peace." Seek "that knowledge of him which is life eternal." And know, that, whilst "they who know him not, and obey not his Gospel, shall be banished from the presence of his glory," his believing and obedient servants shall both serve him, and be served by him, in his kingdom and glory, for ever and ever.]

OUTLINE NO. 68

THE OPPOSITION THAT IS MADE TO RELIGION.

Exod. v. 17, 18. *But he said, Ye are idle, ye are idle; therefore ye say, Let us go and do sacrifice to the Lord. Go therefore now and work.*

MAN prides himself upon his reason: but let him be under the influence of passion or interest, and nothing can be found more unreasonable: his eyes are blinded, his heart is hardened, his conscience is seared, and his actions are nearer to those of a maniac, than of a rational being. Nor is his madness ever carried to a greater extent, than when religion is concerned. Look at the persecutors of God's people, from Cain to this present moment: what have they been, but agents of the devil, fighting against God, and murdering their fellow-creatures with insatiable cruelty? A just specimen of their conduct we have in the history before us. Moses and Aaron were sent of God, to require that the Hebrew nation, who were then in Egypt, should go and offer sacrifices to him in the wilderness; where they might serve him without any fear of offending, or of being interrupted by, the people amongst whom they dwelt. Pharaoh not only refused his permission, but proudly defied Jehovah, and ordered immediately that such burthens should be laid upon the people as it was impossible for them to bear. On their complaining to him of the oppression which they suffered, and of the unmerited punishment that was inflicted on them, he relaxed nothing of his unrighteous decree, but exulted in their miseries, and dismissed them with invectives: "Ye are idle, ye are idle," &c.

In discoursing on these words, it will be profitable to us to consider,

I. What is that sacrifice which God requires at our hands—

We, as well as the Hebrews, are called to sacrifice unto our God.

But is it our flocks and our herds that he requires? No[a]: this is the message which he has sent us; "My son, give me thy heart[b]." The sacrifice that he demands, is,

1. An humble heart—

[Every child of man must, at his peril, present this to God — — — And every one that presents it to him, shall certainly be accepted[c] — — —]

2. A believing heart—

["Without faith it is impossible to please God[d]." It is faith that renders every other offering pleasing and acceptable to him[e]. This he considers as a sacrifice — — — It was not sufficient, that penitents under the law confessed their sins, or that they brought their sin-offering to be presented by the priest: they must lay their hands upon the head of their offering, and thereby profess their faith in that atonement, which in due time was to be made for the sins of the whole world[f]. In like manner we also must not only "acknowledge

[a] Ps. l. 8—15. and li. 16.   [b] Prov. xxiii. 26.   [c] Ps. ii. 17.
[d] Heb. xi. 6.   [e] Heb. xi. 4.
[f] Phil. ii. 17. The lamb that was offered every morning and evening, was to have a meat-offering of fine flour mingled with oil, and a drink-offering of wine poured upon it: and all was to be consumed together: Exod. xxix. 40. St. Paul, referring to this, calls

our iniquity," but must by faith transfer it to the sacred head of Jesus, who atoned for it on the cross, and through whom alone we can ever find acceptance with God[g].]

3. A thankful heart—

[This is a tribute most justly due to Him, who has loaded us with so many benefits, but, above all, has redeemed us by the blood of his only-begotten Son. The command given us is, "Rejoice evermore;" "Rejoice in the Lord alway, and again I say, rejoice." This is a sacrifice peculiarly pleasing to God[h] — — — and "the very stones will cry out against us," if we should refuse to offer it[i].]

4. An obedient heart—

[This is the crown of all. It is the *end* of all. For this we repent; for this we believe; for this we give thanks to God: all without this were only a solemn mockery. It is in order to this that God has vouchsafed to us so many mercies[k] — — — And we may be well assured, that every act of obedience, however small, if only it proceed from an humble, believing, and thankful heart, shall be accepted of him[l].]

Reasonable as such a sacrifice is, we are shocked to see,

II. In what light it is regarded by an ungodly world—

Did Pharaoh contemptuously resist the divine mandate; did he treat the request of the Hebrews as a pretext for idleness; and did he make it an occasion for the most cruel oppression? Here we may see a true picture of the world at this day: it is precisely thus that religion is now opposed;

1. With contempt—

[Pharaoh regarded the proposal of Moses as unworthy of notice. He saw no necessity for either himself or others to obey the commands of God; nor did he believe that any evil consequences would ensue from disobedience[m]. And how are the requisitions, which are now made to us in Jehovah's name, attended to amongst us? Is not this the universal cry; 'There is no need of so much religion; we shall do very well without

---

their faith the sacrifice; and says, that he should rejoice in *offering (in pouring out as a libation)* his own blood, to be presented to God together with it.

[g] John i. 29.   [h] Heb. xiii. 15. Ps. cvii. 22. and cxvi. 17.
[i] Luke xix. 40.   [k] Rom. xii. 1.   [l] Heb. xiii. 16.
[m] ver. 3, 9. He calls the menaces with which God's command was enforced, "vain words."

it; we have nothing to fear, though we live in the neglect of it?' Yes: all our exhortations to serve God with your whole hearts are, by many, considered in no better view than as weak, though well-intentioned, effusions of a heated imagination.]

2. With calumny—

[Men who choose not to obey the calls of God will always revile those who do. They will impute their zeal to hypocrisy, or idleness, or conceit, and vanity. They will presume to judge the motives of religious people, with as much confidence as if they could see the heart. Pharaoh had certainly no reason to ascribe to idleness the request that had been made to him: yet with a malignant triumph he professes to have seen through their motives, which he was determined to counteract. So, at this time, the enemies of true religion will represent the professors of it as heretical and seditious, and the Ministers of it as people that "turn the world upside down."]

3. With oppression—

[It is happy for us that all possess not the power of Pharaoh; and that the law has affixed bounds to the tyranny of man. Were it not so, we should still see, that the natural enmity of man against his God is as fierce as ever. Civilization has altered our habits, but made no change at all in our hearts. Husbands, parents, masters, in numberless instances, obstruct the progress of religion in the hearts of those over whom they have influence; either requiring services that shall interfere with their religious duties, or laying snares to divert their attention from them. And when complaint is made by their injured dependents, they will shew no regard to their consciences, but will exult in tyrannizing over them with their imperious mandate.]

ADDRESS—

1. The opposers of true religion—

[Many who in themselves are serious and devout, are as bitter enemies to spiritual religion as the most abandoned profligate can be. When the Jews wanted to expel Paul and Barnabas from Antioch, they could find no better, or more willing, agents than "devout and honourable women[n]." But it were better for any one to have a millstone about his neck, and to be cast into the sea, than to be found among the opposers of vital godliness[o]. "Their Redeemer is mighty;" and he will avenge their cause. Instead therefore of setting yourselves against them, and calumniating them, inquire what is the reason that you yourselves are not religious. May not your own words be retorted upon you; "Ye are idle, ye are idle; therefore ye say, Let us *not* sacrifice unto the Lord?" Yes; it

[n] Acts xiii. 50. [o] Matt. xviii. 6.

is no calumny to affirm this: "Go therefore now, and work." Go; and instead of obstructing the sacrifices of others, present to God the sacrifice that he demands of *you*.]

2. Those who meet with persecution for righteousness' sake—

["All who will live godly in Christ Jesus are taught to expect persecution:" therefore think it not strange that you are called to suffer; but rather "rejoice that you are counted worthy to suffer for Christ's sake." Are you discouraged, because the relief you have sought for is withheld, and your troubles seem to increase? It was thus that God dealt with the Hebrews in the instance before us; and he not unfrequently deals thus with his people, in order that he may be the more glorified in their ultimate deliverance. If therefore the shadows of the night be still lengthened, you need not despair; for "at evening-time it shall be light;" and in the hour of your deepest distress God will surely interpose for your succour and relief[p]. Take care however that the enemies of religion have no cause to find fault with you for neglecting the duties of your station. It is no little stumbling-block in their way, when you give them occasion to adopt the language of the text. See to it then, that you be active and diligent in every work to which God, in his providence, has called you. The direction given you by God himself combines worldly activity with spiritual fervour, and represents each of them, in its place, as truly acceptable to him; "Be not slothful in business, but fervent in spirit, serving the Lord[q]."]

[p] Deut. xxxii. 36.   [q] Rom. xii. 11.

OUTLINE NO. 69

THE DESPONDENCY OF ISRAEL.

Exod. vi. 9. *And Moses spake so unto the children of Israel: but they hearkened not unto Moses, for anguish of spirit, and for cruel bondage.*

"AS face answers to face in a glass, so does the heart of man to man." We are apt, indeed, to imagine that the Jews were a people of more than ordinary depravity: but it is found that mankind almost universally act precisely as they did, under similar circumstances. We have here a remarkable instance of despondency. The Hebrews had been long groaning under a most cruel oppression: and God had sent his servant, Moses, to deliver them from it. But the effect of his interposition hitherto had been only to augment their troubles. Of this they had bitterly complained, as indeed had Moses himself also: and now, for their comfort, God sent them by Moses a most consolatory message, assuring them, that, however gloomy their prospects might appear to be, a most perfect deliverance was at hand. But they, we are told, "hearkened not unto Moses, for anguish of spirit, and for cruel bondage."

Let us consider,

I. Their conduct on this occasion—

The testimony of Moses was in every respect worthy of credit—

[He had wrought before the people the miracles which God had commissioned him to work, in confirmation of his divine mission[a]: and hitherto, if he had not yet succeeded in his embassy, he had executed his office with fidelity and courage. It might be supposed, indeed, that if Moses himself had fainted under the discouragement which they had experienced, much more might they. But, on the other hand, if God had renewed his commission to Moses, and expressly authorized him to assure them of a speedy and certain deliverance, so that *his* mind was left without any doubt of ultimate success, they might well receive his testimony, and rest upon it with composure.]

Nor could any thing be conceived more suited to their necessities—

[They were under the most "cruel bondage." But Moses declared, that God had entered into covenant with their forefathers, Abraham, Isaac, and Jacob, to deliver them: that he had confirmed this covenant with an oath: that, from compassion to them, he was about to fulfil the engagements he had entered into: that he not only would deliver them from their sore bondage, but would, by the judgments which he would inflict on Pharaoh, make him more anxious to rid himself of them than ever he had been to detain them; and would constrain him, in fact, to "drive them out from his land[b]." He further declared, that God would bring them safely into Canaan, wherein their forefathers had sojourned as pilgrims and strangers, and give it them for their inheritance; and would "take them to him as his peculiar people, and be unto them a God," yea, and " *their* God."

In reporting to them these "great and precious promises," he was careful particularly to make known to them the grounds

[a] Exod. iv. 30.   [b] ver. 1.

on which they might be received with the most implicit affiance; for that God had repeatedly pledged his power and veracity for the performance of them. *Thrice* had God renewed that solemn declaration, " I am Jehovah," the eternal, self-existent, and immutable Jehovah: and, times almost without number, he had undertaken to execute, with his own irresistible arm, the whole that he had promised: " *I will* bring you out; *I will* rid you; *I will* redeem you; *I will* bring you into the land; *I will* give it you; *I will* take you to me for a people, and *I will* be your God[c]."]

Yet would not the people receive, or even " hearken to," his words—

[Their minds were so wholly occupied with their present troubles, that they could think of nothing else: they were altogether overwhelmed with " anguish of spirit:" and so utterly did they despair of relief, that they desired to be left to live and die under their present servitude, rather than run the risk of augmenting their afflictions by any further application to Pharaoh in their behalf[d].]

Without dwelling any longer on their conduct, I beg leave to call your attention to,

II. The instruction to be derived from it—

We may notice from hence,

1. The weakness of the human mind—

[It has been justly said, that " oppression will make a wise man mad[e]:" and the common experience of all is, that " hope deferred maketh the heart sick[f]." In my text, we see both the one and the other strongly exemplified. And, in truth, where afflictions are great and of long continuance, the mind of every man is apt to faint: nor can any thing but divine grace adequately sustain it. Even David, when hunted by Saul as a partridge upon the mountains, forgat for a season the power and fidelity of his Protector, and in a fit of despondency exclaimed, " I shall one day perish by the hand of Saul." So, under various circumstances, the Church of old complained, " My way is hid from the Lord, and my judgment is passed over from my God:" yea, " the Lord hath forsaken me, and my God hath forgotten me." Sometimes her despair has been so entire, that she has even made the justice of it a ground of appeal both to God and man: " Shall the prey be taken from the mighty, or the lawful captive delivered?" But this experience, in whomsoever it be found, is decidedly contrary to the mind and will of God. We are never to limit the power of

[c] ver. 2—8.   [d] Gen. xiv. 11, 12.   [e] Eccl. vii. 7.   [f] Prov. xiii. 12.

God, or to doubt his veracity. We are not to suppose, that, because we see not how deliverance can come, God is at any loss for means whereby to effect it. It is well to "have the sentence of death in ourselves, that we may not trust in ourselves, but in God who raiseth the dead," and has promised to "judge his people and repent himself for his servants, when he seeth that their power is gone, and that there is none shut up or left[g]."]

2. The proper office of faith—

[Faith is to look, above all created things, to God; and to realize, under every dispensation, the presence of him that is invisible. It is to lay hold on God's word, and to rest upon it, and to expect its accomplishment, in defiance of men or devils. It is to hope, even "against hope." Its legitimate exercise may be seen in Abraham, when he was commanded to offer up his son: "I have no fear but that God will fulfil his promise in Isaac: even though I should reduce him to ashes upon an altar, God can raise him up again, yea, and will raise him up again, rather than suffer one jot or tittle of his word to fail." "Being strong in faith, and giving glory to God," he both formed, and acted upon, this assured expectation: and in proportion to the strength of our faith will be our confidence in God, even under the most discouraging circumstances. We shall say, "Though the fig-tree should not blossom, neither shall fruit be in the vines; the labour of the olive shall fail, and the fields shall yield no meat; the flock shall be cut off from the fold, and there shall be no herd in the stalls; yet I will rejoice in the Lord, I will joy in the God of my salvation[h]."

Had Israel on this occasion been able to confide in God, how sweetly composed had their minds been in the midst of all their troubles! Let us learn to exercise this grace of faith, and under the darkest dispensations to say, "Though he slay me, yet will I trust in him."]

3. The excellency of the Gospel dispensation—

[What Moses said to Israel, *we* are authorized and commissioned to declare to you. You are under a bondage far more cruel than that which Israel experienced: but in the name of Almighty God we come to you, and proclaim, that he has entered into covenant with his Son for your redemption; that he has confirmed that covenant with an oath; that he will bring you out from the power of sin and Satan, and conduct you in safety to the heavenly Canaan. For the fulfilment of all this he pledges to you his word, saying, in relation to every part of the work, '*I*, the immutable Jehovah, will do it for you: *I* will work; and who shall hinder?' Only believe in

[g] Deut. xxxii. 36.   [h] Hab. iii. 17, 18.

him: believe that "what he has promised he is able also to perform." You have seen what he did for Israel, notwithstanding their unbelief: what then shall he not do for you, if you will truly believe in Christ as your appointed Saviour? He will not only bring you forth out of the land of your captivity, but will preserve you throughout the whole of this dreary wilderness, and introduce you finally to the full possession of your glorious inheritance. Yes, Brethren, these things we declare unto you in the name of Almighty God: and if, with Caleb and Joshua, you will "follow the Lord fully," like them you shall have your portion assuredly in the realms of bliss.]

OUTLINE NO. 70
GOD HARDENING PHARAOH'S HEART.
Exod. vii. 3. *I will harden Pharaoh's heart.*

AS there are in the works of creation many things which exceed the narrow limits of human understanding, so are there many things incomprehensible to us both in the works of providence and of grace. It is not however necessary that, because we cannot fully comprehend these mysteries, we should never fix our attention at all upon them: as far as they are revealed, the consideration of them is highly proper: only, where we are so liable to err, our steps must be proportionably cautious, and our inquiries be conducted with the greater humility. In particular, the deepest reverence becomes us, while we contemplate the subject before us. We ought not, on the one hand, to indulge a proud and captious spirit that shall banish the subject altogether, nor, on the other hand, to make our assertions upon it with a bold, unhallowed confidence. Desirous of avoiding either extreme, we shall endeavour to *explain* and *vindicate* the conduct of God, as it is stated in the text.

I. To explain it—

We are not to imagine that God infused any evil principle into the heart of Pharaoh: *this* God never did, nor ever will do, to any of his creatures[a]. What he did, may be comprehended in three particulars—

1. He left Pharaoh to the influence of his own corruptions—

[a] Jam. i. 13.

[Pharaoh was a proud and haughty monarch: and, while he exercised a most arbitrary and oppressive power over his subjects, he disdained to respect the authority of Jehovah, who was "King of kings, and Lord of lords."

God, if he had seen fit, might have prevented him from manifesting these corruptions. He might have struck him dead upon the spot; or intimidated him by a dream or vision; or have converted him, as he did the persecuting Saul, in the midst of all his malignant projects: but he left him to himself, precisely as he does other men when they commit iniquity; and suffered him to manifest all the evil dispositions of his heart.

This is no other conduct than what God has pursued from the beginning. When men have obstinately "rebelled against the light," he has "given them up to follow their own hearts' lusts[b]:" and we have reason to expect that he will deal thus with us, if we continue to resist his will[c].]

2. He suffered such events to concur as should give scope for the exercise of those corruptions—

[He raised Pharaoh to the throne of Egypt, and thereby invested him with power to oppress[d]. By multiplying the Jews, he made their services of great importance to the Egyptian empire. The labours of six hundred thousand slaves could not easily be dispensed with; and therefore the temptation to retain them in bondage was exceeding great. Besides, the request made of going to serve their God in the wilderness must appear to him frivolous and absurd; for, why should they not be content to serve him in the land? Moreover, the success of his magicians in imitating the miracles of Moses, would seem to justify the idea, that Moses was no more than a magician, only perhaps of a more intelligent order than those employed by *him*. The frequent and speedy removal of the judgments that were inflicted on him, would yet further tend to harden him, by making him think light of those judgments. Thus the unreasonableness of his opposition would be hid from him; and he would persist in his rebellion without compunction or fear.]

3. He gave Satan permission to exert his influence over him—

[Satan is a powerful being; and, when the restraints which God has imposed upon him are withdrawn, can do great things. He cannot indeed force any man to sin against his will: but he can bring him into such circumstances, as shall have a strong tendency to ensnare his soul. We know from the history of Job, how great things he can effect for the distressing of a most

[b] Rom. i. 24, 26, 28.   Ps. lxxxi. 11, 12.   2 Thess. ii. 10—12.
[c] Gen. vi. 3.   Lev. xxvi. 27, 28.   Prov. i. 24—30.
[d] Rom. ix. 17.

eminent saint: much more therefore may we suppose him to prevail over one, who is his blind and willing vassal[e]. We do not indeed know, from any express declarations, that Satan interfered in this work of hardening Pharaoh: but, when we recollect how he instigated David to number the people; how he prevailed on Peter to deny, and Judas to betray, his Lord; how he filled the hearts of Ananias and Sapphira that they might lie unto God; and finally, how expressly we are told that "he works in all the children of disobedience;" we can have no doubt respecting his agency in the heart of Pharaoh.

Thus, as far as respects a withholding of that grace which might have softened Pharaoh's heart, and a giving him an opportunity to shew his malignant dispositions, and a permitting of Satan to exert his influence, *God* hardened Pharaoh's heart: but as being a perfectly free agent, *Pharaoh* hardened *his own* heart: and this is repeatedly affirmed in the subsequent parts of this history.]

When once we have learned what was the true nature of God's agency, and how far it was concerned in the hardening of Pharaoh's heart, we shall be at no loss,

II. To vindicate it—

We must never forget that "God's ways and thoughts are infinitely above ours;" and that, whether we approve of them or not, "he will never give account of them to us:" yet, constituted as we are, we feel a satisfaction in being able to discern their suitableness to the divine character. Of the dispensation then which we are considering, we may say,

1. It was *righteous*, as it respected the individual himself—

[It was perfectly righteous *that Pharaoh should be left to himself.* What injury would God have done, if he had acted towards the whole human race precisely as he did towards the fallen angels? What reason can be assigned why man, who had imitated their wickedness, should not be a partaker of their punishment? If then none had any claim upon God for the exercise of his grace, how much less could Pharaoh have a title to it, after having so proudly defied God, and so obstinately withstood his most express commands? If there was any thing unjust in abandoning Pharaoh to the corrupt affections of his heart, all other sinners in the universe have reason to make the same complaint, that God is unrighteous in his dealings with them. In that case, God could not, consistently with his own

[e] 2 Cor. iv. 4. 2 Tim. ii. 26.

justice, permit sin at all: he must impose an irresistible restraint on all, and cease to deal with us as persons in a state of probation.

Again, it was righteous in God *to suffer such a concurrence of circumstances as should give scope for the exercise of his corruptions.* God is no more bound to destroy man's free agency by his providence, than he is by his grace. Was it unrighteous in him to let Cain have an opportunity of executing his murderous project against his brother Abel? or has he been unjust, as often as he has permitted others to accomplish their wicked purposes? Doubtless he has interposed, by his providence, to prevent the execution of many evils that have been conceived in our minds[f]: but he is not bound to do so for any one; nor could he do it universally, without changing the nature of his government, and the whole course of the world.

Moreover, it was righteous *to give Satan liberty to exert his influence over Pharaoh.* Pharaoh chose to believe the agents of Satan rather than the servants of the Most High God; and to obey their counsels rather than his. Why then should God continue to restrain Satan, when Pharaoh desired nothing so much as to yield to his temptations? When Ahab sent for all his lying prophets to counsel him and to foster his delusions, God permitted "Satan to be a lying spirit in the mouth of all those prophets," that they might all concur in the same fatal advice[g]. Was this unjust? Was it not agreeable to Ahab's own wish; and was not the contrary counsel of the Lord's prophet rejected by him with disdain? Pharaoh wished to be deceived; and God permitted it to be according to his own heart's desire.

On the whole then, if men are to be left to their own free agency, instead of being dealt with as mere machines; and if God have ordered the general course of his providence agreeably to this rule, resisting the proud while he gives grace to the humble; then was he fully justified in suffering this impious monarch to harden his already proud and obdurate heart[h].]

2. It was *merciful,* as it respected the universe at large—

[We form erroneous conceptions of the divine government, because we view it on too contracted a scale. God, in his dealings with mankind, consults, not the benefit of an individual merely, but the good of the whole. Now this conduct towards Pharaoh was calculated exceedingly to promote the welfare of all succeeding generations. It has given us lessons of instruction that are of the greatest value.

It has shewn us *the extreme depravity of the human heart.* Who would have conceived that a man, warned as Pharaoh was

[f] Hos. ii. 6.   [g] 1 Kings xxii. 21—23.
[h] Compare Deut. ii. 30. and Josh. xi. 20.

by so many tremendous plagues, should continue, to the last, to set himself against the God of heaven and earth? But in him we see what men will do, when their pride, their passions, and their interests have gained an ascendant over them: they will defy God to his face; and, if softened for a moment by the severity of his judgments, they will soon, like metal from the furnace, return to their wonted hardness.

It has shewn us *our need of divine grace.* Widely as men differ from each other in their constitutional frame both of body and mind, they all agree in this, that " they have a carnal mind, which is enmity against God; and which neither is, nor can be, subject to his law[i]." We may all see in Pharaoh a striking portrait of ourselves: and if one be enabled to mortify the evils of his heart, whilst others continue in bondage to their lusts, he must say, " By the grace of God I am what I am." If we have no more grace than Pharaoh in our hearts, we shall have no more holiness in our lives.

It has shewn us *the danger of fighting against God*[k]. "Fools make a mock at sin," and "puff at the threatened judgments" of God. But let any one see in Pharaoh the danger of being given over to a reprobate mind: let any one see in what our hardness of heart may issue: and he will tremble lest God should say respecting him, " He is joined to idols; let him alone."

It has shewn us *the obligations we lie under to God for the long-suffering he has already exercised towards us.* We read the history of Pharaoh: happy is it for us, that we have not been left, like him, to be a warning to others. No tongue can utter the thanks that are due to him on this account. If we know any thing of our own hearts, we shall be ready to think ourselves the greatest monuments of mercy that ever were rescued from perdition.

Now these lessons are invaluable: and every one that reads the history of this unhappy monarch, must see them written in it as with the pen of a diamond.]

ADDRESS—

[We are told to " remember Lot's wife:" and it will be well also to remember Pharaoh. Let none of us trifle with our convictions, or follow carnal policy in preference to the commands of God — — — Let the messages of God be received with reverence, and obeyed with cheerfulness — — — Let us be afraid of hardening our own hearts, lest God should give us over to final obduracy[l]. If God withdraw from us, Satan will quickly come[m]: and if we are left to Satan's agency, better were it for us that we had never been born. — — — Seek of God the influences of the Holy Ghost, who will " take away the heart of stone, and give you an heart of flesh."]

Rom. viii. 7.   [k] Isai. xlv. 9.   [l] Job ix. 4.   [m] 1 Sam. xvi. 14

OUTLINE NO. 71

PHARAOH'S ELEVATION TO THE THRONE OF EGYPT.

Exod. ix. 16. *In very deed, for this cause have I raised thee up, for to shew in thee my power, and that my name may be declared throughout all the earth.*

IT is justly said, in reference to evidence, that it is strong in proportion as it arises out of incidental points, which had no necessary connexion with the fact to be established. The same I may say in relation to the doctrines of our holy religion, especially those doctrines which are most controverted, and most stand in need of evidence for their support. Of this kind is the doctrine of election; which, being extremely opposed to the pride of human nature, meets with strong opposition from the carnal mind. I am far from saying that that doctrine is not extremely objectionable, if viewed as its adversaries, and not a few of its advocates also, are wont to state it; but, if viewed in its true light, and as the Scriptures themselves state it, I conceive that it cannot reasonably be doubted.

In the passage before us, there was no particular intention to establish that doctrine. Moses had laboured in vain to induce Pharaoh to let the people of Israel go to worship Jehovah in the wilderness. He had, as God's appointed instrument, inflicted many plagues on the land of Egypt, and removed them again by his intercessions; and yet neither by the judgments nor the mercies had he prevailed on Pharaoh, who still continued to harden his heart against God. He now assumed a bolder tone; and declared, that not only should the Egyptians be smitten with pestilence, but that Pharaoh himself also " should be cut off from the earth," for his obstinate resistance to God's express commands. And then he delivers to him, from God himself, this awful declaration: " In very deed, for this cause have I raised thee up, for to shew in thee my power, and that my name may be declared throughout all the earth."

This declaration it is my intention, in the present discourse,

I. To explain—

God here asserts, that he had raised up Pharaoh for a special purpose, with which his own glory was intimately connected. He had determined to bring forth his people from Egypt, in such a way as should display most remarkably his own power, and should bring glory to his name throughout all the earth. Some, by the expression "raised up," understand restoring him to health from the disorder inflicted on him in common with his people and the magicians. But it does not appear that Pharaoh had been visited with that disorder: and the threatening in the verse before our text, "I *will* smite thee," rather seems to shew, that he had not yet been smitten in his own person: but, whether we understand the words as relating to his elevation to the throne, or to a restoration to health, the main object of the declaration will be the same; namely, that God, knowing what would assuredly be the result of a further trial of his obedience, had determined so to try him, in order that by the issue of the contest God's glory might be displayed throughout all the earth.

The substance of the declaration, then, may be considered as expressing the following truths—

1. That God allots to every man his station in life—

[Nothing can be more clear, than that the time and place of every man's entrance into life is fixed by God. That we are born in this age and country has in no respect depended on ourselves: we might as well, if God had so ordained, been born of Heathen or Mahometan parents, or never have been permitted to see the light, and perished in our mother's womb. We might have been brought into the world from parents either of the highest or lowest rank, and been doomed to occupy a place in society widely different from that which we at present fill. All this was true of Pharaoh, and it is equally true of every child of man. "Our times are in God's hands[a]," and "he determines the bounds of our habitation[b]."]

2. That he foreknows how every man will act in the situation to which he is called—

[a] Ps. xxxi. 15. [b] Acts xvii. 26.

[He foresaw infallibly how Pharaoh would act in resisting all the means that should be used to bring him to a compliance with the divine command. Nor is there any thing hid from his all-seeing eye: if there were, it would be impossible for him to foretell, as he has done by his Prophets, the minutest circumstances that could occur, and at the distance of many hundred years. The prophecies relating to the death of our blessed Lord specify what should be *said*, as well as *done*, by persons who were least of all aware that they were fulfilling any prediction, and who would rather, if it had been possible, have prevented its accomplishment. We may be sure, therefore, that that testimony respecting him is true, " Known unto him are all things, from the beginning of the world^c."]

3. That, whilst he leaves to every man the free exercise of his will, he overrules the actions of all for the accomplishment of his own eternal purposes—

[God, as we have observed, had decreed to magnify himself in his mode of bringing forth his people from Egypt. But, in order to this, it was necessary that his will should be opposed, and that occasion should be given for the executing of his judgments upon the oppressors of his people. He knew what Pharaoh would do under such circumstances: and he both preserved him in life, and elevated him to the throne, that he might have an opportunity of manifesting what was in his heart, and be able to carry into effect the dictates of his own depravity. In all that he did, he was perfectly a free agent: for though it is said, that " God hardened Pharaoh's heart," he did so, not by infusing any evil principle into him, but by giving him up to the impulse of his own inveterate corruptions. God foresaw how those corruptions would operate, and that they would lead to the accomplishment of his own eternal purpose: and he needed only to leave Pharaoh to the dictates of his own mind, to secure the final execution of all that he himself had ordained. God had determined every thing respecting the crucifixion of our blessed Lord: but he needed not to inspire the Jewish rulers with envy, or the Roman governor with timidity, or Judas with covetousness, or the populace with cruelty: it was sufficient to give them up respectively to the dominion of their own lusts; and they all infallibly concurred to " do what his hand and his counsel had determined before to be done^d." It is precisely in the same way that we are to account for all that is done, whether it be good or evil; except that, in the effecting of what is good, he puts the desire to effect it into the heart of the agent, whilst in the perpetration of evil he merely gives up the person to

^c Acts xv. 18.   ^d Acts iv. 28.

the influence of his own lusts. In either case, the agent is perfectly free, and follows what is the bent of his own heart: only, in the one case, the heart is renewed, and in the other it is left under the power of its own depravity. Josiah and Cyrus both fulfilled the counsels of Heaven; the one by burning men's bones on the altar which Jeroboam had raised, and the other by liberating the Jews from Babylon. Both these events were foretold hundreds of years before they came to pass; and the very names of the agents were declared hundreds of years before any persons of their name were known in the world. Sennacherib also fulfilled the will of Heaven, in punishing God's offending people: "Howbeit he meant not so, neither did his heart think so; it was in his heart only to aggrandize himself at the expense of other nations[e]." But God, by all, accomplished "the counsel of his own will[f]:" and in all things " shall his counsel stand, and he will do all his will[g]."]

4. That by all, whatever their conduct be, he will eventually be glorified—

[That God will be glorified in the obedience of the righteous, is a truth which needs not to be confirmed: whatever they do, it is " to the praise of the glory of his grace:" and at the last day the Lord Jesus will come " to be glorified in his saints, and to be admired in all them that believe." But will he be glorified in the ungodly also? Yes. He declared that he would " get himself honour upon Pharaoh and all his hosts[h]:" and this he did by overwhelming them in the sea: and so he will do, also, in the destruction of the wicked, at the last day: he will then make known the inflexibility of his justice, and " the power of his wrath:" and the whole universe shall be constrained to say, " Even so, Lord God Almighty, true and righteous are thy judgments[i]."]

Having thus explained the declaration in my text, I proceed,

II. To improve it—

All Scripture is said to be " profitable for doctrine, for reproof, for correction, and for instruction in righteousness," or, in other words, for the establishment of sound doctrine, and for the enforcing of a holy practice. For these two ends I will endeavour to improve the subject before us. And,

1. For the establishment of sound doctrine—

[The doctrine which I hinted at, in the commencement of

[e] Isai. x. 7.   [f] Eph. i. 11   [g] Isai. xlvi. 10.
[h] Exod. xiv. 17.   [i] Rev. xvi. 6, 7. and xix. 2.

this discourse, is strongly insisted on by the Apostle Paul; and the words of my text are adduced by him in confirmation of his statement. He is shewing that God, in the exercise of his mercy to the Jewish nation, had acted altogether in a way of grace, according to his own sovereign will and pleasure: that he had entailed his blessings on Isaac and his seed, instead of imparting them to Ishmael and his posterity; and, in like manner, had again limited them to Jacob, the younger son of Isaac, and withheld them from Esau, the elder son. This had God done "in order that his purpose according to election might stand, not of works, but of him that called." Then, knowing that the proud heart of man would rise against this doctrine, and accuse it as "imputing unrighteousness to God," he further confirms his statement by express declarations of God to Moses: "He saith to Moses, I will have mercy on whom I will have mercy; and I will have compassion on whom I will have compassion:" and from thence he draws this conclusion; "So, then, it is not of him that willeth, nor of him that runneth, but of God that sheweth mercy." To this declaration he adds another of a similar tendency, addressed to Pharaoh, even the very words of my text: "For this same purpose have I raised thee up, that I might shew my power in thee, and that my name might be declared throughout all the earth:" from which words he draws again this remarkable conclusion; "Therefore hath God mercy on whom he will have mercy; and whom he will, he hardeneth[k]."

Now here the doctrine of election is stated in the strongest and most unequivocal terms. But let not any one imagine that the doctrine of reprobation is therefore true. God has not said in my text, "I have brought thee into the world on purpose to damn thee, and to get glory to myself in thine everlasting destruction:" no, there is no such assertion as that in all the Holy Scriptures. There is, in the Epistle of St. Peter, an expression which *in sound* has that aspect; but, when properly explained, it has no such meaning. It is said by him, "These stumble at the word, being disobedient; whereunto also they were appointed[l]." But to what were they appointed?— to disobedience? No: but to make that word, which they would not obey, an occasion of falling. God has ordained, that "they who will do his will, shall know of the doctrine, whether it be of God[m]:" but that those who will not do his will, shall stumble at his word, and find the Lord Jesus Christ, as revealed in it, "a rock of offence, yea, a gin also and a snare[n]." This will throw the true light upon our text: God did not

[k] Rom. ix. 7—18.   [l] 1 Pet. ii. 8.   [m] John vii. 17.

[n] Isai. viii. 14, 15, compared with the fore-cited passage from St. Peter.

bring Pharaoh into the world on purpose to destroy him: but, foreseeing the inveterate pride and obstinacy of his heart, he raised him to the throne, where he would have an opportunity of displaying with effect those malignant dispositions, and would thereby give occasion for God to glorify himself, in an extraordinary display of his justice and his power, in the punishment of sin.

Here, then, we see the electing grace of God. God chose Moses, who had been in rank and authority the second person in the kingdom of Egypt, to be the deliverer of his people. Moses, when called to the work, declined it again and again; and might well have been left to reap the bitter fruit of his folly. But God, by his Spirit, overcame his reluctance, and upheld him in the performance of his duty. To Pharaoh he gave not this grace; but left him to the power of his own lusts. In making this distinction, God did no injury to Pharaoh. Neither Pharaoh nor Moses had any claim upon God. If, when Moses declined the honour which was offered him, God had transferred that honour to Pharaoh, and given up Moses to the evil of his own heart, he would have done no injury to Moses: Moses would have brought the punishment upon himself, by his own wickedness: and God had a right to bestow his grace on whomsoever he pleased: and consequently, in leaving Pharaoh to harden his own heart and to perish in his sins, whilst he shewed mercy to Moses, and made him an honoured instrument of good to the Jewish nation, God did no injury to Pharaoh or to any one else: in the exercise of mercy, he acted as an Almighty Sovereign; and in the exercise of judgment, he acted as a righteous Judge, in perfect consistency with justice and with equity. We see at all events the fact, that " God did, after much long-suffering, make known on one his wrath, as on a vessel of wrath that had *fitted itself* for destruction;" and that toward another " he made known the riches of his glory, as on a vessel of mercy which *he himself had prepared* unto glory[o]." The exercise of his mercy was gratuitous and without desert; but the exercise of his displeasure was merited and judicial.

Now what is there here to be offended with? The fact is undeniable: and, if God was at liberty to exercise his sovereignty in such a way *then*, he is at liberty to do it still: and if he may justly do it in *any* case, as that of Ishmael and Isaac, or of Esau and Jacob, or of Pharaoh and Moses, he may with equal justice do it in *every* case. Let us, then, not ignorantly and proudly deny to him a right, which all of us claim for ourselves—even that of dispensing our favours to whom we will. If no one has a claim on him, no one has a right to complain

[o] Rom. ix, 22, 23. See the Greek.

if a favour which he despises is withheld from him: on the other hand, the person on whom that special favour is conferred, must to all eternity adore the sovereign grace that has dispensed it to him.]

2. For the enforcement of a holy practice—

[All of us, whether high or low, rich or poor, are in the station, which God, in his infinite wisdom and goodness, has allotted to us. The rich therefore have no reason to boast; nor have the poor any reason to repine. The different members of our own body have not all the same office: but God has "placed each member in the body, as it has pleased him;" and for purposes which each is destined to accomplish. One great duty is common to us all; namely, that of discharging to the utmost of our power our respective offices, and of bringing to God that measure of glory of which he has made us capable. God is, in reality, as much glorified in the submission of the poor, as in the activity of the rich. The eye, and the foot, equally subserve the interests of the body, whilst discharging their respective functions; and equally display the goodness of our Creator, in so administering to our wants. Let us then simply inquire, what that service is which we are most fitted by capacity and situation to perform; and let us address ourselves to it with all diligence. If placed, like Pharaoh, in a post of great dignity and power, let us improve our influence for God, and account it our honour and happiness to advance his glory. If called, like Moses, to labour for the deliverance of God's people from their spiritual bondage, let us execute our office with fidelity, and never rest till we have "finished the work which God has given us to do[p]." Thus shall we acceptably fulfil the ends of our creation; and God will be glorified in us, both in time and in eternity.]

[p] If there were occasion to speak more fully to *Ministers*, here the subject might be amplified to advantage.

OUTLINE NO. 72

THE DANGER OF DISREGARDING THE WORD OF GOD.

Exod. ix. 20, 21. *He that feared the word of the Lord among the servants of Pharaoh, made his servants and his cattle flee into the houses: and he that regarded not the word of the Lord, left his servants and his cattle in the field.*

THE word of God in every age has met with a very different reception from different people: from the antediluvian scoffers to the present moment, the generality have deemed it unworthy of their attention, while a few have regarded it with reverence and godly fear. Never had any declaration a better title to belief than that to which the text alludes: Moses had already, in the space of a few days, foretold many judgments, which were instantly inflicted or removed according to his predictions; and since they had not been effectual to subdue the stubborn heart of Pharaoh, he announced the determination of God to send another judgment on the land of Egypt, even a storm of hail and lightning, which should destroy every man and beast that should be exposed to its fury. There were many however who despised the threatening, and disdained to send their servants and cattle to a place of shelter; but others, who had profited by past experience, used with eagerness the precaution suggested to them—

From this circumstance we are led to shew,

I. How a regard for God's word will influence men here—

In all temporal concerns men are affected by any report in proportion to its credibility and importance—

[If they hear of any great *good* that is placed within their reach, they feel a desire after it springing up in their minds: if there be some considerable probability of their attaining it, their hopes are excited, and their endeavours multiplied in order to secure it. If the possession of it appear near and certain, they already congratulate themselves on the expected acquisition, though not without a mixture of anxious suspense. On the other hand, do they hear of any great *evil* that may come upon them? they begin to be disquieted: does it approach nearer and nearer? they think how they may avoid it, and use every precaution that prudence can suggest: does it appear imminent and almost unavoidable? their fears and anxieties are proportionably increased. Nor are these effects peculiar to any times, places, or persons: they will be found on examination to be invariable and universal.]

Thus it must also of necessity be with respect to men's spiritual concerns, in proportion as what God has spoken concerning them is believed and felt—

[Suppose a person to be thoroughly persuaded that, "except he repent he must eternally perish;" that, "except he be born again of the Spirit, he cannot enter into the kingdom of heaven;" and that, "he that hath the Son hath life, and he that hath not the Son of God hath not life;" what effect must such momentous truths produce upon his mind? Must he not of necessity begin to inquire into the meaning of these expressions, and feel a solicitude to have these questions satisfactorily determined: 'Am I a real penitent? Am I born again? Have I the Son of God?' If he doubt the truth of these things, and think they may be taken in a lower sense, he will of course be less concerned to attain the experience of them; or, if other things appear to him of superior importance, he will attend to those things in preference. But let him have that faith which gives a present subsistence to things future, and a demonstrable reality to things invisible[a], and it will be impossible for him to trifle with such solemn declarations. It is true, he may sin against the convictions of conscience; but if he continue so to do, it is evident that his convictions are not proportioned in any degree to the importance of eternal things, and that he cherishes a secret hope of escaping by some means or other the judgments denounced against him. Let him but *feel* the worth of his soul *in a degree proportioned to its value;* let him estimate that as men estimate the worth of their natural life, and he could no more resist *habitually* the convictions of his mind, than he could sit composed, while his house and family were ready to be destroyed by fire: he would surely resemble those Egyptians who sought shelter for their servants and cattle; he would "flee from the wrath to come, and lay hold on eternal life."]

Such a practical attention will be given to the word of God by all who truly believe it, because they know,

II. How it will affect their state hereafter—

The distinction put between the believing and unbelieving Egyptians related merely to this present life: but the Scriptures authorize us to declare that a similar distinction will be made between believers and unbelievers in the day of judgment. Yes assuredly,

1. They who have sought the appointed refuge shall be saved—

[Christ is that hiding-place to which all are enjoined to flee: every other covert will be found " a refuge of lies, which the hail shall sweep away[b]:" but Christ is a sure refuge, " to which whosoever runneth shall be safe." Whatever we may have been, and whatever we may have done in past times, we have nothing to apprehend from the wrath of God, provided we be found in Christ." "Believing in him, we are justified from all things," and shall unite for ever with the murderous

[a] Heb. xi. 1. in the Greek. [b] Isai. xxviii. 17.

Manasseh, the adulterous David, the filthy Magdalen, and the persecuting Saul, in singing "Salvation to God and the Lamb!" We must not however be understood to say, that an attention to the faith of the Gospel will save us, while we neglect its practical injunctions: far from it: but this we do say, that the vilest of sinners may find "acceptance in the Beloved;" and that "all who put their trust in him may be quiet from the fear of evil." The declaration of God himself is, "There is no condemnation to them that are *in* Christ Jesus."]

2. They, on the contrary, who have despised the offers of mercy, shall perish—

["Whatsoever men sow, that shall they also reap:" and though God's vengeance may be long delayed, it shall surely come at last. What if we see no symptoms of it now? There was no appearance of a deluge when Noah warned the old world; nor were the fire and brimstone visible, when Lot entreated his sons-in-law to escape with him from Sodom; yet were the predictions relative to these events exactly fulfilled: he who built the ark, and he who fled from the devoted city, were preserved; while they who took not warning, were destroyed. So also shall it be in the last day: "the unbelief of men shall not make the faith of God of none effect." "Their covenant with death shall be disannulled, and their agreement with hell made void: when the overflowing scourge shall pass through, they shall be beaten down by it[c]." Nor shall the excuses, which they now urge with so much confidence, avail them. It is probable that many of the Egyptians might expose themselves to danger in consequence of *urgent business,* or from what they judged a *necessary obedience to the commands of their masters;* but they perished notwithstanding. So shall that word be verified in spite of all excuses, "Whoso despiseth the word shall be destroyed; but he that feareth the commandment, shall be rewarded[d]."]

ADDRESS,

1. Those that disregard the word of the Lord—

[There are, alas! too many who "stumble at the word, being disobedient:" their language is, "As for the word that thou hast spoken unto us in the name of the Lord, we will not hearken unto thee[e]." If they do not avowedly reject the word, they shew by their conduct, that they consider its doctrines as fanatical, its precepts as harsh, its promises as illusory, and its threatenings as vain. But, while "they thus practically reject the word of the Lord, what wisdom is in them[f]?" Doubtless if they who were in the midst of the storm saw any of their neighbours housed, they would cast a wishful look at them:

[c] Isai. xxviii. 18. [d] Prov. xiii. 13. [e] Jer. xliv. 16. [f] Jer. viii. 9

and will not their lot be envied in the last day, who shall have taken refuge in Christ, and found protection from the wrath of God? Let then the remembrance of what took place in Egypt operate powerfully on our hearts. Let us "search the Scriptures, and make them our meditation day and night." Let us take them " as a light to our feet and a lantern to our paths." Let us "treasure them up in our hearts," and labour to follow the directions they give us. Let us "receive the word with meekness," "not as the word of men, but as it is in truth, the word of God." Let us beg of God that it may be " quick and powerful, and sharper than any two-edged sword, piercing to our inmost souls, and discovering to us the very thoughts and intents of our hearts." Let God's blessed word regulate our hearts and lives: then will God look upon us with favourable acceptance[g], and acknowledge us as "his in the day that he shall make up his jewels[h]."]

2. Those who fear the word of the Lord—

[Some there are amongst us, we trust, who having once, like good Josiah, wept on account of the denunciations of God's wrath, now, like holy Job, "esteem God's word more than their necessary food." There is not a threatening in it which they dare to despise, or a promise which they do not desire to enjoy, or a precept which they do not labour to obey. They desire nothing so much as to be "cast into the mould of the Gospel," and to be "sanctified by means of it in body, soul, and spirit." To all of this character I say, Happy are ye; for if "ye tremble at the word" of God, ye have no reason to tremble at any thing else. Ye may look at death with complacency, and at hell itself without terror, since ye are screened under the shadow of your Redeemer's wings. Envy not then the liberty, and the thoughtlessness of sinners; neither let their revilings deter you from your purpose. The time is quickly coming when your God will appear to their shame and to your joy[i]. Then the wisdom of your conduct will be seen in its true colours: and you shall understand the full import of that question, "Doth not my word do good to him that walketh uprightly[k]?"]

[g] Isai. lxv. 2.   [h] Mal. iii. 17.   [i] Isai. lxv. 5.   [k] Mic. ii. 7.

OUTLINE NO. 73

ON DELAYING OUR REPENTANCE.

Exod. x. 3. *Thus saith the Lord God of the Hebrews, How long wilt thou refuse to humble thyself before me?*

IT cannot be denied that Pharaoh was a remarkable character, raised up by God himself to be a monument of God's power throughout all generations[a]. Yet we mistake if we think that the dispositions which he exercised were peculiar to him: the occasions that called them forth into exercise, were peculiar; but the dispositions themselves were the common fruits of our corrupt nature, visible in all the human race. The command given to Pharaoh to permit all the Hebrews to go into the wilderness to offer sacrifice to their God, he chose not to comply with: and all the judgments inflicted on him, and the mercies vouchsafed to him, were ineffectual for the subduing of his rebellious spirit, and for the reducing of him to a willing obedience. And every one who reads the history of these events stands amazed at the pride and obduracy of his heart. But if we would look inward, and see how *we* have withstood the commands of God, and how little effect either his judgments or his mercies have produced on us, we should find little occasion to exult over Pharaoh: we should see, that, however circumstances then elicited and rendered more conspicuous the evils of *his* heart, the very same corruptions, which he manifested, are in *us* also, and that every individual amongst us has the same need as he of the expostulation in the text; "How long wilt thou refuse to humble thyself before me?" And it is remarkable that this very account of Pharaoh was ordered to be transmitted to the latest posterity, in order that the children of all succeeding generations might see in it what his enemies are to expect at His hands, and what his friends[b].

That we may render this subject the more generally useful, we will,

I. Shew wherein true humiliation consists—

A full and abstract investigation of this point would lead us too far: we shall therefore confine ourselves to such particulars as the context more immediately suggests. True humiliation then consists in,

1. A deep and ingenuous sorrow for sin, as contrasted with forced acknowledgments—

[If confessions extorted by sufferings or by fear were

[a] Exod. ix. 16.   [b] ver. 1, 2.

sufficient evidences of humility, Pharaoh would never have received the reproof in our text: for on the plague of hail being inflicted, he sent for Moses and said, "I have sinned this time. The Lord is righteous; and I and my people are wicked[c]." But notwithstanding this, in God's estimation he still, as the text expresses it, "refused to humble himself before God." Yet is this the only humiliation which many amongst ourselves have ever experienced. In a time of sickness perhaps, or under any great and accumulated afflictions, we have been constrained to confess our desert of God's judgments. We have seen, that He has been contending with us; and that yet heavier judgments awaited us, if we did not humble ourselves before him. We have trembled perhaps at the prospect of approaching dissolution, and at the thought of appearing in an unprepared state at the tribunal of our Judge. Hence have arisen some forced acknowledgments of our sinfulness, whilst yet we neither hated our sins, nor lothed ourselves on account of them: and hence, on our restoration to health, we have returned, like fused metal from the furnace, to our wonted hardness and obduracy.

True humiliation is widely different from this. It implies a deep and ingenuous sorrow for sin, not only on account of the judgments it will bring upon us, but on account of its own intrinsic hatefulness and deformity. It leads us to smite on our breasts with conscious shame; and fills us with self-lothing and self-abhorrence: and this it does not only before we have obtained mercy, but afterwards; yea, and so much the more because God *is* pacified towards us[d].

We readily acknowledge that tears are no certain sign of penitence; and that the sensibility that produces them depends rather on the constitutional habit, than on the convictions of the mind. Yet whilst we read so much in the Scriptures respecting men sowing in tears, and going on their way weeping, and whilst we behold the Saviour himself weeping over Jerusalem, and pouring out his soul before God with strong crying and tears, we cannot but think, that those who have never yet wept for sin, have never felt its bitterness: and there is just occasion for us to weep over all who have not yet wept for themselves. It is scarcely to be conceived that any man has a truly broken and contrite spirit, whose sighs and groans have not often entered into the ears of the omnipresent God, and whose tears have not been often treasured up in his vials.]

2. An unreserved obedience to God, as contrasted with partial compliances—

[Pharaoh, under the pressure of his successive calamities,

---

[c] Exod. ix. 27.   [d] Job xlii. 6. with Ezek. xvi. 63.

yielded in part to the commands of God: he resisted altogether at the first; but gradually receded from his determinations, and permitted the Hebrews to offer their sacrifices in Egypt; then to go into the wilderness, provided they did not go very far into it: then he would let the men go: then at last the women and children also: but he would not suffer them to take away their cattle: those he was determined to keep, as a pledge of their return. In all this there was nothing but pride and stoutness of heart. He held every thing fast, till it was wrested from him by some fresh judgment, and conceded nothing but from absolute compulsion. And thus it is that many amongst ourselves part with their sins. They would retain them all, and gladly too, if the indulgence of them would consist with their hope from heaven. If they part with any, they do it as a mariner who casts his goods overboard to lighten his ship and keep it from sinking: but it is with reluctance that he parts with them; and he wishes for them all again, the very instant he is safe on shore. From the same motive flows his performance of certain duties: he engages not in them from any delight that he has in them, but from a self-righteous desire of purchasing heaven by these sacrifices.

But in all this there is nothing of true humiliation, nothing of real piety. The sinner, when his heart is right with God, desires to fulfil all the commandments of his God: "not one of them is grievous unto him:" he would not wish to be allowed to violate any one of them; but desires to " stand perfect and complete in all the will of God." He would not retain a right eye or a right hand, that should be an occasion of offence to his God and Saviour. As it is his prayer that " God's will may be done by him on earth as it is in heaven," so is it his daily endeavour to carry it into effect: and, could he but have the desire of his soul, he would be " pure as Christ himself is pure," and " perfect as his Father which is in heaven is perfect."

This union of deep sorrow for the past, and of unreserved obedience for the future, is marked by God himself as constituting that state of mind which alone will prove effectual for our acceptance with him.]

Having explained the nature of true humiliation, we proceed to,

II. Expostulate with those in whom it is not yet wrought—

There is but too much reason for this expostulation wheresoever we look—

[Their need of humiliation, none, I apprehend, will venture to deny. Let us only look back and see how we have acted towards God, as our Creator, our Governor, our

Benefactor — — — Let us mark our past conduct also towards the Lord Jesus Christ, who assumed our nature, and died upon the cross to save us — — — Let us yet further call to mind all the resistance which we have given to the motions of the Holy Spirit within us — — — and we shall find ground enough for our humiliation before God.

Yet who has humbled himself aright? Who has sought the Lord from day to day " with strong crying and tears?" — — — Who has given up himself wholly and unreservedly to God, determining through grace to have no other will but his? — — —

Does not conscience testify against us in relation to these matters, and warn us that there is yet much, very much wanting, to perfect our humiliation before God? — — —]

We beg leave then, in the name of the Most High God, to expostulate with all whose consciences now testify against them—

[" How long will ye refuse to humble yourselves before God?" Have ye ever fixed a time in your minds? Do ye fix upon old age? What certainty have ye of living to old age? Do ye fix upon a time of sickness and of death? How know ye that ye shall have space then given for repentance, or that the Spirit of God, whom ye now resist, shall be imparted to you for the producing of true repentance? How know ye, that if you do *then* repent, your repentance will proceed any further, or be more effectual for your salvation than Pharaoh's was?

Consider, I pray you, the *guilt*, the *folly*, and the *danger* of delaying your humiliation before God. Will you make the very forbearance of God which should lead you to repentance, the ground and occasion of protracting your rebellion against him? — — — Think ye that God will not overcome at the last? Will ye set briers and thorns in battle against the devouring fire? or did ye ever hear of one who hardened himself against God and prospered? — — —Will not sin harden you in proportion as it is indulged? And " will the Spirit strive with you for ever?" Have you not reason to fear, that, if you continue impenitent under your present circumstances, God will give you up to judicial hardness, and a reprobate mind? — — —

Beloved Brethren, I entreat you to fix some time when you will cast down the weapons of your rebellion, and humble yourselves in truth before God — — —]

Two encouragements I would set before you:

1. It is never too late—

[At " the eleventh hour" those who give themselves up to Him shall be received. Let not the aged, or the sick, say, 'There is no hope.' Let not the vilest of the human race indulge despair. A Manasseh holds forth to every child of man the richest encouragement ——— and an assurance that of those who come to Christ in penitence and faith, "not one shall ever be cast out[e]"———]

2. It is never too soon—

[It was not the men only, but the children also, yea, even "the little ones," whom God required to go forth into the wilderness to offer sacrifice to him[f]: and in the New Testament our blessed Lord says, "Suffer the little children to come unto me, and forbid them not; for of such is the kingdom of heaven." O that young people did but know the blessedness of serving God! Who ever yet regretted that he had begun to repent too soon? Who ever yet made it a matter of sorrow that he "had served the Lord from his youth?" "Remember then, my Brethren, your Creator in the days of your youth." Let not Satan have the best of your time; and the mere dregs be reserved for God: but "to-day, whilst it is called to-day," begin that life, which is the truest source of happiness in this world, and the most certain pledge of glory in the world to come.]

[e] 2 Chron. xxxiii. 12, 13.   [f] ver. 9, 10.

OUTLINE NO. 74
DISTINGUISHING PRIVILEGES OF THE LORD'S PEOPLE.

Exod. x. 23. *But all the children of Israel had light in their dwellings.*

OF all the plagues which in rapid succession were inflicted upon Egypt, not so much as one fell upon the children of Israel: their cattle, and every thing belonging to them, enjoyed the same exemption as themselves. And this distinction was well calculated to convince Pharaoh, that Israel's God was the only true God, and that the idols of the heathen were vanity[a]. But, whilst we admit that this was the primary end of all the judgments, and of the plague of darkness amongst the rest, we cannot but think that this particular plague had something in it more than ordinarily instructive; inasmuch as it served to shew, that between the Lord's people and others there is at all times as great a difference, as there then was between Goshen and the rest of Egypt. We say not, indeed, that this particular application of the subject is anywhere suggested by the inspired writers; but we do say, that it may well be so applied,

[a] Exod. viii. 22

in a way of accommodation at least, to the elucidation of this most important point.

I will take occasion from it then to shew,

I. The difference which God has put between his own people and others—

In their state, and nature, in their relation to God and to each other, in their prospects also, and in their end, the two descriptions of persons are widely different from each other: the one are quickened from the dead, and partakers of a divine nature; united to Christ and to each other in one body and by one spirit; with an heavenly inheritance before them, which they are speedily and for ever to possess; whilst the others are yet "children of the wicked one," with no other prospect than that of a banishment from the divine presence, and an everlasting participation with the fallen angels in their unhappy lot. But without entering into this large view of the subject, I will endeavour to shew what light the children of Israel are privileged to enjoy in,

1. Things temporal—

[In appearance, "all things come alike to all;" or, if there be any particular difference in relation to temporal things, it is rather in favour of the ungodly. But the godly, whether they possess more or less of this world, have an enjoyment of it, of which the world at large are destitute, and in their present state incapable. They taste God's love in every thing; and have a more vivid apprehension of the smallest blessings, than an ungodly man has of the greatest. The "blessings" of the ungodly are, in fact, "cursed to them:" "their table is a snare to them;" and even their bodily health and strength are made occasions of more flagrant transgressions against their God. To God's Israel, on the contrary, their severest afflictions are made sources of good; insomuch that they can "glory in their tribulations[b]," and "take pleasure in their sorest infirmities[c]." Whatever trials assault them, they "all work together for their good[d];" yea, "light and momentary as they are, they work out for them a far more exceeding and eternal weight of glory[e]." The very best portion of the wicked is lighter than vanity; whilst the worst of a good man's lot is received by him not only with "patience

[b] Rom. v. 3.   [c] 2 Cor. xii. 10.   [d] Rom. viii. 25.   [e] 2 Cor. iv. 17.

and long-suffering, but with joy and thankfulness[f]." Though he be the poorest of mankind, he does in effect "inherit the earth;" yea, he "inherits all things."]

2. Things spiritual—

[The ungodly man is truly in darkness with respect to every thing that is of a spiritual nature. He neither does, nor can, comprehend any thing of that kind, for want of a spiritual discernment. But God's highly favoured people "have light in their dwellings," whereby they can discern things invisible to mortal eyes. The evil of sin, the beauty of holiness, the glory of Christ, the blessedness of heaven, are open to their view, and are contemplated by them with a zest which can be conceived by those only who actually experience it in their souls. What shall I say of "the light of God's countenance lifted up upon them," or of "the love of God shed abroad in their hearts by the Holy Ghost?" What shall I say of the Holy Spirit dwelling in them as "a Spirit of adoption," "witnessing with their spirits that they are God's children," and "sealing them unto the day of redemption," and being "an earnest of heaven itself" in their souls? To attempt to describe these things would be only to "darken counsel by words without knowledge." If we should in vain attempt to convey to one immured in a dungeon a just conception of the lustre and influence of the meridian sun; much more must we fail, if we would attempt to give to a natural man a just apprehension of "the things of the Spirit:" for neither have we any language whereby adequately to express them, nor have they any faculties whereby duly to apprehend them.]

3. Things eternal—

[What can an ungodly man see beyond the grave? Truly in relation to the future world he is in darkness, even in "a darkness that may be felt." If he reflect at all, he can feel nothing but "a certain fearful looking-for of judgment and fiery indignation to consume him," and have no prospect but that of "the blackness of darkness for ever." But in reference to eternity, the child of God is seen to the greatest advantage. O, what prospects are open to his view! What crowns, what kingdoms, await him! Truly he stands as on Mount Pisgah, and surveys the Promised Land in all its length and breadth. He joins already with the heavenly hosts in all their songs of praise, and, according to the measure of the grace bestowed upon him, anticipates "the pleasures which are at God's right hand for evermore."]

But, that I may not tantalize you with joys which you can never taste, let me proceed to shew you,

[f] Col. i. 11, 12.

II. How we may secure to ourselves their happy lot—

Can an Egyptian become an Israelite? Yes, he may—

[An Israelite is a descendant of Abraham, in the line of Jacob. But how then can this relation be transferred to a foreigner? After the flesh indeed, an Edomite must remain an Edomite; an Egyptian must continue an Egyptian. But after the Spirit, the transition may be made by all, of whatever nation, provided only they earnestly desire it. Through faith in that blessed Saviour in whom Abraham believed, we may be brought to a participation of all the blessings which were conferred on him. Hear what the Scripture saith: "Know ye, that they who are of faith, *the same are the children of Abraham:*" the same, too, are "*blessed with* faithful Abraham;" yea, "*the blessing of* Abraham comes on them through Jesus Christ:" "if we be Christ's, then are we *Abraham's seed, and heirs* according to the promise[g]."]

And, under this character, we shall be exempted from all the Egyptian plagues, and entitled to all the distinctions that ever were conferred on God's chosen people—

[Truly, however gross the darkness which may have covered us in past times, we shall have "light in our dwellings;" yea, we shall be brought out of darkness into God's marvellous light; and not only "be turned from darkness unto light, but from the power of Satan unto God." Say, Brethren, whether this does not accord with the experience of some amongst you? Say, whether the brightest hours of your former life are comparable even with your darkest now? I well know that in this present life there will be clouds that will occasionally intercept the full radiance of the Sun of Righteousness, and induce a transient gloom over your horizon: but I ask with confidence, whether at such a season you would exchange your portion for that of the happiest worldling upon earth? No: you well know, that though your "darkness may continue for a night, joy will come in the morning[h]:" and even in the darkest night some gleams of light are wont to shine into your soul, according to that sure promise, "Unto the godly there ariseth up light in the darkness[i]." True it is, that sin will bring darkness upon the soul: and true it is, also, that bodily disease may sometimes operate unfavourably in this respect: but, if we be upright before God, "when we walk in darkness, the Lord will be a light unto us[k];" and, in

---

[g] Gal. iii. 7, 9, 14, 29.   [h] Ps. xxx. 5.
[i] Ps. cxii. 4.   [k] Mic. vii. 8.

due season, " our light shall shine in obscurity, and our darkness be as the noonday¹."]

ADDRESS—

1. Those who are walking in the light of their own carnal enjoyments—

[Truly it is but a taper that ye possess, whilst ye are regardless of the radiance of the noonday sun — — — And what does God say to you? " Behold, all ye that kindle a fire, that compass yourselves about with sparks; walk in the light of your fire, and in the sparks that ye have kindled: but this shall ye have of mine hand at last, ye shall lie down in sorrowᵐ." " Behold, my servants shall eat, but ye shall be hungry: behold, my servants shall drink, but ye shall be thirsty: behold, my servants shall rejoice, but ye shall be ashamed: behold, my servants shall sing for joy of heart, but ye shall cry for sorrow of heart, and shall howl for vexation of spiritⁿ."]

2. Those who, though Israelites indeed, are yet walking in somewhat of a gloomy frame—

[We have before said, that such seasons may occur: but the direction given you by God himself is that which must be your consolation and support: " Who is among you that feareth the Lord, that obeyeth the voice of his servant, and yet walketh in darkness and hath no light? Let him trust in the name of the Lord, and stay upon his Godᵒ." There may be reasons for the withdrawment of light from your souls, reasons of which you at present have no conception. Peradventure God has seen that you have not duly improved the former manifestations of his love; or he may see that an uninterrupted continuance of them might give advantage to Satan to puff you up with pride. But, whether you can trace these suspensions of the divine favour to any particular cause or not, learn at all events to justify God in them, and to improve them for the deeper humiliation of your souls: and look forward to that blessed period when you shall " dwell in the light as God is in the light," and enjoy a day that shall never endᵖ.]

¹ Isai. lviii. 10.   ᵐ Isai. l. 11.   ⁿ Isai. lxv. 13, 14.
ᵒ Isai. l. 10.   ᵖ 1 John i. 7. Rev. xxi. 23. and xxii. 5.

OUTLINE NO. 75

GOD PUTS A DIFFERENCE BETWEEN HIS PEOPLE AND OTHERS.

Exod. xi. 7. *Know, how that the Lord doth put a difference between the Egyptians and Israel.*

A PRINCIPAL intent of God in the various dispensations of his providence is, to make himself known unto the world. By some of his works he makes known his natural perfections of wisdom and power; by others, his moral perfections of goodness and truth. In his dealings with Pharaoh in particular, we are expressly told that he had this end in view[a]. The exercise of his sovereignty was in that instance intended to be displayed[b]; as also in the whole of " the difference which he put between the Israelites and the Egyptians:" but if we consider these two nations as types or representatives of the friends and enemies of God, we shall be rather led to contemplate the equity of all his dispensations towards them. It is in this light that we propose to dwell upon the words before us.

" Know ye then that the Lord doth put a difference between his own people and others"—

I. He did so from the beginning—

[Go back to the antediluvian world[c] — — — Consult the patriarchal age[d] — — — Look at the history before us[e] — — — Search the records of all succeeding ages[f] — — — The annals of the whole world conspire to establish this important truth.]

II. He does so at this present hour—

[If we have been attentive observers of what passes around us, or within our own hearts, we shall not need to be told that God does at this time, no less than in former ages, distinguish his people from others. He does so in the dispensations[g]

---

[a] Exod. x. 1, 2.   [b] Rom. ix. 17—20.

[c] How different his conduct towards the two first men that were born into the world! Gen. iv. 3—5. What singular honour did he confer on Enoch! Heb. xi. 5. What distinguished mercy did he vouchsafe to Noah! Gen. vi. 9—13.

[d] How different his regards to Abraham, Isaac, and Jacob, from any that he shewed to those amongst whom they dwelt!

[e] From the latter plagues, the flies, the murrain, the darkness, and the slaughter of the first-born, the Israelites were exempt. The cloud also was dark to one, but light to the other: and the sea was both a passage and a grave.

[f] It is impossible to read the history of David or Elijah in the Old Testament, or of the Apostles in the New, and not see this written as with a sunbeam.

[g] He not unfrequently interposes to screen them from calamities, (Job v. 19—24.) and always to sanctify the calamities he sends. Rom. viii. 28. His very presence with them in trouble is equivalent

of his providence — — — and in the communications of his grace [h] — — —]

III. He will do so to all eternity—

[If we would know the full extent of that difference which he will put between his people and others, we must go up to heaven, and taste all the glories of it — — — and go down to hell, and experience all its miseries — — — Never till then shall we be adequate judges of this momentous subject.]

QUESTIONS—

1. Do you believe this truth?

[Many think that "God will not do good or evil," and that he will neither reward nor punish. Whether they be conscious of such infidelity or not, their life too plainly proves its dominion over them — — — Beware of such atheistical sentiments; and seek that, whatever becomes of others, ye may be monuments of his love and favour — — —]

2. Do you live under the influence of it?

[Happy were it for us, if we could always bear in mind this solemn truth! How importunate would be our prayers, how ardent our praises, how indefatigable our exertions! — — — Let us contemplate the separation which God will make in the day of judgment[i]; and labour incessantly, that we may be numbered amongst his most favoured saints[k] — — —]

to a deliverance from it. Ps. xxxi. 20. (*The full import of that verse will, when discovered, richly repay our meditations upon it.*)

[h] Whence is it that the Lord's people are enabled to triumph, as they do, over the world, the flesh, and the devil? Is it not that they are strengthened by Christ, (Phil. iv. 13.) and that "his grace is sufficient for them?"

[i] Mal. iii. 18. Matt. xxv. 33, 46. [k] Mal. iii. 16, 17.

OUTLINE NO. 76

REDEMPTION CELEBRATED.

Exod. xii. 41, 42. *It came to pass at the end of four hundred and thirty years, even the self-same day it came to pass, that all the hosts of the Lord went out from the land of Egypt. It is a night to be much observed unto the Lord, for bringing them out from the land of Egypt: this is that night of the Lord to be observed of all the children of Israel in their generations.*

THE Lord, for wise and gracious reasons, often delays the execution of his promises; till we, in our impatience, are almost ready to think he has forgotten them. But, however long he may appear to neglect us, "he is not slack concerning his promises, as some men count slackness[a]." He has fixed a time, beyond which there shall be no delay[b]: and at the appointed hour he will shew himself "mighty to save."

To Abraham and his seed God promised to give the land of Canaan. But behold, no less than four hundred and thirty years were ordained of him to pass, and a great portion of that time in extreme suffering, before his seed were permitted to see the long-wished-for period. But at the time fixed from the beginning in the divine counsels, "even the self-same day it came to pass," that all the hosts of Israel were brought forth out of Egypt; and God's promises to them were fulfilled.

In like manner it was promised to Adam that "the seed of the woman should bruise the serpent's head." But four thousand years were suffered to elapse before that promised Seed was sent into the world. "When, however, the fulness of time was come, God sent him, made of a woman, made under the Law, to redeem them that were under the Law, that we might receive the adoption of sons[c]." In effecting this great work, the Messiah was to die[d]. But "he was not to see corruption[e]." On the third day he was to rise again[f]. To prevent this, every expedient was resorted to, that human ingenuity could contrive. But at the appointed moment the Saviour rose; and thus completed the deliverance of a ruined world.

These two events are referred to in the text; the one, historically; the other, typically.

To these events I will *first* call your attention—

Great was the deliverance of Israel from Egypt—

[Sore, beyond conception, was the bondage of the children of Israel; insomuch that "God himself was grieved at it." But, through the judgments executed on their oppressors, Pharaoh was at last prevailed on to dismiss them. The last great judgment that was inflicted on their enemies was the destruction of their first-born throughout all the land of Egypt;

---

[a] 2 Pet. iii. 9.   [b] Hab. ii. 3.   [c] Gal. iv. 4, 5.
[d] Heb. ii. 14, 15.   [e] Ps. xvi. 10.   [f] Matt. xii. 40.

from which the Israelites were protected by the blood of the paschal lamb sprinkled on their dwellings. This was altogether a wonderful deliverance, such as never had been vouchsafed to any other nation under heaven[g].

The end of that deliverance rendered it yet more glorious; because they were now consecrated to the Lord as "a special people above all people upon the face of the earth:" and they were led forth under the immediate guidance and protection of God himself, to "a land flowing with milk and honey," "a land that was the glory of all lands."

This was a redemption which might well be remembered by them, in all future ages, with wonder, and gratitude, and praise.]

But infinitely greater is the deliverance that has been vouchsafed to us—

From how much sorer bondage are we rescued, even from the bonds of sin and Satan, death and hell! ——— And how much more wonderful is the means of our preservation, even the blood of God's only dear Son, once shed on Calvary, and now sprinkled on our souls! ——— To how much higher a state too are we raised, not *nominally*, but *really*, the sons of God, and the inheritors of the kingdom of heaven! ——— What shall we say of this? It surpasses the utmost conception both of men and angels; and has a height and depth, and length and breadth, that is utterly incomprehensible.]

Let me *next* commend to your special observance this[h] day, on which these great events are commemorated—

They deserve well to be commemorated by the whole human race—

[The deliverance from Egypt will be a standing memorial of God's power and grace to the very end of time. But what shall we say of the redemption which that event typified? Should not *that* be held in remembrance by us? Should not that be annually commemorated with the devoutest acknowledgments? Verily, "it is a day much to be observed unto the Lord," even unto the latest generations.

And here I cannot but regret that the stated remembrance of these wonderful events is by a great multitude of religious professors utterly disregarded. Under an idea of avoiding Popish superstition, many have run to an opposite extreme, and cast off the very semblance of gratitude, and put from them the most effectual means of exciting it in the soul. That such memorials may degenerate into form, I readily acknowledge; but that they may be subservient to the greatest

[g] Deut. iv. 32—34.   [h] Preached on *Easter Day*.

spiritual elevation, I have no doubt: and I cannot but lament, that, through a licentious zeal for what they call liberty, many deprive themselves of most invaluable blessings. To us of the Established Church, I thank God, these privileges are preserved: and I would recommend to every one of you a conscientious and devout improvement of them. Nor can I doubt, but that as the memorial of our Lord's death continued to us in the Sacramental Supper is found a blessing, so will the stated remembrance of our Lord's birth, and death, and resurrection, on the days on which they are commemorated, prove a blessing to all who will consecrate the time to a special consideration of those stupendous mercies.]

The way in which they should be observed may be learned from the history before us—

[The Israelites, to their latest generations, were on that day to eat of the paschal lamb, and to renew their dedication of themselves to him as his peculiar people. And in this way should we employ this holy day.

Let us this day *keep a feast unto the Lord*[i]. Let us eat of the Paschal Lamb, and feed on that adorable Saviour who shed his blood for us, to redeem our souls from death — — — But let us " eat it with the bitter herbs" of penitential sorrow, and " with the unleavened bread" of sincerity and truth[k]. Nor is this a suggestion of man; but of the Lord himself, who has given us this very command[l]. Mark well, I pray you, these peculiar circumstances, which alone will ensure a favourable acceptance of your services before God: for without deep penitence and guileless sincerity your services will be only an abomination to the Lord — — —

Let us also *dedicate ourselves to him as his peculiar people*[m]. We are not our own: we are bought with a price: we should therefore glorify our God with our bodies, and our spirits, which are his[n]. Remember how entirely the people of Israel were now separated from the world, and how completely they were made dependent on their God. Remember too, that they had but one object in view, namely, the attainment of the promised land. Thus *in spirit* should we be: *in spirit*, I say; because we have offices to perform, which preclude a possibility of entire separation from the world. But if, whilst we fulfil the duties of our respective stations in the world, we attain *in heart* what the external situation of Israel was designed to represent, we shall do well. *This* should from henceforth be our one labour. Behold them, and God himself at their head—he theirs, and they his! So let us consecrate ourselves this day to him, that " we may be his people, and he our God, for ever and ever."]

[i] ver. 14.   [k] ver. 8. with Deut. xvi. 1—4.   [l] 1 Cor. v. 7, 8.
[m] Exod. xiii. 2. with Numb. viii. 17.   [n] 1 Cor. vi. 19, 20.

OUTLINE NO. 77
THE PASSOVER.

Exod. xii. 3—11. *Speak ye unto all the congregation of Israel, saying, In the tenth day of this month they shall take to them every man a lamb, according to the house of their fathers, a lamb for an house: and if the household be too little for the lamb, let him and his neighbour next unto his house take it, according to the number of the souls: every man according to his eating shall make your count for the lamb. Your lamb shall be without blemish, a male of the first year: ye shall take it out from the sheep, or from the goats. And ye shall keep it up until the fourteenth day of the same month; and the whole assembly of the congregation of Israel shall kill it in the evening. And they shall take of the blood, and strike it on the two side-posts, and on the upper door-post of the houses wherein they shall eat it. And they shall eat the flesh in that night, roast with fire, and unleavened bread; and with bitter herbs they shall eat it. Eat not of it raw, nor sodden at all with water, but roast with fire; his head with his legs, and with the purtenance thereof. And ye shall let nothing of it remain until the morning; and that which remaineth of it until the morning ye shall burn with fire. And thus shall ye eat it; with your loins girded, your shoes on your feet, and your staff in your hand: and ye shall eat it in haste; it is the Lord's passover.*

THE mercies promised to the Lord's people shall be fulfilled to them in due season. Their trials may be long continued, and may increase when the time of their termination is near at hand: but God will not forget his promises, or delay the execution of them beyond the proper time. He had foretold to Abraham that his posterity should be ill treated in Egypt to a certain period; but that they should then be brought out of it with great substance. The appointed period, foretold four hundred and thirty years before, was arrived, and yet the condition of the Israelites was as distressed as ever: but at its conclusion, "*even on the self-same day,*" the promised deliverance was vouchsafed; and an ordinance was appointed to keep up the remembrance of it to all future generations.

From the words of our text we shall be led to notice,
I. The ordinance itself—

This was,

1. Commemorative—

[The deliverance of Israel from the sword of the destroying angel, and from their bondage in Egypt, was great[a], and unparalleled from the foundation of the world[b]. And, in the commemoration of it, God appointed that in all future ages one of the junior members of each family should ask the reason of the institution, and the head of the family should relate what God had done for their nation in *passing over* the houses of the Israelites when he slew the Egyptians, and in bringing them out of their cruel bondage[c]. To this the Apostle refers, when he speaks of the Lord's Supper as an ordinance appointed for "*the shewing forth* of the Lord's death, till he come" again at the end of the world to judgment[d].]

2. Typical—

[Every the minutest particular in this ordinance seems to have been intended to typify the redemption of the world by the death of Christ. "The *lamb*," which was to be "*under a year old*," denotes Christ, "the Lamb of God," in a state of perfect purity[e]. It was to be "*a male*," as being the most perfect of its kind, and "*without blemish*," in order to represent the perfect manhood of Christ, who was indeed "a lamb without blemish and without spot[f]." It was to be *set apart four days before it was slain;* not only to mark God's eternal designation of Christ to be a sacrifice, but to foreshew that Christ, during the four last days of his life, (from his entrance into Jerusalem to his death,) should be examined at different tribunals, to ascertain whether there were the smallest flaw in his character; that so his bitterest enemies might all be constrained to attest his innocence, and thereby unwittingly to *declare, that he was fit to be a sacrifice for the sins of the whole world.* The precise hour of the day wherein Jesus was to die, is thought to have been predicted by *the time appointed for the slaying* of the paschal lamb, which was "between the two evenings," or soon after three o'clock in the afternoon: and it was ordered to be *slain by all the congregation;* to shew that all ranks and orders of men, both of Jews and Gentiles, should concur in his death. Its *blood* was to be *sprinkled on the door-posts and lintels*, to shew that the blood of Christ must be sprinkled upon our hearts and consciences, if we would not fall a prey to the destroying angel: but it was *not* to be sprinkled *on the threshold*, because the blood of Christ is not to be trodden under foot, or counted by

---

[a] Deut. xxvi. 8.   [b] Deut. iv. 34.   [c] ver. 25—27.   [d] 1 Cor. xi. 26.

[e] This seems more suited to its tender age than the explanation generally given, of Christ being cut off in the midst of his years.

[f] 1 Pet. i. 19

any as an unholy thing[g]. Its *flesh* was *to be roasted,* (not to be eaten raw or boiled,) that the extremity of our Saviour's sufferings from the fire of God's wrath might be more fitly depicted. It was to be *eaten by all;* because none can ever be saved, unless they eat of Christ's flesh, and receive him into their hearts by faith. It was to be *eaten whole, and not a bone of it to be broken*[h]; probably to intimate, that we must receive Christ in all his offices and in all his benefits; and certainly to foreshew, that he should be exempt from the common fate of all who died his death, and be marked out thereby with the most undoubted evidence, as the true Messiah. And *none* of it was *to be left till the morning,* lest it should be treated contemptuously by the profane, or become an occasion of idolatry or superstition to mistaken zealots; and to guard us also against similar abuses in the supper of our Lord.]

Some other particulars worthy of observation will occur, while we consider,

II. The manner of its celebration—

In this also was the ordinance both commemorative and typical. The *bitter herbs* and *unleavened bread* were intended to keep up a remembrance of the bitter sorrows which they endured, and the bread of affliction which they ate, in Egypt[i]; and their *standing,* with their *loins girt,* and *shoes on their feet,* and *staves in their hands,* denoted the haste with which they were driven out of the land, as it were, by the Egyptians themselves. As types, these things declared in what manner we should feed upon the Lord Jesus Christ. We know that it is possible enough to strain types and metaphors too far: but in interpreting the import of the paschal sacrifice, though in some smaller matters we may not be able to speak with certainty, the great outlines are drawn by an inspired Apostle; who says, " Christ our passover is sacrificed for us[k]." Taking him then for our guide, we say that we may learn even from the manner in which the passover was celebrated, how we are to feast upon the Lamb of God that has been slain for us. We are to do it

1. With humble penitence—

[The bitter herbs reminded the Israelites of the misery they had endured: but *we* must further reflect upon the guilt

---

[g] Heb. x. 29.   [h] John xix. 36.   [i] Deut. xvi. 4.   [k] 1 Cor. v. 7, 8.

we have contracted. Their bondage was the effect of force and constraint; ours has been altogether voluntary; and therefore has involved us in the deepest guilt —— — When we eat of Christ's flesh, we must recollect that his sufferings were the punishment of our iniquities; and we must "look on him whom we have pierced, and mourn; yea, we must mourn for him as one mourneth for his only son[1]." And the more assured we are of our deliverance from wrath through him, the more must we abhor ourselves for all our iniquities, and for all our abominations[m] — — —]

2. With unfeigned sincerity—

[This is expressly declared by the Apostle to have been intended by the unleavened bread[n]. Sin is a leaven, the smallest portion of which will leaven and defile our whole souls. It must therefore be purged out with all possible care and diligence. If we retain knowingly and wilfully the smallest measure of it, we have nothing to expect but an everlasting separation from God and his people — — — Let us then search and try our own hearts; and beg of God also to "search and try us, to see if there be any wicked way in us, and to lead us in the way everlasting" — — — We must be "Israelites indeed and without guile," if we would enjoy the full benefits of the body and blood of Christ.]

3. With active zeal—

[We are in a strange land, wherein "we have no continuing city; but we seek one to come, even a city that hath foundations, whose builder and maker is God." We are not to take up our rest in this world, but, as pilgrims, with our loins girt, our shoes on our feet, and our staff in our hand, to be always ready to proceed on our journey to the heavenly Canaan. In this state and habit of mind we should feed upon Christ from day to day; commemorating the redemption he has wrought out for us, and receiving from him renewed strength for our journey — — — This weanedness from every thing in this world, and readiness to depart out of it at any moment that our Lord shall call us, constitutes the perfection of a Christian's character, and the summit of his felicity — — —]

APPLICATION—

[Whether we be Israelites feeding on the Paschal Lamb, or Egyptians lying on our beds in thoughtless security, let us remember, that the hour is fast approaching, when God will put a difference between the Israelites and the Egyptians. Let the one rejoice in the safety which they enjoy under the blood sprinkled on their hearts; and let the other tremble at

---

[1] Zech. xii. 10.   [m] Ezek. xvi. 63.   [n] 1 Cor. v. 7, 8.

OUTLINE NO. 78
DELIVERANCE OF THE ISRAELITES FROM THE DESTROYING ANGEL.

Exod. xii. 21—23. *Then Moses called for all the elders of Israel, and said unto them, Draw out, and take you a lamb according to your families, and kill the passover. And ye shall take a bunch of hyssop, and dip it in the blood that is in the bason, and strike the lintel and the two side-posts with the blood that is in the bason; and none of you shall go out at the door of his house until the morning. For the Lord will pass through to smite the Egyptians: and when he seeth the blood upon the lintel and on the two side-posts, the Lord will pass over the door; and will not suffer the destroyer to come in unto your houses to smite you.*

THE office of a Minister is to declare to the people what he himself has received from God to deliver to them[a]. Nothing should be added by him; nothing should be withheld[b]. The direction given to Moses, "See thou make all things according to the pattern shewed to thee in the mount[c]," is that to which all the servants of God should be conformed in all their ministrations. In this consists fidelity. "If we add any thing to the word of God, the plagues contained in it shall be added unto us: if we take away from it, our names shall be taken out of the book of life[d]." It is spoken to the honour of Moses, that "he was faithful in all his house:" and we find invariably, that the messages which he delivered to the people, and the ordinances which he established among them, accorded with the commission which he himself had received from God. In the words before us, he delivers to them a message of terror and of mercy: he informs them of the judgment about to be inflicted on the Egyptian first-born; and of the means which

---
[a] 1 Cor. xv. 3. [b] Acts xx. 27. [c] Heb. viii. 5. [d] Rev. xxii. 18, 19.

God in his mercy had appointed for exempting them from the general calamity.

We propose to consider,

I. The means prescribed—

God might have preserved his people without any particular means; as he did when he sent forth an angel to destroy almost the whole Assyrian army. But he intended this deliverance as a type of a far greater deliverance, which he should afterwards effect through the incarnation and death of his own Son; and therefore he appointed certain observances which should lead their minds to that great event—

1. They must kill the paschal lamb—

[Though the passover differed from all other sacrifices, inasmuch as no part of it was burnt upon the altar, yet it is expressly called a sacrifice[e]; and it was ordered to be represented under that character to all succeeding generations[f]: and St. Paul himself speaks of it as prefiguring, *in that particular view*, the death of Christ[g].

Here then it is most instructive to us, as it teaches us, that, without a sacrifice offered unto God for us, we cannot obtain favour in his sight, or escape the judgments which our sins have merited. We do not presume to say, absolutely, what God might, or might not, have done; because we know nothing of God except as he is pleased to reveal himself to us: but, as far as the revelation he has given us enables us to judge, we are persuaded that a vicarious sacrifice was necessary; and that, without such a sacrifice, God could not have been " just, and at the same time the justifier" of sinful man[h] — — —]

2. They must sprinkle its blood—

[The destroying angel might have been instructed to discern between the Israelites and the Egyptians without any external sign upon the walls: but God ordered that the blood of the lamb should be sprinkled on the lintel, and side-posts of the doors, in order to shew us yet further, that the blood of Christ must be sprinkled on our souls. The blood of the lamb did not save the Israelites by being shed, but by being sprinkled: and, in the same manner, it is not the blood of Christ as shed on Calvary, but as sprinkled on the soul, that saves us from the wrath to come. Hence the Scripture so often speaks of our being " come to the blood of sprinkling, which speaketh better things than the blood of Abel[i]." We must, as it were,

[e] Deut. xvi. 4.   [f] ver. 26, 27.   [g] 1 Cor. v. 7.
[h] Rom. iii. 25, 26.   [i] Heb. xii. 24. and 1 Pet. i. 2.

dip the hyssop in the blood, and by faith apply it to our own hearts and consciences, or else we can have no benefit from it, no interest in it — — —]

3. They must abide in their houses—

[This was appointed, that they might know to what alone they owed their safety, namely, to the blood sprinkled on their houses. If, presuming upon their descent from Abraham, or upon their having killed the passover, any of them had ventured abroad before the morning, they would, in all probability, have perished, as Lot's wife did after her departure from Sodom, or as Shimei afterwards did by going without the walls of Jerusalem[k]. The injunction given to them, teaches us, that we must "*abide* in Christ[1];" and that, to venture for one moment from under the shadow of his wings, will involve us in the most imminent danger, if not in utter ruin. We have no protection from the pursuer of blood any longer than we continue within the walls of the city of refuge[m] — — —]

Let us now take a view of,
II. The deliverance vouchsafed—

The deliverance itself was truly wonderful—

[Throughout all the land of Egypt, the first-born of every person, from the king on his throne to the captive in the dungeon, was slain by an invisible agent. By whatever means the various families were awakened, whether by any sudden impression on their minds, or by the groans of their first-born smitten by the destroying angel, there was at the same hour throughout all the kingdom a cry of lamentation and of terror; of lamentation for their deceased relatives, and of terror on their own account, lest a similar judgment should be inflicted on them also. What dreadful consternation must have prevailed, the instant that the extent of this calamity was seen; when every one, going for relief and comfort to his neighbour, saw him also overwhelmed with similar anguish! But though the first-born of men and cattle was destroyed amongst all the Gentiles, not one, either of men or cattle, suffered amongst the Israelites. How must the whole Jewish nation be struck with wonder at this astonishing display of God's mercy towards them!

But a greater deliverance than this was shadowed forth. There is a day coming when God will put a more awful difference between his friends and enemies; when his enemies,

---

[k] 1 Kings ii. 41—46.
[1] John xv. 4—7. N.B. Five times in four verses is this truth repeated.
[m] Numb. xxxv. 26—28.

384 EXODUS, XII. 21—23. [78.

without exception, shall be smitten with the second death, and his friends be exalted to eternal glory and felicity. What terror will be seen in that day! what weeping, and wailing, and gnashing of teeth among the objects of his displeasure! and what exultation and triumph amongst those who shall be the monuments of his distinguishing favour! *That* deliverance will be indeed wonderful; and eternity will be too short to explore the unsearchable riches of grace and love contained in it.]

The manner in which it was effected also deserves particular attention—

[There was not *one* agent only in this transaction, but *two:* a destroying angel, that went forth to execute judgment indiscriminately on one in every house; and God, who attended him, as it were, to intercept his stroke, and ward off the blow wherever the blood was sprinkled on the houses. This is clearly intimated in the text; and it is as clearly referred to by the Prophet Isaiah, who combines this image with that of a bird darting between her offspring and the bird of prey, in order to protect them from their voracious enemy[n]. Indeed the very name given to the ordinance which was appointed to commemorate this event, was taken from the circumstance of God's leaping forward, and thus obliging the angel to *pass over* every house where the blood appeared.

In reflecting on this, we take comfort from the thought, that, whoever may menace the Lord's people, God himself is their protector; and that, "while he is for them, none can be effectually against them." If all the angels in heaven, yea and all the devils in hell too, were employed to execute vengeance on the earth, we need not fear; since God is omniscient to discern, and almighty to protect, the least and meanest of his believing people.]

We may LEARN from hence,

1. The use and excellence of faith—

[It was "by faith that Moses kept the passover, and the sprinkling of blood, lest he that destroyed the first-born should touch them[o]." It is by faith also, and by faith alone, that we can obtain an interest in the Lord Jesus. In what other way can we present to God his sacrifice? In what other way can we sprinkle our hearts with his atoning blood? In what other way can we "*abide* in him till the morning" of the resurrection? This is not done by repentance, or love, or any other grace, but by faith only. Other graces are good, and necessary in their place; but it is faith only that apprehends Christ, and obtains for us all the benefits of his passion. Let us then

[n] Isai. xxxi. 5. [o] Heb. xi. 28.

"believe in him," and "live upon him," and "dwell in him," as our sure and only deliverer from the wrath to come.]

2. The importance of inquiring into our state before God—

[The generality go to their rest as securely as the Egyptians did, unawed by the threatenings of Almighty God, and unconscious of the danger to which they were exposed. But how many wake in eternity, and find their error when it is too late! Let me then entreat you to inquire whether you have ever dreaded the stroke of God's avenging arm? whether you have been made sensible that God has appointed one way, and one way only, for your escape? whether you have regarded "Christ as your passover that has been sacrificed for you?" whether you have fed upon him, with the bitter herbs of penitence and contrition? Have you dipped the hyssop, as it were, in his blood, and sprinkled your souls with it? And do you feel that it would be at the peril of your souls, if you were to venture for one moment from your place of refuge? Make these inquiries; and be not satisfied till you are assured, on scriptural grounds, that you are out of the reach of the destroying angel. Till then, adopt the prayer of David; "Purge me with hyssop, and I shall be clean; wash me, and I shall be whiter than snow."]

OUTLINE NO. 79

REDEMPTION OF THE FIRST-BORN.

Exod. xiii. 14—16. *And it shall be, when thy son asketh thee in time to come, saying, What is this? that thou shalt say unto him, By strength of hand the Lord brought us out from Egypt, from the house of bondage. And it came to pass, when Pharaoh would hardly let us go, that the Lord slew all the first-born in the land of Egypt, both the first-born of man, and the first-born of beast: therefore I sacrifice to the Lord all that openeth the matrix, being males; but all the first-born of my children I redeem. And it shall be for a token upon thine hand, and for frontlets between thine eyes: for by strength of hand the Lord brought us forth out of Egypt.*

THE works of God deserve to be had in continual remembrance. His interpositions on behalf of our forefathers ought not to be forgotten by us; for we ourselves are greatly affected by them. The whole nation of the Jews at this day, and to the remotest period of time, are deeply interested in the mercy shewn to their ancestors when the Egyptian first-born were slain. If we reckon that every Israelite had two sons, as well as daughters, (which, considering the care that had been taken to destroy all the male children, may be taken as a fair average,) and one out of those sons had been slain, we may calculate, that not above one third of that nation would ever have come into existence. On account of the distinguished greatness of that deliverance, God appointed that it should be kept in remembrance, by means of a variety of ordinances instituted for that purpose. Some of these institutions were to be annually observed, (as the Passover and the feast of unleavened bread,) and others were designed as daily memorials of it. Such was the redemption of the first-born, mentioned in our text. In consequence of the preservation of the first-born, both of men and beasts, among the Jews, God claimed all their future first-born, both of men and beasts, as his property: the clean beasts were to be sacrificed to him; the unclean were to be exchanged for a lamb, which was to be sacrificed; and the first-born children were to be redeemed at the price of five shekels, which sum was devoted to the service of the sanctuary. This ordinance the Jews, to the latest generations, were bound to observe,

I. As a memorial of God's mercy—

In this view, the end of the appointment is repeatedly mentioned in the text. Every time that the redemption-price was paid for the first-born, either of man or beast, it was to be like " a token upon their hands, or a frontlet, or *memorial*, between their eyes[a]," to bring this deliverance to their remembrance.

Now the deliverance vouchsafed to *us*, infinitely exceeds *theirs*—

[Theirs was great, whether we consider the state from which they were brought (a sore bondage), or the means by which they were delivered (the slaughter of the Egyptian first-born), or the state to which they were raised (the service and enjoyment of God, both in the wilderness and in the land of Canaan). But compare ours in these respects, the guilt and

---

[a] See ver. 9.

misery from which we are redeemed ——— the death, not of a few enemies, but of God's only dear Son, by which that redemption is effected ——— and the blessedness to which, both in this world and the next, we are brought forth ——— and all comparison fails: their mercy in comparison of ours is only as the light of a glow-worm to the meridian sun.]

Every thing therefore should serve to bring it to our remembrance—

[God has instituted some things for this express purpose, namely, baptism and the Lord's supper. But why should not the same improvement be made of other things? Why may not the sight of a first-born, whether of man or beast, suggest the same reflections to our minds, that the redemption of them did to the Jews? Why should not the revolutions of days, months, and years, remind us of the darkness and misery from which we are brought through the bright shining of the Sun of Righteousness? What is a recovery from sickness, but an image of the mercy vouchsafed to our souls? As for the Scriptures, I had almost said that we should literally imitate the mistaken piety of the Jews, who wore certain portions of them as bracelets and frontlets; but, if not, we should have them so much in our hands and before our eyes, that the blessed subject of our redemption by Christ should never be long out of our minds.]

But the redemption of the first-born was to be observed also,

II. As an acknowledgment of their duty—

God, in addition to the claim which he has over all his creatures as their Maker, has a peculiar claim to those whom he has redeemed. In this view he called upon the Jews, and he calls upon us also,

1. To consecrate ourselves to him—

[The Jewish first-born of beasts (as has been observed) were sacrificed to God; and his right to the first-born of men was acknowledged by a redemption-price paid for them[b]. The same price too was paid by all (five shekels, or about twelve shillings), to shew that every man's soul was of equal value in the sight of God. With us, there are some important points of difference. All of us, whether male or female, and whether first or last in order of nativity, are accounted as the first-born[c]: nor can any price whatever exempt us from a personal consecration of ourselves to the service of the Lord. The Levites were afterwards substituted in the place of the first-born[d]: but for us no substitute can be admitted. "We are not our own, we are bought

[b] Numb. iii. 46, 47.   [c] Heb. xii. 23.   [d] Numb. iii. 44—50.

with a price," says the Apostle: from whence his inference is, "Therefore we must glorify God with our body and our spirit, which are his^e." And in another place he expresses the same idea in terms still more accommodated to the language of our text; "I beseech you," says he, "by the mercies of God, that ye present your bodies a living sacrifice, holy, acceptable unto God, which is your reasonable service^f."]

2. To serve him with the best of all that we have—

[The poorest among the Israelites, whose cow had enlarged his little stock, must immediately devote that little acquisition in sacrifice to God. If it were an horse or an ass that had produced him a foal, he must redeem the foal with a lamb, or "break its neck^g;" God having decreed, that his people shall derive no comfort or advantage from any thing, with which they are unable, or unwilling, to honour him.

Thus are we bound to "honour God with our substance, and with the first-fruits of all our increase." We must not stay till we have got in our harvest, and then spare to him a pittance out of our abundance; but we must devote to him a portion of what he has already bestowed, and trust him to supply our remaining wants. Strange will it be indeed, if, when "he has not spared his own Son, but delivered him up for us all," we can grudge him any thing that is in the power of our hands to do.]

ADDRESS—

1. Inquire into the nature and ends of God's ordinances—

[The rites of baptism and the Lord's supper are very little understood amongst us: whereas, if we would inquire into the reason of these institutions, we should find them lead us immediately to the great work of redemption: in the former of them we are dedicated to Him who has redeemed us from the bondage of corruption; and in the latter, we renew to him, as it were, our baptismal vows, and derive strength from him for the performance of them. In the common ordinances of divine worship we should see the care which God has taken to make known to us the way of salvation, and to display to us the exceeding riches of his grace in Christ Jesus. If we duly considered God's design in appointing an order of men to minister in his sanctuary, we should not complain that we heard so much of Christ; but rather, we should go up to his house hungering and thirsting after him, as the bread of life and the water of life.

2. Devote yourselves to the service of your God—

[The names of the first-born, and of them only, "are written in heaven^h." If therefore we would partake of the

---

^e 1 Cor. vi. 19, 20.   ^f Rom. xii. 1.   ^g ver. 13.   ^h Note^c.

heavenly inheritance, we must regard ourselves as "an holy nation, and a peculiar people." What the Levites were externally, that must we be in the inward devotion of our souls. We are not loaded, like them, with the observance of many burthensome ceremonies; but the sacrifices of prayer and praise we ought to offer unto God continually; and, in this respect, we are to emulate, as it were, the saints in heaven, who rest not day and night in ascribing glory " to Him who loved them, and washed them from their sins in his own blood." We should distinctly consider ourselves as " his purchased possession," and account it our highest happiness and honour to be in every thing at his disposal[i].]

3. Endeavour to instruct others in the great work of redemption—

[On all the different occasions it was appointed, that children should make inquiries into the reasons of the various institutions which they saw[k]; and that such explanations should be given them, as should tend to perpetuate divine knowledge to the remotest generations. Such inquiries we should encourage amongst our children: and we should cheerfully embrace every opportunity that is afforded us, of instructing them in the things belonging to their eternal peace. If such catechetical instructions were given in our different families, to how much greater advantage would the word of life be dispensed! Our hearers then, being habituated to the consideration of divine truths, would enter more easily into the various subjects that are set before them. They would attend both with pleasure and profit, more especially when they were arrived at years of discretion; whereas now, the greater part of our auditories hear as if they heard not, and continue years under the ministry of the Gospel without ever understanding its fundamental truths. Let this attention then be paid by all parents and masters to their respective families; yea, let the ignorant in general, whether children or adults, be the objects of our affectionate regard: and let us all, in our respective spheres, contribute, as we are able, to impart the knowledge of Christ to others, that they also may behold the salvation of God.]

[i] Rev. xiv. 4. The redeemed are to "follow the Lamb whithersoever he goeth."
[k] Exod. xii. 26. and xiii. 8. and Josh. iv. 6, 7.

OUTLINE NO. 80
GOD'S CONDESCENSION TO HIS PEOPLE'S WEAKNESS.

Exod. xiii. 17, 18. *And it came to pass, when Pharaoh had let the people go, that God led them not through the way of the*

EXODUS, XIII. 17, 18. [80.

land of the Philistines, although that was near; for God said, Lest peradventure the people repent when they see war, and they return to Egypt: but God led the people about, through the way of the wilderness of the Red Sea.

IN whatever light we view God, whether as a God of power or of love, we are constrained to say, "Who is like unto thee, O Lord!" Behold the issue of his contest with the haughty Pharaoh: the very instant that the full time is arrived, the time predicted four hundred and thirty years before, the proud monarch not only consents to the departure of Israel, but urges them to go with all possible expedition; and the whole land of Egypt is become so anxious for their departure, that every person is glad to give his most valuable raiment, together with his jewels or vessels, of silver or of gold, to any Israelitish woman that asks them of him[a]. Yet, though thrust out by the inhabitants, the Israelites do not go out as by flight, but, in an orderly manner, "harnessed," that is, arranged as an army, in five different divisions[b]; yea in a triumphant manner also, laden with the spoils of their vanquished enemies: "nor was there one feeble person among their tribes;" not one was left behind; nor was one single person unfit to undertake the journey. Thus was the power of Jehovah magnified in the completest victory that can possibly be imagined; a victory, not over their arms merely, but over their proud, obstinate, rebellious hearts.

But we are no less called to admire the kindness of God to his people, than his power over his enemies. He knew, that his people were dispirited through their long and cruel bondage; and that, if he led them the

---

[a] Exod. iii. 21, 22. and xi. 2, 3. and xii. 35, 36. The Israelites did not *borrow* them with any promise of returning them; but *asked* for them, and *required* them: and the people, partly through fear, and partly through a temporary willingness to compensate for the injuries they had sustained, hastily gave them whatever they desired.

[b] The marginal reading in the Bible says, *five in a rank*: but this, allowing three feet between each rank, and two thousand ranks in a mile, would make the van and rear to be sixty miles apart: for there were no less than six hundred thousand men, besides women and children.

near way to Canaan through the land of the Philistines, (which was at most only a journey of eight or ten days[c],) they would be intimidated by the hostile appearance of the Philistines, and be ready to return to Egypt, rather than enter on a warfare for which they were unprepared. He therefore condescended to their weakness, and led them another way. This may appear an unimportant circumstance in this astonishing history; but we think it will afford us some useful hints, while we call your attention to the following observations:

I. As long as we are in this world, successive trials must be expected—

[The trials of the Israelites did not cease when they came out of Egypt: whichever way they had proceeded, they would have met with difficulties. Thus it is with those who are redeemed from spiritual bondage: they come not into a state of rest, but of conflict. The fluctuating state of the *world* cannot but place many difficulties in their way——— And Satan, even if he knew that he could not finally prevail against them, would not cease to harass them to the utmost of his power ——— And their own hearts, if they had no other enemy to encounter, would afford them many occasions for labour and sorrow——— To every person that is desirous of reaching the promised land, this life is a state of warfare: and if he would gain the victory, he must " put on the whole armour of God," and " endure hardness as a good soldier of Jesus Christ," and " fight the good fight of faith."]

For these conflicts God fits his people: but,

II. Whatever deliverances we may have experienced in past times, we are ever liable to faint under future trials—

[One would have thought that persons who had so recently seen the irresistible power of Jehovah engaged for them, would not have feared any enemies they might be called to encounter. But God knew that the appearance of new difficulties would soon efface from their minds the remembrance of past deliverances. How just his estimate of them was, appeared, as soon as ever they knew that they were pursued by the Egyptian armies. They instantly murmured against Moses and against God for bringing them out of Egypt; and regretted that they had ever left the land of their captivity[d]. And when they had

---

[c] Gen. xliii. 2, 10.   [d] Exod. xiv. 11, 12. and xvi. 3.

actually reached the borders of the promised land, so terrified were they at the report of their spies respecting the stature of the Canaanites, and the strength of their fortresses, that they proposed even there to appoint a captain over them, to conduct them back again to the land of Egypt[e]. This principle of unbelief is so deeply rooted in our hearts, that even the most eminent saints have yielded to its influence under severe trials: David, notwithstanding God had promised him the throne of Israel, thought he should one day perish by the hands of Saul[f]; Elijah, who had so boldly withstood Ahab, fled from his post through fear of Jezebel[g]; and the Apostles, who had seen on numberless occasions the almighty power of Jesus, expected nothing but death, even while He was in the vessel together with them[h]. No wonder then if *we* find " our spirits fail" in seasons of extraordinary difficulty or danger. Indeed, who amongst us is so firm, that he can enter into a cloud, and not be afraid[i]? Who, when a cloud is ready to burst over his head, can say at all times, " I know whom I have believed, and that He is able to keep that which I have committed to him[k]," and will overrule these troubles for my eternal good[l]? Under great temptations more especially, and under the hidings of God's face, it is not uncommon for truly upright persons to doubt, whether they shall ever get safe to Canaan; and almost to regret, that they have ever turned their backs on Egypt.]

Not that we shall be really and finally deserted: for,

III. God, in condescension to his people's weakness, proportions their trials to their strength—

[What he did to the Israelites on this occasion, he did to the Christian Church in its infancy: the Apostles were screened from persecution till " they had received more power from on high:" and, for a considerable time after the day of Pentecost, they alone were noticed by the ruling powers: opposition, till the death of Stephen, was limited almost exclusively to them; and very little affected the Church at large. In the experience of individuals, the tender mercy of God is often very conspicuous at this day. Whilst they are yet young and feeble, he is pleased to screen them from that fierce opposition, which, at a more advanced period, they will have to encounter: and oftentimes their very corruptions appear to be almost extinct, when, in fact, they are only dormant: their joys also in the Lord are made to abound in such a manner, that they are ready to think they shall never more be called to conflict with sin or sorrow. These are mercies to them from the Lord, to strengthen their resolution, and animate their exertions. God

[e] Numb. xiv. 2—4.   [f] 1 Sam. xxvii. 1.   [g] 1 Kings xix. 1—3.
[h] Mark iv. 38.   [i] Luke ix. 34.   [k] 2 Tim. i. 12.   [l] Rom. viii. 28.

is graciously pleased to hide from them at the present the trials which they will hereafter sustain, well knowing that they would be too much discouraged by a sight of them, and perhaps be tempted to despair. "He does not put new wine into old bottles," but only into vessels capable of enduring the expansive efforts of fermentation[m]. He will not overdrive the lambs, lest they die of fatigue[n]. In the mean time he expressly assures us, that he will not suffer us to be tempted above that we are able, but will, with the temptation, also make a way to escape, that we may be able to bear it[o]; "and that as our day of temptation is, so shall also our strength be[p]."]

On these truths we would ground a word of EXHORTATION—

1. Fear nothing in the way of duty—

[Had the Israelites considered what God had already done for them, they would not have been afraid of any armies that could be brought against them: for, could not the angel that destroyed the Egyptian first-born destroy *them* also? And what have we to fear when once we are enlisted under the banners of Christ? Is not "the Captain of our salvation" at hand to fight for us[q]? and "if He be for us, who can be against us[r]?" Let us not then be afraid, even though earth and hell should combine against us: "let us not cry, A confederacy, a confederacy, or fear like other people; but sanctify the Lord of Hosts himself; and let him be our fear, and let him be our dread[s]." "The waves of the sea may rage horribly; but He that sitteth on high is mightier[t]:" "therefore we should not fear, though the earth were removed, and the mountains cast into the depths of the sea[u]." It is a fixed unalterable truth, sanctioned and confirmed by the experience of millions, that "none can harm us, if we be followers of that which is good[x]." If we be weak as "worms," yet shall we "thresh the mountains," and make them as the dust of the summer threshing-floor[y].]

2. Commit yourselves to the divine guidance and direction—

[God is the same now that he was in the days of old. What he did for Israel in a visible and external manner, he will do invisibly and internally for his Church at this time. Only "acknowledge him in all your ways, and he will direct your paths[z]." We say not that he will guide you by visions, or voices, or revelations; but he will by his word and Spirit: *in*

---

[m] Mark ii. 22. [n] Gen. xxxiii. 13, 14. [o] 1 Cor. x. 13.
[p] Deut. xxxiii. 25. [q] Josh. v. 14. [r] Rom. viii. 31.
[s] Isai. viii. 12, 13. [t] Ps. xciii. 3, 4. [u] Ps. xlvi. 2, 3.
[x] 1 Pet. iii. 13. [y] Isai. xli. 10—16. [z] Prov. iii. 6.

reference to them we may say, "You shall hear a voice behind you, saying, This is the way, walk ye in it, when ye turn to the right hand or turn to the left[a]." If your situation be painful at the present, or even contrary to what you have expected, do not hastily conclude that God has forsaken you. The way in which the Israelites were led was circuitous; but it was "the *right* way[b]." Commit yourselves then to Him, and he shall accomplish for you that which shall ultimately be best for you[c]. "He will lead you by a way that you know not; He will make darkness light before you, and crooked things straight. These things will he do unto you, and not forsake you[d]." He will guide you by his counsel; "even to hoar hairs he will carry you[e];" and after that "receive you to glory[f]."]

[a] Isai. xxx. 21. [b] Ps. cvii. 7. [c] Ps. xxxvii. 5.
[d] Isai. xlii. 16. [e] Isai. xlvi. 4. [f] Ps. lxxiii. 24.

OUTLINE NO. 81

THE PILLAR AND THE CLOUD.

Exod. xiii. 21, 22. *And the Lord went before them by day in a pillar of a cloud, to lead them the way; and by night in a pillar of fire, to give them light; to go by day and night. He took not away the pillar of the cloud by day, nor the pillar of fire by night, from before the people.*

IN reading the Holy Scriptures, we cannot but be struck with the suitableness and seasonableness of the divine interpositions. It might be thought indeed that the Israelites at their departure out of Egypt, amounting to six hundred thousand fighting men, without one single invalid amongst them, would be irresistible: but if we consider, that they were without discipline, without arms, without stores either of clothing or provision, and without any knowledge of the way through "a great and terrible wilderness," and without any possibility of obtaining even so much as bread or water for their sustenance, we shall see, that they needed only to be left to themselves, and they must all quickly perish in the wilderness. But in the hour of need, God came down in a pillar of a cloud by day and of fire by night to guide them in their way, and never left them till they arrived at the promised land. This mercy, and the continuance of it, are the two points to which at present we would call your attention.

I. The mercy vouchsafed to them—
This was,
1. Most signal—

[Never was there any thing like it from the foundation of the world. God had revealed himself to several in dreams and visions, and under the appearances of men and angels: but never in a visible stationary form, like that before us. By this cloud he *guided* them in the way. Without such a direction they could not have found their way through that trackless desert: but by it they proceeded without fear of erring: and all their motions were regulated by it, whether by day or night[a].

By this cloud also they were *protected*. Though this use of the cloud is not noticed in the text, it is in other passages[b]. In that hot sandy desert, it would have been impossible for them to prosecute their journey under the rays of the meridian sun: indeed even without journeying, they could scarcely have endured the intense heat to which they would have been exposed. God therefore graciously protected them by the refreshing shadow of that cloud. And to this the prophet evidently alludes, when describing the superior privileges of the Christian Church[c]]

2. Most significant—

[This cloud was, in the first place, *a symbol of God's presence*. After the Israelites had offended God in worshipping the molten calf, God threatened to leave them, and to commit the care of them to an angel: and on that occasion the cloud removed from the camp, in token that he was about to depart from them[d]. And afterwards, when, in the same spirit of rebellion, they were going up against the Canaanites without the pillar and the cloud, Moses said to them, "Go not up, for the Lord is not among you[e]."

This cloud was also *a seal of his covenant*. Though the covenant, afterwards made on Horeb, was not yet formally declared, yet it was considered as existing, not only because God had actually now taken the Israelites under his protection, but because he had, four hundred years before, engaged to Abraham, that his posterity should be parties in the covenant already made with him. It is true, that circumcision was *the* rite, by which all the descendants of Abraham were to be initiated into the bond of that covenant; but still *this* was *a* (temporary) seal of that relationship, which now existed between God and them: and therefore the Apostle compares it with baptism, by which we are admitted into the Christian

---

[a] Numb. ix. 15—23.
[b] Numb. x. 34. and xiv. 14. and especially Ps. cv. 39.
[c] Isai. iv. 5, 6.   [d] Exod. xxxiii. 2, 3, 7, 9.   [e] Numb. xiv. 42

covenant; and declares that they were "baptized unto Moses in that cloud," as we are "baptized by water unto Christ[f]."

It was, moreover, *an emblem of yet richer mercies.* We cannot suppose that, under that typical dispensation, so important a circumstance as this was destitute of any spiritual meaning. Indeed it is manifest from a fore-cited passage[g], that it was expressly designed to typify the guidance and protection which the Church of Christ should enjoy even to the remotest ages, through the influences of the Holy Spirit.]

We cannot fail of observing, that Moses, in recording this mercy, lays great stress on,

II. The continuance of it—

The cloud abode with them during the whole time of their sojourning in the wilderness. What a glorious view does this give us of our God! and how are we constrained to admire,

1. His inexhaustible patience—

[Truly the Israelites were "a rebellious and stiff-necked people." Nor could either mercies or judgments ever produce on them any thing more than a mere transient effect. Every fresh trial called forth the same murmuring discontented spirit. On some occasions they seemed almost to have exhausted the patience of God himself. But God is slow to anger, though provoked every day: and if they had been less deserving of his wrath, we should never have known (unless perhaps by our own experience) how far the patience of God could extend. If it had not been ascertained by such an undeniable fact, we could not have conceived it possible for God himself to have "borne their manners in the wilderness during the long space of forty years[h]."]

2. His unbounded kindness—

[In reading this history, one is astonished to find, that God attended to that people, as if there had been no other creatures in the universe. He was incessantly occupied (if we may so speak) about their matters. He carried them through the wilderness, as a man would carry his infant son[i]. His conduct towards them is beautifully compared with that of the eagle, teaching its young to fly, and darting under them, when falling, to bear them up again to their nest on her expanded

[f] If we suppose that the cloud occasionally distilled, as it were, a dew upon them, it would be a striking illustration of the sprinkling of water in the rite of baptism. But on this we lay no stress.

[g] Isai. iv. 5, 6.

[h] See this expatiated upon in a most feeling manner, Neh. ix. 16—19.   [i] Deut. i. 31.

wings[k]. But it is thus that God yet watches over his redeemed people[l]. "Lo, I am with you alway," says he, "even to the end of the world[m]."]

3. His inviolable fidelity—

[It was from a regard to the promise which he had made to Abraham, and from a concern for his own honour, that God would not cast them off. He did indeed punish them oftentimes: but yet he continued to the last to acknowledge them as his people: "Thou wast a God that forgavest them," says the Psalmist, "though thou tookest vengeance of their inventions[n]." What a striking proof does this give us, that "God hateth putting away," and that "he will not cast off his people, because it hath pleased him to make us his people." "Faithful is He that hath called us, who also will do it," that is, will "finish in us the work he has begun," and "perfect that which concerneth us."]

We may LEARN from hence,

1. What reason we have for gratitude—

[Let any one who has been brought out of spiritual bondage, and led forward towards the heavenly Canaan, examine attentively his own experience: let him see by what particular means he has been brought to enjoy the guidance and protection of God, and to advance in safety through this dreary wilderness; and he shall see as plain marks of a superintending and all-directing Providence, as are to be found in the history before us: yea, he may see too as wonderful exhibitions of God's patience, kindness, and faithfulness. Let every such person then adore and magnify his God. We all feel how suitable such a frame of mind was for the cloud-directed Israelites: let us all seek to feel and manifest it in our own case.]

2. What grounds we have for faith—

[Has Jesus Christ come into the world to lessen the privileges of his people? Has he not rather extended and enlarged them? In the external manifestations of God's presence we are inferior to the Jews; but we have, what more than counterbalances that loss, the internal and spiritual communications of his grace. Yes, our God will, by his Spirit, "guide us into all truth," and lead us in the way wherein we should go. By the same Spirit also will he protect us from the burning heat of persecution and temptation, and from the assaults of all our spiritual enemies. Of this we may be assured: for he has said, that "he will keep his sheep, and give unto them eternal life; and that none shall ever pluck them out of his hands."]

[k] Deut. xxxii. 11, 12. [l] Isai. xlvi. 3, 4. and xxvii. 4.
[m] Matt. xxviii. 20. [n] Ps. xcix. 8.

OUTLINE NO. 82

THE COMMAND GIVEN TO THE ISRAELITES IN THEIR STRAITS.

Exod. xiv. 15. *Speak unto the children of Israel, that they go forward.*

IT is truly said by the prophet, " He that believeth shall not make haste;" that is, he shall not yield to any fears, so as to be driven by them to adopt any hasty or improper measures for his deliverance. We may say on the other hand, He that believeth shall not delay: he shall, in proportion to the degree in which his faith is exercised, discern the seasons for action, as well as for prayer: nor shall he be so occupied in one duty, as to overlook and neglect another. That Moses believed God's gracious promises of deliverance, we can have no doubt: for he reported them to the Israelites with unshaken confidence: yet it should seem, by the continuance of his urgent petitions after he had received these promises from God, that he was almost afraid that his enemies would be upon him, before the promises could be fulfilled. Doubtless God was pleased with his fervent prayers at other times: but here he gently reproves Moses for remaining occupied in one duty, when there was another which the immediate occasion more urgently required: " Wherefore criest thou unto me?" Go and give the proper directions to the people: go and execute your office as their leader, and command them to " Go forward."

Though this command was given under peculiar circumstances in which it cannot *literally* be applied to us, yet, *in the spirit* of it, it is applicable to all the Lord's people when reduced to difficulties in the way of their duty. And it may, not improperly, suggest to us the following reflections. Difficulties in the way of our duty,

I. May be expected—

God is pleased sometimes to screen his people from trials, so as scarcely to let them suffer at all from persecutions, and very little even from internal conflicts. As he led not the Israelites the near way to

82.] GOD'S COMMAND IN ISRAEL'S DIFFICULTY. 399

Canaan, lest they should, in their unprepared state, be discouraged by entering into immediate contests with the warlike Philistines[a], so he sometimes leads his people now in a comparatively safe and easy path. But generally speaking we must expect difficulties—

[It cannot be thought that Satan will relinquish his vassals without making repeated efforts to reduce them to their former bondage. When commanded to depart from the youth whom he had so long possessed, he cast him down, and tare him in such a manner, that the spectators conceived him to be dead[b]. Thus does he also at this time frequently deal with those, whom by the superior strength of Jesus he is compelled to relinquish[c]: he endeavours to shut them up in despondency, or perhaps even to drive them to suicide. And when he has not prevailed in the first instance, he departs from them (as he did even from our Lord himself), only " for a season." Methinks he is in this the very archetype of Pharaoh; who, having liberated the Israelites only by compulsion, rejoiced in a prospect of wreaking his vengeance on them, and collected all his forces to bring them back again to his dominion. To the latest hour of their lives will he avail himself of every opportunity to assault them, and will use all his wiles, and all his devices, to harass, if he cannot finally destroy, them.

Nor is it to be supposed that the world will sit contented with the loss of their former companions. It is said of Noah, that in building the ark, " he *condemned the world*[d]:" so, in turning from sin to God, we, in fact, condemn the world: our faith condemns their unbelief; our fear, their security; our obedience, their disobedience. This is clearly declared by Solomon; " They that forsake the law, praise the wicked; but such as keep the law, contend with them[e]." Our actions speak, though our lips should be silent: and the more bright our light shines, the more visible must be the surrounding darkness. The world are driven to the alternative of condemning either themselves or us, seeing that it is impossible that such opposite lines of conduct should both be right: we must not wonder therefore if they load *us* with reproach and ignominy, and if " those especially who are of our own household become our greatest foes." This is the natural result of their self-love; I may add too, of their love for us.

Neither can we hope that all our former habits should be at once changed, so that we should feel no difficulty in mortifying our deep-rooted lusts, or in exercising graces, to which till lately we were utter strangers. Old passions will revive; old

---

[a] Exod. xiii. 17.   [b] Mark ix. 26.   [c] Luke xi. 21, 22.
[d] Heb. xi. 7.   [e] Prov. xxviii. 4.

temptations will recur; and our natural indisposition to holy exercises will shew itself; however much we are on our guard, and however diligently we address ourselves to the great work that is before us. If even the Apostle Paul, after so many years spent in the service of his God, had reason to complain of "a law in his members warring against the law of his mind," so that "the things which he would, he did not, and the things that he would not, those he did;" we cannot expect such an entire exemption from conflicts, but that we must sometimes have to cry out with him, "O wretched man that I am! who shall deliver me?"

Thus may all of us take to ourselves the advice that is given in the Book of Ecclesiasticus; "My son, if thou set thy heart to seek the Lord, prepare thy soul for temptation."]

It is well to be aware of the difficulties that are in our way; for they,

II. Must be encountered—

[*We must not dream of neutrality.* It is indeed said by our Lord on one occasion, "He that is not against us is with us[f]:" but *that* referred only to persons really interested in his cause, though not moving exactly in the same way; and was intended to teach candour in judging those who differ from us. On another occasion he said, "He that is not with me is against me; and he that gathereth not with me, scattereth abroad[g]:" and this was to inform us, that His cause admits of no neutrality: we must take a determined part against sin and Satan: and even to deliberate, in such a case, is to be guilty of treason and revolt.

Nor must we give way to fear. Let the trials that threaten us be ever so severe, we must not shrink back, as though we had not counted the cost. We must be prepared to "deny ourselves, to take up our cross, to follow Christ;" we must "be ready not only to be bound, but even to die for him," at any time and in any manner that he shall see fit. If we saw the furnace now before us, and burning with seven times its accustomed fury, and men ready to cast us into it, we must take the same decided part that the Hebrew youths did: "Be it known to thee, O king, that we will not serve thy gods, nor worship the golden image which thou hast set up[h]."

Nor must we be discouraged by difficulties. To what purpose is there a complete set of armour provided for us, and a victorious issue assured to us, if we are to faint as soon as difficulties press upon us? We should rather rise to the occasion. "If the iron be blunt, we must whet the edge, or put to more strength[i]." As soldiers of Jesus Christ, it is our very

[f] Luke ix. 50.   [g] Matt. xii. 30.   [h] Dan. iii. 18.   [i] Eccl. x. 10.

profession to endure hardships[k]. If at any time we find our strength decay, we must go to Him, who has promised to "renew" it to such a degree, that we may "mount up with wings, as eagles" after their plumage is restored, and pursue our course as racers, without weariness or fainting[l]. Whatever be our trials, it is at our peril to draw back from the encounter[m]. "We must not even look back, after having put our hands to the plough." It is "he only that overcometh," who shall possess the crown of victory[n].]

To meet all difficulties thus, we are encouraged by an assurance, that they,

III. Shall be vanquished—

[*Consult the promises of God*, and see what they say: are *they* not as extensive as our necessities? What is there that arrests your progress, or obstructs your way? Is it a mountain? You may say to it, "Who art thou, O great mountain? Before Zerubbabel thou shalt become a plain[o]." Is it a sea? God will "make even *the depths* of the sea a way for the ransomed to pass over[p]." Is it your own weakness that disheartens you? Behold, "one of you shall chase a thousand, and two shall put ten thousand to flight[q]." Is it rather your unworthiness? "It was for his own name's sake that he made you his people; and for his own name's sake he will not cast you off[r]." You will not suppose that there was any great worthiness in the Chaldeans; but see how assured they were of victory when God was on their side[s]. And shall your weakness or unworthiness be any effectual obstruction, if your God fight for you? You would not think there was any great cause for a lion to despair when contending with the defenceless lamb: yet that is the very image by which God has been pleased to designate the contest in which you are engaged, and the victory that awaits you[t].

If you need any thing else to encourage you, *look at "the cloud of witnesses" that are now in heaven,* with palms in their hands, and crowns on their heads, and everlasting songs of triumph in their mouths: were not they once in your state, conflicting with the same enemies, and complaining of the same discouragements? Do you not find amongst them many whose trials were far more severe than you ever experienced? And yet were they not crowned at last? Did not their difficulties yield to their repeated efforts; and was not "the grace of Christ sufficient for them?" Why then should not you

---

[k] 2 Tim. ii. 3.   [l] Isai. xl. 27—31.   [m] Heb. x. 38, 39.
[n] Rev. iii. 21.   [o] Zech. iv. 7.   [p] Isai. li. 10.
[q] Josh. xxiii. 10. with Deut. xxxii. 30.   [r] 1 Sam. xii. 22.
[s] Jer. xxxvii. 10.   [t] Mic. v. 7, 8.

also triumph? "Is God's arm shortened that he cannot save; or his ear heavy that he cannot hear?" Doubt not then but that you also shall see your enemies dead upon the sea-shore, and that, "through the strength of Christ you shall be more than conquerors."]

To you then who have escaped from bondage, and are going under the guidance of your God towards the heavenly Canaan, we say, "Go forward." But, that we may not leave you without some more particular directions, we say, Go forward,

1. Warily—

[Your way is not so manifest, but that you need to explore it with continual care. You have indeed the pillar and the cloud; but it is visible only in the Holy Scriptures; it is to be found only in the precepts of the Gospel, and in the example of our Lord. If, because your views of Christian doctrines be clear, you suppose that you are not liable to err materially in your practice, you are greatly mistaken. The Apostle tells us, that "they who strove in the games were not crowned, unless they strove lawfully[u]," that is, according to the rules prescribed them. So neither shall we be approved by our Judge, if we do not regulate our spirit and conduct altogether by the rules contained in the inspired volume. Hence we need "to walk circumspectly[x];" to look well to our ways; to consult the Scriptures; to mark the footsteps of our blessed Lord; and, above all, to pray, with the Psalmist, "Lead me, O Lord, in the right way, because of my enemies.[y]"]

2. Steadfastly—

[It is not on some particular occasions only that you are to serve the Lord, but at all times, and on all occasions. Whatever advances you have made, we still say, "Go forward." Whatever obstacles are in your way, we repeat the word, "Go forward." Yea, whatever sufferings await you, we say again, "Be not discouraged because of the way[z]," but "Go forward." Only be sure that you are in the way of duty; that you are following the Lord's will, and not your own; and then go forward with all patience and perseverance. You must "know no man after the flesh:" you must, as our Lord says, "hate father and mother, and your own life also[a]," in comparison of him. Having nothing in view but the glory of your God, you must "forget what is behind, and press forward towards that which is before." You must "be steadfast,

---

[u] 2 Tim. ii. 5.   [x] Exod. xxiii. 13.   Eph. v. 15.
[y] Ps. xxvii. 11.   [z] Numb. xxi. 4.   [a] Luke xiv. 26.

immovable, always abounding in the work of the Lord; and then your labour shall not be in vain in the Lord."]

3. Triumphantly—

[In every other contest, men exert themselves with a degree of uncertainty respecting the issue: and to " boast, when girding on their armour, as though they had put it off[b]," would be only a mark of folly and presumption. But things are far otherwise with you. Your victory depends, not on an arm of flesh, but on the power and veracity of God. While therefore you are yet on the field of battle, you may advance with David's confidence against Goliath, even though you are only "a stripling with a sling," and your enemies are deemed invincible. It was thus that Paul triumphed, and hurled defiance against all the foes that could assault him, whether on earth or in hell[c]. Thus also may you anticipate the shouts of victory, and say, " The Lord God will help me: therefore shall I not be confounded: therefore have I set my face like a flint; and I know that I shall not be ashamed. He is near that justifieth me: who will contend with me? Let us stand together: who is mine adversary? let him come near to me. Behold, the Lord God will help me; who is he that shall condemn me? Lo, they all shall wax old as a garment; the moth shall eat them up[d]."]

[b] 1 Kings xx. 11.   [c] Rom. viii. 35—39.   [d] Isai. l. 7—9.

OUTLINE NO. 83

ISRAEL'S DELIVERANCE AT THE RED SEA.

Exod. xiv. 31. *And Israel saw that great work which the Lord did upon the Egyptians: and the people feared the Lord, and believed the Lord, and his servant Moses.*

THE state of man on earth is diversified with trials and deliverances, more or less, to the latest hour of his life. Even when we have the clearest evidence that we are in the Lord's way, we shall yet meet with many things which will involve us in trouble and perplexity. The disciples were ordered by their Lord to cross the sea of Tiberias: but in passing it, they were overtaken with a storm, which threatened them with destruction. It was not possible for the Israelites to doubt, but that they were precisely in the place where God would have them; yet were they menaced with instant death by the proud vindictive monarch, from whose tyranny they had just escaped.

But this grievous affliction was only introductory to a signal deliverance. God now interposed on their behalf, and wrought for them a "great work."

That we may make a profitable use of this part of scripture history, let us consider,

I. The work referred to—

This is justly called "great:" for it was no less than the destruction of all the Egyptian army in the Red Sea. But that we may view it distinctly in all its parts, we observe, that it was,

1. A discriminating work—

[The pillar which had hitherto gone before the Israelites, to lead them in the way, removed, and stood behind them, as soon as their enemies had come within sight of their camp. But to the Egyptians it presented only a dark side, increasing thereby the natural darkness of the night, and preventing them from continuing their march; while to the Israelites it was a light of fire, enabling them to do whatever their situation and safety required.

Again, the sea which was divided by the east wind, opened a secure retreat for all the hosts of Israel: but as soon as the Egyptians attempted to follow them, it resumed its wonted state, and overwhelmed them utterly; thus affording a passage to Israel, but only a grave to Egypt.

Now this manifest distinction which God made between the Israelites and the Egyptians, might well exalt the work in the eyes of those who were so greatly benefited by it.]

2. A judicial work—

[Pharaoh and his courtiers had hardened their hearts against him, so that all the successive plagues could not bring them to submit to his will. Now therefore God gave them an opportunity to harden their hearts yet more against him. Instead of leading the Israelites at once into the wilderness, he led them aside to a situation, from whence apparently there was no escape. Rocks and morasses were on either side, and the Red Sea before them. This seemed a favourable opportunity for Pharaoh to overtake them, and to wreak his vengeance upon them: and Pharaoh, instigated by his resentment, determined not to lose the opportunity: he instantly collected all the chariots and horsemen in his army, and pursued them: and he rushed into the very snare, which God had predicted he would fall into.

Again, Pharaoh had destroyed the male children of the Israelites in the river Nile: and now God visited this iniquity on him, and on all his army, in the Red Sea.

83.] ISRAEL'S DELIVERANCE AT THE RED SEA. 405

Who does not see in these things a judicial infatuation, and a judicial sentence; both of which, when contemplated by the Israelites, must raise this work yet higher in their estimation?]

3. A glorious work—

[God had said, that he would get himself glory on Pharaoh and on all his subjects; and that the Egyptians should at last be constrained to acknowledge Him as the one supreme God of all the earth. And truly this work did bring glory to God[a]; for it displayed and magnified every one of his perfections: his wisdom in so accomplishing his own will, while no restraint whatever was imposed on the will of Pharaoh; his power, in dividing the sea, and making the waters to stand as a wall, while the Israelites passed through "dry-shod;" his justice, in suffering the Egyptians to proceed so far, as that, when enclosed in his net, they might all be destroyed; his truth and faithfulness, in accomplishing to the posterity of Abraham the deliverance which he had promised four hundred years before.

This work did indeed manifest to Egypt and to Israel, that Jehovah " is the Most High over all the earth," " a God, glorious in holiness, fearful in praises, doing wonders."]

Let us now proceed to notice

II. The effect it produced—

Stupid and insensible as that nation had shewn themselves in the midst of all the mercies vouchsafed to them in Egypt, they could not but be affected with this. Accordingly we find that, on seeing the hand of God thus stretched out for them, they began to feel,

1. A regard for his authority—

[Fear is of two kinds, filial and servile; and it is probable that in some of the people the former predominated, and in others the latter. On an occasion somewhat similar, where God, in testimony of his displeasure against his people for desiring a king, sent a tremendous storm of thunder and lightning, we are told that " the people greatly feared the Lord and Samuel[b]." This was certainly a servile fear: and it should seem that the greatest part of the Israelites at the Red Sea were affected with no higher principle; because they even " within a few days forgat this work[c]," and all the others that God had wrought for them. Indeed temporal deliverances, however great, will produce only transient impressions, if not accompanied with the grace of God. But a view of that redemption which we have in Christ Jesus—what will not *that* effect? That will implant a fear in the heart, a fear that shall

---

[a] Isai. lxiii. 12—14. [b] 1 Sam. xii. 18. [c] **Ps. cvi. 12, 13.**

be mighty and uniform in its operation[d], a fear that shall expel all other fear, and "bring the whole soul into a willing captivity to the obedience of Christ"————]

2. Confidence in his protection—

[As fear, so faith also, is of different kinds. We read of many who, when they saw the miracles of Jesus, believed in him; and yet he would not commit himself to them, because he knew that their hearts were yet unrenewed[e]. And Simon Magus is said to have believed[f], whilst yet he remained "in the gall of bitterness and the bond of iniquity." Such in too great a measure, we fear, was the faith which the Israelites now reposed in God, and in his servant Moses. They were struck with an irresistible conviction, that God was all-sufficient for them, and that Moses was infallibly directed by him to manage every thing for their good. In the very next trial, however, they lost the remembrance of their present convictions, and began to doubt and murmur as before. Not so the persons whose faith is truly spiritual; who, being united to Christ, are partakers of his redemption: they "know in whom they have believed;" and, whatever difficulties occur, they "hold fast their confidence," saying with the Apostle, "He that spared not his own Son, but delivered him up for us all, how shall he not with him also freely give us all things?"————]

IMPROVEMENT—

1. Let us take care that our religious affections be sincere and permanent—

[Many good feelings may be excited in the heart by some particular occurrence, or some moving discourse. But "our goodness is apt to be like the morning dew, or the early cloud that passeth away." Such affections however will afford us no support in a trying hour; much less will they benefit us at the bar of judgment. Let us see to it therefore that we obtain, not merely some transient feelings of good, but a new nature: that so our fear of God be such as to make us obedient to his will, and our faith such as shall enable us to commit ourselves entirely to his disposal.]

2. Let us, for the purpose of generating those affections in our hearts, contemplate deeply the great work of Redemption—

[We never improve aright a typical deliverance, unless we turn our thoughts to the deliverance which it prefigured. What was intended by that before us, we can be at no loss to

---

[d] 2 Cor. v. 14, 15.   [e] John ii. 11, 23, 24.   [f] Acts viii. 13.

determine, since God himself has declared it to us[g]. The redemption of the world by Christ's obedience unto death, and our consequent deliverance from death and hell, should never be far from our thoughts. It is so stupendous a work, that it has filled all heaven with wonder; and the "riches" of divine grace contained in it are absolutely "unsearchable." To know this, to feel this, to be interested in this, will produce a change in our hearts, which shall last for ever[h]. And when we shall see our enemies dead upon the sea-shore, and ourselves placed beyond the reach of harm, it will furnish us with an inexhaustible subject of gratitude and thanksgiving.]

[g] Isai. li. 10, 11.
[h] The conversion of the soul is spoken of in terms directly referring to this event. Isai. xi. 15, 16.

OUTLINE NO. 84
THE CHARACTER OF GOD.

Exod. xv. 11. *Who is like unto thee, O Lord, among the gods? who is like thee, glorious in holiness, fearful in praises, doing wonders?*

EXALTED favours may well be repaid in devout acknowledgments: they are the least returns that we can make to our heavenly Benefactor: and so reasonable is this tribute, that persons who are far enough removed from solid piety, will, under a sense of recent obligations, often cordially unite in paying it to the God of their salvation. The hymn before us was composed by Moses, on occasion of the deliverance vouchsafed to Israel at the Red Sea: and it was sung by all the Israelites, probably by the men and women in an alternate and responsive manner, Miriam leading the women, and, together with them, accompanying the song with timbrels and dances[a]. It is the most ancient composition of the kind, that is extant in the world. The two first verses are a kind of preface, declaring the occasion, and the inspired penman's determination to celebrate it[b]. The mercy then is stated in a most animated manner; and afterwards, its effects, both immediate and remote, are circumstantially predicted. But, between the statement of the mercy and its effects, is introduced

[a] ver. 20, 21. [b] Somewhat like that in Ps. xlv. 1.

an apostrophe, addressed to the Deity himself, and ascribing to him the glory due unto his name. To this portion of the hymn we would now direct your more particular attention. It declares that God is,

I. To be admired for his holiness—

God is essentially and supremely holy—

[He is not only called, by way of eminence, " The Holy One," but this attribute is said exclusively to belong to him; " Thou *only* art holy." As for the gods of the heathen, many of them were no other than deified monsters, patrons of lewdness, of theft, of drunkenness, and every kind of iniquity : and among the rest there was not found even the smallest semblance of real universal holiness. Well therefore might the challenge be made in reference to this, " Who among the gods is like unto thee, O Lord?" This attribute is, in fact, the crown of all the other attributes of the Deity; for, without it, no other perfection could be either amiable in itself or worthy of the Supreme Being. But, without entering into the general view of this subject, we need only look at the " wonders done" on this occasion; and there we shall see a display of this attribute in its most striking colours. Behold his indignation against sin, how it burned against the oppressors of his people, and the contemners of his authority! The very elements themselves were made to rise against the proud associates in iniquity, and to execute upon them the vengeance they deserved — — —]

For this he is greatly to be admired and glorified—

[No other perfection more attracts the attention of all the glorified saints and angels in heaven, than this[c]. And, notwithstanding it is hateful and terrific to impenitent sinners, it is an object of the highest admiration amongst those who have learned to appreciate it aright. David was altogether enraptured with it[d]; and every real saint will " give thanks at the remembrance of it[e]" — — —]

Whilst he is thus admired for his unspotted holiness, he is also,

II. To be feared for his power—

God is a God of unrivalled power—

[The gods of the heathen cannot hear, or see, or move : but the power of Jehovah is infinite. What less than omnipotence could have performed the " wonders" which are here

---

[c] Compare Isai. vi. 3. with Rev. iv. 8.   [d] Ps. xcix. 3, 5, 9.
[e] Ps. xxx. 4. See an animated description of their imbecility Jer. x. 3—7.

celebrated? See how easily the expectations of his enemies were disappointed, and their bloody purposes were frustrated, by one blast of his displeasure[g]! — — —]

For this he is greatly to be feared—

[For this exercise of his power indeed he was praised; as well he might be for such a merciful and complete deliverance. But it may truly be said, that he is "fearful in praises[h]:" for this display of his power clearly shews, that "it is a fearful thing to fall into the hands of the living God." Accordingly we find, that the inspired writers generally make this improvement of God's omnipotence, and suggest it as a motive to reverence his majesty, to regard his will, and to tremble at his displeasure[i] — — —]

We may LEARN from hence,

1. How the mercies of God are to be improved—

[All of us have experienced mercies in abundance: and from them we may obtain the brightest discoveries of our God. O what displays of power, of goodness, and of truth, might all of us behold, if we called to mind the various deliverances which God has wrought out for us, and especially that redemption which was prefigured by the history before us! The connexion between the two is expressly marked by God himself; and we are told, what a mixture of admiration and reverence, of love and fear, a just view of these miracles of mercy will assuredly create[k]. Let them then produce these effects on us; and let us now begin, what we hope to continue to all eternity, "the song of Moses and the Lamb."]

2. How every attempt against him or his people shall surely issue—

[Here we see a lively representation of the final issue of every contest which man shall enter into with his Maker. The forbearance of God may be long exercised; and his enemies may appear for a time to have gained their point: but in due time, hell shall open wide its jaws to swallow them up, and they shall become the wretched victims of their own impiety. Against God and his Church, there is no device, no counsel that shall stand.

[g] ver. 9, 10. The picture here is highly finished. The amplification in the former verse, and the conciseness of the latter, form a beautiful contrast; whilst the image that closes the description, strongly marks the completeness of the judgment executed.

[h] The last clause of the text may be understood as limiting and illustrating the two that precede it. Compare Luke i. 49.

[i] Ps. lxxxix. 6—8. Heb. xii. 28, 29. Deut. xxviii. 58, 59.

[k] Rev. xv. 3, 4.

His Church is founded on a rock, and the gates of hell shall not prevail against it. The enemies of our souls may follow us even to the last moment of our lives; but when the appointed moment is arrived for the completion of all God's promises to us, our souls shall be freed from every assault, and " death and hell, with all their adherents, be cast into the lake of fire[1]."]

[1] Rev. xx. 14.

OUTLINE NO. 85
THE WATERS OF MARAH SWEETENED.

Exod. xv. 24, 25. *And the people murmured against Moses, saying, What shall we drink? And he cried unto the Lord; and the Lord shewed him a tree, which when he had cast into the waters, the waters were made sweet. There he made for them a statute and an ordinance; and there he proved them.*

GREAT are the vicissitudes of human life: nor is there any person exempt from them. Even the most favoured servants of God, when moving expressly in the way that he has appointed for them, may be reduced as it were in an instant from the highest pinnacle of earthly prosperity to a state of the deepest distress and anguish. Not to mention an imprisoned Joseph, a dethroned David, an incarcerated Daniel, we notice the whole nation of Israel exulting in the completest deliverance that ever was vouchsafed to any people in the world, and within three days brought down to utter despondency. But from this we may derive much profitable instruction; whilst we notice,

I. Their trial—

This was indeed severe—

[We have no idea in general how much our happiness, and even our very lives, depend on the common bounties of Providence. We acknowledge this indeed in words; but we have by no means a proportionate sense of our obligations to God for a regular supply of water. The Israelites had travelled three days, and had found none; till at last, coming to Marah, they found an abundant supply: but, behold, the water was so bitter, as to be incapable of being turned to any general use. When the Israelites, in addition to their want, were made to experience this painful disappointment, they broke out into murmuring and complaints.]

But their murmuring was wrong—

[Had the question they put to Moses, been nothing more than a simple interrogation, it had been innocent enough: but it was an unbelieving, passionate complaint. (How often are *our* words also, or our actions, inoffensive perhaps as to their external form, while, on account of the spirit with which they are blended, they are most hateful and detestable in the sight of God!) But why should they murmur against Moses? He had not conducted them thither of his own mind, but by God's command. Their displeasure against him was, in fact, directed against God himself. (And it will be well for us to remember, that in venting our wrath and indignation against the instruments by whom God at any time afflicts us, we vent it in reality against him who uses them.) And why should they murmur against God? Had he committed an oversight in leading them into that situation? Had he forgotten to be gracious? Was he so changed within the space of three days, that he could no longer devise a way for their relief? Or was his ear become so heavy that he could not hear, or his hand so shortened that he could not save? Should they not rather have concluded, that now, as on many recent occasions, he had permitted their trial to be great, in order that he might the more abundantly magnify his own power and mercy in their deliverance? Doubtless this would have become them who had seen so many and such stupendous miracles wrought in their behalf.]

We next fix our attention upon,

II. Their deliverance—

Some have thought, that the healing of the waters by casting a tree into them, was intended to typify the sweetening of all our afflictions, and the removing of all our sorrows, by the cross of Christ. It might be so: but we are afraid to venture upon any ground not expressly trodden by the inspired writers. We therefore rather content ourselves with shewing what God indisputably declared by this singular interposition:

1. That he is never at a loss for means whereby to effect his purposes—

[If we cannot see some opening whereby God can come to our relief, we are ready to think that he is quite excluded from us. But what need has he of any means at all? What means did he employ in constructing the universe? Indeed the very means he does use, are generally such, as tend only to evince, by their utter inadequacy, the mighty working of his own power. It was thus when he healed the deleterious waters of a spring, and the barrenness of the land through which they ran, by a single cruse of salt[a]: and thus also when he restored the serpent-bitten Israelites by the mere sight of a brasen serpent. As to the idea of the tree itself possessing qualities calculated to produce the effect, it cannot for one moment be admitted; because the waters were sufficient for the supply of two millions of people, besides all their cattle; and because the effect was instantaneously produced. We therefore say again, that the insufficiency of the means he used, displayed only the more clearly the all-sufficiency of his own power, precisely as when by the voice of a feeble worm he awakens men from their death in trespasses and sins[b].]

2. That he will put honour upon humble and believing prayer—

[There is such "efficacy in the fervent prayer of a righteous man," that God, if we may be permitted so to speak, is not able to withstand it. See persons in any circumstances whatever, and you are sure to find them extricated from their difficulties, and made victorious over their enemies, when once they begin to pray. Even if the people themselves be ever so unworthy, yet, if they have an Advocate and Intercessor for them at the throne of grace, they almost invariably escape the judgments which God had denounced against them; so cordially does "God delight in the prayer of the upright," and so desirous is he to encourage all persons to pray for themselves. The murmuring spirit of the people might well have provoked God to decline all further communication with them: but Moses prayed; and his cry entered into the ears of the Lord of Hosts.]

But both the trial and deliverance were sent with a view to some ulterior good: let us consider,

III. God's design in each—

Amongst other objects which God designed to accomplish, the two following seem to be peculiarly prominent. He sought to bring them to a sense of,

1. Their duty—

[What particular statutes and ordinances God promulged to them at this time, we are not informed. But there is one thing which he certainly made known to them; namely, the conditional nature of the covenant which he was about to make with them, and the suspension of his favours upon their obedience[c]. They had hitherto dwelt only on their privileges, without at all considering their duties: they thought of what

[a] 2 Kings ii. 21. [b] 2 Cor. iv. 7. [c] ver. 26.

God was to be to them; but not of what they were to be to God. *Now* God, having softened their minds by a heavy trial, and conciliated their regards by a miraculous interposition, opens to them the connexion between duty and privilege; and thereby prepares them for becoming " a holy and peculiar people, zealous of good works."]

2. Their sinfulness—

[This mixture of judgment and mercy was well calculated to bring them to a knowledge of themselves. The trial alone would only irritate and inflame their minds: but the deliverance applied a balm to their wounded spirits. By the union of them they would be humbled, and led to acknowledge the heinousness of their ingratitude, their unbelief, their querulousness, and rebellion. This is expressly declared to have been a very principal end of all the dispensations of God towards them in the wilderness[d]: and it is a main object of his diversified dealings with his people at this day.]

Let us LEARN from this subject,

1. To mark the effect of trials and deliverances on our own minds—

[If trials always, instead of humbling, disquiet us; and if deliverances produce only a temporary impression, and not a lasting change on our hearts; can we be right before God? They ought to "work patience, experience, and hope;" and by means of them our faith ought to be so purified, as to tend " to the praise and honour and glory of our God at the appearing of Jesus Christ[e]." By examining into this point we may "*prove* our own selves," and ascertain with considerable precision our true character.]

2. To distrust our religious feelings—

[We may be moved under a sermon or any particular occurrence; we may sometimes be dissolved in tears, and at other times be elevated with joy; and yet have no root in ourselves, nor any inheritance with the saints in light. Who that had heard the devout songs of Israel at the Red Sea, would have thought that in three days they could so totally forget their mercies, and indulge such a rebellious spirit? But look within; and see whether, after an occasional exercise of religious affections, you have not, within a still shorter space of time, been hurried into the indulgence of the most unhallowed tempers, and the gratification of a spirit that is earthly, sensual, and devilish? Ah! think of "the stony-ground hearers, who received the word with joy, and yet in time of temptation fell away." Lay not then too great a stress on some transient

[d] Deut. viii. 2.   [e] 1 Pet. i. 7.

emotions; but judge yourselves by the more certain test of a willing and unreserved obedience.]

3. To place an entire and uniform dependence on God—

[God may see fit to try us, and to delay the relief that we implore. But let us not entertain hard thoughts of him. From the time of Abraham it has passed into a proverb, that "in the mount the Lord shall be seen." Our Isaac may be bound, and the knife actually lifted up to inflict the fatal blow, and all who might interpose to rescue the victim may be at a great distance; but, in the moment of need, God's voice from heaven shall arrest the murderous hand, and deliver us from the impending stroke. "The vision is yet for an appointed time; therefore, though it tarry, wait for it: for at the appointed season it shall come, and not tarry[f]." Whether our afflictions be of a temporal or spiritual nature, we may rest assured of this blessed truth, that "they who wait on him shall never be confounded."]

[f] Hab. ii. 3.

OUTLINE NO. 86

CHRIST THE HEALER OF HIS PEOPLE.

Exod. xv. 26. *I am the Lord that healeth thee.*

SCARCELY had the Jews passed the Red Sea before they began to murmur: as the Psalmist has said, "They provoked him at the sea, even at the Red Sea[a]." True it was that they must have suffered greatly, both they and their cattle, when they were three days without water; and when, on finding water, it was so bitter that they could not drink it. But, when they had been conducted thither by God himself, (for the pillar and the cloud never left them day or night[b],) they might be assured that He, who had so miraculously delivered them hitherto, would, if they cried unto him, supply their wants. They should have had recourse to prayer therefore, and not to murmuring. But this conduct of theirs gave occasion for a rich display of God's mercy towards them, and for an explicit declaration on his part what the rule of his procedure towards them in future should be. They were delivered from the Egyptian

[a] Ps. cvi. 7. [b] Exod. xiii. 22.

yoke: but they were not to cast off obedience to their God. They were, as his redeemed people, to consecrate themselves to him, and to obey his voice in all things: and, according as they performed or neglected their duty to him, he would extend to them his favour, or visit them with his displeasure; either loading them with, or exempting them from, the diseases with which the Egyptians had been visited, and which they greatly dreaded[c].

This declaration of God to them was so important, that the Prophet Jeremiah, a thousand years afterwards, referred to it, to shew, that, from the very first moment of the people having been taken into covenant with God, their sacrifices had been held as of no account in comparison of obedience. "I spake not unto your fathers, nor commanded them in the day that I brought them out of the land of Egypt, concerning burnt-offerings or sacrifices. But this thing commanded I them, saying, Obey my voice, and I will be your God, and ye shall be my people; and walk ye in all the ways that I have commanded you, that it may be well unto you[d]." Nor is it less important to *us*, at this day; for God will still deal with us according as we conduct ourselves towards him. The retribution indeed may not now be so visibly marked by external dispensations; but it shall be maintained in reference to our souls, God either healing our spiritual maladies, or giving us up to the power of them, according as we approve ourselves to him, or walk contrary to his commands. If we offend him by a wilful and habitual disobedience to his will, none shall be able to protect us: but, if we surrender up ourselves unfeignedly to him, "none shall be able to harm us:" whatever we may either feel or fear, we may assure ourselves of his favour; for he is, and ever will be, "The Lord that healeth us."

In further discoursing on these words, we shall be led to point out,

I. The office which God executes in behalf of his people—

[c] ver. 26. with Deut. xxviii. 27, 60. [d] Jer. vii. 22, 23.

As God inflicts judgments on his enemies, so does he administer healing to his people: and this he does,

1. In a way of gracious exemption—

[The Hebrews were exempted from the various calamities with which Egypt was overwhelmed. And this is particularly noticed in the words preceding my text: "I will put none of these diseases upon thee which I have brought upon the Egyptians: for I am the Lord that healeth thee." In like manner, if we are exempt from many diseases under which others labour, and by which their whole lives are imbittered, we should acknowledge God as the Author of this distinction, and receive it as a special mercy at his hands. We know that even under the Christian dispensation bodily diseases are often sent by God, as the punishment of sin[e]: and we cannot but feel that we have merited, on many occasions, such tokens of his displeasure. If therefore we, like the Hebrews, have been more highly favoured than others, we must, like them, be instructed that it is God alone who has healed us.

But in this general description of Jehovah we must not overlook that which, after all, was chiefly intended—his special favour towards his redeemed people, in reference to spiritual disorders. Thousands are given up, like Judas, to an obdurate heart and a reprobate mind; whilst some, like David and Peter, are recovered from their falls. To whom must the recovery of these be ascribed?—to themselves? They had in themselves no more strength or power than the unhappy Judas had. It was to sovereign grace alone that they owed their restoration to the divine favour, and their return to the paths of holiness and peace. And have not we similar obligations to our heavenly Physician? How often have we indulged in our hearts propensities, to which if we had been given up, we should have fallen a prey, and perished for ever! The sins of the most abandoned of the human race were small in their beginning, and by repetition became inveterate. O! what do we owe to God, who, whilst he has left others to follow the imagination of their own hearts, has restrained *us*, "hedging up our way with thorns, and building a wall, that we might not be able to prosecute the paths" which our corrupt hearts so perversely sought! As far then as by his preventing grace he has kept us from evil, we have reason to adore him as "the healer" of our souls.]

2. In a way of effectual interposition—

[On many occasions did God visit his people with severe chastisements; which he as often removed, at the intercession of Moses, or on the humiliation of their souls before him.

[e] 1 Cor. xi. 30. and Jam. v. 14, 15.

And have there not been times when, by disease or accident, *we* have been brought low; and when, if the evil inflicted had been suffered to attain the same resistless power as it has acquired over others, we must have fallen a sacrifice to its assaults? Whence is it, I would ask, that we have been restored to health, whilst others have sunk under the influence of the same disease? Greatly do we err, if we ascribe our recovery to any thing but the gracious favour of our God. He may have made use of medicine as the means: but whatever may have been the secondary cause, the one great primary cause of all has been the good pleasure of God, whose province alone it is " to kill and to make alive, to wound and to heal[f]."

And what shall we say, if we have been healed of *spiritual* disorders? It is well known that man is altogether corrupt; so that we may apply to him that description which is given of the Jewish state, " from the sole of the foot even to the head there is no soundness in him, but wounds, and bruises, and putrifying sores[g]." In every faculty of our souls we are corrupted and debased by sin: our understanding is darkened; our will rebellious; our affections sensual; our very conscience is blind and partial. Now, if God has dealt with us as he did with the springs of Jericho[h], if he has cast the salt of his grace into our souls, and healed us at the fountain-head, have we not cause to bless and magnify his name? It is expressly in reference to such a miracle as this that God assumes to himself the name contained in our text. The waters of Marah being so bitter as to be unfit for use, God directed Moses to cast a certain tree into them, by means of which they were instantly made sweet[i]. And are not we also directed to " a tree, whose very leaves are for the healing of the nations[k]?" Its virtue indeed is not known by thousands, in whose presence it stands; and therefore they continue ignorant of its healing efficacy. But was its virtue ever tried in vain? No: nor ever shall be. Only let Christ be received into the heart by faith, and the whole man will be renewed; the understanding will be enlightened, the will subdued, the affections purified, and the whole soul be " changed into the divine image in righteousness and true holiness. Now, what if God has pointed out this tree to us? What if we have experienced its healing efficacy? Then have we in ourselves an evidence that our blessed Saviour sustains the office claimed by him in our text: and then are we called to acknowledge it with gratitude, and to adore him for this stupendous exercise of his power and grace.]

Such being the office of our blessed Lord, let us consider,

[f] Deut. xxxii. 39.   [g] Isai. i. 6.   [h] 2 Kings ii. 20—22.
[i] ver. 25.   [k] Rev. xxii. 2.

II. The duty which we owe him in reference to it—

This, though already in a measure anticipated, may with great propriety be now more distinctly noticed.

1. We should acknowledge him in the mercies we have received at his hands—

[Sure I am, that his *preventing* goodness is by no means appreciated as it ought to be. We see others sick and dying; and little think to whom we owe it, that their lot has not been awarded to us. We are restored after sickness; and how soon do we forget the hand that has delivered us[1]! Nor are we less insensible of our obligations to God for preservation from great and heinous sins; whereas, if we noticed the falls of others who were in every respect as likely to stand as ourselves, we should be filled with wonder and admiration at the distinguishing mercies vouchsafed unto us. Even *converting* grace, alas! how little gratitude does it excite in our hearts! We can see clearly enough the goodness of God to Israel in bringing them out of Egypt, and in making them a peculiar people to himself, whilst their Egyptian taskmasters were left to perish. But "that deliverance, though glorious, had no glory," in comparison with that which is vouchsafed to us. But I call on all to look at the mercies which they have experienced, and at the means by which they have been procured for a ruined world. The tree that heals us has been felled: the Saviour has been "wounded for our transgressions, and bruised for our iniquities; and *by his stripes we are healed.*" Yes, the Saviour himself has died, that we may live[m]. Shall any one, then, that has experienced the virtue of his blood and the efficacy of his grace, not bless him? O! let every soul stir himself up to praise his God, and break forth like David, " Bless the Lord, O my soul, and all that is within me bless his holy name! Bless the Lord, O my soul, and forget not all his benefits; who *forgiveth all thy sins*, and *healeth all thy diseases*[n]!"]

2. We should apply to him for the mercies which we may yet stand in need of—

[Wherefore does the Saviour proclaim to us his office, but that we may apply to him to execute it in our behalf? That you are all labouring under a mortal disease, is certain: and that there is but one remedy for all, is equally clear. But that remedy is all-sufficient: none ever perished, who applied

---

[1] If this were a *Spital* Sermon, or on occasion of *a deliverance from childbirth*, this would be the place for some appropriate observations.

[m] Isai. liii. 5. with 1 Pet. ii. 24.   [n] Ps. ciii. 1—3.

it to their souls. See our Redeemer in the days of his flesh: was there any disease which he could not cure? Was not even a touch of his garment instantly effectual for one who had spent her all upon physicians, and to no purpose? Methinks I hear one complaining, that sin and Satan have such an entire possession of his soul, as to render his state altogether hopeless. But "is there no balm in Gilead? Is there no Physician there?" Look at the demoniac in the Gospel: so entirely was he possessed by Satan, that no chains could bind him, no restraints prevent him from inflicting deadly wounds upon himself. But a single word from the Saviour expels the fiend, and causes the maniac to sit at his feet, clothed, and in his right mind. Fear not then, thou desponding sinner; for there is nothing impossible with him. And if thou say, 'True; but he has already tried his hand upon me in vain, and given me up as incurable;' hear then what he speaks to thee by the Prophet Isaiah: "For his iniquity I was wroth, and smote him: I hid me, and was wroth; and yet he went on frowardly in the way of his heart." (Here is your very case: and what says he to it? Does he say, 'I have therefore given him up as incurable?' No; but ("I have seen his ways, and will heal him." Heal HIM, does he say? Yes; "I will heal HIM, and will restore comforts to him and to his mourners[o]." Go then to him, thou desponding soul. Say to him, as David did, "Lord, be merciful unto me; heal my soul, for I have sinned against thee[p]." ——— If you reply, 'There is no hope for me, because I have once known the Lord, and have backslidden from him;' be it so; yet, as a backslider, hear what a gracious message he sends thee by the Prophet Jeremiah: "Return, ye backsliding children, and I will heal your backslidings[q]." One thing only would I guard you against, and that is, "the healing of your wounds slightly[r]." Let your wounds be probed to the very bottom: and then, as the waters of Marah were healed so as that the fountain itself was changed, so shall your soul be purified throughout, and "the waters flowing from you spring up unto everlasting life[s]."]

[o] Isai. lvii. 17, 18.   [p] Ps. xli. 4.   [q] Jer. iii. 2
[r] Jer. vi. 14.   [s] John iv. 14. and vii. 38.

OUTLINE NO. 87

SCRIPTURAL EQUALITY.

Exod. xvi. 16—18. *This is the thing which the Lord hath commanded: Gather of it every man according to his eating; an omer for every man according to the number of your persons: take ye every man for them which are in his tents.*

And the children of Israel did so, and gathered, some more, some less. And when they did mete it with an omer, he that gathered much had nothing over, and he that gathered little had no lack.

TO exercise faith, in opposition to all the dictates of sense, is no easy attainment. For instance; the Jews in the wilderness soon found that they had no means of subsistence; and no prospect was before them, but that of speedily perishing by hunger and thirst. Yet they did not well to murmur against Moses and Aaron, who, as God's appointed agents, had brought them forth from Egypt: in fact, their murmuring was against God himself, to whom they should rather have applied themselves in earnest prayer for the relief of their necessities. The wonders which he had already wrought for them were abundantly sufficient to shew them, that, whilst under his care, they had nothing to fear. Doubtless the pressure of hunger and of thirst rendered it difficult for them to believe that God would provide for them; and God therefore mercifully bore with their impatience, and relieved their wants: he gave them water out of a rock; and supplied them with bread from the clouds, even with bread sufficient for them from day to day. In relation to the manna, which was rained every night round about their tents, and which they were commanded to gather for their daily use before the risen sun had caused it to melt away, there was this very peculiar circumstance daily occurring during the whole forty years of their sojourning in the wilderness, that, whilst the head of every family was to gather a certain portion (an omer, about five pints,) for every person dependent on him, "those who had gathered more" found, when they came to measure it, that they "had nothing over; and those who had gathered less, that they had no lack." Now this circumstance being so very peculiar, I shall endeavour to unfold it to you in its proper bearings: in order to which, I shall consider it,

I. As an historic record—

A more curious fact we can scarcely conceive: and

it is the more curious, because it occurred, not occasionally in a few instances, but continually, for forty years, through the whole camp of Israel.

It arose, I apprehend,

1. From God's merciful disposition towards them—

[A variety of circumstances might occur from time to time to prevent some heads of families from making the necessary exertion before the sun should have dissolved the manna, and have deprived them of the portion which they ought to have gathered. Illness, in themselves or their families, might incapacitate them for the discharge of their duty in this matter; or a pressure of urgent business cause them to delay it till it was too late. In this case, what must be done? God, in his mercy, took care that there should be in some a zeal beyond what their own necessities required, and that their abundance should be sufficient to counterbalance and supply the wants of others. In order to this, he needed only to leave men to the operation of their own minds. They did not collect the food by measure, but measured it after they had brought it home; that so they might apportion it to every member of their family, according to the divine command. Hence it would often occur, that one who was young, active, vigorous, and disengaged, would exceed his quota; whilst another who was enfeebled by sickness, or depressed by sorrow, or occupied with some urgent business, as that of attending on his sick wife and family, might collect but little. Neither the one might think of administering relief, nor the other of receiving it; but in all cases where there was excess or defect found in the exertions of one, there was a corresponding want or superfluity in another; so that, on measuring the whole, there was no superfluity or defect throughout the whole camp.

In fact, this, in some respect, obtains throughout the whole world: for though there is doubtless a great disparity in men's possessions, arising from different circumstances, the rich unwittingly supply the necessities of the poor, by dispersing their wealth in return for the comforts or elegancies of life: and thus, to a much greater extent than men in general are aware, is equality produced among them; all having food and raiment, and no one possessing more.]

2. From their bountiful disposition towards each other—

[In this view St. Paul quotes the very words of my text. He is exhorting the Corinthians to liberality in supplying the wants of their poorer brethren: he tells them, however, that he did not mean to burthen them for the purpose of easing others; but only that, by an equality, their present abundance might be a supply for the wants of others; who, in return, might supply their wants, in case circumstances should arise to admit of it and require it; that so there might be, under all circumstances, an equality: as it is written, "*He that had gathered much had nothing over; and he that had gathered little had no lack*[a]." This sense does not at all oppose that which I have before given: on the contrary, it rather confirms the former sense; for it supposes that the overplus was collected *accidentally*, as it were, in the first instance, and without any express intention to dispose of it to others: but on its being found to exceed their own wants, they liberally dispensed it to supply the wants of others; the donors at one time being the recipients at another; and the obligations conferred being mutual, as occasion required.

This, too, is still agreeable to the order of God's providence in the world. No one can tell what change of circumstances may arise, to elevate or depress any child of man: but events continually occur to render a reciprocation of friendly offices both practicable and necessary, and to call forth amongst ourselves the dispositions that were exercised amongst the persons spoken of in our text.]

But, to enter more fully into the design of God in this fact, we must notice it,

II. As a mystical ordinance or appointment—

That the manna was a type of Christ, is beyond a doubt: our blessed Lord himself drew the parallel, in the most minute particulars[b] — — — On this account the manna is called "spiritual meat[c]:" and when, in the bestowment of it, there was so remarkable a circumstance perpetuated throughout the whole camp for forty years, we cannot doubt but that it was intended to convey some particular and very important instruction. Nor does the construction put upon it by St. Paul *in one point of view* at all militate against a different construction of it *in another view*. His interpretation refers to it only as a *temporal* ordinance: but, as it was a *spiritual* ordinance also, we must endeavour to derive from it the instruction which, *in that view*, it was intended to convey[d] — — — I think, then, that we may see in it,

---

[a] 2 Cor. viii. 13—15.   [b] John vi. 31—58.   [c] 1 Cor. x. 3.
[d] St. Matthew's explanation of Isai. liii. 4, 5. (See Matt. viii. 16, 17.) does not invalidate the construction put upon it by St. Peter,

1. Our privilege as Believers—

[Believers now feed on Christ, as the whole Jewish nation fed upon the manna: and from day to day it is found, that "they who gather much have nothing over; and they who gather little have no lack." In the Church of God at this day persons are very differently circumstanced; some having much leisure, and deep learning, and many opportunities of attending ordinances in public, and of acquiring information in private; whilst others are so entirely occupied with temporal concerns, or so remote from opportunities of instruction, that they can gather but little comparatively of the heavenly bread. But have the one therefore any superfluity, or the other any want? No. We will ask of those who are most devoted to the word of God and prayer, whether they find their attainments in knowledge and in grace so abundant, that they have more than their necessities require? No. A blind Papist may boast of his works of supererogation, and of having merits to sell for the benefit of less-favoured people: but " ye, Beloved, have not so learned Christ:" ye know, that if your attainments were an hundredfold more than they are, there were scope enough for the employment of them, without over-burthening your souls: you would still " forget all that was behind, and be reaching forward for that which was before, if by any means you might obtain the prize of your high calling in Christ Jesus[e]." On the other hand, I will ask of those whose attainments are more contracted; Do you not find that your more slender portion is sufficient for you? You feed on the Lord Jesus Christ, as the bread of life: and do you not find that he nourishes your souls; and that pardon, and peace, and holiness, are the fruits of your communion with him? Yes: it is said, " He that believeth" (not he that is very strong in faith) " shall be saved;" yea, and that " *all* who believe (whatever be their stature or growth in grace) are justified from all things." If you be but a child, incapable of digesting strong *meat*, you find that " the sincere *milk* of the word" is sufficient to nourish and support you; and that if you be but a lamb in Christ's flock, " he carries the lambs in his bosom," because " it is not the will of your Father that one of his little ones should perish." This is no reason for your neglecting to exert yourselves to the uttermost: but it is a comfort to you to know, that, though from the peculiarity of your circumstances you have been able to gather but little, you neither have, nor shall have, any occasion to complain that you have " lacked" what was needful for you. If you have

---

1 Pet. ii. 24. Both senses were true: but the *spiritual* sense was the *more important*.

[e] Phil. iii. 13, 14.

had no superabundance of grace, " your strength has been according to your day."]

2. Our duty, as Saints—

[All, whilst they judged their first offices due to those who were immediately dependent on them, considered themselves as members of one great family, and bound to administer help to all whose necessities should require it. Thus should the whole collective mass of believers consider themselves bound to render every possible assistance to every part of Christ's mystical body. Every joint is to supply a measure of nutriment according to its capacity, for the good of the whole body; that so the whole may be strengthened, and edified in love[f]. The command is plain, " Strengthen ye the weak hands, and confirm the feeble knees: say unto them that are of a fearful heart, Be strong; fear not; your God will come and save you[g]." With whatever we be enriched, we should be ready to impart of our stores liberally and without grudging; considering that we are but stewards of all that we possess, and that in dispensing to others the benefits we have received, whether they be of a temporal or spiritual nature, we most resemble our Heavenly Father, and best answer the ends for which those blessings have been committed to us. True, indeed, we have not any thing of our own, which we can impart to others; (we have no more oil in our lamps than is wanted for ourselves[h];) nor can any diligence in the head of a family supersede the necessity of every member gathering for himself; (for " every man must bear his own burthen[i]:") but still, as instruments in God's hands, we may be serviceable to many[k], and may, as golden pipes, convey the golden oil, for the enlightening and edifying of the Church of God[l].]

Having thus marked the *distinct* views in which I conceive the fact before us ought to be regarded, I will now, in conclusion, suggest the INSTRUCTION to be derived from it in a *collective* view. We may LEARN from it, I think,

1. Contentment—

[The whole people of Israel had but this food for forty years; nor, except for use on the Sabbath-day, was any of it to be treasured up, even for a single day. The whole people of Israel were to subsist on God's providence, exactly as the birds of the air and the beasts of the field. Nor was any thing more than food and raiment to be the portion of so much as

[f] Eph. iv. 15, 16.   [g] Isai. xxxv. 3, 4. with Heb. xii. 12, 13.
[h] Matt. xxv. 8, 9.   [i] Gal. vi. 5.   [k] Jam v 19, 20.
[l] Zech. iv. 12. with 1 Thess. v. 11, 14.

one amongst them: with this they were to be content; and with a similar portion should we also be content[m]. Hear St. Paul's experience on this subject: "I have learned in whatsoever state I am, therewith to be content. I know both how to be abased; and I know how to abound: everywhere, and in all things, I am instructed both to be full and to be hungry, both to abound and to suffer need[n]." Precisely such should be the frame of our minds also. We should offer continually, and from our inmost souls, that prayer which our Lord has taught us, "Give us day by day our daily bread:" and we should really be willing to live dependent on our God for every blessing, whether for body or for soul, whether for time or for eternity.]

2. Confidence—

[In parting with any superfluity which they might have attained, the whole people of Israel shewed that they looked to God alone for a supply of their necessities, and that they had no doubt of his continued care even to the end. The same lesson should we also learn. We should "take no thought for the morrow, but seek first the kingdom of God and his righteousness, and rest assured that all needful blessings shall be added unto us[o]." We should regard God as our Parent; who, if he neglect not the birds of the air, or the meanest worm of the earth, will surely not neglect his own children, but will rather feed them with bread from heaven, and cause that bread to follow them in all their journeys, than leave them one day without the supply that is needful for them.]

3. Liberality—

[Certainly, to give away the superabundance which they had gathered, when they had not any thing in hand for their subsistence on the morrow, was a bright example of generosity. I am far from saying that we, under our dispensation, should carry our liberality to the same extent; but I have no doubt but that the spirit which they manifested should be cultivated by us also, and that to a much greater extent than is generally imagined. The instruction given by John the Baptist to the people of his day was, "He that hath two coats, let him give to him that hath none; and he that hath meat, let him do likewise[p]." If it be thought that this was nothing but an Eastern proverb, I answer, that St. Paul, in the very place where he quotes the words of my text, proposes to our imitation the example of the Macedonians, which scarcely fell short of the very letter of St. John's instructions: "For at a time when they were in a trial of great affliction

---

[m] 1 Tim. vi. 8.   [n] Phil. iv. 11, 12.
[o] Matt. vi. 31—34.   [p] Luke iii. 11.

and in deep poverty themselves, they yet abounded unto the riches of liberality; being willing to give not only to their power, but beyond their power, and praying him with much entreaty to take upon him the office of dispensing their alms to their afflicted brethren^q." Nay more, he proposes to us the example of our blessed Lord himself, who "though he was rich, yet for our sakes he became poor, that we through his poverty might be rich^r." Let this mind then be in you, my beloved brethren; and account yourselves rich, not in proportion to what you can consume upon yourselves, but according to what you are able to administer for the benefit of others. "In bearing one another's burthens, ye shall best fulfil the law of Christ^s."]

^q 2 Cor. viii. 1—4.   ^r 2 Cor. viii. 9.   ^s Gal. vi. 2.

OUTLINE NO. 88
SENDING OF THE MANNA.

Exod. xvi. 35. *And the children of Israel did eat manna forty years, until they came to a land inhabited: they did eat manna until they came unto the borders of the land of Canaan.*

THE history of the Israelites in the wilderness contains an uninterrupted series of miracles. It might be well expected, that two millions of people encamped in a barren desert would soon begin to want fresh supplies of food. And so it happened. In a month after their first departure from Egypt, they had exhausted the store that they had brought with them. But God, who had brought them thus far, would not suffer them to remain destitute any longer than was necessary to try their faith and patience. He therefore gave them from the clouds a peculiar kind of food, (such as had never been seen before,) a small white substance, like coriander-seed, which, when ground in a mill and baked or seethed in water, was extremely palatable.

We propose to make some observations upon,

I. The provision he gave them—

Let *the occasion* on which he gave it be first considered—

[Instead of confiding in that God who had so often, and so wonderfully interposed for them, they murmured against him in a most impious manner, wishing that he had involved them in the judgments which had desolated Egypt, rather than that he should have brought them into their present difficulties[a]. And though their complaints were directed professedly only against Moses and Aaron, they were, in fact, against God himself, by whose direction alone any step had been taken[b]. How astonishing was it that God should take occasion from such a grievous act of impiety to give them such tokens of his love and mercy! Might we not have expected rather that he should execute upon them his severest judgments? But thus he has done in all ages, in order to display the sovereignty and the riches of his grace[c] — — —]

Next, let us notice *the directions he gave respecting it*—

[*They were to gather the manna from day to day, reserving none of it for the morrow*[d]. This was to teach them their entire dependence upon God, and impress them with a sense of God's continued care of them. And though *we* are not forbidden, yea rather are commanded, to make suitable provision for our families, yet in the habit of our minds we are to be continually dependent on God, and free from all anxious care or distrust — — —

They were not to gather any on the Sabbath, but to provide a double portion on the day preceding it [e]. How early was the observance of the Sabbath inculcated! The law was not yet given; therefore the observance of the Sabbath was not a mere ceremonial commandment. Nor was the injunction relative to it either given by Moses, or received by Israel, *as a new thing:* it doubtless had been enforced from the beginning of the world: and consequently *we*, no less than the Jews, are bound to lay aside all temporal concerns, as much as possible, on that day, and to consecrate it wholly to the service of our God — — —

They were to preserve some of it in a pot, and lay it up before the Lord as a memorial for future generations[f]. They were not to forget the mercies vouchsafed to them; but rather to transmit to their latest posterity the remembrance of them; in order that they also might be led to serve and trust in the living God. And have not we also memorials of the love of God to us? Search the records of our national history, or let every one consult his own personal experience; and we shall find abundant reason to adore that God, who has interposed

---

[a] ver. 3.   [b] ver. 8.
[c] To Adam, Gen. iii. 6, 12, 15. To Saul, Acts xxvi. 10—16. To ourselves in unnumbered instances, making our sins the occasion of deeper humiliation.
[d] ver. 4, 19.   [e] ver. 29.   [f] ver. 32, 33.

for us in ten thousand dangers, and supplied our continually returning wants — — —]

The peculiar interposition of God in relation to it deserves also particular notice—

[It was so ordered by his providence, that, when the members of the different families had put together the portions which they had severally collected, and measured it out again for the purpose of distributing to each his regular portion, there never was found any redundancy, or any want[g]. What this was designed to teach us, we are at no loss to determine; since God himself has suggested the proper improvement of it. We all are members of one great family. Some, by God's blessing on their diligence, or by some other means, possess much; whilst others, through a variety of circumstances, possess but little: we ought therefore (not indeed to make one common stock, but) to "lay by us for the poor, according as God has prospered us;" that, as far at least as the enjoyment of the necessaries of life are concerned, there may be an equality; the abundance of the rich supplying the necessities of their less-favoured brethren[h]. O that there were in all of us such an heart, and that, instead of scraping together all that we can save, for the purpose of enriching our families, we found our happiness in doing good, being "glad to distribute, and willing to communicate!"— — —]

From viewing the mercies God vouchsafed to the Israelites, let us turn our attention to,

II. The corresponding provision he has given us—

St. Paul tells us, that the manna of which we have been speaking, was "spiritual meat[i]." It was carnal indeed in its immediate use; but it typically shadowed forth the food on which our souls must live: and, to those who partook of it in faith, it was a source of spiritual and eternal blessings. The Lord Jesus Christ has fully explained the subject to us; and drawn a parallel between *the manna* on which the Israelites subsisted, and *himself* as the life of our souls[k]. We shall not trace that parallel here[l], but consider the subject in a more appropriate view.

Three things then we wish you to remark;

1. The freeness of *this* provision—

[g] ver. 16—18.   [h] 2 Cor. viii. 14, 15.
[i] 1 Cor. x. 3.   [k] John vi. 32—58.
[l] The parallel is drawn in Dis. on John vi. 34. and 1 Cor. x. 3, 4.

[What have we done to *merit* the gift of God's dear Son? We were rebels against the Majesty of heaven, and deserved nothing but "wrath and fiery indignation to consume us"— — — The manna rained round the tents of the murmuring Israelites was not more freely given, than Christ is sent to us, and salvation by him is offered us in the Gospel[m]— — —]

2. The suitableness—

[The manna was adapted to nourish equally the infant and adult. And to whom is not Christ suited? The great sinner will find in him precisely such a Saviour as his necessities require — — The weak, the timid, the disconsolate, yea, all persons in all possible circumstances, shall find, that he is as much suited to their individual cases, as if God had sent him for them alone; and to their palate, as though they themselves had chosen what kind of a Saviour they would have — — —]

3. The sufficiency—

[The vigour of all was renewed from day to day by means of the food provided for them; and they were enabled to march or fight, as occasion required. And what cannot he do who feeds upon the Lord Jesus Christ? What conflicts shall not he support; what victories shall not he gain? "The grace of Christ will be sufficient for him;" and he will be "able to do all things through Christ who strengtheneth him"— — —" He that gathers most of this heavenly manna, will indeed have nothing over; but he who gathers ever so little, shall have no lack"— — — *Twice* is it repeated in our text, that they ate of the manna *till they arrived at the promised land:* never did it fail them; nor did they ever need any other food. And thus assuredly shall Christ continue to the end the support of all who feed upon him; and, in possessing "that hidden manna," they shall have all that they can want in this dreary wilderness; they shall have an earnest and antepast of heaven itself[n].]

[m] Isai. lv. 1.   [n] Rev. ii. 17.

OUTLINE NO. 89
MOSES STRIKING THE ROCK.

Exod. xvii. 5, 6. *And the Lord said unto Moses, Go on before the people, and take with thee of the elders of Israel: and thy rod, wherewith thou smotest the river, take in thine hand, and go. Behold, I will stand before thee there upon the rock in Horeb: and thou shalt smite the rock, and there shall come water out of it, that the people may drink. And Moses did so, in the sight of the elders of Israel.*

THE whole of man's pilgrimage on earth is but a succession of trials and deliverances. And God so ordains it to be, because it is for our greatest good: "Trials work patience; and patience, experience; and experience, hope." The frequent recurrence of difficulties to *the Israelites* in their journey through the wilderness may serve as a glass wherein to view the state of the Church in this world, and, more or less, of all the individuals that are in the world: and the interpositions of God on *their* behalf shew, what is the real, though less visible, course of his providence at this time. Scarcely had the waters at Marah been sweetened for their use, and manna been given them for their support, than they again experienced a most afflictive pressure (a want of water for themselves and their cattle); and again a miraculous deliverance, at Massah or Meribah.

We propose to notice in our present discourse,

I. The circumstances of this miracle—

And here there are two things to which we would call your attention:

1. The time—

[The Israelites had renewed their murmurs against God; and were so incensed at a renewal of their difficulties, that they were ready to stone Moses for having brought them into their present trying situation. As for their Divine Benefactor, they even questioned whether he were with them in the camp or not; assured that, if he was, he was unmindful of their necessities, or unable to relieve them.

Yet at the very moment that they were so offending the Divine Majesty, did God interpose for their relief. What an exalted idea does this convey to us of the patience and long-suffering of God! And, if we were to mark the seasons of God's interpositions in *our* behalf, we should find abundant matter for admiration and gratitude — — —]

2. The manner—

[This singularly displays the grace of God. God makes Moses, whom they were ready to kill as their enemy, the instrument of their deliverance. He orders the rod, which had wrought such wonders in Egypt and at the Red Sea, to be used, not for their destruction (as might have been expected), but for the supplying of their necessities. He himself, whose very existence they had questioned, went to preside visibly on the occasion; and the elders, who had so unreasonably doubted his power and love, were suffered to be eye-witnesses of the miracle wrought for their preservation.

How remarkably does this illustrate the precept which God has given us, "not to be overcome of evil, but to overcome evil with good!" And what convincing evidence does it afford us, that, "where sin has abounded, his grace shall much more abound!" — — —]

But though these circumstances are instructive, the chief thing to be noticed in the miracle, is,

II. The hidden mystery contained in it—

We can have no doubt but that this part of sacred history was intended to typify and prefigure Christ[a], as a source of all spiritual blessings to the world; as a spring,

1. Divinely appointed—

[No one would have conceived the idea of looking for water in that rock, any more than in any other spot throughout the plain whereon it stood: nor would it have entered into the mind of man to bring water out of it by the stroke of a rod or cane. But God appointed both the rock and the rod to be means and instruments of communication between himself and his distressed people. And who would ever have thought that God's only dear Son should be given unto us; and that blessings should be made to flow down to us through the wounds inflicted on him both by God and man? Yet "was all this done according to the determinate counsel and foreknowledge of God." "He was smitten, stricken of God, and afflicted," that our souls might be redeemed from death: "He was wounded for our transgressions, that by his stripes we might be healed." Yes, it is a faithful saying, that "the Father sent the Son to be the Saviour of the world." "It pleased the Father that in Christ should all fulness dwell;" and that "we should receive out of his fulness" "every thing that pertaineth to life and godliness."]

2. All-sufficient—

["The water gushed out of the stricken rock, and flowed like a river; so that it abundantly supplied the whole camp of Israel, (both men and beasts,) following them in all their journeyings for the space of eight and thirty years. And who ever lacked, that has once drunk of the water that Christ gives to his Church and people? Never *did* any of them, never *shall* any, thirst again: for "the water that Christ gives them shall be in them a well of water springing up unto everlasting life[b]"— — —]

3. Universally accessible—

[a] 1 Cor. x. 4.   [b] John iv. 13, 14.

[The water from the rock flowed to every quarter of the camp; and the people instantly dug pools for its reception, so that men and cattle were supplied without the least difficulty[c]. And how free is our access to Christ; free to all persons, and at all times! Hear his own invitation, and the invitation of his Spirit, of his Church, and of all that know the value of those living waters[d]— — —As the vilest murmurers in the camp drank of that stream, so may even the most flagrant rebels in the universe drink of this[e]— — — "Christ has within him the residue of the Spirit[f];" and "pours out that Spirit abundantly[g]" upon all who call upon him; upon all, without price[h], without parsimony[i], and without upbraiding[k]— — —]

WE may LEARN from hence—

1. The experience of real penitents—

[Their thirst after the Saviour is urgent and insatiable[l]— — — What a blessed sight would it be to behold a whole congregation as eager in their desires after Christ as the Israelites were after a supply of water for their bodies!— — — The Lord hasten the season when this thirst shall prevail throughout all the world!]

2. The mercy reserved for them—

[They may feel many painful sensations, and be greatly disquieted for a season: but the promise which God has given them shall surely be realized by all[m].— — —]

[c] Numb. xxi. 16—18. [d] Rev. xxi. 6, 7. [e] Ps. lxviii. 18.
[f] Mal. ii. 15. [g] Tit. iii. 6. [h] Isai. lv. 1.
[i] John vii. 37—39. [k] Jam. i. 5. [l] Matt. v. 6.
[m] Isai. xli. 17, 18. and xliii. 20.

OUTLINE NO. 90

THE HISTORY OF THE JEWS TYPICAL OF CHRISTIAN EXPERIENCE.

Exod. xvii. 11. *And it came to pass, when Moses held up his hand, that Israel prevailed: and when he let down his hand, Amalek prevailed.*

IT pleases God, in general, to effect his purposes by certain means; yet the very means he uses are, for the most part, such as tend only to illustrate his power, and to lead our minds up to him as the first great Cause of all. But on no occasion has the truth of this observation more manifestly appeared, than in the history now before us, wherein we are informed, that the success of the Israelites in an engagement with Amalek was made to depend, not on the bravery of the soldiers, or the skill of their commander, but on the holding up of the hands of Moses at a distance from the field of battle.

In discoursing on this remarkable event, we shall consider it as,

I. A typical history—

The whole history of the Israelites, from their deliverance out of Egypt to their establishment in the land of Canaan, was altogether of a typical nature: but we shall limit our observations to the circumstances now under our consideration.

We may notice then a typical reference,

1. In the conflicts which the Israelites maintained—

[The Israelites were scarcely come out of Egypt, before they were attacked by the Amalekites, though no provocation had been given on their part. This represented the opposition which the world and Satan make to the true Israelites, as soon as ever they separate themselves from the ungodly, and set their faces towards the promised land. Though they do nothing to merit persecution, yea, though, in every point of view, they are become more excellent and praiseworthy, and desire nothing but to prosecute their journey peaceably through this dreary wilderness, yet are they hated, reviled, persecuted; nor can they obtain the inheritance prepared for them, without arming themselves for the combat, and " warring a good warfare."]

2. In the commander under whom they fought—

[Joshua was appointed to set the army in array, and lead them out to battle. Now the very name of Joshua is precisely the same with that of Jesus[a], who is " given to us of God to be our leader and commander[b]." He is " the Captain of our salvation," under whom we are enlisted, and under whose banners we fight. Whether we bear more or less the brunt of the battle, it is He who appoints us our respective stations; and it is to Him that we must look for direction and support. And while, " as good soldiers of Jesus Christ, we endure hardness" at his command, we may depend on him for all necessary provision, and for an abundant share of the spoils of victory.]

3. In the means by which they obtained the victory—

[a] Acts vii. 45. Heb. iv. 8.   [b] Isai. lv. 4.

[The rod of Moses was that with which he had wrought his wonders in Egypt; and it was a special emblem of the divine power. This he was to hold up in the sight of Israel on an adjacent hill: and, while he held it up, they prospered; but when, through infirmity, he let it down, their enemies prevailed against them. Now it is thus that we are to obtain the victory against our enemies: we must have our eyes fixed on the power of God exerted in our behalf: as long as we have clear views of this, we shall vanquish every adversary; but, if at any time this cease to be exalted in our eyes, we shall surely faint and fail.

The lifting up of the hands of Moses may further denote the efficacy of prayer. And it is certain that our success will fluctuate, according as our applications at the throne of grace are continued or relaxed.]

But this history may further be considered as affording us,

II. An instructive lesson—

It may well teach us,

1. That, whatever mercies we have received, we must still expect conflicts—

[The Israelites had been brought through the Red Sea, and fed both with manna from heaven, and water from the solid rock; and they might have fondly dreamed of nothing but security and peace: but they were rather called to scenes of difficulty and danger. Thus it is with us, when we commit ourselves to the guidance of the pillar and the cloud. We may think perhaps that, because we are reconciled to God, and made heirs of his kingdom, we are henceforth to enjoy uninterrupted tranquillity: but we shall soon find, that we have to "wrestle; and that too, not only with flesh and blood, but with principalities and powers." We may indeed be screened for a season by the good providence of God; as the Israelites were kept from going through the territory of the Philistines, lest they should be discouraged by the opposition that they would have met with from that warlike people[c]: but we are men of war by our very profession; and, sooner or later, our courage and fidelity will be put to the test. It is through much tribulation that we must enter into the kingdom; and we must "fight the good fight of faith, before we can receive the crown of righteousness from the hands of our righteous Judge."]

2. That we must not despond, though our success for a time should appear doubtful—

[c] Exod. xiii. 17.

[The Israelites in this very first encounter were at times repulsed; and victory was long held in suspense, before it was finally declared in their favour. Thus we must expect, that our enemies, though frequently beaten, will return to the charge, and often threaten our very destruction. But, if wounded, we must apply to Christ for healing; if faint, we must beg him to renew our strength; if driven before our enemies, we must rally, and resume the contest, ever remembering under whom we fight, and how much depends upon a victorious issue. We must also, like Aaron and Hur, *assist each other;* holding up each other's hands, and animating each other's hearts; nor ever terminate our exertions, till God shall scatter all our enemies, and bruise under our feet the vanquished foe.]

3. That a believing use of the appointed means, how inadequate soever, or even useless, they may appear, will be crowned with success at last—

[Nothing can be conceived less connected with the event, than the means which were used by Moses; yet were they necessary: for if, when through infirmity the use of them was intermitted, the scale of victory was instantly turned in favour of the Amalekites, much more, if he had disregarded them altogether, would the most fatal effects have followed: but the persevering use of them procured at last the desired success. Thus the attending of public ordinances, and waiting upon God in secret, may seem but ill calculated to produce such great effects as are said to depend upon them: but, as the occasional and unallowed neglect of these duties is attended with many painful consequences, so a wilful contempt of them would infallibly terminate in our destruction. On the other hand, a diligent and continued attention to them will and must prevail: our prayer shall go up with acceptance before God, and the word we hear shall prove " the power of God to the salvation of our souls." Only let us " lift up holy hands without doubting," until the evening of life, and we shall be " more than conquerors through him that loved us."]

ADDRESS,

1. Those who know nothing of spiritual conflicts—

[If they, who are at ease in Zion, and experience no spiritual conflicts, were real Christians, there would be no resemblance at all between them and the Israelites, by whom they were typically represented; and all that is spoken about the Christian warfare, the armour provided for us, and the General under whom we fight, would be altogether without a meaning. But in vain shall the true Israelites expect peace, as long as there are any Amalekites in the world. Our Lord "came not to send peace on earth, but a sword:" and though he may, in some instances, cause our enemies to be at peace with us, yet will they never be so much at peace, but that we shall have many to contend with: or, if men should cease from troubling us, we shall have enough, both from Satan and our own lusts, to call forth all our exertions, and to make us fervent in imploring help from God. Let those, then, who feel not these conflicts, inquire whether their peace be not the consequence of a captivity to their enemies, instead of a victory over them: nor let them ever expect to reign with Christ, unless they first enlist under his banners, and fight after his example.]

2. Those who are ready to faint by reason of their conflicts—

[Your insufficiency to withstand your enemies often discourages and disquiets you: but the Israelites prevailed, notwithstanding their inexperience in the art of war, because they had God on their side. Fear not then ye, "whose hands are weak, whose knees are feeble, and whose hearts are faint; for, behold, your God shall come and save you[d]." Behold, his power is now exalted in your sight: look at it; remember what it has effected in the days of old: and know, that it shall be exerted in your behalf, if you do but trust in it. Nor forget, what a Captain you are fighting under: the world, which molests you, has been overcome by him; and "the prince of this world has been judged" by him. Fight on then a little longer, assured that you shall ere long put your feet upon the necks of your enemies, and enjoy the fruits of victory for ever and ever.]

[d] Isai. xxxv. 3, 4.

OUTLINE NO. 91

MOSES' MESSAGE TO THE ISRAELITES.

Exod. xix. 3—6. *And Moses went up unto God: and the Lord called unto him out of the mountain, saying, Thus shalt thou say to the house of Jacob, and tell the children of Israel; Ye have seen what I did unto the Egyptians, and how I bare you on eagles' wings, and brought you unto myself. Now therefore, if ye will obey my voice indeed, and keep my covenant, then ye shall be a peculiar treasure unto me above all people: for all the earth is mine. And ye shall be unto me a kingdom of priests, and an holy nation. These are the words which thou shalt speak unto the children of Israel.*

WE cannot but admire God's condescension in noticing our fallen race. When we see him renewing to them his acts of kindness after repeated instances of ingratitude, we are yet more amazed: but when we behold him entering into covenant with the most rebellious of his creatures, and binding himself by promises and oaths to load them with his richest benefits, we are altogether lost in wonder. Since the time that Israel were liberated from their bondage in Egypt, about six weeks had now elapsed; during which time every successive trial had evinced, that they were a rebellious and stiff-necked people. But, instead of casting them off, God commissioned Moses to propose to them a covenant, wherein they should engage to be obedient to his will, and he would engage to make them truly prosperous and happy. The same condescension does God manifest to us; as will appear if we consider,

I. The mercies God has already vouchsafed us—

Those enumerated in the text were *distinguishing* mercies—

[God had inflicted the heaviest judgments on the Egyptians; but had brought out his people safely and triumphantly[a] to the mountain, which he had long before marked as the place where they should worship him and enjoy his presence[b]. This "they saw;" and therefore could not question the goodness of God towards them — — —]

And have *we* no distinguishing mercies to call forth our gratitude?

[What though we have never experienced such *miraculous* interpositions; have we not, both individually and collectively, unbounded reason for thankfulness on account of the *peculiar* favours conferred on us?

Think how many millions of the human race are sitting in darkness and the shadow of death, without the smallest knowledge of a Saviour, or even of the one true God! But *we* are favoured with the light of revelation, and, we hope we may say too, a faithful ministration of the word of life — — — Reflect further, how many, under distress of mind, or body, or estate, are sinking under the insupportable load of their afflictions, whilst we have experienced but little trouble, perhaps so much only as to display more clearly the goodness of God in our

---

[a] The eagle, to rescue her young from impending danger, will bear them upon her pinions to a place of safety. Compare Deut. xxxii. 11.   [b] Exod. iii. 12.

repeated deliverances — — — Consider also, how many have within a few months or years been summoned into the presence of their God, whilst we have yet our lives prolonged, and further space given us for repentance — — — Could we but realize these thoughts, we should see that not even the Israelites themselves had more reason for gratitude than we.]

Let us from the consideration of God's past mercies extend our views to,

II. Those which he has yet in reserve for us—

Those which he promised to the Israelites were exceeding great—

[" All the earth was the Lord's ;" and therefore he might have taken any other people in preference to them[c]: but he had chosen them in preference to all others[d]; and promised to exalt them above all others in *national honour*, and *individual happiness*.

What an unspeakable *honour* was it to them to be made " an holy nation," consecrated in a peculiar manner to the service of their God! to be " a kingdom of priests," all having access to God, to offer to him the sacrifices of prayer and praise! and to be regarded by God as " his peculiar treasure," which he prized above all, and would secure to himself for ever!

What an *happiness* too to all of them, as far as worldly prosperity could make them happy ; and, to those who could discern the spiritual import of these promises, what a source it was of unutterable peace and joy! — — —]

But the mercies promised to them were only shadows of those which are reserved for us—

[These promises have their chief accomplishment under the Gospel dispensation[e]. And O! how inconceivably "great and precious" are they! Believers are at this time amidst the ungodly world, what the Israelites were in Egypt, " a chosen generation," objects of God's sovereign and eternal choice. They are " a royal priesthood," even " kings and priests unto their God[f]," having dominion over sin and Satan, and " yielding up themselves to him a living sacrifice, acceptable to him through Jesus Christ." As embodied under one head (the Lord Jesus), and living under the same laws, and enjoying the same privileges, they are also " an holy nation ;" and as differing from all others in their views and principles, their spirit and conduct, they are " a peculiar people," " a peculiar people zealous of good works[g]."

[c] This is evidently the meaning of the text ; and it should not be overlooked.
[d] Deut. vii. 6—8. [e] 1 Pet. ii. 9. [f] Rev. i. 6. [g] Tit. ii. 14.

These are the blessings promised to men under the Gospel; and it will be utterly our own fault if we be not partakers of them.]

But these blessings must be sought for in God's appointed way. Let us therefore consider,

III. The terms upon which he will bestow them upon us—

The promises of God to Israel were altogether conditional—

[We have seen what he engaged to do for them: but it was upon the express condition, that they "obeyed his voice, and kept his covenant." They must take him for their God, and devote themselves to his service—and then he would make them his people, and give them incessant and increasing tokens of his love and favour. This covenant was not wholly legal, nor wholly evangelical, but a mixture of both. Inasmuch as it prescribed conditions, it was legal; and inasmuch as it secured to them a remission of sins upon their returning unto God, it was evangelical: but on the whole the legal part was far the more prominent; and the promises were made void by their neglecting to perform the stipulated conditions.]

Those made to us, though absolute in some respects, are conditional in others—

[Under the Christian dispensation, all is of grace: grace is not only the predominant feature, but the sum and substance of the New Covenant: and repentance, faith, and holiness, are not merely required, but bestowed[h]; and *that* freely unto all who ask for them at the hands of God[i]. "By the grace of God we are what we are;" and "by grace are we saved" from first to last. Yet are faith and obedience indispensably necessary to our eternal salvation: nor need we be afraid of speaking of them as *conditions* of our salvation, provided we be careful to divest them of all idea of *merit*, or of being *a price* whereby ulterior blessings are to be purchased. God has given us a covenant of grace; and that covenant we must embrace: and it will be in vain to hope for acceptance with God, if we do not found all our hopes of happiness on Christ the Mediator of that Covenant. God has also given us a revelation of his will: and that will we must do; nor will that "grace of God ever bring salvation unto *us*, if it do not lead us to deny ungodliness and worldly lusts, and to live righteously, soberly, and godly in this present world[k]." These then

---

[h] Acts v. 31. Heb. xii. 2. Rom. vi. 14.   [i] Ezek. xxxvi. 37.
[k] Tit. ii. 11, 12.

are *the terms* on which we shall enjoy all the privileges of God's chosen people: and, though it is true that "without Christ we can do nothing," it is also true, that the only way in which we ever can attain happiness, is, by repentance towards God, and faith in our Lord Jesus Christ. Christ is ready to save us *all;* but he will ultimately prove a Saviour to those only who obey him— — —]

In APPLYING this subject to ourselves, we shall,

1. Deliver God's message to you—

[Observe how solemnly God's injunction to Moses respecting the delivery of this message is *twice repeated* in the text. *In reference to this,* God twice says by the prophet, that "he protested, yea protested earnestly," to this people[1]. But you have already seen that the promises in our text refer principally to the dispensation under which we live. To you therefore must this message be addressed, in the name, and by the command, of God himself. And, as Moses "*laid before the faces* of that people the words which God commanded him[m]," so also would we "use great plainness of speech," whilst we are delivering to you the message of the Most High.

The terms on which alone you can be saved have been already stated to you[n]— — —We ask you then, is there any thing unreasonable in them? Are you not rather so convinced of their reasonableness, that, if we were to tell you that you were at liberty to disregard God's covenant, and to violate his will, — — — you would cry out against us as impious blasphemers?—Behold, then, we have a testimony in your own consciences in favour of the message which we have delivered to you: and, if you continue to expect heaven on any other terms, you will be self-condemned to all eternity[o].]

2. Inquire what answer we must return to God—

[Moses received the people's answer, and reported it to God[p]. And O that we could hear the same answer from you all, "All that the Lord hath spoken will we do!" It is true, they spake in their own strength, and therefore failed to execute their promises: but surely it was good to form the determination; it shewed that they saw the equity of God's commands: and, had they sought strength from God to fulfil his will, their resolution would have produced the best effects. But are not many of you disposed rather to reply, "As for the word that thou hast spoken unto us in the name of the Lord, we will not hearken unto thee[q]?" Perhaps you are not yet hardened

---

[1] Jer. xi. 7.   [m] ver. 7.
[n] A recapitulation of them here would be proper.
[o] See Jer. xi. 1—5.   [p] ver. 8.   [q] Jer. xliv. 16.

enough to make this reply in words; but is it not the language of your hearts and lives?— — — Must we not carry this report to God[r]? — — — O that you would hearken to God's voice, before it be too late[s]! — — —

But we trust there are some of a better mind amongst us, some who cordially assent to whatever God has been pleased to propose — — — On behalf of them we pray, that God may fix this pious disposition abidingly in their hearts[t]. Happy are we to see the rising purpose to obey God! but we must caution all not to adopt the purpose lightly, or to carry it into execution in a partial or listless manner. The message of God in the text is, "If ye will obey my voice *indeed*." Our obedience must be sincere, habitual, and unreserved. We must not be satisfied with purposes and resolutions, but must carry them into effect: nothing must divert us, nothing intimidate us, nothing retard us. But let us hold fast the covenant of grace, and uniformly obey the commands of God, and then all the blessings of grace and glory shall be ours — — —]

[r] Put their conduct into words. [s] Jer. xiii. 15—17.
[t] 1 Chron. xxix. 18.

OUTLINE NO. 92

THE GIVING OF THE LAW.

Exod. xx. 18, 19. *And all the people saw the thunderings and the lightnings, and the noise of the trumpet, and the mountain smoking: and when the people saw it, they removed, and stood afar off. And they said unto Moses, Speak thou with us, and we will hear: but let not God speak with us, lest we die.*

THE law of God was originally written on the heart of man: but by sin it was almost obliterated, so that scarcely any traces of it remained. When therefore it pleased God to separate to himself a peculiar people, who should know his will, and enjoy his presence, and subserve his glory, it was necessary, if we may so speak, that he should republish his law, and record it in some way, which might give it a permanent establishment in the world. This he was pleased to do on Mount Sinai, after having conducted his people thither in safety, and shewn, by the wonders he had wrought, that he was indeed the only true God. What were the particulars of that law, we do not now stop to inquire[a]: that to which we would draw your attention is, *the manner of its promulgation.* In the preceding chapter we are informed of all those particulars which are briefly recapitulated in our text. On contemplating that tremendous scene, we are naturally led to inquire, *Why did God publish his law in that manner?* The answer to this question is important; and will prove highly instructive to us all. He did it,

I. To impress their minds with a fear of his Majesty—

[God is a great God, and greatly to be feared[b]. But though the Israelites had seen ample demonstrations of this in Egypt, they had a very inadequate sense of it upon their minds. Hence arose their murmurings and distrust as often as any fresh difficulty occurred. And what is at the root of all *our* disobedience? Is it not that "we do not fear that great and fearful name, THE LORD OUR GOD[c]?"— — —

To beget in the minds of those whom he was bringing into covenant with himself a just sense of his greatness, he appeared to them in a thick cloud, with thunderings, and lightnings, and the sound of a trumpet most terrific. The effect was produced, insomuch that Moses, though terrified beyond measure himself, was forced to administer comfort and encouragement to them[d]. We find somewhat of a similar effect upon ourselves in a violent tempest: and, if we could realize the scene that was exhibited on Sinai, we should say indeed, "It is a fearful thing to fall into the hands of the living God"— — —]

II. To shew them the nature of that dispensation—

[The dispensation of the law, though suited to the Jews at that time, and even glorious, as a type or figure of the Gospel dispensation, was yet in fact "a ministration of death[e]." It required perfect obedience to the law, and denounced a curse for every instance of disobedience; and required all the people, not only to accept it, but to approve of it, in that particular view[f]. Who can contemplate such a covenant, and not tremble to have his hopes founded on it? There was indeed much of the Gospel contained in the ceremonial law; and the penitent Israelite found refuge there. But the law published on Sinai was "a fiery law," "a ministration of condemnation:" and the terrors which were infused into the people by the thunders of Sinai, fitly represented the terrific nature of that

[a] See Disc. on Rom. iii. 20. [b] Deut. x. 17. [c] Deut. xxviii. 58.
[d] ver. 20. [e] 2 Cor. iii. 7, 9.
[f] Compare Gal. iii. 10. with Deut. xxvii. 26.

covenant.—Happy would it be for us, if we availed ourselves of these instructive intimations, to renounce that covenant which consigns us over unto death, and to embrace that better covenant which is revealed to us in the Gospel!]

III. To make them feel their need of a Mediator—

[The people, who but just before had been with difficulty restrained from breaking through the bounds that had been assigned them, were now so alarmed, that they fled from their station, and entreated, that God would no more deliver his commands to them in that way, lest they should die. They desired that Moses might be appointed as a Mediator between God and them, and that all future intimations of God's will should be given them through him. Of the full meaning of their own request they themselves were not aware: for, inasmuch as Moses was a type of Christ, it was, in fact, a desire that *Christ* might be their Mediator, and that all their intercourse with the Deity might be through *Him*. This was the construction which God himself put upon it; and in this view he approved of, and applauded it [g] — — — To the same effect also the Apostle speaks. He tells us that the law was not designed to give us life, but to shew us our need of **Christ, and** to bring us unto him as our only hope [h] — — —]

INFER,

1. How thankful should we be for the Christian covenant!

[It is to *this* that *we* are come, if we have truly believed in Christ. And oh! how different is our state from those who are yet under the law [i] ! — — — Instead of being prohibited from drawing nigh to God, we are permitted and commanded to come unto him. Let us avail ourselves of the blessed privilege, and seek closer fellowship with our God, and brighter views of his glory — — —]

2. How careful should we be not to revert to the Jewish covenant!

[We do, in fact, revert to it, if we seek justification by the law of works. If we do *any* thing in order to be justified by it, we instantly become debtors to do the whole law.—Let it not then appear to us a light matter to indulge a self-righteous spirit; for if we do, we renounce all hope from the grace of the Gospel, and " Christ, with respect to us, is dead in vain [k]."]

3. How studiously should we cultivate the fear of God!

---

[g] Compare Deut. v. 27, 28. and xviii. 15—18.   [h] Gal. iii. 24.
[i] Heb. xii. 18—24.   [k] Gal. v. 1—4.

[Terrible as the appearance and the voice of God were on that occasion, his appearance in the day of judgment will be infinitely more tremendous — — — "Knowing therefore the terrors of the Lord, we would persuade you" to turn unto him, ere it be too late. We wish however to produce in you, not a *slavish*, but a *filial* fear: *that* will only drive you from God; and therefore in relation to it we say with Moses, "Fear not:" but *this* will make you happy in the service and enjoyment of God; and therefore we add, "Let his fear be ever before your faces, that ye sin not[1]."]

[1] ver. 20.

OUTLINE NO. 93

ON CIRCUMSPECTION.

Exod. xxiii. 13. *In all things that I have said unto you, be circumspect.*

IF we were about to prosecute a journey through an extensive forest, where the path was exceeding intricate, where we were in hourly danger of treading upon serpents and scorpions, and where there were declivities so steep and slippery that it was almost impossible but that we must fall down some tremendous precipice, we should feel it necessary to get the best information, and to use the utmost caution in all our way. Such is really our state: in our journey towards heaven we may easily mistake the road; and, even when we are walking in it, we are encompassed with so many dangers, and obstructed by so many difficulties, that we need to exercise continual vigilance and circumspection. Hence, in tender love to us, our heavenly Guide puts us on our guard, and says, "In all things that I have said unto you, be circumspect."

In discoursing on these words we shall consider,

I. The injunction—

It is our duty and our happiness to have all our actions conformed to the mind and will of God: but, in order to this, we must attend diligently to the *matter,* the *manner,* and the *end* of them:—

1. The matter—

[Notwithstanding we have the written word, which, when

duly followed, will suffice to direct our conduct; yet we must have a very considerable knowledge of the Scriptures, and a well-regulated mind, in order to ascertain clearly the will of God. It not unfrequently happens that one duty seems to interfere with another; as when a work of mercy calls for a violation of the Sabbath, or a command of an earthly parent militates against the command of God. In the former case we are to " prefer mercy before sacrifice:" in the latter, we must " obey God rather than man:" but how to discriminate aright at all times, is very difficult: and a well-intentioned person may grievously err, if he do not bring his actions to the touchstone of God's word, and determine, through grace, to regulate them according to that standard[a].]

2. The manner—

[It is by no means sufficient that the *matter* of our actions be right, for they may be so debased by the *manner* of performing them, as to be rendered hateful in the sight of God. Prayer is a duty plainly enjoined: but if it be cold and formal, or offered with an unbelieving heart, it will find no acceptance with God: in vain do persons worship God in such a manner[b]; they shall receive nothing at his hands[c]. Nothing could have been more pleasing to God than David's attempt to bring up the ark to Mount Zion, after it had been at least fifty years in a state of obscurity: but David was inattentive to the manner in which God had appointed the ark to be carried; he put it on a new cart, instead of ordering it to be borne upon the shoulders of the Levites; and *therefore* God manifested his displeasure against him, and against all the people, by striking Uzza dead upon the spot for presuming to touch the ark[d]. We ourselves are not satisfied to have our commands obeyed, unless a due attention be paid also to the manner of executing our will; much less therefore will God be pleased, if we be not as studious to " serve him acceptably," as to serve him at all.]

3. The end—

[Our end or motive in acting determines more than any thing the quality of our actions. Not that a good end will sanctify a bad action; but a bad end will vitiate every action connected with it. If, for instance, in our religious services we seek the applause of men, we must expect no reward from God: the gratification of our pride and vanity is all the reward that such polluted services can obtain[e]. In the account which is given us of Jehu, we find that the very same action, which was rewarded on account of its outward conformity with God's

---

[a] Acts xxvi. 9—11. Gal. ii. 13. and John xvi. 2.
[b] Matt. xv. 7—9. [c] Jam. i. 6, 7. [d] 1 Chron. xv. 13.
[e] Matt. vi. 1—5, 16.

command, was punished on account of the base principle by which he was influenced in performing it. He did well in extirpating the seed of Ahab, and was rewarded for it to the fourth generation[f]: but forasmuch as he was actuated by vanity and ambition, the blood which he shed was imputed to him as murder[g]. Nor is there any thing more common than for even religious persons to mistake the path of duty through an inattention to their own spirit. The disciples doubtless thought themselves under the influence of a commendable zeal, when they would have called fire from heaven to consume a Samaritan village; as did Peter also, when he cut off the ear of Malchus. We should therefore be peculiarly cautious with respect to this, lest by the mixture of any selfish motive or base affection we offend Him, whom it is our desire and endeavour to please.

God having prescribed rules for a just ordering of our whole *spirit* and *conduct*, we must, " *in all things* that he has said unto us, be circumspect."]

The importance of this injunction will appear, while we consider,

II. The reasons of it—

Surely it is a necessary injunction, and no less reasonable than necessary: for,

1. The same authority exists in every commandment—

[It is God who issued a prohibition of adultery and murder: and it is the same Almighty Being who forbids us to entertain a selfish wish or covetous desire[h]. Shall we then acknowledge his authority in our actions, and disregard it in our principles? Shall we think ourselves at liberty to deviate from *any* part of his revealed will? If so, we cease to act as his creatures, and become a God unto ourselves.]

2. Without circumspection we cannot perform any duty aright—

[We cannot find out the real motives of our actions without daily self-examination, and earnest prayer to God for the teachings of his Spirit. However simple the path of duty may appear, there are ten thousand ways in which we may depart from it. And, as long as our hearts are so deceitful, and we have such a subtle adversary striving to mislead us, we shall be in perpetual danger of mistaking our way. If therefore we

---

[f] 2 Kings x. 30.   [g] 2 Kings x. 16. with Hos. i. 4.
[h] Jam. ii. 10, 11.

would serve God aright in *any* thing, we must be circumspect in *every* thing.]

3. An inattention to smaller duties will lead to a violation of the greatest—

[Who shall say, where we shall stop, if once we begin to trifle with God? Eve little thought to what she should be brought by only listening to the suggestions of the tempter: nor did David foresee what would result from the wanton look which he cast on Bathsheba. It was on account of the danger arising from the smallest approach to sin, that God, *in the words following our text*, forbade his people even to "mention the name" of a heathen deity: and on the same account he requires *us* to "abstain from the very appearance of evil." And if we will not "watch in all things," we shall soon have to eat the bitter fruit of our negligence: yea, it will be well, if from *walking* in the *counsel* of the *ungodly*, we do not soon *stand* in the *way* of *sinners*, and at last *sit* in the *seat* of the *scornful*[i].]

4. The greater our circumspection, the more shall we adorn our holy profession—

[There are multitudes on the watch to find out the smallest faults in those who profess religion; and to condemn religion itself on account of them. But a circumspect walk "cuts off occasion from those who seek occasion;" and "by well-doing we put to silence the ignorance of foolish men." It can scarcely be conceived what an effect the conduct of religious people has upon the world, either to recommend religion to them, or to harden them against it. Should not this then make us circumspect? Should we not be careful that we "give no occasion to the adversary to speak reproachfully?" Should we not endeavour to "be wise as serpents, and harmless as doves?" Let us then "so make our light to shine before men, that they may be constrained to glorify our Father that is in heaven."]

5. The whole of our conduct will be reviewed in the day of judgment—

[The most secret springs of action will be brought to light in that awful day, and "the counsels of the heart be made manifest[k]:" God will weigh, not our actions only, but our spirits[l]. "Men judge according to appearance; but He will judge righteous judgment." If this consideration will not make us circumspect, what can we hope to prove effectual? O that we could bear in mind the strictness of that scrutiny, and the awfulness of that decision!]

---

[i] Ps. i. 1. Every word in this verse rises in a climax: "*walk, stand, sit;*" "*counsel, way, seat;*" "*ungodly, sinners, scornful.*"
[k] 1 Cor. iv. 5. Eccl. xii. 14.   [l] Prov. xvi. 2.

ADDRESS,

1. Those who ridicule the circumspection of others—

[To what end has God commanded us to be circumspect, if we are not to regard the injunction? Do you suppose that you are to annul his commands, and to establish rules of conduct that are contrary to his? Or, if you are presumptuous enough to do so in reference to yourselves, do you think that you are to prescribe for others also? You affect to pity the Lord's people as weak enthusiasts: but know that *you* are the true objects of pity, who can rush blindfold in such a manner to your own destruction. Yes; over such as you the Saviour wept: and if you knew your guilt and danger, you would weep for yourselves. Repent, ere it be too late: for, however wise you may imagine yourselves to be, the time is coming when you will change your voice, and say, " We fools counted their life madness [m]." Take care that you yourselves be righteous *enough*, before you ridicule others as " righteous *over-much*."]

2. Those who, in spite of scoffers, are endeavouring to please their God—

[Blessed be God, who enables you to stem the torrent, and to serve him in the midst of a wicked world! But, be on your guard against that scrupulosity, which makes those things to be sins which are no sins; and that superstition, which makes things to be duties which are no duties. Be as careful of adding to the word of God as of detracting from it. Let the different parts of Scripture be compared with each other: and learn your duty not so much from any detached passage, as from a collective view of all those passages which may reflect light upon it. Nevertheless in doubtful matters, you will do well to lean to the safer side.

Yet while you are thus circumspect yourselves, do not presume to judge others. Things may be right in others, which would be wrong in you; and right in you under some circumstances, which under different circumstances would be highly improper. Do not then bring others to your standard, or try them at your bar: " it is to their own Master that they must stand or fall."

Lastly, let not your circumspection fill you with self-preference and self-esteem. However accurately you may walk, there will be still enough to humble you in the dust. You must to your latest hour go to Jesus as the chief of sinners, and seek acceptance with God through his blood and righteousness.]

[m] Wisd. v. 4.

OUTLINE NO. 94

THE DANGER OF WILFUL AND OBSTINATE DISOBEDIENCE.

Exod. xxiii. 20—22. *Behold, I send an angel before thee, to keep thee in the way, and to bring thee into the place which I have prepared. Beware of him, and obey his voice, provoke him not: for he will not pardon your transgressions: for my name is in him. But, if thou shalt indeed obey his voice, and do all that I speak, then I will be an enemy unto thine enemies, and an adversary unto thine adversaries.*

IT is but too common for men to cast the blame of their own negligence on God. But they who labour so much to exculpate themselves now, will one day be silent; and God will finally be justified in every sentence that he shall pass. His kindness to the church of old may shew us what his conduct is towards *us*. And they who are thus guided, warned, and encouraged, must, if they perish, ascribe their condemnation to themselves alone. The words before us contain,

I. The work and office of Christ—

Christ is here called an angel or messenger—

[He is often called by this name in the Holy Scriptures[a]. Nor does he disdain to assume it himself[b]. In his essential nature indeed he is equal with the Father. But in his mediatorial capacity he sustains the office of a servant.]

As the angel of the covenant, he leads and keeps his people—

[He is represented as a leader and commander, like Joshua, his type[c]. He went before them in the wilderness in the pillar and the cloud. And still, though invisibly, guides them in their way to heaven[d].]

Nor does he leave them till he brings them safely to glory—

[He did not forsake the Israelites, till he had accomplished all his promises[e]. Having "*prepared the land for them,*" he preserved them for it. Thus has he " prepared

---

[a] He is the angel that was in the pillar and the cloud, Exod. xiv. 19. That angel was Jehovah, Exod. xiii. 21. That Jehovah was Christ, 1 Cor. x. 9. See also Mal. iii. 1.

[b] John xii. 49.   [c] Isai. lv. 4.

[d] Ps. xxv. 9. and xxxii. 8.   [e] Josh. xxiii. 14.

mansions for us" also[f]; and will surely bring us to the full possession of them.[g]]

But as this office of Christ implies a correspondent duty in us, God suggests,

II. A caution against neglecting him—

We are much in danger of displeasing him—

[As our guide, he expects implicit obedience. Nor can we rebel against him without "provoking" his indignation[h]. Hence we need continual circumspection[i].]

The consequence of displeasing him will be very terrible—

[Doubtless to penitents he is full of mercy and compassion. But to impenitent offenders he will manifest his wrath[k]. Nor will he suffer any to continue in their sins with impunity[l].]

His power and dignity are a certain pledge to us that he will avenge the insults that are offered him—

[By "the name of God" we understand not his authority only, but his very nature[m]. And this union with the Father is a pledge to us, that he will act as becomes the divine character. Nor will any consideration of mercy ever tempt him again to sacrifice the honour of the Deity to the interests of man.]

It is not however by terror only that God would persuade us; for he adds,

III. An encouragement to obey him—

Obedience is in some sense the condition of God's favour—

[We know that there is nothing meritorious in man's obedience. Yet is there an inseparable connexion between that and the divine favour. Nor is it a partial obedience only that he requires at our hands. It must be earnest, unwearied, uniform, and unreserved.]

And to those who yield him this obedience he will shew himself an active friend, and an almighty protector—

[His favour consists not in a mere inactive complacency. It will manifest itself in a constant and powerful interposition

[f] John xiv. 2.   [g] 1 Pet. i. 4, 5.   [h] Isai. lxiii. 10.
[i] ver. 13.   [k] Ps. vii. 11—13.   [l] Ezek. xxiv. 13, 14.
[m] John xiv. 10, 11. and x. 30.

on their behalf[n]. He will not fail to secure them the victory over all their enemies.]

ADDRESS,

1. Those who disregard the voice of this divine Messenger—

[From what is spoken of his mercy you are ready to think him destitute of justice. And from the depth of his condescension you conclude he will not vindicate his own honour. But where God most fully proclaims his mercy he declares his justice also[o]. Make not him then your enemy who came from heaven to save you. Consider what means he has used to guide you to the promised land. Consider what great things he would do for you, if you would obey his voice. Consider what certain and terrible destruction your rejection of his mercy will bring upon you[p]. And instantly surrender up yourselves to his direction and government.]

2. Those who, though they submit to his government, are doubtful of success—

[The Israelites, notwithstanding all the miracles they had seen, were afraid they should not finally attain the object of their desires. Thus amongst ourselves, many tremble lest their expectations should never be realized. But is not God able to beat down your enemies before you? Or will he forget the promise he has so often renewed? If he be incensed against you, it is not owing to unfaithfulness in him, but to instability in you[q]. Only be vigilant to obey his will, and to *follow him fully:* and you need not doubt but that he will preserve you unto his heavenly kingdom[r].]

3. Those who are following him with cheerfulness to the heavenly land—

[Blessed be God, there are some of you like-minded with Joshua and Caleb[s]. And are not you living monuments of the power and grace of God? Have you not on many occasions proved his readiness to pardon sin? And do you not daily experience his paternal care and protection? Go on then with increasing vigilance and an assured hope. Know that all the power and perfections of God are engaged for you: and that "having guided you by his counsel, he will finally bring you to glory."]

[n] 2 Chron. xxxii. 8. Isai. xlix. 25.   [o] Exod. xxxiv. 7.
[p] Heb. xii. 25.   [q] Jer. ii. 17.   [r] 2 Tim. iv. 18.
[s] Numb. xiv. 24. and xxxii. 12.

OUTLINE NO. 95

THE VICTORIES OF ISRAEL GRADUAL AND PROGRESSIVE.

Exod. xxiii. 29, 30. *I will not drive them out from before thee in one year, lest the land become desolate, and the beast of the field multiply against thee. By little and little will I drive them out from before thee, until thou be increased and inherit the land.*

THE more we investigate the dispensations of Providence, the more we shall see, that "God's ways are not as our ways, nor his thoughts as our thoughts." If we had been left to form conjectures respecting man in his first creation, who would have conceived that God should suffer the work of his hands to be so marred as Adam was by the fall, and so large a portion of his creatures to perish in everlasting misery? Nor, if we were told that God would take to himself, from amongst the fallen sons of Adam, a peculiar people, and rescue them by so many signs and wonders from their bondage in Egypt, should we have imagined that he would, after all, keep them in the wilderness for the space of forty years, till the whole generation were swept away; and suffer two individuals only, of the whole nation, to enter the promised land. But "his ways are in the great deep; and his footsteps are not known." When, at last, he had brought his people into Canaan, we should then at least suppose that he would give them a speedy and quiet possession of the land. Yet, behold, he tells them, beforehand, that he will "not drive out the inhabitants at once, but only by little and little."

We propose to inquire into,

I. The design of God in the dispensation here referred to—

It was intended,

1. As an act of mercy, to preserve his people—

[The people altogether amounted to about two millions; and the country which they were to occupy extended from the Red Sea to the Euphrates[a]. But, if so small a population were spread over so wide a space, the wild beasts would

---

[a] ver. 31. with Gen. xv. 18.

quickly multiply, and speedily desolate the whole land. True, indeed, God could, if it should so please him, interpose by miracle to change the ferocity of the most savage animals: but that was no part of his plan. He permitted, therefore, vast multitudes of the devoted nations yet to live, that so they might, for their own sake, prevent the increase and incursions of the wild beasts, till Israel should have multiplied so as to be able, in every part, to protect themselves.]

2. As an act of righteousness, to try them—

[All the trials with which God's people were visited in the wilderness were sent " to prove them," whether they would serve the Lord or not. Not that God needed any such information, as the result of experiment; because "he knew what was in man," whose heart and reins were open to him from the foundation of the world: but it was desirable, for their own sakes, that they should have an insight into their own hearts, and be able to appreciate the whole of God's dealings with them. By the continuance of the devoted nations amongst them, they would see how prone they were to seek their own carnal ease and interests, by mingling themselves among them, when they should have been labouring with all their might to effect their utter extirpation. By observing also the success or failure of their efforts against these enemies, they would be able to judge, with accuracy, how far they were in favour with God, or under his displeasure; and would consequently be led to approach him with suitable emotions of gratitude or contrition. This is the view which the Scripture itself gives us of this very dispensation: "These were the nations which the Lord left *to prove Israel* by them — the Philistines, Canaanites, Sidonians, and the Hivites; it was TO PROVE ISRAEL BY THEM, to know whether they would hearken to the commandments of the Lord, which he commanded their fathers by the hand of Moses[b]."]

3. As an act of judgment, to punish them—

[Though there were good ends to be answered, by a gradual execution of the judgments denounced against the seven nations of Canaan, it was the fault of the Israelites themselves that the extirpation of them was not more rapid and complete. They gave way to sloth, when they should have been in full activity; and yielded to fear, when they should have gone forth in assured dependence on their Lord. By this, they greatly increased their own trials, and multiplied their own afflictions. God had told them by Moses, saying, "If ye will not drive out the inhabitants of the land from before you, then it shall come to pass, that those whom ye let

[b] Judg. iii. 1—4.

remain of them shall be pricks in your eyes, and thorns in your sides, and shall vex you in the land wherein ye dwell. Moreover, it shall come to pass, that I shall do unto you, as I thought to do unto them[c]." Joshua also, at the close of his life, reminded them, that " no man had been able to stand before them:" and then assured them, that " one man of them should be able to chase a thousand, if only they would take heed to themselves to love the Lord their God: but that, if they did in any wise go back, and cleave unto the nations which remained among them, and make marriages with them; then know for a certainty," says he, " that the Lord your God will no more drive out any of these nations from before you; but they shall be snares and traps unto you, and scourges in your sides, and thorns in your eyes, until ye perish from off this good land which the Lord your God hath given you[d]." Accordingly, this prediction was soon verified; and God punished them, as he had said: for, on their " making leagues with the inhabitants of the land," they were induced at last to "forsake the Lord, and worship Baal and Ashteroth:" and " the Lord's anger was kindled against them; and he sold them into the hands of their enemies round about, so that they could not any longer stand before their enemies: and they were greatly distressed. Therefore the Lord left those nations, without driving them out hastily; neither delivered he them into the hand of Joshua[e]."

Thus in this dispensation there was a mixture of mercy and of judgment: of mercy primarily; of judgment through their own fault.]

This view of God's dealings with his people of old affords us a fit occasion to inquire into,

II. His design in a corresponding dispensation towards his people at this day—

The redemption which he has vouchsafed to us through the blood of his only dear Son might justly lead us to expect, that when once we are truly brought out from the dominion of sin and Satan, our triumphs over them would be complete. But it is not so: for though the yoke with which we were oppressed is loosened, a measure of our bondage still remains: there is yet " the flesh lusting against the spirit, so that we cannot do the things that we would[f];" yea more, "there is yet a law in our members

[c] Numb. xxxiii. 55.   [d] Josh. xxiii. 9—13.
[e] Judg. ii. 2, 12—15, 23.   [f] Gal. v. 17.

warring against the law in our minds, and too often bringing us into captivity to the law of sin which is in our members[g]." Now whence is it, that God suffers his people to be yet harassed with the remains of sin? He suffers it,

1. For our deeper humiliation—

[The sins of our unconverted state may well humble us in the dust, and cause us to "go softly," in the remembrance of them, to our dying hour. But the views of our depravity, which we derive from them, are as nothing in comparison of those which we gain from the workings of corruption in our converted state. These are the views which cause us to cry out, "O wretched man that I am! who shall deliver me[h]?" These were the views which constrained Job to exclaim, "Behold, I am vile:" "I repent, and abhor myself in dust and ashes[i]." And, in proportion as they are discovered to us, they will constrain every living man to "lothe himself for his iniquities and abominations[k]." Now this is a feeling that well becomes our sinful race: and though the acquisition of it is obtained through much painful experience, yet does it, in the issue, well repay all that we have suffered in the attainment of it.]

2. For our ultimate advancement—

[A child has all the members of a perfect man; yet are they in a very feeble and imperfect state: and it is by the exercise of his powers that he has those powers strengthened and enlarged. And thus it is with every child of God. He is born a babe: and, though every gracious principle exists within him, he is so feeble as scarcely to be able to withstand temptation, or to exercise his powers to any great extent. But, through the remains of sin within him he is led to frequent conflicts with it: by exercise, his powers are increased; and by progressive increase, they are perfected. Thus, from "a babe," he grows up to maturer age and stature, and becomes "a young man;" and from "a young man," "a father."

Nor is it in this world only that the believer is benefited by his conflicts; for in proportion as he grows in the knowledge of the Saviour and in a conformity to his image, will be the weight of glory bestowed on him in the realms of bliss. The improvement of the talents committed to him will bring a corresponding recompence, at the time that he shall give up his account to God. If no corruption had remained in his heart "*to prove him,*" he would have had scarcely any opportunity

---

[g] Rom. vii. 23.   [h] Rom. vii. 24.
[i] Job xl. 4. and xlii. 6.   [k] Ezek. xxxvi. 31.

of shewing his fidelity, his zeal, his love, his gratitude: but being called " to fight a good fight," and having approved himself " a good soldier of Jesus Christ," he shall receive together with the approbation of his Lord, a brighter crown, and a more glorious inheritance, than could have been awarded to him at the period of his first conversion.]

3. For his own eternal glory—

[Doubtless the first exercise of mercy towards a repenting sinner brings much glory to God: and if at the first moment of his conversion every saint were translated to glory, he would have abundant reason to adore and magnify the grace to which he was so greatly indebted. But of the patience, the forbearance, the long-suffering, the compassion, and the faithfulness of God, he would have a very indistinct and inadequate conception. It is by his inward trials and conflicts that he acquires the fuller discovery of these perfections, and is prepared to give God the glory of them in a better world. The shouts of one who is but a babe in Christ will, on his introduction to the divine presence, no doubt be ardent: but what will be the acclamations of a soul that has passed through all the eventful scenes of arduous and long-protracted warfare! Of what wonders will he have to speak! or rather, how may we conceive of him as prostrating himself in silent adoration through his overwhelming sense of the divine goodness, whilst the less-instructed and less-indebted novice rends the air with acclamations and hosannahs! Yes verily: if the angels stand round about the saints, as not having so near an access to God as they, so we may conceive of the less-privileged saints as standing round about the elders, in whom " God will be more admired," and by whom he will be more " glorified[l]."]

We must not however DISMISS this subject without adding a few words,

1. Of caution:—

[It is, as we have said, the fate of man in this world still to carry about with him a corrupt nature, which proves a source of much trouble and distress: nor can any man hope to get rid of it, till he shall be liberated by death itself. Nevertheless, it is our own fault that the corruptions which remain within us are not more weakened and subdued. Let any one read the account given of the different tribes, in the first chapter of the book of Judges, and say whether he does not impute blame to the Israelites themselves, for suffering the nations, whom they were ordered to extirpate, to retain so formidable a power in the midst of them[m]? Had they

[l] 2 Thess. i. 10. with Rev. vii. 9—12. [m] Judg. i. 21, 27, 29—35.

persevered with the same zeal and diligence as they exercised on their first entrance into Canaan, and pursued with unrelenting energy those whom they had been commanded to destroy their occupation of the land had been far more peaceful and entire. And so, if we, from our first conversion to God, had maintained with unremitting zeal our warfare with sin and Satan, as it became us to do, we should have had all the corruptions of our nature in more complete subjection, and should have enjoyed a far greater measure of tranquillity in our own souls. Let not any one, then, delude himself with the thought that the strength of his corruptions is a subject rather of pity than of blame: but let all know, that they are called to maintain a warfare; that armour, even "the whole armour of God," is provided for them, in order that they may prosecute it with success; and that, if only they will "quit themselves like men," the Captain of their salvation has assured to them a complete victory. Gird on your armour then, my Brethren; and, if your enemy has gained any advantage over you, return to the charge; and never cease to fight, till Satan, and all his hosts, are "bruised under your feet."]

2. Of encouragement—

[The doom of your enemies is sealed[n]; and, if you "go forth in the strength of your Lord," "you shall be more than conquerors through him that loveth you ." Let it not be grievous to you that such a necessity is imposed upon you. Did your Saviour himself enter the lists, and fight against all the powers of darkness till he had triumphed over them and despoiled them all; and will not you, at his command, go forth, to follow up, and complete, his victory[p]? Fear not on account of the strength or number of your enemies: for "they shall be bread for you;" and your every victory over them shall nourish and strengthen your own souls. And let all animate one another to the contest. See the happy effect of this amongst God's people of old. We are told, "Judah said unto Simeon his brother, Come up with me into my lot, that we may fight against the Canaanites; and I likewise will go with thee into thy lot. So Simeon went with him. And Judah went up: and the Lord delivered the Canaanites and the Perizzites into their hand[q]." True it is, indeed, that we cannot aid each other precisely in the same way that they did: but we may encourage one another, and strengthen one another, and by our example animate one another to the combat; and may thus contribute, each of us, to the success of those around us. And it is but a little time that we have to fight: for soon we

[n] Deut. vii. 22, 23.   [o] Rom. viii. 37.
[p] Col. ii. 15. with John xvi. 11.   [q] Judg. i. 3, 4.

shall come to that better land, where "there shall no more be the Canaanite in the house of the Lord of Hosts." Even in this world we are taught that such a period shall arrive [r]: but, if not permitted to behold it here, we shall assuredly behold it in the world above, where "former things shall have passed away, and sin and sorrow shall be found no more [s]." "Wherefore comfort ye one another with these words."]

[r] Zech. xiv. 21.   [s] Rev. xxi. 4.

OUTLINE NO. 96
GOD'S COVENANT WITH ISRAEL.

Exod. xxiv. 6—8. *And Moses took half of the blood, and put it in basons; and half of the blood he sprinkled on the altar. And he took the book of the covenant, and read in the audience of the people: and they said, All that the Lord hath said will we do, and be obedient. And Moses took the blood, and sprinkled it on the people, and said, Behold the blood of the covenant, which the Lord hath made with you concerning all these words.*

OF such terrible majesty is God, that none could behold his face and live. Even in his most condescending intercourse with men, he has made them to feel, that he is "a God greatly to be feared, and to be had in reverence of all them that are round about him." When he descended on Mount Sinai, to proclaim his law, all the people of Israel entreated that he would not speak to them any more, except through the intervention of a Mediator. He was graciously pleased to make further communications to his people, and to enter into a covenant with them: but here a select number only were permitted to approach him, and of them none but Moses was suffered to "come near unto him."

The covenant which he made with them, is the subject now before us: and we shall consider it in a two-fold view:

I. As made with Israel—

An altar being built, together with twelve pillars, the one to represent Jehovah, and the other the twelve tribes of Israel, the covenant was,

1. Made—

[God, as the author of that covenant, declared by Moses the terms on which he would acknowledge Israel as his peculiar people. Moses had written in a book the laws which God had made known to him, the *moral*, the *ceremonial*, the *judicial;* and all these he read in the audience of the people. To these, in the name of God, he required a cheerful and uniform obedience: and, upon their obedience to these, God promised on his part to favour them with his continued protection, and with the ultimate and peaceful enjoyment of the promised land. Thus was care taken that they should know to what they were to subscribe, and that their future welfare depended on their fidelity to their own engagements.

The people on their part gave their consent to the terms prescribed: and this they did in the most solemn manner. In declaring their acceptance of the covenant they were *unanimous, cordial, unreserved.* There was not one dissentient voice. They had repeatedly before engaged to do whatever the Lord should enjoin[a]; but here they do it with additional force and emphasis[b]. Nor do they make the least exception to any one thing as burthensome or oppressive. In the most unqualified manner they bind themselves to a perfect and perpetual obedience; " All that the Lord hath said will we do, and be obedient."]

2. Ratified—

[From the very time that God first set apart Abraham to be the progenitor of his peculiar people to the time when that people were carried captive to Babylon, it seems to have been customary to confirm covenants by sacrifices; which, when slain, were divided into parts placed opposite to each other; and then the parties covenanting passed between those parts, and thereby pledged themselves to a faithful observance of the covenant[c]. But in this instance solemnities were used, which shewed that the sacrifices were essential to the covenant itself. God could not enter into covenant with sinners till an atonement had been offered for their sins. And now that this atonement was offered, one half of the blood of the sacrifices was poured upon the altar, to evince that God was reconciled to them; and the remainder was sprinkled upon the book and upon the people, in order to seal upon their hearts and consciences his pardoning love, and to remind them, that all their hope in that covenant depended on the blood of atonement with which it was sprinkled.]

---

[a] Exod. xix. 8. and xxiv. 3. [b] " We will do, *and be obedient.*"
[c] In Abraham's time, Gen. xv. 9, 10, 17; in David's, Ps. l. 5; in Jeremiah's, Jer. xxxiv. 18—20. A similar custom obtained also among the Greeks.

After having duly considered this covenant as made with Israel, it will be proper to view it,

II. As typifying that under which we live—

That it was a type of the Christian covenant we are sure, because St. Paul quotes the very words of our text, to prove that the death of Christ was necessary to give efficacy to his mediation, and to secure to us the blessings of his covenant[d]. He mentions also some additional circumstances not related in the history: but of them we forbear to speak, that our attention may be confined to the point immediately before us. The connexion between the two is that which we assert, and which we wish to illustrate. Let us then return to the covenant made with Israel, and notice more particularly,

1. The nature of it—

[The covenant made with Israel was a *mixed* covenant; partly *legal*, for it contained the law of the ten commandments delivered on Mount Sinai; partly *evangelical*, for it comprehended many ceremonial institutions whereby the people were to obtain remission of their sins; and partly *national*, because it comprised many civil restrictions which were peculiar to that people. But the covenant under which we are, is *purely evangelical*, having not the smallest mixture of any thing else with it. Our covenant does not prescribe laws, by obedience to which we are to obtain mercy; but offers mercy freely as the gift of God through Christ, and promises grace, whereby we shall be enabled to fulfil the will of God. Sanctification is not required of us as a ground for our justification, but is promised to us as a fruit and evidence of our justification. In this covenant we are not to obey *in order that* God may give, but to obey *because he has given*, and will give. We are not first to give to God that he may afterwards give to us; but he gives all, and we receive all.]

2. The ratification of it—

[The blood of sprinkling used by Moses was a mere shadow; it had of itself no value whatever: it could neither satisfy the justice of God, nor bring peace into the consciences of men. But the blood with which our covenant is ratified is called "the blood of God[e]," because it was the blood of Him who was God as well as man. That blood has indeed an

---

[d] Heb. ix. 17—19.   [e] Acts xx. 28.

efficacy that transcends all conception. It has reconciled God to a guilty world: and, when sprinkled on the hearts of men by faith, it fills them with "a peace which passeth all understanding." And as Moses, in the quality of God's high-priest, sprinkled the blood both upon the altar and the people, so does our "great High-Priest," the Lord Jesus, now sprinkle his blood for us before the throne of God, and sprinkle it also on our hearts, whensoever we go to him for that purpose. The covenant too itself is continually exhibited to us as sprinkled with his blood; so that we may be certain that God will fulfil it to us in all its parts. If only we accept it, and rely upon it, all its blessings shall be ours, both in time and in eternity.]

3. The acceptance of it—

[There was much in the people's acceptance of that covenant worthy of our imitation: but there was also much which it becomes us carefully to avoid.

In the first place, guard against their *ignorance*. They were evidently not acquainted with the requisitions of the covenant to which they subscribed. They heard its contents read to them indeed; but they did not enter into their full meaning, neither had they duly considered them. Let not this be the case with us, lest we "begin to build without counting the cost." Let us consider that it requires us to receive every thing as persons wholly destitute, and to receive it in every part without the smallest partiality or reserve. Let us remember, that though it does not require holiness as a *meritorious* condition of our acceptance, it promises holiness as one of its chief blessings[f]: and that, if we do not *desire*, and *strive*, to be "holy as God is holy," and "perfect as God is perfect," all our professed hope in the covenant is vain and delusive. We can no more be saved by the covenant without holiness, than we can without faith. Let this be known, and weighed, yea and be wrought into the soul as a fixed principle, before we presume to think that we have any interest in Christ, or in the covenant which he has sealed with his blood.

In the next place, guard against their *self-righteousness*. They imagined that they could so fulfil their obligations as to earn and merit all the blessings of the covenant. Let not us make so fatal a mistake. Let us rather acknowledge, that "if we had done all that is commanded us, we should be only unprofitable servants." But who will say that he has done *all* that is commanded him, or indeed *any one thing*, in which God could not discern some imperfection and defect? If this be so, then do we need *mercy* and *forgiveness* even for our best actions; and consequently can never merit by them the salvation of God. Let this then be also engrafted in our minds,

[f] Ezek. xxxvi. 25—27.

that we may be accepted with the publican, and not be rejected with the Pharisee.

Lastly, let us guard against their *self-dependence.* They never doubted but that they were able to do all that was commanded them. They thought it was as easy to perform as to promise. But in a very few days they provoked God to jealousy with their golden calf: so little did they remember the precepts that had been given them, or the vows that were upon them. Let it not be so with us. Let us bear in mind, "we have not of ourselves a sufficiency even to think a good thought;" and that "without Christ we can do nothing." If we embrace the covenant as they embraced it, we shall fail as they failed.]

We cannot better CONCLUDE this subject than by addressing you as Moses addressed the Israelites: "Behold the blood of the covenant which the Lord hath made with you,"—or, as St. Paul quotes the words, "the covenant which God hath *enjoined* unto you!"

1. Behold the covenant itself—

[It is "ordered in all things and sure:" there is not a want which a human being can feel, for which ample provision is not made in it. And it is free for every creature under heaven. Whatever you may have been in times past, you may at this moment partake of all the blessings of this covenant, if only you be willing to receive them freely, and without reserve. On the other hand, if you disregard this covenant, and "count the blood of it an unholy thing," "there remains no other sacrifice for sin, but a certain fearful looking for of judgment and fiery indignation to consume you." God has shut you up to this, and *enjoined* it unto you by an irreversible decree. Receive it therefore, and live; reject it, and perish.]

2. Behold the blood of the covenant—

[What *instruction* does that blood convey! Did the Israelites see their bleeding sacrifices, and not discern *the desert of sin?* How much more then must we discern it in the precious blood of our incarnate God! And surely we may also see in it *the* transcendent *love of Christ*, who submitted to "make his soul an offering for sin," that, the covenant being sealed with his blood, we might be partakers of its richest blessings.

What *comfort* too does it convey to the soul! Look on that blood, thou doubting Christian, and then say whether God will not fulfil all the promises that he has ever made: say whether, in such a mode of ratifying his covenant he has not provided "strong consolation for all who flee to the refuge set before them" in the Gospel.

Finally, What *a stimulus* does it give *to all holy and heavenly affections!* Shall not that question be continually upon thy mind, "What shall I render unto the Lord?" Look on that blood, and grudge God your services, if ye can. Think much of any duties you can perform, or of any sufferings you can endure for him, if ye can. Only keep your eye fixed upon that blood, and you shall be irresistibly constrained to exult and glory in God, and to consecrate unto him all the faculties and powers of your souls.]

OUTLINE NO. 97

A SIGHT OF GOD IS A FEAST TO THE SOUL.

Exod. xxiv. 11. *They saw God, and did eat and drink.*

GOD is every where present, but no where visible, unless he please to draw aside the veil, and reveal himself to us. It is in heaven alone that his unveiled glory is continually seen. There have however in former times been many occasions whereon he has discovered himself to men, sometimes in human, sometimes in angelic form, and sometimes in a bright appearance, in which no similitude could be traced, and of which no representation can be made. The manifestation of which the text speaks, seems to have been of the last kind. It was vouchsafed to a great many persons at once: and while they beheld his presence, they feasted before him.

In discoursing upon this interesting event, we shall notice,

I. Their vision—

The circumstances of the vision are particular, and deserve an attentive consideration—

[*The persons* to whom it was vouchsafed were Moses, and Aaron with his two eldest sons, Nadab and Abihu, and seventy of the "elders of Israel," who are also called "nobles." Who these nobles were we cannot absolutely determine; but it is most probable that they were persons of consequence in the different tribes, who were selected to represent the nation at large; and, if six were taken out of each tribe, they might in round numbers be called seventy, though strictly speaking they would amount to seventy-two.

The time at which they were thus favoured, was after they had consented to the covenant which God had made with them. Subsequent to the publication of the moral law from Mount Sinai, God ordained a variety of statutes, which were peculiar to Israel as a nation; and at the same time made with them *a national covenant*, partaking of a covenant of works, and partly of a covenant of grace. In this, they undertook to serve God; and God undertook to protect and bless them. This covenant had been confirmed by a sacrifice, in which the different parties had met, as it were, and given their consent to it. God was represented by the altar; and the twelve tribes were represented by the twelve pillars which Moses had erected near the altar[a], as well as by the seventy elders, who had been chosen out from among them. The blood of the sacrifice had been sprinkled on them all; on the altar, the pillars, and the people. The book of the covenant also had been sprinkled with it[b], to shew, that, though God did not relax the demands of his law, he would not be extreme to mark the unallowed violations of it. *After this covenant had been thus made and ratified*, God called Moses and the others to come up higher on the mountain; and revealed to them his glory.

The manner also in which God revealed himself, is worthy of notice. There had been a manifestation of the Deity prior to this: but O! how different from it! That display which God made of himself at the giving of the law was in "blackness and darkness, and tempest; and attended with such tremendous thunderings and lightenings, that all the people, yea, and "Moses himself, exceedingly trembled and quaked." But, in *this* vision all was light and serene, and calculated to inspire the beholders with joy and confidence. The appearance of the Deity was beyond the brightness of the meridian sun; and underneath it "the pavement, as it were, upon which he stood, was like the sapphire" stone, or like the azure sky, bespangled with stars[c].

Thus the vision altogether was suited to a new-covenant state, wherein the people were introduced into communion with their God, and honoured with these astonishing tokens of his love and favour.]

Such a vision is now vouchsafed to us under the Gospel—

[We shall not indeed behold God precisely as they did; for such visions have long since been discontinued. But there is a spiritual view of the Deity, which we may, and must, partake of; and which, we are authorized to say, was typified by the vision before us. In the Epistle to the Hebrews, the

---

[a] ver. 4.   [b] Heb. ix. 18—23.   [c] ver. 10.

preceding context is expressly quoted, and that too with some additional circumstances not related by Moses[d]: and we are told that the event there referred to, was "a pattern of the heavenly things," which we enjoy under the Gospel. The view which we have of the Deity, prior to our embracing the new covenant, inspires us with nothing but terror: but when we have accepted the covenant of grace, which was confirmed by the sacrifice of Christ, and have sprinkled on our consciences the blood of that sacrifice, *then* we shall be admitted to a more clear, but less terrific, view of God: his justice will appear more awful in the sacrifice which it demanded, than even in the curses it denounced: but it will be seen tempered with mercy; and ready to harmonize with mercy in every act of love. This vision we are to enjoy, not through the medium of representatives, but every one of us for himself. It is of Christians in general, and not of some distinguished favourites only, that the Apostle says, "God hath shined in our hearts to give the light of the knowledge of the glory of God in the face of Jesus Christ[e]." Here, by the way, we see *where* we are to have this vision: it is to be "*in our hearts:*" it is an object of contemplation to the mind; and not of sight to our bodily organs.]

Together with their vision, it will be proper to notice also,

II. Their feast—

It was generally supposed that none could see God and live[f]: but here the seventy elders, as well as Moses and Aaron, beheld him, and yet "he laid not his hand on any one of them" to hurt them[g]. On the contrary,

They feasted on their sacrifice in the divine presence—

[They had sacrificed burnt-offerings, and peace-offerings. Of the latter, the offerers were allowed to eat, in token of their acceptance with God. Indeed it had long before been customary for parties covenanting with each other, to feast together at the ratification of their covenant[h]. And here, if we may so speak, the different parties feasted together: God's part of the sacrifices had been consumed upon his altar; and the remainder was eaten by the offerers. And doubtless it must have been a precious feast to those, who had so lately trembled at the thunders of Mount Sinai. Their souls must

[d] Heb. ix. 18—23.   [e] 2 Cor. iv. 6.   [f] Gen. xxxii. 30.
[g] This is the meaning of the words preceding the text.
[h] Gen. xxxi. 54.

have been yet more refreshed with a sense of the divine favour, than their bodies by the provision thus allotted for their support.]

But their feast was no less typical than their vision—

[Christ, who is our sacrifice, calls all his people to "eat his flesh, and to drink his blood." But we must not imagine that this refers to corporeal food: our Lord speaks of spiritual food, of which our souls are to partake by the exercise of faith on him. Yes, his atonement is indeed a feast to the soul: in this sense it may be truly said, " His flesh is meat indeed; and his blood is drink indeed[i]." On this we are to feed in the immediate presence of our God. However "far off we are, we may draw nigh by the blood of Jesus[k]," yea, "we may have boldness to enter into the holiest by the blood of Jesus[l]:" we may see God reconciled to us in him; and may rejoice in him as our God and portion for ever. The wonders of his love are to be the continual banquet of our souls. His "exceeding great and precious promises" are "a feast of fat things, of wines on the lees well refined[m]." Of these we are to "eat freely, and abundantly[n]:" we are to "sit under his shadow; and his fruit will be sweet unto our taste[o]:" yea, " we shall be satisfied as with marrow and fatness[p];" enjoying a "peace that passeth all understanding," and being "filled with joy unspeakable and glorified[q]."]

ADDRESS,

1. Those who are afar off from God—

[The prohibition given to the Israelites, is cancelled with respect to you. The veil of the temple was rent in twain at the death of Christ, in token that a new and living way was opened to all, and that all who believed, were constituted " a royal priesthood[r]." Will ye then decline the invitation that is sent you? We are commissioned to go forth into the highways and hedges to call you to the feast, which a God of infinite love has prepared for you. O come, and partake of it. But remember that, in order to enjoy it, you must first accept the new covenant, and submit to be saved by the free mercy of God in Christ Jesus. Sprinkle yourself with the blood of Christ, your all-atoning sacrifice; and then you may have fellowship both with the Father and the Son, and feast before God for ever on the provisions of redeeming love.]

[i] John vi. 53—56.   [k] Eph. ii. 13.   [l] Heb. x. 19.
[m] Isai. xxv. 6.   [n] Cant. v. 1.   [o] Cant. ii. 3.
[p] Ps. lxiii. 5.   [q] 1 Pet. i. 8.   [r] 1 Pet. ii. 9.

2. Those who are inclined to rest in external privileges—

[Such was the case with the greater part of those to whom the text refers. One would have supposed that they could never have forgotten their obligations to God, or have ceased to serve him: but, alas! in a very little time, Nadab and Abihu were struck dead for their impiety; and of the seventy elders, not one, as far as we know, held fast his integrity. They were ready, as indeed were all the people also, to profess their allegiance to the Deity; "All that the Lord hath said, will we do, and be obedient:" but they soon forgat their pious resolutions, and revolted from their duty. Beware, Brethren, lest it be so with you. It will be to very little purpose to say at last, "Lord, Lord, have we not eaten and drunk in thy presence[s]?" If you have "not been steadfast in his covenant," your outward professions, or past experiences, will avail little. Maintain therefore continually your dependence upon Christ; and, in his strength, exert yourselves to fulfil his holy will.]

3. Those who are coming to the table of their Lord—

[We ask not whether you have a deep experience of divine truth, but whether you have fled to Christ from the terrors of the law? Have you seen yourselves condemned by the covenant of works; and are you seeking mercy through the covenant of grace? Are you really sprinkling yourselves with the blood of Christ, your great sacrifice, and coming to God through him alone? If so, behold, there is a table spread, and you are called to come and feast upon your sacrifice in the presence of your God. Come thither in faith; and your God will make his glory to pass before your eyes; yea, Christ will "reveal himself to you in the breaking of bread[t]," "and fill you with "his loving-kindness, which is better than life itself." Thus shall you be strengthened for all future services, till at last you shall be called to "eat and drink at Christ's table in the kingdom of your Father.[u]"]

[s] Luke xiii. 26.   [t] Luke xxiv. 31, 35.   [u] Luke xxii. 30.

OUTLINE NO. 98

THE COMMAND TO BUILD THE TABERNACLE.

Exod. xxv. 8, 9. *Let them make me a sanctuary; that I may dwell among them. According to all that I shew thee, after the pattern of the tabernacle, and the pattern of all the instruments thereof, even so shall ye make it.*

THE more minutely we consider the Mosaic economy, the more we find it fraught with the richest instruction: and we are persuaded, that, if the lovers of literature had any idea what inexhaustible treasures of wisdom and knowledge are contained in it, they would not be so regardless of it, as they too generally are. We cannot read a single chapter without seeing ample ground for this remark. To go no further than the text; wherein we have the command of God to build a tabernacle for him, and to fit it up in a peculiar manner. Even upon the face of this command there is something that invites inquiry: but, when we have explored its hidden sense, we shall discover in it a deep mystery, and derive from it much important information.

Let us consider then the direction,

I. As given to the Jews—

In order to obtain a clear and just view of the subject, it will be proper to notice,

1. The general direction—

[God delights in the exercise of mercy. Mercy prompted him to separate for himself a peculiar people in the midst of a ruined world. Mercy led him to reveal himself to them in such a way as to impress them with an awful sense of his majesty; and afterwards to give an order respecting the making of a sanctuary for him, where they might obtain more easy and familiar access to Him, and He might the more abundantly display unto them the riches of his grace. It was not for his own accommodation that he gave the order, (for "the heaven of heavens cannot contain him,") but for their benefit; that, by seeing him continually in the midst of them, they might know that he was in a peculiar manner their God. It was an honour to them that he would accept their offerings, and that he would condescend to dwell in an habitation, such as his poor and sinful creatures could provide for him.]

2. The particular limitation of it—

[Such things only as he appointed were to be used either in the framing, or the furnishing, of the tabernacle: and, that every thing might be formed agreeably to his mind, he not only gave to Moses a general description of what was to be done, but shewed him a model of every individual thing that was to be made; and enjoined him to make it exactly according to the pattern shewn to him in the mount. This order was given to

Moses *repeatedly*, and with very peculiar force and emphasis[a]: and his strict adherence to it in every particular is, in the last chapter of this book, mentioned no less than eight times, once after every separate piece of furniture that was made[b]. In the New Testament too his compliance with the command is repeatedly noticed, and the very order itself expressly quoted[c]. Now what was the reason of this limitation? Why must only such and such things be made; and they of such precise materials and shape? The reason was, The whole was intended to typify things under the Gospel dispensation: and as none but God could know all the things which were to be prefigured, so none but he could know infallibly how to designate them to the best effect. Had Moses been left to contrive any thing out of his own mind, there might have wanted a correspondence between the type and the antitype: but when a model of every thing was shewn him by God himself, the whole must of necessity accord with the mind and purpose of him for whom they were made.

We forbear to particularize the correspondence between the shadows and the substance, because that cannot be profitably done without entering more fully into the subject than our time at present will admit of: but that the correspondence was designed of God, and actually exists, and was the end for which such precise orders were given, is beyond all doubt. "The first tabernacle," says St. Paul, "while it was yet standing, was a figure for the time then present;" "and served unto the example and shadow of heavenly things," that is, of things under the Gospel dispensation[d].]

But the direction in our text had not *merely* a typical reference; for it may properly be considered,

II. As applicable to us—

The tabernacle typified, not only the Lord Jesus, "in whom dwelt all the fulness of the Godhead bodily," but *us* also—

["The Church of God is his house[e]," "the habitation of God through the Spirit[f]." Yea, every believer is himself "the temple of the living God; as God hath said; I will dwell in them, and walk in them; and I will be their God, and they shall be my people[g]." Moreover, God himself, commending the fidelity of Moses in constructing every thing according to his order, draws for us the parallel between the tabernacle erected by him, and that which Christ possesses in our hearts: "Moses verily was faithful in all his house as a servant, for a

---

[a] See ver. 40. and ch. xxvi. 30.   [b] Exod. xl. 16—33.
[c] Acts vii. 44. Heb. viii. 5.
[d] Heb. ix. 8, 9. with viii. 5. before cited.   [e] 1 Tim. iii. 15.
[f] Eph. ii. 21, 22.   [g] 2 Cor. vi. 16.

testimony of those things which were to be spoken after; but Christ as a Son over his own house: *whose house are* we[h]." The truth is, that "God dwelleth not in temples made with hands." Even while his tabernacle and temple were yet standing, God testified respecting them, that the temple which alone he regarded, was a broken and contrite spirit[i].]

To us therefore may the direction fitly be addressed—

[Make ye, my Brethren, a sanctuary for the Lord, that he may dwell among you: let every one willingly present unto him his heart, and entreat him to fill it with his presence. Let his habitation too be furnished with every thing suited to the worship which you have to offer. You are not called to carnal ordinances, and therefore have no need of such things as were wanted under the Jewish dispensation. It is with the gifts and graces of the Spirit that you are to serve and honour God. Abound ye therefore in them. Grudge no expense whereby you may obtain them. Let them all be formed according to the model shewn you in the mount. In Christ Jesus you have a perfect pattern of them all. "Look to it," that your graces accord with his. Let none be wanting, none be different. Let the command of God be the *reason* of all that you present unto him, the example of Christ the *pattern*, and the glory of God the *end*. Whatever you have brought with you out of Egypt (out of your unconverted state) honour God with it: let it be gold and silver, or talents of any kind, consecrate them to the Lord: make use of them for the building of his tabernacle, and the exalting of his glory in the world. Remember too more especially to be conformed to the pattern *in this respect;* his tabernacle was most glorious *within:* on the outside were rams' skins, and badgers' skins; but *within*, all was of gold and linen exquisitely wrought. O that our *interior* might be such, as *most* to glorify our God! We are far from saying that the *exterior* should be neglected: but it should be modest and unassuming: and they who from their connexion with us can penetrate within the veil, should see that our hidden virtues are the most eminent, and that God is most honoured in those dispositions and habits of ours, which are most concealed from public view.

In vain are you baptized into the name of the Sacred Trinity, if you do not "observe and do all things whatsoever Christ has commanded you:" nor indeed can you in any other way hope for the accomplishment of that promise, "Lo, I am with you alway, even unto the end of the world[k]." Let me therefore

[h] Heb. iii. 5, 6.   [i] Isai. lvii. 15. and lxvi. 1, 2. with Acts vii. 47—50.
[k] Matt. xxviii. 19, 20.

entreat you to seek for "*grace*," whereby you may serve God acceptably; and to make the blessed resolution of the Psalmist, that " you will give neither sleep to your eyes, nor slumber to your eye-lids, till you have found a place (in your own hearts) for the Lord, an habitation for the mighty God of Jacob[1]."]

[1] Ps. cxxxii. 2—5.

OUTLINE NO. 99
AARON'S BREAST-PLATE.

Exod. xxviii. 29, 30. *And Aaron shall bear the names of the children of Israel in the breast-plate of judgment upon his heart, when he goeth in unto the holy place, for a memorial before the Lord continually. And thou shalt put in the breast-plate of judgment the Urim and the Thummim; and they shall be upon Aaron's heart, when he goeth in before the Lord: and Aaron shall bear the judgment of the children of Israel upon his heart before the Lord continually.*

LITTLE do men in general imagine what treasures of knowledge are contained in the Old Testament. There is not any thing revealed concerning Christ in the New Testament, which was not prefigured in the Mosaic ritual. As every thing relating to his life and death may be clearly seen in the prophets, so every thing relating to his office and character may be learned from the ceremonial law. Even the ornaments of the high-priest were intended to shadow forth some of the most important offices which our blessed Lord sustains. That particular ornament which we propose to notice at present, is the breast-plate of judgment: respecting which we shall point out,

I. Its primary use—

It will be proper, before we speak of its use, to shew what the breast-plate was—

[The priest wore an ephod, (a kind of short coat without sleeves,) made of fine linen, richly embroidered. The breast-plate was a piece of fine linen, which, when doubled, was a span square. Upon that were placed twelve precious stones, each of them having the name of one of the tribes (according to their seniority) engraven upon it. This was worn upon the breast, over the ephod: and the high-priest was to wear it whenever he went into the presence of God: and it was called " the breast-plate of judgment," because God, by means of it, communicated his mind and judgment to him respecting the children of Israel.

Within this breast-plate were placed the Urim and the Thummim. What these were, we are not informed. Many have thought, that they were not distinct from the stones: and that the terms Urim and Thummim merely designated the use to which those stones were applied. But the language of the text, especially when confirmed by Levit. viii. 8, leaves no doubt, but that the Urim and Thummim were distinct from the breast-plate, and were " put into " it after it was made. It is no objection to say, that the one is sometimes mentioned without the other, or, that we know not who made the Urim and Thummim, or what they were. It is sufficient for us to know, that they were added to the breast-plate, and that they were appointed for a very important purpose.]

The particular use of the breast-plate shall now be distinctly declared—

[The breast-plate thus formed, was to be worn by the high-priest, whenever he performed the duties of his office. It was suspended from his shoulders by two golden chains, fixed to two onyx-stones; on which, as well as on the twelve stones, were engraven all the names of the twelve tribes of Israel, six on each stone; and both the one and the other were " for a memorial before the Lord continually[a]." We must understand this as spoken after the manner of men. We are not to suppose that God *needs* to be reminded of his people; but the sight of their names, whenever the high-priest came into his presence, was (so to speak) to remind him, that he had a people who were to be the objects of his peculiar care.

The Urim and Thummim were for a different purpose. They were, in some way or other, to communicate answers to the high-priest, whenever he consulted God upon any matter relating to the civil or religious concerns of the nation. To inquire how the answers were given, whether by a secret suggestion to the mind of the high-priest, or by an audible voice, or in any other way, is vain: we should be contented to be ignorant about those things whereon God has not seen fit to inform us. That the Urim and the Thummim were consulted, and not only by the high-priest, but by others without him; and that specific answers were obtained from God; is certain. Joshua[b], and those who succeeded him in the government of Israel[c], sought instruction from God through the medium of these. The eleven tribes had the mind of God repeatedly made known to them in the same way, when they desired to be informed, whether they were to wage war against the offending

---

[a] ver. 12.   [b] Numb. xxvii. 21.   [c] Judg. i. 1.

tribe of Benjamin[d]. David in various straits took counsel of God in this way, and had such information conveyed to him as was impossible for any but the omniscient God to impart[e]. Saul asked counsel in the same way; but could not obtain an answer, because he had provoked God to cast him off[f]. At the time of the Babylonish captivity the Urim and the Thummim were lost, and were never afterwards recovered[g]; till Christ, whom they typified, came to instruct us in all things that can at all conduce to our real welfare.

The very names, Urim and Thummim, serve in a great measure to designate their particular use. Their import is, *Lights* and *Perfections:* and they were for the express purpose of conveying *light* to those who consulted them, even such light as would *perfectly* and infallibly direct their way.

Thus, as the breast-plate of judgment consisted of two different parts, so it was intended for two different uses; the stones in it were *for a memorial before God;* and the Urim and Thummim that were in it, were *for the obtaining of instruction from God.*]

But we shall have a very inadequate notion of the breast-plate, unless we understand,

II. Its typical intent—

Few are so ignorant as to need to be informed, that Christ is our great High-Priest. Now the breast-plate, of which we have been speaking, was designed to represent,

1. What Christ *is doing for* us—

[Christ, in the execution of his priestly office, was to "enter into the holy place," there "to appear in the presence of God for us." Accordingly, after his resurrection, he ascended to heaven, that he might there complete the work he had begun on earth. On his heart are engraven the names of all his people: on his shoulders he also bears them all: not one of them is forgotten by him: he presents them all before his Father, and is "their memorial before God continually." God cannot even look upon his Son without being reminded, that there is in this lower world a people who need his incessant care. He sees at one view all their states, and all their circumstances. He sees how dear they are to his Son, who bears them ever on his heart; who sympathizes with them in their afflictions, and desires to have them extricated from all their difficulties. Were he disposed to be unmindful of them, he

---

[d] Judg. xx. 18, 23, 27, 28.   [e] 1 Sam. xxiii. 9—12. and xxx. 7. 8.
[f] 1 Sam. xxviii. 6.   [g] Ezra ii. 63. Neh. vii. 65.

could not cast them out of his thoughts, or be deaf to the intercessions of our great High-Priest.

Here then is the security of all the children of Israel: "they have a great High-Priest, who is passed into the heavens, Jesus, the Son of God," who has undertaken their cause, and is their Advocate with the Father, and "who is *therefore* able to save them to the uttermost, *because* he ever liveth to make intercession for them."]

2. What Christ *will do in* us—

[In Christ " are hid all the treasures of wisdom and knowledge." There is no case wherein we may not consult him; nor any, wherein he will not vouchsafe to direct our steps. *How* he will answer us, we will not presume to say: he has ten thousand ways of making known his will, and of overruling our purposes, without at all infringing the liberty of our will, or altering the general dispensations of his providence. It is sufficient for us to know, that " the meek he will guide in judgment, the meek he will teach his way;" and that " whatsoever we ask of him he will do, that the Father may be glorified in the Son." From the consideration of his being our great and compassionate High-Priest, we are encouraged to come boldly to the throne of grace, that we may obtain mercy, and find grace to help us in the time of need[h]; and we are sure, that, if we come unto God through him, " we may ask what we will, and it shall be done unto us." We need not say, This is so great a matter, that it would be presumptuous in me to ask it; nor, This is so small, that it would be unworthy of his attention: for, whether it be great or small, he would spread it before his heavenly Father, and obtain for us an answer of peace: his *light* should dispel our darkness, and his *perfections* dissipate our fears: the weakest should not be left to faint[i], nor the most ignorant to err[k].]

In this subject we may find abundant matter,

1. For reproof—

[When we come into difficult circumstances, we are too apt to imagine, like the Church of old, that " God hath forsaken and forgotten us." But if God reproved *them* by declaring, that " a nursing mother could sooner forget her sucking child than he could forget them, since they were engraven on the palms of his hands[l]," how much more are *we* reproved by this typical representation of Christ, on whose shoulders we are supported, and on whose heart we are engraven! O let such unbelieving fears be put away! Let us " know in whom we

---

[h] Heb. iv. 14—16.   [i] Isai. xl. 29—31.   [k] Isai. xxxv. 8.
[l] Isai. xlix. 14—16.

have believed, that He is able to keep that which we have committed to him." Let us remember, that, whilst he retains his priestly office, and his Father retains his regard for him, " he will not suffer one of his little ones to perish."]

2. For encouragement—

[Our trials may be numerous, and our difficulties urgent: but our High-Priest is ever at hand, to inquire of God for us. Nor does he need to be informed by us, what to ask; for he "knoweth what is in man," and sees at the same time all the devices of our enemy. If only we lift up our hearts to him, his effectual aid shall be instantly obtained; for he is *with us*, to know our desires; and *with God*, to interest him in our favour. Let us then be encouraged to cast our care on him: and let us make him, what God has intended he should be to us, " our *wisdom*, and righteousness, our *sanctification*, and redemption[m]."]

[m] 1 Cor. i. 30.

OUTLINE NO. 100
AARON'S MITRE.

Exod. xxviii. 36—38. *And thou shalt make a plate of pure gold, and grave upon it, like the engravings of a signet,* HOLINESS TO THE LORD. *And thou shalt put it on a blue lace, that it may be upon the mitre: upon the fore-front of the mitre it shall be. And it shall be upon Aaron's forehead, that Aaron may bear the iniquity of the holy things, which the children of Israel shall hallow in all their holy gifts: and it shall be always upon his forehead, that they may be accepted before the Lord.*

IF it were once ascertained that God had imposed a number of ordinances upon his people, we should be ready to conclude that his institutions were not mere arbitrary and insignificant laws, but that they had some occult meaning, worthy of their divine Author. But when we are informed by God himself, that many things, apparently most indifferent, were intended to shadow forth the great mystery of redemption, we are persuaded that not even the minutest ordinance among them was without some appropriate and important signification. But though we believe this, we do not presume to assign the meaning of each, any further than we are warranted by the Scriptures themselves. Instead of wandering into the regions of conjecture, we judge it more for general edification to confine ourselves to matters which are obvious and acknowledged.

The whole dress of the high-priest was unquestionably typical; and designated either the office of our great High-Priest, or his qualifications for the discharge of it. That part to which we would now direct your attention, is his mitre. This, as the text informs us, was a covering for his head (somewhat like the turbans worn in the East at this day): it was made of fine linen, and had, in the front of it, a gold plate, with this inscription, HOLINESS TO THE LORD. It was worn by him whenever he officiated in the temple. Through this the high-priest was considered as holy, and was the appointed means of expiating the defects that were in the services of the people, and of procuring acceptance for their persons. Now, whilst *the end for which it was worn* manifests, beyond a doubt, that the appointment was typical, it enables us to declare with certainty the true intention of the type.

This institution then was intended to foreshew,

I. The holiness of our great High-Priest—

[*Christ was* in truth "the HOLY ONE of Israel." *It was necessary that he should be spotless* himself; for had he not been so, he could not have made atonement for us; yea, he would have needed an atonement for himself[a]. The utmost care was taken respecting the typical offerings, to ascertain that they were without blemish: *and it seems to have been particularly ordained* of God *that the innocence of Jesus should be established* by every possible proof, (and by the repeated testimony even of the judge that condemned him,) in order that his fitness, as our sin-offering, might appear. *Thus was* the type accomplished in him; and *a sure foundation was laid for all the hopes that are built upon him.*]

II. The need we have of an interest in it—

[The high-priest, so habited, was to "bear the iniquity of the holy things, which the people should hallow." Their best services were imperfect, in manner at least, if not in the matter of them also: and they were to seek acceptance through the holiness of their high-priest alone. Thus it is with us also. All that we do is imperfect. The best service we ever

[a] Heb. vii. 26, 27. 1 John iii. 5.

performed was mixed with sin, and needed an atonement to be made for it. Without an atonement, it could never have been regarded by a holy God. This was strongly marked in the ordinance before us, and ought to be remembered by us as a ground for the deepest humiliation.]

III. Its efficacy in our behalf—

[The people's services were, through this typical holiness of their high-priest, accepted of God, notwithstanding the imperfection of them: nor shall ours be despised, if we trust in the merits and mediation of the Lord Jesus. This was beautifully represented under the Mosaic dispensation by the acceptance of *leavened* bread[b], and *mutilated* beasts[c], when offered as thank-offerings, and not as offerings for sin: and the same encouraging truth is plainly asserted in the New Testament[d]. Let us only be interested in "the spotless Lamb of God," and all that we do in his name shall find acceptance before God.]

This subject is well CALCULATED,

1. To humble the self-righteous—

[What room can there be for trusting in our own righteousness, when the most righteous act we ever performed had an iniquity in it which needed to be borne by our great High-Priest? Lay aside your proud thoughts, and "seek to be found in Christ, not having your own righteousness, but his."]

2. To encourage the desponding—

[Be it so; you are a sinner: "but if any man sin, we have an Advocate with the Father, Jesus Christ *the righteous:*" and through him you may draw nigh to God with boldness and confidence[e].]

3. To direct and animate the godly—

[You are now "priests unto God;" and are to have HOLINESS TO THE LORD written upon your foreheads[f], that it may be visible to God and man. Remember that "God will be sanctified in all that draw nigh unto him[g];" and that "as He who hath called you is holy, so must ye be holy in all manner of conversation[h]."]

b Lev. ii. 11. with vii. 13. and xxiii. 17.   c Lev. xxii. 21—23.
d Heb. xiii. 15.   1 Pet. ii. 5.
e Eph. iii. 12. Heb. x. 19—22.   f Zech. xiv. 20.
g Lev. x. 3. Ps. xciii. 5.   h 1 Pet. i. 15, 16. and ii. 9

OUTLINE NO. 101
THE ALTAR OF INCENSE.

Exod. xxx. 7—10. *And Aaron shall burn thereon sweet incense every morning: when he dresseth the lamps, he shall burn incense upon it. And when Aaron lighteth the lamps at even, he shall burn incense upon it; a perpetual incense before the Lord, throughout your generations. Ye shall offer no strange incense thereon, nor burnt-sacrifice, nor meat-offering; neither shall ye pour drink-offering thereon. And Aaron shall make an atonement upon the horns of it once in a year with the blood of the sin-offering of atonements: once in the year shall he make atonement upon it throughout your generations. It is most holy unto the Lord.*

THE little acquaintance which Christians in general have with the Mosaic Law, unfits them for the reception of that instruction which the Law is well calculated to convey. Doubtless, to find the precise import of all its ordinances is beyond the power of man. But there is much of it explained in the New Testament; and much may not improperly be explained from analogy; and the light which it reflects on the truths of Christianity would richly repay any efforts that were made for the discovery of it.

In the altar of incense, in its *materials,* for instance, or its *structure,* we are not aware that any mystery of practical importance is contained, except indeed that it was preeminently holy, and therefore required peculiar sanctity in those who should approach it. Its *situation* too, as immediately before the mercy-seat, and separated from it only by the vail which divided the sanctuary from the holy of holies, marked in a peculiar way, that those who burnt incense upon it were to consider themselves as more than ordinarily nigh to God, and to have in exercise every disposition that became them in so high and holy an employment. The *use* to which it was ordained, is the point to which I would more particularly call your attention. And we may consider it,

I. As a typical institution—

And here are two things particularly to be noticed in relation to it; namely,

1. Its daily use—

[Aaron himself in the first instance, and afterwards other priests in their courses[a], was to trim the lamps every morning and evening, and to light any of them that might have gone out. At these seasons, he was to take fire from the altar of burnt-offering, and to put it on a censer, and to burn incense with it upon the altar of incense. This, I say, he was to do every morning and evening; and that was called "a perpetual incense before the Lord."

This, beyond all doubt, was intended to typify the Lord Jesus Christ, who, as our great "High-Priest, is set on the right hand of the throne of the Majesty in the heavens, *a Minister of the sanctuary, and of the true tabernacle,* which the Lord pitched, and not man[b]." To him is assigned the office of interceding for his Church and people; and he has ascended up into the more immediate presence of his God for that end: as says the Apostle; "Christ is not entered into the holy places made with hands, *which are the figures of the true,* but into heaven itself, now *to appear in the presence of God for us*[c]." There he superintends the lamps of his sanctuary, "walking amongst the seven golden candlesticks, which are the seven Churches[d]," and either trimming or furnishing them with supplies of oil, as their various necessities may require. At the same time he offers up to God his intercessions for them, pleading with him in behalf of every individual, and obtaining for them all those blessings which they more particularly stand in need of.

To the Aaronic priests God had said, "There will I meet with thee:" and no doubt he did, in numberless instances, as well as in that of Zacharias[e], vouchsafe to them there more peculiar answers to their prayers. Our Great Intercessor could say, "I know that thou hearest me always[f]:" nor can we doubt but that myriads of his people are either preserved from falling, or restored after their falls, purely through "his intercession for them, that their faith may not ultimately fail[g]."]

2. Its annual expiation—

[It was enjoined that "an atonement should be made upon the horns of this altar once a year with the blood of the sin-offering of the atonements." And this, I apprehend, was to shew that without the blood of atonement no intercession could be of any avail. An atonement must be made for sin: and "without it there could be no remission[h]." The blood, too, that must be put on this altar must be the blood of

---

[a] Luke i. 8, 9.   [b] Heb. viii. 1, 2.   [c] Heb. ix. 24.
[d] Rev. i. 13, 20. and ii. 1.   [e] Luke i. 11—13.   [f] John xi. 42.
[g] Luke xxii. 32.   [h] Heb. ix. 22.

bullocks, and not either of goats or lambs: for *in the very same offering* which was made for sins of ignorance, the blood of bullocks which was shed for *a priest*, and for *the whole congregation*, was put upon the horns of *the altar of incense;* whereas that which was shed for *a ruler*, or *a common person*, which was of goats and lambs, was put upon *the altar of burnt-offering;* by which the sins of priests were marked as of greater enormity than the sins of others; and the altar of incense as of higher sanctity than the altar of burnt-offering[i]. This is very strongly expressed in the New Testament, there being always a superior efficacy ascribed to the intercession of Christ than even to his death. Thus when, to the question, "Who is he that condemneth?" the Apostle answers, "It is Christ that died," he adds, "*yea rather*, that is risen again, who is even at the right hand of God, who also maketh intercession for us[k]." Again, in the Epistle to the Hebrews he lays the greatest stress on the intercession of Christ as being the most effectual for the salvation of his people: "He is able to save to the uttermost all that come unto God by him, seeing he ever liveth to make intercession for them[l]." And to the same effect, also, in his Epistle to the Romans: "If when we were enemies we were reconciled to God by the death of his Son, *much more*, being reconciled, we shall be saved by his life[m]." Whether this was intended to be marked by the atonement being only annual, whilst the offering of incense was daily, I pretend not to say. I should apprehend not. I should rather think that that part of the appointment signified that Christ would make the expiation but once, whilst his intercession would be continual: but, at all events, the union of the two is absolutely indissoluble; as St. John intimates, when he says, "If any man sin, we have an Advocate with the Father, Jesus Christ the righteous, *who is also the propitiation for our sins*[n]." In fact, his atonement is the very plea which he offers in our behalf. When the high-priest entered within the vail, immediately after burning the incense he sprinkled the blood of the sacrifice upon the mercy-seat and before the mercy-seat[o]; intimating thereby, that all his hope of acceptance, whether for himself or others, was founded on the sacrifice which he had offered. And precisely thus does the Lord Jesus Christ prevail: for it is in consequence of his having offered his soul a "sacrifice for sin," that he is authorized to expect a spiritual seed to be secured to him; and in consequence of his "having borne the sins of many," that he confidently and with effect "maketh intercession for the transgressors[p]."]

[i] Compare Lev. iv. 7, 18. with Lev. iv. 22, 25, 27, 30, 34.
[k] Rom. viii. 34.   [l] Heb. vii. 25.   [m] Rom. v. 10.
[n] 1 John ii. 1.   [o] Lev. xvi. 11—14.   [p] Isai. liii. 10, 12.

I have observed, that we may yet further consider this ordinance,

II. As an emblematic rite—

In this view it marks,

1. The privilege of Christians—

[We have before said, that common priests were ordained to officiate at this altar. And are not we "a royal priesthood[q]?" Are not we "made kings and priests unto our God[r]?" Yes; and "the prayers we present to God come up before him as incense; and the lifting up of our hands is as an evening sacrifice[s]." In this manner are we privileged to draw nigh to God. We, every one of us, "have, through Christ, access by one Spirit unto the Father[t]:" yea, "we have boldness to enter into the holiest by the blood of Jesus[u]," and to prostrate ourselves at the very footstool of God himself. Did God say to Aaron, "I will meet thee there?" so says he to us also: "Draw nigh to me; and I will draw nigh to you[x]." Nor need we go to Jerusalem, or to his tabernacle to find him: for he has said, that "*in every place* incense should be offered to him, and a pure offering[y]." And, that we may feel ourselves more at liberty to approach him, his altar under the Christian dispensation is represented as *of wood*, and not *of gold*, and as being four times the size of that which was made for his tabernacle[z]; to denote, I apprehend, the greater simplicity of Gospel worship, and the admission of all nations to the enjoyment of it.

We must indeed pay particular attention to that caution given to Aaron in the text: "Ye shall offer no strange incense thereon, nor burnt-sacrifice, nor meat-offering; neither shall ye pour drink-offering thereon." The incense was to be that alone which God had appointed; and special care was taken to make no confusion between the offerings belonging to the altar of burnt-offering, *which were for an atonement*, and that which was proper to the altar of incense, which was *for acceptance only*. Thus, when drawing nigh to God in prayer, we must not bring the fervour of mere animal spirits, which are so often mistaken for true devotion; but a broken and contrite spirit, which alone sends forth an odour that is well pleasing to God[a]. Nor must we imagine that by our prayers, or by any thing else that we can bring to God, we can atone for sin, or contribute in the least degree towards the efficacy of Christ's atonement: these must be kept quite distinct: and whilst our

---

[q] 1 Pet. ii. 9. [r] Rev. i. 5, 6. [s] Ps. cxli. 2.
[t] Eph. ii. 18. [u] Heb. x. 19. [x] Jam. iv. 8.
[y] Mal. i. 11. [z] Compare ver. 2—5. with Ezek. xli. 22.
[a] Ps. li. 17.

prayers are offered on the altar of incense, our pleas must be taken solely from the altar of burnt-offering, even from the sacrifice of the Lord Jesus Christ, "by whom alone our offerings can ascend to God[b]," and "through whom alone they can be acceptable in his sight[c]."

In this manner we are to approach God, whilst we go in before him to trim our lamps, and to have them duly supplied with oil. Every morning and evening at the least must the odours of our incense ascend up before God; or, as the Apostle says, we must "pray without ceasing[d]:" and we may be sure that "God will meet with us," and bless us in all that we solicit at his hands: "However wide we open our mouth, he will fill it[e]:" yea, "he will do for us exceeding abundantly above all that we can ask or think[f]."]

2. The ground of their acceptance in the use of it—

[This is strongly marked in the annual atonement made on this altar. Day and night was the priest to officiate there: yet, after he had presented incense on that altar for a whole year, he must make atonement on the altar with blood. And however much or devoutly we pray, we must trust, not in our prayers, but in the great Sacrifice that has been offered for us. Yea, our very prayers need that sacrifice: the very best service we ever offered, needed an atonement; nor could it come up with acceptance before God, if it were not washed in the Redeemer's blood, and presented to God by him. Hear what St. John says, in the book of Revelation: "Another angel came, (the Angel of the Covenant, the Lord Jesus,) and stood at the altar, having a golden censer: and there was given unto him much incense, that he should offer it with the prayers of all saints upon the golden altar that was before the throne: and the smoke of the incense, which came with the prayers of the saints, ascended up before God, out of the angel's hand[g]." "Were God to call us into judgment for the very best prayer we ever offered, we could not answer him for one of a thousand[h];" no, nor for one during our whole lives: but when cleansed in the Redeemer's blood, both our persons and our services shall be regarded by God as pure, even "without spot or blemish[i]."

Of course, it is here supposed that we harbour no wilful sin within us: for, "if we regard iniquity in our hearts, God will not hear us[k]:" our very "incense will be an abomination to him[l];" and, in offering it, "we shall be as though we offered swine's blood, or blessed an idol[m]." But, if we "draw nigh

[b] Heb. xiii. 15.   [c] 1 Pet. ii. 5.   [d] 1 Thess. v. 17.
[e] Ps. lxxxi. 10.   [f] Eph. iii. 20.   [g] Rev. viii. 3, 4.
[h] Job ix. 3.   [i] Eph. v. 25—27.   [k] Ps. lxvi. 18.
[l] Isai. i. 13.   [m] Isai. lxvi. 3.

to God with a true heart, we may also approach him with full assurance of faith[n]."]

Let us SEE here,

1. How highly we are privileged under the Christian dispensation—

[The Jews were privileged, and highly too, in comparison of all the nations of the earth, in that they had ordinances of divine appointment, in the due observance of which they might find favour with God. But how infinitely are we distinguished above the Jews themselves! We have not to seek the intervention of *a man*, a *sinful* man, yea, and a *dying* man, who must soon leave his office to another, and be followed by an endless succession of sinners like himself. We have an High-Priest, who is " Emmanuel, God with us; " " who needed not to offer first for his own sins, and then for the people's; " and " who, having an unchangeable priesthood, continueth for ever," and " is consecrated for evermore[o]." Moreover, we are not like the Jews, to whom all access to God in their own persons was prohibited; and who, if they had presumed to invade the priestly office, would have been made monuments of God's vengeance on the very spot. No: we may draw nigh to God, every one of us for himself: even to God's throne may we go, and offer him our sacrifices with a certainty of acceptance. The way prepared for us is " a new and *living* way: " and whilst going to him in that way, " we may ask what we will, and it shall be done unto us; " yea, even " before we ask, he will answer; and whilst we are yet speaking, he will hear[p]." Reflect on these privileges, Brethren, and be thankful for them; and improve them diligently in the way prescribed————]

2. What a holy people we should be unto the Lord—

[What the priests were in their attendance on the altar, yea, what the Lord Jesus Christ himself is before the throne of God, that should we be, to the utmost of our power. We should be ever delighting ourselves in the exercise of prayer and praise, and dedicating our whole selves to the service of our God. Let our " lamps " be ever kept burning bright before the Lord. Let us obtain " from the sacred olive-branches fresh supplies of golden oil through the golden pipes " of his word and ordinances[q]; and let our whole deportment shew, that we correspond with the description given us, " a people near unto the Lord[r] " ————]

[n] Heb. x. 22.   [o] Heb. vii. 23—28.   [p] Isai. lxv. 24.
[q] Zech. iv. 11, 12.   [r] Ps. cxlviii. 14.

OUTLINE NO. 102
THE ATONEMENT-MONEY.

Exod. xxx. 14—16. *Every one that passeth among them that are numbered, from twenty years old and above, shall give an offering unto the Lord: the rich shall not give more, and the poor shall not give less, than half a shekel, when they give an offering unto the Lord, to make an atonement for your souls. And thou shalt take the atonement-money of the children of Israel, and shalt appoint it for the service of the tabernacle of the congregation; that it may be a memorial unto the children of Israel before the Lord, to make an atonement for your souls.*

IT is always profitable to mark the accomplishment of the divine promises, that, from discovering the faithfulness of God, we may learn to acknowledge his providence, and depend upon his care. He had promised to Abraham, that "his seed should be as the stars of heaven for multitude:" and, though their increase for about three hundred years was but small, yet, previous to their departure from Egypt, they were become exceeding numerous: and God appointed that they should be occasionally numbered, and a stated tax be levied on every individual, that so the fulfilment of his word might be made manifest. In this appointment there were some circumstances peculiarly instructive, especially the equality of the tax, and the application of it to the service of the sanctuary.

Let us notice,

I. The tax levied—

The tax being "a ransom, and an atonement for their souls," had evidently a spiritual import; and from the same being levelled upon all, we observe,

1. That the souls of men are of equal value in the sight of God—

[The half-shekel was equal to about fifteen-pence of our money; and this was to be paid by every one that was numbered, without any regard to his station or ability: "The rich were not to pay more, nor the poor less." Now as this was "a ransom and atonement for their souls," it is manifest, that all their souls were of equal value in the sight of God. And who is there that does not feel this? There are many things in this world the value of which is purely imaginary, and depends upon the taste of the possessor: but the worth of the soul is *real:* the poorest of men has as deep an interest in the welfare of his own soul as the richest: heaven is as desirable, and hell as terrible, to the one as to the other: and God has an equal respect for both[a]. Let not any one despise others, as though their eternal interests were not to be consulted; or imagine that they themselves are overlooked by God, as though he did not will their salvation as much as that of any other person in the universe[b].]

2. That all equally need reconciliation with God—

[A ransom and an atonement were required for all: and as all of *them* needed mercy at God's hands, so do all of *us.* We are far from saying that all are equally sinful; for there doubtless are different degrees of guilt, and will be corresponding degrees of punishment: but this we say, that all have sinned and come short of the glory of God; and consequently all are obnoxious to "that wrath of God, which is revealed against all ungodliness and unrighteousness of men." We know that many conceive so highly of themselves, as to imagine that God would be unjust if he should consign them over to destruction. But such persons have never considered what the law of God requires, or what it denounces against those who have violated its commands[c]. We willingly concede, that, in the eyes of men, some may be comparatively innocent: but, "before God, every mouth must be stopped, and all the world become guilty."]

3. That all must seek it on the same terms—

[Here again we remark, that no difference was put between one and another: all were to offer the half-shekel as an atonement for their souls. It is by an atonement too that we also must seek acceptance with God. None can *merit* forgiveness at his hands; none can do any thing towards meriting it: the atoning blood of Christ is that which alone can satisfy divine justice; and it is his obedience unto death which must constitute the justifying righteousness of all mankind[d]. Any thing of our own, blended with that, or added to it, will invalidate it altogether. Salvation must be wholly of works or of grace[e]: and if we cannot earn it by our works, (which no created being can,) then must we accept it altogether as "the gift of God through Jesus Christ our Lord[f]." It is evident that so small a sum as half a shekel could not *purchase* the divine favour: it was a mere acknowledgment that they needed an atonement, and were willing to accept the favour of God on any terms that he should propose: so, our humili-

---

[a] Job xxxiv. 19.   [b] 1 Tim. ii. 4.   [c] Gal. iii. 10.
[d] Isai. xlv. 24, 25. Jer. xxiii. 6.   [e] Rom. xi 6.   [f] Rom. vi. 23

ation and faith can *purchase* nothing; but *only manifest* our cordial acquiescence in the way of salvation provided for us.]

It will be yet further instructive to consider,

II. The use and application of the tax—

The tax was intended,

1. To obtain acceptance for the offerers—

[The very terms "ransom," and "atonement," clearly shew, that the offerers were considered as in a state of guilt and bondage: and they were warned, that, if they refused to pay "the atonement-money," they would bring upon themselves the divine displeasure [g]. It was certainly an aggravation of David's sin in numbering the people, that, while he gratified his own pride and creature-confidence, he neglected to honour God by levying for him the appointed offering: and no less than seventy thousand of his subjects were destroyed in three days by a pestilence sent from God. This may give us some little idea of the vengeance that will overtake those who despise the atonement of Christ; and of the glorious deliverance which *they* shall obtain, who believe in him. The protection, the peace, the plenty, which his obedient people enjoyed in the wilderness, and their final possession of the promised land, represented the spiritual blessings which all "the ransomed of the Lord" shall eternally inherit.]

2. To convey instruction to the rising generation—

[The money, we are told, was to be "a memorial unto the children of Israel before the Lord." We read of different memorials in the Scriptures. The censers in which Korah and his company offered incense were taken out of the fire wherewith the offerers were consumed, and were made into plates for the covering of the altar, "to be a memorial, that none but the seed of Aaron come near to offer incense before the Lord [h]." The jewels and bracelets of which the Israelites spoiled the slaughtered Midianites were presented to the Lord, "as a memorial unto the children of Israel," that not one of their own army fell, though the whole Midianitish kingdom was utterly destroyed [i]. Now such memorials were the half-shekels at the numbering of the people: they served to remind the whole nation of Israel, that, as sinners, they stood in need of an atonement, and that none who consecrated themselves to the service of their God should ever perish. Such memorials too are all who now seek for mercy through the atoning blood of Christ. They are as lights in a dark world: they unwittingly instruct all around them: as Noah by building the ark "condemned the world," and tacitly admonished them of the impending judgments, so

---

[g] ver. 12. [h] Numb. xvi. 36—40. [i] Numb. xxxi. 48—54

do they who flee to Christ for refuge, testify to all around them, that there is salvation in Him, and in him alone.]

3. To give honour unto God—

[It was by these offerings, that the various services of the tabernacle (by which above all things God was honoured) were maintained. And who are they that now honour God in the world? Who are they that truly and spiritually maintain his worship? We fear not to say, that God is more acceptably served by his penitent and believing people, than by all the world besides. The gift of his only-begotten Son to die for us is that which he himself most commends to our attention; nor can he be more glorified on earth, or even in heaven itself, than in acknowledgments of our obligations to him for this stupendous effort of his love.]

APPLICATION—

Amongst the Israelites there were several classes exempt from the payment of this tax: but none amongst us can plead any exemption from that which is required of us, the tribute of a broken and contrite spirit—

1. Not the Levites—

[These were not numbered for war, and therefore were not included in the tax[k]. But the Levites amongst *us* should be the very first to devote themselves to God, and to render to him that tribute, which they demand from others — — —]

2. Not old people—

[These for the same reason were omitted both in the numbering and the taxation. But who have so much cause to bear in mind the atonement of Christ as they who are on the borders of eternity, and are so soon to stand at his judgment-seat? It is to be lamented, that people advanced in years too generally take for granted that all is well with them, though they have never sought "a ransom, or an atonement, for their souls." But let the aged amongst us be diligent in working out their salvation, and "so much the more as they see the day approaching."]

3. Not women—

[These were considered as included in the men; and therefore were not personally either taxed or numbered. But our offerings must be personal: nothing can be done by proxy: as there is "neither Jew nor Greek amongst us, so is there neither male nor female:" all must be judged by their own works, and all must be accepted through their own faith.]

[k] Numb. i. 47.

4. Not children—

[Persons under twenty years of age were not deemed strong enough for war, and therefore were passed over. But who shall say at what age our responsibility to God begins? Who shall assign the limit at which God will "wink at," or condemn, the transgressions of his law? Surely this were presumptuous and dangerous ground: let not any of you dare to stand upon it. If the services of a Samuel or a Timothy can be acceptable to God, the iniquities of childhood may be provoking. The tax required from you is not burthensome to any: seek not therefore, nor desire, an exemption from it. It is your heart, and not your property, that God requires: present it to him as purchased by the blood of his dear Son, and you shall be numbered amongst his people to all eternity.]

OUTLINE NO. 103

THE ANOINTING OIL.

Exod. xxx. 25—31. *Thou shalt make an oil of holy ointment, an ointment compound after the art of the apothecary: it shall be an holy anointing oil. And thou shalt anoint the tabernacle of the congregation therewith, and the ark of the testimony, and the table and all his vessels, and the candlestick and his vessels, and the altar of incense, and the altar of burnt-offering with all his vessels, and the laver and his foot. And thou shalt sanctify them, that they may be most holy: whatsoever toucheth them shall be holy. And thou shalt anoint Aaron and his sons, and consecrate them, that they may minister unto me in the priest's office. And thou shalt speak unto the children of Israel, saying, This shall be an holy anointing oil unto me throughout your generations.*

OF the Ceremonial Law in general we may say, it was intended to shadow forth the Lord Jesus Christ in the whole of his work and offices. The Epistle to the Hebrews admirably illustrates it in this peculiar view, shewing with minuteness and precision the scope and object of it as relating to him, and as fulfilled in him. To his priesthood, in particular, the ordinance which we here read of more especially referred; for in the fortieth chapter, where the words of my text are again almost literally repeated, it is said, "Their anointing shall surely be an everlasting priesthood throughout their generations[a]."

[a] Exod. xl. 10—15.

THE ANOINTING OIL.

But it is remarkable, that after the Babylonish captivity this ointment, so far as we are informed, was never made. And this seems to have been permitted of God, in order to direct their minds to that richer unction, which they were to receive from their Messiah. Previous to the time of Christ, the Holy Spirit was very sparingly and partially bestowed; as it is said, "The Holy Spirit was not yet given, because that Jesus was not yet glorified[b]:" but after the ascension of our Lord and Saviour to heaven, "the Spirit was shed forth abundantly" upon God's Church[c]; and from that time, multitudes, both of priests and people, have been wholly sanctified unto the Lord. Under this dispensation it is our happiness to live; so that, with a special reference to ourselves, I may well proceed to shew,

I. The universal need there is of the Holy Spirit's influence—

There was nothing *under the Law* so holy, but that it needed this divine unction—

["The tabernacle" itself, the immediate residence of the Deity; and "the ark," wherein the tables of the Law were placed, and which was a preeminent type of the Lord Jesus Christ, who fulfilled the Law for us; these, I say, were anointed; as were also "the table" of shewbread, and the candlestick, the one representing Christ as the bread of life, and the other "as the light which lighteneth every man that cometh into the world." Now, whence was it that these needed such purification? They were used in the service of sinful man, and therefore were polluted, and needed to be so purified; as heaven itself, the abode of all the glorified hosts, is said to be: for "the patterns of things in the heavens were purified with these earthly sacrifices, whilst the heavenly places themselves were purified with better sacrifices than these[d]."

That "Aaron and his sons" needed this holy ointment, we do not wonder, since they were sinners like unto us. But taking the whole together as used for sinful man, they serve to shew us, that there is not a *thing* or *person* in the universe that must not be so sanctified, before God can find pleasure in any services presented to him.]

Nor is there any thing *under the Gospel* which does not need it—

[b] John vii. 39.   [c] Tit. iii. 6.   [d] Heb. ix. 23.

[What are the ordinances of religion, or what the souls of men, without the Holy Spirit? The one are an empty form; and the other, "a cage of every unclean bird." Regard us *as men*, and every thing we do is defiled before God. But consider us *as priests*, for into that office every true Christian in the universe is brought[e], and how can we approach the Most High God, and offer any acceptable sacrifice unto him, unless we be first consecrated with that divine unction, which God has promised to all who seek him in spirit and in truth[f]? It is the duty of the greatest of men, and the privilege of the meanest, to get himself anointed with this holy oil. Even our Lord Jesus Christ himself, *as man* and *as Mediator*, needed it. We are informed, that "God anointed *him* with the Holy Ghost and with power[g]:" much more, therefore, must *we*, corrupt and sinful creatures, need, under all circumstances, his gracious communications: indeed we are expressly told, that, "if any man have not the Spirit of Christ, he is none of his[h]."]

II. His sufficiency for all to whom that influence is applied—

This appears,

1. From the preciousness of the ointment which was used—

[The spices were peculiarly rare and odoriferous; and the oil with which they were blended was most pure. And was this appointed for nought? Doubtless this was intended to shadow forth the excellency of the Spirit's gifts: for on whomsoever he was poured, whether on the Saviour himself or on any of the sons of men, he was "a spirit of wisdom and understanding, a spirit of counsel and of might, a spirit of knowledge and of the fear of the Lord, and he made the person of quick understanding in the fear of the Lord[i]." There is not a faculty in man to which the Spirit's influence does not extend, or which it will not sanctify: it imparts light to the understanding, flexibility to the will, purity to the affections, tenderness to the conscience, and holiness to the entire man: it makes us altogether "a new creation," and sanctifies every offering which we present to God; so that "God smells a sweet savour from it[k]," and is well pleased with services which could not otherwise be accepted of him.]

2. From the virtue infused into every thing anointed with it—

[e] 1 Pet. ii. 9. Rev. i. 6.   [f] Luke xi. 13.   [g] Acts iv. 27. and x. 38.
[h] Rom. viii. 9.   [i] Isai. xi. 2, 3.   [k] Phil. iv. 18.

[Every vessel that was anointed with that ointment, imparted a sanctity to every thing with which it came in contact[1]. And thus, in like manner, every true Christian communicates to others, so far as his influence extends, the same divine principles which he himself has imbibed. As it was said of the Saviour, so may it be said of all the Lord's anointed, " Their garments smell of myrrh, aloes, and cassia[m]:" and wherever they come, they diffuse around them " *the savour* of the knowledge of Christ." We cannot have a more complete idea of its efficacy, than the Corinthian Church, through the instrumentality of St. Paul, exhibited. In their unconverted state, many of them had been of a most abandoned character: yet, having drawn that character in all its most degraded forms, he says of them, " Such were some of you: but ye are washed, but *ye are sanctified*, but ye are justified, in the name of the Lord Jesus, and *by the Spirit of our God*[n]." Only let the Spirit of God accompany the word to the hearts of men, and the day of Pentecost fully shews us what effects it will produce.]

I ENTREAT you then, my brethren—

I. Seek the Holy Spirit for your own souls—

[There is " an unction of the Holy One," which every one of you may obtain, and which will operate upon you to your complete salvation[o]——— But I must guard you against every counterfeit that may be mistaken for it. There is such a thing as enthusiasm: and it is by no means uncommon for persons to mistake some feelings or conceits of their own for the sanctifying influences of the Spirit of God. And I must warn you, that, as any person compounding for himself an ointment similar to that which was made for God was to be cut off from his people[p], so a substitution of any thing in the place of God's Holy Spirit will infallibly issue in your destruction. You shall not however err, if you go to your great High-Priest, and ask for the Holy Spirit at his hands: for he has been anointed with " the Spirit without measure[q];" and the Spirit that has been poured so largely upon him shall " descend to the skirts of his garments[r]," and to the very meanest of all his members.]

2. Guard against every thing that may reflect dishonour upon him—

[The high-priest under the Law was forbidden to display those feelings which were incident to common men, because " the crown of the anointing oil was upon him[s]." And you

---

[1] ver. 29.   [m] Ps. xlv. 8.   [n] 1 Cor. vi. 9—11.
[o] 1 John ii. 20, 27.   [p] ver. 32, 33.   [q] John iii. 34.
[r] Ps. cxxxiii. 2.   [s] Lev. xxi. 10—12.

likewise, my brethren, if you have been indeed anointed with the Spirit of God, must shew that superiority to earthly things, which would be in vain looked for from the natural and unconverted man. Very striking is that expression of Solomon, " Dead flies cause *the ointment of the apothecary* to send forth a stinking savour: so doth a little folly him that is in reputation for wisdom and honour[t]." There is a sanctity about the Christian character which should be kept inviolate. If you are "sons of God, you should be blameless and harmless in the midst of a crooked and perverse nation, shining among them as lights in the world[u]." The Spirit of God may be soon "grieved;" yea, he may be even " vexed," and " quenched" by any deliberate sin: for sin in *you* will " cause the very name of God himself to be blasphemed." I pray you, then, walk circumspectly, and in a way " worthy of your high calling," yea, " worthy also of Him who hath called you unto his kingdom and glory." O " may the Spirit of God sanctify you wholly! and I pray God that your whole spirit and soul and body may be preserved blameless unto the coming of our Lord Jesus Christ."]

[t] Eccl. x. 1.   [u] Phil. ii. 15.

OUTLINE NO. 104
GOD THE SOURCE OF ALL WISDOM.

Exod. xxxi. 6. *In the hearts of all that are wise-hearted I have put wisdom.*

WHEN the time is come for carrying into effect the purposes of God, difficulties, which appeared insurmountable, vanish, and " mountains become a plain." The obstacles which opposed the deliverance of Israel from Egypt, were only augmented till the precise hour for its accomplishment arrived: but at the appointed hour, even " the self-same night," they not only went out unmolested, but were actually thrust out by their oppressors. At the Red Sea, an interposition equally seasonable was vouchsafed to them; as was also a supply both of bread and water in the wilderness, in the hour of need. Those who looked only to second causes judged the various blessings unattainable: but, on all the occasions, God shewed that there was nothing impossible to him; and that whatever he had ordained, should not fail for want of means and instruments whereby to effect it. Having brought his people into the wilderness he commanded a tabernacle to be reared, and to be furnished with a great diversity of vessels proper for his service. The most costly materials were to be used, and the most exquisite workmanship employed, in the structure of the whole. But where should all the materials be found? Behold! the Egyptians themselves had loaded the Israelites with them to an immense amount, no one throughout the whole land of Egypt refusing to an Israelite any thing that he required. Still, though gold and silver and precious stones and other things were found amongst them, and were granted by them with a liberal hand, who was there amongst the whole nation that could fashion them according to the model shewn to Moses in the mount? They had been so oppressed, that it would be in vain to look for persons sufficiently skilled in works of gold and jewellery and embroidery, to execute all that was required for the occasion. But was the work therefore delayed? No: God, by his Spirit, instructed two persons, Bezaleel and Aholiab, with a perfect knowledge of the whole work; and, under their superintendence, others were speedily qualified for executing every one the office assigned to him; so that the whole was finished within the short space of nine months. Every one performed his part aright, because " in the heart of all that were wise-hearted God had put wisdom."

From this remarkable expression I shall take occasion to point out, in reference to " *wisdom*,"

I. Its only source—

The wisdom here spoken of, proceeds from God—

[Whatever difference may be occasioned in men by education, the original faculty of understanding is our Creator's gift. Some, indeed, are born into the world destitute of any rational powers: if, therefore, we have been favoured with them, we are the more indebted to the goodness of our heavenly Father. It is probable that amongst the poor, or even amongst the uncivilized part of mankind, many possess by nature as much strength of intellect as the most learned philosopher; whilst, for want of the advantages of education, they have never been able to turn it to any good account. If, therefore, we have enjoyed the means and opportunities of cultivation which have been withheld from others, we must ascribe that also to God, who in this respect, also, has made us to differ. The Scriptures trace to this same source the wisdom manifested by the husbandman in ploughing his ground and threshing out the corn: "Doth the plowman plow all day to sow? doth he open the clods of his ground? His God doth instruct him to discretion, and doth teach him. . . . The fitches are beaten out with a staff, and the cummin with a rod. This also cometh forth from the Lord of Hosts, who is wonderful in counsel, and excellent in working[a]." We wonder not, therefore, that the skill so suddenly given to Bezaleel, and to all who worked under him, is ascribed to God; for that was indeed truly miraculous. But the declaration which traces it to God, extends to every kind and every measure of wisdom; and consequently constrains us to give God the glory of every faculty we possess, and of all the improvement that we have made of it. We are not left in any respect to "sacrifice to our own drag, or to burn incense to our own net:" the whole honour must be given to God, and to God alone.]

But to the same source must we yet more eminently trace the attainment of spiritual wisdom—

[Of this, no measure whatever is born with man, or is natural to man. "He is born like a wild ass's colt." As for "the things of the Spirit of God, they are foolishness unto him: neither can he know them, because they are spiritually discerned." Nor is wisdom the product of mere human instruction: for "the world by wisdom knew not God." The Apostles, when instructed in divine knowledge, traced the acquisition to the only true source: "We have received, not the spirit of the world, but the Spirit which is of God, that we may know the things that are freely given to us of God." Even the Messiah himself was instructed for the discharge of his office by the very same Spirit who wrought in Bezaleel for the forming of the tabernacle. Of Bezaleel it is said, "I have filled him with the Spirit of God, in wisdom, and in understanding, and in knowledge, and in all manner of workmanship[b]:" and of Jesus it is said, "The spirit of the Lord shall rest upon him, the spirit of wisdom and understanding, the spirit of counsel and of might, the spirit of knowledge and of the fear of the Lord; and shall make him of quick understanding in the fear of the Lord[c]." And the same Spirit will be given to us also, to enlighten our minds with saving knowledge: for St. Paul says, "I pray always for you, that God may give unto you the spirit of wisdom and revelation in the knowledge of him, the eyes of your understanding being

---

[a] Isai. xxviii. 24—29.   [b] ver. 3.   [c] Isai. xi. 2, 3.

enlightened, that ye may know what is the hope of his calling[d]." To him, then, must every man look for wisdom: and from him shall every man receive it, who seeks it in a becoming way[e]. As Bezaleel and Aholiab were instructed at once how to *perform all manner of work;* and as the disciples of Christ, poor uneducated fishermen, were enabled at once to *speak different kinds of tongues;* so shall the Spirit impart to us also, according to our respective necessities, that we may both *know* and *do* all that God has required of us.]

In the works to which this consummate wisdom was to be applied, we may see,

II. Its most appropriate use—

For the formation of the tabernacle was this wisdom given—

[For that work it was indispensably necessary: for the things which were to be formed had never been seen before; no, nor any thing like them: and for such sacred vessels the most exquisite skill was required. Had even angels been employed in the formation of this structure, their utmost abilities would have been well employed.]

And have not we a similar use for the wisdom bestowed on us?

[Behold " the tabernacle of David which is broken down!" does not that need to be reared again[f]? Are not the whole race of mankind to be formed as " vessels of honour meet for their Master's use?" But who can discharge this office? If St. Paul, with all his endowments, was constrained to ask, " Who is sufficient for these things[g]?" how much more must we? For, who amongst us has such an insight into the deep mysteries of the Gospel, as to be fully assured that he shall in no respect deviate from " the pattern shewn" to Prophets and Apostles " in the mount?" Or who shall undertake to fashion the rude materials of the human heart after the perfect image of our God? Who that knows any thing of Jewish prejudice or Gentile superstition, shall attempt to cope with them in his own strength, or hope to reduce them to the obedience of faith? Verily the Preacher of the Gospel needs to be endued with wisdom from above, with wisdom too of no ordinary measure, for the work to which he is called: and all the talents that the most distinguished philosopher can possess, will find ample scope for exercise in this great work. In comparison of rearing a tabernacle for the Lord, what is there under

---

[d] Eph. i. 17, 18.   [e] Prov. ii. 1—6.
[f] Amos ix. 11, 12. with Acts xv. 16, 17.   [g] 2 Cor. ii. 16.

heaven that deserves a thought? If the forming of *the shadows* of divine truth was a just employment of supernatural skill, doubtless an exhibition of *the substance* may profitably engage all the talents that were ever confided to mortal man.]

To all, then, I would SAY,

1. Acknowledge God in all the talents you possess—

[Not only Bezaleel and Aholiab, but all who were employed in the different departments of the work, were taught of God. So, whatever furniture we have for the constructing of God's spiritual tabernacle, we have received it from the same heavenly source, and must ascribe the glory of it altogether to our God. Let this be borne in mind, and none will envy those who are endowed with richer talents than themselves, or despise those who are called to occupy a humbler post. The eye in the natural body vaunts not itself above the hand, nor the hand above the foot; but each is satisfied with executing the work for which it is fitted and ordained: so let it be with us; every one doing what God has called him to, and every one seeking the glory of God in all that he performs.]

2. Improve your talents for the end for which they have been committed to you—

[At the formation of the tabernacle, every one engaged, according to his ability, to expedite the work. Men, women, rulers, all accounted it their honour to be employed for God[h]: and "*so*," we are told, "it became one tabernacle[i]." And who can say what the effect would be, if all, men, women, and rulers, engaged heartily in the work of God, and laboured to advance his glory in the world? Beloved Brethren, let us not sit down in despair, because the work is too great and arduous. God can fit us for it, however ignorant we be; and can bless us in it, however unequal we may be for the task assigned us. Only let it be said of every one amongst us, "He has done what he could," and we shall yet see glorious days amongst us; and God will rear his tabernacle, and glorify himself, as in the days of old.

But, for this end, it is necessary that you "stir up your hearts;" for, by nature, they are sadly averse to it. Nor need we fear that any exertions of ours will exceed the demand for them. The materials for the tabernacle, and the work, were soon supplied, when a whole nation were willing and active in the cause: but there is no fear that we shall have to bid you to cease either from your offerings or your labours[k]. The whole world is the tabernacle which you are to rear; and every soul within it is a vessel you are to form for God's

---

[h] Exod. xxxv. 21, 24, 25—27.   [i] Exod. xxxvi. 13.
[k] Exod. xxxvi. 5—7.

honour. Go on then, all of you, both in your individual and collective capacity, without intermission and without weariness: so shall the work proceed to the honour of our God, and a rich recompence be treasured up for your own souls.]

OUTLINE NO. 105
MOSES' INDIGNATION AGAINST THE WORSHIPPERS OF THE GOLDEN CALF.

Exod. xxxii. 19, 20. *And it came to pass, as soon as he came nigh unto the camp, that he saw the calf, and the dancing. And Moses' anger waxed hot, and he cast the tables out of his hands, and brake them beneath the mount. And he took the calf which they had made, and burned it in the fire, and ground it to powder, and strawed it upon the water, and made the children of Israel drink of it.*

IT is painful to reflect how transient is the effect of the most laborious ministry, and in how many instances hopeful appearances of piety come to nought. If ever man was faithful, it was Moses; of whom God himself says, "He was faithful in all his house." And if ever there was reason to expect that the work of conversion had taken place upon many hundreds of thousands of people, it was when Israel were singing praises to their God on occasion of their deliverance at the Red Sea. It might well be supposed, that their gratitude to God on that occasion, deepened by the awe impressed upon their minds at the thunders of Mount Sinai, would never be forgotten. But, behold! Moses, summoned as he was by God into the holy mount, in order that he might receive from Jehovah a written copy of that Law which had been just proclaimed, had not been absent from the people forty days, before they all concurred in desiring Aaron to make for them a god whom they might worship, and who should go before them in their way to the promised land: and even Aaron himself became an active confederate in this horrible apostasy. As for Moses, they seem to have lost all respect for him, as well as all becoming reverence for Jehovah, whose minister he was. Of this, God apprised Moses; and at last sent him down in haste to the people, that he might see with his own eyes what impiety they were committing. Moses, therefore, hastened down from the mount: and, filled with indignation against them for their wickedness, he testified his displeasure in the way recorded in our text.

Let us consider,

I. The grounds of his indignation—

The worshipping of the golden calf was a sin of most extraordinary enormity—

[Such interpositions in their behalf had that people seen, as never had been witnessed by any other people under heaven. And they were still within sight of that burning mount where Jehovah himself, their great Deliverer, yet vouchsafed to them his visible presence. They had but just before, too, received an express command to make no symbol of the Deity[a], nor to keep in existence any of the gods of the heathen, but to "destroy their altars, and break down their images, and cut down their groves, and burn their graven images with fire;" and not so much as to "desire the silver or gold that was on them, or to take it unto them, lest they should be snared therein; but they were utterly to detest and abhor it, as an accursed thing[b]." Yet, behold! within less than forty days, they desire Aaron to make them a golden image, similar, probably, to what they had seen in Egypt[c]; and they take the ear-rings from their sons and from their daughters for the purpose of forming it; and, having formed it, they offer sacrifices to it, and ascribe to it the honour of all their past deliverances, saying, "These be thy gods, O Israel, which have brought thee up out of the land of Egypt[d]."

This was plain and unequivocal idolatry. Perhaps they might be ready to deny this charge, just as the Papists have since done; and to say, that they only looked to the calf as a symbol, to remind them of the Deity, to whom alone they had respect in all the worship that they paid. They might say, that they could not be supposed to ascribe their deliverance to that, which but a few days before was in their own ears, and had no collective existence till it was cast into a mould and made a calf. But *God declares it to have been idolatry*, as all the worship paid to images and crucifixes by the Church of Rome also is; as the Apostle, in reference to this very transaction, says; "Neither be ye idolaters, as were some of them: as it is written, The people sat down to eat and to drink, and rose up to play[e]."

[a] Exod. xx. 4.   [b] Deut. vii. 5, 25, 26.   [c] Ezek. xx. 8.
[d] ver. 1—8.   [e] Compare ver. 6. with 1 Cor. x. 7.

Here, then, was ample occasion for the hot displeasure of Moses.]

And is there no similar evil prevalent amongst us?

[As Protestants, we have discarded the idolatrous practices of the Church of Rome. But we may "set up idols in our hearts[f]," as well as in our houses: we may have the love of money there; and that is expressly designated by the opprobrious name of idolatry: " Covetousness," says the Apostle, "is idolatry[g]." We may be addicted to sensual appetites: and then we make, as we are told, "a god of our belly[h]." " The loving and serving of the creature more than the Creator[i]," in whatever way we do it, is the very essence of idolatry; and " provokes the Lord to jealousy[k]," as much without an external symbol, as with one. God says, " My son, give me thy heart:" and if that be withheld from him, he is justly filled with indignation against us.

Let me, then, bring home this matter more closely to your hearts and consciences. The Israelites professed to celebrate their redemption from Egypt: and having presented their sacrifices of burnt-offerings and peace-offerings, " they sat down to eat and to drink of the portion of the peace-offerings which was allowed to them, and rose up to play." And, when Moses came down from the mount, he heard, whilst yet at some distance, their carnal revelry; which they judged a becoming mode of honouring their great Deliverer. Now at this season[l] we profess to commemorate the Redemption, not of a single nation, but of the whole world; and not by power only, but by price, even the precious blood of God's only dear Son: we commemorate, I say, the Incarnation of the Son of God, for the deliverance of our souls from sin and Satan, death and hell. And in what way do we commemorate it? Is not this season even proverbially devoted to carnal mirth? We present our offerings, if I may so say, on the day appointed; and throughout the whole season, with the exception of two or three hours, " we sit down to eat and to drink, and rise up to play." *Such is our religion,* precisely like that of those impious idolaters. To the honour of the Levites, it must be acknowledged that they did form an exception to this national transgression. Would to God the like could be said of our Levites! or even of our Aarons! But, with us, Levites and Aarons too are found, for the most part, sanctioning, by their presence and example, these sad enormities; as if Christ had come for no better purpose than to give us a more ample occasion for carnal indulgence.

[f] Ezek. xiv. 3. [g] Col. iii. 5. [h] Phil. iii. 19. [i] Rom. i. 25.
[k] 1 Cor. x. 22. [l] Sermon for *Christmas.*

Judge ye, then, whether God may not well be filled with indignation against us, as he was against his less enlightened and less indebted people of that day?]

Having seen the grounds of Moses' indignation, let us proceed to mark,

II. His expressions of it—

1. He broke before their eyes the tables of the Law, which God had committed to him—

[Was this done in a paroxysm of rage? No:[m] it was a significant action, declaring, in effect, to the whole people, that they had made void all their solemn engagements with the Deity[n]; and that therefore the covenant he had made with them, of which "these tables were a testimony[o]," was utterly annulled.

And are not all the provisions of the Gospel, too, made void by wilful and deliberate sin? They *are:* and all hope in the Gospel, whilst our hearts are alienated from God, and fixed on earthly vanities, is nothing but delusion. Our Lord has faithfully warned us, that it is in vain for us to "cry, Lord! Lord! if we do not the things which he says:" and that however we may debate the matter with him in the last day, saying, "Lord, have we not prophesied in thy name, and in thy name cast out devils, and in thy name done many wonderful works? he will reply, I never knew you: depart from me, ye who work iniquity[p]." Whoever then ye be, who, instead of delighting yourselves in God, are addicted to carnal mirth, I break the tables of the covenant before your faces this day; and declare, that "whoso doeth not righteousness, is not of God;" but that, on the contrary, "whosoever committeth sin, is of the devil[q]." It is needful that we declare this faithfully: for, whilst dancing about your golden calf, you conclude that all is well, and little think in what light your conduct is viewed by a holy and jealous God. And to learn it, first, when your Lord shall descend from His holy mount to judge the world, will be too late: for, as the Levites passed through the camp, and avenged the cause of God on the offenders without favouring even their nearest relatives, so will the angels at that day inexorably and irresistibly execute on all the violators of God's covenant the judgments denounced against them[r]. Let all, then, bear in mind, that "God is a jealous God;" and that "he will neither give, nor suffer us to give, his glory to another."]

---

[m] The manner in which Moses, forty years afterwards, relates it, sufficiently proves this. See Deut. ix. 16, 17.   [n] Deut. v. 27.
[o] ver. 15.   [p] Matt. vii. 21—23.   [q] 1 John iii. 6, 8, 9.
[r] Compare Isai. xxxvii. 36. with Matt. xiii. 41, 42.

2. He ground the calf to powder, and constrained the people to swallow it with their drink—

[We need not look for any recondite mystery in this, because the obvious effect of the act itself was sufficiently instructive. No greater indignity could be offered to this worthless idol, than that which he devised; nor any more humiliating punishment be inflicted upon the people, than to compel them to *swallow their god*, and to " cast him out into the draught" with their common food.

And shall not we, also, be made ashamed of the gods that we have chosen? Yes: if we will choose " vanity, we must have vanity for our recompence." Do I say, We *must?* Let me rather change the word, and say, We *have:* for I may ask of all the votaries of earthly gain or pleasure, " What fruit have ye ever had of those things, whereof ye are *now* ashamed ? What have ye done, but " filled your belly with the east wind?" I must warn you, then, that ye shall all " eat of the fruit of your own ways," and " be filled with your own devices." The day is quickly coming, when you shall be as much ashamed of those things which you now regard with idolatrous affection, as ever the Israelites were of their golden calf: yea, and when you yourselves also "shall wake to shame and everlasting contempt[s]."]

From this subject we may fitly LEARN,

1. The danger of sanctioning the evils around us—

[Aaron should have rejected with abhorrence the measure proposed to him: but he acquiesced, and even made himself a ringleader in this vile apostasy. With such a sanction as his, it is not to be wondered at if the people went forward with unsuspecting alacrity, and sacrificed with readiness their most valuable ornaments for the furtherance of their plans. But who does not see how aggravated his guilt was, in comparison of theirs? He, from his nearer intercourse with God, had far greater information than they; and, from the high office which he sustained, he was bound to use his influence for the suppression of evil, and the enforcing of God's commands. The same I must say of all who are possessed of influence amongst ourselves. Whether it be magisterial or ministerial influence that we possess, or only that which is connected with our respective situations in life, we are bound to exert it for God; and, if we neglect to do so, the blood of those who perish through our neglect may well be required at our hands.

I know that we have excuses without number to offer in our behalf; just as Aaron had when reproved for his conduct on this occasion. But, behold, what a pitiful figure he made, when attempting to justify himself before his reprover! " Let

---

[s] Dan. xii. 2.

not the anger of my Lord wax hot: thou knowest the people, that they are set on mischief." (This was a reason why he should have withstood them, and not a reason for concurring with them.) Again, "The people said to me, Make us gods who shall go before us. Then I said to them, Whosoever hath any gold, let him break it off. So they gave it me: and I cast it into the fire; and there came out this calf[t]:"—came out accidentally, I suppose, and without any mould prepared for the formation of it! What a tissue of folly and of falsehood! See to what a state this man was reduced, even he who was so eloquent, that he was appointed to "be a mouth to Moses." But thus it will be with sinners in the last day, with Aarons as well as others; (for official dignity is of no account in the sight of God;) or rather, their mouths will be shut through their utter incapacity to offer the smallest vindication of their folly[u]. Remember this, Brethren; and "have no fellowship with the unfruitful works of darkness, but rather reprove them[x]."]

2. In what way we should be affected with them—

[See what a contrast there was between the conduct of Moses and of Aaron on this occasion! Whilst Aaron was uniting with the people in their transgression, Moses was filled with indignation against the sin, and with pity for the sinners. His indignation we have seen: and no sooner had he expressed it in the way that became him, than he returned to God, to implore mercy in their behalf. Forty days and forty nights had he already fasted: and he went up to the mount and fasted forty more days and forty nights, wrestling with God in fervent intercession, if that by any means he might prevail to obtain pardon for their sin[y]. Here was a man of God indeed! This, then, is the way in which we should act in reference to the sins around us. We should weep over them before God: yea, "rivers of tears should run down our eyes, because men keep not God's law." Such men as he are blessings to the world: for, as "God hearkened unto him at that time also[z]," so will he do to us, if we "stand in the gap before him, to avert his wrath" from an ungodly world[a]. Little did that people think to whom the preservation of their lives was owing: and little do an ungrateful world know to whom they are indebted for the forbearance that is yet daily exercised towards them[b]. But let it be sufficient for us, that God knows and approves our labours of love; and that, whether we prevail for others or not, our prayers shall surely return into our own bosom, to the everlasting benefit of our own souls.]

[t] ver. 21—24.   [u] Matt. xxii. 12.   [x] Eph. v. 11.
[y] Deut. ix. 18, 19.   [z] Deut. ix. 18, 19.
[a] Ps. cvi. 23. with Ezek. xxii. 30.   [b] Matt. xxiv. 22

OUTLINE NO. 106
THE LORD'S PEOPLE TO BE DECIDED AND FIRM.

Exod. xxxii. 26. *Who is on the Lord's side? let him come unto me.*

THESE are the words of Moses: and they were spoken on a very particular occasion. Whilst he had tarried on the top of Mount Sinai for the space of forty days, Aaron and the people of Israel, despairing of his return, had made a golden calf to represent Jehovah, and had worshipped that as their God. Moses, on his return, found them in the very act of performing their idolatrous rites; and, filled with indignation against them, he broke the two tables of the Law which he had received from Jehovah, in token that the covenant which God had made with them was altogether dissolved: and he reduced the golden calf to powder, and strewed it upon the water, and made the people to drink of it; that so they might have within themselves a testimony of their folly, and be assured that a cup of merited affliction should one day be put into their hands. And it is remarkable, that the Jews in general conceive that, in all their afflictions, there are, as it were, some grains of this golden calf even to this very day. For Aaron, Moses interceded, and obtained forgiveness[a]. And on behalf of the people, too, he so far prevailed, that only the ringleaders in this rebellion should be punished in the first instance; though, at a future period, this sin should surely be visited upon them all. To punish those who were most bold and daring in this impiety, and were walking abroad as not ashamed of it, Moses called to him those who were zealous for God's honour, and ordered them to go through the camp and indiscriminately slay all they met with, without regarding even their nearest and dearest relatives. This was doubtless a most painful service to all who were engaged in it: but they executed it with fidelity, and brought thereby a blessing on their own souls.

[a] Deut. ix. 20.

Now, let it not for a moment be imagined that God's faithful servants are called to any such office now. Christianity provides no such bloody employment for its votaries: it consigns the sword altogether to the civil magistrate, who alone is empowered to use it for the punishment of evil-doers. Still, however, there will arise many profitable lessons from this passage· to elicit which, I shall make some observations upon,

I. The inquiry instituted—

Amongst the people of Israel there were, especially of the tribe of Levi, some who had not joined in the idolatrous rites, but had remained faithful to their God: and Moses, standing in the gate of the camp, called them to his assistance, saying, "Who is on the Lord's side?" Now from hence we observe,

1. That there are two classes, and two classes only, into which the whole world must be divided—

[There are some who are "on the Lord's side;" and there are others who are on the side of sin, and the world, and Satan. That in these two great parties there may be many subdivisions, I grant: but there is no third party. Amongst the godly there may be persons of different sentiments and different habits: and among the ungodly there may also be many different degrees of impiety, and different states of mind: but, still, the great leading features of both parties sufficiently and infallibly attest to which they belong. The distinguishing marks of each I shall trace presently: at present I have only to shew, that two parties do actually exist, and must of necessity exist, as long as there continues an ungodly man on earth. They may be very unequal in their numbers, as was the case in the history before us: an immense multitude, with Aaron at their head, were on the side of idolatry; and a little remnant, with Moses at their head, were "on the Lord's side." It is probable, that, at that time, the friends of idolatry poured contempt on the godly as *a party*, just as the ungodly world do at this day on the advocates of true religion; forgetting that they themselves also are *a party*, no less than their opponents. But whose fault is it if the godly are *a party*? Are *they* to blame for adhering to their duty, and siding with their Lord? No, surely: the blame must attach altogether to those who turn from their God, and are disobedient to his will. And if the godly be but "a little flock" in comparison of their opponents, it may be their misfortune, but it is not their fault, any more than it was the fault of Noah, or of Lot, or of Elijah, that they were so circumstanced in the ages and places wherein they lived. Let it not be thought that I am justifying what is usually called a party spirit; for I cannot but reprobate *that* as a very great evil: but I do, and must maintain, that to serve our God with fidelity is our bounden duty, even though the whole world, with Aaron at their head, should depart from him: and, if they choose to designate us as *a party*, I would have no man ashamed of belonging to a party, of which our Lord and Saviour is himself the Head.]

2. That it is of great importance to ascertain to which class we belong—

[Both are alike in this respect, that they are rational and nmortal beings: but in many respects they differ widely from each other: the one are "partakers of a divine nature" through the influence of the Spirit of God upon their souls; the others are altogether carnal, possessing nothing but what they brought into the world with them. The one live altogether for God; the others, for themselves. The one are in favour with God; the others are under his just and heavy displeasure. The one will, ere long, stand at the right hand of their Judge; the others will be turned to his left hand, differing as widely from the former as goats from the sheep. The one will be exalted to heaven, and be seated for ever on the throne of God; the others will be cast down to hell, and take their portion in the lake of fire and brimstone for ever and ever. Can these differences be contemplated for a moment, and any doubt remain whether we ought to examine to which class we belong? Methinks the matter should not be left in suspense one single moment; more especially since the means of ascertaining the point are close at hand, and easy to be used. The blessed word of God, if studied with prayer, will enable us to form a very correct judgment. True it is, that we cannot determine the question in relation to each other, because we know not what passes in the hearts of men, and can therefore judge of each other by the outward conduct alone: but we have an internal monitor, that will faithfully discharge its office, if we will listen to it, and will declare to us all that it has seen in the inmost recesses of our hearts: and, if we will but lay, to our own souls, "judgment for a line, and righteousness for a plummet," we shall soon discover " whose we are," and with whom we must expect our everlasting abode.]

To this I will add some observations on,

II. The direction given—

Moses, in calling to him the faithful servants of the Lord, shewed, that the Lord's people should on all occasions manifest,

1. A readiness to confess him—

[Neither the authority of Aaron, nor the rage of all Israel, was to deter any one from shewing himself on the Lord's side. So neither should any of us be afraid to confess Christ openly in the face of an ungodly world. We err exceedingly if we fancy that there is any third party to which we may adhere with safety to our souls. There are but two governors, to one or other of which we must adhere; "the god of this world," and the God of heaven. The servants of Satan are bold in serving him; and the servants of the Lord Jesus must be bold in confessing him: and if, from any motive whatever, we deny him, he will be ashamed of us, and deny us, in the presence of his Father and of the holy angels. I mean not to say, that Christians are to distinguish themselves by foolish singularity in matters of indifference: but in matters of plain duty they are to differ from the ungodly as widely as light from darkness : " they are to come out from among them, and be separate, and not to touch the unclean thing," if they would have " God for their Father," and approve themselves to him as " his sons and daughters"— — —]

2. A determination of mind to sacrifice every thing for him—

[Moses, in his farewell discourse, at the distance of forty years, particularly commends this conduct of Levi, in that " he said unto his father and his mother, I have not seen him, neither did he acknowledge his brethren, nor know his own children: but he had observed God's word, and kept his covenant[b]." And this shews, that, though we are not called to follow his *act*, we are to imbibe and manifest his *spirit*, so far at least as to sacrifice every thing *to*, and *for*, our God. Our blessed Lord distinctly and frequently inculcates this important lesson : "We are to forsake all for him—father, mother, brother, sister, houses, lands, yea, our very life also, if we would be his disciples:" yea, we are to " *hate* them all for him," that is, in comparison of him[c]. Doubtless, in the execution of this duty, we may appear unkind, undutiful, and cruel; but we must be firm, and suffer nothing to divert us from the path of duty : however painful it may be to discharge it, we must proceed, and, in dependence on divine strength, endure firmly unto the end. No doubt, if we are called to advance in opposition to the will of those who have the rule over us, we should be much on our guard, that we give them no unnecessary offence. We are to take great care that we contend for nothing but what is of vital importance, and that in our necessary conflicts we manifest nothing of an unhallowed

---

[b] Deut. xxxiii. 9.   [c] Luke xiv. 26.

spirit. But proceed we must in obedience to our God; and if called to an account for it by any human authority whatever, our answer must be, "Whether it be right to hearken unto you more than unto God, judge ye; for we cannot but do what is commanded us by our God."]

As a further IMPROVEMENT of this subject, we will proceed,

1. To *prosecute* the inquiry—

["Who amongst you is on the Lord's side?" I have before said, that this is easy to be ascertained: and now let us address ourselves to the inquiry. By nature, we are all "enemies to God," and "children of wrath." It is by grace alone that our state can be changed, so that we can with justice be numbered as the servants of the Lord. Who then, amongst you, has been made sensible of his guilty and undone state? Who, amongst you, has fled to the Lord Jesus Christ for refuge from the wrath of God? and who is yet daily imploring mercy at the hands of God in his name? Who has given up himself unreservedly to God, as his reconciled God in Christ Jesus? and who is living altogether to the glory of his holy name? These are questions to be asked, and answered, in order to ascertain the point in hand. You must remember, that your having been baptized into the name of Christ will by no means determine the point: for all the Israelites had been circumcised, and had been "baptized also unto Moses in the cloud and in the sea:" and as their profession was insufficient to prove them the Lord's, so also is ours. Nor will any transient impressions of joy and gratitude prove the point: for such emotions had been lately experienced by all Israel at the Red Sea, though now, alas! they were altogether forgotten. It is the daily life and conversation that alone can determine this all-important point. "Examine yourselves then, my Brethren, and prove your own selves." Try whether you are ready to obey the call of God, and to abandon all for Christ. See whether you resemble your Lord and Saviour in the whole of his spirit and deportment. See whether, whilst you profess to be on the Lord's side, you are really "walking as he walked," and giving up yourselves entirely to him. Decide not the question on any doubtful or insufficient grounds, lest you deceive your own souls, and perish amidst the enemies of God. One thought only I will leave upon your minds; and it is this: 'If you be not on the Lord's side, can you reasonably hope that ever he should be on yours? And if you have not him for your friend and portion in the day of judgment, how awful will be your condition!' But an hour before, the whole camp of Israel was filled with the noise of joy and shouting: and in another hour, thousands were smitten down by the swords of their own brethren. So in a few more hours may the most thoughtless amongst you be consigned over to the jaws of death, by the hands of an angry and avenging God. Oh! may God awaken you to your condition ere it be too late! and may you be found of that party, of which God himself is the acknowledged and eternal Head!]

2. To *enforce* the direction—

["Come unto me," says Moses: and I also would say, "Go unto him." If you belong truly to the Lord, you must go and learn from Moses what the will of the Lord is. The tables of the Law must be to you a rule of life and duty. "The whole Law is comprehended in these two commandments, To love God with all your heart, and mind, and soul, and strength, and To love your neighbour as yourselves." This is "the law of charity, which if you fulfil, you will do well." This is the law of Christ, which every follower of Christ is bound to obey. Go then, daily, and sit at the feet of Moses. For your *principles* and *motives* you must go to Christ alone: but for your directory in the path of duty, you must go to the law of Moses, which is a perfect transcript of God's mind and will. Never can I enforce this too strongly, and especially after what I have said of sacrificing all for Christ. The command to honour your father and your mother is "the first commandment with promise:" and this shews how high it stands in the estimation of your God. Let it not be less high in your estimation also: and remember, that, except in those things which are directly contrary to God's revealed will, the commands of earthly superiors should be regarded by you as the commands of God. A sword is indeed put into your hands; but it is for the purpose of slaying, not men, but sin, and Satan, with whom you are to contend, till they are "bruised under your feet." Gird yourselves, therefore, for the occasion; and go through the whole camp of your spiritual enemies, and spare neither small nor great. So shall the blessing of God come upon you, both in time and in eternity.]

OUTLINE NO. 107
MOSES INTERCEDES FOR ISRAEL.

Exod. xxxii. 31—33. *And Moses returned unto the Lord, and said, Oh! this people have sinned a great sin, and have made them gods of gold! Yet now, if thou wilt forgive their sin—; and if not, blot me, I pray thee, out of thy book which thou hast written. And the Lord said unto Moses, Whosoever hath sinned against me, him will I blot out of my book.*

WELL may it be said, "Lord, what is man?" Truly "his goodness is as a morning cloud, and as the early dew that passeth away." If we did not see it verified in fact, one would scarcely conceive it possible that man should be so frail and mutable as both history and experience attest him to be. The Israelites were now at the very mount where they had beheld Jehovah shining forth in all his terrific majesty, and had heard him proclaiming in most tremendous sounds his holy law. They beheld also upon the mount that very same cloud, the symbol of the divine presence, which had led them in their way from the land of Egypt to that place: yet, because Moses, when summoned by God to come up to the mount, abode there longer than they expected, they cast off him, and God also; and desired visible gods to be made for them, that they might in future commit themselves to *their* guidance and protection. It is this, which Moses so pathetically laments in the words before us.

The whole history is very instructive. That we may have a concise, but comprehensive, view of it, let us notice,

I. The sin of Israel—

This was a dreadful compound of ingratitude, folly, and impiety—

[The people had already forgotten the numberless mercies which they had received from God, through the ministration of his servant Moses: they thought that they themselves could form an image which should supply the place of all other benefactors, human and divine: and in direct opposition to the most express commands[a], to which they had so recently promised the most faithful adherence, they made a golden calf, and appointed it as the representative of the Deity, and offered sacrifices to it as their deliverer and their guide: yea, so bent were they upon having a *visible* god to go before them, that they at the very first proposal gave up their ornaments, in order that of them an image might be formed, which they might worship after the manner of Egypt. But most of all are we surprised, that Aaron, the divinely appointed colleague of Moses, should, at the first mention of such a device, assent to it, and be the very person to form the image, and to proclaim a feast unto Jehovah in honour of it: and that, when reproved for his wickedness, he should attempt to justify it by such

[a] Exod. xx. 4, 23.

frivolous and even false excuses[b]. Well might Moses lament before God, "Oh! this people have sinned a great sin!"]

But the greatness of the sin will be more easily imagined from the indignation which both God and Moses expressed against it—

[The wrath of God, we are told, was "fierce, and waxed hot" against the offending people; and he threatened instantly to destroy them. The anger of Moses also "waxed hot" as soon as ever he beheld their impiety: and the indignation he manifested clearly shewed his opinion at least of their conduct.

First, having in his hands *the tables of stone*, whereon God had with his own finger written the precepts of his law, *he dashed them in pieces before their eyes*. This was no rash expression of intemperate wrath, but a holy and significant emblem, representing to them the crime they had committed. God had condescended to enter into covenant with them to be their God; and they had covenanted to be his people: and these tables of stone contained, as it were, the terms of the agreement; and were a pledge, that God would fulfil to them all that he had spoken. But this covenant they had entirely annulled; and all their expectations from God were utterly destroyed.

Next, *he reduced the idol to dust, and cast it on the water, that all the people might be compelled to drink of it*. This was well calculated to shew them how much they had debased themselves, in submitting to worship that as a god, which they must swallow with their food, and cast off together with it.

But lastly, he made them feel, as well as see, the marks of his displeasure. *He called the Levites*, who notwithstanding the defection of Aaron had remained faithful to their God, *and commanded them to* go through the camp, and without favour or pity to *slay all the ringleaders with the sword*. Thus were three thousand of them punished on the spot: there needed no formality of trial: they were caught in the fact; and the judgment of zeal was deservedly executed upon them.]

That no part of Moses' anger was of a sinful kind, or expressed with undue severity, is evident from his tender compassion for the offenders, whilst he hated and abhorred their offence. To elucidate this, we notice,

II. The intercession of Moses—

No sooner did he see how God was displeased with them, than, notwithstanding the prohibition given him, he began to intercede for them—

---

[b] ver. 24.

[The prohibition, "Let me alone," operated on his mind rather as an encouragement to intercede; because it seemed to say, If you intercede for them, my hands are tied; and I cannot execute upon them my threatened vengeance. He fell down instantly before God, and urged in their behalf every plea which was suited to the occasion.

He reminded God *of his relation to them*. Though God had appeared to disclaim them in that he had called them Moses' people, Moses pleaded, that God himself had brought them out of Egypt, and had signally marked them as his peculiar people. He reminded God also of *his promise to their fathers*, which, if they were utterly destroyed, would be violated. As for having another nation raised up from his loins, he did not desire that honour: all he wanted was, to avert from this offending people the judgments they had merited. He further expressed his concern to God respecting *his honour among the heathen*. Lord, what will the Egyptians say? What opinion will they form of thee? Will they not represent thee either as weak, and incapable of carrying this people to the promised land; or as cruel, and bringing them out hither on purpose to slay them? Lord, if thou regardest not *them*, have regard for thine own honour, and spare the people for thy great name's sake.]

After reproving their iniquity, he returned again unto the Lord, to renew, more fervently than ever, his intercession for them—

[*He confesses humbly the greatness of their sin;* well knowing, that for the obtaining of mercy, nothing is so efficacious as humiliation before God. *He then implores pardon for them*, if pardon can be extended to so rebellious a people. But, if some atonement must be made, and if some signal mark of his displeasure must be given, then he entreats that the judgment may fall on *him*, and not on them. *He desires* to be excluded from Canaan, and, as far as relates to this life, *to be blotted out of the list of God's peculiar people, in their stead:* that so the enormity of their sin, and God's abhorrence of it, might be made manifest, and yet the transgressors themselves be living monuments of God's mercy [c].

What a bright pattern is here of zeal for God, and compassion for men! And how desirable is such an union of them, as will keep us from palliating sin on the one hand, or hating and despising the sinner on the other.]

How far this intercession prevailed will be found in,
III. The reply of God—

[c] It were absurd to think that he proposed to subject himself to *eternal* misery for them: for this would be more than even Christ himself has done for us.

God condescended to remit the punishment of their iniquity—

[At the very first intercession of Moses, God repented of the evil which he had thought to do unto his people[d]; and, in answer to the last, he renewed his commission to Moses to lead them to the promised land: and, though he withdrew himself from them in a measure, he commanded a created angel to guide them in the way[e]. He declared indeed, that, if by a continuance of their rebellions they compelled him to punish them, he would then visit for this sin together with the rest; but, if they were truly penitent, and observant of his will in future, he would remember it against them no more.

What an amazing view does this give us of the condescension of God, and the efficacy of fervent prayer! The prayer of one single person availed for the procuring of pardon for two millions of people, and for Aaron at their head, notwithstanding the peculiar enormity of his sin[f]: yea, it prevailed at a time when God was so incensed against them as to forbid any intercession in their behalf, and to declare that he would "blot out their name from under heaven." Surely the remembrance of this single instance is sufficient to encourage all the world to implore mercy for themselves, and to make continual intercession also for others.]

He declared, however, that at his future tribunal justice should be strictly administered to all—

[Rewards and punishments are often national in this world, and consequently partial: sometimes the innocent are involved in the punishment of the guilty; and sometimes the guilty escape without any punishment at all. But at God's tribunal in the last day no such inequalities will be found: there every one will answer for his own personal transgressions, and stand or fall according to his own personal conduct: "The wicked will go into everlasting punishment; but the righteous into life eternal." Multitudes in that day will be found, who, in name and profession, were the Lord's people: but, inasmuch as they "had only a name to live, and were really dead," God will blot them out of his book, and disclaim all relation to them or regard for them. Solemn indeed, and most worthy to be impressed upon our minds, is this declaration of God: it relates, not to that people only, but to all that dwell upon the face of the whole earth. Intercession may prevail in this world for the averting of temporal judgments even from the impenitent: but, in reference to the eternal world, nothing will prevail but

---

[d] ver. 14. [e] Compare ver. 34. with ch. xxxiii. 2, 3.
[f] Deut. ix. 20. Read that whole chapter.

personal repentance, and humble affiance in the Lord Jesus Christ.]

From this subject we may LEARN,

1. What an evil and bitter thing sin is—

[The Israelites might have excused themselves by saying, as the Papists do respecting their images, that they did not intend to make a god of the golden calf, but only to use it as the means of bringing the true God more forcibly to their minds. But what would such sophistry have availed them? Would either God or Moses have altered their estimate of the crime, because *they* chose to veil it under specious names[g]? And to what purpose is it for us to extenuate our crimes? We have soft imposing names whereby to conceal the evil of covetousness and sensuality; but does not God declare both the one and the other to be idolatry[h]? Does he not speak of men having "idols in their heart[i]?" and is not this the essence of all idolatry, to "love and serve the creature more than the Creator, who is blessed for evermore?" We may attempt also to extenuate our guilt, as Aaron did, from our acting under the influence of others, and not *designing* to do exactly all that we did: but this could not deceive Moses; much less can it deceive God. Moreover, both the people and Aaron might even think that they were honouring Jehovah; for they kept the feast professedly unto *him:* and when they had eaten and drunk of their sacrifices, they might think it well became them to indulge in mirth. We too may keep our feasts, and fasts, and Sabbaths, professedly to the Lord; and may conclude we have ground for cheerful security: but God may, all the while, be as wroth with us, as he was with them, and may have determined to blot out our unworthy names from the book of life. O that we would duly reflect on these things! O that we would consider that sin, however extenuated by us, is hateful to God; that he sees it wherever it is transacted, and under whatever veil it may be concealed; and that, finally, the time is quickly coming, when he will execute judgment upon all according to their works! Then will sin appear in its real colours; not in the temporal destruction of a single nation, but in the everlasting destruction of all, who have died in impenitence and unbelief.]

2. How much we are indebted to the Lord Jesus Christ—

[The intercession of Moses for the Jewish nation was typical of the yet more effectual intercession of our great Advocate, the Lord Jesus Christ. We may in a measure picture

---

[g] It is expressly called idolatry, 1 Cor. x. 7.
[h] Eph. v. 5. Phil. iii. 19.   [i] Ezek. xiv. 3, 4, 7.

to ourselves the benevolent exercise of Moses, whilst the thoughtless Israelites were revelling in security. In *that* then let us view what has been taking place in heaven on our behalf. We have been sinning against God, a stiff-necked and rebellious generation: and many times has the decree gone forth, " Cut them down; why cumber they the ground?" But the Lord Jesus, presenting that most efficacious of all pleas, his own atoning blood, has said, " Spare them, O my Father! spare them yet another year." Yes; had it not been for his intercession, we should not have been now in this place, but in that place of torment from whence there is no return. O that we might learn to estimate our obligations to him! O that we might go to him ourselves, and entreat him to obtain for us converting grace, and everlasting glory! Were but our eyes duly turned to him, our expectations could not be too large, or our confidence too strong.

But we must remember that nothing can supersede our own repentance: not even the blood and intercession of Christ will avail for those who die impenitent. The declaration of God shall never be reversed, " Whosoever hath sinned against me, him will I (if he die impenitent) blot out of my book." There are two fatal errors which pervade the great mass of nominal Christians: the one is, that they shall be saved by their repentance, though they trust not in Christ; and the other is, that they shall be saved by Christ, though they do not personally repent. But neither of these things can ever take place. The impenitent may be spared for a time; but they shall perish for ever: but the penitent, who believe in Christ, " shall never come into condemnation, but shall have everlasting life."]

OUTLINE NO. 108

REPENTANCE OF THE ISRAELITES.

Exod. xxxiii. 5, 6. *Therefore now put off thy ornaments from thee, that I may know what to do unto thee. And the children of Israel stripped themselves of their ornaments, by the Mount Horeb.*

THAT which is principally required of Ministers, is fidelity[a], to dispense the word of God aright, without courting the applause of men, or fearing their displeasure. Of hearers it is required, that they receive the word of God with all readiness of mind, and obey it without reserve. Where such Ministers and such people are, happy will they be in each other, and happy also in their God. Of the descrip-

[a] 1 Cor. iv. 1, 2.

tion we have mentioned was Moses; but not so the people of Israel: they were stiff-necked and rebellious throughout the whole course of his ministry among them. On some few occasions, however, they seemed to be of a better mind; particularly on the occasion now before us. Moses had declared to them a message from God; in which their true character was drawn, and his judgments against them were awfully denounced[b]: and the effect, for the present at least, was such as was reasonably to be expected: they trembled at the divine judgments, and humbled themselves instantly in the mode prescribed. This is declared in the text; for the elucidating of which we observe,

I. God is not able to exercise mercy towards an impenitent transgressor—

God certainly is "rich in mercy," and delights in the exercise of it; and would gladly manifest it towards all the human race[c]. But impenitence presents an insurmountable obstacle in his way, so that he cannot shew mercy towards any who abide in it. He cannot,

1. Because it would be inconsistent with his own perfections—

[He is a God of inflexible justice, unspotted holiness, and inviolable truth. But what evidence would there be that any one of these perfections belonged to him, if he, in direct opposition to his own most positive declarations, put no difference between the proud contemner of his authority, and the humble repenting suppliant? — — —]

2. Because it would be ineffectual for the happiness of the persons themselves—

[Annihilation indeed would be a benefit, if that were granted to them; because they would then be rescued from the sufferings that await them: but to raise them to heaven would be no source of happiness to them. Having still a carnal mind which is enmity against God, they must hate him though in heaven: either God, or they, must change, before they can have fellowship with each other. As little comfort could they find in the society or employment of the heavenly hosts. The

---

[b] See the former part of ver. 5. [c] 1 Tim. ii. 4. Ezek. xxxiii. 11.

glorified saints and angels could not unite with those who had no one sentiment or feeling in unison with their own[d]: nor would they who hate the exercises of prayer and praise in this world, find any satisfaction in such exercises in the world above. I say therefore again, that to an impenitent sinner heaven would be no heaven: for while sin reigns within him, he has a hell in his own bosom, and carries it with him wheresoever he goes.]

3. It would introduce disorder into the whole universe—

[What sensations must it occasion *in heaven!* for if God can so change his very nature as to love an unholy creature, who can tell but that he may go one step further, and hate an holy one? As for the effect of it *on earth*, no one from that moment would either hate or fear sin: not hate it, because they would see that God does not hate it; and not fear it, because they would see that he will not punish it. Even *in hell* the effect of it would be felt: for, if God takes an impenitent *man* to his bosom, why may he not an impenitent *spirit* also; and what hinders but that the fallen angels may yet become as happy as those who never fell? Could such a thought as this be cherished in that place of torment, hell would from that moment cease to be the place it is.]

Here then is ample reason why God, notwithstanding his delight in mercy, cannot find how to exercise it towards impenitent sinners. But,

II. Where humiliation is manifested, mercy may be expected—

This appears,

1. From the very mode in which repentance is here enjoined—

[When we speak of God as embarrassed in his mind, or perplexed in his counsels, we must not be understood to intimate that such things *actually* exist: for "known unto God are all his works from the beginning of the world:" nor can any occasion possibly arise, wherein he can be at a loss how to act. But he is pleased to speak in this kind of language respecting himself, in order to accommodate himself to our feeble apprehensions: "Put off thy ornaments, *that I may know* what to do unto thee." Thus in various other places he speaks as perplexed in his mind about the line of conduct he shall pursue[e], and as wishing to shew mercy, but not knowing

---

[d] They would be ready to "*thrust him out*" of their society. Luke xiii. 28.   [e] Hos. vi. 4.

how to do it consistently with his own honour[f]. Let us not then be misunderstood, as though, in accommodating ourselves to the language of our text, we deviated at all from that reverence which is due to the Supreme Being.
It is here intimated then, that, whilst impenitence continues, *he knows not how* to exercise mercy to the sinner: but it is also intimated, that, when once persons are humbled for their wickedness, he is at no loss at all how to act towards them: he can then give full scope to the merciful disposition of his own heart, and can pour out all his benefits upon them without any dishonour to his own name. Yes; that point attained, the law is honoured by the sinner himself; the atoning blood of Christ may be applied freely to cleanse him from his guilt; the mercy vouchsafed to him will not be abused; the heavenly hosts will be made to shout for joy; and God himself will be glorified to all eternity. There is no obstacle whatever to the freest and fullest exercise of love towards such a Being; and therefore God knows both what to do, and how to do it to the best effect.]

2. From the experience of penitents in all ages—

[Look at *those in our text:* God had threatened that he would go with them no more, but commit them to the guidance of a created angel. This had produced upon them a very deep impression: the fear of being deserted by him had wrought more powerfully upon them than the slaughter of three thousand of their number on the day before[g]. They humbled themselves in the way that God had commanded; and, behold! the mercy, so ardently desired by them, and by Moses, was granted: " My presence shall go with thee, and I will give thee rest[h]."
Look at *all other penitents* from the foundation of the world: was ever so much as one spurned from the footstool of divine grace? Was ever one sent empty away? Even where the repentance was far from genuine, considerable respect was paid to it, and the blessing sought for was bestowed[i]. How much more where the repentance itself has been deep, and the contrition manifest! Not even the greatest accumulation of guilt that ever was known, was suffered to outweigh the tears of penitence, or to shut up the tender mercies of our God from a contrite soul[k]. The Saviour was sent into the world for the very purpose of saving them that are lost; and he assures " all who are weary and heavy laden with a sense of their sins, that, on coming to him, they shall find rest unto their souls."]

APPLICATION—

[f] Jer. iii. 19.   [g] ver. 1—4.   [h] ver. 14.   [i] 1 Kings xxi. 27—29.
[k] 2 Kings xxi. 16. with 2 Chron. xxxiii. 1—13.

1. Consider what obstructions you have laid in the way of your own happiness—

[Had you not sinned, or, after your sins, continued impenitent, you would have been happy long since in the enjoyment of your God. He has been long "waiting to be gracious" unto you, but you would not suffer him to be so. He has been longing "to gather you, even as a hen gathereth her chickens under her wings, but you would not." Say then, what alternative is left to God? He has called, but you have refused: he still calls, and you still continue to reject his counsels. Truly, "he knows not what to do:" if he spare you, you only add sin to sin; and if he cut you off, you perish without the smallest hope of mercy. Who can tell but that he is deliberating at this moment, and just about to form his ultimate decision? Who can tell but that this very night he may determine, as he did respecting his people of old; "Go to, I will tell you what I will do to my vineyard: I will take away the hedge thereof, and it shall be eaten up; I will tread down the wall thereof, and it shall be trodden down[1]:" or, as he elsewhere says, "I swear in my wrath that they shall never enter into my rest?" Know, beloved, that if this calamity fall upon you, the fault is utterly your own: nothing but "iniquity can separate between you and your God; nothing but sin unrepented of can hide his face from you[m]."]

2. Endeavour instantly to remove them—

[Methinks I see your impenitence, like a dam, barring out from you those streams of mercy, which would refresh and fertilize your souls. O remove it without delay! But take care that your repentance is genuine and unreserved. External and temporary repentance will avail only for the removal of temporal judgments. That which is required in order to the final remission of your sins, must be deep, spiritual, and abiding: it must shew itself in the whole of your conduct and conversation. You will put away those pleasures, those vanities, those companions, that have been to you an occasion of falling; and you will "walk mournfully before the Lord of Hosts" to the latest hour of your lives: "you will lothe yourselves for all your iniquities and abominations," as well after that God is pacified towards you, as before[n]. Let this then be begun *immediately*, even as "the Israelites put off their ornaments *on the very mount of Horeb.*" Let there be no delays; no waiting for a more convenient season. And let not the loss of heaven be the only object of your fear: fear also *the loss of the divine presence. This*, as you have seen, was peculiarly dreaded by the

---

[1] Isai. v. 5.   [m] Isai. lix. 2.   [n] Ezek. xxxvi. 31. with xvi. 63.

Israelites: let it also be peculiarly dreaded by you: and never cease to humble yourselves before God, till you have attained a sweet assurance of his guidance through this wilderness, and of his blessing in Canaan at the termination of your way.]

OUTLINE NO. 109
PAST MERCIES PLEADED BEFORE GOD.

Exod. xxxiii. 12, 13. *Thou hast said, I know thee by name, and thou hast also found grace in my sight. Now therefore, I pray thee, if I have found grace in thy sight, shew me now thy way that I may know thee, that I may find grace in thy sight.*

NOTHING is more profitable than to be brought, as it were, into the secret chamber of the saint, and to be a witness of his intercourse with God. His humble confidence, his holy boldness, his fervent supplications, his almost irresistible pleadings, give us a juster view of man's *present* salvation, than any declarations, however strong, could convey. The blessedness of true religion is there embodied, and is therefore seen in all its fair proportions and magnificent dimensions.

The prayer which we have just heard, was uttered on occasion of the transgression of Israel in the matter of the golden calf. God had threatened to destroy the whole nation: but, at the intercession of Moses, he so far forgave them, as to suspend his judgments, and to promise, that though HE would conduct them no longer by his *immediate* presence, he would send an angel with them, who should lead them to the promised land. This, however, Moses could not endure: if God should not go with them, he judged it undesirable to be guided thither at all: and therefore he renewed his pleadings with God in their behalf, hoping to prevail to the full extent of his wishes. God had offered to destroy that whole nation, and to raise up another from the loins of Moses: and this token of God's good-will towards him he laid hold of as a ground of hope, and urged it as a plea with God to grant him his full desire: "Thou hast said, I know thee by name, and thou hast found grace in my sight. Now therefore, I pray thee, if I have found grace in thy sight, shew me now thy way that I may know thee, that I may find grace in thy sight."

Let us notice here,

I. The fact pleaded—

God had given him the assurances here spoken of—

[We are not told exactly either when, or how, God had declared to him these glad tidings. It is probable, however, that it was by an audible voice during their late extraordinary intercourse, wherein, we are told, "The Lord spake unto Moses face to face, as a man speaketh unto his friend[a]." The import of the declaration, however, is clear. It could not mean that God merely knew the name of Moses; for he knew the name of every human being as well as his: it means, that from all eternity he had ordained Moses to his high station, and had appointed him to be a vessel of honour, in whom he would be glorified. I say not, but that the conduct of Moses, as contrasted with that of Aaron and the people of Israel, might bring down upon him more special tokens of God's favour: for I can have no doubt but that God, who rewardeth every man according to his works, did confer upon him many blessings as the reward of his piety, according to that established rule of his, "Them that honour me, I will honour:" but the primary source of all his blessedness was God's electing love and sovereign grace; though the manifestations of that love, by an immediate assurance from heaven, might be given him as a recompence for his fidelity.]

And are not similar assurances vouchsafed to God's faithful people at this day?

[If we examine the Holy Scriptures, we shall find, that neither electing love, nor the manifestation of it to the soul, are confined to Moses. To Jeremiah this declaration was vouchsafed: "Before I formed thee in the belly, *I knew thee;* and before thou camest forth out of the womb, I sanctified thee, and I ordained thee a prophet unto the nation[b]." Here the very same expression, "I knew thee," is explained as equivalent to a fore-ordination of him to the prophetic office. And the same sovereign grace is exercised towards men in reference also to their everlasting concerns; as it is said, "Whom God did foreknow, he also did predestinate to be conformed to the image of his Son[c]." Nor must we understand this foreknowledge as forming *the ground* of God's future mercies to the persons foreknown, but rather as constituting *the source* from

---

[a] ver. 11.   [b] Jer. i. 5.   [c] Rom. viii. 29.

whence those blessings flow: as the Apostle says, "God has chosen us in Christ before the foundation of the world, that we should be holy (not because he foresaw that we should be holy, but in order that we might be holy) and without blame before him in love[d]." And it is on this electing love of his, and not on any merits or strength of ours, that our security, in reality, depends: for it is said, "The foundation of God standeth sure, having this seal, The Lord knoweth them that are his[e]."

But does God manifest this his electing love to any now, as he did to Moses? Yes: not indeed by an audible voice, but by other means sufficiently intelligible both to themselves and others. What else is meant by the Witness of the Spirit? for, now, as well as in former days, "The Spirit itself beareth witness with our spirit, that we are the children of God[f]." Nor is it in that way only that he makes known our relation to him, but by a work of grace upon our souls: for it was from the "work of faith, and labour of love, and patience of hope in the Lord Jesus Christ," which St. Paul saw in his Thessalonian converts, that he "*knew their election of God*[g]."

The fact, then, which Moses pleaded with God is no other than what all his saints are at liberty to plead: for as it is true, that "he knows them by name, and that they have found grace in his sight," so is it true, also, that he has, more or less evidently, declared it to them all; not indeed to any by an audible voice; but to some by the secret influences of his Spirit, and to all by the visible operations of his grace.]

The next point for our consideration is,

II. The petition urged—

It is thought by many, that an assurance of our acceptance with God would render us careless and supine: but—

The very reverse was its effect on Moses—

[The mercies vouchsafed to him, only stimulated him to a more earnest desire after further blessings. He does not say, "If I have found grace in thy sight, I am content: but, if I have found grace in thy sight, shew me thy way, that I may know thee, and that I may find further grace in thy sight."]

And such will be its effect on all God's chosen people—

[Blessings will be regarded by them, not as gifts wherein to rest, but as pledges and earnests of future blessings. It was a wise and truly spiritual argument which was offered by

---

[d] Eph. i. 4.   [e] 2 Tim. ii. 19.   [f] Rom. viii. 16.   [g] 1 Thess. i. 3, 4.

Manoah's wife for the pacifying of her husband's mind: "If the Lord were pleased to kill us, he would not have received a burnt-offering or a meat-offering at our hands, neither would he have shewed us all these things, nor would, as at this time, have told us such things as these[h]." Past mercies are rather urged by them in prayer as *pleas* for further blessings. It was thus that David regarded them: "Thou hast delivered my soul from death: wilt not thou deliver my feet from falling, that I may walk before God in the light of the living[i]?" And in this way will God's special favour operate on every ingenuous mind. Instead of being satisfied with a taste of his love, we shall hunger and thirst after the full banquet; and never cease from aspiring after a further growth in grace, till we have attained the full measure of the stature of Christ, and our graces are perfected in glory.

Nor shall we be anxious about our own advancement only: we shall feel for God's honour also; and for the welfare of those around us. This appears, in a striking point of view, in the conduct of Moses on this occasion: for, not content with finding grace himself, he adds, "And consider that this nation is thy people;" in which words he combines a tender regard for God's honour with an anxiety for his people's welfare. His further pleading also deserves attention: "Wherein shall it be known here, that I and thy people have found grace in thy sight? Is it not in that thou goest with us[k]?" Now this shews us the true effect which a sense of God's love will produce: it will make us not only anxious to obtain richer communications of grace and peace to our own souls, but more earnest also to promote to the utmost of our power the good of all around us.]

The answer given to this petition leads us to notice,

III. The plea admitted—

God, in his mercy, vouchsafed to Moses an answer of peace—

[The plea peculiarly honoured God, in that, whilst it acknowledged his sovereign grace in the blessings already bestowed, it regarded him as a God of unbounded goodness, able and willing to fulfil all his petitions. And God's answer to it shewed how greatly it was approved by him: "The Lord said unto Moses, I will do this thing also that thou hast spoken, for thou hast found grace in my sight, and I know thee by name[l]." Here, I say, God not only grants the petition, but specifically founds the grant upon the very plea that had been urged.]

[h] Judg. xiii. 23.
[k] ver. 16. with ch. xxxiv. 9.
[i] Ps. lvi. 13.
[l] ver. 17.

And when did he ever refuse to hear a petition so enforced?

[God loves to be addressed with confidence, provided the confidence be grounded on his power and grace. He bids us to come to him " with a full assurance of faith;" to " ask what we will:" and he gives us reason to hope, that, if we come in faith, he will " do for us not only what we ask, but exceeding abundantly above all that we can ask or think." It might be feared, that the importunity of Moses would offend him. But it did not: nor was he angry with Jacob, who " wrestled with him in prayer all night," and boldly said, " I will not let thee go until thou bless me." On the contrary, he commands us to wait on him with unwearied importunity, and to " continue instant in prayer," till he bestow upon us all that our hearts can wish. " The wider we open our mouths in prayer, the more he will fill them."]

To IMPROVE this subject, I would say,

1. Bear in mind the tokens of God's love—

[Look at what he " has said to you" in his word: take his " exceeding great and precious promises," and tell me whether you can ever want a plea to urge at the throne of grace. You admire his condescension and grace to Moses: but it is no other than what he will manifest to you, if, like Moses, you consecrate yourselves to his service. You cannot, indeed, expect to converse with God face to face, as a man converseth with his friend: but by faith you may approach him no less certainly, and no less nearly; and may be sure of obtaining from him an answer of peace. Only take with you his words of promise, and spread them before him; and every jot and tittle of them shall be fulfilled to your souls.]

2. Let the effect of his distinguishing grace be to make you more earnest in your desires after him—

[When David said, " O God, thou art my God," he added, " early will I seek thee." In truth, this is our great encouragement to seek him: for, if he " loved us with an everlasting love," what may we not expect his loving-kindness to do for us? If once you could bring yourselves to say, ' I am one of God's elect, and therefore am at liberty to relax my efforts in his service;' you would need no further evidence, that you are " yet in the gall of bitterness," and have no part or lot in his salvation. If you have a good hope that you are his children indeed, then will you " walk worthy of your high calling," and " purify yourselves even as he is pure."]

3. Improve your interest in God for the good of others—

[In this Moses greatly excelled: he was willing and desirous even to "be blotted out of God's book" himself, if that, by means of it, he might obtain mercy for his offending nation. See to it, Brethren, that your religion operate thus on you. Behold the state of those around you; how many thousands there are dying in their sins! And will you not interest yourselves in their behalf, and labour to obtain for them the mercy that has been vouchsafed to you? Will you suffer your very friends and relatives to perish, without any serious effort in their behalf? Oh! pity them, and pray for them; and "give unto God no rest," till you have obtained some evidence that you have not laboured altogether in vain.]

OUTLINE NO. 110
GOD'S PRESENCE WITH HIS CHURCH.

Exod. xxxiii. 14. *And he said, My presence shall go with thee, and I will give thee rest.*

IT is not in the power of words to express, or of any finite imagination to conceive, the extent and riches of divine grace. The instances in which it was manifested to the Israelites of old, inasmuch as they were obvious to the eye of sense, are more calculated to excite our admiration; but the church at this time, and every believer in it, experiences equal tokens of God's kindness, if we can but view them with the eye of faith. It was under circumstances, wherein the Israelites had justly incurred God's heavy displeasure, that the promise in the text was made to them: and to *us*, if we do but use the proper means of attaining an interest in it, is the same promise given, notwithstanding our heinous backslidings, and innumerable provocations.

That we may be stirred up to improve it, we shall point out,

I. The blessings here promised—

Though the promise was given immediately to Moses, yet it was not *literally* fulfilled either to him or to the people of that generation; since both he, and they, died in the wilderness. This circumstance alone would lead us to look for some mystical accomplishment, which it should receive; and while the

Scripture warrants, it will also fully satisfy, our inquiries on this head. The promise has relation to us, as well as to the Israelites; and teaches us to expect,

1. God's presence in our way—

[God had refused to proceed any further with the Israelites, on account of their worshipping the golden calf. In answer however to the supplications of Moses, he had condescended to say, that he would "send an angel" in his stead. But when Moses would not be satisfied with that, and continued to plead for a complete restoration of his favour to Israel, God, overcome, as it were, by his importunity, promised to go before them still in the pillar and the cloud[a]. More than this they did not need; and less than this could never satisfy one, who had ever experienced the divine guidance and protection. And has not our blessed Lord made the same promise to *us?* Has he not said, "Lo, I am with you alway, even to the end of the world[b]?" Has not his prophet assigned this as a reason why we should dissipate our fears, and look forward to the eternal world with confidence and joy[c]? On this promise then let us rely; and let us know, that if we have God for our guide, our protector, and provider, we have all that can be necessary for us in this dreary wilderness.]

2. His glory as our end—

[Canaan was a place of rest to the Israelites after the many difficulties that they sustained in their way to it: and heaven will be indeed a glorious rest to us after our weary pilgrimage in this world. Now as the prospect of the land flowing with milk and honey, sweetened all the fatigues and dangers of their journey in the wilderness, so the hope of "that rest which remaineth for God's children," encourages us to persevere in our labours to attain it: and this rest is promised us, in spite of all the exertions of men or devils to deprive us of it. Our conflicts may be many, and our trials great; but our rest is sure; for God hath said, "I will never leave thee, nor forsake thee[d]".]

These blessings being so necessary, we should anxiously inquire into,

II. The means of attaining them—

Moses is here to be considered in a double view, as a type of Christ, and as an example to us: and, in these two capacities, he teaches us to look for these blessings,

1. Through the intercession of Christ—

---

[a] Exod. xxxii. 34. with the text. [b] Matt. xxviii. 20.
[c] Isai. xli. 10.   [d] Compare Josh. i. 5. with Heb. xiii. 5, 6.

[Christ, like Moses, has immediate access to that Divine Being who is wholly inaccessible to us[e]; and it is owing to his entrance *within the tabernacle* to "appear in the presence of God for us," that the wrath of the Almighty has not burst forth upon us on numberless occasions, and consumed us utterly[f]. It is not only at our first return to God that we must seek the mediation of Jesus Christ; we must apply to him continually as our advocate with the Father, expecting nothing but through his prevailing intercession. This is the way pointed out for us by the beloved disciple, especially in seasons, when fresh-contracted guilt has excited just apprehensions of the divine displeasure; "If any man sin, we have an advocate with the Father, Jesus Christ the righteous[g]." Whether therefore we desire grace or glory, let us seek it through Christ, as the purchase of his blood, and the consequence of his intercession.]

2. Through our own importunate supplications—

[While the Israelites put off their ornaments in token of their unfeigned humiliation, Moses, as their representative, importuned God for mercy, and urged his requests with the most forcible and appropriate pleas[h]. In this manner should we also cry unto our God for pardon and acceptance, not enduring the thought of being left by him, lest we come short of that rest to which he has undertaken to lead us[i]. Nor should we cease to plead, till we have an assured hope that he is reconciled towards us, and a renewed prospect of his continued presence with us to the end of life. It is in this way that his people have prevailed with him in every age[k]; and he has pledged himself to *us*, that, when our uncircumcised hearts are humbled, he will remember his holy covenant, and return in mercy to us[l].]

INFER,

1. How greatly are we indebted to Jesus Christ!

[Where shall we find one who has not made to himself some idol, and "provoked the Lord to jealousy?" And how justly might God have sworn in his wrath that we should not enter into his rest! But our adorable Saviour has sprinkled the mercy-seat with his precious blood, and offered up the incense of his own prevailing intercession on our behalf. Surely he is well called "*Our peace*[m]," since he alone procures it, maintains it, perfects it. Let us bear in mind then our obligations to him, and ascribe to him the glory due unto his name.]

2. How earnest ought we to be in intercession for each other!

[e] 1 Tim. vi. 16.   [f] Heb. ix. 24.   [g] 1 John ii. 1.
[h] ver. 12, 13.   [i] Heb. iv. 1.   [k] Dan. ix. 7, 8, 17, 18, 19.
[l] Lev. xxvi. 40—42.   [m] Eph. ii. 14.

[In the history before us we behold one man interceding for a whole nation, and *that* too under circumstances where there could be scarcely any hope to prevail: yet he not only obtains a revocation of the sentence which God had passed, but a renewal and continuance of his wonted favours towards them. Shall we then neglect the duty of intercession, or intercede for each other merely in a formal way, as though we expected no answer to our petitions? Let us not so greatly dishonour God, and so wickedly slight our own privileges[n]. We are expressly commanded to pray one for another, yea, and to make intercessions for all men[o]: let us not doubt therefore but that, by pleading earnestly with God, we may obtain blessings for our friends, for our country, and for all whose cause we plead. "The effectual fervent prayer of a righteous man availeth much."]

3. How happy are they who are enabled to live upon the promises!

[Were we to consider the length and difficulty of our way, the enemies we have to encounter, and our utter insufficiency for any thing that is good, we should utterly despair of ever reaching the heavenly Canaan. But God promises to us his presence in the way, and his rest at the end of our journey; and "he who has promised is able also to perform." Let our trust then be in him, "with whom is no variableness, neither shadow of turning." Let us "cast our care on him who careth for us." Let our discouragements, yea, our very iniquities, bring us nearer to him, and cause us to rely more simply on his word. Thus shall we experience his faithfulness and truth, and be monuments of his unbounded mercy to all eternity.]

[n] 1 Sam. xii. 23.   [o] Jam. v. 16.

OUTLINE NO. 111
GOD'S GOODNESS HIS GLORY.

Exod. xxxiii. 18, 19. *And he said, I beseech thee, shew me thy glory. And he said, I will make all my goodness pass before thee.*

NO man can have ever contemplated the intercession of Abraham in behalf of Sodom and Gomorrha, without being astonished at the condescension of God, who would permit a worm of the earth so to encroach upon his goodness, and so to make every fresh concession a foundation for yet further petitions. Somewhat of the same kind we behold in Moses when interceding for Israel, when God had threatened to destroy them for worshipping the golden calf. He had, by his importunity, prevailed on God to promise that he would suspend the execution of his judgments on them; and that, though he could no longer vouchsafe to conduct them himself, he would send an angel, who should lead them in safety to the promised land. Having succeeded so far, he prosecuted his work of intercession, till he had prevailed on God yet further to bear with them, and to continue to them his presence and guidance as he had hitherto done. And now, having found Jehovah so infinitely condescending to him when importuned for others, he determined to urge a petition for himself; a petition, which, under any other circumstances, he could never have dared to ask: and it was no less than this, "I beseech thee, shew me thy glory."

His success in this petition will form *the first part* of our present subject: and some reflections arising out of that success will *close* it. Let us notice,

I. His success in this petition—

The petition itself must be first explained—

Respecting its import, commentators have differed: some having imagined that it proceeded from weakness and infirmity, as if he had needed further evidence of God's presence and favour. But a due attention to God's reply will remove all doubt respecting the precise meaning of his servant's request. Moses had enjoyed many visible tokens of God's presence: in the burning bush; in the bright cloud which conducted Israel out of Egypt; on the burning mount, where he had been admitted into the immediate presence of the Deity; and at the door of the tabernacle of the congregation, whither God had descended on purpose to honour him in the sight of all Israel, and "spoken with him face to face, as a man speaketh to his friend[a];" Jehovah had appeared to him. How, then, after so many manifestations of the divine presence, could he say, "Shew me thy glory?" I answer, In all those manifestations he had seen only *a symbol* of the Deity: now therefore he desired a sight of *the Deity himself*. He knew that the Deity was visibly seen in heaven: and he did not know but that he *might* also be visibly seen on earth: and therefore he made *this* the subject of his request.

[a] ver. 9—11.

111.] GOD'S GOODNESS HIS GLORY. 529

God's gracious reply to him shews clearly that *this* was the thing desired: for he said to Moses, "Thou *canst not* see my face: for there shall no man see me, and live [b]." Human nature, in its present shape, is incapable of sustaining so bright a vision; as the unprotected eye is of gazing upon the meridian sun. And therefore, whilst God approved of the petition as proceeding from an ardent desire after a more perfect knowledge of him, he told him that in its full extent it could not be granted; not because of any want of condescension in the Deity to grant it, but for want of a capacity in Moses himself to sustain it.]

The answer of God to it will be now clear—

["I will make all my goodness pass before thee;" so that, though the full effulgence of my glory will be veiled, all that can be endured by thee, and that will profitably correspond with thy petition, shall be granted. In respect of the effulgence of my glory, I will favour thee with such a view of my *back parts* (for *my face* thou *canst not* see) as shall give thee as full a conception of my glory as thou art capable of in thy present state; and, by an audible voice, will make known to thee my perfections, which thou art more concerned to know, and by an acquaintance with which thy soul will be far more enriched, than it could be by any manifestation of my Godhead, however clear or bright! Accordingly, God put him into a clift of a rock, and covered him there with his hand whilst he was passing by; and then withdrew his hand, that he might have such a distant and mitigated view of his back parts, as might be seen without the utter destruction of the beholder [c].

This vision God accompanied with a distinct and audible annunciation of his own attributes, as a God of infinite majesty, of almighty power, of unbounded mercy, and of immaculate and inexorable justice; all of which perfections were illustrative of his goodness [d]. Here it is of importance to observe, that God's justice, no less than his mercy, is an essential part of his goodness. As in human governments the exercise of justice, however painful to those who by their violations of the law have incurred a sentence of condemnation, is beneficial to the whole community; so is it in the divine government, which, if it allowed impunity to transgressors, would be disparaged and dishonoured.

The particular perfection of *sovereignty* is supposed by many to be in direct opposition to the attribute of *goodness;* and is therefore denied by them as having any existence, or at least any exercise, in the divine government. But, the very moment that God says to Moses, "I will make all *my goodness* pass

[b] ver. 20.   [c] ver. 20—23.   [d] Exod. xxxiv. 5--7.

before thee," he adds, "and I will proclaim the name of the Lord before thee, and *I will be gracious to whom I will be gracious, and will shew mercy to whom I will shew mercy.* This perfection, therefore, in conjunction with all the rest, must be considered as constituting an essential part of the divine character, and as properly illustrating his "goodness."

And here let me remark, that it is not in any single perfection that God's glory consists, but in the united and harmonious exercise of all. "God is light," we are told[e]. Now light consists of many different rays, some of a more brilliant, and others of a more sombre aspect: and we can no more detach from it those which are of a darker hue, than those which are more bright and vivid. It is in the union and just admixture of all, that light consists. And so it is with respect to the divine glory; to which all God's perfections—the more forbidding or terrific attributes of sovereignty and justice, no less than the more endearing perfections of love and mercy—are necessary. And this view of the divine glory fully answered the wishes of Moses, which a more literal compliance with his petition, even if it could have been endured, would not so well have satisfied.]

A more distinct explanation of the particulars contained in this answer to Moses will more properly arise, whilst we make,

II. Some reflections arising out of his success—

Behold here,

1. The excellence of the Gospel—

[In the Gospel, all that was vouchsafed to Moses is imparted to us with tenfold advantage: because, whilst a fuller insight into the revelation itself is granted to us than was ever vouchsafed to him, we can contemplate it at our leisure, and without any such emotions as would tend to embarrass our minds. Behold then, I say, that Almighty God, "who dwelleth in the light which no man can approach unto, whom no man hath seen or can see[f]," is become visible to us in the person of his Son: as it is said, "No man hath seen God at any time: the only-begotten Son, who is in the bosom of the Father, he hath declared him[g]." The Lord Jesus Christ, "having in himself all the fulness of the Godhead[h]," is, on this very account, called "the image of the invisible God[i];" because Jehovah, who in his own essence is invisible to mortal eyes, is become visible to us in the person of his Son, who is "the brightness of his Father's glory, and the express image

[e] 1 John i. 5.   [f] 1 Tim. vi. 16.   [g] John i. 18.
[h] Col. ii. 9.   [i] Col. i. 15.

of his person[k];" insomuch, that "whoso hath seen him, hath seen the Father[l]." In truth, this was the mystery, which Moses probably did not understand at the time; the mystery, I mean, of his being put into the clift of the rock. For, "that rock was Christ[m]:" and it is in Christ only that God's perfections can find scope for exercise towards sinful man, and be all displayed in united splendour. But in Christ, "mercy and truth meet together, and righteousness and peace kiss each other[n]." Come then, Beloved, come to the Gospel, even to "the glorious Gospel of the blessed God!" come there, and "behold in it, as in a glass, the glory of the Lord, that you may be changed by it, even as Moses was, into the same image, from glory to glory, even as by the Spirit of the Lord[o]!" You are privileged beyond all the prophets, not excepting even the Baptist himself: for St. Paul says, that "what no eye had seen, nor ear heard, neither had it entered into the heart of man to conceive, (no, not even the eye, or ear, or heart of Moses himself,) God had revealed unto the Christian Church by his Spirit[p]." And by that same Spirit, working *in* and *by* the word, will God reveal it unto you also, even all "the glory of God in the face of Jesus Christ[q]."]

2. The power of faith—

[Faith is justly called "the substance of things hoped for, and the evidence of things not seen[r]." It penetrates into the highest heavens, and "beholds Him that is invisible[s]." It "sees God, and Jesus standing at the right hand of God[t]," able to succour, and ready to reward, his faithful people. Yes; "though now we see not our adorable Saviour with our bodily eyes, yet, believing in him, we rejoice with joy unspeakable, and full of glory[u]." We need not envy Moses: for, great as his privilege was, it was not to be compared with ours. His eyes were gratified with a glorious sight, no doubt; and his mind was instructed with audible sounds: but he saw not the truths realized; nor did he fully comprehend the things revealed to him[x]. But we have seen our God incarnate; and have "beheld his glory, the glory as of the Only-begotten of the Father[y]." We have seen in his atonement all the perfections of God harmonizing and glorified: and we understand clearly, how God can be "just, and yet the justifier of sinful men[z]." We know him to be "a just God, and yet a Saviour[a]:" and live in the sweet assurance, that he is not only merciful,

[k] Heb. i. 3.   [l] John xiv. 9.   [m] 1 Cor. x. 4.
[n] Ps. lxxxv. 10.   [o] 2 Cor. iii. 18.   [p] 1 Cor. ii. 9, 10.
[q] 2 Cor. iv. 6.   [r] Heb. xi. 1.   [s] Heb. xi. 27.
[t] Acts vii. 55.   [u] 1 Pet. i. 8.   [x] 1 Pet. i. 10—12.
[y] John i. 14.   [z] Rom. iii. 26.   [a] Isai. xlv. 21.

but "faithful also, and just to forgive us our sins, and to cleanse us from all unrighteousness[b]." The world at large, indeed, and multitudes even of the Christian world, have no experimental sense of these things: and the reason of their blindness is, they have not faith (for "all men have not faith[c]"): but to believers, "Christ manifests himself as he does not unto the world[d];" and so enables them to "behold his glory, that they are changed by it into the same image, from glory to glory, even as by the Spirit of the Lord[e]." Blush, then, ye who "see in Christ no beauty nor comeliness for which he is to be desired[f]:" know, that it is the result of "unbelief, by which the devil has blinded you[g]:" and that, "if ye will believe, ye shall see the glory of God[h];" ye shall see it, not only in the exercise of his power, but also in the display of "all his goodness."]

3. The efficacy of prayer—

[Wonderfully is this illustrated in the passage before us. But shall we suppose that God is less condescending now than in the days of Moses, or that he will not answer prayer at this time as well as then? Know ye, that God is the same gracious God as ever: "with him is no variableness, neither shadow of turning[i]:" "The prayer of the upright is still his delight[k]," as much as at any period of the world: and that "those who come to him in his Son's name, he will in no wise cast out." On the contrary, he tells us, that "we may ask what we will; and it shall be done unto us[l]." There is no limit to his answers to believing prayer, except such as his own glory, or our capacity, have imposed. "It is not in him that we are straitened, but in our own bowels[m]." How, then, should we urge the petition of Moses, and say, "O Lord, I beseech thee, shew me thy glory!" Let us have but "one thing to desire of the Lord;" and let that be, that we may behold his glory[n]: let us go into his presence: and say, with David, "O God, thou art my God; early will I seek thee: my soul thirsteth for thee; my flesh longeth for thee in a dry and thirsty land, where no water is; to see thy power and thy glory[o]:" and God will draw aside the veil that intercepts our views of him; yea, "he will come down from the habitation of his holiness and his glory[p]," and present himself before us, saying, "Here I am[q]." He would even fulfil to us his promise, "hearing us before we ask, and answering whilst yet we

[b] 1 John i. 9.   [c] 2 Thess. iii. 2.   [d] John xiv. 22.
[e] 2 Cor. iii. 18.   [f] Isai. liii. 2.   [g] 2 Cor. iv. 4.
[h] John xi. 40.   [i] Jam. i. 17.   [k] Prov. xv. 8.
[l] John xv. 7.   [m] 2 Cor. vi. 12.   [n] Ps. xxvii. 4.
[o] Ps. lxiii. 1, 2.   [p] Isai. lxiii. 15.   [q] Isai. lviii. 9.

are speaking to him^r." O that we would plead with him as he has commanded us to do^s, and "give him no rest^t," till he answer us in the desire of our hearts! And let us not imagine, that he will be offended at the largeness of our petitions: for he is as willing, as he is "able, to do exceeding abundantly for us above all that we can ask or think^u." Let us "open our mouths ever so wide, he will most surely fill them^x."]

4. The blessedness of heaven—

[When Peter beheld his Lord transfigured upon Mount Tabor, he said, "It is good to be here." And if such a view of Christ's glory, with his bodily eyes, was so delightful, what must it be for our disembodied spirits to be introduced into his immediate presence, and to "see him as he is^y!" What views shall we then have of the perfections of the Godhead all uniting and glorified in the work which he accomplished on the cross! Truly that heavenly city, where he abides, "has no need of the sun or moon to lighten it; for he will be the light thereof^z," and with his glory shall every soul be filled. If we account Moses happy when favoured with his transient visions of God, what shall we be, when around his throne we behold him in all his glory, and look forward to a never-ending duration of our bliss! O that we could contemplate more the blessedness of that state; and live more in an habitual preparation for it! Lift up your hearts, Brethren; for the blessed period is nigh at hand. Be "looking for it, and hasting to it^a:" and let "nothing short of that have any glory in your eyes, by reason of the glory that excelleth." Take now already the golden harps into your hands; and begin "the blissful song." Emulate to the utmost of your power those who are gone before you: and soon you shall join the countless choir in singing "the song of Moses and the Lamb."]

^r Isai. lxv. 24.   ^s Luke xviii. 1, 7.   ^t Isai. lxii. 7.
^u Eph. iii. 20.   ^x Ps. lxxxi. 10.   ^y 1 John iii. 2.
^z Rev. xxi. 23.   ^a 2 Pet. iii. 12.

OUTLINE NO. 112
THE PERFECTIONS OF GOD.

Exod. xxxiv. 5—7. *And the Lord descended in the cloud, and stood with him there, and proclaimed the name of the Lord. And the Lord passed by before him, and proclaimed, The Lord, the Lord God, merciful and gracious, long-suffering, and abundant in goodness and truth, keeping mercy for thousands, forgiving iniquity and transgression and sin, and that will by no means clear the guilty.*

THE voice of inspiration says to every one of us, "Acquaint thyself with God, and be at peace." An acquaintance with ourselves (which indeed is equally necessary to our salvation) will only lead us to despair, unless its effects be counteracted with a proportionable knowledge of our God. The more we discern of our own depravity, the more must we see of our guilt, our danger, and our helplessness: nor can any thing pacify our consciences, and allay our fears, but a view of the divine perfections, as united and harmonizing in the work of redemption. But *that* once obtained, our minds will be serene and happy: and the more complete our view of God is, the more firm will be our confidence in him, and the more sublime our joy. Moses, well aware of this, prayed to God to shew him his glory. To this request God graciously condescended, and appointed him a place where he would meet him, and make this discovery unto him. In discoursing upon this marvellous event, we shall notice,

I. The situation in which Moses was placed—

We are told that "God stood with him THERE:" but this not being a prominent feature in the text, we shall premise some observations as introductory to our remarks upon it—

[In the first place, we would observe that, in interpreting the Holy Scriptures, we are not at liberty to indulge our own fancy; we must approach them with sacred awe and reverence; and give such explanations of them only, as we verily believe to be agreeable to the mind of that blessed Spirit, through whose inspiration they were written.

Next, we observe, that the whole of the Mosaic economy was of a typical and mysterious nature; and that, though it is sometimes difficult to ascertain the precise import of some events, yet the meaning of those which are more striking is clear and obvious, and may be stated without any fear of deviating from the truth.

Further, there are many events, of which we should have made only a general improvement, which God himself has marked as conveying very minute and particular instruction. For instance, the miracle wrought by Moses, when he struck the rock, and thereby gave the whole nation a supply of water, which followed them all through the wilderness, might be supposed to teach us only, that God will supply the wants of his people who put themselves under his guidance: but St. Paul teaches us to look deeper into that miracle, and to find in it the great mysteries of redemption. He tells us that "that rock was Christ;" and, that the water which they drank of was "*spiritual* drink;" or, in other words, that the miracle denoted, that Christ, being struck with the rod of the law, becomes unto us a never-failing source of all spiritual blessings[a].

We only observe further, that there was no occasion whatever, in which we might more certainly expect to find something typical and mysterious, than in that before us. God was about to reveal himself to Moses in a manner that he never did, either before or since, to any mortal man: and the directions which he gave previous to this discovery of himself, and which were necessary for the safety of his favoured servant, were so minute and significant, that we cannot doubt, but that the whole transaction was replete with mysterious import, and most valuable information.]

We come now to notice the situation in which Moses was placed—

[God commanded Moses to go up to Mount Sinai, and stand upon a rock; and promised that he would there pass by him in a visible manner: but, because it was not possible for him to behold the splendour of the divine glory, God told him, that he would put him into a clift of the rock, and discover to him such a view of his glory as his frail nature could sustain. Accordingly, having put him into the clift of the rock, and covered him with his hand, to prevent him from getting any sight of his face (which he could not have seen consistently with the preservation of his life), he passed by, and then, withdrawing his hand, he permitted him to see his "back parts," that is, to have such an indistinct view of him as we have of a person who has passed by us[b].

Now Sinai and Horeb, it appears, were two tops of the same mountain. We are told in the context[c], that God called Moses to come up unto Mount *Sinai:* yet the preceding chapter informs us that the Israelites were at that time encamped by the Mount of *Horeb*[d]. The whole nineteenth chapter of Exodus informs us that the intercourse which Moses had with God at the time of the giving of the law, was on Mount *Sinai:* whereas Moses elsewhere informs us, that he stood before the Lord in *Horeb*[e]; and that the Lord made a covenant with them in *Horeb*[f]; and that the people provoked the Lord to wrath in *Horeb*[g]. Hence it is manifest, that the terms Horeb and Sinai

---

[a] 1 Cor. x. 4.   [b] Exod. xxxiii. 20—23.   [c] ver. 2.
[d] Exod. xxxiii. 6.   [e] Deut. iv. 10, 15.   [f] Deut. v. 2.
[g] Deut. ix. 8. with x. 1—5. *which was the very period alluded to in the text.*

are used as nearly, or altogether, synonymous; because the same transactions are represented indifferently as having taken place on the one, or on the other.

Now it has already appeared that the rock in Horeb is declared by God himself to have been a lively representation of Christ: and therefore we may well suppose, that *this* rock, which was certainly in the same mountain, if not the very identical rock, was intended also to prefigure him; more especially as the putting of Moses into the clift of it exactly represents the benefits we receive by virtue of an interest in Christ. To those who are not "in Christ," "God is a consuming fire[h]:" and, if he were to pass by any persons who have not "fled to Christ for refuge[i]," he would instantly "burn them up as thorns[k]," and "consume them with the brightness of his coming[l]." Besides, it is in Christ only that we can have even the faintest view of God; because it is in Christ only that his perfections are displayed to man; and it is only when we are in Christ, that we have any eyes to behold them.

Here then we see, not only that there is something mysterious in the situation of Moses, but that a due consideration of it is necessary to a full understanding of the passage before us.]

In considering this singular favour conferred on Moses, we proceed to notice,

II. The revelation which God gave of himself to him—

Though the terms in which God described his perfections are many, yet they may be reduced to three heads;—

1. His majesty—

[God, in calling himself "the Lord, the Lord God," intimated that he was that eternal, self-existent Being, who gave existence to every other being, and exercised unlimited authority over the works of his hands. His dominion is universal, his power irresistible, his sovereignty uncontrolled: "He doth according to his will in the armies of heaven, and among the inhabitants of the earth;" "nor can any stay his hand, or say unto him, What doest thou?"

Such a manifestation of his majesty was peculiarly necessary, in order that our obligations to him might appear in their proper light: for never, till we have learned to acknowledge and adore his sovereignty, shall we be able rightly to appreciate his love and mercy.]

2. His mercy—

[Many expressions are heaped together upon this subject,

[h] Heb. xii. 29.   [i] Heb. vi. 18.   [k] Isai. xxvii. 4.   [l] 2 Thess. ii. 8

because mercy is the attribute in which God peculiarly delights; and because he desires to impress our minds with right apprehensions of it.

God first, in general terms, declares himself to be "merciful and gracious;" by which we are to understand, that he is ever ready to pity the miserable, and relieve the needy. He is in his own nature propense to love and kindness, and forward to exercise his benevolence, whenever he can do it in consistency with his other perfections.

The first-fruit of his mercy is "long-suffering." And how long did he bear with the antediluvian world! for the space of one hundred and twenty years did he wait, to see if by the ministry of Noah he could turn them from their evil ways. What can we conceive more insufferable than the conduct of the Israelites in the wilderness? they were always murmuring and rebelling against God, who had done such great things for them: yet did he bear with them forty years. But we need not look back to the Antediluvians or the Jews: what monuments have we ourselves been of his patience and long-suffering! How have we provoked him to anger every day of our lives! yet we are here at this moment on praying ground, instead of being, where we most richly deserve to be, in the very depths of hell.

Nor has he merely borne with us: he has shewn himself also "abundant in goodness and truth." He has been doing us good from the first moment of our existence to this present hour. He has "made his sun to shine, and the rain to descend upon us," and "given us fruitful seasons, filling our hearts with food and gladness." But he has done infinitely more for us than this: for he has given his only dear Son to die for us, and " his good Spirit to instruct us," and has been calling us by the ministrations of his servants to receive all the blessings both of grace and glory. Many "great and precious promises also has he given us;" not one of which has he ever falsified, or shewn the least reluctance to fulfil.

Moreover, this kindness of his extends to the latest generations; for he is "keeping mercy for thousands" that are yet unborn. One reason why he bears with many proud rebels is, that he has mercy in reserve for many who are to proceed from their loins, who would never be brought into existence, if he were to execute on their offending parents the judgments they deserved. Who can tell? he may have "kept mercy" for some of *us* to this present hour; and the time may now be come, wherein he shall make us willing to accept it. Would to God it might be so!

But the completion of his mercy is seen in his "forgiving iniquity, and transgression, and sin." Search the sacred records, and see what sins he has forgiven! what sins before conversion! what sins after conversion! and you will find, that there is no species or degree of sin which he has not pardoned, even though it have been often repeated, and long continued in. Let any one attempt to enumerate his own transgressions, and he will find them more in number than the sands upon the sea-shore, and sufficient, if visited according to their desert, to sink the whole world into perdition: yet, if he be a believer in Christ, they are all forgiven. How many iniquities then is God continually pardoning in every quarter of the globe! But this is the habit which most characterizes his nature and perfections. Though he cannot look upon iniquity without the utmost abhorrence of it, yet is "judgment his strange work," and mercy is his delight.]

3. His justice—

[The concluding sentence of our text is understood by some to mean, that when he begins to punish "he will not make a full end," but "in judgment will remember mercy:" and it is certain that it will bear this sense, because, literally translated, it stands thus, "Clearing he will not clear." But then, in this description of his attributes, God would wholly omit his justice, which we cannot suppose he would: nor would the words, in this sense, at all agree with the words that follow them. We take them therefore as they are in our translation; and, according to their obvious meaning, they convey to us a most important truth. God does indeed take pleasure in the exercise of mercy: but still he will never violate the rights of justice: he will pardon; but not the impenitent or unbelieving: it is to those only who repent, and believe the Gospel, that he will finally approve himself a reconciled God. Nothing shall ever prevail upon him to "clear one guilty" person, who holds fast his iniquities, or will not wash them away in the Redeemer's blood. It may be asked, Will he not have respect to the multitude of those who are in that predicament? or will he not be softened when he shall see them weeping, and wailing, and gnashing their teeth, in hell? We answer, No: he will *by no means* clear the guilty: if they will live and die in sin, they must "eat the fruit of their own doings."

It is worthy of particular notice in this place, that Moses desired to see God's *glory;* and that God said, he "would make all his *goodness* pass before" him: from whence we are assured, that God's *goodness*, and his *glory*, are as much seen in his justice, as in any other attribute whatever. Indeed, if God were destitute of this perfection, he would cease to be either glorious or good: he could not be glorious, because not perfect; nor could he be good, because he would give licence to his creatures to violate his law, to throw his whole government into confusion, and to render themselves miserable: for not God himself could make them happy, while sin lived and reigned in their hearts. It is by his justice that he deters men from sin; and teaches them to flee from that which would imbitter even Paradise itself: and therefore justice, however severe may be its aspect upon sin and sinners, is indeed a part of the divine goodness, and a ray of the divine glory.]

INFER,

1. How wonderful is the efficacy of prayer—

[Moses, notwithstanding an apparent prohibition, had interceded with God on behalf of the idolatrous Israelites, and had prevailed[m]. Still however, God, to mark his displeasure, refused to go with the people any more; and said he would commit the guidance of them to an angel[n]. But Moses, having thus far obtained a favourable audience, requested and urged, that God himself should still go with them, as he had hitherto done. Nothing would satisfy him but this[o]. When he had succeeded in this, he grew bolder still; and asked, what no living creature had ever dared to ask, "O God, I beseech thee, shew me thy glory!" God approved of his boldness, and granted him this also. And what would he not grant to us, if we would ask in humility and faith? He says himself, "Open thy mouth wide, and I will fill it[p]." O Brethren! see in this instance the efficacy of prayer; and know, that if you asked forgiveness for the vilest of all sins, and prayed to have the presence of God with you all through this wilderness, and even begged to have the glory of God himself pass before your eyes, it should be given you: your iniquities should be forgiven; you should have God for your constant protector and guide; and he would "shine into your hearts, to give you the light of the knowledge of the glory of God in the face of Jesus Christ[q]." O pray without ceasing, and without doubting.]

2. Of what importance is it to obtain an interest in Christ—

[All, except the true Christian, have erroneous views of God: some are led by his majesty or justice to give way to desponding fears: others from a sight of his grace and mercy are induced to cherish presumptuous hopes. It is the Christian alone that sees his majesty tempered with mercy, and his mercy harmonizing with the demands of justice. No man can have this sight of God, till he be put into the clift of the rock. What we said at the beginning, we now repeat, that to all who are not in Christ, God will be a consuming fire. Seek then, my

---

[m] Exod. xxxii. 10—14. [n] Exod. xxxii. 34. [o] Exod. xxxiii. 15
[p] Ps. lxxxi. 10. [q] 2 Cor. iv. 6.

Brethren, to be "found in Christ." Then "shall you see the King in his beauty[r]:" then shall you behold him transfigured, as it were, before your eyes[s]; and have a foretaste of that blessedness which you shall enjoy, when " you shall see him as you are seen, and know him even as you are known[t]."]

[r] Isai. xxxiii. 16, 17.   [s] Matt. xvii. 1, 2.
[t] 1 John iii. 2. with 1 Cor. xiii. 12.

OUTLINE NO. 113
JEHOVAH A JEALOUS GOD.

Exod. xxxiv. 14. *The Lord, whose name is Jealous, is a jealous God.*

PRACTICAL religion is altogether founded on the character of God. If he were, as many foolishly imagine him to be, "a Being like unto ourselves," a very small measure of duty and service would be all that he could reasonably require. But being a God of infinite majesty, and unbounded mercy, it is not possible to exercise towards him too great a measure of fear and love; nor can he be too strict in exacting at our hands the utmost that we are able to pay. In this view, the feeling of jealousy, which seems at first sight not to comport well with our notions of the Supreme Being, may very properly be ascribed to him; and we may justly say, as in our text, "The Lord, whose name is Jealous, is a jealous God."

Let us contemplate,

I. The character of God, as here described—

Jealousy does exist in the bosom of Jehovah—

[Jealousy in man is a painful feeling, arising from a suspicion that a measure of the regard due to us is transferred to another, who is in no respect entitled to it. And so deep is the wound which it inflicts, especially on a husband who conceives himself to have been dishonoured by his wife, that nothing can ever heal it. "Jealousy," says Solomon, "is the rage of a man: therefore he will not spare in the day of vengeance: he will not regard any ransom; neither will he rest content, though thou givest many gifts[a]." In God, also, does it burn with a most vehement flame: "They have moved me to jealousy," says God; "and a fire is kindled in mine anger, and

[a] Prov. vi. 34, 35.

it shall burn unto the lowest hell, and shall consume the earth with her increase, and set on fire the foundations of the mountains. I will heap mischiefs upon them, and will spend mine arrows upon them[b]." To the same effect the Prophet Nahum also speaks: " God is jealous; and the Lord revengeth: the Lord revengeth, and is furious; the Lord will take vengeance on his adversaries; and he reserveth wrath for his enemies[c]."]

Nor is this unworthy of his character—

[On account of his own inconceivable excellency he deserves to stand without a rival in our affections. On account of what he has also done for us in creation, in providence, and in grace, especially in the gift of his only dear Son to die for us; and, I may add, on account of the relation in which he stands as " the Husband of his Church[d]," he has additional claims to our supreme regard: and if he see that we are in any respect suffering any thing to stand in competition with him, he may well be jealous. In truth, he could not, consistently with his own perfections, dispense with these obligations, even for a moment. " He cannot give his glory to another[e]:" he would cease to be God, if he could suffer his own inalienable rights to be withheld from him, and not express his indignation against the idolatrous offender. It is his very " *name*" and nature to be jealous: as to those who love him, he is a God of love and mercy; so is he, of necessity, to those who alienate their affections from him, " a jealous God, and a consuming fire[f]."]

From this view of his character, let us proceed to notice,

II. Our duty, as arising from it—

We must not act in any way inconsistent with the relation which we bear to him. We must not suffer,

1. Any alienation of our affections from him—

[We are bound to love him with *all* our heart, and *all* our mind, and *all* our soul, and *all* our strength. Nothing is to be loved by us but in subordination to him, and for his sake. If any thing under heaven be permitted to share our regards with him, we are guilty of idolatry[g]. Nothing is excepted, when the Apostle says, " Set your affections on things above, and not on things on the earth[h]." We must take care, therefore, not only not to love any thing above him, but to "*hate* even father and mother, and our own lives also," in comparison of him.]

2. Any abatement in our attentions to him—

---

[b] Deut. xxxii. 21—23. [c] Nah. i. 2. [d] Isai. liv. 5. [e] Isai. xlii. 8.
[f] Deut. iv. 23, 24. [g] Col. iii. 5. [h] Col. iii. 2.

[God speaks of our espousals to him as a season of peculiar love[i]. And at that season we are, for the most part, delighted with every thing that may bring us into nearer communion with him, and express the feelings of our heart towards him. Then the reading of his word, and secret prayer, and an attendance on the public ordinances of religion are to us sources of the sublimest joy. But if we become cold in these respects, and the ardour of our love abate, can we suppose that he will be pleased with us? Will he not say to us, as to the Church at Ephesus, "I have somewhat against thee, because thou hast left thy first love[k]?" Surely, if an earthly husband will not endure a declension in his wife's regards, much less will the God of heaven and earth endure a diminution of ours.]

3. Any unnecessary intercourse with things which have a tendency to draw us from him—

[*This* is particularly marked in the preceding context. God requires his people not to form alliance with their heathen neighbours, nor to accept invitations to their idolatrous feasts: he commands them to "destroy their altars, and break down their images, and cut down their groves," and to forbear even the mention of the gods whom they worshipped. He knew how soon "evil communications would corrupt good manners:" and therefore he forbade any unnecessary intercourse with the heathen. And has he not given a similar injunction to us also? Has he not declared, that, as soon may "light and darkness have communion with each other, or Christ with Belial, as a believer with an unbeliever;" and that, therefore, we must come out from the ungodly world, and be separate, and not touch the unclean thing, if we would have him for "a father unto us, and act as becomes his sons and daughters[1]?" This is a gracious and merciful warning, similar to what an affectionate husband would give his wife in relation to the society of one who was seeking to seduce her. And we must carefully attend to it; and be no more "of the world, than Christ himself was of the world." We must endeavour to "keep our garments clean" amidst the pollutions that are around us[m], and "hate even the garment spotted by the flesh[n]." We must not be contented with avoiding evil, but must "abstain even from the appearance of it[o]."]

ADDRESS—

1. Those who think it an easy matter to serve God—

[Though a woman may without any great difficulty perform her duties to an affectionate husband, where the bias of

[i] Jer. ii. 2.   [k] Rev. ii. 4.   [l] 2 Cor. vi. 14—18.
[m] Rev. iii. 4.   [n] Jude, ver. 23.   [o] 1 Thess. v. 22.

her natural affections is on the side of duty, it is not so easy to execute all that our God requires: for there we stem the current of nature, instead of being carried forward by it. Hence, when the whole people of Israel were so ready to bind themselves to serve their God, Joshua warned them, that they could not do it without divine aid[p]. So let me say to you, that, if you will indeed give yourselves to the Lord, and take him as your portion, you must not engage in your own strength; but must look unto your "God, who alone can work in you either to will or to do."]

2. Those who are unconscious of having given occasion to God to be jealous of them—

[Look, not merely at your *acts*, but at *the dispositions of your mind;* and then judge. He says, " Give me thy heart." Now see whether your affections have not strayed; yea, whether you have not been like the wild ass in the wilderness, whom none can overtake or keep from her mate, till the time for parturition has nearly arrived[q]? This is an humiliating, but a just, image of our conduct; and if we will not acknowledge it, and humble ourselves under a sense of it, "God will surely plead with us" to our confusion[r].]

3. Those who are ashamed of their past ways—

[Amongst men, the unfaithfulness of a wife may have been such as to preclude a possibility of her restoration to the station she once held: but no departures, however grievous, shall prevent our restoration to the divine favour, if, with sincerity of heart, we humble ourselves before him[s]. In the name of God himself, I am commanded to proclaim this, and to invite the most abandoned of you all to return to him[t]. "Return, then, unto him, and so your iniquity shall not be your ruin[u]."]

[p] Josh. xxiv. 18, 19.   [q] Jer. ii. 23, 24.   [r] Jer. ii. 35.
[s] Jer. iii. 1.   [t] Jer. iii. 12—14.   [u] Ezek. xviii. 30.

OUTLINE NO. 114

THE THREE YEARLY FEASTS AT JERUSALEM.

Exod. xxxiv. 23, 24. *Thrice in the year shall all your men-children appear before the Lord God, the God of Israel. For I will cast out the nations before thee, and enlarge thy borders: neither shall any man desire thy land, when thou shalt go up to appear before the Lord thy God, thrice in the year.*

BESIDES the weight of evidence arising from the accomplishment of prophecy, and the working of miracles, to prove the divine origin of the Mosaic dispensation, there is a great abundance of internal evidence in the dispensation itself, that corroborates and confirms our conclusions respecting it. What impostor that ever lived would have been weak enough to put his religion to such a test as this which we have now read? No one would have done it even for a few years, whilst he himself might be at hand to execute his own plans; much less would any man transmit such an ordinance to posterity, when one single instance of failure would be sufficient to subvert his whole religion. But, not to dwell on this, we will,

I. Draw your attention to the institution itself—

It was, that all the males should go up to Jerusalem thrice in the year, from every quarter of the land, to keep a feast there unto the Lord. Now consider,

1. Of what nature this appointment was—

[It was partly *political*, and partly *religious*. As a *political ordinance*, it was intended to cement the people together, and to keep them united in love. Had they had no common centre of union, no appointed means of communion, the different tribes might in process of time have forgotten their relation to each other, and have sought their own separate interests, instead of acting in concert with each other for the good of the whole. But by this expedient, all who had the greatest influence among them were brought frequently into the closest fellowship with each other, and, on their return to their respective homes, diffused the same brotherly affection through the land. As *a religious ordinance*, it was of singular importance, not only for the preserving of the people from idolatry, (to which they were always prone,) but for the impressing of their minds with a love to vital godliness. The times appointed for their assembling at Jerusalem were at *the feast of unleavened bread*, to commemorate their deliverance from Egypt and from the sword of the destroying angel; at *the feast of Pentecost*, to commemorate no less a mercy, the giving of the law; and at *the feast of tabernacles*, or of *in-gathering* (as it was called), to commemorate their living in tents in the wilderness, and to render thanks for the fruits of the earth which they had gathered in[a]. Thus at the returning seasons of *spring*, of

---

[a] See Deut. xvi. 1—16.

summer, and of *autumn*, they were required to commemorate the mercies which had been vouchsafed to their nation, and with *joy* and *gratitude* to acknowledge their obligations to Jehovah[b] — — — What a blessed tendency had such seasons to keep alive in their minds a sense of their high privileges, and to spread a savour of true religion through every family in the land!]

2. What care God took to guard against the objections to which it was liable—

[It would of necessity occur to all, that, by their observance of this ordinance, their land on every side would be exposed to the incursions of their enemies, who would not fail to take advantage of their absence, and to retaliate upon them the injuries they had sustained. In this view it should seem, that they would be highly criminal in leaving the women, the children, the aged, and the sick, in such a defenceless state, and that it would be more advisable to depute some from every quarter to represent the rest. But God would not be served by deputy: he commanded all to keep the feasts at the place prescribed: and, to remove all apprehensions about their property or their families, he pledged himself to protect their frontier, and so to overrule the minds of their enemies, that they should not even "*desire*" to invade their land at any of those seasons. They had seen how able he was to turn the minds of their enemies in Egypt, who had just before sent, yea even "*thrust*," them out of the land, laden with spoil; and he engaged that, to the remotest period of their existence as a nation, he would interpose for them with equal effect, if only they would trust their concerns to him, and serve him in his appointed way.]

We indeed have nothing to do with the institution before us: nor do we much admire the formal custom (which seems to have arisen from it) of attending at the Lord's supper on the three great festivals of our Church, while we live in the neglect of that ordinance all the year besides. Nevertheless the institution is far from being uninteresting to us; as will be seen, while we,

II. Suggest some observations founded upon it—

Much might we speak respecting *the providence of God,* who so miraculously wrought upon the minds of their enemies, that no infidel could ever adduce

---

[b] They were ordered to *rejoice* before the Lord, and to make freewill offerings to him: "None were to come empty." Mark especially, Deut. xvi. 10, 15, 16.

one single instance wherein this promise failed. We might speak also respecting *the happiness of true religion;* and draw a parallel between the Jews assembling for their solemn feasts, and Christians universally uniting in the same grateful acknowledgments and heavenly joys. But there are two observations, to which, as arising clearly out of the subject, and as being of singular importance, we would limit your attention :—

1. The service of God is of paramount obligation—
[We have seen what strong objections might have been made to the ordinance before us, which yet was required punctually to be observed. And we know that carnal reason has much to suggest in opposition to the commands of God, much that is founded in fact and in the experience of mankind : ' If I serve my God according to the requisitions of his word, I shall be forced to deny myself many things that are pleasing to flesh and blood: I shall also be singular, and shall expose myself to the derision and contempt of those who are hostile to true religion : my very friends may turn against me ; and I may suffer materially in my temporal interests.' All this, and more than this, is very true : but it affords no reason whatever for disobeying the commands of God. The Jews would doubtless on many occasions have preferred their domestic ease and comfort, or the occupations in which they were engaged, to the fatigue and trouble of a long expensive journey. But the command was positive: and so is ours; it admits of no excuses: we are expressly required to " deny ourselves, to take up our cross daily, and to follow Christ:" and it is on these terms only that we can be his disciples. If called to "forsake father and mother, and houses and lands, for the Gospel's sake," we must forsake, yea and " hate them all," if they stand in competition with Christ, or would draw us from our allegiance to him. We must not love even life itself in comparison of him, but cheerfully sacrifice it at any time, and in any way that our fidelity to him may require. " It is not necessary that I should live," said a great general, "but it is necessary that I should proceed." Thus must the Christian say, ' Tell me not of difficulties, or dangers : it is not necessary that I should be rich, or honoured, or even that I should live ; but it is necessary that I should obey my God : a heated furnace, or a den of lions, is nothing to me : duty is all. If I die for conscience sake, I rejoice that I am counted worthy to suffer in so good a cause.' This was the mind of Paul : " None of these things move me," says he, " neither count I my life dear unto me:" " I am ready not **only** to be bound, but also to die at Jerusalem for the Lord's

sake." O that we might be like him; men of piety, men of principle, men of firmness and decision!]

2. They who serve the Lord shall be saved by him—

[The trust which the Jews at those stated seasons reposed in God was never disappointed. Nor shall ours be, though all the hosts both of men and devils were confederate against us. The challenge is justly given us, " Who ever trusted in the Lord, and was confounded?" There is a great fault amongst religious people in relation to this: many are distressing themselves with doubts and fears, ' Shall I persevere to the end? shall I be saved at last?' A holy caution is doubtless very becoming in every state; but not a slavish fear. Our concern should be to serve God: it is his concern, if I may so speak, to save us. Even from temporal trials he can, and will, protect us, as far as is for our good[c] ———— As for spiritual and eternal evils, he will assuredly protect us from them. " Who is he that shall harm us, if we be followers of that which is good?" Satan, it is true, will never for a moment relinquish his *desire* to assault us: that roaring lion will never intermit his wish to devour: but God will be as " a wall of fire round about us," and "his grace shall be at all times sufficient for us:" " nor shall any temptation take us beyond what we are able to bear, or without a way to escape from it." " Know ye then, Brethren, in whom ye have believed; that he is able to keep that which you have committed to him." Know that, if only your eyes were opened, you might at this moment see horses of fire and chariots of fire all around you, and an host of angels encamped around you for your protection. Invade not any longer the province of your God. Leave to him the care of preserving you; and confine your solicitude to the serving and honouring of him. This is your duty; it is also your privilege: the direction of God himself is this; " Commit your souls to him in well-doing as into the hands of a faithful Creator." Be assured that he will not fail you; and that " He who hath promised, is able also to perform."]

[c] See a most striking illustration of this truth in Acts xviii. 9—18. To allay Paul's fears, God promised to protect him in a city proverbially abandoned. He preached there eighteen months unmolested. At last a violent assault was made upon him by all the Jews in the city: but the judge would take no cognizance of their complaints, and drove them away from his judgment-seat. The Greeks, who had joined with the Jews, being irritated by this conduct, laid hold on Sosthenes, whom they conceived to be a friend of Paul's, and beat *him* in the very presence of the judge: but Paul, on whose account the clamour was raised, escaped unhurt, and continued in the city a good while longer without any injury whatever; and at last departed from it in peace. So faithful are the promises of God!

OUTLINE NO. 115
THE VEIL OF MOSES.

Exod. xxxiv. 35. *And the children of Israel saw the face of Moses, that the skin of Moses' face shone. And Moses put the veil upon his face again, until he went in to speak with him.*

IT is an established and invariable truth, that "those who honour God shall surely be honoured by him." We have the clearest evidence of this, both in the antediluvian and patriarchal ages. Did Abel honour God by his offering, Enoch by his walk, and Noah by his faithful warning of an ungodly world? they also were blessed with signal manifestations of the divine favour. Did Abraham, Lot, or Job display singular piety? they were as singularly protected, delivered, and exalted by their God. The same we observe of Moses. He was faithful to his God, when all Israel, not excepting Aaron himself, revolted from him; and to him did God vouchsafe so bright a glory, that none of his countrymen were able to fix their eyes upon him; insomuch that he was constrained to put a veil upon his face, in order to facilitate their access to him, and restore his wonted opportunities of conversing with them. This veiling of his face is to be the subject of our present consideration: and we shall notice it in a two-fold view:

I. As a kind expedient—

The face of Moses shone with a dazzling and overpowering splendour—

[He had for forty days and nights been communing with God upon Mount Sinai: and it pleased God, for the confirmation and increase of his authority among the people, to send him down to them with a lustre upon his countenance, that should at once convince them whose servant he was, and whose authority he bare.

At the first sight of him, both Aaron and all the people were affrighted. This was the natural effect of that guilt which they had so recently contracted. They feared that he was sent as an avenger to punish their iniquity. When they found that their organs of sight were too weak to behold the bright effulgence of his glory, they felt how unable they must be to withstand the terror of his arm.

As the brightness of Moses' face was supernatural, so the effect of it on the people was peculiar to that occasion. But there is an awe inspired by the presence of every good man, in proportion to the weight of his character and the eminence of his piety. Herod, though a king, " feared John, because he knew that he was a just and holy man." And Job tells us, that at his presence " the aged rose, and the young men hid themselves."]

To facilitate their access to him, he adopted the expedient mentioned in the text—

[He was not conscious of the splendour with which his countenance was irradiated, till their inability to behold him convinced him of it. Nor is it ever found that those who bear much of the divine image are conscious of their own superiority: their minds are fixed on their own defects rather than on their excellencies, and, from their deep views of their remaining corruptions, they are ready to count themselves " less than the least of all saints." When he perceived the effect which the sight of him produced, instead of being elated with the honour conferred upon him, or desiring to employ it for the maintenance of his own authority, he put a veil upon his face to conceal its brightness, and called them to him that he might impart unto them the instructions he had received from God. As often as he returned to commune with his God, he took off the veil, as not either necessary or befitting in the divine presence: but in all his intercourse with the people, he covered his face. On this point many useful thoughts occur; but we shall reserve them for the close of our subject, where they will be more advantageously suggested in a way of practical improvement.]

We pass on to notice this act of Moses,

II. As an instructive emblem—

Whether Moses himself understood the full signification of his own act, we cannot say: it is probable he did not: for certain it is, that the prophets in many instances could not see the full scope of their own prophecies. But, whether he understood it or not, we are assured, on infallible authority, that his covering his face with the veil was intended by God to represent,

1. The darkness of that dispensation—

[The Mosaic dispensation was " a shadow of good things to come:" but what the substance was, none could exactly ascertain. The very tables which at this time Moses had brought down from God, contained a law, the *nature, intent.*

or *duration* of which none of them could understand. They could not discern its spiritual import, but judged of it only by the letter. They thought it a covenant of life; whereas it was not at all designed " to give life," but rather to be " a ministration of condemnation and death." They supposed it was to continue to the end of time; when it was merely given for a season, till the things which it prefigured should be accomplished. Its splendour was veiled from their sight, as was the brightness of Moses' face: and St. Paul informs us, that the expedient to which Moses resorted, was intended to shew, that the law was in itself " glorious[a]," but that " the children of Israel could not steadfastly look to the end of it[b]."]

2. The blindness of the human mind—

[There were in the Jews of those days, and there are at this hour, a blindness of mind, and an obduracy of heart, which render them almost invincibly adverse to the truth of God. We see it, and wonder at it, in *them;* but are unconscious of it in *ourselves,* and insensible of it as a matter of personal experience: yet are we, in fact, greater monuments of obduracy than they; because there was a veil over their dispensation, which is removed from ours. Did they continue stiff-necked and rebellious, amidst all the mercies and judgments with which they were visited? so do we: the " god of this world hath blinded us:" "our understanding is darkened;" " we are alienated from the life of God through the ignorance that is in us, and because of the blindness of our hearts:" we "hate the light, and will not come to it, lest our deeds should be reproved." Now this propensity in human nature to reject the truth, and to " account it foolishness," was intended to be marked by this significant action of the Jewish lawgiver. St. Paul explains it in this very way[c]: " Their minds," says he, " were blinded: for until this day remaineth the same veil untaken away: even unto this day, when Moses is read, the veil is upon *their heart.*"]

3. The benefit to be expected from their promised Messiah—

[The occasional removal of his veil when he went into the presence of his God, shewed, that it was not always to continue on the dispensation, but that at a future period it should be removed, and the dispensation itself " abolished." The Messiah, to whom they were constantly directed to look, as to that promised seed in whom all the nations of the earth should be blessed, was to take away both the foregoing veils; the one, by fulfilling the law in all its parts; and the other, by communicating his Holy Spirit to all his followers. Then the true nature of that

---

[a] 2 Cor. iii. 7. [b] 2 Cor. iii. 13. [c] 2 Cor. iii. 14, 15.

law would be fully understood; and Christ would be recognised as "the end of the law for righteousness to every one that believeth." Then should the glory of that dispensation be clearly seen, and the incomparably brighter glory of the Christian dispensation be seen also.

For this view of the subject we are also indebted to the Apostle Paul; who tells us that the Gospel, as "a ministration of the Spirit" and "of righteousness," was to succeed, and to eclipse, the law; and that "when the Jews should turn to the Lord, the Messiah would take away that veil" from their hearts, and bring them into the light and "liberty" of the children of God[d].]

In the former part of our discourse we forbore to make several remarks, which we reserved for this place; and which, while they elucidate the subject, will afford rich INSTRUCTION,

1. To Ministers—

[We have seen what Moses did; and in some respects we should imitate him; but in others we should adopt a directly opposite conduct.

It was truly amiable in him to condescend to the infirmities of the people, and to veil his own glory for their good. Thus should every minister prefer the instruction of his people to the display of his own talents, or the aggrandizement of his own name. It is pitiful indeed to court applause for our learning, when we should be converting souls to Christ. St. Paul, qualified as he was to astonish men with his parts and talents, "would rather speak five words to the understandings of men, than ten thousand words in an unknown tongue." Our blessed Lord "spake as men were able to hear it;" and reserved his fuller instructions till his hearers were better qualified to receive them. Paul also gave only "milk to babes," whilst "to those who were of full age he administered meat." Thus should we do, lest we blind or dazzle men by an unseasonable display even of truth itself. But are we, like Moses, to use concealment? No: the Apostle expressly guards us against imitating Moses in this particular: "NOT as Moses," says he; "NOT as Moses, who put a veil over his face;" but, on the contrary, we must "use great plainness of speech[e]." There is nothing in the Gospel that requires concealment, nor any thing that admits of it: we must "declare unto men the whole counsel of God." We must discriminate so far as to judge what will, and what will not, "be profitable to men;" but the truth we must declare without the smallest mixture or reserve;

---

[d] 2 Cor. iii. 7—11, 16, 17. [e] 2 Cor. iii. 12, 13.

and "by manifestation of the truth must commend ourselves to every man's conscience in the sight of God[f]." It must be our labour to rend away the veil from the hearts of our hearers: for "if our Gospel be *veiled*, it is *veiled* to them that are lost[g]." "The glory of God shines in the face of Jesus Christ;" and to shew them that glory in all its brightness, is to be the one object of our labour, as it is the unwearied effort of the devil to conceal it from their view[h].]

2. To hearers—

[You should be aware that there is a veil upon your hearts, else you will never pray unto the Lord to remove it. Even the Apostle Paul, learned as he was in all biblical knowledge, had, "as it were, scales fall from his eyes," when God was pleased to lead him to a clear view of his Gospel. So must "the eyes of your understanding also be enlightened," before you can "discern aright the things of the Spirit." But though God has appointed ministers to instruct you, you are all at liberty, yea you are required, to go yourselves, like Moses, into the presence of your God. Do not however veil your faces before him, but go exactly as you are. Your fellow-creatures could not endure to see all that is in your hearts; nor would it be of any use to reveal it to them: but "to God all things are naked and open;" and the more fully you unbosom yourself to him, the more will his blessing come upon you. It is by putting off the veil from your own hearts, that you shall with "open *unveiled* face behold his glory;" and, by beholding it, "be changed into the same image from glory to glory, by the Spirit of the Lord." Truly you shall, in a measure, experience the same benefit as Moses did: you shall be "beautified with salvation;" "the beauty of the Lord your God shall be upon you;" and all that behold you shall be "constrained to acknowledge, that God is with you of a truth." When this effect is produced, "let your light shine before men." You are not called to veil it, but rather to display it; not indeed for your own honour (*that* were a base unworthy motive), but for the honour of your God, that they who "behold your good works may glorify your Father that is in heaven."]

[f] 2 Cor. iv. 2.

[g] Compare the language in the original. It is the same word throughout: κεκαλυμμένον. 2 Cor. iii. 13. to iv. 6.

[h] 2 Cor. iii. 13. to iv. 6. The beauty of the passage is lost if the two chapters be not read together.

OUTLINE NO. 116
THE OFFERINGS FOR THE TABERNACLE.

Exod. xxxvi. 5—7. *And they spake unto Moses, saying, The people bring much more than enough for the service of the work, which the Lord commanded to make. And Moses gave commandment, and they caused it to be proclaimed throughout the camp, saying, Let neither man nor woman make any more work for the offering of the sanctuary. So the people were restrained from bringing: for the stuff they had was sufficient for all the work to make it, and too much.*

THE followers of Christ are supposed to regard this as their favourite maxim, 'The greater the sinner, the greater the saint:' they are considered also as approving an inference that may be deduced from it, namely, that it is advisable to commit some gross crime, in order to augment our future piety. We trust however, that such calumnies, though often affirmed, are not really credited. The least consideration would convince a man, that such a sentiment could find no place in a religious mind. But though we disclaim any such licentious tenets, (yea, and utterly abhor them,) yet we must say, that "he who has been forgiven much, will love much;" and that "godly sorrow," in proportion as it exists in the soul, "will work indignation and revenge" against all our spiritual enemies, and will lead us invariably to "bring forth works meet for repentance." This truth is strongly illustrated in the history before us. The whole nation of the Jews had revolted from God, and worshipped the golden calf. For this God had threatened them with utter destruction; but, upon the intercession of Moses, had reversed his decree, and had received them again to his favour. Instead of forsaking them utterly, he had even determined to dwell among them as their God; and had ordered a tabernacle to be made for him, with every thing else which would be wanted for the services they were to present unto him. For the constructing of this he relied on the liberality of his people: and the event proved that his reliance was well placed; and that their sense of the obligations conferred upon them was sufficiently powerful for the occasion. The account given us of *their zeal* is truly edifying. It will be proper to notice,

I. The object of it—

[They had lately shewn an unhappy zeal in the service of a false god; and now they laboured to evince their gratitude to Jehovah, and to exalt the honour of his name. This desire filled the whole nation, and was the main-spring of those exertions which they now made.

And who must not acknowledge this to have been an object worthy their supreme attention? Survey the objects which occupy the minds of men, and to the pursuit of which they willingly devote their wealth and labour: the gratifications of sense, how mean are they, in comparison of that which now animated the Jewish people! the attainment of honour, or the acquisition of wealth, how empty are they in comparison of that nobler end which Israel pursued! Theirs was worth ambition, and might well provoke them all to holy emulation. To have Jehovah resident among them—to provide for him a suitable habitation—to have proper means of access to him, and of communications from him—and, finally, to possess before their eyes a pledge of his continued care, and his eternal love—*this* was as much beyond the poor objects of common ambition, as the contemplations of reason and philosophy exceed the dreams of children.

Happy would it be for us, if we all formed the same judgment, and were all penetrated with the same desire!— — —]

II. The operation—

[There are two things in their conduct which we cannot fail to notice, and admire; namely, their liberality and their diligence. No sooner did they know what things would be accepted, than they vied with each other in supplying them. Whatever any man possessed that could be applied to the projected structure, he deemed it instantly, *Corban;* and without hesitation consecrated it to the service of his God. Their ornaments, of whatever kind, were stripped off; all, both men and women, being more desirous to beautify the sanctuary of their God, than to adorn themselves. Each seemed to think himself rich, not in proportion to what he retained for his own use, but to the supplies he was able to contribute. The poorest among them were as glad to give their wood, their rams' skins, or their brass, as the richest were their jewels and their gold.

Nor were they less solicitous to work, than to supply materials for working. The women engaged in spinning the goats' hair and in embroidering the linen, while the men were occupied in forming the wood and metals for their respective uses. Those who could teach were as glad to instruct others, as others were to receive instruction: and all desired, in whatever way they could, to advance the work.

Now it is in this way that genuine religion always operates. The converts in every age are represented as coming unto God, " their silver and their gold with them[a]:" and it is characteristic of them all, that they are " a peculiar people, zealous of good works" — — —]

III. The effect—

[Such was the conduct of all who were " wise-hearted," and " whose spirits made them willing" to glorify their God[b]: and the effect was, that, in a very few days, the abundance of the gifts exceeded the occasion for them; and it became necessary to issue through the camp a prohibition against adding any thing further to the store.

O what might not be done for the honour of God and the benefit of mankind, if all exerted themselves according to their ability! How easy would it be to erect places for the worship of God; to provide accommodations for the poor; to administer instruction to the ignorant, consolation to the troubled, relief to the distressed! Such an union of zealous exertions as we see exhibited on this occasion, would in a great measure drive affliction from the world, and turn into a paradise this vale of tears — — —]

IMPROVEMENT—

1. Let the cause of God be dear unto our souls—

[We have not, it is true, any such edifice to raise, and therefore may be supposed to have no such call for zeal and diligence. But is there not a spiritual temple which God desires to have erected for him, and wherein he may be glorified? Yea, is not that temple infinitely more dear to him than any which can be formed by human hands? The material tabernacle was only a shadow of that better habitation wherein God delights to dwell. Should not *that* then be an object of our concern? Should not the manifestations of his presence, and the establishment of his kingdom in the world, call forth our zeal, as much as the erection of that fabric in the wilderness did the zeal of Israel? Well may it shame the world at large, that every trifle occupies their minds, more than this: and even the people of God themselves have reason to blush, that their feelings are so acute in reference to their own interests and honour, and so dull in what regards the honour and interests of their God.]

2. Let us cordially and universally co-operate for the advancement of it—

[a] Compare Isai. lx. 17. Acts ii. 44, 45. 2 Cor. viii. 1—4.

[b] Mark how often these expressions occur in this and the preceding chapter.

[It is generally thought that the duty of propagating Christianity pertains to Ministers alone. But it is very little that a Minister can do without the co-operation of his people. Multitudes will never come to hear him, or afford him any opportunities of benefiting their souls: and the greater part even of those who do attend his ministry, gain little from it, for want of having the subjects which they hear impressed upon their minds in a way of private instruction. All should contribute, according to their ability, to advance the salvation of those around them. Masters should take the superintendence of their families, and parents of their children. The more enlightened among the people should endeavour to instruct their unenlightened neighbours. The visiting of the sick, the relieving of the needy, the conducting of Sunday schools for the benefit of the poorer classes, these, and such like works, should be regarded by all, both men and women, as their common province, and followed by all according to their respective abilities[c]. The people of Israel deemed it not so much their duty, as their privilege, to contribute to the raising of the tabernacle: and this is the light in which we should view our calls to exertion. Do any account it hard to sacrifice somewhat of their time and interest in such a cause? O "tell it not in Gath; publish it not in the streets of Askelon!" "Let not the redeemed of the Lord say so, whom he hath redeemed from the hand of the enemy." Let us rather unite, all of us, with willing hearts, in the service of our God; and, "whatever our hand findeth to do, let us do it with all our might."]

[c] See Rom. xvi. 3, 12. and Phil. iv. 3.

OUTLINE NO. 117
THE TABERNACLE SERVICE COMMENCED.

Exod. xl. 1, 2. *The Lord spake unto Moses, saying, On the first day of the first month shalt thou set up the tabernacle of the tent of the congregation.*

THE beginning of a new year is, not without reason, considered by Christians in general as a fit occasion for more than ordinary attention to religious duties. I say not, indeed, that the generality of Christians actually so employ that hallowed time: for, in fact, the whole season wherein we commemorate the incarnation of our blessed Lord is by the generality made rather a time for carnal mirth. But still, this is acknowledged by all to be rather an abuse of our religious privileges than a suitable improve-

117.] THE TABERNACLE SERVICE COMMENCED. 557

ment of them. There is in the minds of all a consciousness, that to review our past errors with penitence, and to prepare for a more diligent performance of our duty in future, is the proper employment of that period, when we are entering, as it were, upon a new scene of things. In my text, "the first day of the first month" was appointed by God himself as the time for commencing the services of the tabernacle, after the Israelites had abode in the wilderness nearly a whole year. Doubtless, both Moses and the various artificers had used great diligence to get every vessel ready for the service which it was destined to perform: and great exertion must have been made on the day here spoken of, wherein the tabernacle and all the vessels of it were not only got ready for their destined use, but were employed in the very service for which they had been formed. But the command of Jehovah animated the people on this occasion: and, I hope, their conduct will encourage us also to prosecute with becoming earnestness the labours which this season calls for at our hands.

For the advancement of this blessed object, I will set before you,

I. The work here assigned to Moses—

He was ordered now to set up the tabernacle with every thing belonging to it, and to commence the service of it. A pattern of every part of it had been shewn to him on Mount Sinai, and according to that pattern had every thing been formed. No less than eight times in this one chapter is it said, that he did every thing "*as the Lord had commanded him.*" For all this care, both in relation to the pattern given him, and to the execution of it by himself and all under his command, there was, no doubt, a very important reason. The very injunction given him at the time of shewing to him the pattern, "See thou make all things according to the pattern shewn to thee in the mount[a]," strongly marked, that, in the divine mind, there was some very important end to

[a] Exod. xxv. 40.

be accomplished by it. What that end was we are informed in the Epistle to the Hebrews: The tabernacle itself, and all its vessels, were intended to be "an example and shadow of heavenly things," that is, of the things revealed to us under the Christian dispensation. In a word, the law and its ordinances were intended to give a just representation of the Gospel and its mysteries; and the two were to accord with each other in every the minutest part, even as an impression with the seal by which it was made [b].

Behold, then, here was the work assigned to Moses, namely, to give to the Jewish people such an exhibition of the Gospel and its mysteries as should suffice for them under that shadowy dispensation, and prepare them for that fuller manifestation which should be vouchsafed to the Church by the ministry of Christ and of his holy Apostles.

[The tabernacle itself was a representation of Christ, "in whom dwelt all the fulness of the Godhead bodily [c]," and who in his incarnate state "dwelt (tabernacled) amongst us [d]." The priests, the altar, and the sacrifices, shadowed him forth as "the Great High-Priest," through whom alone we can come to God [e]; and who, being himself the altar that sanctified the gift [f], "offered himself a sacrifice for the sins of the whole world [g]," even "an offering and a sacrifice to God of a sweet smelling savour [h]." The altar of incense also designated that same divine Saviour as ever living to make intercession for us [i]. The candlestick also, and the table of shewbread, represented him as "the light of the world [k]," and as "the bread of life, of which whosoever eats shall live for ever [l]." The lavers too represented him as "the fountain opened for sin [m]," in which every one "who washeth is cleansed from all sin [n]." The same may be said of every the minutest vessel in the sanctuary: they all shadowed forth the Lord Jesus in some part of his Mediatorial office. But I must by no means omit to mention the ark, in which the tables of the Law were placed, and which was covered by the mercy-seat of precisely the same dimensions, and which represented him as fulfilling the Law for us [o], and as obtaining mercy for all who should

[b] Heb. viii. 5.   [c] Col. ii. 9.   [d] John i. 14. ἐσκήνωσεν
[e] Heb. x. 19—22.   [f] Heb. xiii. 10.   [g] Heb. x. 12.
[h] Eph. v. 2.   [i] Heb. ix. 24.   [k] John viii. 12.
[l] John vi. 48, 58.   [m] Zech. xiii. 1.   [n] Rev. i. 5.
[o] Rom. x. 4.

come to God by him[p]. Now all of these, whether the vessels, or the persons who officiated in the use of them, "were anointed with oil[q]," to shew, that even Christ himself, "being anointed with the oil of gladness above his fellows[r]," had "the Spirit given to him without measure for the performance of his work[s];" and that no person or service can ever be "acceptable to God," unless it be "sanctified by the Holy Ghost[t]."]

Let us next turn our attention to,

II. The corresponding work that is now called for at our hands—

We are now called, every one of us,

1. To realize in our minds the things here shadowed forth—

[The wonders of Redemption should occupy our attention every day: but on this day especially should we be coming to God in "that new and living way which Christ has opened for us through the veil." We should go to the Lord Jesus Christ as our sacrifice, and as the altar that sanctifies that sacrifice, and as the priest that offers it. Under all the characters that have been before contemplated concerning him, we should apply to him — — — "receiving every thing out of his fulness[u]." From day to day, as long as the Jewish polity existed, were the various sacrifices and services of the Mosaic ritual renewed: and as long as the world shall stand, must we look to Jesus as here shadowed forth, feeding on him as our bread, washing in him as our laver, and living altogether by faith on him[x]. Would to God that every one of you would this very day begin these services, if you have hitherto been strangers to them; or prosecute them with redoubled ardour, if you have already entered on this life of faith! — — —]

2. To get them spiritually wrought within our own souls—

[We have said that *Christ* was *mystically* shadowed forth in all the services of that day. And this is true. But it is also true that *the life of God in our own souls* was *spiritually* represented. Yes, Brethren, "we are temples of the Holy Ghost[y];" and "God will come down and dwell in us[z];" yea, "Christ will dwell in our hearts by faith[a]." And in us are "the sacrifices of prayer and praise to be offered to him continually[b]." In truth, we ourselves are to be living sacrifices

[p] Heb. vii. 25.   [q] ver. 9, 13—15.   [r] Ps. xlv. 7.
[s] John iii. 34.   [t] Rom. xv. 16.   [u] John i. 16.
[x] Gal. ii. 20.   [y] 1 Cor. vi. 19.   [z] 2 Cor. vi. 16.
[a] Eph. iii. 17.   [b] Heb. xiii. 15.

to him^c; and, as an holy priesthood, we are to be offering ourselves to him^d. Every faculty of our souls is to be sanctified to his service by the Holy Spirit, *lightened* by his light, and *nourished* by his grace. We are, in fact, to be "lights in this dark world^e," and "witnesses for Jehovah, that he alone is God^f." My dear Brethren, this conformity to Christ is at once our duty and our privilege: and to "grow up into him in all things as our living Head," is the work of every day throughout our whole lives^g. Now, then, I call you to commence this work, if it be not yet begun; or to proceed in it with augmented ardour, if, through the grace of God, it be already begun in your souls. And for your encouragement, I will venture to affirm, that the tokens of God's approbation which were vouchsafed to Moses, shall as really, if not so sensibly, be renewed to you; for "the glory of the Lord shall fill" your souls, and the most signal manifestations of his love shall abide with you, both in this world, and in the world to come^h ———]

And now I APPEAL to you, whether this will not be a good employment for the season on which we have just entered?

[Who does not regret that he has lost so much time already? Moses, considering how many months had been consumed in the wilderness before he began his work, could not have well completed it before. But who amongst you might not have begun long before, and been now both serving and enjoying God in a tenfold greater degree, if he had duly improved his time, and prosecuted his work with unremitting care? Well; let it then be your endeavour now to "redeem the time;" that, if this be the destined period that is to put an end to your earthly existence, you may enter with joy into the presence of your Lord, and be for ever happy in the bosom of your God.]

^c Rom. xii. 1.   ^d 1 Pet. ii. 5.   ^e Phil. ii. 15.
^f Isai. xliii. 12.   ^g Eph. iv. 15.   ^h ver. 34, 35.

OUTLINE NO. 118

ERECTING OF THE TABERNACLE.

Exod. xl. 33, 34. *So Moses finished the work. Then a cloud covered the tent of the congregation, and the glory of the Lord filled the tabernacle.*

AN union of many hands and much zeal must of necessity expedite any work that is undertaken. So it proved in the constructing of the tabernacle; the whole of which, notwithstanding the exquisite skill and workmanship with which every part of it was formed, was in about the space of seven months completely finished, so as to be capable of being all erected, and brought into use in one single day. Such activity could not but be highly pleasing to God, in whose service it was employed. Accordingly we find that he immediately testified his approbation of it by a most astonishing act of condescension and grace.

That we may see the subject in its true light, let us inquire into,

I. The work here referred to—

This was the constructing of the tabernacle; a work of singular excellency and importance, whether it be considered in itself, or in its typical design. Let us view it,

1. In itself—

[It will be proper to notice briefly its *form*. There was a court about sixty yards long, and thirty broad, enclosed by linen curtains, suspended about nine feet high on brasen pillars. Within that, at the west end of it, was a structure, about eighteen yards long, and six broad, made with boards of Shittim wood, covered with gold, and fastened together by bars of the same materials. The boards were forty-eight in number, fixed in ninety-six sockets of silver, each of them about an hundred pounds weight. The whole was covered first with curtains of fine embroidered linen, and then with three other coverings, one of goats' hair, another of rams' skins dyed red, and another of badgers' skins. This structure was divided into two apartments, called the holy place, and the holy of holies; the former being about twelve yards by six; and the latter six yards square, and as many high. The entrance to each of these was from the east, (as was that of the outward court also,) each leading to the other through a veil of embroidered linen.

The *furniture* of the whole was quite appropriate. In the outer court, (to which all *clean* Hebrews and proselytes had access,) was the brasen altar, on which the sacrifices were offered, and the brasen laver, in which the priests and Levites were to purify themselves. In the holy place (into which the priests were admitted) was the candlestick, the table of shewbread, and the altar of incense. In the holy of holies (where the high-priest alone entered, and that only on one day in the year,) was the ark, covered by the mercy-seat; on which abode the Shechinah (the bright cloud, the symbol of the Deity), between cherubim. In the ark the tables of the law were deposited: and at a subsequent period, Aaron's rod that budded, and the golden pot that had the manna, were laid up before it[a].

We need not enter minutely into these things: it will be more instructive, after taking this summary view of the whole, to notice it,]

2. In its typical design—

[In interpreting the types, we must bear in mind that the greater part of them had reference to Christ in one view, and to his Church and people in another view. This was particularly the case with respect to the tabernacle.

It typified, in the first place, *the Lord Jesus* Christ. Our Lord himself, speaking of his own body, says, " Destroy this temple, and in three days I will raise it up again[b]." And in the Epistle to the Hebrews, his body is represented as that " more perfect tabernacle in which he ministered, and which was not made with hands, as the other was, but by the immediate agency of the Holy Ghost[c]." The correspondence between the two is obvious: for " in Him dwelt all the fulness of the Godhead bodily:" and through his atoning sacrifice, and sanctifying grace, and prevailing intercession, we all are brought into a state of acceptance with God. On the other hand, as there was no way to the Mercy-seat but through the Holy Place, " so no man can now come unto the Father but by him."

It further typified *the Church*, which, though mean without, " is all glorious within." In that alone is any acceptable sacrifice offered unto God. In that alone are the sanctifying operations of the Spirit experienced. In that alone is the bread of life administered, or the light of truth exhibited. In that alone does God manifest his glory, or communicate his saving benefits. Hence the beloved disciple, speaking of the Church in the latter days, says, " The tabernacle of God is with men, and he will dwell with them, and they shall be his people, and God himself shall be with them, and be their God[d]."

Once more, it typified *heaven* also. Remarkable is the language of the Apostle, who says, " Christ is not entered into the holy places made with hands, *which are the figures of the true*, but into *heaven itself*, now to appear in the presence of God for us[e]." There, not the symbol of the Deity, but all the glory of the Godhead, is unveiled. There the sacrifices of praise and thanksgiving ascend up with a sweet odour unto

---

[a] Compare Heb. ix. 4, 5. with 1 Kings viii. 9.   [b] John ii. 19, 21.
[c] Heb. viii. 2. and ix. 9—11.   [d] Rev. xxi. 3.   [e] Heb. ix. 24.

God continually. There the illumination, the nourishment, the purity of every soul is complete. No veil obstructs the view, or forbids the access, of any individual: the beatific vision is vouchsafed to all, and the full fruition of their God is the portion of all the saints.]

If we judged only from the minuteness of the orders which God gave respecting this work, we should conceive highly of its importance: but still more shall we see it, if we consider,

II. The testimony of his approbation with which God honoured it—

[We must bear in mind that Israel had sinned a grievous sin; that, at the intercession of Moses, God had turned away from his holy indignation, and promised to continue with them as their God. In token of his reconciliation, he ordered this tabernacle to be made for him; and the very day it was erected, he came down visibly to take possession of it as his peculiar residence, and so filled it with his glory, that Moses himself could no longer stand to minister there[f]. Now whilst this testified his approbation of their work, and of those who had been engaged in it, it shewed to all future generations, that *He will return to those in love and mercy, who return to him in a way of penitence and active obedience.*

In this view, we are led to consider this event, not as relating to the Israelites merely, but as speaking to us. Where is the nation, where the church, where the individual, who has not given just occasion to the Lord to shut up his loving-kindness in displeasure? — — — Yet where is there to be found, in the annals of the world, one single instance, wherein God has turned a deaf ear to the supplications of a real penitent? Instances to the contrary are without number — — — And God, as in the history before us, has seemed ambitious, as it were, to make "his grace abound, not only where sin had abounded," but (I had almost said) in proportion as sin had abounded — — —We must be careful not to "limit the Holy One of Israel," whose "ways and thoughts are as far above ours, as the heavens are above the earth." We are apt to forget that he is the same God now, as he was in the days of old: but "he changeth not:" and if his manifestations be less visible than formerly, they are not a whit less real, or less gracious[g]]

APPLICATION—

[The day on which this work was finished was the first day of the year[h]. What a blessed commencement was it of

[f] ver. 35.   [g] 2 Cor. vi. 16. and John xiv. 21.   [h] ver. 2.

the new year! How sweet must have been the retrospect to all who had been engaged in the work, when they saw that they had not spent the preceding year in vain! Each could call to mind some sacrifices which he had made for God, or some exertions used in his service: and they would enter on the new year with a determined purpose to serve and honour God more than they had ever yet done. Beloved Brethren, is it so with you? Have you in your consciences an evidence that you have lived for God, and made it a principal object of your life to serve and honour him?———But, however the past year may have been spent, bethink yourselves now what work you have to do for him, and how you may perfect it with expedition and care. And O that we may speedily have such a day amongst us as the Israelites enjoyed; all of us presenting to him our souls and bodies for his habitation, and receiving from him undoubted tokens of his favourable regard!]

LEVITICUS.

OUTLINE NO. 119

THE BURNT-OFFERING.

Lev. i. 3, 4. *If his offering be a burnt-sacrifice of the herd, let him offer a male without blemish: he shall offer it of his own voluntary will, at the door of the tabernacle of the congregation, before the Lord. And he shall put his hand upon the head of the burnt-offering; and it shall be accepted for him, to make atonement for him.*

THE institution of sacrifices may be considered as nearly coeval with the world itself. As soon as man had fallen, he needed an atonement; and an atonement was provided for him by God himself; who promised, that "the seed of the woman should bruise the serpent's head:" nor can we reasonably doubt, but that God himself, who, we are told, "clothed our first parents with skins," appointed the beasts, whose skins were used for that purpose, to be offered up first in sacrifice to him. Whence, if God had not originally sanctioned it, should Abel think of offering up "the firstlings of his flock?" and why should that very sacrifice receive such a signal testimony of the divine approbation? Even the distinction between clean and unclean animals was known before the flood; and an additional number of the clean were taken into the ark, that there might be wherewith to offer sacrifice unto the Lord, when the deluge should be abated. Abraham also, and Melchizedec, and Job, all offered sacrifices, before the Mosaic ritual was known: so that Moses did not so much introduce new institutions, as regulate those which had existed before; and give such directions respecting them, as should suit the dispensation which his ritual was intended to prefigure.

Sacrifices are of two kinds, *propitiatory*, and *eucharistical;* the one to make atonement for sins committed; the other to render thanks for mercies received. Of the *propitiatory* sacrifices we have an account of no less than six different sorts; (all of which are stated in the seven first chapters of Leviticus;) "the burnt-offering, the meat-offering, the sin-offering, the trespass-offering, the offering of consecrations, and the peace-offering[a]." It is of the first of these that we are to speak at this time.

We shall notice,

I. The offering itself—

[The *burnt-offering* was the most ancient and dignified of all the sacrifices, and at the same time the most frequent; there being two every day in the year, except on the Sabbath-days, when the number was always doubled. The things of which it consisted, varied according to the ability of the offerer: it might be taken from among the herd, or the flock, or of fowls[b]: that so no one might have any excuse for withholding it at its proper season. By this accommodation of the offering to the circumstances of men, it was intended, that every one should evince the sincerity of his heart in presenting unto God the best offering that he could; and that no one should be discouraged from approaching God by the consideration that he was not able to present to him such an offering as he could wish. "The turtle-dove or young pigeon" was as acceptable to God as the "ram" or "bullock," provided it was offered with a suitable frame of mind. Indeed the directions respecting the poor man's offering were as minute and particular as any[c]: which shewed, that God has no respect of persons; and that his Ministers also must at their peril be as anxious for the welfare, and as attentive to the interests, of the poorest of their flock, as of the most opulent.

One thing was indispensable; that the offering, whether of the herd or of the flocks, must be "a male, and without blemish." It was to be the most excellent of its kind, in order the more fitly to shadow forth the excellencies of our incarnate God; who alone, of all that ever partook of our nature, was truly without sin. Had the smallest imperfection attached to him, he could not have been a propitiation for our sins. The utmost care therefore was to be taken in examining the offerings

---

[a] Lev. vii. 37. They were not *altogether* propitiatory; but are numbered with the propitiatory, because they were *in part* burnt upon the brasen altar.

[b] ver. 3, 10, 14.   [c] ver. 14—17.

which prefigured him, that they might, as far as possible, exemplify his spotless perfection.]

II. The manner in which it was presented—

Here also we notice very minute directions respecting,

1. The offerer—

[He must bring his sacrifice "of his own voluntary will." He must feel his need of mercy, and be very desirous to obtain it. He must see that no mercy can be found, except by means of a sacrifice: and he must thankfully embrace the opportunity afforded him; not accounting God his debtor for the sacrifice offered to him, but himself a debtor to God, for his permission to approach him in such a way.

He must bring his sacrifice to "the door of the tabernacle of the congregation, before the Lord." Whilst, in doing this, he acknowledged that the Lord dwelt there in a peculiar manner, he publicly, before all the people, acknowledged himself a sinner like unto his brethren, and needing mercy no less than the vilest of the human race. Not the smallest degree of self-preference could be allowed; but all must be made to see and feel that there was but one way of salvation for ruined man.

Further, he was to "put his hand upon the head of his offering." By this significant action, he still more plainly declared, that he must perish, if ever his sins should be visited upon him; and that all his hope of acceptance with God was founded on the vicarious sufferings of this devoted victim.]

2. The offering itself—

[This must be "slain," (whether by the offerer or the priest, is uncertain[d],) and its "blood be sprinkled round about upon the altar." The slaughtered animal was then to be "flayed," and "cut into pieces," according to a prescribed rule: "the inwards and the legs," which might be supposed to need somewhat of purification, were "washed," and, together with the *whole* body, "burnt upon the altar." The skin alone remained, as a perquisite of the priest[e]. Do we not see in these things a striking exhibition of the sufferings of the Son of God, who was in due time to become a sacrifice for the sins of the whole world? Death was the wages due to sin, and that too under the wrath of an offended God. True it is, that the consuming of an animal by fire was but a faint representation of that

---

[d] We apprehend it was by the priest, or some Levite assisting him. See ver. 15. The same ambiguity as to the meaning of the word, "*they,*" may be seen in 2 Chron. xxix. 22; but it is plain, from ver. 34. of that chapter, that neither the priests nor the offerers killed the sacrifices; but the Levites killed them, and the priests received the blood. [e] Lev. vii 8.

misery, which we must to all eternity have endured; and of that which our blessed Lord sustained, both in his body and in his soul, when he died under the load of our iniquities.

The partial washing of the sacrifice might probably denote the perfect purity of Christ; or perhaps it might intimate the concurrence of the Holy Spirit, through whose divine agency he was fitted for a sacrifice, and by whose almighty aid he was enabled to offer himself up to God: for it was " *through the eternal Spirit* that he offered himself without spot to God."]

III. The benefits resulting from it—

[" It was accepted for the offerer, to make an atonement for him." As there were two kinds of guilt, ceremonial and moral, so there were two kinds of absolution, one actual in the sight of God, the other merely external and shadowy. We observe then in relation to these sacrifices, that they cleansed from *ceremonial* defilement *really*, and from *real* defilement *ceremonially*. There were certain things, not evil in themselves, but made so by the special appointment of God, (such as the touching of a grave or a dead body;) and the persons who had done them were to be accounted unclean, till they were purified in the way prescribed: and their observance of the prescribed forms did really purge them from the defilement they had contracted, so that no guilt would be imputed to them, nor any punishment inflicted, either in time or eternity. On the other hand, there were things really evil, (as theft or perjury,) which subjected the offender to punishment by the laws of man: now the guilt of these crimes was not purged away by the appointed sacrifices, any further than the exempting of the person from the punishment denounced by law: his conscience still remained burthened with guilt; and he must, notwithstanding all his sacrifices, answer for his crimes at the tribunal of God. This is the distinction made for us by God himself, who says, that "the blood of bulls and of goats, and the ashes of an heifer sprinkling the unclean, did really sanctify to the purifying of the flesh:" but they "never could make a man perfect as pertaining to the conscience:" in that sense, "it was not possible that the blood of bulls and of goats could take away sins."

It may be asked then, What benefit was there to counterbalance the cost and trouble of the sacrifices? I answer, that an exemption from temporal judgments, whether inflicted by God or man, was a great benefit: but to be encouraged to come to God as a merciful and gracious God, and to have Christ so clearly and constantly exhibited before their eyes, was an unspeakable benefit, which would have been cheaply purchased by the cattle on a thousand hills.]

In this ordinance we may find,

1. Much for our instruction—

[Of all the subjects that can be offered to our view, there is not any that can bear the least comparison with that leading subject of the Gospel, Christ crucified: and I had almost said, that the New Testament itself scarcely unfolds it more clearly, than the ordinance before us. What would the most ignorant of the Jews imagine, when he saw the sacrifice led forth, the offerer putting his hand upon it, and the priest slaying it, and afterwards reducing it to ashes? Would he not see that here was a manifest substitution of an innocent creature in the place of the guilty, and that that very substitution was the means of reconciling the offender to his God? I will grant, that a person ignorant of the typical nature of those ordinances, might be led to ascribe the benefit to the ordinance itself, without looking through it to the sacrifice which it shadowed forth; but he could not be so blind as not to see, that acceptance with God was by means of a vicarious sacrifice. Yet, behold, we Christians, who live under the meridian light of the Gospel, need to be told, that we must be saved entirely through the atonement of Christ: yea, after all that a minister, or God himself, can say, the great majority of us will seek acceptance, in whole or in part, by our own righteousness. Go back to the Law: ask a Jew to teach you: let those whom you despise for their ignorance, be your preceptors. It is a shame and scandal that salvation by Christ is so little known amongst us[f], and that the preachers of it are yet represented as setting forth a "*new doctrine*[g]." Be instructed then, ye opposers of Christ crucified, who are yet ignorantly "seeking to establish your own righteousness:" learn, even from the Law itself, to embrace the Gospel: and "kiss the Son, lest he be angry, and ye perish from the way."]

2. Much for our imitation—

[Every one whose conscience convicted him of sin, offered, "of his own voluntary will," the best sacrifice he could; grudging nothing whereby he might honour God or promote his own salvation. An irreligious man might have asked, 'Wherefore is all this waste of cattle, which, instead of being consumed by fire, might be sold, or given to the poor?' But the man who fears God, would reply, that nothing can be wasted which is in any way conducive to God's honour and our salvation. This is the spirit that should animate us. We may be called to make sacrifices for God: our reputation, our interest, our liberty, our very lives, may be called for in his service: and shall we be backward to make the sacrifice? Alas! too many of us are rather for a *cheap* religion; and their chief anxiety is, to get to heaven at as cheap a rate as possible, and to sacrifice for God as little as they can: if they are poor,

---

[f] 1 Cor. xv. 34.   [g] Acts xvii. 19.

Their little can't be spared; and if they are rich, Their victim is too costly. Away with such low and niggardly thoughts: let the large and liberal spirit of Christianity possess your souls: let nothing that you have endured, move you; nor any thing that you can endure: be willing to be bound, or even to die, for the Lord's sake. As for your lusts, let them be sacrificed, and utterly consumed: the sooner they are mortified, the better. And those things, which, if not called for by God in the way of his providence, you might innocently retain, bring to the altar with your own hands, and, *of your own voluntary will,* offer them to God: spare not any thing one moment, if it stand in competition with your duty, and the maintenance of a good conscience before God. In a word, " present your own selves to him a living sacrifice; for that is your reasonable service; and it shall be accepted of your God[h]."]

[h] Rom. xii. 1.

OUTLINE NO. 120
THE MEAT-OFFERING.

Lev. ii. 1—3. *And when any will offer a meat-offering unto the Lord, his offering shall be of fine flour: and he shall pour oil upon it, and put frankincense thereon: and he shall bring it to Aaron's sons, the priests: and he shall take thereout his handful of the flour thereof, and of the oil thereof, with all the frankincense thereof; and the priest shall burn the memorial of it upon the altar, to be an offering made by fire, of a sweet savour unto the Lord: and the remnant of the meat-offering shall be Aaron's and his sons': it is a thing most holy of the offerings of the Lord made by fire.*

IN order to a judicious exposition of the types, it is necessary that we should have certain canons of interpretation, to which we should adhere: for, without them, we may wander into the regions of fancy, and cast an obscurity over those Scriptures which we undertake to explain. Now it must be remembered, that Christ and his Church, together with the whole work of salvation, whether as wrought by him, or as enjoyed by them, were the subjects of typical exhibition. Sometimes the type pointed more immediately at one part of this subject, and sometimes at another; and sometimes it applied to different parts at the same time. The tabernacle, for instance, certainly represented Christ, " in whom dwelt all the fulness of the Godhead bodily:" and it represented the Church also in which God's presence is more especially manifested, and his service more eminently performed. The types being expressly instituted for the purpose of prefiguring spiritual things, have a determinate meaning in their minutest particulars: and it is highly probable that they have always a two-fold accomplishment, one in Christ, and the other in the Church. For instance; every sacrifice undoubtedly directs our views to Christ: yet we ourselves also, together with our services, are frequently represented as sacrifices acceptable to him: which shews, that the sacrifices have a further reference to us also. But here, it is of great importance that we distinguish between those expressions of the New Testament which are merely metaphorical, and those which are direct applications of the types. St. Paul, speaking of the probability of his own martyrdom in the cause of Christ, says, " If I be *offered* upon the sacrifice and service of your faith, I joy and rejoice with you all." Here he alludes to the drink-offerings, which were always *poured out* upon the sacrifices; and intimates that he was willing to have his blood *poured out* in like manner for the Church's good. This, *as a metaphor*, is beautiful; but if we were to make the sacrifices *typical* of faith, and the drink-offerings *typical* of martyrdom, and from thence proceed to *explain the whole type in like manner*, we should bring the whole into contempt. The rule then that we would lay down is this; to follow strictly the apostolic explanations as far as we have them; and, where we have them not, to proceed with extreme caution; adhering rigidly to the analogy of faith, and standing as remote as possible from any thing which may appear fanciful, or give occasion to cavillers to discard typical expositions altogether.

The foregoing observations are particularly applicable to the subject of our present consideration. We apprehend that the meat-offering *might* be applied in every particular both to Christ and his Church: but in some instances the application would appear forced; and therefore we think it better to omit some things which may possibly belong to the subject, than to obscure the whole by any thing of a doubtful nature. Besides, there are in this type such a multitude of particulars, that it would not be possible to speak satisfactorily upon them all in one sermon, if we were to take them in the most comprehensive view: we shall therefore confine ourselves to such observations as will commend themselves to your judgment, without perplexing you by too great a diversity on the one hand, or by any thing fanciful or doubtful on the other.

That we may prosecute the subject in a way easy to be understood, we shall distinguish the meat-offering by its great leading feature, and consider it in that view only. The *burnt-offering* typified exclusively the atonement of Christ: the *meat-offering* typified our sanctification by the Spirit.

As for the meat-offerings which accompanied the stated burnt-offerings, they, together with their attendant drink-offerings, were wholly consumed upon the altar; but those which were offered by themselves, were burnt only in part; the remainder being given to the priests for their support. It is of *these* that we are now to speak. The different materials of which they consisted, will serve us for an easy and natural distribution of the subject.

The first thing to be noticed is,
"The fine flour"—

[Whatever we see burnt upon the brasen altar, we may be sure was typical of the atonement of Christ: whether it were the flesh of beasts, or the fruits of the earth, there was no difference in this respect: it equally typified his sacrifice. This appears not only from the meat-offering being frequently mentioned together with the burnt-offering in this very view[a], but from its being expressly referred to as a means of expiating moral guilt[b]. It is on this account that we number it among the *propitiatory* sacrifices, notwithstanding its use in other respects was widely different. There is indeed, in the mode of treating this fine flour, something well suited to shadow forth the sufferings of Christ: it was *baked* (in a pan or oven) or *fried*, and, when formed into a cake, was *broken* and *burnt*

[a] See Ps. xl. 6—8. and Heb. x. 5—8.
[b] 1 Sam. iii. 14. and xxvi. 19. The mincha is the offering spoken of in both these places.

upon the altar. Who can contemplate this, and not see in it the temptations, conflicts, and agonies of the Son of God? We cannot but recognise in these things, HIM, " who was wounded for our transgressions and bruised for our iniquities;" who himself tells us, that " He was the true bread, of which whosoever ate, should live for ever."

In the close of the chapter we are told, that, notwithstanding the first-fruits, *when offered as the first-fruits*, might not be burnt upon the altar[c], yet, *if offered as a meat-offering*, they would be accepted[d]; and that in that case the ears must be dried by the fire, and the corn be beaten out, to be used instead of flour. The mystery in either case was the same: the excellency of Christ was marked in the quality of the corn, and his sufferings in the disposal of it.]

The next thing that calls for our attention is,

" The oil"—

[Though the sacrifice of Christ is the foundation of all our hopes, yet it will not avail for our final acceptance with God, unless we be " renewed in the spirit of our minds," and be rendered " meet for the heavenly inheritance." But to effect this, is the work of the Holy Spirit, by whose gracious operations alone we can " mortify the deeds of the body," and attain the divine image on our souls. Hence, in approaching God with their meat-offering, they were to mingle oil with the flour, or to anoint it with oil, after having previously made it into a cake. We do not deny but that this part of the ordinance might represent, in some respect, the endowments of Christ, who was anointed to his work, and fitted for it, by a superabundant measure of the Holy Ghost[e]: but, as it seems designed more particularly to mark the sanctification of our souls, we the rather confine it to that sense. And in this we have the sanction of two inspired persons, a Prophet, and an Apostle, both of whom refer to the mincha as expressive of this very idea. Isaiah, speaking of the conversion of the Gentiles in the latter days, says, " Men shall bring them for an offering (a mincha) unto the Lord, as the children of Israel bring an offering (a mincha) in a clean vessel into the house of the Lord[f]." And St. Paul, speaking of that event as actually fulfilled under his ministry, goes yet further into the explanation of it, and says, that the sanctification of their souls by the Holy Ghost corresponded with the unction wherewith that offering was anointed: " I am," says he, " the minister of Jesus Christ to the Gentiles, that the *offering up* of the Gentiles might be acceptable, *being sanctified by the Holy Ghost*[g]."

[c] ver. 12.   [d] ver. 14—16   [e] Luke iv. 18. and John iii. 34
[f] Isai. lxvi. 20.   [g] Rom. xv. 16.

Here then we are warranted in saying, that all who would find acceptance with God, must "have an unction of the Holy One, even that anointing which shall abide with them and teach them all things[h]." We should "be filled with the Spirit, and "live and walk under" his gracious influences[i].]

In a subsequent part of this chapter there is an especial command to add to this, and indeed to every sacrifice, a portion of
"Salt,"—

[Here we have no difficulty; for the very terms in which the command is given, sufficiently mark its import: "Thou shalt not suffer the *salt of the covenant of thy God* to be lacking from thy meat-offering[k]." Had salt been mentioned alone, we might have doubted what meaning to affix to it; but, being annexed to the covenant of God, we do not hesitate to explain it as designating the *perpetuity of that covenant.* It is the property of salt to keep things from corruption: and the Scriptures frequently apply it to the covenant, in order to intimate its unchangeable nature, and duration[l]. In this view of it, we are at no loss to account for the extreme energy with which the command is given, or the injunction to use salt in *every* sacrifice: for we cannot hope for pardon through the sacrifice of Christ, nor for sanctification by the Spirit, but according to the tenour of the everlasting covenant. Nay, neither the one nor the other of these, nor both together, would have availed for our salvation, if God had not *covenanted* with his Son to accept his sacrifice for us, and to accept us also as renewed and sanctified by his Spirit. We must never therefore approach our God without having a distinct reference to that covenant, as the ground and measure, the pledge and earnest, of all the blessings that we hope for. Even Christ himself owed his exaltation to glory to this covenant: it was "through the blood of the *everlasting covenant* that his God and Father brought him up again from the dead[m]." And it is because "that covenant is ordered in all things and sure," that we can look up with confidence for all the blessings both of grace and glory.]

Together with these things that are enjoined, we find some expressly prohibited: there must be
"No leaven, nor honey[n]"—

[Leaven, according to our Lord's own explanation of it, was considered as an emblem of corruption either in doctrine or in principle[o]: and honey seems to have denoted sensuality. Now these were forbidden to be blended with the meat-offering.

[h] 1 John ii. 20, 27.   [i] Eph. v. 18. Gal. v. 25.   [k] ver. 13.
[l] See Numb. xviii. 19. 2 Chron. xiii. 5.   [m] Heb. xiii. 20.
[n] ver. 11.   [o] Matt. xvi. 12. Luke xii. 1.

There were occasions, as we shall see hereafter, whereon leaven at least might be offered; but in this offering not the smallest measure of either of them was to be mixed. This certainly intimated, that, when we come before God for mercy, we must harbour no sin in our hearts. We must put away evil of every kind, and offer him only " the *unleavened* bread of sincerity and truth." The retaining " a right hand or a right eye," contrary to his commands, will be as effectual a bar to our acceptance with God, as the indulgence of the grossest lusts. If we would obtain favour in his sight, we must be " Israelites indeed, and without guile."]

There was however one more thing to be added to this offering, namely,

" Frankincense"—

[The directions respecting this were singularly precise and strong. This was not to be mixed with the offering, or strewed upon it, but to be put on one part of it, that, while a small portion only of the other materials was put upon the altar, *the whole of this* was to be consumed by fire[p]. Shall we say, that this was enjoined, because, being unfit for *food*, it was not to be kept for mere *gratification* to the priests, lest it should be brought into contempt? This by no means accounts sufficiently for the strictness of the injunction. We doubt not but that its meaning was of peculiar importance; that it was intended to intimate " the delight" which God takes in the services of his upright worshippers[q], of those especially who come to him under the influences of his Spirit, trusting in the Saviour's merits, and in the blood of the everlasting covenant. Yes, their every prayer, their every tear, their every sigh and groan, comes up with acceptance before him, and is to him " an odour of a sweet smell," " a sacrifice pleasing and acceptable unto him through Jesus Christ." As the sacrifice of Christ himself was most pleasing unto God, so are the services of all his people for Christ's sake[r].]

There is yet one thing more which we must notice, namely, that a part only of this offering was burnt, and that

" The remnant" was given to the priests[s]—

[The handful which was burnt upon the altar, is repeatedly called " a memorial:" and it was justly called so, especially by those who had an insight into the nature of the offering which they presented: for it was a memorial *of God's covenant-engagements,* and *of their affiance in them.* Such also is, in

[p] ver. 2, 16. *"all, all."*   [q] Prov. xv. 8.
[r] Compare Eph. v. 2. with Heb. xiii. 16. Phil. iv. 18. and 1 Pet. ii. 5.   [s] ver. 3, 10.

fact, every prayer which we present to God: we remind God (so to speak) of his promises made to us in his word; and we plead them as the grounds of our hope, and the measure of our expectations.

"The remnant was given to Aaron and his sons." This, to *the Israelites,* would intimate, that all who would obtain salvation for themselves, must at the same time be active in upholding the interests of religion, and promoting the glory of their God. To *us,* it unfolds a deeper mystery. *We* are frequently spoken of in the New Testament as being ourselves "made priests unto God[t]." Since the veil of the temple was rent in twain, there is a way, "a new and living way, opened for *us* into the Holy of Holies[u];" and all of us, as "a kingdom of priests," have free and continual "access thither with boldness and with confidence[x]:" and we also have a right to all the provisions of God's house. It is our blessed privilege to feed upon that bread of life, the Lord Jesus, who has emphatically said, "My flesh is *meat* indeed, and my blood is *drink* indeed[y]." We may richly participate all the influences of the Spirit, and claim all the blessings of the everlasting covenant. Indeed, "if we feed not on these things, there is no life in us; but if we live upon them by faith, then have we eternal life."

Behold then, Brethren, "the remnant" of the offering: here it is, reserved for us in this sacred treasury, the book of God. Take of it; divide it among yourselves; eat of it; "eat and drink abundantly, O beloved[z];" eat of it, and live for ever. It is that "feast of fat things," spoken of by the prophet, which all of you are invited to partake of[a]. Only let not any hidden abomination turn it into a curse. If the bread be received even from the Saviour's hands, and you partake of it with an unsanctified heart, it will only prove an occasion of your more entire bondage to Satan, and your heavier condemnation at the last[b]. But, if you "draw nigh to God with a true heart, and full assurance of faith," "he will abundantly bless your provision[c]," and "your soul shall delight itself in fatness[d]."]

[t] Isai. lxvi. 21. with 1 Pet. ii. 5. and Rev. i. 6. and xx. 6.
[u] Heb. x. 19—22.   [x] Eph. iii. 12.   [y] John vi. 51—57.
[z] Cant. v. 1.   [a] Isai. xxv. 6.   [b] John xiii. 26, 27.
[c] Ps. cxxxii. 15.   [d] Isai. lv. 2.

OUTLINE NO. 121

THE MEAT-OFFERING A TYPE OF CHRIST.

Lev. ii. 13. *Every oblation of thy meat-offering shalt thou season with salt; neither shalt thou suffer the salt of the covenant of thy God to be lacking from thy meat-offering: with all thine offerings thou shalt offer salt.*

THERE certainly is need of much sobriety and caution in interpreting the typical parts of Scripture, lest, instead of adhering to the path marked out for us by the inspired writers, we be found wandering in the regions of fancy and conjecture. But there are some types, which, notwithstanding they be soberly explained, appear at first sight the mere creatures of one's own imagination; which, however, on a more full investigation, evidently appear to have been instituted of God for the express purpose of prefiguring the truths of the Gospel. Of this kind is the ordinance now under our consideration: for the elucidating of which, we shall,

I. Explain the meat-offering—

The directions respecting it were very minute—

[Meat-offerings were annexed to many of the more solemn sacrifices, and constituted a part of them [a]. But they were also frequently offered by themselves. They were to consist of fine flour, *mixed* with oil, and *accompanied* with frankincense [b]. The quantity offered was at the option of the offerer, because it was a free-will offering. The wheat might be presented either simply dried and formed into flour, or baked as a cake, or fried as a wafer [c]: but, in whatever way it was presented, it must by all means have salt upon it [d]. It was on no account to have any mixture in it, either of honey, or of leaven [e]. A part, or a memorial of it, was to be taken by the priest (but with *all* the frankincense), and to be burnt upon the altar [f]: and the remainder was for the maintenance of the priest himself, as holy food [g]. When it was duly offered in this manner, it was most pleasing and acceptable to God [h].]

And this was altogether typical of things under the gospel dispensation.

It was typical,

1. Of Christ's sacrifice—

[The meat-offering, or *mincha*, is often spoken of in direct reference to Christ, and his sacrifice. In the Epistle to the Hebrews, we have a long passage quoted from the Psalms, to shew that neither the meat-offering (mincha) nor any other sacrifice was to be presented to God, after that Christ should have fulfilled those types by his one offering of himself upon the cross [i]. And it is of great importance in this view to

[a] Numb. xxviii. throughout. [b] ver. 1, 2, 5. [c] ver. 4, 7, 14.
[d] ver. 13. [e] ver. 11. [f] ver. 16. [g] ver. 3.
[h] ver. 9. [i] Compare Ps. xl. 6—8. with Heb. x. 5—10.

remember, that though the meat-offering was for the most part eucharistical, or an expression of thankfulness, it was sometimes presented *as a sin-offering, to make an atonement for sin:* only, on those occasions, it was not mixed with oil, or accompanied with frankincense, because every thing expressive of joy was unsuited to a sin-offering[k]. This is a clear proof, that it must typify the sacrifice of Christ, who is the true, the only propitiation for sin[l].

Now there was a peculiar suitableness in this offering to represent the sacrifice of Christ. Was it of the finest quality, mixed with the purest oil, and free from any kind of leaven? this prefigured his holy nature, anointed, in a superabundant measure, with the oil of joy and gladness[m], and free from the smallest particle of sin[n]. Its destruction by fire on the altar denoted the sufferings he was to endure upon the cross; while the consumption of the remainder by the priests, marked him out as the food of his people's souls, all of them being partakers of the sacerdotal office, a kingdom of priests[o]. The frankincense also, which ascended in sweet odours, intimated the acceptableness of his sacrifice on our behalf.]

2. Of our services—

[The services of Christians are also frequently mentioned in terms alluding to the mincha, or meat-offering. *Their alms* are spoken of as a sacrifice well pleasing to God[p], an odour of a sweet smell[q]. *Their prayers* are said to be as the evening sacrifice, that was always accompanied with the meat-offering[r]: and the prophet Malachi, foretelling that, under the Gospel, "all men," Gentiles as well as Jews, "should pray everywhere[s]," uses this language; "I have no pleasure in you (Jews) saith the Lord, neither will I receive an offering (a mincha) at your hand: for from the rising of the sun even to the going down of the same, my name shall be great among the Gentiles, and in every place incense shall be offered unto my name, and a pure offering (mincha); for my name shall be great among the heathen, saith the Lord of hosts[t]." In a word, *the conversion of sinners, and their entire devoting of themselves to God,* is represented under this image: "They shall bring all your brethren, says the prophet, for an offering (mincha) unto the Lord, as the children of Israel bring an offering (mincha) in a clean vessel unto the Lord[u]." And St. Paul (alluding to the flour mixed with oil) speaks of himself as ministering the Gospel to the Gentiles, "that the offering up

---

[k] Lev. v. 11, 13. See also 1 Sam. iii. 14.   [l] 1 John ii. 2.
[m] Ps. xlv. 7.   John iii. 34.   [n] 1 Pet. ii. 22.
[o] Exod. xix. 6. with 1 Pet. ii. 9.   [p] Heb. xiii. 16.
[q] Phil. iv. 18.   [r] Ps. cxli. 2. with Numb. xxviii. 4, 5.
[s] 1 Tim. ii. 8.   [t] Mal. i. 10, 11.   [u] Isai. lxvi. 20.

of the Gentiles might be acceptable, being sanctified by the Holy Ghost[x]."

Nor is it without evident propriety that our services were prefigured by this ordinance. Was the flour to be of the best quality, and impregnated with oil? we must offer unto God, not our body only, but our soul; and *that* too, anointed with an holy unction[y]. Was neither honey, nor leaven, to be mixed with it? our services must be free from carnality[z], or hypocrisy[a]. Was a part of it, together with *all* the frankincense, to be burnt upon the altar, and the remainder to be eaten as holy food? thus must our services be inflamed with divine love, and be offered *wholly* to the glory of God; and, while they ascend up with acceptance before God, they shall surely tend also to the strengthening and refreshing of our own souls[b].]

There is, however, one circumstance in the meat-offering, which, for its importance, needs a distinct consideration; which will lead us to,

II. Notice the strict injunction respecting the seasoning of it with salt—

It surely was not in vain, that the injunction respecting the use of salt *in this, and in every other offering*, was so solemnly *thrice* repeated in the space of one single verse. But not even that injunction should induce one to look for any peculiar mystery (at least, not publicly to attempt an explanation of the mystery) if the Scriptures did not unfold to us its meaning, and give us a clew to the interpretation of it.

The whole ordinance being typical, we must consider this injunction,

1. In reference to Christ's sacrifice—

[Salt, in Scripture, is used to denote *savouriness* and *perpetuity*. In the former sense, our Lord compares his people to good salt, while false professors are as "salt that has lost *its savour*[c]." In the latter sense, God's covenant is often called "a covenant of salt[d]." Apply then these ideas to the sacrifice of Christ, and the reason of this reiterated injunction will immediately appear.

How savoury *to God*, and how sweet *to man*, is the atone-

---

[x] Rom. xv. 16.   [y] 1 Thess. v. 23.   1 John ii. 20, 27.

[z] If we are to annex any other idea than that of *leaven* to "honey," that of carnality seems the most appropriate. Prov. xxv. 16, 27.

[a] Luke xii. 1.   1 Cor. v. 7, 8.   [b] Isai. lviii. 10, 11.

[c] Matt. v. 13   [d] Numb. xviii. 19. and 2 Chron. xiii. 5

ment which Christ has offered! In the view of its acceptableness *to God*, and *in direct reference to the meat-offering*, it is thus noticed by St. Paul; "He gave himself for us, an offering and a sacrifice *to God* for a sweet smelling savour[e]." And, as having laid, by his own death, the foundation of his spiritual temple, he is said to be "*precious* unto *man* also, even unto all them that believe[f]."

Moreover the efficacy of his atonement is as immutable as God himself. In this, as well as in every other respect, "Jesus Christ is the same yesterday, to-day, and for ever[g]." The virtue of his blood to cleanse from sin, was not more powerful in the day when it purified three thousand converts, than it is at this hour, and shall be to all who trust in it[h].]

2. In reference to our services—

[Let the ideas of savouriness and perpetuity be transferred to these also, and it will appear that this exposition is not dictated by fancy, but by the Scriptures themselves.

A mere formal service, destitute of life and power, may be justly spoken of in the same humiliating terms as a false professor, "It is not fit for the land, nor yet for the dunghill[i]." Hence our Lord says, *in reference to the very injunction before us*, "Every sacrifice shall be salted with salt. Salt is good: but if the salt have lost its saltness, wherewith will you season it? HAVE SALT WITHIN YOURSELVES[k]." What can this mean, but that there should be a life and power in all our services, an heavenliness and spirituality in our whole deportment? We should have in ourselves[l], and present to God[m], and diffuse on all around us[n], a "*savour* of the knowledge of Christ."

Nor is the continuance or perpetuity of our services less strongly marked: for in addition to the remarkable expressions of our Lord before cited[o], St. Paul directs, that our "speech be ALWAY with grace, *seasoned with salt*[p]." There never ought to be one hour's intermission to the divine life, not one moment when we have lost the savour and relish of divine things.]

In order to a due IMPROVEMENT of this subject, let us reduce it to practice—

1. Let us take of Christ's sacrifice, and both present it to God, and feed upon it in our souls—

[All the Lord's people are "kings and *priests* unto God[q]:" all therefore have a right to present to him this offering, and to feed upon it: both of these things may be done by faith;

[e] Eph. v. 2.　　[f] 1 Pet. ii. 7.　　[g] Heb. xiii. 8.
[h] 1 John i. 7.　　[i] Luke xiv. 34, 35.　　[k] Mark ix. 49, 50.
[l] Matt. xvi. 23.　　[m] 2 Cor. ii. 15.　　[n] 2 Cor. ii. 14.
[o] Mark ix. 49, 50.　　[p] Col. iv. 6　　[q] Rev. i. 6.

and both *must* be done by us, if ever we would find acceptance with God. Let us think what would have been the state of the Jewish priests, if they had declined the execution of their office. Let us then put ourselves into their situation, and rest assured, that a neglect of this duty will bring upon us God's heavy and eternal displeasure[r]. On the other hand, if we believe in Christ, and feed on his body and blood, we shall be monuments of his love and mercy for evermore[s].]

2. Let us devote ourselves to God in the constant exercise of all holy affections—

[All we have is from the Lord; and all must be dedicated to his service. But let us be sure that, with our outward services, we give him our hearts[t]. What if a man, having good corn and oil, had offered that which was damaged? Should it have been accepted[u]? Or, if he had neglected to add the salt, should it have had any savour in God's estimation? So neither will the form of godliness be of any value without the power[x]; but, if we present ourselves[y], or any *spiritual* sacrifice whatever, it shall be accepted of God through Christ[z], to our present and eternal comfort.]

[r] John vi. 53. [s] John vi. 54. [t] Prov. xxiii. 26.
[u] Mal. i. 8. [x] 2 Tim. iii. 5. [y] Rom. xii. 1. [z] 1 Pet. ii. 5.

OUTLINE NO. 122

GREEN EARS OF CORN TO BE OFFERED.

Lev. ii. 14—16. *If thou offer a meat-offering of thy first-fruits unto the Lord, thou shalt offer for the meat-offering of thy first-fruits green ears of corn dried by the fire, even corn beaten out of full ears. And thou shalt put oil upon it, and lay frankincense thereon. It is a meat-offering. And the priest shall burn the memorial of it, part of the beaten corn thereof, and part of the oil thereof. It is an offering made by fire unto the Lord.*

AS there was a great variety of offerings under the Law, such as burnt-offerings, peace-offerings, trespass-offerings, sin-offerings, meat-offerings, so was there a variety of those which I have last mentioned—the meat-offerings. Some of these were constantly offered with and *upon* the burnt-offerings: some of them were offered separately by themselves: and these also were of two different kinds; some of them being *ordinary*, and appointed on particular occasions; and others of them *extraordinary*, and altogether *optional*, and presented only when persons particularly desired to "honour God with their substance." The *ordinary* and *appointed* meat-offerings are spoken of in the beginning of this chapter[a]: the *extraordinary* and *optional* are spoken of in my text. It is to the latter that I would draw your attention at this time. And for the purpose of bringing the ordinance before you in the simplest and most intelligible manner, I will set before you,

I. Its distinguishing peculiarities—

In some respects this meat-offering agreed with those which were common—

[It consisted of corn: it was accompanied with oil: frankincense also was put upon it. A part of it and of the oil were burnt upon the altar, together with *all* the frankincense, as a memorial to the Lord: and the remainder of the corn and oil was given to the priests, for their subsistence.

Thus far it was an expression of gratitude to God for the mercies he had begun to impart, and of affiance in him for a complete and final bestowment of the blessings so conferred.]

In other respects it differed from those which were common—

[In the common meat-offerings the corn used was ripe, and ground into flour: but in this the corn was unripe, and incapable of being ground into flour, till a certain process had been used in relation to it. "The ears of corn were" cut when "green:" they were then to be "dried with fire:" and *then* were they to be offered in the way appointed for common meat-offerings[b].]

Contenting myself with barely specifying the peculiarities under my first head, I proceed to explain them under my second head; and to mark, in relation to this ordinance,

II. Its special import—

As far as its observances accorded with those of the common meat-offering, its import was the same—

[Burnt-offerings referred entirely to Christ, and shadowed forth him as dying for the sins of men. But the meat-offerings represented rather the people of Christ *gathered out from the world, anointed with the Holy Spirit*, and *offered up upon God's*

---

[a] Compare ver. 1—3. with chap. xxiii. 9—14.
[b] Compare ver. 2, 3. with the text.

altar, as consecrated to his service, and inflamed with holy zeal and love, for the advancement of his glory in the world. In this view the Prophet Isaiah speaks of the whole Gentile world, who shall be consecrated to the Lord in the last day: "They shall bring all your brethren *for an offering* unto the Lord out of all nations, upon horses, and in chariots, and in litters, and upon mules, and upon swift beasts, to my holy mountain Jerusalem, saith the Lord, as the children of Israel bring an offering in a clean vessel into the house of the Lord[c]." (The Mincha, or meat-offering, is that which is here particularly referred to.) To the same effect St. Paul also speaks in the New Testament of this very conversion as actually begun under his ministry: "I am," says he, "the minister of Jesus Christ to the Gentiles, ministering the Gospel of God, that *the offering up* of the Gentiles might be acceptable, being sanctified by the Holy Ghost[d]." Here is not only the same mention of the meat-offering as we observed in the Prophet Isaiah, but a more distinct reference to it as accompanied with oil, and as denoting the sanctification of believers by the gift of the Holy Ghost. This, then, may be considered as marking the import of this ordinance, so far as it agreed with the common meat-offerings.]

But so far as this meat-offering was peculiar, its import was peculiar also—

[We cannot, indeed, speak with the same confidence on this part of our subject as respecting the meat-offerings in general; because the inspired writers of the Old and New Testament are silent respecting it: yet I cannot but feel assured in my own mind, that "the green ears" are intended to denote the younger converts, who by reason of their tender age seem almost incapable of being so dedicated to the Lord. God would have such to be presented to him: and, that their *supposed* incapacity to serve him might be no discouragement either to them or us, they are ordered to be gathered in, that so they may be prepared for the honour that is to be conferred upon them. Additional pains are to be taken with them, in order to supply by artificial means, as it were, what nature has not yet done for them; and to God are they to be presented, without waiting for that maturity which others at a more advanced period of life have attained. They are not to be desponding in themselves, as though it were not possible for them to find acceptance with God; nor are they to be overlooked by others, as though it were in vain to hope that any converts should be gathered from amongst them. God would have it known, that he is alike willing to receive all; and that

[c] Isai. lxvi. 20. [d] Rom. xv. 16.

he will be glorified in all, " the least as well as the greatest[e]," in " little children, as well as in young men and fathers[f]."]

Having elsewhere explained the different parts of the meat-offering, I forbear to dwell on them[g], having no intention to speak of that ordinance any further than it is peculiar, and appropriate to the present occasion[h]. But, as in that view it is very interesting, I proceed to point out,

III. The instruction to be derived from it—

Assuredly it is highly instructive,

1. To Parents—

[Does it not shew you, that you should present your children to the Lord in early life? Yes; you should dedicate them to him even from the womb. See the examples of Hannah[i], and Elizabeth[k], and Lois, and Eunice[l]: are not these sufficient to guide and encourage you in this important duty? And is it no encouragement to you to be assured by God himself, " Train up a child in the way he should go; and when he is old he will not depart from it[m]?" I say, then, labour with all diligence to promote the spiritual edification of your offspring; and whilst they are yet so green and young as to appear incapable of serving God with intelligence and acceptance, devote them to him, in the hope that, with the oil and frankincense put upon them, they may prove an offering well pleasing to God, and may come up with a sweet savour before him.]

2. To Ministers—

[" The pastor after God's own heart" will " feed the lambs," as well as the sheep, of Christ's flock. And we rejoice in the increased attention that of late years been paid to the rising generation. But, after all, there is abundant occasion for augmented efforts in their behalf. Even the Apostles themselves had but very inadequate views of their duty in reference to persons in early life. When parents brought their children to Christ that he might bless them, the Apostles, judging that this was an unprofitable wasting of their Master's time, forbade them. But our blessed Lord was much displeased with them, and said, " Suffer the little children to come unto me, and forbid them not: for of such is the kingdom of God. And he took them up in his arms, put his hands upon them,

[e] Jer. xxxi. 34.
[f] 1 John ii. 12—14.
[g] See the Discourse on Lev. ii. 1—3.
[h] *Confirmation*, or *Sunday Schools*.
[i] 1 Sam. i. 22, 24, 28.
[k] Luke i. 15.
[l] 2 Tim. i. 5.
[m] Prov. xxii. 6.

and blessed them[n]." And who can tell what a blessing may attend the efforts of ministers, in reference to young people, even whilst the older and more intelligent reject their word? Certainly the appointment of the ordinance which we have been considering proclaims loudly the duty of ministers, and affords them all the encouragement that their hearts can desire.]

3. To young people—

[Persons in early life, though taken to God's house that they may serve the Lord in his instituted ordinances, rarely imagine that they have any personal interest in any part of the service. They think that religion is proper for those only who have attained a certain age; and that it will be time enough for them to serve the Lord, when their understandings are more matured. But the corn cannot be too green, provided only " the ears be full[o]." There must be *integrity*, whatever be the age: for an hypocrite can never find acceptance with God. But as to intellectual capacity, God both can and will supply that to the youngest child in the universe that has a desire to surrender himself up to him: yea, " the things which are hid from the wise and prudent, he will reveal to babes; for so it seemeth good in his sight[p]." Nay more, to those in early life God has given an express promise, a promise made exclusively to them: " They that seek me early shall find me[q]." Why, then, should young people despond, as though they were incapable of serving God? I have no hesitation in saying, that they are as acceptable an offering as can possibly be presented to the Lord: yea, in some respects God is more glorified in them than in persons at a more adult age; because the power of divine grace is more conspicuous in proportion as it is seen to be independent of man. Nor am I sure that such early monuments of divine grace do not render peculiar service to the Church; because their exhortations and examples are preeminently calculated to affect both the old and young: the old, as putting them to shame; and the young, as shewing them the practicability of God's service even at their tender age. I say, then, that this ordinance is particularly instructive to the young, and should inspire them with a holy zeal to surrender up themselves to God at the earliest period of their lives.]

ADDRESS—

1. The young—

[Methinks I see you with your heads erect, and yourselves in all the greenness of early life; and I hear you saying,

[n] Mark x. 13—16.   [o] ver. 14.   [p] Matt. xi. 25, 26.   [q] Prov. viii. 17.

'Leave me to myself; at least leave me till many more suns and showers have brought me to a maturity better suited to your use.' But no, my young Brethren; I would not leave you another day. God has appointed that the green ears be dried by the fire, and so be fitted for his use: and gladly would I use all possible means to qualify you for the honour to which he calls you: nor can I doubt but that, if you be willing, you shall be accepted of him. And think, I pray you, of the advantage of being consecrated to the Lord in early life: think how many sins you will avoid: think what an advance you may hope to have made in the divine life, whilst others are only beginning their Christian course. Above all, think what an honour it will be to serve the Lord; and what happiness to be regarded by him as his peculiar people. O, let me not speak in vain: but now vie, as it were, with each other, who shall be foremost in this blessed race, and who shall consecrate himself to God at the earliest period of his life. Happy am I to assure you, that the oil and frankincense are ready, and that the fire is already kindled on God's altar. Only be willing to be the Lord's, and this very hour shall your offering come up with acceptance before him.]

2. Those who are more advanced in life—

[If the green ears be sought for the Lord, surely you can have no doubt respecting the proper destination of those that are more matured. Affect, then, the honour which is now offered you, of being the Lord's. And remember, that, as a part only of the offering was consumed upon the altar, and the rest was given to the priests for their subsistence, so must ye gladly give yourselves to the Lord for the advancement of his glory, and the establishment of his kingdom in the world. It is for this that so many suns have shone upon you, and so many showers have been vouchsafed: and know, that in giving to God, ye give only what ye have received from him; and that, instead of conferring any obligation upon him, the more you do for him, the more you are indebted to him. Yes, know, that if the honour to which we call you were duly appreciated, there is not an ear in the whole field of nature that would not be anxious to attain it. May the meat-offerings, then, this day be multiplied on God's altar; and his name be increasingly glorified amongst us, for Christ's sake! Amen and Amen.]

OUTLINE NO. 123

THE SIN AND TRESPASS-OFFERINGS COMPARED.

Lev. v. 5, 6. *And it shall be, when he shall be guilty in one of these things, that he shall confess that he hath sinned in that*

123.] SIN AND TRESPASS-OFFERINGS COMPARED.

thing. And he shall bring his trespass-offering unto the Lord for his sin which he hath sinned, a female from the flock, a lamb, or a kid of the goats, for a sin-offering; and the priest shall make an atonement for him concerning his sin.

IN the words before us, the terms "sin-offering." and "trespass-offering" are used as signifying precisely the same thing: and in the 11th and 12th verses the trespass-offering is thrice mentioned as "a sin-offering." But they are certainly two different kinds of offering; though learned men are by no means agreed respecting the precise marks of difference between them. Indeed, almost all who have undertaken to explain them, confess, that they are not satisfied with what others have written upon the subject. The difficulty seems to lie in this; that the sin-offering seems to have respect to a lighter species of sin, and yet to require the more solemn offering; whilst the trespass-offering relates to considerably heavier offences, and yet admits of an easier method of obtaining forgiveness: for in the trespass-offering, pigeons or turtle-doves might be offered, or, in case of extreme poverty, a measure (about five pints) of flour: but in the sin-offering no such abatement, no such commutation, was allowed. This leads many (contrary to the plain letter of the Scripture) to represent the sin-offering as relating to the lighter, and the trespass-offering to the heavier, transgressions. But we apprehend that sufficient stress has not been laid on some peculiarities respecting the trespass-offering, which give by far the most satisfactory solution to the difficulties that occur in it. As for those things which the sin-offering has in common with the burnt-offerings or peace-offerings, we forbear to touch upon them, they having been already noticed in our discourses on those subjects: nor shall we enter very fully into the trespass-offering, because that is reserved for a future occasion[a]. We shall contract our present discussion into as short limits as possible, by omitting all that would lead us over ground already trodden, and fixing our attention on those few

[a] See Discourse on Lev. v. 17—19.

points, which will mark the peculiar features of these offerings, together with their distinctive differences.

We will,

I. Compare them together—

They agree in many things, each requiring that the blood of an animal should be shed and sprinkled as an atonement for sin. But they also differ very materially,

1. In the occasions on which they were offered—

[The sin-offerings were evidently presented on account of something done amiss through *ignorance* or *infirmity*[b]: but the trespass-offering was for sins committed through *inadvertence* or *the power of temptation*. Among these latter were sins of great enormity, such as violence, and fraud, and lying, and even perjury itself[c]. There must of course be very different degrees of criminality in these sins, according to the degree of information the person possessed, and the degree of conviction against which he acted. It might be that even in these things the person had sinned through ignorance only: but, whatever circumstances there might be to extenuate or to aggravate his crime, the trespass-offering was the appointed means whereby he was to obtain mercy and forgiveness.]

2. In the circumstances attending the offerings—

[*In the sin-offering*, there was particular respect to the rank and quality of the offender. If he were a priest, he must offer a bullock; which was also the appointed offering for the whole congregation: if he were a ruler or magistrate, he must offer a kid, a male; but if he were a common individual, a female kid or lamb would suffice. The blood of the victim, in the priest's offering, was to be sprinkled before the veil, and to be put upon the horns of the altar of incense; whilst the blood of the ruler's, or common person's sacrifice, was not sprinkled at all, nor put on the horns of the *golden* altar, the altar of incense; but was put on the horns of the altar of burnt-offering only, (that is, the *brasen* altar,) and poured out at the bottom of that altar.

In the trespass-offering, no mention is made of a bullock for any one, but only of a female kid or lamb: even turtle-doves or young pigeons might be presented; or, in the event of a person not being able to afford them, he might offer about five pints of flour, which would be accepted in their stead[d]. This is the excepted case which St. Paul refers to, when he says, "*Almost*

---

[b] See the whole fourth chapter. [c] ver. 1, 4. and chap. vi. 2, 3
[d] ver. 6, 7, 11.

123.] SIN AND TRESPASS-OFFERINGS COMPARED. 589

all things are by the law purged with blood[e]." Now thus far it does appear, that the heavier sins were to be atoned for by the lighter sacrifices: and *this is the source of all the difficulty that expositors find in the subject.* But there were three things required in this offering, which had no place in the sin-offering, namely, confession of the crime, restitution of the property, and compensation for the injury. Suppose a person had "robbed God" by keeping back a part of his tithes, (whether intentionally or not,) as soon as it was discovered, he must present his offering, confess his fault[f], restore what he had unjustly taken, and add one-fifth more of its value[g], as a compensation for the injury he had done. The same process was to take place if by fraud or violence he had injured a man[h]. This gives a decided preponderance to the trespass-offering: and shews, that the means used for the expiation of different offences bore a just proportion to the quality of those offences.]

We shall now proceed to state,

II. What they were both designed to teach us—

The spiritual instruction to be derived from the sacrifices themselves, and the particular rites that accompanied them, we pass over, for the reasons before assigned. But there are some lessons of an appropriate nature which we may dwell upon to great advantage:—

1. Sin, however venial it may appear to us, is no light evil—

[There are many branches of moral duty which are regarded as of but little importance. *Truth*, though approved and applauded as a virtue, is almost universally violated in the way of trade, and that too without any shame or remorse. Who that has ever bought or sold a commodity of any kind, has not seen that character realized, "It is naught, it is naught, saith the buyer; but when he is gone his way, then he boasteth" of the good purchase he hath made[i]? He must know little of the world, or of himself, who does not know, that "as a nail sticketh between the joints of the stones, so does lying between buying and selling[k]." Nor is *honesty* deemed at all more sacred than truth. Persons who would not rob or steal, will yet run in debt, when they know that they have not the means of satisfying their creditors. They will also defraud the revenue

---

[e] Heb. ix. 22.   [f] ver. 5.   [g] Lev. vi. 5.

[h] If the person injured could not be found, restitution was to be made to the priest, as God's representative. Numb. v. 6—8.

[i] Prov. xx. 14.   [k] Ecclus. xxvii. 2.

by every device in their power; purchasing goods that have not paid the customs, avoiding stamps where they are positively enjoined, and withholding, where they think they can do it without detection, the taxes which by law they are bound to pay. Such is the morality of many, who yet would be very indignant to be called thieves and liars. But God has given them no such licence to dispense with his laws; nor do they applaud such conduct when they themselves are the victims of deceit and fraud. Let them know therefore, that however partial they may be in estimating *their own* character and conduct, God " will judge righteous judgment:" and that, if sins of ignorance and infirmity were not pardoned without an atonement, much less shall such flagrant sins as theirs. It is true, they may plead custom; but before they venture to rest upon that plea, let them be well assured that God will accept it.]

2. There may be much guilt attaching, where there is but little suspicion of it—

[It is supposed in the sin-offering, that *priests*, and *rulers*, and *common individuals*, and *whole congregations*, may have committed sins, without being aware that they have done so. And may not the same thing occur amongst us? Let *ministers*, the priests of God, look back; let them consider the nature of their office, the responsibility attaching to it, the multitudes who have been, and yet are, committed to their care; the consequences of a faithful or unfaithful discharge of their duty; let them then compare their lives and ministrations with the lives and ministry of Christ and his Apostles, or with the express injunctions of Holy Writ; will *they* find no sins which they have overlooked? Will they see no occasion for the atonement of Christ? Truly, if it were not for the hope of mercy which we have through his atoning blood, we should be of all men most miserable; so great is the guilt which the most diligent amongst us has contracted by his defective ministrations. Let *rulers* proceed to make similar inquiries respecting their diligence, their impartiality, their zeal: let them see whether they might not have promoted in many instances a more active co-operation for the suppression of evil, and for the propagation of true religion: will *they* see no cause for shame and sorrow, when they see how little they have done for God, and in what a degree they have borne the sword in vain? Let any *private individual* institute a similar inquiry into all the motives by which he has been actuated, the dispositions he has manifested, the tempers he has exercised, and the use he has made of his time, his property, his influence: will *he* find nothing to condemn? Lastly, let *whole congregations* or communities be made to examine the maxims embraced, the habits countenanced, and the conduct pursued among them: will there be no room for them to acknowledge a departure from the ways of God? Is society in such a state, that all which we see and hear will stand the test, if tried by the requisitions of God's holy law?

Yet where are the consciences that are burthened with guilt? Where are the penitents applying to the blood of atonement? Are not the great mass of mankind, whether rulers or subjects, whether ministers or people, blessing themselves as having but little, if any, occasion to repent? Ah! well might David say, and happy would it be for us if it were the language also of our hearts, "Lord, who can understand his errors? cleanse thou me from my secret faults[1]!" And let none think that his ignorance is any excuse for him before God: for our ignorance arises only from inconsideration: and God expressly warns us, that that plea shall avail us nothing[m].]

3. The moment we see that we have sinned, we should seek for mercy in God's appointed way—

[As soon as the fault or error was discovered under the law, the proper offering (whether sin, or trespass, offering) was to be brought: and, if the offender refused to bring his offering, his sin became presumptuous; and he subjected himself to the penalty of death[n]. To infinitely sorer punishment shall we expose ourselves, if we neglect to seek for mercy through the atoning blood of Christ[o]. The declaration of God is this; "He that covereth his sins, shall not prosper; but whoso confesseth and forsaketh them shall have mercy[p]."

But let us beware of one delusion which proves fatal to thousands: we are apt to content ourselves with general acknowledgments that we are sinners, instead of searching out our particular sins, and humbling ourselves for them. Doubtless it is right to bewail the whole state of our souls: but he who never has seen any individual evils to lament, will have but very faint conceptions of his general depravity. We should therefore "search and try our ways;" and not only say with Achan, "I have sinned against the Lord God of Israel," but proceed with him to add, "*Thus* and *thus* have I done[q]." This is the particular instruction given in our text: the person who had transgressed any law of God, whether ceremonial or moral, was, as soon as he discovered it, to "confess, that he had sinned *in that* particular *thing*." O that we were more ready to humble ourselves thus! But we love not the work of self-examination: and the evils which we cannot altogether hide from ourselves, we endeavour to banish from our minds; and hence it is that so many of us are "hardened through the deceitfulness of sin."]

[1] Ps. xix. 12. See also Ps. cxxxix. 23, 24.   [m] Eccl. v. 6.
[n] Compare Numb. xv. 27—31. with Heb. x. 28.
[o] Heb. x. 29.   [p] Prov. xxviii. 13.   [q] Josh. vii. 20.

4. We never can be truly penitent for sin, if we are not desirous also to repair it to the utmost of our power—

[Certain it is that no reparation for sin can ever be made to God. It is the precious blood of Christ, and that only, that can ever satisfy the offended Majesty of heaven. But injuries done to our fellow-creatures, may, and must, be requited. If we have defrauded any, whether individuals or the public, it is our bounden duty to make restitution to the full amount: and, if we cannot find the individuals injured, we should make it to God, in the persons of the poor. To pretend to repent of any sin, and yet hold fast the wages of our iniquity, is a solemn mockery: for the retaining of a thing which we have unjustly acquired, is, in fact, a continuation of the offence. Let us make the case our own, and ask, Whether, if a man had defrauded us, we should give him credit for real penitence, whilst he withheld from us what he had fraudulently obtained? We certainly should say, that his professions of repentance were mere hypocrisy: and therefore the same judgment we must pass on ourselves, if we do not to the utmost of our power repair every injury we have ever done. Look at Zaccheus, and see what were the fruits of penitence in him: "Lord, half of my goods I give to the poor; and if I have wronged any man, I restore him four-fold[r]." See also the effect of godly sorrow in the Corinthian Church; "What indignation against themselves, yea, what zeal, yea, what revenge, yea, what a determination to clear themselves" of the evil in every possible way[s]! Look to it, beloved, that the same proofs of sincerity be found in you. Yet do not presently conclude that all is right, because you have made restitution unto man: (this is a mistake by no means uncommon:) the guilt of your sin still remains upon your conscience, and must be washed away by the atoning blood of Christ: *that* is the only "fountain opened for sin and uncleanness," nor, till you are washed in that, can you ever behold the face of God in peace.]

[r] Luke xix. 8. [s] 2 Cor. vii. 11.

OUTLINE NO. 124

THE TRESPASS-OFFERING A TYPE OF CHRIST.

Lev. v. 17—19. *If a soul sin, and commit any of these things which are forbidden to be done by the commandments of the Lord; though he wist it not, yet is he guilty, and shall bear his iniquity. And he shall bring a ram without blemish out of the flock, with thy estimation, for a trespass-offering unto the priest: and the priest shall make an atonement for him concerning his ignorance wherein he erred, and wist it not; and it shall be forgiven him. It is a trespass-offering: he hath certainly trespassed against the Lord.*

THE ceremonial law was intended to lead men to Christ, and was calculated to do so in a variety of ways. It exhibited Christ in all his work and offices, and directed every sinner to look to him. Moreover, the multitude of its rites and ceremonies had a tendency to break the spirits of the Lord's people, and to make them anxiously look for that period, when they should be liberated from a yoke which they were not able to bear, and render unto God a more liberal and spiritual service. It is in this latter view more especially that we are led to consider the trespass-offering, which was to be presented to God for the smallest error in the observation of any one ordinance, however ignorantly or unintentionally it might be committed. In order to elucidate the nature and intent of the trespass-offering, we shall,

I. Shew the evil of sins of ignorance, and the remedy prescribed for them—

It is often said that the intention constitutes the criminality of an action. But this principle is not true to the extent that is generally supposed.

It is certain that ignorance *extenuates* the guilt of an action—

[Our Lord himself virtually acknowledged this, when he declared that the opportunities of information which he had afforded the Jews, greatly enhanced the guilt of those who rejected him[a]. And he even urged the ignorance of his murderers as a plea with his heavenly Father to forgive them; "Father, forgive them; for they know not what they do[b]." St. Peter also palliated their crime upon the very same principles; "I wot that through ignorance ye did it, as did also your rulers[c]." And St. Paul speaks of himself as obtaining mercy *because* what he had done was done ignorantly and in unbelief[d]: whereas if he had done it, knowing whom he persecuted, he would most probably never have obtained mercy.

But it is equally certain that ignorance cannot *excuse* us in the sight of God—

[a] John ix. 41. and xv. 22. [b] Luke xxiii. 34.
[c] Acts iii. 17. [d] 1 Tim. i. 13.

[A man is not held blameless when he violates the laws of the land because he did it unwittingly: he is obnoxious to a penalty, though from the consideration of his ignorance that penalty may be mitigated. Nor does any man consider ignorance as a sufficient plea for his servant's faults, if that servant had the means of knowing his master's will: he rather blames that servant for negligence and disrespect in not shewing greater solicitude to ascertain and perform his duty.

With respect to God, the passage before us shews in the strongest light, that even the slightest error, and *that* too in the observance of a mere arbitrary institution, however unintentionally committed, could not be deemed innocent: on the contrary, it is said, "He shall bring his offering; he *hath certainly trespassed against the Lord*." Much more therefore must every violation of the *moral* law be attended with guilt, because there is an inherent malignity in every transgression of the moral law; and because man's ignorance of his duty, as well as his aversion to duty, is a fruit and consequence of the first transgression. Hence is there an eternal curse denounced against *every* one that *continueth* not in *all* things that are written in the book of the law to *do* them[e].

It is yet further evident that ignorance is no excuse before God, because St. Paul calls himself a blasphemer, and injurious, and a persecutor, yea, the very chief of sinners, for persecuting the Church, notwithstanding he thought he *ought* to do many things contrary to the name of Jesus[f]. And God declares that men perish for lack of knowledge[g], and that, *because* they are of no understanding, he will therefore shew them no favour[h].]

The only remedy for sins, how light soever they may appear to us, is the atonement of Christ—

[The high-priest was appointed particularly to offer for the *errors* of the people[i]. And as soon as ever an error, or unintentional transgression, was discovered, the person guilty of it was to bring his offering[k], and to seek for mercy through the blood of atonement. There was indeed a distinction in the offerings which different persons were to bring; which distinction was intended to shew that the *degrees* of criminality attaching to the errors of different people, varied in proportion as the offenders enjoyed the means of information.

If a priest erred, he must bring a bullock for an offering[l]; if a ruler erred, he must offer a male kid[m]; if one of the

---

[e] Gal. iii. 10.   [f] Acts xxvi. 9. with 1 Tim. i. 15.   [g] Hos. iv. 6.
[h] Isai. xxvii. 11.   [i] Heb. ix. 7. with Ezek. xlv. 19, 20.
[k] The offering was to be of proper value according to the priest's "estimation." Lev. xxvii. 2—8.
[l] Lev. iv. 3.   [m] Lev. iv. 22, 23.

common people erred, he must bring a *female* kid, or a *female* lamb[n], or, if he could not afford that, he might bring two young pigeons[o]. And, to mark yet further the superior criminality of the priest, his offering was to be *wholly* burnt, and its blood *was to be sprinkled* seven times before the veil of the sanctuary, and to be put upon the horns of *the altar of incense;* whereas the offerings of the others were to be *only in part* consumed by fire; and their blood was *not to be sprinkled* at all before the veil, and to be put only on the horns of *the altar of burnt-offering*[p]. Further still, if a person were so poor as not to be able to afford two young pigeons, he might be supposed to have still less opportunities of information, and was therefore permitted to bring only an ephah of fine flour; part of which, however, was to be burnt upon the altar, to shew the offerer what a destruction he himself had merited[q]. And *this is the excepted case* to which the Apostle alludes, when he says, with his wonted accuracy, that "*almost* all things are by the law purged with blood[r]."

But, under the Gospel, there is no distinction whatever to be made. We must now say, *without any single exception,* that "without shedding of blood there is no remission." We need Christ as much to bear the iniquity of our holy things, as to purge our foulest transgressions[s]: there is no other fountain opened for sin[t], no other way to the Father[u], no other door of hope[x], no other name whereby we can be saved[y]. Christ is "*the Ram*[z]," "caught in the thicket[a]," if we may so speak, who must be our substitute and surety, whether our guilt be extenuated by ignorance, or aggravated by presumption.]

This point being clear, we proceed to,

II. Suggest such reflections as naturally arise from the subject—

A more instructive subject than this cannot easily be proposed to us. It leads us naturally to observe,

1. What a tremendous load of guilt is there on the soul of every man!

[Let but the sins, *which we can remember,* be reckoned up, and they will be more than the hairs of our head. Let those be added, *which we* observed at the time, but *have now forgotten,* and oh, how awfully will their numbers be increased! But let all the trespasses, which we have committed through

[n] Lev. iv. 27, 28, 32. [o] ver. 7.
[p] Lev. iv. 6, 7, 12. comp. with Lev. iv. 25, 26, 30, 31.
[q] ver. 12. [r] Heb. ix. 22. [s] Exod. xxviii. 38.
[t] Zech. xiii. 1. [u] John xiv. 6. [x] John x. 9.
[y] Acts iv. 12. [z] See the text. [a] Alluding to Gen. xxii. 13.

ignorance, be put to the account; all the smallest deviations and defects which the penetrating eye of God has seen, (all of which he has noted in the book of his remembrance,) and surely we shall feel the force of that question that was put to Job, "Is not thy wickedness great? are not thine iniquities infinite[b]?" If we bring every thing to the touchstone of God's law, we shall see, that "there is not a just man upon earth who liveth and sinneth not[c];" and that "in many things we all offend[d];" so that there is but too much reason for every one of us to exclaim with the Psalmist, "Who can understand his *errors?* O cleanse thou me from my secret faults[e]!" Let none of us then extenuate our guilt, or think it sufficient to say, "It was an error[f]:" but let us rather humble ourselves as altogether filthy and abominable[g], as a mass of corruption[h], a living body of sin[i].]

2. How awful must be the state of those who live in *presumptuous* sins!

[The evil of sins committed ignorantly, and without design, is so great, that it cannot be expiated but by the blood of atonement: what then shall we say of *presumptuous* sins? how heinous must *they* be! Let us attend to the voice of God, who has himself compared the guilt contracted by unintentional, and by presumptuous sin; and who declares that, though provision was made under the law for the forgiveness of the former, there was no remedy whatever for the latter: the offender was to be put to death, and to be consigned over to endless perdition[k]. Let none then think it a light matter to violate the dictates of conscience, and the commands of God; for, in so doing, they pour contempt upon God's law, yea, and upon God himself also[l]: and the time is quickly coming, when God shall repay them to their face[m]; and shall beat them, not like the ignorant offender, with few stripes, but, as the wilful delinquent, with many stripes[n]. Let this consideration make us cry to God in those words of the Psalmist, "Keep thy servant from presumptuous sins; let them not have dominion over me; so shall I be undefiled and innocent from the great offence[o]."]

3. How desperate is the condition of those who make light of Christ's atonement!

[Under the law, there was no remission even of the smallest error, but through the blood of atonement. Nor can any sin

[b] Job xxii. 5.   [c] Eccl. vii. 20.   [d] Jam. iii. 2. Prov. xxiv. 16.
[e] Ps. xix. 12.   [f] Eccl. v. 6.   [g] Ps. xiv. 3.
[h] Rom. vii. 18. Isai. i. 5, 6.   [i] Rom. vii. 14, 24.
[k] Numb. xv. 27—31.   [l] Numb. xv. 27—31.
[m] Deut. vii. 10. Eccl. xi. 9.   [n] Luke xii. 48.   [o] Ps. xix. 13.

whatever be pardoned, under the gospel dispensation, but through the sacrifice of Christ. Yet, when we speak of Christ as the only remedy for sin, and urge the necessity of believing in him for justification, many are ready to object, 'Why does he insist so much on justification by faith?' But the answer is plain: 'You are sinners before God; and your one great concern should be to know how your sins may be forgiven: now God has provided a way, and only one way, of forgiveness; and *that* is, through the atonement of Christ: therefore we set forth Christ as the one remedy for sin; and exhort you continually to believe in him.' Consider then, I pray you, what the true scope of such objections is: it is to rob Christ of his glory, and your own souls of salvation. Remember this, and be thankful, that the atonement is so much insisted on, so continually set before you. Pour not contempt upon it: for, if "they who despised Moses' law died without mercy," " of how much sorer punishment, suppose ye, shall he be thought worthy, who hath trodden under foot the Son of God, and counted the blood of the covenant, wherewith *he* was sanctified, an unholy thing[p]?" Yes, to such wilful transgressors, " there remaineth no more sacrifice for sin, but a certain fearful looking for of judgment, and fiery indignation to consume them [q]."]

4. How wonderful must be the efficacy of the blood of Christ!

[Let only *one* man's sins be set forth, and they will be found numberless as the sands upon the sea-shore: yet the blood of Christ can cleanse, not him only, but a whole world of sinners, yea, all who have ever existed these six thousand years, or shall ever exist to the very end of time: moreover, his one offering can cleanse them, not merely from sins of ignorance, but even from presumptuous sins, for which no remedy whatever was appointed by the law of Moses[r]. What a view does this give us of the death of Christ! O that we could realize it in our minds, just as the offender under the law realized the substitution of the animal which he presented to the priest to be offered in his stead! Then should we have a just apprehension of his dignity, and a becoming sense of his love. Let us then carry to him our crimson sins[s], not doubting but that they shall all be purged away[t]; and we may rest assured that, in a little time, we shall join the heavenly choir in singing, " Unto him that loved us, and washed us from our sins in his own blood, be glory and dominion for ever and ever [u]."]

[p] Heb. x. 28, 29.   [q] Heb. x. 26, 27.   [r] Acts xiii. 39.
[s] Isai. i. 18.   [t] 1 John i. 7.   [u] Rev. i. 5, 6.

OUTLINE NO. 125
FIRE ON THE ALTAR NOT TO GO OUT.

Lev. vi. 13. *The fire shall ever be burning upon the altar: it shall never go out.*

IT is a matter of deep regret that religious persons do not enter more fully into the Jewish Ritual, and explore with more accuracy the mysteries contained in it. And I am not sure that Ministers, whose office properly leads them to unfold the sacred volume to their people, are not chargeable with a great measure of this remissness, in that they are not more careful to bring forth to their view the treasures of wisdom that are hid in that invaluable mine.

Of course, it will not be expected that on this occasion I should attempt any thing more than to illustrate the subject that is immediately before me. But I greatly mistake, if that alone will not amply suffice to justify my introductory observation; and to shew, that an investigation of the Law in all its parts would well repay the labours of the most diligent research.

The point for our present consideration is, *the particular appointment, that the fire on the altar should never be suffered to go out.* I will endeavour to set forth,

I. Its typical import, as relating to the Gospel—

Every part of the Ceremonial Law was "a shadow of good things to come." This particular ordinance clearly shews,

1. That we all need an atonement—

[This fire, which was to be kept in, was given from heaven[a]: and it was given for the use of all; of all Israel without exception. There was not one for whom an atonement was not to be offered. Aaron himself must offer an atonement for himself, before he can offer one for the people[b]. Who then amongst us can hope to come with acceptance into the divine presence in any other way? Our blessed Lord has told us, "No man cometh unto the Father, but by me." And St. Paul assures us, that "without shedding of blood there is no remission of sins." We must all, therefore, bring our offering to

---

[a] Lev. ix. 24.   [b] Heb. vii. 27.

the altar; and lay our hands upon the head of our offering; and look for pardon solely through the atoning blood of Jesus. The fire, too, was for the *daily* use of all. And daily, yea, and hourly, have all of us occasion to come to God in the same way. There is not an offering that we present to God, but it must be placed on his altar: and then only can it ascend with a sweet smell before God, when it has undergone its appointed process in that fire.]

2. That the sacrifices under the Law are insufficient for us—

[Thousands and myriads of beasts were consumed on God's altar; and yet the fire continued to burn, as unsatisfied, and demanding fresh victims. Had the offerings already presented effected a complete satisfaction for sin, the fire might have been extinguished. But the repetition of the sacrifices clearly shewed, that a full atonement had not yet been offered. In fact, as the Apostle tells us, they were no more than "remembrances of sins made from year to year;" and "could never take away sin," either from God's register of crimes, or from the conscience of the offender himself[c]. Thus, under the very Law itself, the insufficiency of the Law was loudly proclaimed; and the people were taught to look forward to a better dispensation, as the end of that which was, after a time, to be abolished.]

3. That God would in due time provide himself a sacrifice, with which he himself would be satisfied—

[From the beginning, God had taught men to look forward to a sacrifice which should in due time be offered. It is probable that the beasts, with whose skins our first parents were clothed, were by God's command first offered in sacrifice to him. We are sure that Abel offered in sacrifice the firstlings of his flock: and it is probable that fire was sent from heaven, as it certainly was on different occasions afterwards, to consume it: and that it was this visible token of God's acceptance of Abel's sacrifice, that inflamed the envy and the rage of Cain[d]. From Noah's offerings, also, "God smelled a sweet savour," as shadowing forth that great sacrifice which should in due time be offered[e]. To Abraham the purpose of God was marked in a still more peculiar manner. He was commanded to "take his son, his only son, Isaac," and to offer him up upon an altar, on that very mountain where the Temple afterwards was built, and where the Lord Jesus Christ himself was crucified. The fire, therefore, that was burning upon the altar, and the wood with which it was kept alive,

[c] Heb. x. 1—4, 11. and ix. 9.   [d] Gen. iv. 4, 5.   [e] Gen. viii. 20, 21.

did, in effect, say, as Isaac so many hundred years before had done, "Behold the fire and the wood; but where is the lamb for a burnt-offering?" Yea, it gave also the very answer which Abraham had done, "My son, God will provide himself a lamb for a burnt-offering [f]." Thus, by keeping up the expectation of the Great Sacrifice which all the offerings of the Law prefigured, it declared, in fact, to every successive generation, that in the fulness of time God would send forth his own Son, to "make his soul an offering for sin," and, by bearing in his own person the iniquities of us all, "to take them away from us[g]." In short, this fire, and every offering that was consumed by it, directed the attention of every true Israelite to that adorable "Lamb of God, that taketh away the sins of the world[h]," and who in actual efficiency, as well as in the divine purpose, has been "the Lamb slain from the foundation of the world[i]."]

4. That all who should not be interested in that great sacrifice must expect His sorest judgments—

[The victims consumed by that fire were considered as standing in the place of men who deserved punishment. This was clearly marked, not only by their being set apart by all Israel, and offered with that express view, but by the offenders themselves putting their hands on the heads of their victims, and transferring their sins to the creatures that were to be offered in sacrifice to God[k]. The fire that consumed them was expressive of God's indignation against sin, and declared the doom which the sinner himself merited at God's hands; yea, and the doom, too, which he himself must experience, if sin should ever be visited on him. It declared, what the New Testament also abundantly confirms, that "God is a consuming fire[l];" and that they who shall be visited with his righteous indignation, must be "cast into a lake of fire[m]," where "their worm dieth not, and *the fire never shall be quenched*[n]." Methinks, then, the fire burning on the altar gave to every person that beheld it this awful admonition; "Who can dwell with the *devouring fire?* Who can dwell with *everlasting burnings*[o]?"]

In considering this ordinance, it will be proper yet further to declare,

II. Its mystical import, as relating to the Church—

The different ordinances of the Jewish Law had at least a two-fold meaning, and, in many instances, a

---

[f] Gen. xxii. 7, 8.   [g] Isai. liii. 6, 10.   [h] John i. 29.
[i] Rev. xiii. 8.   [k] Lev. iv. 4, 15, 24, 29, 33.   [l] Heb. xii. 29.
[m] Rev. xx. 15.   [n] Mark ix. 43, 44, 45, 46, 48. *five times.*
[o] Isai. xxxiii. 14.

still more comprehensive import. The tabernacle, for instance, prefigured the body of Christ, "in which all the fulness of the Godhead dwelt;" and the Church, where God displays his glory; and heaven, where he vouchsafes his more immediate presence, and is seen face to face. So the altar not unfitly represents the cross on which the Lord Jesus Christ was crucified[p]; and the heart of man, from whence offerings of every kind go up with acceptance before God[q]. In the former sense we have its *typical*, and in the latter its *mystical* import.

Now in this mystical, and, as I may call it, emblematical sense, the ordinance before us teaches us,

1. That no offering can be accepted of God, unless it be inflamed with heavenly fire—

[When Nadab and Abihu offered incense before God "with strange," that is, with common, "fire," they were struck dead, as monuments of God's heavy displeasure: "There went out fire from the Lord, and devoured them; and they died before the Lord[r]." And shall we hope for acceptance with God, if we present our offerings with the unhallowed fire of mere natural affections? Our blessed Lord has told us, that he would "baptize us with the Holy Ghost and *with fire*[s]:" and every sacrifice which we offer to him should be inflamed with that divine power, even the sacred energy of his Holy Spirit, and of his heavenly grace. Let us not imagine that formal and self-righteous services can be pleasing to him; or that we can be accepted of him whilst seeking our own glory. Hear the declaration of God himself on this subject: "Behold, all ye that kindle a fire, that compass yourselves about with sparks! walk in the light of your fire, and in the sparks that ye have kindled: but this shall ye have of mine hand, ye shall lie down in sorrow[t]."]

2. That if God have kindled in our hearts a fire, we must keep it alive by our own vigilance—

[I well know that this mode of expression is objected to by many: but it is the language of the whole Scriptures; and therefore is to be used by us. We are "not to be wise above what is written," and to abstain from speaking as the voice of inspiration speaks, merely from a jealous regard to human systems. True it is, we are not to attempt any thing

[p] ɔ. xiii. 10—12.   [q] Heb. xiii. 15, 16.   [r] Lev. x. 1, 2.
[s] Matt. iii. 11.   [t] Isai. l. 11.

in our own strength: (if we do, we shall surely fail:) but we must exert ourselves notwithstanding: and the very circumstance of its being "God alone who can work in us either to will or do," is our incentive and encouragement to "work out our own salvation with fear and trembling[u]." If *we cannot work without God, neither will God work without us.* We must "give all diligence to make our calling and election sure[x]." We must "keep ourselves in the love of God[y]:" we must "stir up (like the stirring of a fire) the gift of God that is in us[z]:" we must from time to time "be watchful, and strengthen the things that remain in us, that are ready to die[a]." In a word, we must be "keeping up the fire on the altar, and never suffer it to go out."

This, indeed, was the office of the priests under the Law; and so it is under the Gospel: and this is, indeed, the very end at which we aim in all our ministrations. We never kindled a fire in any of your hearts; nor ever could: *that* was God's work alone. But we would bring the word, and lay it on the altar of your hearts; and endeavour to fan the flame; that so the fire may burn more pure and ardent, and every offering which you present before God may go up with acceptance before him. But let me say, that, under the Christian dispensation, ye all are "a royal priesthood:" there is now no difference between Jew and Greek, or between male and female: ye therefore must from morning to evening, and from evening to morning, be bringing fresh fuel to the fire; by reading, by meditation, by prayer, by conversation, by an attendance on social and public ordinances, by visiting the sick, and by whatever may have a tendency to quicken and augment the life of God in your souls. The sacred fire must either languish or increase: it never can continue long in the same state. See to it, then, that you "grow in grace," and "look to yourselves that ye lose not the things that ye have wrought, but that ye receive a full reward[b]."]

3. That every sacrifice which we offer in God's appointed way shall surely be accepted of him—

[There is the fire: see it blazing on the altar. Wherefore is it thus kept up? kept up, too, by God's express command? Wherefore? that ye may know assuredly that God is there, ready to accept your every offering. You think, perhaps, that you have no offering worthy of his acceptance. But do you not know, that he who was not able to bring a kid, or a lamb, or even two young pigeons, might bring a small measure of fine flour; and that *that* should be burnt upon the altar for him,

---

[u] Phil. ii. 12, 13.   [x] 2 Pet. i. 10.   [y] Jude, ver. 21.
[z] 2 Tim. i. 6. See the Greek.   [a] Rev. iii. 2.   [b] 2 John 8.

125.] FIRE ON THE ALTAR NOT TO GO OUT. 603

and be accepted as an atonement instead of a slaughtered animal[c]? Be assured, that the sigh, the tear, the groan shall come up with acceptance before him, as much as the most fluent prayer that ever was offered; and that the widow's mite will be found no less valuable in his sight, than the richest offerings of the great and wealthy. Only do ye " draw near to God;" and be assured, " He will draw near to you:" and, as he gave to his people formerly some *visible* tokens of his acceptance, so will he give to you the invisible, but not less real, manifestations of his love and favour, " shedding abroad his love in your hearts," giving you " the witness of his Spirit" in your souls, and " sealing you with the Holy Spirit of promise as the earnest of your inheritance, until the time of your complete redemption."]

In CONCLUDING this subject, I would yet further say,

1. Look to the great atonement as your only hope—

[I wish you very particularly to notice when it was that God sent down this fire upon the altar. It was when Aaron had offered a sacrifice for his own sins, and a sacrifice also for the sins of the people. It was, then, whilst a part of the latter sacrifice was yet unconsumed upon the altar, that God sent down fire from heaven and consumed it instantly[d]. When this universal acknowledgment had been made of their affiance in the great atonement, then God honoured them with this signal token of his acceptance. And it is only when you come to him in the name of Christ, pleading the merit of his blood, and " desiring to be found in him, not having your own righteousness but his," it is then I say, and then only, that you can expect from God an answer of peace. It is of great importance that you notice this: for many persons are looking *first* to receive some token of his love, that they may afterwards be emboldened to come to him through Christ. But you must *first* come to him through Christ; and *then* " he will send the Spirit of his Son into your hearts, whereby you shall cry, Abba, Father."]

2. Surrender up yourselves as living sacrifices unto God—

[On the Jewish altar *slain beasts* were offered: under the Christian dispensation you must offer *yourselves*, your whole selves, body, soul, and spirit, a *living* sacrifice unto the Lord. This is the sacrifice which God looks for; and this alone he will accept. This too, I may add, is your reasonable service[e]. *This* must *precede* every other offering[f]. A divided heart God

[c] Lev. v. 5—13.   [d] Lev. ix. 8, 13, 15, 17, 24.
[e] Rom. xii. 1.   [f] 2 Cor. viii. 5.

will never accept. Let the whole soul be his; and there shall not be any offering which you can present, which shall not receive a testimony of his approbation here, and an abundant recompence hereafter: for, "if there be only a willing mind, it shall be accepted according to that a man hath, and not according to that he hath not."]

OUTLINE NO. 126
THE PEACE-OFFERING.

Lev. vii. 11. *This is the law of the sacrifice of peace-offerings.*

IN the order in which the different offerings are spoken of, the peace-offering occurs the third; but, in the third chapter, the law of the peace-offerings is no further stated than it accords with the burnt-offering; and the fuller statement is reserved for the passage before us. Hence in the enumeration of the different offerings in verse 37, the peace-offering is fitly mentioned last. That we may mark the more accurately its distinguishing features, we shall state,

I. The particular prescriptions of this law—

Many of them were *common* to those of the burnt-offering; the sacrifices might be taken from the herd or from the flock: the offerer was to bring it to the door of the tabernacle, and to put his hands upon it: there it was to be killed; its blood was to be sprinkled upon the altar, and its flesh, in part at least, was to be burnt upon the altar. Of these things we have spoken before; and therefore forbear to dwell upon them now.

But there were many other prescriptions *peculiar* to the peace-offering; and to these we will now turn our attention. We notice,

1. The matter of which they consisted—

[Though the sacrifices might be of the herd or of the flock, they could *not be of fowls:* a turtle-dove or pigeon could not on this occasion be offered. In the burnt-offering, males only could be presented; but here it might be *either male or female.* In the meat-offering, either cakes or wafers might be offered; but here must be *both cakes and wafers:* in the former case, *leaven* was absolutely prohibited; but here it *was enjoined;*

leavened bread was to be used, as well as the unleavened cakes and wafers[a].]

2. The manner in which they were offered—

[Particular directions were given both with respect to the *division* of them, and the *consumption*. The meat-offering was divided only between the altar and the priests: but, in the peace-offering, the offerer himself had far the greatest share. God, who was in these things represented by the altar, had the fat, the kidneys, and the caul, which were consumed by fire[b]. The *priest* who burned the fat was to have the breast and the right shoulder: the breast was to be waved by him to and fro, and the shoulder was to be heaved upwards by him towards heaven. By these two significant actions, God was acknowledged both as the Governor of the universe, and as the source of all good to all his creatures: and from them these portions were called "the wave-breast, and the heave-shoulder[c]." One of the cakes also was given to the priest who sprinkled the blood upon the altar, who, after heaving it before the Lord, was to have it for his own use[d]. All the remainder of the offering, as well of the animal as the vegetable parts of it, belonged to *the offerer;* who together with his friends might eat it in their own tents. Two cautions however they were to observe; the one was, that the persons partaking of it must be "clean," (that is, have no ceremonial uncleanness upon them;) and they must eat it within the time prescribed.

We will not interrupt our statement by any practical explanations, lest we render it perplexed: but shall endeavour to get a clear comprehensive view of the subject, and then make a suitable improvement of it.]

Let us proceed then to notice,

II. The occasions whereon the offering was made—

There were some *fixed* by the divine appointment, and some altogether *optional.* The fixed occasions were, at the consecration of the priests[e]; at the expiration of the Nazarites' vow[f]; at the dedication of the tabernacle and temple[g]; and at the feast of firstfruits[h]. But besides these, the people were at liberty to offer them whenever a sense of gratitude or of need inclined them to it. They were offered,

1. As acknowledgments of mercies received[i]—

[a] Lev. iii. 1. and vii. 12, 13.   [b] Lev. iii. 3—5.
[c] ver. 30—34.   [d] ver. 14.   [e] Exod. xxix. 28.
[f] Numb. vi. 14.   [g] Numb. vii. 17. 1 Kings viii. 63.
[h] Lev. xxiii. 19.   [i] ver. 12.

[It could not fail but they must sometimes feel their obligations to God for his manifold mercies: and here was a way appointed wherein they might render unto God the honour due unto his name. In the 107th Psalm we have a variety of occurrences mentioned, wherein God's interposition might be seen: for instance, in bringing men safely to their homes after having encountered considerable difficulties and dangers: in redeeming them from prison or captivity, after they had by their own faults or follies reduced themselves to misery: in recovering persons from sickness, after they had been brought down to the chambers of the grave: in preserving mariners from storms and shipwreck: in public, family, or personal mercies of any kind. For any of these David says, " Let them sacrifice the sacrifice of thanksgiving, and declare his works with rejoicing[k]."]

2 As supplications for mercies desired—

[These might be offered either as free-will offerings, or as vows[l]; between which there was a material difference; the one expressing more of an ingenuous spirit, the other arising rather from fear and terror. We have a striking instance of *the former*, in the case of the eleven tribes, who, from a zeal for God's honour, had undertaken to punish the Benjamites for the horrible wickedness they had committed. Twice had the confederate tribes gone up against the Benjamites, and twice been repulsed, with the loss of forty thousand men: but being still desirous to know and do the will of God in this matter, (for it was God's quarrel only that they were avenging,) " they went up to the house of God, and wept and fasted until even, and offered burnt-offerings and *peace-offerings* unto the Lord:" and then God delivered the Benjamites into their hand; so that, with the exception of six hundred only, who fled, the whole tribe of Benjamin, both male and female, was extirpated[m]

Of *the latter* kind, namely, the vows, we have an instance in Jonah and the mariners, when overtaken with the storm. Jonah doubtless had proposed this expedient to the seamen, who, though heathens, readily adopted it in concert with him, hoping thereby to obtain deliverance from the destruction that threatened them[n]. And to the particular vows made on that occasion, Jonah had respect in the thanksgiving he offered after his deliverance[o].

Between the peace-offerings which were presented as *thanksgivings*, and those presented in *supplication* before God, there was a marked difference: the tribute of love and gratitude was far more pleasing to God, as arguing a more heavenly frame of mind: and, in consequence of its superior excellence, the

[k] Ps. cvii. 22.   [l] ver. 16.   [m] Judg. xx. 26.
[n] Jonah i. 16.   [o] Jonah ii. 9.

sacrifice that was offered as a thanksgiving must be eaten on *the same* day; whereas the sacrifice offered as a vow or voluntary offering, might, as being less holy, be eaten also on *the second* day. But, if any was left to the third day, it must be consumed by fire P.]

Having stated the principal peculiarities of this law, we shall now come to its PRACTICAL IMPROVEMENT. We may find in it abundant matter,

1. For reproof—

[The Jews, if they wished to express their humiliation or gratitude in the way appointed by the law, were under the necessity of yielding up a part of their property (perhaps at a time when they could but ill afford it) in sacrifice to God. But no such necessity is imposed on us: " God has not made us to serve with an offering, nor wearied us with incense:" the offerings he requires of us are altogether spiritual: it is " the offering of a free heart," or " of a broken and contrite spirit," that he desires of us; and that he will accept in preference to " the cattle upon a thousand hills." Well therefore may it be expected that we have approached God with the language of the Psalmist, " Accept, I beseech thee, the free-will offerings of my mouth q." But has this been the case? Have our sins brought us unto God in humiliation; our necessities, in prayer; our mercies, in thankfulness? What excuse have we for our neglects? These sacrifices required no expense of property, and but little of time. Moreover, we should never have brought our sacrifice, without feasting on it ourselves. Think, if there had not been in us a sad aversion to communion with God, what numberless occasions we have had for drawing nigh to him in this way! Surely every beast that was ever slaughtered on those occasions, and every portion that was ever offered, will appear in judgment against us to condemn our ingratitude and obduracy!— —]

2. For direction—

[Whether the peace-offering was presented in a way of thanksgiving or of supplication, it equally began with a sacrifice in the way of atonement. Thus, whatever be the frame of our minds, and whatever service we render unto God, we must *invariably fix our minds on the atonement of Christ*, as the only means whereby either our persons or our services can obtain acceptance with God. Moreover, having occasion to offer sacrifice, we must *do it without delay*, even as the offerers were to eat their offerings in the time appointed r — — We must

---

P ver. 15—18.   q Ps. cxix. 108.
r Heb. iii. 13—15. Ps. cxix. 60. 2 Cor. vi. 2.

be attentive too *to our after-conduct*, " lest we lose the things that we have wrought, instead of receiving a full reward[s]." However carefully the offerers had observed the law before, yet, if any one presumed to eat the smallest portion of his offering on the third day, instead of being accepted of God, his offering was utterly rejected; and he was considered as having committed a deadly sin[t]. O that those who spend a few days in what is called 'preparing themselves' for the Lord's supper, and after receiving it return to the same worldly courses as before, would consider this! for no service can be pleasing to God which does not issue in an immediate renunciation of every evil way, and a determined, unreserved, and abiding surrender of the soul to God. In coming to God, we must, at least in purpose and intention, be " clean;" else we only mock God, and deceive our own souls[u]: and, after having come to him, we must proceed to " cleanse ourselves from all filthiness both of flesh and spirit, perfecting holiness in the fear of God[x]."]

3. For encouragement—

[On these occasions a female offering was received, as well as a male, and leavened bread *together with* the unleavened. What a blessed intimation was here, that " God will not be extreme to mark what is done amiss!" A similar intimation is given us in his acceptance of a mutilated or defective beast, when presented to him as a free-will offering[y]. Our best services, alas! are very poor and defective: corruption is blended with every thing we do: our very tears need to be washed from their defilement, and our repentances to be repented of. But, if we are sincere and without allowed guile, God will deal with us as a Parent with his beloved children, accepting with pleasure the services we render him, and overlooking the weakness with which they are performed[z].]

[s] 2 John, ver. 8. [t] ver. 18. [u] ver. 20. [x] 2 Cor. vii. 1.
[y] Lev. xxii. 23. [z] Prov. xv. 8. Ps. cxlvii. 11.

OUTLINE NO. 127

GOD'S ACCEPTANCE OF THE SACRIFICES.

Lev. ix. 23, 24. *And Moses and Aaron went into the tabernacle of the congregation, and came out, and blessed the people: and the glory of the Lord appeared unto all the people. And there came a fire out from before the Lord, and consumed upon the altar the burnt-offering and the fat: which when all the people saw, they shouted, and fell on their faces.*

WHEN we see the great variety of ordinances instituted by Moses, and the multitudes of sacrifices

127.] GOD'S ACCEPTANCE OF THE SACRIFICES. 609

that were, either in whole or in part, to be consumed upon the altar, we are ready to ask, Of what use was all this? and what compensation could be made to the people for all the expense and trouble to which they were put? But in the text we have a ready, and a sufficient answer. God did not long withhold from them such communications, as would abundantly recompense all that they did, and all that they could, perform for his sake : he gave them such testimonies of his acceptance as made all their hearts to overflow with joy.

Let us consider,

I. The testimonies of his acceptance—
Of these there were different kinds;
1. Ministerial—

[Moses and Aaron, having finished all that they had to do within the tabernacle, came forth, and "blessed the people:" and in this action they were eminent *types of Christ*, and *examples to all future ministers* to the end of time.

As types of Christ, they shewed what he should do as soon as he should have completed his sacrifice. The acceptance of all his believing followers being now certain, he blessed them; and was in the very act of blessing them, when he was taken up from them into heaven[a]. Scarcely had he taken possession of his throne, before he "sent down upon them the blessing of the Father," even the Holy Ghost[b], to be their Guide and Comforter : and, when he shall have finished his work of intercession within the veil, he will come forth to pronounce upon them his final benediction, "Come, ye blessed of my Father! inherit the kingdom prepared for you from the foundation of the world." When on earth, he offered himself a sacrifice, and died as a sinner under the malediction of the law : but at the day of judgment he will, "unto those who look for him, appear the second time, without sin, to their complete salvation[c]."

As examples to ministers, they shewed what all ministers are authorized and empowered to declare unto those who rely on the great sacrifice. They are to stand forth, and, in the very name of God, to proclaim pardon and peace to every one of them without exception[d] — — —]

2. Personal—

[In two ways did God himself, without the intervention of

[a] Luke xxiv. 50, 51.   [b] Acts ii. 33. and iii. 26.
[c] Heb. ix. 28.   [d] Acts xiii. 38, 39.

any human means, condescend to manifest his acceptance of the sacrifices which were now offered.

He first *displayed his glory* before all the people. This on some occasions was done in testimony of his displeasure, and in support of his servants who acted under his authority [e] : but here, as also on other occasions, it was altogether a token or his favour. In what precise manner this was done, we are not informed: but we are well assured, that it must have been in a way suited to his own glorious majesty, and in a way that carried its own evidence along with it.

Of course, such exhibitions of the divine glory are not now to be expected: but there are others, which, though not visible to mortal eyes, are very perceptible by the believing heart; and which shall be vouchsafed to those who come to God by Jesus Christ. Our blessed Lord has assured his believing followers, that "he will manifest himself unto them as he does not unto the world:" which promise would be nugatory, if the manifestations referred to did not carry their own evidence along with them. It is not easy indeed to mark with precision the agency of the Holy Spirit, so as to distinguish it from the operations of our own mind: but *in the effects* we can tell infallibly, what proceeds from God, and what from ourselves. The views which we may have of God and his perfections, may, as far as relates to the speculative part, arise from human instruction; but the humility, the love, the peace, the purity, with all the other sanctifying effects produced by those views upon the soul, can proceed from God alone: they are the fruits of the Spirit, and of him only. Hence, though no man can conceive aright of the manifestations of God to the soul, unless he have himself experienced them, nor can know exactly what it is to have "the Spirit of God witnessing with his spirit," or "shedding abroad the love of God in his heart," yet we are in no danger of error or enthusiasm, whilst we look for these things as purchased for us through the sacrifice of Christ, and judge of them, not by any inexplicable feelings, but by plain and practical results.

In addition to this display of his glory, God *sent fire from heaven* to consume the sacrifice. By this he shewed the people what fiery indignation they themselves merited, and that he had turned it from them, and caused it to fall on the sacrifice which had been substituted in their stead.

The observations just made, will apply also to this part of our subject. We are not to expect such a visible token, that our great sacrifice is accepted for us: but all the assurances of it which God has given us in his word, shall be applied with power to our souls, and be impressed with as strong a

---

[e] Numb. xiv. 10. and xvi. 19, 42.

conviction upon our minds, as if we had seen a demonstration of it exhibited before our eyes.]

From the testimonies themselves let us turn our attention to,

II. The effects produced by them—

It is common to visible objects to affect us strongly. Accordingly the people were deeply impressed by what they now saw. They were filled,

1. With exalted joy—

[Had they not been taught to expect some extraordinary expressions of God's regard, they would probably have been terrified, as Gideon and Manoah were[f]: but being prepared[g], they were filled with triumphant exultation, and rent the air with their shouts[h].

How far a similar mode of expressing our religious feelings at this time would *in any case* be proper, we will not absolutely determine: but we apprehend that *in the general* it would not. Such manifestations as those we are considering, are calculated to make a strong impression on the mind, and to call forth the affections into violent and immediate exercise: but the truths of the Gospel, and the communications of God to the soul, affect us rather through the medium of the understanding; and, consequently, are both more slow, and more moderate, in their operation. Yet doubtless somewhat of the same emotions must be right, especially in our secret chamber, where our communion with God is usually most intimate; and where others who are strangers to our feelings, cannot be offended by what they would deem enthusiastical or hypocritical expressions of them. The inward triumph of the Apostle Paul seems more suited to our dispensation[i]: and *that* it is both the privilege and duty of every one of us to enjoy.]

2. With profound reverence—

["They fell upon their faces," in humble adoration of their God and King. This union of humility and joy was exactly what one would have wished to see in them: and happy would it be if some who talk most of spiritual joys would learn of them! Even the seraphim before the throne cover both their faces and their feet, from a consciousness of their unworthiness to behold or serve their God: and the glorified saints, from similar feelings, cast their crowns at his feet. How much more therefore should *we* have our most exalted joys tempered with humility! This should never for one moment be forgotten:

[f] Judg. vi. 21, 22. and xiii. 19—22. [g] ver. 6.
[h] See a similar instance, Ezra iii. 11. [i] Rom. viii. 31—39.

our affiance, our love, our gratitude, our assurance, our very triumphs, will all prove vain, if they be not chastised and softened with humiliation and contrition. If we look at the most eminent saints, and mark the effects of God's condescension to them, we find them invariably expressing their acknowledgments in a way of reverence and self-abasement[k]: and the more our devotion resembles theirs, the more acceptable it will be to the Supreme Being.]

Let us LEARN from this subject,

1. To lay no stress on transient affections—

[One would have thought that such a frame of mind as the people experienced at this time, must have issued well; and that they would henceforth approve themselves faithful to their God. But these were mere transient emotions, which were forgotten as soon as any temptation arose to call forth their unsubdued corruptions. And thus it is with multitudes under the Gospel; whom our Lord compares to seed sown upon stony ground, which springs up with great rapidity, but withers away as soon; because it has no deepness of earth to grow in, nor any roots to nourish it[1]. We ought indeed to have our affections called forth into exercise; nor is that religion of any value that does not engage them in its service: but that religion which is seated only in the affections, will never be of any long duration. The understanding must be informed, the judgment convinced, and the will determined, upon the subject of religion; and then the affections will operate to advantage; but, unless the *whole* heart and the *whole* soul be engaged in the work, it will come to nought.]

2. To be thankful for the advantages that we enjoy—

[We are apt to envy the Jews their exalted privileges, and to imagine, that, if we had enjoyed the same, we should have made a better improvement of them: but we see how fleeting and inefficacious are the impressions made by sensible manifestations, when of that whole nation two only were admitted into the promised land. *They* "walked by sight:" but *we* are " to walk by faith." This is the principle which we are to cultivate: we must look by faith to the great sacrifice: we must see our great High-Priest entered within the veil for us, and coming forth to "bless us with all spiritual blessings." Then shall we find, that, in proportion as this principle is brought into exercise, it will work by love, and purify the heart, and overcome the world, and render us meet for our everlasting inheritance.]

[k] Gen. xvii. 3. Exod. iii. 6.   [1] Matt. xiii. 5, 6, 20, 21

OUTLINE NO. 128

DEATH OF NADAB AND ABIHU.

Lev. x. 1—3. *And Nadab and Abihu, the sons of Aaron, took either of them his censer, and put fire therein, and put incense thereon, and offered strange fire before the Lord, which he commanded them not. And there went out fire from the Lord, and devoured them; and they died before the Lord. Then Moses said unto Aaron, This is it that the Lord spake, saying, I will be sanctified in them that come nigh me, and before all the people I will be glorified. And Aaron held his peace.*

IN all that we behold around us there is a great degree of obscurity, so that we can judge but very imperfectly either of the actions of men, or of the dispensations of God. For want of an insight into the motives of men's conduct, we cannot form a correct estimate of their character; nor can we, without a revelation from heaven, distinguish those events which come directly from God, and those which, though ultimately referable to him, proceed rather from secondary causes. But in the Bible we find certainty. We learn the principles by which men are actuated; and see the hand of God accomplishing his own unerring purpose. We behold sin in all its diversified forms; virtue in all its various degrees; mercies in all their rich extent; and judgments in all their tremendous consequences. Had the event, of which we read in our text, happened in our day, we should probably have admired the zeal of Nadab and Abihu, and have represented their death as a translation from the service of God in an earthly tabernacle to the enjoyment of him in the tabernacle above. It is possible too that we might have ascribed the silence of Aaron to a want of parental affection. But, through the light which the Scripture casts upon these things, we behold in the death of the former, *a judgment inflicted;* and, in the silence of the latter, *a virtue exercised.*—Under these two heads we shall consider the history before us.

I. The judgment inflicted—

Nadab and Abihu were the two eldest sons of Aaron. They had been just consecrated, together with their father, to the priestly office: but,

They committed a grievous sin—

[It should seem that they were elated with the distinction conferred upon them, and impatient to display the high privileges they enjoyed. Hence, without waiting for the proper season of burning incense, or considering in what manner God had commanded it to be done, they both together took their censers (though only one was ever so to officiate at a time) and put common fire upon them, and went in to burn incense before the Lord.

Now this was a great and heinous sin: for God had just before sent fire from heaven, which he commanded to be kept always burning on the altar for the express purpose of being exclusively used in the service of the tabernacle. Their conduct therefore shewed, that they had made no just improvement of all the wonders they had seen; and that they were unconscious of the obligations which their newly-acquired honours entailed upon them. It even argued a most criminal contempt of the Divine Majesty, in opposition to whose express commands they now acted.]

For this, they were visited with a most awful judgment—

[God, jealous of his own honour, punished their transgression, and marked their sin in their punishment. They had slighted the fire which God had given them from heaven; and he sent fresh fire to avenge his quarrel. They neglected to honour God; and He got himself honour in their destruction. They, by their example, encouraged the people to disregard the laws that had been promulged; and He, by executing judgment on the offenders, shewed the whole nation, yea and the whole world also, that " he will by no means clear the guilty." Thus did God maintain the honour of his law, as he afterwards did the authority of his Gospel[a].]

Whilst in them we behold with grief the enormity and desert of sin, in their afflicted father we are constrained to admire,

II. The submission exercised—

Doubtless the affliction of Aaron was exceeding great—

[These were his own sons, just consecrated to the high office they sustained. In them he had promised himself much

[a] Acts v. 1—11.

comfort; and had hoped, that the whole nation would receive permanent advantage from their ministrations. But in a moment he beholds all his hopes and expectations blasted. He sees his sons struck dead by the immediate hand of God, and that too in the very act of sin, as a warning to all future generations. If they had died in any other way, his grief must have been pungent beyond expression: but to see them cut off in this way, and with all their guilt upon their heads, must have been a trial almost too great for human nature to sustain.]

But he submitted to it without a murmuring word or thought—

[The consideration suggested to him by Moses, composed his troubled breast. God had given repeated warning that he would punish with awful severity any wilful deviations from his law[b]. Now, as a Sovereign, he had a right to enact what laws he pleased; and they, as his creatures, were bound to obey them. It became him to enforce the observance of his laws, and to vindicate the honour of his insulted majesty, if any should presume to violate them. What would have been the effect if such a flagrant violation of them, in those who were to be examples to the whole nation, were overlooked? Would not a general contempt of the divine ordinances be likely to ensue? For prevention then as well as punishment, this judgment was necessary. And the consequence of it would be, that God would henceforth be honoured as a great and terrible God, and that the whole assembly of the people would learn to tremble at his word, and to obey it without reserve. Thus, however painful the stroke was to him, he submitted humbly to it, because it was necessary for the public good, and conducive to the honour of his offended God.

It is not improbable too that he would recollect the forbearance exercised towards him in the matter of the golden calf; and that, while he deplored the fate of his children, he magnified the mercy that had spared him.]

From this subject we may LEARN,

1. To reverence God's ordinances—

[Well may all, both ministers and people, learn to tremble when they approach God in the institutions of his worship. Were this example of divine vengeance duly considered, surely ministers would never dare to seek their own glory when they stand up to address their audience in the name of God. They would look well to their ministrations, and be sure that they presented before God no other fire than what they had previously taken from his own altar —— The people too would

[b] Exod. xix. 22. Lev. viii. 35. and xxii 9.

never venture to come to the house of God in a thoughtless or irreverent manner, but would reflect on the holiness and majesty of the Supreme Being, and endeavour to approve themselves to him in all the services they offered[c]— — —Beloved Brethren, it is no *legal* argument which we offer, when we remind you that God is jealous of his own honour, and exhort you from that consideration to take heed to yourselves whensoever you approach his house, his altar, or his throne of grace: it is the very argument urged by an inspired Apostle, and that too in reference to the history before us; "Let us have grace, whereby we may serve God acceptably with reverence and godly fear; for *our God is a consuming fire*.[d]"]

2. To submit to his dispensations—

[It pleases God sometimes to try in a peculiar manner his most favoured saints. But from whatever quarter our trials come, we should view the hand of God in them, and say, " It is the Lord, let him do what seemeth him good[e]." It becomes not us to "reply against God;" or "the clay to strive with the potter." As a Sovereign, he has a right to do with us as he will: and, if only he be glorified, we should be content, whatever we may suffer for the attainment of that end. The recollection of our own deserts should always stop our mouths, or rather prevent even the rising disposition to murmur against him. He never did, nor can in this world, punish us more than our iniquities deserve: and therefore a *living* man can never have occasion to complain[f]. Let us then, whatever our afflictions be, submit with meekness to his chastising hand: "let us be still, and know that he is God:" yea, let us be thankful that "he is magnified in our body, whether it be by life or by death[g]."]

[c] Ps. lxxxix. 7.   [d] Heb. xii. 28, 29.   [e] 1 Sam. iii. 18. See also Ps. xxxviii. 13. and Job i. 21.   [f] Lam. iii. 39.   [g] Phil. i. 20.

OUTLINE NO. 129

THE LAWS RELATING TO LEPROSY.

Lev. xiii. 45, 46. *And the leper, in whom the plague is, his clothes shall be rent, and his head bare, and he shall put a covering upon his upper lip, and shall cry, Unclean, Unclean. All the days wherein the plague shall be in him he shall be defiled; he is unclean: he shall dwell alone; without the camp shall his habitation be.*

AMONG the various disorders with which the Jews were afflicted, the leprosy was marked as the most odious and disgraceful; and the rules for distinguishing it from all similar disorders were laid down by God himself with very extraordinary accuracy and precision. As existing in garments and in houses, it seems to have been peculiar to the Jews; and to have entirely vanished with their dispensation. But there doubtless was some important end for which God visited them with this disorder: and what that was, may be gathered from the various ordinances relating to it. In all the differences which God commanded to be put between things clean and unclean, he designed to teach us the *evil* and *bitterness* of sin: but from the leprosy more particularly may these things be learned. We may learn, I say,

I. The evil of sin—

Whatever resemblance the leprosy might bear to some other disorders, it differed materially from all others. It was,

1. Universally judicial—

[This disorder was not, as some have thought, acquired by contagion; for it was not at all infectious: but it proceeded immediately from the hand of God; and was always considered as a punishment for sin. Miriam was smitten with it for her rebellion against Moses[a]: and Gehazi, for his covetous and dishonest conduct towards Naaman the Syrian[b].

In this light also should sin be viewed. True, it first entered through the device of Satan: but from that time has it been, more or less, judicially inflicted by God, on those who have disregarded the divine commands. Frequently is God said to "blind the eyes," and "harden the hearts" of men. We must not indeed suppose, that he ever does this by a positive infusion of sin into the soul: *this* would not consist with his own glorious perfections: but he abandons men to the evil of their own hearts, and withholds from them that grace whereby alone they can overcome their corruptions. Multitudes are "given up by him to a reprobate mind, because they like not to retain him in their knowledge[c]." And he tells us plainly, that this punishment shall be inflicted on us, if we do not guard against sin in its first beginnings: "The backslider in heart shall be filled with his own ways; he shall eat of the fruit of his own ways, and be filled with his own devices[d]." Who indeed has not found the truth of these declarations? Who does not see, that, if we harbour pride, covetousness,

[a] Numb. xii. 10—15. [b] 2 Kings v. 27. [c] Rom. i. 28.
[d] Prov. i. 30, 31. and xiv. 14

impurity, sloth, or any other evil principle in our hearts, it will gain such an ascendant over us, as at once to chastise us for our folly, and to augment our guilt? The truth is, that the very heaviest judgment which God can inflict upon us in this world, is, to give us over to the evil of our own hearts, and to say, "He is joined to idols; *let him alone*[e]."]

2. Pre-eminently hateful—

[If there were but the smallest appearance of the leprosy on any one, he must instantly have it examined with all possible care. He must not trust to his own judgment, but must apply to those whom God had authorized to determine the point, according to the rules prescribed for them. If the disorder existed, though in ever so low a degree, the person was instantly visited with all its painful consequences: and if only a doubt of its existence was entertained, he must be shut up, and re-examined, week after week, till the point could be determined. Surely nothing could more strongly declare its odiousness in the sight of God.

In this respect it most emphatically marks the hatefulness of sin. "Sin is that abominable thing which God hateth[f]." He charges us to abhor it[g], and to abstain from all appearance of it[h]. He solemnly assures us, that, if we harbour it in our hearts, it shall not go unpunished[i]. He requires us to "search and try our ways;" and to bring every thing to the touchstone of his word[k]: nor would he have us satisfied with our own judgment, lest our self-love should deceive us: we must come to our great High-Priest, "whose eyes are a flame of fire;" and beg of him to "search and try us, and to see if there be any wicked way in us[l]." However clear we may be in our own eyes, we must say with St. Paul, "I judge not mine own self: for I know nothing by myself; yet am I not hereby justified; but he that judgeth me is the Lord[m]."]

3. Absolutely incurable—

[There was nothing prescribed, nor indeed any thing to be attempted, for the cure of this disorder. Nothing but the hand that inflicted it, could remove it. Hence the removal of it is most generally expressed by the term *cleansing;* and those who were relieved from it are said to have been *cleansed*[n].

And certain it is that none but God can deliver us from sin. No superstitious devices have ever been able to root it out, no human efforts to subdue it. The blood of Christ alone can wash away its guilt; and the grace of Christ alone can suppress its operation.]

[e] Hos. iv. 17. [f] Jer. xliv. 4. [g] Rom. xii. 9. [h] 1 Thess. v. 22.
[i] Exod. xxxiv. 7. and Prov. xi. 21. [k] Isai. viii. 20.
[l] Ps. cxxxix. 23, 24. [m] 1 Cor. iv. 3, 4. [n] Luke xvii. 14, 17.

Clearly as the evil of sin is seen in this disorder we behold yet more strongly marked,

II. The bitterness of it—

The person afflicted with the leprosy was put out of the camp or city in which he had dwelt, and was forced to live alone, being cut off from all intercourse with his dearest relatives°. How inexpressibly painful must this have been!———

Here then we see shadowed forth the miserable state of men by reason of sin. When it shews itself only in unallowed infirmities, it will consist with the divine favour; just as the leprosy, when it was turned to a kind of scurf that covered the whole body from head to foot, was considered as no longer rendering the person ceremonially unclean[p]: but, as long as it continues " deeper than the skin," with " quick raw flesh rising," and " white or yellow hair;" in other words, while it reigns within, and produces its accustomed fruits, it incapacitates us for,

1. Fellowship with God's Church on earth—

[Social intercourse indeed with the Lord's people is not prohibited: but that fellowship which the saints enjoy with each other in spiritual exercises is altogether beyond the reach of those who live in wilful sin. The Apostle justly asks, " What communion hath light with darkness, or righteousness with unrighteousness, or he that believeth with an unbeliever[q]?" The views, desires, and pursuits of the ungodly are altogether different from those which characterize the children of God; and they make for themselves that separation, which under the law was the subject of an express command. Strictly speaking perhaps, the separation begins on the side of the Lord's people, because they are commanded to " come out from the world, and be separate, and *not to touch the unclean thing*[r]:" but the effect is the same: in the one case, the unclean were but few, and therefore were separated from the mass; but in the other case, the mass are the unclean; and the clean are separated from them.]

2. Admission into his Church in heaven—

[St. Paul appeals to us respecting this as a thing plain, obvious, and undeniable[s]: and our blessed Lord repeatedly

---

[o] 2 Kings vii. 3. and xv. 5.   [p] ver. 12, 13.   [q] 2 Cor. vi. 14, 15.
[r] 2 Cor. vi. 17.   [s] 1 Cor. vi. 9.

affirms it with the strongest asseverations that it was possible for him to utter [t]. When king Uzziah was smitten with the leprosy in the temple, all the priests with one accord rose upon him, and *thrust him out* of the temple; yea, and he himself also *hasted to go out* [u]. And thus it would be in heaven, if by any means an unrenewed sinner were admitted there: he would be *thrust out* [x], as unworthy of a place among that blessed society; and he would haste to flee out, from a consciousness that nothing but redoubled misery could await him there [y] ———]

ADDRESS—

1. Let us entertain a godly jealousy over ourselves—

[Men are very apt to " think themselves something, when they are nothing." But we should diligently " prove our own work, that we may have rejoicing in ourselves alone, and not in another [z]." As in the leprosy, so in the dispositions of the heart, it is often difficult to distinguish with certainty: the lines of distinction between unbelief and fear, presumption and faith, worldliness and prudence, and between a variety of other principles existing in the mind, are more easily defined on paper, than discerned in the heart: truth and error often so nearly resemble each other, that none but our great High-Priest can enable us to discern them apart. Yet if an evil principle be admitted into the mind, it will produce a thousand evils in the life. Hence a peculiar stigma was put upon the leprosy, when detected in the *head:* then the person was declared " *utterly* unclean [a]." Be on your guard therefore, beloved Brethren; and beg of God, that you may never be permitted to deceive your own souls. When doubts arose about the leprosy, the person was shut up for seven days; and this was repeated, till the point could be ascertained. And if you would occasionally retire from the world, and spend a day in fasting and self-examination, you would detect many evils of which at present you have very little conception, and acquire a perfection of character not to be attained in any other way.]

2. Let us humble ourselves for our remaining imperfections—

[However we may have been cleansed from our leprosy, there is, as was before observed, the leprous scurf still over us from head to foot [b]. We still therefore have occasion to cry with the prophet, " Woe is me! for I am a man of unclean lips [c]." " Our very righteousnesses are, in fact, but filthy

[t] John iii. 3, 5.   [u] 2 Chron. xxvi. 20.   [x] Luke xiii. 28.
[y] Ps. i. 5.   [z] Gal. vi. 3—5.
[a] ver. 44. This expression does not occur anywhere else.
[b] ver. 12, 13.   [c] Isai. vi. 5.

130.] PURIFICATION OF THE LEPER. 621

rags[d];" so that we still have reason, like holy Job, to "lothe and abhor ourselves in dust and ashes[e]." The external signs of sorrow which were prescribed to the leper, we should commute for those which indicate true contrition: "Rend your *heart*," says the prophet, "and *not your garments*[f]." We should "walk humbly with God," and so much the more when we find that "he *is* pacified towards us[g]." And, as they who had only been suspected of the leprosy were required to wash their garments[h], so let us, who yet retain such awful memorials of it, "wash ourselves from day to day in the fountain opened for sin and for uncleanness" — — —]

[d] Isai. lxiv. 6. [e] Job xlii. 6. [f] Joel ii. 13. [g] Ezek. xvi. 63. [h] ver. 34.

OUTLINE NO. 130
PURIFICATION OF THE LEPER.

Lev. xiv. 4—9. *Then shall the priest command to take for him that is to be cleansed, two birds alive and clean, and cedarwood, and scarlet, and hyssop. And the priest shall command that one of the birds be killed in an earthen vessel, over running water. As for the living bird, he shall take it, and the cedar-wood, and the scarlet, and the hyssop, and shall dip them and the living bird in the blood of the bird that was killed over the running water: and he shall sprinkle upon him that is to be cleansed from the leprosy seven times, and shall pronounce him clean, and shall let the living bird loose into the open field. And he that is to be cleansed shall wash his clothes, and shave off all his hair, and wash himself in water, that he may be clean: and after that he shall come into the camp, and shall tarry abroad out of his tent seven days. But it shall be on the seventh day, that he shall shave all his hair off his head, and his beard, and his eye-brows, even all his hair he shall shave off: and he shall wash his clothes; also he shall wash his flesh in water, and he shall be clean.*

THERE is an indissoluble connexion between duty and privilege, though that connexion is, for the most part, but little understood. Our privileges are in general supposed to arise out of the performance of our duties; whereas the reverse of this is more generally true: privileges are freely bestowed upon us by God according to his own sovereign will and pleasure; and these operate as incentives to love and serve him. The blessings of election and vocation are not vouchsafed to us on account of our antecedent merit, but in order that we may shew forth the praises of Him that hath called us.

We see this exemplified in the laws relating to the leprosy. Nothing was prescribed whereby people should first of all heal themselves: but, when God of his infinite mercy had first healed them, then were they to come and offer their acknowledgments in the way appointed.

The ordinances to be observed by them are here laid down: and from them we see, that the purification of the leper was two-fold;

I. Incipient—

[Two birds were to be taken; one of which was to be killed over a vessel of spring-water; and the other, dipped in the bloody water, was to be let loose. Some interpret this as signifying, that Christ should die for us, and that the sinner, dipped as it were in his blood, should be liberated from sin and death, and be enabled to soar above this lower world, both in heart and life. But we apprehend that both the birds equally designate Christ. And, inasmuch as the living bird was dipped in the blood of that which was killed, this intimated, that all that Christ should do for us after his resurrection, was founded upon the atonement which he had offered; by which he obtained a right to justify us, and to send us his Holy Spirit, and to save us with an everlasting salvation[a]. As for the cedar-wood, the scarlet wool, and the hyssop, which were also dipped in the bloody water, and used in sprinkling the leper, we forbear to specify the spiritual import of each, because it must rest on mere conjecture, and will not prove satisfactory after all. But the circumstance of the blood being mixed with living water, most assuredly was designed to teach us, that Christ saves us no less by his Spirit than by his blood; by his Spirit, from the power of sin; and by his blood, from its guilt. Moreover, these are never separated. When his side was pierced, "there came out (as John, who was an eye-witness, testifies) both blood and water[b]." On which circumstance he lays great stress; assuring us, that "Christ came not by water only, but by water and blood[c]." These two then being sprinkled upon the sinner, "the priest of God is fully authorized to pronounce him clean" — —

In confirmation of this statement we need only to refer to the two goats offered on the great day of annual expiation: that which was slain, and that which carried the sins of the people

[a] Heb. ix. 12. Rom. v. 10.   [b] John xix. 34, 35.   [c] 1 John v. 6.

into the wilderness, equally prefigured Christ[d]; the one, as "dying for our sins; and the other, as rising again for our justification[e]." The two birds presented by the leper were in this respect precisely similar; and equally point us to that blessed Jesus, who says, "I am He that liveth, and was dead; and behold I am alive for evermore.[f]"

We only add further on this point, that it was the "sprinkling" of this blood and water upon the leper, that rendered the ceremony effectual for his good. In vain would the one bird shed his blood, or the other be dipped in it and let loose, unless there were an application of that blood and water to the leper himself. But being "sprinkled *seven* times," he was *perfectly* clean; so far at least as to be brought into the camp, and put into a train for that sanctification which was,]

II. Progressive—

[The leper was to wash both himself and his clothes, and to shave off all his hair, and then to come into the camp. But he was not fully restored to his place in society at once: he was not admitted into his tent, but was to live in some place alone for seven days more; and then, after again washing his body and his clothes, and shaving off all his hair, even to his eyebrows, he was reinstated in all his former privileges and comforts.

This was designed to shew, that the defiling effects of sin yet remain, even after that we are cleansed in the blood of Christ, and renewed by the Spirit. We need still to be renewed, both in our outward and inward man, day by day. Sin cleaves to us, yea, it spontaneously rises up in us; so that though we be washed ever so clean, we shall need to be washed again; and though we be shaved ever so close, we shall not be many days without manifesting that the work of sanctification is not yet perfect. Besides, there are higher degrees of holiness to which the regenerate are to be constantly aspiring. They are "not to account themselves to have yet attained; but, forgetting the things which are behind, they are to press forward for that which is before[g]." They are to be continually "putting off the old man, and putting on the new, even till they be renewed after the very image of their God in righteousness and true holiness[h]." Instead of regarding their restoration to the divine favour as a reason for resting satisfied with their attainments, they are to make their interest in the promises an occasion, and a stimulus, to "cleanse themselves from all filthiness both of flesh and spirit, and to perfect holiness in the fear of God[i]." "Having this hope in them," they are to stop short of nothing

[d] Lev. xvi. 21, 22.   [e] Rom. iv. 25.   [f] Rev. i. 18.
[g] Phil. iii. 12—14.   [h] Eph. iv. 22—24.   [i] 2 Cor. vii. 1

that can be attained in this life, but to "purify themselves even as God is pure[k]."]

Amongst Israel of old, the great mass of the population had never been infected with the leprosy at all: but that is not the case with us: the leprosy of sin has infected every human being: and there are now but two classes, under the one or the other of which we must all be arranged.

We will therefore ADDRESS ourselves,

1. To those who are yet infected with the leprosy—

[What was done at the time of *pronouncing* the lepers clean, is the very thing which must be done to *make* you clean. You must be sprinkled with the blood and Spirit of Christ, even of " Him who died for you and rose again." This is *necessary;* nor can any human being be saved without it: and it shall be *effectual;* so that no human being shall ever perish, provided he apply to his soul this divinely appointed remedy: " The blood of Jesus Christ shall cleanse him from all sin[1];" and the Spirit of Christ shall " cleanse him from all his filthiness and uncleanness[m]." The priests of old could not *heal* the leper, but only *declare* him healed: but our High-Priest can heal us. Only cry to him, as the lepers did in the days of his flesh, " Jesus, Master, have mercy on us!" and God himself shall acknowledge and pronounce you clean. The hyssop is even now at hand, wherewith you may sprinkle your own souls. Use it now by faith, and you shall experience with David both its incipient and progressive efficacy : " Purge me with hyssop, and I shall be clean ; wash me, and I shall be whiter than snow[n]." But sprinkle not yourselves once or twice only, but ' seven times;" then shall you be " washed *thoroughly* from your iniquity, and be cleansed from your sin[o]."]

2. To those who have been cleansed from it—

[Your state is beautifully represented by that of the healed leper. You are not yet admitted to your home, where your more perfect brethren enjoy without any intermission their Father's smiles : but you are brought into the camp; you are acknowledged as clean, notwithstanding your remaining imperfections : and there is yet only a single week before you will be brought into the full " liberty of the children of God." True, the intervening time must be spent in humiliating and painful exercises: but those exercises are all preparing you for the richer enjoyment of the promised bliss: " they are rendering you *meet* for the inheritance of the saints in light[p]."

[k] 1 John iii. 3.   [1] 1 John i. 7.   [m] Ezek. xxxvi. 25.
[n] Ps. li. 7.   [o] Ps. li. 2.   [p] Col. i. 12.

Look forward then to the happiness that awaits you: and carefully attend to every thing that God has enjoined; lest, when the appointed time shall arrive, you shall be found to have neglected the duties of the present moment. Labour then to the uttermost to get rid of sin: " Wash ye, make you clean q." As for the deep-rooted evils that spring up within you from time to time, if they cannot be eradicated, let them be shaved off the very moment that they appear. And let the time now appropriated to mortification and self-denial, be sweetened by the anticipation of that blessed hour, when you shall enter into the joy of your Lord, and rest for ever in the bosom of your God.]

q Isai. i. 16.

OUTLINE NO. 131
THE CLEANSING OF THE LEPER.

Lev. xiv. 14—18. *And the priest shall take some of the blood of the trespass-offering, and the priest shall put it upon the tip of the right ear of him that is to be cleansed, and upon the thumb of his right hand, and upon the great toe of his right foot. And the priest shall take some of the log of oil, and pour it into the palm of his own left hand: and the priest shall dip his right finger in the oil that is in his left hand, and shall sprinkle of the oil with his finger seven times before the Lord. And of the rest of the oil that is in his hand shall the priest put upon the tip of the right ear of him that is to be cleansed, and upon the thumb of his right hand, and upon the great toe of his right foot, upon the blood of the trespass-offering. And the remnant of the oil that is in the priest's hand he shall pour upon the head of him that is to be cleansed; and the priest shall make an atonement for him before the Lord.*

IF persons sought nothing more than entertainment in their studies, we know of no book that would afford them so much gratification as the Bible. Not to mention any particular beauties, such as the sublimity of its poetical parts, or the simplicity of the historical, there is something inexpressibly grand in the general harmony of the whole, and the fitness of every part to answer the ends for which it was designed. The great edifice that was to be erected, was Christianity: the model that was formed for the purpose of exhibiting it to the world in types and shadows, was Judaism: and the correspondence between the model and the structure in all its parts affords an inexhaustible fund of pleasing and useful instruction. Let us take, for example, the ceremonies observed at the cleansing of the leper; and we shall find that they set forth in a very striking light the most essential doctrines of the Gospel. They teach us more particularly,

I. The *ends* for which the blood and Spirit of Christ are to be applied to our souls—

It is scarcely needful to observe, that the blood of the sacrifices typically represented the blood of Christ; or that the oil which was used on various occasions with the sacrifices, represented the Spirit of Christ, with which every true Christian is, and must be, anointed[a].

The end for which they were put upon the leper is said to be, to "make an atonement for him[b]." But, in order to understand this aright, we must consider the state of the leprous person: he was banished from the house of God, and from all communion with his dearest friends: but, when he was healed, and the ceremonies appointed for his purification were performed, then he was restored completely to fellowship with God, and with his Church. The word atonement therefore is here used in a lax sense: strictly speaking, it was the blood of the sacrifice alone that made atonement: but the whole ceremony is said to make an atonement, because it was *that* which availed for the *complete* restoration of the leper to the enjoyment of all his privileges.

Moreover, he is said "to be cleansed" by these ceremonies, when, in fact, he was healed of his leprosy before any of these ceremonies could be used: so this was not an *actual*, but a *declarative* cleansing of his leprosy. Nevertheless it was intended to typify that which is *actually* effected by the blood and Spirit of

[a] 2 Cor. i. 21. 1 John ii. 20, 27.
[b] We might suppose from the concluding words of the text, that the priest was to make some *other* atonement for him: but in ver. 29. the matter is put beyond a doubt; for there it is expressly said, that these ceremonies were performed " *to make* an atonement for him."

Christ: these *really* cleanse our souls, and restore us perfectly to the service and enjoyment of God. The two together have a combined effect, to bring us to God: but they have separate and very distinct offices, which we ought carefully to notice:—

1. The blood of Christ must be applied to purge away our guilt—

[There is no possibility of cleansing our souls from guilt by any thing that we can do. As the blood of bulls and of goats cannot take away sin, so neither if we could shed rivers of tears, would they suffice to expiate one single offence; much less could they wash out the stain which we have contracted by a whole life of sin. It was because of the insufficiency of all other means, that God sent his only dear Son to die for us. The blood of Him who was " Jehovah's fellow," was an ample satisfaction for the sins of the whole world. No other atonement was necessary: nothing can add to the perfection of it. By means of it, God is reconciled to sinners; and nothing is wanting, but that the sinner himself should dip the hyssop in that precious blood, and sprinkle it upon his own conscience[c]. *This is the use which we are to make of the blood of Christ:* and if we apply it thus to our souls in faith, it will " purge us thoroughly from our iniquity, and cleanse us from our sin."]

2. The Spirit of Christ must be applied to renovate our nature—

[As the leprosy defiled the whole man, so does sin pollute our whole souls. Our nature is altogether corrupt: and we must be renewed in every part, before we can enter into the kingdom of God[d]. In our present state, we should not be capable of enjoying the divine presence, even if we were admitted to it. But how can this new nature be obtained? We can no more create ourselves anew, than we could create ourselves at first. We can no more give ourselves a spiritual nature, than vegetables can endue themselves with animation, or animals with reason. The spiritual life is, if we may so speak, a higher scale of existence: for though our faculties remain the same, they acquire a totally new direction as soon as ever the spiritual life is infused into our souls. Hence the true Christian is unequivocally called " a new creature[e]: " and hence arises our need of a divine Agent to bring us to this state. For this purpose therefore the Holy Spirit, the third Person in the ever blessed Trinity, is given to us: he is offered to us, to sanctify us throughout[f]. *To this end we must seek*

[c] Heb. ix. 12—14.   [d] John iii. 3, 5.   [e] 2 Cor. v. 17.   [f] Tit. iii. 5.

his *influence, and submit to his operations.* Thus shall the effectual working of his power transform our souls into the divine image^g, and make us " meet for the inheritance of the saints in light^h."]

But these points will receive additional light, while we consider,

II. The *manner* in which the blood and Spirit of Christ are to be applied, in order to their being effectual for the ends proposed—

From the rites used in cleansing the leper, we learn, that the application both of the blood and Spirit of Christ must be,

1. Particular—

[Doubtless our whole man needs purification both from the guilt and pollution of sin. But the application of the blood and oil to the ear, the thumb, and the toe of the leper, seems to intimate, that every member of the body, and every faculty of the soul, whereby we either receive or execute the will of God, needs a *special* purification from guilt and corruption. Great is the guilt we have contracted in hearing, since we have not been obedient to the voice of God. Great is the guilt we have contracted in the whole of our walk and conduct, since we have walked in our own way rather than in God's, and done our own will rather than his. Now it is proper that we should call these things to mind, and humble ourselves before God on account of them, imploring mercy for every particular offence, and seeking a renovation of every particular faculty and member; that so our powers may all become " instruments of righteousness unto Godⁱ." Not that we are to be so occupied with the consideration of our particular offences as to forget that we need a thorough renovation: no; after having put the blood and oil on the parts which seem most to need their influence, we should " pour the remainder of the oil upon our head," that it may flow over our whole body^k, and that we may " be sanctified wholly in body, soul, and spirit^l."]

2. United—

[Neither the blood nor the oil were on any account to be omitted in the purification of the leper: nor can either of them be omitted in the restoration of our souls to God. In vain shall we profess to be justified by the blood of Christ, if we be not also sanctified by his Spirit: and in vain shall we profess to have experienced a renovation of our souls by the influences of the

^g Eph. iv. 23, 24.   ^h Col. i. 12.   ⁱ Rom. vi. 13
^k ver. 18.   ^l 1 Thess. v. 23.

131.] THE CLEANSING OF THE LEPER. **629**

Spirit, if we do not trust entirely in the blood of Christ for pardon and acceptance. In the consecrating of Aaron and his sons to the priesthood, almost the same services were performed as at the purification of the leper: the blood was to be put on their ears, thumbs, and toes, and then, *together with the oil,* to be sprinkled on their bodies and their garments[m]. The same idea was suggested by the sprinkling of blood mixed with water in the preparatory part of the leper's purification[n]: and it was also intimated by the effusion of blood and water from our Saviour's side, when he was pierced by the spear[o]. St. John, who alone records that remarkable fact, lays great stress upon it in his first epistle, reminding us that "he came by water and blood, not by water only, but by water and blood[p]." Doubtless these things were designed to teach us, that God has united the pardoning virtue of Christ's blood, with the sanctifying operations of his Spirit; and that "what he has joined together, no man should presume to put asunder."]

3. Orderly—

[It is by no means an indifferent matter what order we observe in applying the blood and Spirit of Christ to our souls, or, in other words, whether we seek justification or sanctification in the first place. It is true, that, in speaking of them, our words need not always be placed with accuracy and precision; for even St. Paul himself, when speaking to the Corinthians, says, "Ye are washed, ye are sanctified, ye are justified in the name of the Lord Jesus, and by the Spirit of our God[q]." But it is highly necessary that we should have clear and determinate ideas on the subject. The order relative to the leper was, that the oil should be put (on the ear, thumb, and toe) "upon the blood of the trespass-offering[r]:" and to prevent our imagining this to mean only that it should be applied *in addition to* the blood, it is added afterwards, that the oil must "be put upon *the place* of the blood of the trespass-offering[s]." Surely this was not so minutely ordered for nought: it plainly shews us that the blood of Christ must be *first* applied for our justification; and that *then* the Spirit will be given for our sanctification. And this is the more carefully to be observed, because it is the very reverse of what men, of themselves, are disposed to do. We are apt to seek sanctification first; and then to make our proficiency in it the ground (in part at least) of our justification: but we must come to God as sinners to be "justified *freely by his grace* through the redemption that is in Christ Jesus[t];" and, being united thus by faith to Christ as the living

---

[m] Exod. xxix. 20, 21. [n] ver. 5—7. [o] John xix. 34, 35.
[p] 1 John v. 6. [q] 1 Cor. vi. 11. [r] ver. 17.
[s] ver. 28. [t] Rom. iii. 24.

vine, we shall derive virtue from him for the bringing forth the fruits of righteousness and true holiness[u].]

4. Believing—

[At the purification of the leper the priest was to "sprinkle the oil seven times before the Lord." This denoted that, while in the performance of these ceremonies they sought the glory of the Lord, they expected from him an abundant supply of those blessings which were typically represented by them. Thus in applying the blood and Spirit of Christ to our souls, we must feel a persuasion that we are using the instituted means of our salvation; and that, in the use of them, we shall receive from God the blessings we stand in need of. Such a confidence is not to be called presumption. Presumption is the expectation of benefits in a way wherein God has not warranted us to expect them: but the most assured expectation of them, when accompanied with a diligent discharge of our duty, and a humble dependence on his promises, is in the highest degree pleasing to God, and profitable to man. The "stronger we are in faith, the more do we give glory to God[x]," and ensure the accomplishment of his promises to our souls[y].]

ADDRESS—

1. To those who are conscious of their leprous state.

[The lepers were not left to judge of their own state: they were examined by the priest, and necessitated to abide by his decision. Think ye then, that, when our great High-Priest shall inspect your souls, he will not find out the marks of leprosy that are upon you? Be assured that, however they may be covered from the eye of man, they are all "naked and open (as the sacrifices were when flayed and cut down the back-bone) before the eyes of Him with whom we have to do[z]." O search out your iniquities, and "rend your hearts, and cover your lips, and, with the convicted leper, cry, Unclean, unclean[a]!" If you be not conscious of your disorder, you will never feel your need of purification from it; and consequently you will neglect the means prescribed for your recovery, and perish in your sins. May God avert from you so heavy a calamity, and incline you to accept with gratitude his proffered mercy!]

2. To those who desire deliverance from it—

[The lepers, though in a most afflicted state[b], had reason to be resigned to their lot, because their disorder came from

---

[u] John xv. 5. Rom. vii. 4.   [x] Rom. iv. 20.
[y] John xi. 40. 2 Chron. xx. 20.
[z] Γυμνὰ καὶ τετραχηλισμένα. Heb. iv. 13.
[a] Lev. xiii. 45. with Isai. vi. 5.
[b] For the true state of a leper, see Numb. xii. 12.

the hand of God. But your disorder comes from yourselves; and therefore you should not be satisfied with its continuance one day or hour. You do well to be solicitous about the removal of it; and we entreat you never to relax your solicitude about it, till the desired healing has been imparted to your souls. Know ye then for your comfort, that the blood and oil are already prepared, and that your great High-Priest is at this moment ready to apply them to your souls. Only go to him, and he will rejoice to minister to your necessities. Go humbly, yet boldly to him: present your ear, your hand, your foot, yea, and your whole person before him, that he may put upon them the blood and oil: and doubt not but that instantly you shall be restored to God, and stand "faultless before his presence with exceeding joy[c]."]

[c] Jude, ver. 24.

OUTLINE NO. 132

THE SCAPE-GOAT A TYPE OF CHRIST.

Lev. xvi. 21, 22. *And Aaron shall lay both his hands upon the head of the live goat, and confess over him all the iniquities of the children of Israel, and all their transgressions in all their sins, putting them upon the head of the goat, and shall send him away by the hand of a fit man into the wilderness. And the goat shall bear upon him all their iniquities, unto a land not inhabited.*

OF all the types, under the Mosaic dispensation, there was not one more plain in its import, or more useful in its tendency, than that before us. Most other types receive light from their accomplishment in Christ; this reflects light on the Gospel itself. The high-priest, having before offered a bullock and a ram, was to take two goats; and, having determined by lot which of them should be killed, and which be kept alive, was to kill the one, and to sprinkle its blood, with the blood of the bullock, within the sanctuary, and then to present the other before the Lord in the manner described in the text: he was to confess over it the sins of the people, and, by putting his hands upon its head, to transfer to it the people's sins; and then to send it into the wilderness that it might never more be seen of men. This ceremony **pointed out to them the true and proper *object* of** faith: the *operation* of it on the believer's mind; and the *fruit and benefit* of it to his soul.

I. The true and proper object of faith—

[When the high-priest put his hands on the head of the scape-goat, the eyes of all present must of necessity be turned towards that devoted creature. They indeed who were endued with a spiritual discernment, would look through the type unto Christ the great Antitype: but still the goat would be regarded by all as the immediate instrument used by God for the removal of their sins: their faith terminated on *that* as the instituted means of their deliverance.

Thus is Christ the one object to whom the eyes of all must be directed. He has been *chosen of God* from all eternity to bear in his own person, and to take away from his people, all their sins[a]. In due time he was *exhibited to the world* in this very character[b]: the iniquities of all mankind were *laid upon him*[c]: and his command to every living creature is, Look unto *Me* and be ye saved[d].

There was indeed under the law another goat, whose blood was shed for the remission of their sins; which was therefore to be considered by them as a joint object of their faith. But the two together were, in fact, but one sacrifice, the one representing the death of Jesus, and the other his resurrection. While therefore we view Christ as dying for our offences, we must also, in conformity with the type before us, regard him as rising again for our justification[e].]

II. Its operation on the believer's mind—

[The high-priest confessed over the scape-goat the sins of all Israel with their several aggravations, at the very time that he transferred them to him by the imposition of his hands. By this significant ordinance he clearly shewed how faith always operates. It leads us in the first place to transfer all our guilt to the sacred head of Jesus. While we see the impossibility of removing our sins in any other way, faith will incline us to avail ourselves of that inestimable privilege of carrying them to the Saviour, and thereby securing to ourselves an everlasting deliverance from them. But will it therefore cause us to think lightly of our iniquities, because they may be cancelled by such means? No: it will rather make them to appear exceeding sinful; and will dispose us to humble ourselves for them in dust and ashes. A true believer will not so much as desire pardon without being made to feel the evil and bitterness of sin: and the more sincerely he looks to Christ,

---

[a] Rev. xiii. 8.   [b] Rom. iii. 25. See also John i. 29. 2 Cor. v. 21.
[c] Isai. liii. 6.   [d] Isai. xlv. 22.   [e] Rom. iv. 25.

the more unfeignedly will he bewail his manifold transgressions [f]. While, with Mary, he boldly confesses Christ, with her he will kiss his feet, and wash them with his tears [g].]

III. The fruit and benefit of it to his soul—

[No sooner was the ordinance before us duly performed, than the sins of all Israel were taken away, and God was reconciled to his offending people. This indeed being only a typical institution, the pardon obtained by means of it was neither perfect nor durable, except to them who looked through the type to Christ himself. But faith in Christ, whether exercised by them or us, will obtain a full and everlasting remission of all our sins. Under the law indeed, there were some sins for which no sacrifice was appointed, and which therefore could not be purged away by any ceremonial oblations whatever. But there is no sin from which we shall not be justified by faith in Jesus [h]. From the very instant that we are enabled to lay them upon his head, they shall be carried into the land of oblivion, and never more be remembered against us [i]: yea, they shall be cast into the very depths of the sea [k], and be put away from us far as the east is from the west [l].]

From hence we may LEARN,

1. The different offices of repentance and faith—

[Repentance can never make atonement for sin. However penitent we be, we must lay our hands upon the head of the scape-goat, and transfer our guilt to him. On the other hand, faith does not supersede repentance, but rather encourages and invites us to it. We must repent, in order to prepare our hearts for a grateful acceptance of pardon, and a diligent improvement of it in our future life: but we must believe in order to obtain pardon; *that* being bestowed solely on account of Christ's vicarious sacrifice. Repentance stirs us up to exercise faith on Christ; and faith stimulates us to further acts of penitence, for the honouring of the law, the justifying of God, the exalting of Christ, the purifying of the heart, the adorning of our profession, and the rendering of us meet for glory. To be in a state pleasing to God, we must be believing penitents, and penitent believers.]

2. The folly of delaying to repent and believe—

[Impenitence and unbelief keep us from Christ, and rivet our sins upon us. We must all resemble either the oblation, or the offerer: we must either, like the goats, die under the wrath of God, and be for ever banished, as accursed creatures,

[f] Ezek. xvi. 63.   [g] Luke vii. 37, 38.   [h] Acts xiii. 39.
[i] Isai. xliii. 25. Heb. viii. 12.   [k] Mic. vii. 19.   [l] Ps. ciii. 12

from his presence; or we must go with penitence and contrition to our living Surety, and cast our iniquities on him. And can there be a doubt which state we should prefer? Or would we continue another hour under the guilt of all our sins, when there is such a way provided for the removal of them? Let us then behold the Scape-goat, as in our immediate presence, and go instantly to lay our sins on him. It cannot, as under the law, be done by the priest for us; it must be done by every one of us for himself. Let us then go to him with penitence and faith, and rest assured that we shall not repent or believe in vain.]

OUTLINE NO. 133
DUTIES REQUIRED ON THE GREAT DAY OF ATONEMENT.

Lev. xvi. 29, 30, 33. *And this shall be a statute for ever unto you, that in the seventh month, on the tenth day of the month, ye shall afflict your souls, and do no work at all, whether it be one of your own country, or a stranger that sojourneth among you. For on that day shall the priest make an atonement for you, to cleanse you, that ye may be clean from all your sins before the Lord..... And he shall make an atonement for the holy sanctuary, and he shall make an atonement for the tabernacle of the congregation, and for the altar; and he shall make an atonement for the priests, and for all the people of the congregation.*

THE wisdom and piety of the Church in early ages appointed, that a considerable portion of time at this season of the year should be devoted annually to the particular consideration of our Saviour's sufferings; and that the day on which he is supposed to have died upon the cross, should be always observed as a solemn fast. In process of time many superstitious usages were introduced; which, however, in the Reformed Churches, have been very properly discontinued. But it is much to be regretted, that, whilst we have cast off the yoke of Popish superstition, we have lost, in a very great measure, that regard for the solemnities which our Reformers themselves retained; and which experience has proved to be highly conducive to the spiritual welfare of mankind. The Nativity of our Lord indeed, because it is a *feast*, is observed by almost all persons with a religious reverence; but the day of his death, being

133.] DUTIES ON THE GREAT DAY OF ATONEMENT. 635

to be kept as a *fast*, is almost wholly disregarded; insomuch that the house of God is scarcely at all attended, and the various vocations of men proceed almost without interruption in their accustomed channel. We are well aware that the Jewish institutions are not to be revived: but, though the ordinances themselves have ceased, the *moral ends* for which they were instituted should be retained; nor should any *means*, whereby they may, in perfect consistency with Christian liberty, be attained, be deemed unworthy of our attention.

The great day of annual expiation was the most solemn appointment in the whole of the Mosaic economy. Its avowed purpose was to bring men to repentance, and to faith in the atonement which should in due time be offered. Now these are the sole ends for which an annual fast is observed on this day: and, if they be attained by us, we shall have reason to bless God for ever that such an appointment has been preserved in the Church.

In considering the passage before us there are two things to be noticed;

I. The objects for which atonement was made—

To have a just view of this subject, we must not rest in the general idea of an atonement for sin, but must enter particularly into the consideration of the specific objects for which the atonement was made. It was made,

1. For the High-Priest—

[The persons who filled the office of the priesthood were partakers of the same corrupt nature, as was in those for whom they ministered: and, being themselves sinners, they needed an atonement for themselves[a]: nor could they hope to interpose with effect between God and the people, unless they themselves were first brought into a state of reconciliation with God. Hence they were necessitated to "offer first of all for their own sins."

And this is a point which reflects peculiar light on the excellency of the dispensation under which *we* live. Our High-Priest was under no such necessity: He had no sin of his own to answer for[b]: and hence it is that his atonement becomes effec-

[a] Heb. v. 1—3.   [b] 1 Pet. ii. 22.

tual for us[e]: for, if he had needed any atonement for himself, he never could have procured reconciliation for us [d] ———]

2. For the people—

["All the people of the congregation" were considered as sinners; and for all of them indiscriminately was the atonement offered. None were supposed to be so holy as not to need it, nor any so vile as to be excluded from a participation of its benefits.

But here again we are reminded of the superior excellency of the Christian dispensation. For though, among the Jews, the atonement was offered for all, it did not suffice for the removal of guilt from all: it took off the dread of punishment for ceremonial defilements; but left the people at large, and especially all who had been guilty of presumptuous sin, under the dread of a future reckoning at the tribunal of God. "It could not make any man perfect as pertaining to the conscience[e]." The very repetition of those sacrifices from year to year shewed, that some further atonement was necessary[f]. But under the Gospel the reconciliation offered to us is perfect: it extends to all persons and all sins, in all ages, and quarters, of the world. No guilt is left upon the conscience, no dread of future retribution remains, where the atonement of Christ has had its full effect[g]: there is peace with God, even "a peace that passeth all understanding:" He "perfects, yea, perfects for ever, all them that are sanctified[h]."]

3. For "the sanctuary itself and the altar"—

[Even the house of God, and the altar which sanctified every thing that was put upon it, were rendered unclean by the ministrations of sinful men. The very touch or presence of such guilty creatures communicated a defilement, which could not be purged away but by the blood of atonement. The high-priest, even while making atonement for the holy place, contracted pollution, from which he must wash himself, before he could proceed in his priestly work[i]. In like manner, the person who led away the scape-goat into the wilderness, and the person who burnt the sin-offering without the camp, must wash, both their persons and their clothes, before they could be re-admitted into the camp[k]. What an idea does this give us of the corruption of human nature, when even the most holy actions, performed according to the express appointment of God, were, by a painful necessity, the means and occasions of fresh defilement!

From the atonement required for the sanctuary we learn, that heaven itself, so to speak, is defiled by the admission of

[e] 1 John iii. 5. 2 Cor. v. 21.   [d] Heb. vii. 26—28.
[e] Heb. ix. 9, 10.   [f] Heb. x. 1—4.   [g] Heb. ix. 14.
[h] Heb. x. 14, 17, 21, 22.   [i] ver. 24.   [k] ver. 26—28.

sinners into it; and that on that very account it could not be a meet habitation for the Deity, if it were not purified by the atoning blood of Christ[1].]

A just view of these things will discover to us the connexion between the atonement itself, and,

II. The duty especially enjoined at the time of that atonement—

To afflict the soul is our duty at all times—

[As for the penances which men have contrived for the afflicting of *the body*, they are neither acceptable to God, nor beneficial to man: they tend to keep men from true repentance, rather than to lead them to it. Doubtless such a measure of fasting and bodily self-denial as shall aid the soul in its operations, is good: but still it is *the soul* chiefly that must be afflicted. *That* is the principal seat of sin, and therefore should be the principal seat of our sorrows. Indeed, it is the soul alone which possesses a capacity for real and rational humiliation.

Now as there is "no man who does not in many things, yea, in every thing (to a certain degree) offend," there is no man who does not need to afflict his soul, and to humble himself before God on account of his defects.

But it may be asked, How is this to be done? How can we reach our soul, so as to afflict it? I answer, By meditating deeply on our sins. We should call to mind all the transactions of our former lives, and compare them with the holy commands of God. We should, as far as possible, make all our sins pass in review before us: we should consider their number and variety, their constancy and continuance, their magnitude and enormity: we should search out all the aggravating circumstances with which they have been committed, as being done against light and knowledge, against mercies and judgments, against vows and resolutions, and, above all, against redeeming love. We should contemplate our desert and danger on account of them, and our utter loathsomeness in the sight of God. This is the way to bring the soul to "a broken and contrite" state: and this is the duty of every living man.]

But it was peculiarly proper on the great day of atonement—

[The exercise of godly sorrow would further in a variety of views a just improvement of all the solemnities of that day. *It would dispose the person to justify God in requiring such services.* Those who felt no sense of sin would be ready to complain of the ordinances as burthensome and expensive: but those who were truly contrite, would be thankful, that God had appointed *any* means of obtaining reconciliation with him———

[1] Heb. ix. 23.

It would prepare the person for a just reception of **God's** *mercy*. An obdurate heart would reject the promises, just as the trodden path refuses to receive the seed that is cast upon it. The fallow ground must be broken up before the seed can be sown in it to good effect — — —

It would lead the person to acknowledge with gratitude the unbounded goodness of God. A person, unconscious of any malady, would pour contempt on any prescription that was offered him for the healing of his diseases: but one who felt himself languishing under a fatal, and, to all appearance, incurable disorder, would accept with thankfulness any remedy which he knew would restore his health. Thus it is the penitent sinner, and he only, that will value the offers of mercy through the blood of atonement — — —

Lastly, *it would stimulate him to greater watchfulness and diligence in future*. Suppose a person pardoned; if he felt not the evil and bitterness of sin, he would be as remiss and careless as ever: but, if his heart had been altogether broken with a sense of sin, if he had groaned under it as an intolerable burthen, he would be doubly careful lest he should subject himself again to the same distress and danger: and the more assured he was of pardon and acceptance with God, the more desirous he would be to "render unto God according to the benefits received from him" — — —]

The REFLECTIONS to which this subject will naturally give rise, are such as these:

1. How vain is the idea of "establishing a righteousness of our own!"

[If the most holy actions of the most holy men, done expressly according to the divine appointment, rendered the persons unclean, yea and the very sanctuary of God and the altar itself unclean, so that the washing of water and the sprinkling of blood were necessary for their purification, who are *we*, that we should be able so to live as to claim a reward on the ground of *merit*? Let us lay aside this vain conceit, which, if not corrected, will infallibly issue in our own destruction. We need one to "bear the iniquity of our holy things[m]," no less than the iniquity of our vilest actions: and, from first to last, we must receive "eternal life as the free unmerited gift of God through Jesus Christ[n]."]

2. How transcendent must be the efficacy of our Redeemer's blood!

[All these sacrifices which were repeated from year to year could never purge the conscience of one single individual: but

---

[m] Exod. xxviii. 38   [n] Rom. vi. 23

the blood of Jesus Christ, once shed on Calvary, is sufficient to cleanse the whole world. Stupendous thought! Let us endeavour to realize it, and to get the evidence of it in our own souls — — —]

3. How blessed is the issue of true repentance!

[Men imagine that to afflict the soul is the way to be miserable: but the very reverse is true: to "sow in tears is the sure way to reap in joy[o]." How beautifully was this represented on the day of atonement! It was on *that day* (every fiftieth year) that the Jubilee was to be proclaimed[p]. What a blessed termination of the day was this! What a balm to every afflicted soul! Think of the joy which pervaded the whole country, when every man was rendered free, and all returned to their lost inheritance[q]! Such shall be the happy experience of all who afflict their souls for sin, and rely upon the atoning blood of Christ. "They that go on their way weeping, bearing precious seed, shall doubtless come again with rejoicing, bringing their sheaves with them[r]."]

[o] Ps. cxxvi. 5.   [p] Lev. xxv. 9.   [q] Lev. xxv. 10.   [r] Ps. cxxvi. 6.

OUTLINE NO. 134

THE PROHIBITION TO EAT BLOOD.

Lev. xvii. 10—12. *Whatsoever man there be of the house of Israel, or of the strangers that sojourn among you, that eateth any manner of blood, I will even set my face against that soul that eateth blood, and will cut him off from among his people. For the life of the flesh is in the blood; and I have given it to you upon the altar, to make an atonement for your souls: for it is the blood that maketh an atonement for the soul. Therefore I said unto the children of Israel, No soul of you shall eat blood; neither shall any stranger that sojourneth among you eat blood.*

THERE were many ordinances amongst the Jews, of which we cannot see the reason, though doubtless there was not one which Infinite Wisdom did not institute for some gracious end. But the particular enactment before us was of much longer standing than most others, having been given to Noah directly after the flood. The flesh of beasts and of fowls was then given to man for food: but he was at the same time forbidden to eat the blood of either[a]. In the

[a] Gen. ix. 4.

foregoing parts of this book also the prohibition had been repeatedly renewed[b]: and here the reason for such a repeated enactment of the same statute is assigned. Indeed from the peculiar strictness with which the law is here enforced, we might be sure that there was some very important reason for it, though none had been specified. But God, in this passage, has condescended to state the grounds of this solemn charge; namely, that "the blood was the life of the flesh, and that it had been given to man to make an atonement for his soul."

To elucidate this ordinance, I shall,

I. Confirm the fact here stated—

God had from the beginning appointed the blood of animals to be offered by man as an atonement for his soul.

This appears throughout all the Mosaic history—

[If we go back to the time of Cain and Abel, we shall find Abel offering of the firstlings of his flock, and of his receiving on that account a testimony of God's acceptance, which was denied to Cain, who offered only of the fruits of the ground[c]. This, we are assured, was done " in faith;" which shews, that it was done in consequence of an ordinance to that effect having been previously given by God, with a promise of acceptance annexed to it[d]. Noah likewise after the flood offered of every clean beast, and of every clean fowl, upon an altar; and in that act was approved of his God[e]. The Patriarchs also built altars to the Lord from time to time, and presented their offerings upon them. Job also lived in the habitual practice of the same rite[f]. As for Moses, the whole of his law was one continued system of sacrifices, appointed as means of obtaining forgiveness with God; every kind of sin having its distinct sacrifices appointed to atone for it. In all of these, blood was shed, and poured out before the altar, and sprinkled on the altar; and on the great day of annual expiation, was carried within the sanctuary, and was sprinkled before the mercy-seat, and upon the mercy-seat. With one exception only, " there was no remission of sins without shedding of blood[g]." If a man was so poor as not to be able to offer a lamb or a pair of turtle-doves for his transgression, he was to offer some fine flour; a part of which was to be burnt

[b] Lev. iii. 17. and vii. 26.   [c] Gen. iv. 3—5.   [d] Heb. xi. 4.
[e] Gen. viii. 20, 21.   [f] Job i. 5.   [g] Heb. ix. 21, 22.

upon the altar, in token that he had merited destruction by his iniquities, and that he escaped destruction only by that being destroyed in his stead[h].]

The same is found throughout the whole New Testament—

[It had been foretold by Daniel, that Jesus should "make an end of sin, and make reconciliation for iniquity." But how was this to be done? It was, as another prophet testifies, by being "wounded for our transgressions, and bruised for our iniquities," or, in a word, by "making his soul an offering for sin[i]." Accordingly our blessed Lord himself tells us that he came to "give his life a ransom for many." And, when he instituted his last supper, he took the cup, and said, "This is my blood of the New Testament which is shed for many for the remission of sins[k]." The Apostles continually represent the blessings of salvation as being solely the purchase of his blood. "He hath made peace for us through the blood of his cross," and "we have redemption through it, even the forgiveness of sins[l]." Are we "washed from our sins?" it is "by his blood[m]." Do we wash our robes and make them white? it is in the blood of the Lamb[n]. Do we overcome our enemies? it is by the blood of the Lamb[o]. Are we justified? it is by his blood[p]. In a word, all on earth and all in heaven bear testimony to this blessed truth, that "Jesus hath redeemed us to God by his blood[q]."]

This fact then being undeniable, that "God has given us the blood as an atonement for the soul," we proceed to,

II. Consider the prohibition as founded on it—

Scarcely is such energy to be found in any other prohibition throughout the whole Scriptures, as in that before us. And how is it to be accounted for? What is there in the fact alleged that can justify such tremendous menaces as are annexed to this injunction? I answer, The prohibition was most salutary for them, as tending,

1. To excite in them reverence for their sacrifices—

[The Jews saw continually the same animals slaughtered for their own use as were slain for sacrifice: and, if no restraint had been imposed upon them in relation to the blood, they

[h] Lev. v. 11.   [i] Isai. liii. 5, 10.   [k] Matt. xxvi. 28.
[l] Col. i. 14, 20.   [m] Rev. i. 5.   [n] Rev. vii. 14.
[o] Rev. xii. 11.   [p] Rom. v. 9.   [q] Rev. v. 9.

would soon have lost their reverence for the sacrifice altogether. Even the daily repetition of the same sacrifices had of itself a tendency to familiarize their minds with the offerings, and to weaken the reverence which a more sparing use of them might have generated. But when they were so strictly charged to abstain from the use of the blood themselves, and saw the blood of the sacrifices consecrated exclusively to the Lord, they could scarcely fail to reverence the blood, and consequently to reverence those ordinances in which the welfare of their souls was so deeply concerned.]

2. To bring continually to their remembrance the way of salvation—

[With the prohibition was communicated the reason of it, namely, that the blood was the life, and was given as an atonement for their souls. Now we are but too prone to forget the concerns of our souls: the mind naturally revolts from them, and puts the consideration of them far away. But this ordinance brought continually to their recollection, that they were sinners, needing an atonement; and that they were to be saved only through the intervention of a vicarious sacrifice. Of what incalculable value was the prohibition in this point of view! Not a day, or scarcely an hour, could pass, but they were reminded of these most essential articles of their faith, and taught how alone they were to obtain favour in the sight of God. Various other ordinances were appointed of God for reminding them of the way in which they should serve him; but here one was instituted for bringing constantly to their remembrance the way in which they were to *be saved by him.*]

3. To direct their attention to the great sacrifice—

[All the more intelligent and pious among the Jews saw that their sacrifices shadowed forth some sacrifice that was of infinitely greater value. It is true, their notions respecting Christ's sacrifice were not distinct: yet they could not but see that the blood of bulls and of goats was insufficient to take away sin; and that consequently they must look forward to some other atonement which these typical sacrifices prefigured. To these views they would be further led by the prophecies which represented Christ as bearing on himself, and taking away from us, the iniquities of us all. And even at this hour, I conceive that the prohibition, which is strictly observed by every religious Jew, is well calculated to lead the minds of the Jewish nation to the contemplation of their Messiah, and to the acknowledgment of Jesus in that character.]

From the foregoing subject then we may SEE,

1. How plain is the way of salvation!

[A Jew who had any reflection at all, could not be ignorant that he must be saved by blood, by blood shed in a way of atonement for his sins. He would not dream that he was to make an atonement by his own tears, or alms-deeds, or observances of any kind. Every sacrifice which he saw offered, yea, and every meal which he made on the flesh of animals, would remind him, that his soul could be saved by nothing but an atonement made for sin. Yet, strange as it must appear, Christians without number are ignorant of this fundamental article of our religion, and have no better hope towards God than that which is founded on their own repentances and reformations. Alas! that any who have the Christian Scriptures in their hands should be thus ignorant! and yet thus it is even with many who in other respects are well instructed and intelligent. But know ye assuredly, that there is but one way of salvation either for Jews or Gentiles; and that, the shadowy sacrifices having all passed away, " Christ is now set forth as a propitiation for sin through faith in his blood," and that he is " a propitiation, not for our sins only, but also for the sins of the whole world."]

2. How awful is the state of those who reject it!

[We tremble for those who despised Moses' law, and in contempt of the divine command ate of blood. But how much more must we tremble for those who make light of Christ! For, " if they who despised Moses' law died without mercy, of how much sorer punishment suppose ye shall he be thought worthy, who has trodden under foot the Son of God, and counted the blood of the covenant wherewith he was sanctified a *common* thing[r]!" The command given to us to drink of the blood of our great sacrifice is not a whit less urgent than the prohibition given to the Jews. Our Lord expressly tells us, that " except we eat his flesh and drink his blood, we have no life in us:" and St. Paul gives us this solemn warning, " How can we escape, if we neglect so great salvation!" Verily, if God set his face against the disobedient Jew, much more will he against the disobedient and unbelieving Christian. I charge you then, my brethren, to comply with the divine command in this respect: for if ye do not, O consider " what shall the end be of them that obey not the Gospel of Christ!" Verily, God has told us, and plainly too, that " when the Lord Jesus shall be revealed from heaven in flaming fire, it shall be to take vengeance on them that know not God, and that obey not the Gospel of our Lord Jesus Christ." Let us now then avail ourselves of the opportunity afforded us, and both take of the blood of Christ, and " sprinkle it on our consciences, that it may purge us from dead works to serve the living God."]

[r] Heb. x. 28, 29. κοινόν.

OUTLINE NO. 135

FEAST OF FIRST-FRUITS.

Lev. xxiii. 15—17. *And ye shall count unto you from the morrow after the Sabbath, from the day that ye brought the sheaf of the wave-offering; seven Sabbaths shall be complete: even unto the morrow after the seventh Sabbath shall ye number fifty days; and ye shall offer a new meat-offering unto the Lord. Ye shall bring out of your habitations two wave-loaves, of two tenth deals: they shall be of fine flour; they shall be baken with leaven; they are the first-fruits unto the Lord.*

THERE is no blessing which is not enhanced by a sense of reconciliation and acceptance with God. An ungodly man has his very provisions cursed to him[a]; whilst to the righteous " God hath given all things richly to enjoy." Indeed, it is to present, no less than to future, happiness, that God calls his people. He bids us weep, it is true; but he no-where bids us to be *always* mourning: on the contrary, he commands us to " rejoice in him always, yea, to " rejoice *evermore:*" and assures us, that, though our " weeping may endure for a night, joy shall come in the morning." We have this beautifully exemplified in the appointments under the law. One day in the year was appointed for national humiliation, namely, the day of atonement, wherein all were commanded to afflict their souls: but the very next day, and the whole week following it, was appointed for a feast[b]; by which appointment it was clearly intimated, that they who had obtained reconciliation with God through the atonement of Christ, had reason to rejoice throughout the whole remainder of their lives.

The week succeeding the Passover was called " the feast of unleavened bread:" on the first day of which they were to present to God a sheaf of newly reaped barley; and, fifty days after that, two loaves of wheaten bread; both of them being the first-fruits, the one of the barley harvest, and the other of the wheat. Hence these two periods were called the feasts of " first

---

[a] Deut. xxviii. 16—19. [b] ver. 5, 6.

fruits:" and the appointment of them may be considered in a three-fold view; as,

I. Commemorative—

[The day on which the sheaf of barley was to be presented unto God, was that on which they had come out of Egypt: and it was to be kept in commemoration of that event; that, when they were enjoying the peaceful fruits of industry, they might call to mind the labour and travail they had endured in the land of their captivity.

The fiftieth day after that, was the day on which the law of God had been delivered to them from Mount Sinai. This was no less a mercy than the former: for whilst by the former they were rescued from bondage to men, by the latter they were brought into the service of God[c].

Both of these events were to be remembered on the days thus set apart[d], in order that He who had done such great things for their bodies and their souls, might have the glory due unto his name.

And here we cannot but observe, how beneficial it is to the Church to have particular times set apart for the special remembrance of the various wonders of redemption. If indeed the observance of such institutions were required of us as necessary to salvation, or inculcated as contributing to work out for us a justifying righteousness, or represented as superseding the necessity of a more frequent remembrance of them, or enjoined, as Jeroboam's was, in opposition to the commands of God[e], we should be ready to join with those who reprobate such appointments. But experience proves, that the appointment of seasons for the distinct consideration of particular subjects, has been productive of the greatest good; and that the more solemnly those seasons are devoted to the special purposes for which they are set apart, the more will humility, and every Christian grace, flourish in the soul. And, if the annual remembrance of an earthly deliverance was pleasing and acceptable to God, there can be no reasonable doubt, but that the annual commemoration of infinitely richer mercies (provided only that we guard against self-righteousness and superstition) must be pleasing to him also.]

But these feasts derived a still greater importance from being,

II. Typical—

[Two of the greatest events which ever happened from the foundation of the world, and which are the source and warrant of all our hopes, occurred on the days appointed for these feasts, and were typically prefigured by them.

---

[c] The two are spoken of precisely in this way, as equalled by each other, but by nothing else. Deut. iv. 32—35.
[d] Deut. xvi. 9, 12.   [e] 1 Kings xii. 33.

On the former of those days, that I mean on which the Israelites came out of their graves in Egypt, (which was the first-fruits of their deliverance, as the wave-sheaf was of the barley harvest,) Christ rose from the dead, and rose, not as an individual, but " as *the first-fruits* of them that slept[f];" and has thereby assured to us the resurrection of all his people to a life of immortality and glory[g].

On the latter of those days, namely, the fiftieth day, on which the law was given, (which, like the first-fruits of the wheat harvest, was the pledge and earnest of those mercies which they were afterwards to enjoy under the immediate government of God,) on that day, I say, the Holy Ghost was poured out upon the Apostles[h], who then " received *the first-fruits* of the Spirit[i]." As on that day God had proclaimed his law, so on that day he promulged his Gospel; and gathered to himself three thousand souls, who were *the first-fruits* of that glorious harvest[k], which shall in due time be reaped, when " all shall know the Lord from the least even to the greatest," and " all the kingdoms of the world become the kingdom of the Lord and of his Christ."

In these views the feasts of which we are speaking become exceedingly important. It is true, they were but shadows, and very obscure shadows too: but to us who have the substance, and on whom " the true light shineth," they are worthy of most attentive consideration; as being the first rude drafts or models of that glorious edifice which we inhabit.]

But these feasts are of further use to us, as,

III. Instructive—

[There is not any thing which we are more interested to know than our *obligations to God*, and our consequent *duty towards him:* yet these are clearly and strongly represented to us in the ordinances before us.

Behold our *obligations* to God. In each of these feasts the first-fruits were " *waved*" before God[l], in token that every earthly blessing was derived from him. This was done *in the name of the whole congregation;* so that, whatever diligence or skill any had used in the cultivation of their land, they did not arrogate any thing to themselves, but gave glory to Him " from whom alone proceeds every good and perfect gift." Happy would it be for us, if we also learned this lesson, so as to have our minds duly impressed with the goodness of our God! — — —]

[f] 1 Cor. xv. 20.   [g] 1 Cor. xv. 21—23.
[h] Acts ii. 1. " Pentecost" means the fiftieth day; for which, it is evident, the communication of this blessing was reserved: and it was communicated when that day " was fully come."
[i] Rom. viii. 23.   [k] Rev. xiv. 4.   [l] ver. 11, 17.

FEAST OF FIRST-FRUITS. [135.

Corresponding with our obligations to God is our *duty* towards him. If we have received every thing from him, it is our bounden duty to devote every thing to him, and improve every thing for the honour of his name. And, as at the former of these feasts they offered only *one* sheaf, and *one* lamb, but at the latter they presented *two* loaves, and *seven* lambs[m], so, in proportion as God has multiplied his mercies towards us, we also should enlarge our exercises of gratitude, liberality, and devotion.

Shall these sentiments be thought an undue refinement on the subject before us? They are the very sentiments which God himself suggests in reference to these very institutions. We are expressly told in this view to honour him with all that we *have*, and all that we *are*. Have we *property?* We must "honour the Lord with our substance, and with the *first-fruits* of all our increase:" and, lest that should be thought likely to impoverish us, and it should be deemed advisable rather to gather in our harvest *first*, and then give him out of our abundance, he particularly guards us against any such covetous and distrustful thoughts, and tells us that a believing and thankful dedication of our *first-fruits* is the most likely way to ensure to ourselves an abundant harvest[n]. Alas! how melancholy it is that, when we are receiving so many *harvests* at God's hands, not a few of us are found to grudge him even a *sheaf!*

But it is not our property only that we should devote to God; we should give him *our whole selves*. We are told that "God hath set apart him that is godly for himself[o]," exactly as he did the first-fruits of old, of which it would have been sacrilege to rob him: and every one that professes a hope in Christ is called upon to consider himself in that very view, namely, "as a kind of *first-fruits* of his creatures[p]." Yes, Beloved, "we are not our own; we are redeemed, and bought with a price; and therefore are bound to glorify God with our bodies and our spirits, which are his [q]."

Only let these instructions be impressed upon our minds, and exemplified in our lives, and then we shall make the best possible improvement of these typical institutions. Yea, whether we contemplate the types or the things typified, the improvement of them must be the same. From the resurrection of Christ we must learn to rise again to newness of life; and from the outpouring of the Spirit we must learn to cherish and obey his sanctifying operations. Thus will both Law and Gospel be transcribed into our lives, and God be glorified in all his dispensations.]

[m] ver. 12, 18. [n] Prov. iii. 9, 10. [o] Ps. iv. 3.
[p] Jam. i. 18. [q] 1 Cor. vi. 19, 20.

OUTLINE NO. 136
THE FEAST OF TRUMPETS.

Lev. xxiii. 23—25. *And the Lord spake unto Moses, saying, Speak unto the children of Israel, saying, In the seventh month, in the first day of the month, shall ye have a Sabbath, a memorial of blowing of trumpets, an holy convocation. Ye shall do no servile work therein; but ye shall offer an offering made by fire unto the Lord.*

THE ordinances of the Mosaic law, though dark in themselves, are, for the most part, rendered luminous by the Gospel: their true meaning is opened to us by inspired expositors; and little room is left for the exercise of fancy or conjecture. This however is not universally the case: the ordinance before us is a remarkable exception to the general rule: Moses himself does not inform us on what occasion, or for what particular end it was appointed: nor do the New-Testament writers give us any explanation of the subject. But as it was one of the great annual feasts among the Jews, it must of necessity be instructive. We shall endeavour therefore to search out the meaning as well as we can; and to shew,

I. For what end this feast was instituted—

Some have referred it to the blowing of the trumpet on Mount Sinai: and others have supposed that it referred to all the different occasions whereon the trumpet was blown. But the former of these does not appear a proper foundation for a joyful feast; (when it made all Israel, not excepting Moses himself, to " tremble and quake:") and the latter opinion refutes itself: for if they were used on a variety of occasions, as the summoning of the people to the tabernacle, the directing of them in their journeys, the stirring of them up against their enemies, and the proclaiming of the year of jubilee, it is reasonable to suppose, that the appointment of a feast, called the feast of trumpets, was for some special and peculiar purpose. Accordingly, though the purpose is not specified, we may form a good judgment respecting it, from the peculiar day on which it was to be observed That which in our text is called the seventh month, had been always deemed the first month of the year; but when God brought his people out of Egypt, he ordered them, in remembrance of that event, to reckon their year differently, and to begin it in the spring, instead of the autumn[a]. Still however, in their civil and political matters, they retained the original mode of reckoning; and, except in their ecclesiastical concerns, this continued to be the first month in the year. This day then was *the first day in the new year;* and the feast of trumpets was to them " a memorial;" a memorial of *mercies received,* and of *mercies promised:*

1. Of mercies received—

[It is possible that the creation of the world, which was supposed to have been in the autumn, (when so many of the fruits are ripe,) was then particularly commemorated. But we apprehend that the mercies of the preceding year were then reviewed; and grateful acknowledgments were made to God for them. This seems to be a fit employment for the commencement of a new year; and every succeeding year must of necessity bring with it many renewed occasions for praise and thanksgiving. Even though the nation should have been visited with judgments, still those judgments are so disproportioned to men's ill desert, and are always blended with so many mercies, that there could not fail of being always abundant reason for joy and gratitude.

The blowing of the trumpets would awaken the attention of the people to the duties of the day, and bring to their recollection some at least of those mercies, which they were now called upon to acknowledge.]

2. Of mercies promised—

[In this sense the term "memorial" is often used in Scripture. The stones on Aaron's breast-plate were a "memorial," to remind the people, that God regarded them as his peculiar care, and bore them upon his heart[b]. The atonement-money, which was to be paid on numbering the people, was also a "memorial" of the security which was assured to them under God's protecting hand[c]. The frankincense which from week to week was put upon the shew-bread[d], was of a similar nature; for whilst it reminded God of his people and their necessities, it was a pledge to them that he would supply their wants. Moreover, the Psalmist, expressly referring to this feast, says,

[a] Exod. xii. 2.   [b] Exod. xxviii. 12, 29.
[c] Exod. xxx. 16.   [d] Lev. xxiv. 7.

"it was ordained *for a testimony*[e]." Now when this "memorial" sounded in their ears, the various temporal mercies which they would need, would of course occur to their minds. But there were spiritual blessings, which probably came but little into the contemplation of the people, which yet were of principal importance in the sight of God, and were particularly shadowed forth on this occasion; I mean, the prosperity of Zion, and the enlargement of the Church of Christ.

That this was intended, an inspired Apostle assures us; for speaking of this very feast amongst others, he says, "Which things are a shadow of good things; but the body is of Christ[f]."

The language used in reference to the Gospel, strongly confirms this truth. It is emphatically called, "the joyful sound;" and they who preach it are said, to "lift up their voice as a trumpet:" and when the fulness of time shall come for the universal establishment of Christ's kingdom in the world, the sound of this trumpet shall be heard to the remotest corners of the earth, and all, from the least even to the greatest, shall come up to his temple. Even "Assyria and Egypt," the most determined enemies of God's people, shall be stirred up by it to "come and worship in the holy mount in Jerusalem[g]."

Such a prospect was a solid ground of joy. We rejoice in the partial accomplishment of this event that has already taken place: and we look forward with joy to its full and final accomplishment.]

Let us proceed to consider—

II. In what manner it was to be observed—

The three great feasts, the Passover, the feast of Pentecost, and the feast of tabernacles, were greater than this; because, on them, all the males were required to assemble at Jerusalem: but next to them was the feast of trumpets. It was more holy than a common Sabbath; because no servile work at all might be done on this day; whereas on common Sabbaths an exception was made for preparing their necessary provision. Moreover on this day they were to be fully occupied in offering sacrifices to God. Besides the daily sacrifices, and those appointed at the beginning of every month, there were many peculiar to this occasion: and an express order was made, that neither the daily nor monthly offerings should be superseded, but that those for this day should be presented in addition to all the others[h].

[e] Ps. lxxxi. 1—5. Comp. also Numb. x. 9, 10.   [f] Col. ii. 16, 17.
[g] Isai. xxvii. 13. *Mark this passage.*   [h] Numb. xxix. 1—6.

Now from this feast, so peculiarly prefiguring the Gospel, and being observed with such extraordinary strictness, we may LEARN,

1. The scope and tendency of the Gospel—

[When it reaches the ears and hearts of men, it calls them from the world to serve and delight in God, and *that* without intermission, from the morning to the evening of their lives. Not that it forbids all servile work; on the contrary, it requires "every man to abide in the calling wherein he is called," and to fulfil the duties of his station with assiduity: but, while it leaves our *hands* at liberty, it forbids that our *hearts* should be enslaved: *they* must be reserved for God, and fixed on him alone. The one occupation of our lives must be to offer to him the sacrifices of prayer and praise[i]: "Rejoice in the Lord always," says the Apostle, "and again I say, Rejoice." Every blast of the trumpet should remind us of the infinite obligations conferred upon us, and of the assurances which God has given us of final and everlasting happiness. It is not a deliverance from temporal bondage, or victory over earthly enemies, that we have to rejoice in, but in deliverance from the wrath of God, and in victory over sin and Satan, death and hell. All this, too, is given us, not by a mere exertion of God's power, but by the death of his Son, and the influences of his Spirit. Shall not *we* then rejoice? Again I say, that the Gospel trumpet sounds these things in our ears continually; and therefore we should keep throughout our whole lives a feast unto the Lord.]

2. The duty of those who embrace it—

[We have already seen what abstraction from the world, and what devotedness to God, were required of the Jews on that day. If they then, who had only the shadow of heavenly things, were to serve God in this manner, how ought *we*, who enjoy the substance! Surely we should serve him *without grudging, without weariness,* and *without distraction.* If they grudged their numerous and costly sacrifices, or were weary of their long and lifeless services, or had their minds diverted from these poor and "beggarly elements," we should not wonder at it: their very feasts, though suited to the ends for which they were appointed, were burthensome in the extreme. But ours is a spiritual service. True, it may require some sacrifices; but none that are worthy of a thought, when we consider for whom they are made. As for sin, the mortifying of that should be deemed no sacrifice at all: it is rather like the removal of a leprosy, or the healing of a wound. As for time, or interest, there is nothing to be sacrificed in relation to these, that will

[i] Heb. xiii. 15.

not be repaid an hundred-fold even in this life, and with everlasting life in the world to come. And, if we engage heartily in the Lord's service, we shall find, that the more we are employed in it, the more delightful it will be: it is wearisome only to those who are formal and hypocritical in their duties. Doubtless " the flesh will often evince its weakness, even when the spirit is most willing:" but the more we *seek* to rejoice in God, the more we *shall* rejoice in God. Let us be on our guard against those worldly cares or pleasures that are apt to divert the mind from its proper duties. St. Paul particularly tells us, that " he would have us without carefulness;" and recommends us so to order our matters, that we may " attend upon the Lord without distraction[k]." These things then are our duty: *duty*, do I say? they are our *privilege*, our *highest* privilege. So David thought, when he said, " Blessed are the people that know the joyful sound ; they shall walk, O Lord, in the light of thy countenance: in thy name shall they rejoice all the day ; and in thy righteousness shall they be exalted[1]."]

[k] 1 Cor. vii. 35.   [1] Ps. lxxxix. 15, 16.

OUTLINE NO. 137

THE FEAST OF TABERNACLES.

Lev. xxiii. 39—43. *Also in the fifteenth day of the seventh month, when ye have gathered in the fruit of the land, ye shall keep a feast unto the Lord seven days: on the first day shall be a Sabbath, and on the eighth day shall be a Sabbath. And ye shall take you on the first day the boughs of goodly trees, branches of palm-trees, and the boughs of thick trees, and willows of the brook; and ye shall rejoice before the Lord your God seven days. And ye shall keep it a feast unto the Lord seven days in the year: it shall be a statute for ever in your generations; ye shall celebrate it in the seventh month. Ye shall dwell in booths seven days; all that are Israelites born shall dwell in booths; that your generations may know, that I made the children of Israel to dwell in booths, when I brought them out of the land of Egypt: I am the Lord your God.*

CHRISTIANS in general are deterred from the study of the ceremonial law, by the consideration that there is not sufficient light thrown upon some parts to determine their spiritual import, whilst in other parts we are distracted through the diversity of senses which the New Testament appears to affix to them. Certainly these are difficulties in our way; nor can we expect entirely to overcome them: but still there is much that is clear; and even that which is in some respects dubious, will be found in other respects highly edifying.

The feast of tabernacles was one of the three great feasts, at which all the males throughout the nation were to assemble at Jerusalem. Its importance therefore cannot be doubted. But, in our inquiries after the truths which it shadowed forth, we must be guided in some measure by conjecture; and consequently, cannot speak with that full confidence that we maintain where the inspired writers have led the way. Taking care however to distinguish what is doubtful from what is clear and certain, we shall proceed to consider this feast, and to open to you,

I. Its peculiar rites—

Whilst it had some rites common to other occasions, it had some peculiar to itself:

1. The sacrifices offered—

[These were very peculiar, and such as were offered on no other occasion. The feast lasted eight days: on the first of which, thirteen bullocks, with two rams, fourteen lambs, and one kid, and certain meat-offerings, were presented; and, on the six following days, there were the same sacrifices, except that the number of the bullocks, and of their appropriate meat-offerings, was one less every day: this went on to the eighth day, when there was only one bullock, one ram, seven lambs, and a goat, offered[a]. The precise reason of this gradual diminution is not known, unless that it was to shew, that the Mosaic dispensation would gradually decay, and at last vanish away, being terminated by that one great Sacrifice which should in due time be offered.]

2. The services enjoined—

[All were to leave their houses for seven days, and to live in booths constructed of the branches of trees, which they had previously cut down for that purpose. This would doubtless be attended with much inconvenience to them: but they were to rise superior to such consideration, and to spend the time in holy joy. Part of the command was, that they should " rejoice before the Lord their God." After the time of Joshua, when the piety of the nation had begun to decline, the observance of this ordinance was discontinued; or if it was now and then repeated for a single year, the institution was regarded only in

[a] Numb. xxix. 12—39.

a partial and formal way; till Nehemiah, after the return of the people from Babylon, revived and enforced the practice of former days[b].]

The next thing to be noticed in reference to this feast, is,

II. Its primary end—
This was two-fold:
1. Commemorative—
[All the time that the people sojourned in the wilderness, even forty years, they dwelt in booths or tents; in remembrance of which this feast was instituted[c]. We are apt to forget the mercies which God has vouchsafed to us, and especially those vouchsafed to our forefathers at a remote period. But we ourselves inherit the benefits conferred on them: the descendants of those who were delivered from Egypt, owed all their liberty to God's miraculous interposition, no less than their fathers; and therefore were equally bound to keep God's goodness to them in remembrance: and by leaving their houses for a week, and living in booths, they would know precisely the situation of their ancestors, and learn to be thankful for their own more comfortable habitations.]

2. Eucharistic—
[This feast was after the harvest and vintage were finished; and it was intended to be a season of thanksgiving for the fruits of the earth. Hence it was called " the feast of in-gathering[d];" which shews, that the *time* of keeping the feast was illustrative of one thing, and the *manner*, of another. Not but that there was a close connexion between the two; for in the wilderness they had nothing but manna; but, in the land of Canaan, they enjoyed all the fruits of the earth in the richest abundance: and, consequently, whilst they glorified God for miraculously supplying the daily wants of their ancestors by food from heaven, they were called upon to bless and adore his name for the continued blessings imparted to themselves.]

Thus far the intention of the feast is manifest. Our ground is not so clear in what remains: yet we utterly disclaim all idea of giving loose to our imagination on sacred subjects: we propose to you what, though we cannot prove, we think highly probable; and leave you to judge for yourselves, whilst we point out,

III. Its mystical design—

[b] Neh. viii. 13—17.   [c] ver. 43.
[d] Exod. xxiii. 16. Deut. xvi. 13—15.

That this was a shadow, we have no doubt: **and that Christ is the substance**, is equally clear and certain: this point is determined by God himself in reference to the feasts and Sabbaths in general[e], and therefore much more in relation to this, which was as sacred a feast as any, perhaps the most so of any, in the whole year. We apprehend then that this feast was intended to shadow forth,

1. The incarnation of Christ—

[The three great feasts were, the Passover, or feast of unleavened bread, the feast of Pentecost, and the feast of tabernacles. In the first, the death of Christ was typified: in the second, the out-pouring of the Spirit: and in this last, the incarnation of Christ. It was highly probable that this great event would be shadowed forth by some feast, as well as the other two: and there is good reason to think it was referred to in the feast before us. The very term used by the Evangelist in declaring the incarnation of our Lord, seems to mark this reference[f]: and the conduct of the people, when they were persuaded that he was the Christ, corresponds very much with the rights prescribed at this feast: " They cut down branches from the trees, and strawed them in the way, and cried, Hosanna to the Son of David! Blessed is he that cometh in the name of the Lord; Hosannah in the highest[g]!" It is true, this was at another feast: but still it marks the connexion in their minds between the feast of tabernacles, and the advent of the Messiah. There was a remarkable circumstance which took place *at the feast of tabernacles*, which throws some additional light on this subject. The eighth day was "the great day of the feast." And though the dwelling in booths was discontinued, the people observed the season as a feast unto the Lord. They had indeed substituted a rite or ceremony on that day, bringing water from the pool of Siloam, and pouring it out as a libation to the Lord. The idea was perhaps adopted from that expression of the prophet, " With joy shall ye draw water out of the wells of salvation[h]." On this day, in the place of public concourse, our Lord stood and cried with a loud voice, " If any man thirst, let him come unto ME and drink[i]." This was in fact, as if he had said, You expect at

[e] Col. ii. 16, 17.
[f] John i. 14. ἐσκήνωσεν. And though custom has led us to regard December as the time of his birth, the arguments to prove that he was born in the autumn are far more probable. Could this point be perfectly ascertained, it would strongly confirm the supposed reference of this feast to that event.
[g] Matt. xxi. 8, 9.   [h] Isai. xii. 3.   [i] John vii. 2, 37, 38.

this time the advent of your Messiah, from whom you will derive all spiritual blessings: behold, I am he: and, if you will come unto me, you shall receive more than tongue can utter, or imagination conceive.

We say not that these things amount to a proof of the point in question: but we suggest them for your consideration, and leave you to form your own judgment upon them.]

2. The duty of his people—

[Here we can speak with more decision. No one who knows the figurative nature of the Jewish ritual can doubt, but that this feast was designed to teach us, that " we are strangers here, and sojourners, as all our fathers were[k]." When fixed in our habitations and enjoying every comfort of life, we are apt to think that this is our *home:* the language of our hearts is, " Soul, take thine ease; eat, drink, and be merry." But " this is not our rest." We are here only in a wilderness; and we must *in the spirit of our minds* resemble the patriarchs of old, " who, though in the land of promise, dwelt in tabernacles, declaring that here they had no continuing city, but that they sought another country, that is, an heavenly[l]." This is to be the character of all the Lord's people[m], who, " though *in* the world, are not *of* the world," and who " are looking for a city that hath foundations, whose builder and maker is God"————]

APPLICATION—

[It may be asked, What is all this to *us?* I answer, Read what the prophet says, and you will have more satisfactory information than you are aware of[n]. Beyond all doubt he is speaking of those who live under the Gospel: and the repeated injunctions which he gives relative to our observance of this feast, are a strong confirmation, that there was in it a mysterious and most important meaning. I call upon you then to keep this feast, to keep it with holy joy unto the Lord. Think of the incarnation of our blessed Lord! What a stupendous mystery! God, even the most high God, leaving his blest abodes, and sojourning here in a tabernacle of clay! Is not this worthy to be commemorated? Does it not demand our most ardent praise?———— Think of the harvest of blessings which we obtain through him! Our corn and wine and oil are but shadows of that heavenly food which is prepared for us, and on which, if it be not our own fault, we are feeding from day to day. Let earthly things then not engross your affections, but lead you to seek those which are spiritual and eternal[o]———— And whether your temporal comforts be

[k] Ps. xxxix. 12. [l] Heb. xi. 9, 13, 14, 16. [m] 1 Pet. ii. 11.
[n] Zech. xiv. 16—19. [o] Col. iii. 2.

increased or diminished, ever remember where your home is; and that when your week is finished, " you have an house not made with hands, eternal in the heavens^p" — — —]^q

p 2 Cor. v. 1.
q If this subject were taken on a *Christmas-day*, or for a *Harvest* Sermon, the more appropriate idea must be most expanded.

OUTLINE NO. 138
THE GOLDEN CANDLESTICK.

Lev. xxiv. 1—3. *And the Lord spake unto Moses, saying, Command the children of Israel, that they bring unto thee pure oil-olive beaten, for the light, to cause the lamps to burn continually. Without the veil of the testimony, in the tabernacle of the congregation, shall Aaron order it from the evening unto the morning before the Lord continually: it shall be a statute for ever in your generations.*

TO engage actively in the service of God is a duty that should not be delayed: nor should any expense or trouble that may be incurred, be regarded as any obstacle to the performance of our duty. The tabernacle being erected, and the sacred vessels prepared, an order was given that the appointed services should instantly commence; and the people were directed to bring such things as were necessary for the maintenance of divine worship. That part of the tabernacle which was covered in, consisted of two parts, the holy place, and the holy of holies. In the former of these, the daily services were performed: the latter was never entered but on one day in the year. The part devoted to the service of God was lighted by a candlestick with seven lamps, which were kept continually burning[a]. The whole furniture of the tabernacle, no less than the tabernacle itself, was typical: some things were more illustrative of Christ and his

[a] Doubts indeed have been entertained whether they were kept alight by day; because some passages of Scripture seem to intimate that they were not: see Exod. xxx. 7. 2 Chron. xiii. 11. 1 Sam. iii. 3. but the order that they should "burn continually," seems plain; and the occasion for it was perpetual; and, above all, Josephus, who could not but know the practice of his day, affirms that three lamps were kept burning by day, and all of them by night.

character; and others more applicable to the Church: and some things referred to both. It is possible that the candlestick might be intended to represent Christ as "the light of the world:" but we are sure that it shadowed forth his Church; and therefore without nesitation we shall consider it as typically representing the Church;

I. In its privileges—

The Church was justly exhibited under that figure—

[Of what materials and form the candlestick was, we are distinctly informed[b]. That it was designed to represent the Church, is declared by Christ himself[c]. And, if we consider of what it was composed, and how it was supplied, and for what purposes it was used, we shall see a striking correspondence between the Church and that. It was formed of pure gold; in which respect it characterized the saints, who are not polished over for the purpose of glittering in the sight of men, but are really "renewed in the spirit of their minds," and "made partakers of a divine nature[d]" — — — It was supplied with the purest oil; which fitly represented that "unction of the Holy One which we have received[e]," for the enlightening of our minds, and the sanctifying of our souls — — — Its use was obvious: it was to shine in darkness, that all who were engaged in the service of their God might fulfil their duties aright; and that God might be glorified in them[f]. Such lights are the saints to be in the midst of a dark world, that through their instrumentality others may be directed into the way of peace, and be constrained to "glorify their heavenly Father" — — —]

The priest, whose duty it was to trim the lamps, prefigured Christ—

[This is a point on which there can be no doubt, it being affirmed on the authority of Christ himself[g]. He is constantly employed in inspecting and trimming the lamps: there is not a saint on whom his eyes are not fixed, and whose declensions, however secret, he does not behold — — —When necessary, he i terposes, by his providence or grace, to correct their dulness, and to restore them to their wonted splendour[h] — — —]

Whilst the Church was thus characterized in its privileges, it was also shadowed forth,

[b] Exod. xxv. 31—38.   [c] Rev. i. 20.   [d] 2 Pet. i. 4.
[e] 1 John ii. 20, 27.   [f] Rev. i. 12, 13.   [g] Heb. iv. 14, 15.
[h] John xv. 2.

II. In its duties—

The duties of the saints are,

1. To shine—

[It is justly observed by our Lord, that "no man lights a candle, to put it under a bushel or a bed; but sets it in a candlestick, that all who are in the house may see the light." It is not for themselves alone that the saints are endued with the gifts and graces of the Holy Spirit, but for God, and for their fellow-creatures; for God, that his power and grace may be magnified on earth; and for their fellow-creatures, who are to be benefited by their instructions, their influence, and their example[i] ——— Our responsibility in this respect is not sufficiently considered. But if we are stewards even of our earthly possessions, and bound to lay them out for God, much more are we "stewards of the manifold grace of God[k]," and bound to administer freely unto others what we ourselves have freely received[l] ———]

2. To be receiving more grace from Christ in order to their shining with yet brighter lustre—

[It is from Christ that the Holy Spirit must be derived. It is "He who has the residue of the Spirit[m]." "The Father gave not the Spirit to him by measure[n]," but in all his immeasurable fulness; and "out of that fulness must we all receive, even grace for grace[o]." This is strikingly represented by the prophet Zechariah, who, speaking *apparently* of the civil and ecclesiastical governors of his Church, Joshua and Zerubbabel, represents Christ *in reality* (for *he* is both the King and Priest of his Church) as the inexhaustible source of that golden oil, which is continually communicated by him to every lamp in his sanctuary[p] ——— By prayer and faith we must keep that communication open, and entreat him, that, "as he has given us life, so he would give it us more abundantly" ———]

We would take occasion from this subject to SUGGEST to you,

1. An important inquiry—

[Are you Christians indeed? If this question be too indefinite, then I ask, Are you as lights shining in a dark place? Surely this matter is not difficult to determine. You may easily see whether you are living like the world around you, or whether you are reproving others by the brightness of your example. This idea is proposed by our Lord under the figure of a "broad and a narrow way;" the one easy and much trodden, the

---

[i] Matt. v. 14—16. [k] 1 Pet. iv. 10. [l] Matt. x. 8. [m] Mal. ii. 15.
[n] John iii. 34. [o] John i. 16. [p] Zech. iv. 2—4, 11—14.

other difficult and unfrequented; the one terminating in destruction, the other leading to everlasting life. St. Paul expresses the same in language more accommodated to our text[q]. Judge yourselves, Brethren, in reference to this matter: and never think that you are Christians indeed, unless you have an evidence in your own souls, that, through the influences of the Holy Spirit, you are exhibiting a light, which both instructs and "condemns the world" around you.]

2. A solemn admonition—

[If we profess ourselves to be the Lord's people, let us consider somewhat more distinctly what we profess. As lamps in God's sanctuary, we profess to be "of pure gold," truly, inwardly, substantially holy, and formed altogether according to the pattern which was shewn to Moses in the mount[r]. What that pattern was, we are at no loss to say: it is set before us with all possible clearness in the person of Jesus Christ. Let every one of us reflect on this, and search into our own hearts to see whether there be in us this resemblance? The inquiry before instituted is a comparison of ourselves with others: the inquiry I now propose, is a comparison of ourselves with that great exemplar, the Lord Jesus Christ. We should examine, not whether we resemble him in those actions which he performed as a prophet, but whether "the same *mind* be in us, as was in him[s]." Our views, our principles, our habits, the great scope and end of our lives, these are the things that are to be inquired into, if we would have a solid evidence in our own souls that we are the Lord's. "We must be like Him," *here* as well as *hereafter*, "if we would be with him" for ever. He himself warns us what will be the consequence of allowing ourselves in any deviation from the path of duty[t]: and therefore, if we would not have "our candlestick removed," let us repent of every known defect, and seek to be "pure as He is pure," and "perfect as He is perfect."]

3. An encouraging reflection—

[How often has our great High-Priest, when he has seen us burning dim and languishing, revived us by seasonable communications, or merciful rebukes! Truly we are living witnesses for him, that "he will not quench the smoking flax[u]" — — May we not then hope, that he will yet bear with us, and administer to us whatever, in a way of influence or correction, we may stand in need of? Surely we may look up to him with joyful confidence, and say with David, "Thou wilt light my candle; the Lord my God will enlighten my darkness[x]." Many

[q] Phil. ii. 15, 16.   [r] Numb. viii. 4.   [s] Phil. ii. 5.   [t] Rev. ii. 1, 5.
[u] Matt. xii. 20. not extinguish the wick, the flame of which has been blown out.   [x] Ps. xviii. 28.

are the storms to which we are exposed in this dreary wilderness, which threaten our extinction; but he is able to preserve us: and as he has made it our duty to "burn continually," so he will give us "supplies of his Spirit" for that purpose: he will "keep us by his power through faith unto everlasting salvation.[y]" "He will keep the feet of his saints; but the wicked shall be silent in darkness[z]"— — —]

[y] 1 Pet. i. 5.   [z] 1 Sam. ii. 9.

OUTLINE NO. 139
THE SHEW-BREAD.

Lev. xxiv. 5—9. *And thou shalt take fine flour, and bake twelve cakes thereof: two tenth-deals shall be in one cake. And thou shalt set them in two rows, six on a row, upon the pure table before the Lord. And thou shalt put pure frankincense upon each row, that it may be on the bread for a memorial, even an offering made by fire unto the Lord. Every Sabbath he shall set it in order before the Lord continually, being taken from the children of Israel by an everlasting covenant. And it shall be Aaron's and his sons'; and they shall eat it in the holy place: for it is most holy unto him of the offerings of the Lord made by fire, by a perpetual statute.*

WHEN God appointed a dwelling-place to be erected for him in the wilderness, he ordered it to be furnished with such appendages as are common in the dwellings of men. There was in the sanctuary, as St. Paul observes, a candlestick, a table, and bread, called the shew-bread[a]. But there was an infinitely higher purpose to be answered by these things, than a mere accommodation of them to the habits of men: they were typical; every one of them was typical; "they were shadows of good things to come." The mystical import of some is much clearer than that of others. Where the writers of the New Testament have explained them, we are able to speak with confidence: but where they are silent, we must proceed in our explanation of them "with fear and trembling." The mystery of the shew-bread is applied by some to Christ, who called himself "the true bread," and, at the institution of his last supper, "took bread, and

[a] Heb. ix. 2.

brake it, and said to his disciples, Take, eat, this is my body." The New-Testament writers give us little, if any, insight into this subject: but they speak so fully and plainly on the subject of the candlestick, that we can easily by analogy trace the import of the shew bread also. It has been shewn, that the candlestick represented the Church, and that the priests who trimmed the lamps represented Christ[b]. The same might therefore well be supposed in relation to the shew-bread: and the circumstance of the flour " being taken from all the children of Israel," and made into " twelve cakes," gives us sufficient reason to conclude, that those cakes did represent the twelve tribes, that is, the Church of God. Nor can we adopt a more satisfactory method of explaining the whole mystery, than that used in reference to the candlestick. Agreeably to the plan then which we pursued on the former subject, we observe, that the shew-bread shadowed forth the people of God,

I. In their privileges—

To elucidate this, consider what is here spoken respecting the twelve cakes;

1. Their solemn presentation before God—

[They were consecrated to God in an orderly and solemn manner, and deposited on his table that they might be always before him. Being piled one upon another in two rows, frankincense was placed on each row, which at the appointed time was burnt " for a memorial, as an offering made by fire unto the Lord." Here we see the Church and people of God consecrated to him according to the terms of " his everlasting covenant," to be unto him a holy and peculiar people. As such they are esteemed by him; and " his eyes are upon them day and night for good:" and, as the frankincense was to God an odour of a sweet smell, so their persons and services shall be accepted by him———True it is that they are mean and worthless in themselves; yet, being *" set apart for him*[c]*,"* he will acknowledge them as his, and look upon them with complacency and delight.]

2. Their periodical renewal—

[Whilst one generation of men is passing away, another arises to fill their place; and amongst them all, God will have

[b] See the preceding Discourse.   [c] Ps. iv. 3.

139.] THE SHEW-BREAD. 603

some, who shall be objects of his peculiar regard. The change of the loaves every Sabbath-day was intended to illustrate this: and in reference to it they were expressly called "the continual bread[d]." The regard shewn by God to those who were first brought out of Egypt, shall be perpetuated to the end of time: never shall any be removed but others shall be ready to succeed; nor shall there ever be a period when God will not have a people truly and entirely consecrated to his service. Sometimes, as in the primitive ages, his saints may be swept away by thousands at a time, so as to threaten their utter extinction: but others shall always be found ready to "be baptized *for* (that is, *in the room of*) the dead," as soldiers instantly come forward, to fill up the ranks which the devouring sword has thinned[e]: nor shall the power of men or devils ever be able to extirpate the Christian name: "the Church is built upon a rock; and the gates of hell shall not prevail against it"— — —]

3. Their ultimate destination—

[The loaves at the close of the week were the property of the officiating priests[f]; and were to be eaten by them in the holy place, as being in themselves most holy. Now we are sure that the priests who attended on the lamps, prefigured Christ: and therefore we have no doubt but that he was equally prefigured by those who attended on the bread. Here then we see, that the saints, when they have abode their appointed time on earth, are the property of Christ: to which purpose it is written in the book of Deuteronomy, "The Lord's portion is his people; Jacob is the lot of his inheritance[g]." This is the high destiny of all who have given up themselves to God. Happy they are in the place which they are allowed to occupy in God's temple below; but happier far at their removal hence, when Christ shall claim them as "his peculiar treasure," and enjoy them for ever as "his purchased possession"— — —]

We may further contemplate the shew-bread as representing the Lord's people,

II. In their duties—

Well may this ordinance teach us,

1. To consecrate ourselves entirely to God—

[Let us contemplate the state of those loaves: they were "taken from the children of Israel," made on purpose for God, and presented to him that they might be wholly and for ever his. And what says God respecting us? "This people have I formed for myself; they shall shew forth my praise[h]." Yes; we should

[d] Numb. iv. 7.
[e] That is most probably the true meaning of 1 Cor. xv. 29.
[f] ver. 9.   [g] Deut. xxxii. 9.   [h] Isai. xliii. 21.

every one of us "subscribe with our hands, and say, I am the Lord's[i]." We should "give up ourselves to him by a perpetual covenant that shall not be forgotten[k]." We should consider ourselves as "separated from mankind" for this very purpose[l], that we may be "wholly sanctified unto him, in spirit, soul, and body[m]." This St. Paul declares to be "our reasonable service[n]." Not that we are to be inactive in the common duties of life, or to spend our days in nothing but contemplation and devotion: this would be to strain the parallel too far: but, in the spirit and habit of our minds, we are to be entirely given up to God, so that "whether we eat or drink, or whatever we do, we should do all to his glory[o]"— — —On the Sabbath especially should this dedication of ourselves be repeated and confirmed. We should come up to the house of God with the same mind as the priests who brought the loaves: their purpose was known and fixed; and they went into the sanctuary determined not to leave it till they had executed their high office. O that we might go to God's house on purpose to consecrate ourselves to him afresh; and never leave our work dubious or incomplete!— — —]

2. To be much occupied in prayer and intercession—

[The loaves were, so to speak, representatives of the tribes of Israel; and the frankincense ascended up as a memorial to God for them. Thus should we consider ourselves interested, not for ourselves only, but for all the Church of God. As for ourselves, we are commanded to "pray *always*," to "pray *without ceasing*," and to "offer unto God the sacrifice of praise *continually*, giving thanks to his name;" so, for others are we required to "make supplications, prayers, intercessions, and thanksgivings for all men." Moreover, this duty is inculcated on all: the prophetic declaration is, that, wherever God is known, "from the rising to the setting sun, even there shall *incense* be offered unto his name, and a pure offering[p]:" "all who make mention of the Lord," will be thus occupied; they "will not keep silence, nor give God any rest, till he establish his Church, and make it a praise in the earth[q]." How prosperous would individuals and churches be, if such a spirit prevailed more amongst them! O that "God would pour out upon us more of a spirit of grace and of supplication!" We should not long remain without manifest tokens of his approbation and love— — —]

3. To wait patiently for our removal hence—

[The loaves were left in the sanctuary till the time appointed

---

[i] Isai. xliv. 5. [k] Jer. l. 5. [l] Lev. xx. 24.
[m] 1 Thess. v. 23. [n] Rom. xii. 1. [o] 1 Cor. x. 31.
[p] Mal. i. 11. [q] Isai. lxii. 6, 7

for their removal. Thus we should " abide with God," performing diligently the work assigned us, till he shall be pleased to dismiss our souls in peace. Our week of life at all events is wearing fast away: but, whether its close be somewhat earlier, or later, than we expect, we should say, like Job, " All the days of my appointed time will I wait, till my change come." If there were no future state of existence, we might wish to have our present lives terminated or protracted, according as our sorrows or joys abound: but as death will introduce us into the more immediate presence of our God, and into a more perfect union and communion with Christ, we may well be contented either to live or die. In some sense indeed we may rather " desire to depart;" yea we may be "looking for, and hasting to, the coming of the day of Christ:" but as it respects impatience or discontent, we may well tarry the Lord's leisure, doing and suffering his holy will, till he shall take us hence, to "rest from our labours," and to " be for ever with the Lord"———]

OUTLINE NO. 140

THE BLASPHEMER STONED.

Lev. xxiv. 13—15. *And the Lord spake unto Moses, saying, Bring forth him that hath cursed without the camp; and let all that heard him lay their hands upon his head, and let all the congregation stone him. And thou shalt speak unto the children of Israel, Whosoever cursed his God shall bear his sin.*

SPIRITUAL subjects are generally most relished by a spiritual mind: and hence it is that in some places of worship they are exclusively brought forward for public discussion; and other subjects, which might be very instructive, are entirely overlooked. We consider it as one great advantage attending a course of sermons on the Holy Scriptures, that every subject must find a place in our discourses, and at some time or other be brought under the view of our hearers. The history before us would at first sight appear so ill calculated for general edification, that we should probably never fix upon it, if left to ourselves. But, occurring as it does in our present course, we shall turn your attention to it: and we trust, that, how unpromising soever it may seem, it will be found replete with very important instruction. There are two things in it which we seem particularly called to notice; namely

I. The danger of ungodly connexions—

To caution us against contracting an intimacy with the ungodly, we are told, that "evil communications corrupt good manners;" and that "the companion of fools shall be destroyed." But in the marriage union such a connexion is peculiarly dangerous, because its influence is incessant, and operative to the latest hour of our lives.

1. It is injurious to the person himself—

[It is from a hope of drawing over their partner to the same views and sentiments with themselves, that multitudes enter into engagements, which prove fatal to their happiness through life. Whatever were the views of this Israelitish woman, she seemed to have succeeded beyond all reasonable expectation in the alliance she had formed: for, instead of being detained in Egypt by her husband, she brought him out with her. But as it was an injury, rather than a benefit, to the Church, that a mixed multitude were united to it[a], so the society of a heathen could never render an Israelite happy. Supposing that the woman had any regard for God, how could she endure to see her husband pouring contempt upon him, and bowing down to idols of wood and stone?——— It is precisely thus when a believer amongst ourselves becomes united to an unbeliever. However suitable in other respects the union may be, it cannot possibly be productive of happiness; for, in all those things which are most important, their views, their feelings, and their conduct must be dissimilar, or rather at variance with each other. The unconverted party can have no sympathy with the converted in the various exercises of mind peculiar to the Christian state; he cannot understand them; the hopes and fears, and joys and sorrows experienced by the believer, appear foolishness in the eyes of an unbeliever; and consequently, there can be no communion between them on those subjects which are most nearly connected with their eternal welfare——— Hence that solemn injunction to form no such alliance[b], but to marry "only in the Lord[c]"———]

2. It is injurious to their offspring—

[Doubtless a true Christian will endeavour to give a right bias to the minds of his children. But the silent and unstudied influence of the ungodly person will operate far more forcibly than the most laboured exertions of the godly. The natural bent of our affections is towards sin: and we are far more ready

---

[a] Exod. xii. 38. with Numb. xi. 4.   [b] 2 Cor. vi. 14, 15.
[c] 1 Cor vii. 39.

to justify what is wrong from the examples of others, than to follow what is right. We all know how much easier a thing it is to go with the stream than against it; or to spread contagion than to cure it. The son of this Israelitish woman, though in the midst of Israelites, did not become a worshipper of the true God, but remained to his dying hour a profane despiser of him. And in like manner it is to be expected, that, where one of the parents is ungodly, the children will follow his example, and tread in his steps —— — It is true, that the most godly parents cannot always prevail on their children to yield to their advice: but, if they have done what they could towards bringing them up in the nurture and admonition of the Lord, they will have the comfort of a good conscience to support them in their trials: but if a believer unites himself to an unbeliever, and his children turn out ill, he will always have himself to blame: and the children themselves will have to reproach them in the last day for having formed a connexion which afforded so bad a prospect in relation to their offspring.]

The history before us naturally leads us also to contemplate,

II. The danger of ungodly habits—

It is manifest that the habits of this man were altogether bad—

[What was the subject of controversy between this man and the Israelite we know not; nor in what manner he blasphemed the God of heaven. But it is evident that he was under the influence of a contentious spirit, and habituated to indulge himself in disparaging the God of Israel. Moreover, his dispute with the Israelite was the very occasion of his blaspheming God. Conceiving that he was injuriously treated by the Israelite, he was not satisfied with reviling *him*, but must revile his religion also, and his God. This is what was wont to be done in the days of old, when the heathen blasphemed the name of God on account of David's misconduct: and the same is done continually in the present day: men cast the blame of every evil, whether real or supposed, which they see amongst Christians, on Christianity itself. They make the Gospel answerable for all that profess it: which is just as absurd, as to condemn Christ and his Apostles, together with Christianity itself, for the treachery of Judas. Had this man been of a meek and quiet spirit, forbearing and forgiving, he would never have yielded to such a paroxysm of wrath: and, if he had cultivated the smallest regard for the Most High God, he would never have waged open war against him by his blasphemy and profaneness.]

The consequences of them proved fatal to him—

[Little did he think what would be the issue of those habits which he was so ready to indulge. The persons who heard his blasphemy, informed against him: and Moses, being as yet uninstructed by God how such iniquity was to be punished, sought direction from him: and was told that "the persons who heard him should lay their hands upon his head," and that "all the congregation of Israel should stone him." And from thence it was made a standing law that every similar offence should be visited with the same punishment. It was too late for the offender now to make excuses: the word was passed; the guilt was contracted; the sentence was fixed. It is thus that our evil habits also, if not repented of, will terminate, and we shall begin to bewail our misery when it is past a remedy ———Even in this world many bring distress and ignominy both on themselves and families by their unhallowed tempers and their unbridled appetites: and in the world to come, every man, however light he may make of sin now, shall find it a burthen too heavy to be borne.]

The ADVICE which we would suggest from this subject, is, to check evil,

1. In ourselves—

[It is said of strife, that it is "like the letting out of water," which having once made a breach in a bank, soon defies all endeavours to restrain it, and inundates the whole country. It is thus with sin of every kind: when it is once permitted to act, none can tell where it will stop. Impiety is generally to be found in the train of ungoverned passions: and, from "walking in the way of sinners," it is no uncommon thing to "sit in the seat of the scornful." Let us be aware of this, and endeavour to oppose sin in its very first rise; ever remembering, that, "if he who despised Moses' law died without mercy under two or three witnesses, a much sorer punishment awaits us," if we become the slaves and victims of any evil propensity ———]

2. In others—

[The people gave information of the man's profaneness, and Moses, by God's direction, gave orders for the whole assembly to unite in executing judgment on him. This draws a profitable line of distinction for us. The magistrate did not use any compulsory measures to make the man an Israelite; but he did interfere to prevent his God and his religion from being exposed to derision. This is the proper province of a magistrate; he must not use the power of the sword to make men religious; but he may use it to keep them from being openly profane: and it is the duty of every man to lend his aid in this matter, and to co-operate for the maintenance of external order and decorum[d]. Let us then not only "have no fellowship with the unfruitful works of darkness, but rather reprove," and, if possible, suppress them.]

[d] If this were a subject taken either for an *Assize Sermon*, or a sermon for *the suppression of vice*, this idea should be enlarged upon.

OUTLINE NO. 141
THE JUBILEE A TYPE OF THE GOSPEL.

Lev. xxv. 9—11. *Then shalt thou cause the trumpet of the jubilee to sound, on the tenth day of the seventh month, in the day of atonement shall ye make the trumpet sound throughout all your land. And ye shall hallow the fiftieth year, and proclaim liberty throughout all the land unto all the inhabitants thereof: it shall be a jubilee unto you; and ye shall return every man unto his possession, and ye shall return every man unto his family. A jubilee shall that fiftieth year be unto you.*

IN order that our Lord's descent from Judah and from David should be clear and acknowledged, it was necessary that the various tribes and families should be kept distinct. With this view many ordinances were appointed for the continuing of every man's inheritance in his own family[a]. This seems to have been the primary intent of that ordinance which is mentioned in the text. A variety of circumstances in a length of time might produce alienations of property; and if this had been suffered to continue, a confusion of the families and tribes would have at last ensued. To prevent this therefore, God commanded that on every fiftieth year every inheritance should revert to its original possessor. This season was called the Jubilee; which, while it answered many other important purposes, served in a very eminent manner to typify the Gospel.

We may observe a very strict agreement between the jubilee and the Gospel:

I. In the time and manner of their proclamation—

The jubilee was proclaimed with the sound of trumpets—

[a] A difficulty on this subject having occurred, God himself decided it, and grounded a new law on that decision. See Numb. xxxvi. 6, 7.

[The tendency of great reverses of fortune is, in many instances at least, to produce a torpor of mind, and a stupid indifference to the things we once highly valued. Hence it was but too probable, that they, who had alienated their inheritance and reduced themselves to the lowest ebb of misery, might sink into such a state of ignorance or indolence, as to let the period appointed for their restoration pass unnoticed. To prevent this, God commanded the trumpets to be sounded throughout all the land; that so the attention of all being awakened, and their spirits exhilarated, every individual might be stirred up to claim the privileges to which he was entitled.]

The precise time on which this sacred year commenced, was " the day of atonement"—

[The day of atonement was the most solemn season in the whole year: the people were required to afflict their souls for sin; and peculiar sacrifices were to be offered for the iniquities of the whole nation. It should seem at first sight that this was an unfit season for the proclamation of such joyful tidings; but it was indeed the fittest season in the whole year: for, when could masters and creditors be so properly called upon to exercise mercy, as when they themselves had been obtaining mercy at the hands of a reconciled God? Or when could debtors and slaves so reasonably be expected to receive their liberties with gratitude, and improve them with care, as when they had been bewailing the sins, by which, in all probability, they had been deprived of them?]

The Gospel also is to be publicly proclaimed in every place—

[One would have imagined that it were quite sufficient for God once to make known the way in which he would pardon sinners, and that from that time every sinner would of his own accord exert himself to obtain the proffered mercy. But experience proves that our bereavement of heaven is not felt as any evil; our bondage to sin is not at all lamented; and, if no means were used to awaken men's attention to their misery, and to stir them up to embrace the blessings of salvation, the greater part of mankind would rest satisfied with their state, till the opportunity for improving it was irrevocably lost. God therefore sends forth his servants to " preach the Gospel to every creature," and commands them to " lift up their voice as a trumpet."]

This too has its origin in the great atonement—

[If, as some contend, the year of our Lord's death was the year of Jubilee, the coincidence was indeed very singular and important. But, however this might be, certain it is, that, " without shedding of blood, there could be no remission;"

nor, till our Lord had expiated the sins of the whole world, could the Gospel be universally proclaimed. But no sooner was his sacrifice offered, than God was reconciled to his guilty creatures; and from that time must the commission given to his Apostles be dated. A very few days had elapsed, when they sounded the Gospel trumpet in the ears of that very people who had crucified the Lord of glory; and had the happiness to find thousands at a time " brought from the bondage of corruption into the glorious liberty of the children of God." Thus clearly was the connexion marked between the atoning sacrifice of Christ, and the deliverance of sinners that was purchased by it.]

But the agreement between the two is yet more manifest,

⁷I. In the blessings conveyed by them—

The privileges imparted by the jubilee were many and of great value—

[There was, in the first place, an universal *exemption from* every kind of agricultural *labour*. None were either to reap the produce of the last year, or to sow their land with a view to a future crop; but all were to gather from day to day what had grown spontaneously; and every person had an equal right to all the fruits of the earth[b]. A better mode of improving their time was provided for them: *public instruction* was to be given to all, men, women, and children; in order that none, however their education had been neglected, might remain ignorant of God, and his law[c]. Now also *debts*, in whatever way they had been contracted, and to whatever amount, were to be freely *remitted*[d]. But, besides these privileges which were common to other sabbatical years, there were others peculiar to the year of jubilee. If any persons had, by their own voluntary act, or by the inexorable severity of some creditor, been sold, they were to *receive their liberty*, and to be restored to their families, as soon as ever the appointed trumpets should sound[e]. Yea, if they had formerly possessed an *inheritance* in the land, they were to be instantly reinstated in the possession of it[f]: so that in a moment they *reverted to* their former condition, with all the advantage of their dear-bought experience.]

Analogous to these are the blessings imparted by the Gospel—

[Varying their order, we shall first mention *the forgiveness of sins*. Though the debt we owe to God exceeds all possible calculation, it is all freely, and for ever remitted, as soon as ever the Gospel trumpet is heard, and its glad tidings are

---

[b] ver. 4—7, 11   [c] Deut. xxxi. 10—13.   [d] Deut. xv. 1, 2.
[e] ver. 39—41.   [f] ver. 10, 28.

welcomed to the soul[g]. *Our bondage to sin and Satan* is *reversed;* so that nothing shall ever lead us captive, provided we assert our liberty, and claim our privilege[h]: being made free by Christ, we shall be free indeed[i]. And, notwithstanding we have sold out heavenly inheritance, and alienated it for a thing of nought, yet are we called to take possession of it: we are *restored* to our father's house; we are brought again into the family of saints and angels; and, with our title to heaven, have the enjoyment of it renewed[k]. Now too are we commanded to *rest from all the works of the law, and from all the works of the flesh;* and, every one of us, to subsist from day to day upon the bounties of divine grace[l]. As we sowed them not, so neither are we to reap them as our own, but to receive them on the same footing as the poorest and meanest of the human race; all of us being alike pensioners on the divine bounty. Nor are we to lay up in store of what God gives us; but every day to gather our daily bread. To all these blessings is added that of *divine instruction:* as we are taught how to improve our leisure, so are eyes given us to see, and ears to hear, and hearts to understand[m]: and henceforth it is to be our daily labour to "grow in grace and in the knowledge of our Lord Jesus Christ." Such are the blessings bestowed by the Gospel; nor can any unworthiness in us deprive us of them, provided we thankfully accept them as the purchase of Christ's blood, and the gifts of his grace[n].]

INFER,

1. In what way it is that sinners are to be converted to God—

[The priest might have expostulated with the Jewish debtors or bond-slaves on the folly of their past conduct; but it was the sound of the trumpet alone that could bring them to liberty. So we may represent to sinners the evil of their past ways, and denounce against them the judgments threatened in the word of God; but it is the sweet voice of the Gospel alone that will enable them to throw off their yoke, and lead them to the enjoyment of eternal glory. This is told us by the prophet; who, speaking of the conversion of the world in the latter day, says, "In that day the great trumpet shall be blown, and they shall come who were ready to perish, and shall worship the Lord in the holy mount at Jerusalem[o]." O

[g] Acts x. 43.   [h] Rom. vi. 14.   [i] John viii. 36.
[k] Eph. ii. 19.   [l] Heb. iv. 10. Gal. ii. 20.   [m] 1 John ii. 20.

[n] For most congregations it would be more edifying to pass over briefly what was common to the sabbatical years, and to insist only on the blessings *peculiar to the year of Jubilee,* namely, deliverance from bondage, and restoration to one's inheritance.

[o] Isai. xxvii. 13.

that this were duly considered by all who go forth as the Lord's ambassadors! It is not to preach a scanty morality that we are called; but to publish the glad tidings of a full and free salvation; a salvation founded in the blood of Christ, and suited to those who are weeping for their sins. Behold then, " this is the accepted time; this is the day of salvation:" now the trumpet sounds in our ears; let us all arise, and bless our Deliverer; and improve the privileges so richly bestowed upon us. Then, when the last trumpet shall sound, and the time, which God has fixed for the redemption of *his* purchased possession, " shall be fully come," we shall be claimed by him as his property, his portion, his inheritance for ever.]

2. How solicitous is God to counteract the folly and wickedness of man!

[A subordinate end of the Jubilee was, to counteract the cupidity of some, and the prodigality of others. But it is a very principal end of the Gospel to remedy the miseries, which men have entailed upon themselves. Well might God have said to the whole human race, "Ye have sown the wind, and ye shall reap the whirlwind:" but instead of that, He says, " Ye have sold yourselves for nought, and ye shall be redeemed without money ᵖ:" " I have no pleasure in the death of a sinner; turn ye, turn ye, why will ye die?" Let not then these gracious declarations reach our ears in vain; Behold, " the year of the Lord's redeemed is come ᑫ;" " the perfect law of liberty" is now proclaimed: the Lord himself now preaches " deliverance to the captives, and the opening of the prison to them that are bound ʳ:" he says to the prisoners, " Go forth and shew yourselves." The Lord grant that none may put from them these words of life, or receive this grace of God in vain!]

3. How blessed are they who embrace the glad tidings of the Gospel!

[We can easily conceive the blessedness of one, who is in an instant restored from poverty and cruel bondage to the possession of liberty and affluence. But who can estimate aright the happiness of those who are freed from the curses of the law, the fears of death, the bondage of sin, and the damnation of hell? Who can fully appreciate the joy of a trembling and condemned sinner, who by the sound of the Gospel is enabled to call God his father, and heaven his rightful inheritance? Well does the Psalmist, in reference to this very ordinance or the Jubilee, exclaim, " Blessed are the people that know the joyful sound ˢ." Surely there is no state on earth to be compared with this. May we seek it as our supreme felicity; and may we all enjoy it as an antepast of heaven!]

ᵖ Isai. lii. 3.　ᑫ Isai. lxiii. 4.　ʳ Luke iv. 18, 19.　ˢ Ps. lxxxix. 15.

OUTLINE NO. 142
THE SABBATICAL YEAR.

Lev. xxv. 20—22. *And if ye shall say, What shall we eat the seventh year? behold, we shall not sow, nor gather in our increase: Then will I command my blessing upon you in the sixth year, and it shall bring forth fruit for three years. And ye shall sow the eighth year, and eat yet of old fruit until the ninth year; until her fruits come in ye shall eat of the old store.*

MANY of the commands of God to his people of old appear to be mere arbitrary impositions, without any other use than that of subjecting their wills to his. But I doubt whether there be one single law that will fairly bear this construction. The reasons of many are not known to us, and perhaps were not fully understood by the Jews themselves: yet we cannot doubt but that if God had been pleased to explain them fully to us, we should have seen as much wisdom and goodness displayed in those which are at present unintelligible to us, as in others which we understand. The command to give rest to the land every seventh year, when the extent of country was so disproportionate to its population, must appear exceeding strange to those who have not duly considered it. The generality of persons would account for it perhaps from its being conducive to the good of the land, which would be too much exhausted, if it were not permitted occasionally to lie fallow. But this could not be the reason: for then a seventh part of the land would most probably have been kept fallow every year, and not the whole at once. Moreover, it would not have been suffered to produce any thing which would tend to counteract the main design; whereas all the seed that had been accidentally scattered on it during the harvest, was suffered to grow up to maturity. Nor can the idea of lying fallow be applied with any propriety to the olive-yards and vineyards, which, though not trimmed and pruned that year, were suffered to bring all their fruit to maturity. We must look then to some other source for the reasons of this appointment. Those which appear the most probable and most important, it is the object of this discourse to set before you.

The ordinance itself is more fully stated at the beginning of the chapter[a]: and it was given,

I. To remind them that God was the great Proprietor of all—

[In the verse following the text, God says to his people "The land is mine." And it was his: he had dispossessed the former inhabitants, and had given it to his own people, assigning to every tribe its precise district, and to every family their proper portion. This they would have been likely to forget in the space of a few years; and therefore, as the great Proprietor, he specified the terms on which he admitted them to the possession of his land, reserving to himself the tithes and first-fruits, and requiring the whole to be left uncultivated and common every seventh year. Thus the people would be reminded from time to time that they were only tenants, bound to use the land agreeably to the conditions imposed on them.

Instructive as this thought was to them, it is no less so to us. Indeed, we should never for one moment lose the remembrance of it. "The whole world is mine," says God, "and the fulness thereof[b]." Nay more, our very "bodies and spirits are his[c]:" and consequently, all that we are, and have, should be used for him, and be entirely at his disposal. Of what incalculable benefit would it be to have our minds duly impressed with this truth! How would it lay the axe to the root of all those evils which arise within us from the diversity of our states and conditions in the world! Pride in the attainment of earthly things, anxiety in the possession, and sorrow in the loss of them, would be greatly moderated ——— Instead of being agitated with the keen sensibilities of an owner, we should feel only a subordinate interest, like that of a steward: we should be neither elated with prosperity, nor depressed with adversity, but in every change should be satisfied, if only we were sure that we had done our duty, and that no blame attached to us.]

II. To keep them from earthly-mindedness—

[When our corn and wine are multiplied, we are apt to be thinking how we may treasure them up, rather than how we shall employ them to the honour of God. To counteract this sordid disposition, God provided, that, when he had given his people the richest abundance, they should think only of the temperate and grateful use of it, and not of amassing wealth. By this ordinance he said to them, what he says to us also, "If

[a] ver. 1—7. (Read it.) See also Exod. xxiii. 10, 11.
[b] Ps. xxiv. 1. and l. 12.   [c] 1 Cor. vi. 20.

riches increase, set not your hearts upon them[d]." He would have us live above this vain world; and not, when running for such a prize, be "loading our feet with thick clay[e]." If we could have the reasons of God's dispensations fully revealed to us, I have no doubt but that we should find that he has this end in view, when he sends us one bereavement after another: he does it, I say, that we may learn to "set our affections on things above, and not on things on the earth"— — —]

III. To lead them to trust in him—

[Like the rich fool in the Gospel, they would have been ready to say, "Soul, thou hast much goods laid up for many years; eat, drink, and be merry." But God is jealous of his own honour. He will not endure that we should "say to gold, Thou art my hope; or to the fine gold, Thou art my confidence." Indeed, he not only denounces against such conduct his heaviest judgments, but sets forth in most beautiful terms its practical effects[f]— — — The cares of this world are as thorns and briers, which choke the seed which God has sown in our hearts, and prevent it from bringing forth any fruit to perfection. They also weigh down the spirits, and oftentimes prove an insupportable burthen to the soul: whereas the person who has learned to confide in God, is always happy: "he knows in whom he has believed," and is assured that "he shall want no manner of thing that is good." Hence David not merely affirms that such persons are happy, but appeals to God himself respecting it; "O Lord God of hosts, blessed is the man that trusteth in thee." This was the state to which God designed to bring his people of old; and in it he would have all his people live, even to the end of the world. "I would have you," says he, "without carefulness:" "Be careful for nothing; but in every thing by prayer and supplication with thanksgiving let your requests be made known unto God; and the peace of God which passeth all understanding shall keep your hearts and minds through Christ Jesus."]

IV. To make them observant of his providential care—

[When they saw that the sabbatical year was at hand, how forcibly would they be struck with the provision which God had made for it! They would have "*three* years" to live on the produce of one single year[g]. But when they saw

---

[d] Ps. lxii. 10.   [e] Hab. ii. 6.   [f] Jer. xvii. 5, 6.

[g] Commentators appear to me to mistake in supposing that the sabbatical year began, like their civil year, in autumn: for then, the sowing and reaping being brought within *one* year, the loss of that whole time would be felt only for two years: but if their year began, like their ecclesiastical year, in the spring, then they would of course not sow in the sixth year, nor reap in the eighth year; because

142.] THE SABBATICAL YEAR. **677**

their barns overflowing with the produce of the earth, and their presses bursting out with new wine, methinks they would say, This is the hand of God: we *will* love him; we *will* serve him; we *will* trust in him: we *will* shew, that we are not insensible of all his love and kindness.

Such sentiments and conduct would tend exceedingly to exalt and honour God; and would conduce very much to the happiness of all. We are apt to think that there is great comfort annexed to the idea of wealth and plenty: but the comfort which a poor man has in receiving his pittance as from the hand of God, far outweighs all that the rich ever felt in their unsanctified abundance — — — The more we enjoy God in the creature, the more we enjoy the creature itself — — —]

V. To typify the felicity of heaven—

[Canaan was an acknowledged type of heaven: and this ordinance fully represented the blessedness there enjoyed. All the land was common during the seventh year; and every person in it, whether rich or poor, a native or a foreigner, had an equal right to every thing in it. None were to assert an exclusive claim to any thing: none were to reap or treasure up the fruits of the earth; but all were to participate with equal freedom the bounties of heaven. What a delightful picture does this give us of that blessed state, in which there will be no distinction of persons, no boast of exclusive rights, no want of any thing to the children of God; but all will have a fulness of joy at God's right hand, and rivers of pleasure for evermore! — — — Even in the Church below there was a little of this, when the disciples had all things common, and none said that any thing he possessed was his own; but in the Church above, this will universally prevail, and endure to all eternity.]

This subject, in its different bearings, affords ample matter of INSTRUCTION to,

1. The doubtful and undetermined Christian—

[The Jews were required to sacrifice their worldly prospects for the Lord: and were threatened, that, if they did not obey this ordinance, God would expel them from the land. This threatening too was executed in the Babylonish captivity, according to the number of sabbatical years which they had neglected to observe[h]. Shall Christians then be backward to

---

they could not reap or sow in the seventh year: consequently, they could only sow in the eighth year what they were to reap in the ninth. The language of the 22d verse seems to require this interpretation. Next to this interpretation, I should prefer that of making the words "three years" to signify "one year, and parts of two."

[h] Lev. xxvi. 33—35. with 2 Chron. xxxvi. 20, 21.

exercise self-denial, or to sacrifice their temporal interests for their Lord and Saviour? Let them not hesitate between duty and interest: the calls, though apparently opposite, are indeed the same: if we sacrifice any thing for the Lord, he will repay us an hundred-fold. If we will lose our lives for his sake, we shall find them: but if we will save them here, we shall lose them in the eternal world.]

2. The careful and worldly-minded Christian—

[If the Jews, whose principal rewards were of a temporal nature, were taught not to place their affections on earthly things, how much less should we! It is really a disgrace to Christianity, when persons who profess godliness are as anxious after this world as those who have no prospects beyond. Yet how common is this character! Happy would it be for them if they would study our Lord's sermon on the mount; and learn from the very birds of the air to live without anxiety for the morrow[1]. Not that they should neglect their earthly business, whatever it may be: but, in the habit and disposition of their minds, they should " be content with such things as they have," and realize the prayer which they profess to approve, " Give us day by day our daily bread!"]

3. The fearful and unbelieving Christian—

[On the command being given respecting the observance of the sabbatical year, some are represented as asking, " What shall we eat the seventh year?" Now thus it is with many Christians, who are anticipating evils, and questioning with themselves what they shall do under such or such circumstances? and fearing, that, if they proceed in the way of duty, they shall not be able to stand their ground. But the answer to such persons is, " Sufficient for the day is the evil thereof." We have no right to anticipate evils; at least, not so to anticipate them as to distress ourselves about them. All that we need to inquire, is, What is the way of duty? True, to carnal minds we may appear to act absurdly, and to thwart our own interests: but the path of duty will always be found the path of safety. God is the same God as ever he was: and, if he call us to exercise faith on him, he will never disappoint us. Justly did Jesus reprove his disciples for fearing, when they had him in the same vessel with them. Let us remember, that he is embarked with us, and that they who trust in him " shall not be ashamed or confounded world without end."]

4. The humble and believing Christian—

[Did you ever, when exercising faith in God, find yourself disappointed of your hope? Did he ever leave you or forsake

[1] Matt. vi. 25—30.

you? If the command have appeared formidable at a distance, have you not always found that your strength was increased according to your day, and that His grace was sufficient for you? Have you not found also, that, though your obedience might be self-denying, it has always been productive of happiness? In short, are you not living witnesses of the truth and faithfulness of your Lord? Go on then, and be examples of a holy self-denying obedience. Prefer the performance of duty before worldly prospects, how lucrative soever they may appear; and let it be seen in you, what it is to " live by faith on the Son of God, who has loved you, and given himself for you."]

OUTLINE NO. 143

GOD'S PROMISES TO PENITENTS.

Lev. xxvi. 40—42. *If they shall confess their iniquity, and the iniquity of their fathers, with their trespass which they trespassed against me, and that also they have walked contrary unto me; and that I also have walked contrary unto them, and have brought them into the land of their enemies; if then their uncircumcised hearts be humbled, and they then accept of the punishment of their iniquity; then will I remember my covenant with Jacob, and also my covenant with Isaac, and also my covenant with Abraham will I remember; and I will remember the land.*

WE are apt to feel a jealousy respecting the divine mercy, as though a free and full exhibition of it would cause men to make light of sin. But the inspired writers seem never apprehensive of any such effects. In the passage before us God has set forth his promises to his people, if they should continue obedient to them; and the most tremendous threatenings, in case they should become disobedient. Yet even then though he foreknew and foretold that they would depart from him and bring upon themselves his heavy judgments, he told them, that, if even in their lowest state they should return to him with humiliation and contrition, he would restore them to his favour, and to the land from whence they should have been expelled. What encouragement the pious Nehemiah derived from these declarations, may be seen in the prayer he offered; in which he reminded God of them, and sought the accomplishment of them to his nation in a season of deep distress[a]. May the contemplation of them be attended with similar effects to our souls, while we consider,

I. What is that repentance which God requires—

We find in the Scriptures a great variety of marks whereby true repentance may be known: but we shall confine our attention to those which are set forth in the text. It is there required,

1. That we should acknowledge our guilt—

[Our fathers' sins, as well as our own, are just grounds of *national* humiliation: in the repentance that is purely *personal*, our own sins, of course, are the chief, if not the exclusive, sources of sorrow and contrition. But our sins should be viewed in their true light, not as mere violations of our duty to man, but as acts of hostility against God. Sin is "a walking contrary to God," or, in other words, a wilful, persevering, habitual opposition to his holy will: nor do we ever appreciate our own character aright, till we see our whole lives to have been one constant scene of rebellion against God——— Even adultery and murder, though so directly militating against the welfare of society, were considered by David as deriving their chief aggravations from this source; "Against Thee, Thee only, have I sinned[b]."]

2. That we should justify God in whatever judgments he may inflict—

[Though we think *ourselves* at liberty to "walk contrary to God," we do not consider *him* as at liberty to "walk contrary to us," but murmur and repine if at any time he punish us for our iniquities. But whatever judgments he may have inflicted on us, we must say, "Thou hast punished us less than our iniquities deserved[c]"——— We should even view his denunciations of wrath in the future world as no more than the just desert of sin; and be ready to acknowledge the justness of the sentence, if we ourselves be consigned over to everlasting misery on account of our sins ——— I know that, when we consult only our proud reasonings on the subject, it is hard to feel entirely reconciled to the declarations of God respecting it: but a sight of sin in its various aggravations will silence us in a moment, and compel us to cry out, "Lord God Almighty, true and righteous are thy judgments[d]!"]

3. That we should be thankful for any dispensation that has been the means of "humbling our uncircumcised hearts"—

[a] Neh. i. 5–9.   [b] Ps. li. 4.   [c] Ezra ix. 13.   [d] Rev. xvi. 7.

[This is one of the most decisive evidences of true repentance. Nothing but real contrition can ever produce this. We may submit to afflictive dispensations with a considerable degree of patience and resignation, even though we have no just view of our guilt before God: but we can never be thankful for them, till we see that sin is the greatest of all evils, and that every thing is a mercy which leads us to repent of sin. Till we are brought to this, we can never be truly said to "accept the punishment of our iniquity." We must accept it as a fatherly chastisement, a token of love, a blessing in disguise: we must say from our hearts, "It is good for me that I have been afflicted"— — —]

These marks sufficiently characterize the repentance which God requires. We now proceed to mark,

II. The connexion between that and the exercise of mercy—

It is strange that any should imagine repentance to be *meritorious* in the sight of God. Our blessed Lord has told us, that obedience itself can lay no claim to *merit;* and that "when we have done all that is commanded us, we should confess ourselves unprofitable servants." Who does not see that an acknowledgment of a debt is a very different thing from a discharge of that debt; and that, if a condemned criminal be ever so sorry for his offences, and acknowledge ever so sincerely his desert of punishment, his sorrow cannot cancel the debt which he owes to the laws of his country; much less can it give him a claim to great rewards? It is not then on a ground of *merit,* that God pardons a repenting sinner. Nevertheless there is a connexion between repentance and pardon: there is a meetness and suitableness in the exercise of mercy towards the penitent;

1. On God's part—

[Repentance glorifies God, as much as any action of a creature can glorify him. It expresses an approbation of his law, and of the penalties annexed to it: it exalts the goodness and mercy of God, by the hope which it entertains of ultimate acceptance with him. There is not any perfection of the Deity which repentance does not honour — — — Hence Joshua said to Achan, "My son, give glory to the Lord God of Israel, and make confession unto him[e]."]

* Josh. vii. 19.

2. On the part of the penitent himself—

[If a man were pardoned without repentance, he would feel little, if any, obligation to God: and would be ready to commit the same iniquities again, from an idea that there was no great enormity in them. But when a person is truly penitent, he admires and adores the riches of that grace that is offered him in the Gospel — — — and, having tasted the bitterness of sin, he is desirous to flee from it, as from the face of a serpent — — —]

Hence it is that so great a stress is laid on repentance, in the text: "If they be humbled, *then* will I pardon:" *then* I can do it consistently with my own honour; and *then* will they make a suitable improvement of the mercy vouchsafed unto them.—It will be profitable yet further to inquire into,

III. The ground and measure of that mercy which penitents may expect—

[The expressions in the text are very peculiar. Thrice is mention made of that covenant which God made with Abraham, and renewed with Isaac and Jacob. And wherefore is this repetition used, but to shew that that covenant is the *ground* and *measure* of all God's mercies towards us? As far as it related to the Jewish nation, it assured to them the enjoyment of the promised land. But it relates also to the spiritual children of Abraham; and assures to them all the blessings of grace and glory. It is that covenant whereby God engaged that "in Abraham's Seed should all the nations of the earth be blessed." Of that covenant Christ was the Mediator and Surety. He undertook to fulfil the conditions of it, that *we* might partake of its benefits. These conditions he did fulfil: "he made his soul an offering for sin;" and now claims the accomplishment of the promise, that "he should see of the travail of his soul and be satisfied." This covenant God remembers on behalf of penitent transgressors; and all his engagements contained in it he will perform. It is not because penitents *deserve* mercy, that he will impart it to them, but because he has promised it in that covenant: and for the very same reason will he impart unto them all the blessings of salvation. All the riches of his glory shall be given them, because they lay hold of that covenant, and look to him to approve himself faithful to his own engagements — — —]

As an IMPROVEMENT of this subject, we would suggest to you two things:

1. Be thankful that you are yet within the reach of mercy—

[The state represented in the text is such as might be thought altogether hopeless. But God says, " If THEN they be humbled, and they *then* accept the punishment of their iniquity, He will even *then* remember his covenant." Surely this shews us that none should despair of mercy, but that, whatever be our state of guilt or misery, we may yet " cry unto God, even as Jonah did, from the belly of hell [f]." But how many are there who are now beyond the reach of mercy! God does not say, that, if we cry unto him in another world, he will regard us. No: we shall then cry in vain for " a drop of water to cool our tongues." O that we might improve this day of grace, this day of salvation! — — —]

2. Have especial respect unto the Covenant of Grace—

It is to that that God looks: and to that should we look also. It is that alone which is the real ground of all our hopes. This matter is by no means sufficiently understood amongst us: we do not consider, as we ought, the stupendous plan of salvation revealed to us in the Gospel. If we saw more clearly the nature and necessity of the covenant which God entered into with his only dear Son for the redemption of a ruined world, we should form a far better estimate of the malignity of sin, and of our obligations to the mercy of God. Beloved brethren, remember this covenant, both for the humiliation and encouragement of your souls. Independent of that, you must expect nothing: but by pleading it before God, you shall obtain what " neither eye hath seen, nor ear heard, nor heart conceived" — — —]

[f] Jonah ii. 2.